NEW TESTAMENT EPISTLES

1 & 2 TIMOTHY
TITUS

A CRITICAL AND EXEGETICAL COMMENTARY

_____ *by* _____

GARETH L. REESE

HEAD OF NEW TESTAMENT DEPARTMENT
CENTRAL CHRISTIAN COLLEGE OF THE BIBLE
MOBERLY, MISSOURI

Scripture Exposition Books, LLC
803 McKINSEY PLACE
MOBERLY, MISSOURI
65270

ACKNOWLEDGMENT

The Scripture quotations contained herein, unless otherwise noted, are from the *New American Standard Bible*, copyrighted 1960, 1962, 1963, 1968, 1971, 1972, 1973, 1975, 1977, by the Lockman Foundation.   Used by permission.

ISBN: 978-0-9984518-3-1

Dedication

This book is dedicated to the first
of two sons God has given to
Kathleen and me, and whom we
named after the young man to
whom two of the Pastoral Epistles
were sent.

TIMOTHY MICHAEL REESE

Preface

"Letters to Young Preachers" is a good way to designate the New Testament writings of 1 Timothy, 2 Timothy, and Titus. The churches where these young preachers were ministering were of different ages (the Ephesian church was about twelve years old, while those on the isle of Crete were more recently planted), but both faced certain similar needs if they were to continue growing. These letters contain timeless instructions to young preachers about what to emphasize in their ministries so the churches they serve and to whom they preach will be what Christ wants them to be. Leaders who want growing churches, and churches who want solid and lasting growth, would do well to hear these directives.

It may not be polite to read other people's letters – unless those letters are included in the New Testament canon. We are then expected to read them and to hear what the Spirit is saying to the churches. Just as the churches to whom Timothy and Titus were ministering were expected to learn from these letters to their evangelists, so we look over their shoulders and discover that what was written then applies to us, especially as we look for directions, exhortations, and warnings concerning church administration and leadership.

The Restoration Movement, which delights to restore things the way they were done in the ideal church we read about in the New Testament, surely needs to hear what these letters say about public worship, the "must" of qualified elders and deacons, sound doctrine, Christian lifestyles, opposition to false teachers, and the qualifications and work of an evangelist. One also finds guidelines concerning the lifestyle the preacher is to live. The epistle to Titus even offers a series of topics the preacher should address as he fills the pulpit and tries to nourish and help individual Christians and the congregation to grow.

This commentator is aware that our Restoration Movement churches have never settled the issue of the relationship between the evangelist (preacher) and the elders of the local congregation. Nor have we come to consensus concerning the qualifications of elders and deacons. Even more troubling has been the question of the role that women may play in church activities and ministry. Is it possible to harmonize the New Testament passages concerning women's role in the life of the church? Some guidelines and directions on these vexing issues will be offered in this commentary, with the prayer that we shall be able to let the Scriptures guide our thoughts and behavior in these matters, as in all others, as we attempt to restore and emulate the way things were done in the New Testament.

If preachers, elders, deacons, and church members will do things like the letters to these young preachers suggest, then perhaps the church in our century will have fewer spots and blemishes, and will be closer to the holy and blameless bride whom Jesus would present in all her glory to Himself (Ephesians 5:27). To that end this work is dedicated.

TABLE OF CONTENTS

INTRODUCTORY STUDIES

COMMENTARIES AND SPECIAL STUDIES

THE PASTORAL EPISTLES

Introductory Studies

I. PRELIMINARY MATTERS

A. Why are these letters (1 Timothy, 2 Timothy, and Titus) called "Pastoral Epistles"?

These letters have to do with what the denominational world calls "pastoral duties," though for only a little over 250 years have they been known as such. P. Anton, at Halle, in his work *Exegetische Abhandlung der Pastoralbriefe*, first suggested the term in 1726 AD.[1] Before that time, these three letters were called "Paul's Letters to Individuals." Paul's letters were divided into two groups: "Letters to churches" and "Letters to individuals." Only in recent times have we called the former "Prison Epistles" and the latter "Pastoral Epistles."

B. Are these letters intended for individuals or for churches?

How long had Timothy been traveling with Paul?   We will discuss the dating of the Pastorals later, but suffice it here to say that the earliest 2 Timothy can be dated is AD 64.   Timothy began traveling with Paul on the second missionary journey, about AD 51, so by the time Paul writes these letters to Timothy, they had been traveling together for 12 or 15 years.   We can easily suppose that within those years Paul likely had told Timothy about elders and deacons, etc.

Are not these pastoral duties, then, intended to be made known to all people for all times?   That is, they are intended for the churches as much as for the individuals to whom they were originally addressed.   Paul writes these things down so that the elders, the deacons, and the members of the various congregations, too, can know Paul is behind what Timothy has been preaching.   It wasn't just a "young preacher" saying these things and who could therefore be safely ignored!

C. Why study the Pastoral Epistles?[2]

A thorough study of the Pastorals is necessary for the following reasons:

1. They shed needed light on the important problem of **church adminis-tration**.   For example, do these letters contain any directions regarding

---

[1] JETS 28:2, p.141.

[2] The following ideas are from Wm. Hendriksen, *Exposition of the Pastoral Epistles*, p.3ff.

public worship which we will need to heed? What qualities must a man possess in order to be a good elder or a conscientious deacon? To what extent should women be employed in the leadership work of the church? Who has the primary responsibility of caring for the needy? How should a minister deal with aged men who are in need of pastoral counseling? With aged women? With young men? With young women?

2. They stress **sound doctrine**. Is it true that it makes no difference *what* a person believes as long as he is sincere in what he believes? Is the Bible "the Word of God" as it lies there, or does it merely *become* the Word of God when it 'touches' you? How must one deal with heretics? Is it possible to pay too much attention to their errors?

3. They demand **consecrated living**. Is it possible for a person to be doctrinally *sound* but corrupt in practice? Must evil men be disciplined? How soon? With what purpose in mind?

4. They answer the question, **"Are creeds of any value?"** Did the early church have any creedal statements? Were the "faithful sayings" early summaries of Christian doctrine? Were there any hymns sung? Did the words of those early hymns then become early creeds? (If this was the order of development, what can we say about the divine origin of the creedal contents?) Or were early creeds turned into hymns? (If this was the order of development, what can we say about the divine origin of the early church's doctrinal standards?) Or was the Holy Spirit the author of both the 'creeds' and the lyrics of the 'early hymns'? (Did they develop independently of each other?)

5. They tell us about **the closing activities in the life of Paul**.[3]

6. In these epistles, as well as in others, **God speaks to us**.

Why should we be interested in Introductory Studies? Why not just start with an exegetical study of 1 Timothy 1:1? Without pausing to learn what we can about the historical situation to which and from which this letter is written, it will not be possible to interpret a number of the verses we find in the letter. It is to learn this historical information, so we can use the historical-grammatical method of interpretation, that we take time to do careful Introductory Studies.

---

[3] See the epilogue in the author's *New Testament History: Acts*, "The Last Labors and Letters of Paul," for the details of these activities.

II. HISTORICAL ALLUSIONS IN THE PASTORALS

A. Historical Allusions in 1 Timothy

1. At the beginning of the letter, 1:1ff.

    a. 1:1 – Paul signs the letter.
    b. 1:2 – Destination ["to Timothy"] and Greetings.
    c. 1:3 – Timothy has been left at Ephesus while Paul journeyed on into Macedonia.

        1) Apparently, Paul has recently been in Ephesus and asked Timothy to stay on there, while he himself went on to Macedonia.
        2) Has Timothy asked permission to leave Ephesus, to which Paul responds, "as I urged you to remain at Ephesus, (continue to do so)"?

2. In the concluding paragraphs of this letter, 6:20ff.

    a. The ending of the epistle provides no historical allusions.

    b. The Subscription

        1) In the KJV, one finds these words in small type at the close of the letter, "The first to Timothy was written from Laodicea, which is the chiefest city of Phrygia Pacatiana."
        2) Where did these subscriptions come from? How accurate are they? Is this one correct?

3. Other historical allusions in 1 Timothy

    a. 3:14,15 – Paul plans to return to Timothy shortly, but may be delayed.
    b. See also 4:13, "Till I come ..."

B. Historical Allusions in 2 Timothy

1. At the beginning of the letter, 1:1ff.

    a. 1:1 – Paul signs the letter.
    b. 1:2 – Destination ["to Timothy"] and Greetings.

c. 1:4 – "I recall your tears." On what occasion were these tears shed? Had it been hard for the two to separate the last time they had parted? Was it on some other occasion that Timothy was brokenhearted over what had happened?

d. 1:6 – "the gift (*charisma*) of God ... through the laying on of my hands." Timothy had supernatural powers (spiritual gifts) of the Holy Spirit, powers he had received through the laying on of an apostle's hands.

    Paul had bestowed powers on both Titus and Timothy. Did these men therefore have powers which today's evangelists do not? If we can't do everything they did, is it proper to compare today's preacher to the office of evangelist we find in the New Testament?

e. 1:8 – Paul is a prisoner when he writes this letter. There is no indication in 1 Timothy or in Titus that Paul is a prisoner at the time he writes those letters. In those letters, instead, we find Paul in the midst of traveling from church to church.

f. 1:11 – The writer is an apostle and a teacher of the Gentiles.

g. 1:15 – "All who are in Asia turned away from me, among whom are Phygellus and Hermogenes." Does this reflect conditions among the churches in the whole Roman province of Asia, or just among certain "Asians" in the town where Paul is imprisoned?

h. 1:16-18 – Onesiphorus sought out Paul while Paul was in Rome, just as had ministered to Paul when Paul was in Ephesus.

    The language in these verses indicates Paul is in Rome when 2 Timothy was written.

2. Historical allusions in the concluding statements of 2 Timothy, 4:6ff.

    a. 4:6 – "The time of my departure has come." Paul realizes he is to be put to death; "departure" is a euphemism for "executed."

    b. 4:10 – "Demas ... has deserted me and gone to Thessalonica."

    c. 4:10 – "Crescens has gone to Galatia, Titus to Dalmatia." Galatia is likely a reference to the country we call France, while Dalmatia was the ancient name for the land we call Yugoslavia.

We hope these men left because Paul had sent them to preach, not because they deserted (as did Demas).

d. 4:11 – Only Luke is with Paul.

e. 4:11b-13 – Tychicus has been sent by Paul to Ephesus. Compared with verse 9, the implication is that Tychicus has been sent to Ephesus as their new preacher so that Timothy could be freed from the work there to come to Paul.

Paul wished Timothy to bring Mark, the cloak, and parchments.

> Mark – John Mark, who went home on the first missionary journey, and whom Paul refused to take with him on the second missionary journey. Paul later recommended Mark to the Colossian brethren (Colossians 4:10).

> Cloak – The word has been variously interpreted as "cloak," "book-cover," "brief case," etc. J. Russell Morse, arrested by Chinese communists while standing in front of his house, was not allowed to go back inside. Perhaps Paul was arrested in like manner, and so was without his personal effects. Or perhaps, Paul had stored his coat at Troas, expecting to return to Troas before winter (i.e., Paul was arrested in the summer; now winter is coming on, and he will need his winter clothes).

> Parchments – The reference is likely to the Old Testament Scriptures. The Jews put the OT Scriptures on parchment.

It is implied Paul had been to Troas since he left his "cloak" there.

Perhaps Tychicus is carrying this second letter from Paul to Timothy ("I have sent Tychicus" would be an epistolary aorist).

f. 4:14,15 – "Alexander the coppersmith did me much harm." Several attempts have been made to identify this "Alexander." Some appeal to Acts 19:33, where an Alexander, a Jew, is named. At the time of the riot at Ephesus, the Gentiles didn't differentiate between the Christians and the Jews, because both condemned idols. Alexander, the Jew, perhaps planned to clarify the Gentiles' thinking; perhaps he was going to show that Christians and Jews were different, but the mob did not listen. Or, since the Jews had protection of the Roman government, perhaps Alexander was going to show that "Christians" weren't "Jews" – so the Gentiles could treat them as they wished, and not be breaking Roman law about legal religions.

Another man named "Alexander" is referred to in Mark 15:21. When Mark identifies for his Roman readers the "Simon of Cyrene" who was impressed to help carry Jesus' cross to Calvary, that Simon is identified as "the father of Alexander and Rufus" (men whom the Roman readers evidently knew). Is there a possibility the Alexander of 2 Timothy 4 and the Alexander of Mark 15 are the same man? Has this son of Simon gone bad, while Rufus (Romans 16:13) is a Christian leader? Or does the Alexander of Mark (who evidently lives in Rome) refer to a different Alexander than 2 Timothy 4 (who evidently lives in Ephesus)?

The Alexander named in 2 Timothy seems to live at Ephesus. Timothy, who is ministering in Ephesus, is to deal with him.

g. 4:16,17 – "At my first defense no one supported me, but all deserted me... but ... I was delivered out of the lion's mouth."

When was this trial ("defense", or as in the KJV, "answer")?

1) Some apply it to Paul's *first* Roman imprisonment. Those who apply it to the first imprisonment say Paul was tried after the record in Acts closes, and that he was released ("delivered out of the mouth of the lion"). Others, also applying it to the first imprisonment, say Paul was tried and at the first trial was acquitted, but yet held for another trial. On this latter view, Paul was never released from his first Roman imprisonment.

2) Some apply it to a *second* Roman imprisonment. It is conjectured Paul was arrested in AD 66 and taken back to Rome. (After Paul's release from his first imprisonment, he had taken up traveling among the churches again. Rome was burned before Paul was arrested the second time. Nero turned against the Christians, accusing them of burning Rome.) Paul wasn't executed immediately after his second arrest. Instead, he faced several trials. By the time he writes 2 Timothy, he has had one trial ("at my first defense") and is expecting another.

Perhaps we   can give a more   definitive answer to this question once we have examined the other evidence as to the time and place of writing of the Pastorals, especially 2 Timothy.

"Delivered from the lion's mouth" – Does that indicate Paul will not have to face the lions in the Circus Maximus, as did many Christians who were persecuted after the burning of Rome? Or shall we take the term "lion" in a figurative sense?

h. 4:19 – "Greet Prisca and Aquila, and the household of Onesiphorus." The last we saw this couple, they were living in Rome (Romans 16:3). Now, here they are back in Ephesus.[4] They were well-travelled. Before this, we've met them in Corinth (Acts 18:2) and earlier at Ephesus (Acts 18:24ff).

Where is Onesiphorus? Is he at home? Has he died, leaving only his household?   Is he still with Paul in Rome (2 Tim. 1:17)?

i. 4:20 – "Erastus remained at Corinth." The language implies Paul has recently visited Corinth. When he left to continue his journey, Erastus remained at Corinth.

"Trophimus I left sick at Miletus." The language implies this was recent. Paul and Trophimus (and others?) were traveling, came to Miletus, and Trophimus was too sick to continue on. (Why didn't Paul heal him since Paul had miraculous powers?)

j. 4:21 – "Make every effort to come before winter!" Paul, the prisoner, will need his winter clothes. He is not to be executed ("the time of my departure") until some time passes, he believes.

"Eubulus, Pudens, Linus, Claudia, and all the brethren greet you." The people named here are apparently in Rome with Paul. Are they members of the church at Rome?

Alford gives evidence that Pudens and Claudia were important Britishers held hostage in Rome. Claudia is said to be the daughter of the Roman ruler (king) in Britain. Pudens was a centurion who became an equestrian, and had been stationed in England in the capacity of adjutant to the King. According to an

---

[4] This comment assumes the conclusion to be reached later about the date of writing for 2 Timothy.

ancient inscription found in Chichester, England,[5] Pudens and Claudia married.

k. 4:22 – "Grace be with you." The "you" is plural, and this has some bearing on the destination of the letter. More readers than just Timothy are involved.

l. Subscription
In the KJV, one finds these words in small type at the close of the letter: "The second epistle unto Timotheus, ordained the first bishop of the church of the Ephesians, was written from Rome, when Paul was brought before Nero the second time."

Is this correct? To what does "the second time" refer? The second time in the first imprisonment or the second time of the second imprisonment? And is "evangelist," which Timothy evidently was, the same office as "bishop"?

3. Other Historical Allusions in 2 Timothy

a. 2:9 – "I suffer hardship even to imprisonment as a criminal." Here is further evidence Paul is a prisoner as he writes 2 Timothy.

b. 3:11 – "persecutions, sufferings …." Paul speaks of persecutions and afflictions which happened to him at Antioch, Iconium, and Lystra. This sounds very much like the events of the first missionary journey, Acts 13,14.

C. Historical Allusions in Titus

1. At the beginning of the letter, 1:1ff.

a. 1:1 – Paul signs the letter.

b. 1:4 – Destination ["to Titus"] and Greetings.

c. 1:5 – Titus was left in Crete to set things in order. The events behind the epistle to Titus are very similar to 1 Timothy. Paul is pictured as traveling from place to place, setting things in order, leaving trusted helpers behind in each community as evangelists.

---

[5] H. Alford, "Prolegomena on the Pastoral Epistles," Vol.3 of *The Greek Testament* (London: Rivingtons, 1870), p. 104-105.

During these travels, Paul has been to Crete, leaving Titus behind to provide leadership and to set in order what remains.

2.   Historical allusions in the closing verses of Titus, 3:12ff.

   a.   3:12 – "When I send Artemas or Tychicus to you ...." Artemas or Tychicus will come to Crete, then Titus can leave his ministry on Crete and join Paul at Nicopolis. (Cp. 2 Timothy 4:11ff. Tychicus was sent to Ephesus so Timothy could leave and go to Rome.)

   b.   3:12 – "Make every effort to come to me at Nicopolis, for I have decided to spend the winter there." Paul was planning to spend the coming winter in Nicopolis. But which Nicopolis? There were as many as 13 cities and towns in the Roman Empire with this name during Paul's time.

   Probably it is the one in Epirus, across the Adriatic Sea from the heel of the "boot" of Italy.

Did Paul get to spend that next winter in Nicopolis?

   1)   Perhaps Paul wintered in Nicopolis, then went toward Troas in the spring and stored his winter clothes there, and was later arrested and taken to Rome the following summer.

2) Perhaps he was arrested in Troas before he got to Nicopolis, and in Rome would then write, "bring my cloak from Troas" and "make every effort to come before winter" (2 Timothy 4:13,21).

In any case, it doesn't appear Paul is in prison as he writes to Titus.

c. 3:13 – "Help Zenas ... and Apollos on their way ...." These two are to be received by Titus and outfitted for the continuation of their journey. They were likely the bearers of this letter to Titus.

d. 3:15 – "All who are with me greet you. Greet those who love us ...." When we compare these greetings with 2 Timothy 4:11 ("only Luke is with me"), we get the idea Paul is travelling, preaching, and training young preachers (apprenticeship-like training) as was his custom.

e. 3:15 – "Grace be with you all." This final greeting from Paul is written to the whole church since "you all" is plural.

f. Subscription
In the KJV, one finds these words in small type at the close of the letter: "It was written to Titus, ordained the first bishop of the church of the Cretians, from Nicopolis of Macedonia." Is this correct?

D. Summary of the Historical Allusions

1. These letters are written by the same person, at about the same time. a) Their style and diction, the motives which they furnish, the state of the church, and the progress of the heresy they describe, are the same in all three letters. So we should assign them to one and the same period in Paul's life. We cannot consent to separate these epistles widely from one another, setting one earlier and the others in the later years of the Apostle's ministry. b) There is a close resemblance in matter and words in Titus and 1 Timothy. The same enemies and the same difficulties are pictured in both letters to Timothy.[6]

---

[6] "They presuppose the same false teachers, the same organization, and entirely similar conditions in the community. They move within the same relative theological concepts and have the same peculiarities of language and style." W.G. Kummel, *Introduction to the New Testament* (Nashville: Abingdon, 1975), p.367.

Again, we say the letters are written not long apart. The three Pastorals present so much similarity that they must be attributed to one writer. It is significant that almost all commentators either reject or retain all three together.

2.   Note the places visited by Paul.

We find evidence Paul has recently visited Ephesus, Miletus, Troas, Crete, possibly Corinth, Nicopolis (of Epirus), Macedonia, and Rome. Paul apparently is traveling when he writes 1 Timothy and Titus.

3.   According to 2 Timothy, Paul is in prison in Rome as he writes.

Paul was a prisoner (2 Timothy 1:8, 2:9) in Rome (2 Timothy 1:15-18). He has already had one trial, making one defense (2 Timothy 4:16,27). He expects execution after the next trial (2 Timothy 4:6).

4.   Paul hopes for Timothy to come to Rome to see him before the end (2 Timothy 4:9,21).

Some insist 2 Timothy is full of contradictions. One passage has Paul saying he is about to die; in another he says, "bring me my books and my coat." Yet the same kind of imprisonment happened to a Christian Church missionary in China, and he asked for almost the same things. It is both understandable and possible to express both discouragement and hope in the same letter.

5.   Timothy is to bring Mark with him.

Colossians 4:10 provides a recommendation of Mark to the Colossian church. The Colossian reference, which we date about AD 62 or 63, is an indication Mark is coming from Rome to Colossae. When 2 Timothy is written (say 5 years or so after Colossians), perhaps Mark is still ministering to the church in Colossae. If he were, it would be easy to send for him from Ephesus to accompany Timothy to Rome.

III. AUTHORSHIP AND ATTESTATION

A. Internal evidence[7]

---

[7] Any discussion of the authorship of the Pastoral Epistles must account for the pertinent information contained in the Pastoral Epistles themselves. See "Historical Allusions" above.

1. **Paul signs all three** of the Pastoral Epistles.

   In agreement with this, the biographical notes in the letters speak of the writer having once been a blasphemer and persecutor (1 Timothy 1:12-17), as now being a preacher and apostle to the Gentiles (1 Timothy 1:1,11, 2:7; 2 Timothy 1:1,11; Titus 1:1), and speak of the journey through Antioch, Iconium, and Lystra, which fits Paul's first missionary journey (2 Timothy 1:12,13, 3:10,11).

2. There are **many vocabulary words** in the Pastorals that are similar to Paul's language as recorded in the ten acknowledged Pauline letters[8] and in the speeches recorded in Acts. These vocabulary terms have been listed in Alford, "Prolegomena on the Pastoral Epistles," p.81, and in *Pulpit Commentary*, p. ii-iv.

3. We find the Pastorals full of **digressions**.

   This is exactly in the manner of Paul. From that which belongs to the general object of the epistle, Paul is ever given to digress to general truths. He then comes back to the general object of the letter – only to digress again at another point.

4. If these Pastorals are forgeries (as some teach), **for what purpose were they written**?

   The object of these letters appears to be the well-being of the Christian societies to which they refer. Who can believe letters calculated to promote such well-being were written with a pen steeped in lies and falsehood? There is a marked and striking difference in the vocabulary of these epistles which a forger certainly would have avoided (see below, *Critical Problems*). Would a forger have ventured to create the great historical difficulties these epistles have given rise to (see below, *Time and Place of Writing*)? When we consider the Divine glow of the Pastorals, the evidence of their genuineness is overwhelming. Placed beside the Epistle of Clement of Rome to the Corinthians, or the Epistles of Ignatius and Polycarp, or the "Epistle of Barnabas," you feel an immeasurable difference between them.

---

[8] When we refer to the "generally acknowledged" or "generally accepted" letters of Paul, we are referring to the other letters of the Pauline Corpus, ten in number, found in the New Testament and bearing the name of Paul as their author. They are Romans through 2 Thessalonians, plus Philemon, in our New Testament collections. (The debate concerning the Pauline authorship of Hebrews is another matter, since Hebrews is not signed. See the writer's commentary *New Testament Epistles: Hebrews* concerning the possibility of the Pauline authorship of that letter.)

5. A number of the **same workers** associated with Paul in Acts and the ten generally accepted epistles of Paul also appear in the Pastorals.

    We find Timothy, Titus, Luke, Apollos, Tychicus, Trophimus, Demas, Mark, Priscilla and Aquila. At the same time, as is to be expected with the passing of years, some of Paul's workers are not with him when these letters were written – e.g., Sopater, Aristarchus, Gaius, Secundus, Tertius, Quartus, Onesimus, Justus, Epaphras, Epaphroditus, Sosthenes, Lucius, etc. We also have new workers introduced – e.g., Phygellus, Hermogenes, Onesiphorus, Crescens, Carpus, Eubulus, Linus, Pudens, Claudia, Artemas, Zenas, and others.

6. We have the **old familiar scenes** of Paul's apostolic labors pictured in the Pastorals.

    Familiar places, like Miletus, Ephesus, Troas, Macedonia, Corinth, still come before us. At the same time, some new places appear – Crete, Nicopolis, Dalmatia.

7. All the **historical and chronological marks** which we can discover in these epistles agree with the theory of their being written in the reign of the emperor Nero.

8. These letters are similar **in structure** to the ten generally accepted Pauline letters. As an example, let us take 2 Timothy and see how it fits with the usual form of Paul's letters.
    a. The mention of the writer's name and office. 1:1
    b. The destination is given. 1:2
    c. The opening salutation. 1:2
    d. The thanksgiving, blending into the body of the letter, comes next. 1:3ff
    e. The concluding salutation, in the present instance rather detailed. 4:19-21
    f. The benediction. 4:22

9. All three close with **the formula** "Grace be with you" that marks all of Paul's letters. The wording in the Pastorals is the abbreviated form that first made its appearance in Paul's letter to the Colossians.

10. Knight very succinctly summarizes what is the thrust of the internal testimony of the Pastorals as to their own authorship:

These three letters certainly claim to be by Paul the former persecutor of Christians who was called to be Christ's apostle, who traveled far and wide in the Mediterranean world preaching the gospel and suffering for it, who continued to feel responsibility for the churches ... (cf. Phil. 2:18-23), and who continued to deal with actual situations and individuals in specific places. The self-testimony of the letters is most explicit in the identification of the author in the first verse of each letter, but it is also found in the repeated and pervasive personal references the author makes about himself and about his relationships with the addressees and other individuals. On this background, it is not difficult to understand why the almost unanimous consensus of the church until the 19th century was that the letters were from Paul the apostle.[9]

B. External Evidence

1. Allusions

   a. Clement of Rome, AD 96. Has allusions to 1 Timothy 2:8 [I Clement 29], 3:13 [I Clement 54], 5:4 [(I Clement 7], 2 Timothy 1:3 [I Clement 45], and Titus 3:1 [I Clement 2].[10]

   b. Ignatius, AD 110. Has allusions to 2 Timothy 1:16-18 [*Ad Eph.* ch.2], and 2:4 [*Ep. to Polycarp*, ch.6].[11]

   c. Polycarp, AD 110. In his letter *Ad Philippians*, he has allusions to 1 Timothy 2:1,2 [ch.2], 3:8, 6:7,10 [ch.4], 2 Timothy 2:11,12,15 [ch.5] and 4:10 [ch.9].[12]

   d. Hegesippus, AD 170. Has allusions to 1 Timothy 6:3,20 [Eusebius, *H.E.* iii.22].[13]

   e. Athenagoras, AD 176. Has allusions to 1 Timothy 5:1,2, 6:16.[14]

   f. Theophilus of Antioch, AD 180. Has allusions to 1 Timothy 2

---

[9] George W. Knight, *Commentary on the Pastoral Epistles* in NIGNT (Grand Rapids: Eerdmans, 1992), p.6.

[10] These can be studied in detail in Homer Kent (*The Pastoral Epistles*, Chicago: Moody Press, 1958), p.24, or Hendriksen, p.32,33. Bernard ("1 Timothy" in the *Cambridge Greek Testament for Schools and Colleges*, p.xix) presents I Clement and the Pastorals in parallel columns.

[11] See Kent, p.25, or Hendriksen, p.32, to see these allusions in detail.

[12] See Kent, p.25,26, and Hendriksen, p.31,32, for details.

[13] See Kent, p.31.

[14] See Lardner, *Works*, vol.1, p.380. See also Kent, p.29, and Hendriksen, p. 31.

verses 1,2 [*Ad Autolyc.* iii.14], and Titus 3:1,3-7.[15]

2. Canonical Lists

   a. Muratorian Canon, AD 170.
       Includes 13 epistles of Paul (the Muratorian Canon excludes
       Hebrews entirely), so it recognizes Paul's authorship of the Pas-
       torals. The language of the Muratorian Canon is, "the blessed
       Paul ... writes ... out of affection and love one to Philemon, one to
       Titus, and two to Timothy ... held sacred in the honorable esteem
       of the church universal in the regulation of ecclesiastical disci-
       pline."

   b. Peshito Syriac, translated in the 2nd century.
       Includes 14 letters of Paul (including Hebrews). Thus the
       Pastorals are included as Pauline.

   c. The letters we call the Pastorals were never doubted by any church
       witness for centuries, but have held their place in all the canons of
       the Eastern and Western churches.

   d. It is to be noted that several of the heretics, at times, did not
       recognize the canonical position of the Pastorals.

      1) Marcion, the Gnostic heretic, AD 140, did not include the
          Pastorals in his canon. Three explanations for this have been
          suggested: (a) The Pastorals did not exist when Marcion
          lived (as many negative critics in a previous generation were
          wont to affirm).[16] (b) Marcion did not know of their exis-
          tence, perhaps because they were addressed to individuals.
          (However, Marcion includes the much shorter letter to the
          individual Philemon.) (c) The Pastorals were disliked by
          Marcion. Since he arbitrarily rejected other books, why not
          these? The Pastorals are anti-Gnostic and anti-ascetic. For
          Marcion, who preached the strictest asceticism, who denied
          the lawfulness of marriage, and who issued rigid rules for
          fasting, a rejection of the Pastorals is altogether to be
          expected. A heretic does not like any writings which direct-
          ly or indirectly condemn his or a somewhat similar heresy.

---

[15] See Kent, p.30.

[16] See below for more on the date of writing for the Pastorals. But a date in the middle or late
2nd century cannot be accepted given the "allusions" already noted from as early as AD 96.

2) Tatian, 2nd century. He rejected both letters to Timothy, but accepted Titus, in his canonical listing.

3) Not all the heretics rejected the Pastorals. Tertullian tells us that many false teachers in his day used the Pastorals to support their false teaching.

e. P46 (one of the Chester Beatty Papyri, from the early 200's AD[17]) presents a bit of a question. It contains a collection of ten of the Pauline epistles (with Hebrews included second), but it does not contain the Pastorals.

How shall we explain the fact that the Pastorals were not included in this collection? Did the scribe run out of space[18] before he could copy the Pastorals? Did the manuscript at one time contain the Pastorals and Philemon, only to have since been lost to us? Did the scribe deliberately include only those letters of Paul to churches (since Philemon as well as the Pastorals are missing)? Until these questions are answered convincingly, it would be improper to appeal to the Chester Beatty Papyrus as proof against the Pauline authorship of the Pastorals.

3. Quotations

a. **Irenaeus** (AD 180) repeatedly quotes all three epistles by name.

1) "Whereas some rejecting the truth bring lying words, and vain genealogies, which minister questions, as the apostle says, rather than godly edifying which is in faith ..." (cp. 1 Timothy 1:4). *Contra Haeres.* i, Proem.

2) He also quotes 1 Timothy 1:9 [*ibid*, IV.xvi.3], 2:5 [V.xvii.1], 3:15 [III.i.1], 4:2 [II.xxi.2].

3) "Of this Linus, Paul makes mention in the epistle to Timothy" (cp. 2 Timothy 4:21). *Contra Haeres.* III. preface 3.

4) "As Paul says, 'A man that is a heretic ... reject'" (cp. Titus 3:10). *Contra Haeres.* I.xvi.3 and III.iv.

---

[17] A recent writer has dated the Chester Beatty Papyri as early as AD 85. See Y.K. Kim, "Paleographical dating of P46 to the Later First Century," *Biblica* 69:2 (1988), p.248-257.

[18] Some students of the old manuscripts have noted that the scribe began to write smaller toward the end of the present collection, so as to include more on the page than he did at the beginning of his copying. One has only to compare the pages from the earlier and later parts of the manuscript to see this phenomenon.

b. **Clement of Alexandria** (AD 190) repeatedly quotes all three Epistles, and says the heretics reject them because their errors are confuted in them.

    1) "Of which the apostle writing says: O Timothy, keep that which is committed to thy trust, avoiding profane and vain babblings and oppositions of science" (cp. 1 Timothy 6:20). *Stromata* II.xi.

    2) "In the second epistle to Timothy the noble Paul commands ...." *Stromata* III.

    3) "Others speak of Epimenides the Cretan ... whom the apostle Paul has mentioned in the epistle to Titus, speaking thus: The Cretans are always liars" (cp. Titus 1:12). *Stromata* I.

c. **Tertullian** (AD 200) quotes again and again by name both epistles to Timothy and the one to Titus.

    1) "And this word Paul has used in writing to Timothy: O Timothy, keep that which is committed to thy trust. And again: That good thing which was committed to thee, keep" (cp. 1 Timothy 6:20 and 2 Timothy 1:14). *De Praescript Haeret.* XXV.

    2) "But of this no more need be said, if it be the same Paul, who writing to the Galatians, reckons heresies among the works of the flesh, and who directs Titus to reject a man that is a heretic, after the first admonition; knowing that he is such an one is subverted, and sinneth, being condemned of himself" (cp. Titus 3:10,11). *De Praescript Haeret.* VI.

d. **Origen** (AD 210) quotes many passages from the Pastorals.

    1) In his work against Celsus, Origen quotes 1 Timothy 2:1,2, 3:15,16, 4:1-5,10, 17,18, 6:20; 2 Timothy 1:3,10, 2:5, 3:6-8, 4:7,11,15,20,21; and Titus 1:9,10,12, 3:6,10, 11; and ascribes them to Paul.[19]

    2) "Moreover, Paul, who himself also subsequently became an apostle of Jesus, says in his epistle to Timothy: This is a faithful saying, that Jesus Christ came into the world to save sinners, of whom I am chief" (cp. 1 Timothy 3:15). *Against Celsus* I.lxiii.

e. **Eusebius** places all three letters in the *homologoumena* (the letters universally accepted as Pauline and as canonical).

4. The authorship of the Pastoral Letters was never seriously doubted un-

---

[19] See Hendriksen, page 29.

til the 1800's. Schmidt in 1804 denied the genuineness of 1 Tim-othy. Schleiermacher in 1807 denied 1 Timothy, and suggested all three would have to be denied before the critics could make their case stand. Eichhorn in 1826 accordingly denied all three.

IV. TIME AND PLACE OF WRITING

A. Review of Information Gained from the Historical Allusions

(1) It has been shown that the letters were written from the same general period in Paul's life. It is not proper to assume one was written early in his ministry, another five years later, and the third, say, ten years later still. (2) The historical allusions tell us Paul was traveling among the churches. In 1 Timothy we learned Paul had recently left Ephesus and gone into Macedonia. In Titus we saw Paul had left Crete and was traveling toward Nicopolis. (3) The three letters come from the latest period of Paul's life. The concluding notices of 2 Timothy forbid giving any date earlier than toward the end of Paul's life. The question then for us is, "What is the latest period of Paul's life?" Was Paul put to death at the end of the first Roman imprisonment (the imprisonment recorded in Acts 28)? Was he liberated from the imprisonment recorded in Acts 28, such that he could resume his apostolic labors, and then later was re-arrested, convicted, and executed?

B. Do the Pastorals Fit into the Book of Acts?

(According to the first hypothesis above, Paul was executed at the end of the first Roman imprisonment. Therefore, it should be possible to fit the historical allusions found in the Pastorals into the life of Paul as recorded in Acts. Can it be done? Also remember, according to the allusions in the epistles, we must find a time when Paul visited Ephesus before going into Macedonia, and a time when he visited Crete.)

1. Paul was in Ephesus at the close of the **2nd missionary journey** (Acts 18:18ff). Some say this is where the Pastorals fit into Acts.

   Evidence: (a) It is supposed that when Paul left Corinth (Acts 18:18) to go to Ephesus, either voluntarily or by stress of weather, he went around by Crete, leaving Titus there. (b) He then pursued his jour-ney to Ephesus, where he wrote the Epistle to Titus, recommending Apollos to him, who he knew was going on to Crete from Corinth (Acts 18:27; Titus 3:13). Priscilla and Aquila were left at Ephesus.

All this would give a date of about AD 53 for the writing of Titus, since we have determined the dates AD 51-54 for the second missionary journey.[20] (c) Paul then proceeded to Caesarea, Jerusalem and Antioch as the second journey concluded. (d) From there, he passed through Galatia and Phrygia, returning to Ephesus (Acts 18:22,23, 19:1), having wintered at Nicopolis in Cilicia, a city lying between Antioch and Tarsus. (e) According to this theory, 1 Timothy was written on the third missionary journey (see below). (f) Also, according to this theory, 2 Timothy was written from the Roman imprisonment recorded in Acts 28. Specifically, 2 Timothy was written after Ephesians, and before Colossians and Philemon.[21]

Objections: (a) The narrative of Paul's passage from Cenchrea to Ephesus with Priscilla and Aquila is quite incompatible with a sojourn at Crete by the way. (b) It seems unlikely an event as important as the evangelization of Crete would be omitted from the record in Acts, had such actually occurred. (c) The haste in Paul's movements from Corinth, in order to enable him to reach Jerusalem by the feast (probably Pentecost), makes the idea of a sojourn in Crete unreasonable. (d) Nicopolis in Cilicia is the most unlikely place imaginable for him to winter in. It was an obscure city, and it is obvious to suppose that Paul would rather have wintered at Antioch or, if so near his home, at Tarsus. (e) Apollos was not yet converted at the time of the second missionary journey. The language of Acts 18 indicates Apollos was not converted until after Paul left Ephesus, so it would be impossible for Paul to recommend him to Titus (as per Titus 3:13).

It becomes evident that the account of the second missionary journey is not reconcilable with the historical allusions in the Pastorals.

2. Paul was also in Ephesus on the **3rd missionary journey** (Acts 19,20).

Evidence: (a) When Paul left Ephesus after the riot of Demetrius and the silversmiths, he went into Macedonia. This fits the allusions concerning Paul's movements just prior to the writing of 1 Timothy,[22] leading us to date 1 Timothy about AD 56. (b) Further support for

---

[20] See the "Chronology of the Apostolic Age" in the author's *New Testament History: Acts* to see how these dates are determined.

[21] The careful student will note that not all writers have the "Prison Epistles" (Ephesians, Colossians, Philippians, and Philemon) written from the first Roman imprisonment. The comment just made does indeed assume that Rome was the place of writing of the Prison Epistles.

[22] Barnes, in his commentary, defends this time and place for the writing of 1 Timothy.

the theory that the Pastorals fit the 3rd missionary journey is found in the words Paul spoke to the Ephesian elders (Acts 20:25ff). Paul says, "I **know** that you shall see me no more." It is argued that it is difficult to reconcile this language with a later visit by Paul to Ephesus – e.g., a visit after a release from the imprisonment in Rome, on which he left Timothy behind. Perhaps Paul's plans were changed for him, as his plans were changed on other occasions. Others say a brief visit to Ephesus is not excluded by the language "I know ...." Rather, what is excluded by this language is an evangelistic work comparable to the three years of day-by-day kingdom-activity in the Ephesus region.

Objections: (a) The information about Timothy given in the Pastorals does not seem to fit the record of Acts 19-20. Per Acts 19:22, Timothy was sent off from Ephesus *before* Paul's departure. Even if Timothy, as has sometimes been thought from 1 Corinthians 16:11 and 2 Corinthians 1:1, returned to Ephesus before Paul left, and in this sense might have been left behind there on Paul's departure, we must suppose that he almost immediately deserted the charge entrusted to him. Just a month or so later, he is with Paul in Macedonia (2 Corinthians 1:1) and six months later is with Paul in Corinth (Romans 16:21), from whence he returned with Paul to Asia (Acts 20:4).[23] (b) If Paul wrote 1 Timothy just a short time after he left Ephesus following the riot, then 1 Timothy 3:14,15 is a flat contradiction of Paul's declared purpose (Acts 19:21, 20:3) of going from Macedonia to Achaia and then to Jerusalem. Only because his plans were changed by a plot of the Jews did he even come anywhere near Ephesus on his subsequent trip to Jerusalem with the offering for the poor saints at Jerusalem. (c) This theory fails to adequately account for the allusions in Titus. The only time Acts records Paul in Crete before AD 61 is on the trip to Rome (Acts 27:7-15). There, the apostle is pictured as a prisoner; he is not carrying on evangelistic work on the island, and he has nothing whatever to say about the place where he expects to spend the next winter or where he desires Titus to meet him. (Note that until the storm, the centurion guarding Paul and the captain of the ship both refused to listen to Paul.)

It becomes evident that the account of the third missionary journey is not reconcilable with the historical allusions in the Pastorals.

---

[23] Nevertheless, some place the writing of 1 Timothy here on the third journey. They state Timothy stayed behind at Ephesus, but for some unknown reason he left sooner than originally expected and joined Paul in Macedonia before 2 Corinthians was written. However, it is difficult to see how the instructions of 1 Timothy could have been carried out quickly enough to allow Timothy to join Paul in Macedonia so soon.

3. Since not every trip of Paul's is recorded in Acts – **perhaps the allusions in the Pastorals would fit a trip not recorded in Acts.**

Paul's "intermediate trip to Corinth" is not recorded in Acts. Perhaps this was the occasion for the writing of the Pastorals.

Evidence: (a) There is the time, unrecorded in Acts, when Paul left Ephesus to go to Corinth. The trip was made between the writing of 1 & 2 Corinthians (see the Introductory Studies to those two books.[24]). (b) It is conjectured that Timothy was left at Ephesus during this trip, and that 1 Timothy dates from this "intermediate trip," about AD 56. (c) In Corinthians and Acts, we have suggested this "intermediate trip" to Corinth and back to Ephesus was a quick trip, just across the Aegean and back. If we were to believe 1 Timothy was written during this trip, we will have to adjust our comments, and admit the trip may have been longer. Instead of a quick round trip across the Aegean Sea and back, Paul would have gone through Macedonia to Corinth, and while passing through Macedonia wrote to Timothy. From Corinth, instead of going east across the Aegean Sea to Ephesus, Paul went to Crete, founding the Cretan churches and leaving Titus to set things in order. From Crete, it is conjectured Paul spent the winter in Nicopolis of Cilicia, from whence he wrote the letter to Titus. (Thus, Titus would be dated AD 56 also.) From Nicopolis, Paul returned through Galatia to Ephesus. (d) It is suggested the trip lasted 9 months – to account for the difference between "two years and three months" of Acts 19:8,10 and the "three years" of Acts 20:31.

Objections: (a) The great and fatal objection to this hypothesis is the insertion of so long a journey between Acts 19:12 and 19:13, or between Acts 19:20 and 19:21. (b) Would Paul make a *prediction* of coming false teachers to the Ephesian elders *after* such a letter as 1 Timothy had been sent to them? When Paul spoke to the Ephesian elders (Acts 20), the apostasy was yet future. In 1 Timothy, the apostasy was already present.[25] (c) According to this view, 2 Timothy was written at the end of the first Roman imprisonment (c. AD 63). But it is most difficult to reconcile the concluding notices of 2 Timothy with such a view.

---

[24] See also the author's *New Testament History: Acts*, p. 685-686, for information about this "intermediate trip."

[25] Some who hold the theory that 1 Timothy was written from the third missionary journey say that the false teachers spoken about in 1 Timothy are *outside* the church, whereas the false teachers of Paul's farewell speech to the Ephesian elders were to come from *inside* the church.

i) In 2 Timothy 4:20 we read, "Trophimus I left sick at Miletus." Assuming the suggested 9-month trip, and allowing two years for the Caesarean imprisonment and two years for the Roman imprisonment, the last time Paul would have been to Miletus was *five years earlier*. What value would it be to tell Timothy that "five years ago I left Trophimus at Miletus"? Furthermore, when Paul passed through Miletus on his way to Jerusalem, Trophimus did not stay at Miletus, for he was with Paul in Jerusalem at the time of Paul's arrest (Acts 21:29).

ii) 2 Timothy 4:13 indicates Paul's winter coat had been left at Troas. Assuming 2 Timothy was written from the close of the imprisonment recorded in Acts 28, it would have been *six years* since Paul had been through Troas. It seems probable that Paul would have needed his winter coat at some time during that six-year period.

(d) Were we to try to show that the Pastoral Epistles come from some time in Paul's life as recorded in Acts, we would have to relate 2 Timothy (which is written from a Roman imprisonment) both to Acts 28 and to the Prison Epistles.[26] This will never do!

i) The Prison Epistles exhibit an expectation of a speedy deliverance[27] from imprisonment. But in 2 Timothy, Paul's tone is wholly different. He writes with a feeling that his work is done, and his departure is near at hand (2 Timothy 4:6-8,19). Unlike the Prison Epistles, there is not a word in the Pastorals about being delivered in answer to the readers' prayers, nor of any expectation of being set free.

ii) In the Prison Epistles, Paul includes Timothy's name in the salutations. But in 2 Timothy, also written from the prison in Rome, Timothy is in Ephesus and is asked to come to Paul.

In the face of these objections and difficulties, we conclude that the Pastorals were *not* written during the "intermediate trip" to Corinth.

---

[26] Observe, again, that this "objection" is based on the studied conclusion that the Prison Epistles were written from Rome, during the imprisonment recorded in Acts 28. Historically, this has been the time and place assigned to the writing of the Prison Epistles (see Guthrie, *Introduction*, on each of the Prison Epistles -- Ephesians, Philippians, Colossians, and Philemon). Should this conclusion be in error, then the argument just presented would no longer be valid.

[27] Philippians 1:19,25,26, 2:24; Philemon 22.

Others suggest a trip, unrecorded in Acts, furnishes the historical situation for the Pastorals. For example, some think Paul made the trip to Crete during the three-month period of Acts 20:2,3. But would Paul undertake a voyage in winter, when sailing on the Mediterranean was so dangerous? It hardly seems likely a trip to all the places mentioned in the Pastorals would be omitted from the book of Acts.

We are driven, therefore, to accept one of two hypotheses: either the hypothesis which denies the Pauline authorship of the Pastorals, or the one[28] which assigns these epistles to a time posterior to that embraced in the Acts narrative.

C. Shall We Then Deny the Pauline Authorship of the Pastorals?

Liberal theologians deny that Paul wrote the Pastorals. Therefore they need not be concerned with fitting them into the life of Paul as recorded in Acts. (1) The negative critics claim that because the Pastorals cannot be fitted into the Book of Acts, Paul didn't write them. Someone else is said to have written them, forging Paul's name in the first verse of each letter. The Pastorals were dated about AD 150 by many of the negative critics, after they had denied the Pauline authorship, and after they had accepted an evolutionary scheme of development for Christian doctrine and polity. (2) Paul, they tell us, was killed in the Neronian persecution immediately following the burning of Rome, and that he was never released from the confinement recorded in Acts 28. Any mention of his death is omitted from the Book of Acts because the writer deliberately closed the record without telling what happened to the "hero," lest the book end in "defeat." (3) In addition, a number of technical arguments are used to deny the Pauline authorship of the Pastorals. (See below, under "Critical Problems.")

There are several weighty objections to the conclusions drawn by liberal scholarship: (1) In the Prison Epistles, Paul expects to be released from the imprisonment during which those letters were written (Ephesians 6:21,22, Philippians 2:24, Colossians 4:8, Philemon 22). The negative higher critics answer that the Prison Epistles were written from Ephesus or Caesarea, not Rome. They say Paul never expected to be released from the Roman imprisonment recorded in Acts 28, although he did ex-

---

[28] It is just a working hypothesis, not a proven fact. Attempts are still being made to fit the Pastorals into the book of Acts. Bo Reicke, "Chronologie der Pastoralbriefe," TLZ 101 (1976), p.81-94, is one such attempt. J.A.T. Robinson, *Redating the New Testament* (Philadelphia: Fortress, 1976) makes extensive use of Reicke's work as he tries to fit the Pastorals into the history of Acts.

pect release from the Caesarean or Ephesian confinements. So the arguments about "Which imprisonment?" that are contained in the Introductory Studies to the *Prison* Epistles have a bearing on the denial of the Pauline authorship of the *Pastoral* Epistles. (2) On what evidence is it asserted that Paul died at the time of the imprisonment recorded at the close of Acts? No evidence at all is given, except the needs of their destructive theories. We should not be awed just because one of the negative critics says Paul was killed in AD 64. (3) Internal and external evidence (see above) point to the Pauline authorship of the Pastorals.

A denial of the Pauline authorship of the Pastorals provides no help in determining the time and place of the writing of the letters. The best answer, therefore, to the question of how we fit the Pastorals together with the Book of Acts is this:

D. Events Alluded to in the Pastorals Occur *After* the Close of Acts

If this be true, we must conclude that Paul was released from the Roman imprisonment recorded in Acts 28. What evidence is there that Paul was released from the first Roman imprisonment? (1) He expected to be released, so the Prison Epistles tell us (see note #27 above). (2) The Roman judicial custom was to release prisoners if their accusers didn't appear within two years.[29] By the time Luke wrote Acts, the two years were ended (Acts 28:30). (3) There is tradition to the effect that Paul was released and resumed his missionary work among the Gentiles:

a.   Clement of Rome

"Let us set before our eyes the illustrious apostles ... After preaching both in the east and west, [Paul] gained the illustrious reputation due to his faith, having taught righteousness to the whole world, and **having come to the extreme limits of the west**, suffered martyrdom under the *prefects*. Thus he was removed from the world, and went into the holy place, having proved himself a striking example of patience." I Clement 5:7

Explanation:

"Prefects" – A.C. Cox, the author of footnotes in the *Ante-Nicene Fathers*, writes, "That is, under Tigellinus and Sabinus, in the last year of the emperor Nero: but some think Hellius and Polycletus are referred to. Some regard the word translated 'prefect' as simply the witness borne by Peter and Paul to the

---

[29] See the author's *New Testament History: Acts*, p.xxxvi, for documentation of this matter of Roman jurisprudence.

truth of the Gospel before the rulers of the earth."

"Limits (bounds) of the west" – Since Clement lived in Rome, most writers interpret the "limits of the west" to refer to Spain; for how could Clement say that Rome was as far west as a man could go? If Paul ever did make a trip to Spain (a desire he expressed in Romans 15:24,28), that trip would have to come after the close of the events recorded in Acts.[30] Thus Clement's statement leads us to believe Paul was freed from the first Roman imprisonment.

b. Muratorian Canon

The Latin text is very difficult to translate or understand, but the part about Paul going to Spain is very clear.

"Luke relates [individual events] for the most excellent Theophilus because in his presence the individual events transpired, as he clearly declares by omitting the passion of Peter as well as the departure of Paul when the latter proceeded from the city [Rome] **to Spain**."

If this is the correct reading of the text, the Muratorian Canon speaks clearly about Paul's "departure ... from the city" and about his being able to resume his labors as an apostle and missionary.

c. Eusebius

"Luke also, who handed down the Acts of the apostles in writing, brought his narrative to a close by the statement that Paul spent two whole years in Rome in freedom, and preached the Word of God without hindrance. Tradition has it that the apostle, having defended himself, was again **sent upon the ministry of preaching, and coming a second time to the city, suffered martyrdom under Nero**. While he was being held in prison, he composed the second epistle to Timothy, at the same time signifying that his first defence had taken place and that his martyrdom was at hand ... We have said this to show that Paul's martyrdom was not accomplished during the sojourn in Rome that Luke describes [Acts 28]." *Ecc. Hist.* II.xxii.1,2

Eusebius is relating the common view ("tradition has it") held by those writers before him. The common view was that Paul was released from the first Roman imprisonment.

d. Theodoret (AD 425) says of Paul that "he came to Spain."

---

[30] Paul has not been to Spain before Romans was written. Romans was written in AD 58, toward the close of Paul's third missionary journey. There is no place for a trip to Spain in the journeys of Paul between the third missionary journey (Acts 18-21) and the voyage to Rome (Acts 27,28). Therefore, any trip to Spain would have to come after the events of Acts 28.

e. Jerome (AD 400) places Paul's martyrdom in the 14th year of Nero (AD 67-68), 3-4 years after liberation from his first imprisonment.[31]

f. Venantius Fortunatus (6th century) says Paul went to Cadiz, Spain.[32]

g. Chrysostom (AD 398) mentions as an undoubted historical fact, "that St. Paul after his residence in Rome departed to Spain."

(4) The tradition that Paul was martyred in Nero's last year implies a release from the first Roman imprisonment. (See Jerome, Eusebius, etc.) The last year talked about in Acts 28 is AD 63. Nero's last year would cover the last part of AD 67 and the early part of AD 68. It is doubtful Paul would be held in prison this whole five years, and therefore the tradition as to the date of Paul's martyrdom (14th year of Nero) is evidence that he was released from the first Roman imprisonment.

It would be fair to list the objections to the idea that the Pastorals represent a period after the close of Acts 28, but we have not found any.[33]

E. Conclusions as to the Time and Place of Writing

1. The simplest explanation is that Paul was released from the first Roman imprisonment and the Pastorals are dated after the close of Acts. The last writing we possess from Paul during that first Roman imprisonment is the epistle to the Philippians, c. AD 63. There (1:26), Paul evidently intends to visit the Philippians, and he is confident the intended visit will not be long delayed (2:24). This same anticipation occurs in Philemon 22. We may safely ascribe to Paul the intention, pending his release, of visiting the Asiatic and Macedonian churches.

2. There is traditional evidence that Paul suffered martyrdom in the last year of Nero's reign. The last year of Nero's reign began in October AD 67, and stretched to July AD 68, when Nero committed suicide. If Paul's death were in Nero's last year, it could not have been before late AD 67 or early AD 68.

---

[31] *Lives of Illustrious Men*, ch.5. See also *Nicene and Post-Nicene Fathers*, Series 2, Vol. 3, p.362-63. Jerome relates "Paul was dismissed by Nero that he might preach Christ's gospel in the West."

[32] This writer is very late, and so the weight to be given to his testimony is slight.   Nevertheless, Cadiz was habitually described as the extreme western point of the Roman Empire.   One Roman writer, Pindar, speaks of Cadiz as the point beyond which no mortal could advance.

[33] We have found no testimony from the early church that contradicts the idea that Paul was released from the first Roman imprisonment, or that has him killed at the end of the imprisonment described in Acts 28.   Furthermore, the traditions about a release and a second imprisonment begin very early – within 30 years of the events they record.

3. What events filled the five-year interval between Paul's last epistle (AD 63) and Paul's death (AD 68)? Perhaps he went to Spain;[34] some even say to Britain. According to the Pastorals, he visited Macedonia and Asia Minor.

4. **The chronological order of the writing of the Pastorals** depends on whether Paul's travels alluded to in the letters cover one trip or two.

    (a) Some conjecture the Pastorals were **all written from one journey**. (1) As noted above, the evidence indicates the Pastorals were written not long apart. (2) Paul's supposed last journey is reconstructed in this fashion: From Crete (Titus 1:3) to Miletus (2 Timothy 3:20) to Ephesus (1 Timothy 1:3) to Troas (2 Timothy 3:13). From Troas, Paul went to Nicopolis (in Epirus) to spend the winter.[35] From Nicopolis, Paul was taken to Rome (2 Timothy 1:17, 4:15-17). (3) When were the letters written? Leaving Titus on Crete would come first on such a trip as the one proposed, so it would be natural for the epistle to Titus to be written first, from Asia Minor (see above), since the instructions would be needed immediately. According to this theory, Titus is dated c. AD 66. Timothy would be left in Ephesus when Paul left that city, so 1 Timothy would be written second, sometime after Paul left Ephesus, perhaps from Macedonia. It would be dated c. AD 66. 2 Timothy would be written last, from the second Roman imprisonment, dated c. AD 67 or 68.

    Objection to the one trip theory: Per 2 Timothy 4:20, Paul visited Miletus *after* writing 1 Timothy. How is 1 Timothy 3:14,15 then to be explained? Did Paul plan a return to Ephesus after wintering in Nicopolis, but his plans were dashed by being arrested?

    (b) Because the conjecture that the Pastorals were written while Paul was on the same trip through the region does not fit all the historical allusions, other authors suggest the letters were written **at various times during the interval between Paul's imprisonments**, and from several journeys. (1) The evidence that the letters were written not long apart fits a span of 2 or 3 years, as well as an interval of only 1 year. (2) Paul's journeys between imprisonments would be reconstructed in this fashion: upon his release after the spring of AD 63, Paul journeyed eastward, visiting perhaps Philippi and then passing

---

[34] Under "Critical Problems" below, this question of a "Spanish Crusade" is discussed.

[35] Some say he went from Troas to Corinth (2 Timothy 3:20) and from thence to Nicopolis. Others give the more probable suggestion that Paul went from Troas to Philippi (Macedonia, 1 Timothy 1:3), and thence to Nicopolis (Titus 3:12).

into Asia Minor.[36]   During this 5-year period, he visited Ephesus, leaving Timothy there, and then went on to Macedonia, intending a future return to Ephesus (1 Timothy 3:14,15).   From Macedonia[37] he wrote 1 Timothy, c. AD 65.   Some time between the imprison-ments, perhaps toward the close of the 5-year interval (if the winter spoken of in Titus 3:12 and 2 Timothy 4:20 is the same winter[38]), Paul visited Crete, leaving Titus behind on the island to set things in order.   Paul's final journey, leading to Rome, would be much the same as given above (from Crete to Miletus [2 Timothy 4:20], to Ephesus [2 Timothy 1], to Troas [2 Timothy 4:13], to Nicopolis [Titus 3:12], to Rome [2 Timothy 1:17]).   The general opinion is Titus was written from Asia Minor.[39]   Paul was on his way to winter in Nicopolis, and would have to travel north from Crete.   2 Timothy agrees with this conjecture.   In 2 Timothy, since last communicating with Timothy, we find Paul had been to Miletus and Troas.   It is also probable Paul spent time in Ephesus.   Perhaps Paul was sick again.   2 Timothy 1:19 says Onesiphorus cared for Paul, and Ephesus was Onesiphorus' hometown (2 Timothy 4:19).   Titus would be dated c. AD 65 or 66.   At length, Paul came to Nicopolis.   Nicopolis was a Roman colony.   There he would find a certain safety against tumultuary violence.   But at the same time, he would be more open to arrest by Roman authorities.   The supposition of Conybeare that Paul, known in Rome as the leader of the Christians, would be likely at any time after AD 64 to be arrested and implicated in causing the burning of Rome, is attractive.   There is no hint in Scripture, or in any history, as to the place or circumstances of Paul's arrest.   But knowing he intended to go to Nicopolis to spend the winter there, and that very shortly after that he was a prisoner in Rome, the natural inference is that he was arrested by the authorities in Epirus and sent from Nicopolis to Rome.

---

[36] He would thus carry out his desires and intentions as indicated in the Prison Epistles by visiting the churches in Asia Minor (Philippians 1:26, 2:25; Philemon 22).

[37] It has generally been assumed 1 Timothy was written from Macedonia.   The Subscription would be wrong as to the place of writing, if this be true.   However, some contend the language of 1 Timothy 1:3 conveys the impression Paul was not in Macedonia at the time of writing, that Paul speaks of the trip to Macedonia as one already past, and succeeded by other circumstances.   If this impression is correct, it would be quite impossible to assign with any certainty the place of writing.

[38] It has been argued that these two passages refer to two different winters.   If they refer to the same winter, and if Paul is going to spend that winter in Nicopolis, why leave his winter clothes at Troas when Nicopolis is his next stop?

[39] In truth, it is not possible to document either the time or the place of writing of 1 Timothy and Titus, any more than it is possible to reconstruct Paul's itinerary at this point in his life; there are not enough references to decide the matter absolutely.   We have followed the view that 1 Timothy was written before Titus, though some writers opt for the converse.   All that is clear from the historical allusions in the Pastorals is that 2 Timothy is the last to be written.

(3) Paul would be sent to Rome to stand trial, for his crime was alleged to have been committed there. The great fire of Rome, supposedly the work of Nero himself, took place on the night of July 19, AD 64. According to the well-known narrative of Tacitus,[40] Nero laid the blame of the fire upon the Christians to divert suspicion from himself, and inflicted the most atrocious punishments upon them. The persecution at first affected only the Christians at Rome, but was afterward extended to Christians in the provinces. Professing the Christian faith was made criminal.[41] In Rome this second time, Paul was thrown in prison. No longer a person charged with matters of Jewish Law, he was treated as a common criminal (2 Timothy 2:9). His Asiatic friends avoided him (2 Timothy 1:15) except Onesiphorus, who sought Paul out and was not ashamed of his chains (2 Timothy 1:16). Demas, Crescens, and Titus had, for various reasons (2 Timothy 4:10) left him.[42] Tychicus had been sent to Ephesus. Of his usual companions, only Luke remained. Under these circumstances, Paul writes 2 Timothy. Timothy is most likely at Ephesus.[43] Tychicus carries the letter (2 Timothy 4:12). Paul urges Timothy to come to him before winter (2 Timothy 4:21), i.e., the next winter after the one he spent in Nicopolis (Titus 3:12). As Paul writes from prison this time, he is expecting execution. How different from his expectations at the close of the first imprisonment. He is brought before the authorities and makes his first defense (2 Timothy 4: 16,17). During his final year, Nero was absent from Rome, being in Greece, and so would not have tried Paul in person. Thus would be explained the notice in I Clement (see above) that Paul was tried before the "prefects." 2 Timothy dates from after Paul's first trial. We date it AD 67 (before the winter of AD 68).

5. After the writing of 2 Timothy, as far as Paul's life is concerned, we must turn to tradition. That he underwent execution by sword is the constant tradition of antiquity, and agrees with the fact of his Roman citizenship, which would exempt him from torture. The traditions on Paul's death are:

---

[40] *Annals* XV.44.

[41] See Tacitus, Sulpitius Severus, and Orosius. It is probable the frequent allusions to perse-cution and suffering in 1 Peter (2:12, 3:16, 4:1,12-16, 5:8,9) refer to this general persecution.

[42] Titus, who was in Crete when Paul wrote to him, rejoined Paul and was then sent to Dalma-tia. At least, we hope this journey was made at Paul's direction, rather than that Titus apostatized.

[43] The evidence that Timothy is still at Ephesus is this: in 2 Timothy 2:17 we find Hymenaeus stigmatized as a teacher of error, and he can hardly be other than the Hymenaeus of 1 Timothy 1:20. Now 1 Timothy was addressed to Ephesus; therefore, so is 2 Timothy. Again, one Alexander is mentioned in 2 Timothy 4:14, and seems to be the same as mentioned in 1 Timothy 1:20.

a) Clement of Rome is most provokingly indefinite.

> "Paul, after many sufferings, having come to the boundary of the west, and having testified before the prefects, so departed from this world." I Clement 5

b) Dionysius of Corinth (AD 170) tells us Peter and Paul both taught in Italy, suffering martyrdom there at the same time. Ap. Eusebius ii.25.

c) Caius (Gaius) of Rome tells us that the "trophies[44] of those who founded the Church of Rome (i.e., Peter and Paul) may be seen both at the Vatican and on the Via Ostia."[45]

d) Tertullian (quoted by Eusebius) tells us Nero was the first emperor to persecute Christians, that he was led on to the slaughter of the apostles, that Paul's head was cut off at Rome itself, and Peter in like manner was crucified in Nero's reign.   Eusebius adds this narrative is confirmed by the inscription (*prosresis*) still extant on their respective tombs at Rome.

e) Eusebius

He adds to the above testimony that Paul, having preached the gospel from Jerusalem to Illyricum, at last suffered martyrdom at Rome, under Nero, and quotes Origen as his authority.

Also in *Chronic. Apos.*, under *Anno Abrah.* 2083 (AD 67), Eusebius says Paul suffered martyrdom in the 14th year of Nero's reign.[46]

f) Jerome (see above) says Paul was martyred in Nero's 14th year.

g) Tradition even has it that June 29 was the date of Paul's martyrdom (though this date may be right or it may be wrong).

6. Summary notes on the date and place of writing of the Pastorals:

1 Timothy – written about AD 65, from Macedonia.
Titus – written about AD 66, from Asia Minor.
2 Timothy – written about AD 67, from Rome.

---

[44] "Trophies" may mean "churches," "monuments," "bones," etc.

[45] Ap Euseb. ii.25.

[46] Zahn, *Introduction*, V.2, p.78. The 14th year extended from October AD 67 to October 68.

V. OCCASION OF THE WRITING OF THE PASTORALS

A. 1 Timothy

The epistle declares its own occasion. The apostle had left Timothy in charge of the Ephesian church, and though he hoped to return soon, was apprehensive that he might be detained longer than expected. He therefore dispatched these written instructions to Timothy.

B. Titus

Titus had been left to work as evangelist on the island of Crete. This letter was written to instruct Titus in his work.

C. 2 Timothy

The immediate occasion seems to have been that Paul was anxious that Timothy come to him in Rome, bringing Mark. Paul wanted to see Timothy once more before his execution.

VI. PURPOSE OF THE WRITING OF THE PASTORALS

Generally, Paul is coming to the end of his life. He realizes he will not have many more years to serve. He is an old man (about as many years old as the year AD you are talking about). He wishes to have these regulations written down for all time. Two broad concerns seem to permeate all three letters: 1) Personal words of encouragement and exhortation are offered to Timothy and Titus, Paul's converts (he calls each of them "my son"[47]) and fellow workers, concerning the imperative of continuing to make a stand against false teaching. 2) The instructions concerning "how to behave in the church of God" contained in the letters are intended as much for the churches in Ephesus and on Crete as they are for Paul's fellow laborers.

The purpose of 1 Timothy seems to be to encourage Timothy and to give instructions[48] to the church, both about the heresies faced and about the government of the church itself.

---

[47] 1 Timothy 1:2, 2 Timothy 1:2, Titus 1:4.

[48] The letters may be addressed to certain individuals (Timothy, Titus), but there is evidence the church as a whole also was addressed. This conclusion is based on the fact that the "you" in the benediction of each letter is plural (1 Timothy 6:21; 2 Timothy 4:22; Titus 3:15).

The purpose of 2 Timothy was to give final counsel and instruction to Timothy, to urge him to continue to suffer (with Paul) for the gospel, and to insist that Timothy pass the gospel on to faithful men who will be able to teach others also. It is an instruction to make provisions for future generations to know the gospel message.

The purpose for the letter to Titus was to instruct Titus respecting the duties he was to perform among the Cretan churches, particularly the appointing of elders over these churches and the combating of false teachers.

These letters were written not because Timothy and Titus were weak, but to give an apostle's weight to their instructions. Paul wasn't asking Timothy or Titus to change. He was asking the people to accept the preaching and leadership and guidance of Timothy and Titus.

> The question might be raised why Timothy should need information concerning the qualifications of elders and deacons, the warning against false teaching, as well as the other material concerning Christian conduct and church organization. Timothy had been associated with Paul for many years, having met him more than fifteen years prior to the writing of this epistle. Timothy had been under Paul's direct guidance most of this time. Why then, it may be asked, was it necessary for Paul to send Timothy the basic information we find in the Pastoral Epistles. This is not evidence of Timothy's ignorance, but rather of the deeper significance of these epistles. They were sent not just for the instruction of Timothy, nor to grant him written assurance of his authority and the content of his message. They were sent with the whole church in mind, that they might know that what the young evangelist was teaching had apostolic authority behind it. This epistle is important not only to the church at Ephesus, but to all churches throughout the generations of time. Paul was presenting the duties of Christian leadership, the duties of the church, the duties of the followers of Christ that are to be observed until the end of time.[49]

Weakness of the church, not on the part of the evangelists, calls forth these letters.

VII. CONTENTS OF THE LETTERS

1 Timothy and Titus contain practical instructions concerning the doctrine, polity, and life of the churches.

2 Timothy contains encouragement to Timothy under the new danger which had come upon the church through the spreading Neronian persecutions, a brief statement of his present conditions, an entreaty to Timothy to hasten to Rome,

---

[49] Adapted from Lewis A. Foster, *1964 Standard Lesson Commentary*, p.344.

and instructions to Timothy about how to carry on after Paul is dead.

> The two letters to Timothy contain Paul's last charge, his dying wishes to the son of his love, who knew so well his mind, his very thought and aspiration. We may well conceive that almost every thought in these letters, every charge, every exhortation, was a reminiscence of some bit of public teaching already well known to Timothy, of some solemn conversation between the master and the pupil, of some grave counsel in which Paul and his trusted pupil and friend had shared. These two letters were the old master's last words, and as the master wrote, or more probably dictated them, he was conscious of this, and strove to compress into the necessary short compass of a brief epistle a summary of what he had already put forth as his teaching on the question of church doctrine, church order, and church life. This is the reason why the charges concerning the life to be led are so repeated, but at the same time so brief; why the directions respecting church order are so concise; why the doctrinal statements are simply urged, and never, as was his old custom in some epistles, argued out and discussed. "We see here," as one has eloquently described it, "rather the succession of brilliant sparks than the steady flame; burning words indeed, and deep pathos, but not the lower of his firmness, as in his discipline of the Galatians – not the noon of his bright warm eloquence, as in the inimitable psalm of love (I Cor. 13)."[50]

VIII. CRITICAL PROBLEMS

For over seventeen centuries, the Pastoral Epistles were believed to have been written by Paul, and in all the churches the letters were received among the divinely inspired Scriptures of the New Testament canon. Beginning about 1800, the genuineness of the Pastoral Epistles has been attacked by negative higher critics.[51] The arguments presented by the negative critics can be summarized under four points: historical arguments, theological arguments, ecclesiastical arguments, and literary arguments.

A. **Historical Arguments** adduced against the genuineness of the Pastorals.

1. The fact that the events alluded to in the Pastorals do not fit into the account in Acts (see above) has been used as an argument against the Pauline authorship of the Pastorals.

---

[50] Adapted from H.D.M. Spence, *The Epistles to Timothy* in Layman's Handy Commentary, (Grand Rapids: Zondervan, 1957), p.175-176.

[51] As noted earlier, Schmidt (1804), Schleiermacher (1807), and Eichhorn (1826) denied the Pauline authorship of the Pastorals. F.C. Baur (1835) and the Tubingen School took the matter further. They concluded that of the letters that carry Paul's signature in our New Testaments, only four were genuine (1 and 2 Corinthians, Galatians, and Romans). Holtzmann (1880) then produced a thoroughgoing rejection of the Pauline authorship of the Pastorals, as did Harrison (1921) in his well-known book, *The Problem of the Pastorals*.

2.   "Let no one look down on your youthfulness" (1 Timothy 4:12) has been used as a historical argument against the genuineness of the Pastorals.   Supposing Timothy to have been about 20 years old when Paul took him for a companion (2nd missionary journey, AD 51-54), he would be 34 or 35 years old when Paul addresses him as a "youth" in 1 Timothy.   In Jewish thinking, a man was "young" until he reached the age of 40, at which time he became an "elder."   It is argued that age 35 would be too young to be given responsibility as the evangelist for a church like Ephesus.   At such an age, a church officer, whose duty was to rebuke elders, would be liable to be slighted and set aside for his youth unless he comported himself with irreproachable modesty and gravity.

3.   The existence of churches on Crete is said to show a later time than Paul for the Pastorals.   Since nowhere in Acts is there any mention of the founding of churches on Crete, this letter is said to present an anachronism.   But what might be the origin of the Cretan churches?   While Paul touched the island several times, he apparently was never there long enough to found any churches.   So it is probable churches were on Crete before Paul got there.   Yet this is no argument against the Pauline authorship of the Pastorals; no one has ever said Paul founded all the churches in the Roman Empire, nor that he could address a letter only to those he personally founded.[52]   We find no objection to the hypothesis someone else planted the churches on the isle of Crete.   Many believe the Cretan churches were founded by men who heard the gospel elsewhere, and then returned to Crete; e.g., Cretans were present at Jerusalem on the Pentecost birthday of the church (Acts 2:11).   Paul would not be overstepping the bounds of his authority if, as an apostle of Jesus, he were to supervise and direct churches he had not planted.   The authority of an apostle was not limited to certain local congregations; it was universal in scope.   We have no way of knowing whether any apostle other than Paul ever visited the Cretan churches before Paul visited them toward the end of his life.   In some commentaries on Titus, the instruction to "set in order" the churches (Titus 1:5) has been used to prove no apostle was there before Paul, otherwise "the churches would have been organized."   Students of the New Testament must be careful about such statements.   Did an apostle have to be present before a church could be "organized"?   If so, how are churches to be "organized" after the last apostle of Jesus is dead?   Did elders and deacons have to be appointed before a church could be called "organized"?   We have the suspicion that already accepted notions of what church polity ought to be have influenced some of the comments made on certain verses in the Pastorals.

4. The planned trip to Spain (Romans 15:24,25) does not match the historical notes found in the Pastorals.   Since the Pastorals do not reflect a trip to Spain, it is argued someone other than Paul must have written the Pastorals.   But did Paul

---

[52] Paul founded neither the church at Rome nor at Colossae, yet he wrote letters to both.

ever make his planned trip to Spain?   The affirmative evidence is given above under "Time and Place of Writing."   But remember, the evidence he did go to Spain is traditional, and traditions are not always correct.   Those recording these traditions were not Holy Spirit-inspired writers, kept free from error as they wrote.

Three alternative answers have been suggested to the question "Did Paul ever get to Spain?"   (a) Paul went to Spain immediately after his release from the first Roman imprisonment, and then came to Crete, to Ephesus, then to Macedonia (as the historical allusions in the Pastorals suggest).   Assuming Paul's first confinement at Rome terminated in the spring of AD 63, and that he immediately, according to his original intention (Romans 15:24), went to Spain, we may assign two years to his visit to Spain, and possibly to Britain, and place his return to Cadiz in the early spring of AD 65.   He proceeded thence to the scene of his former labors, Macedonia and Asia Minor.   (b) Paul went to Crete and Ephesus and Macedonia first, then went to Spain, and from there he returned to Asia Minor and Macedonia before being arrested and returned to Rome.[53]   (c) Paul went to Crete and Ephesus and Macedonia, *and did not go to Spain*.

The evidence adduced that Paul never got to Spain includes: (i) Paul's plans, as expressed in the Prison Epistles, indicate an expectation of going to Macedonia (Philippi) and Asia Minor (Philemon) when he is released.   The Prison Epistles do not indicate (as the earlier Romans letter did) that Paul hopes to go to Spain.   Perhaps the Roman imprisonment changed his mind.   (ii) The historical records know of no churches in Spain at this early period (AD 60-100).[54]   The key objection to the idea Paul never went to Spain is this: the traditions, especially the statement in I Clement, are difficult to harmonize with such an idea.   Clement wrote 30 years after Paul's alleged trip to Spain.   If Paul never went to Spain, how did the tradition get started that he did?[55]   While this commentator doubts Paul went to Spain, he admits it is not completely outside the realm of possibility.

In any case, we have studied the historical arguments often alleged to prove that Paul could not have written the Pastorals, and we have found none of them to be of more weight than the internal evidence in the letters, or the testimony of the church for centuries.

---

[53] So says Thiessen, *Introduction to the New Testament*, p.257.

[54] Other explanations are offered for the absence of any historical record of churches in Spain. The lack of information may reflect the paucity of the historical records.   Or perhaps Paul met with no success in his efforts to plant churches in Spain, if indeed he did get there.

[55] Those who deny a "Spanish Crusade" contend the tradition initially arose, not from historical knowledge of such a trip, but simply from a reading of the Roman letter in which Paul expressed his intentions of going to Spain (Romans 15:24).   Later writers, who continued the tradition, simply repeated what they read in earlier sources without checking the historicity of those sources.

B. **Theological Arguments** adduced against the genuineness of the Pastorals.

1. Heresies of a date later than the period included in Paul's lifetime are allegedly combated in the Pastoral Letters, therefore indicating someone later than Paul wrote them. The negative critics assert the Pastorals controvert 2nd century Gnosticism, especially Marcionism. Marcion was expelled from the Roman church in AD 144; hence, the Pastorals must have been written not earlier than AD 150. If true, Paul could not have been the author. To support the view that whoever wrote the Pastorals is combating the views of 2nd century Gnostics, six points are usually emphasized: (a) The "genealogies" (1 Timothy 1:4; Titus 3:9) are said to be the 2nd century Gnostic "aeons" which emanate from the bosom of God. (b) The "fables" or "myths" (Titus 1:14) represent 2nd century Gnostic speculations. (c) The ascetic practices against which the author issues a warning when he condemns the views of those who forbid marriage and who enjoin abstinence from certain foods (1 Timothy 4:3) point to Marcion, who practiced the strictest asceticism, revolting from marriage, meat, and wine. (d) The denial of a physical resurrection (2 Timothy 2:18) was a feature of 2nd century dualism. (e) The affirmation that *all* Scripture is inspired and useful (2 Timothy 3:16), and that there is only *one* God (1 Timothy 2:5) cannot fail to remind one of Marcion, who rejected all the books of the Old Testament and drew a sharp antithesis between the merely *just* Jehovah of the Old Testament and the *gracious* God of the (i.e., of Marcion's mutilated edition of the) New Testament. (f) That the "very title of Marcion's book" (*Antitheses*[56]) is found in 1 Timothy 6:20 clinches the argument. Surely one who mentions the title of the work of an author who flourished in the *2nd* century cannot have been Paul, who died in the *1st* century.

Indeed, it is strange that this six-point argument which has been so often and so ably refuted is still repeated by some, either in whole or in part, as if it contained a considerable element of value. The answers are simple. (a) The "genealogies" are clearly Jewish[57] in character. Nowhere in Gnostic literature is the term "genealogy" used as a synonym for "aeon." Further, Marcion does not speak of aeons; this confuses his teaching with that of Valentinus. (b) The "fables" and "myths" are definitely called "Jewish" (Titus 1:14). It simply is not fair to equate them with the vagaries of 2nd century Gnosticism. (c) Paul also warned against similar ascetic tendencies in Colossians 2:16-23. Must we conclude that Colossians also belongs to the 2nd century? We readily agree that 1 Timothy 4:3 warns against ascetic Gnosticism, but Marcion wasn't the first or only Gnostic! One of the heresies faced in the latter half of the 1st century AD was quite possibly

---

[56] The Greek word *antitheseis* is translated "opposing arguments" in the NASB of 6:20.

[57] The false teachers referred to in the Pastorals certainly had a *Judaistic* strain in their teaching (see for instance, 1 Timothy 1:7, 4:3; Titus 1:10-14, 3:9). In contrast to this, the Gnostic teachers of the second century were strongly *anti*-Judaistic.

incipient Gnosticism. But note the word "incipient"; it was not the full-blown variety encountered in the 2nd century AD.[58] (d) Denial of a physical resurrection is as "old as the hills." As above, we may agree that this refers to a well-known Gnostic error without agreeing that it speaks of Marcion's particular brand of Gnosticism. (e) When we read the passages to which reference is made in light of their own specific contexts, it becomes clear that when the author speaks of *one* God, he is not contrasting a New Testament God with an Old Testament "demiurge." Neither is he placing the Old Testament in antithetical relationship to the New when he uses the expression "*all* Scripture." Rather, he is contrasting the wrong with the right *use* of Scripture. (f) Surely, a merely verbal coincidence cannot do duty as a convincing argument with respect to authorship.

In addition to what has been said in answer to the arguments of the critics, note the following: (1) It is increasingly recognized today that Gnosticism did not simply emerge full-blown in the 2nd century; it had origins much farther back in history. Gnosticism is not an organically unified system, but is instead a speculative religious syncretism or accretion made up of elements drawn from Platonic philosophy, Oriental mysticism, Cabalistic Judaism, and Christianity. Hence, though it is certainly true that the heresy condemned in the Pastorals had certain traits in common with 2nd century Gnosticism, this by no means identifies the two.[59] (2) The teaching in the Pastorals is best understood as marking a state of transition between Judaism and Gnosticism as the chief foe of Christianity. There are still traces of the Jewish religious influences (1 Timothy 1:7, 6:4,5; 2 Timothy 4:4; Titus 1:14, 3:9). But we also find traces of the beginnings of Gnosticism. (3) Even Baur confessed, after examining Paul's farewell discourse to the Ephesian elders (Acts 20:29,30), "Here we see the Apostle anticipating just

---

[58] The various kinds of false doctrines and heresies counteracted in the later New Testament books differ widely from those which the church of the 2nd century had to struggle. In the New Testament books we find the seeds, but only the seeds, of the later Gnostic doctrines. Dean Alford in his *Prolegomena to the Pastoral Epistles* has well-painted the development of heresy in the early days of Christianity. In Paul's first two groups of letters (Thessalonians, Corinthians, Galatians, and Romans) the principal enemies of the church were "Judaizers." The false teachers against whom Paul warns in his last two groups of letters (Prison and Pastoral Epistles) seem to have held a position intermediate to Christianity's former Judaizing adversaries and the subsequent Gnostic heretics. The general characteristics of the heresies spoken of in the Pastoral Epistles certainly would *not* appear to belong to a period after the destruction of Jerusalem, AD 70.

[59] Paul opposes a form of incipient Gnosticism as early as the writing of Colossians. The error of the 19th century higher critics was their belief that *no* Gnostic ideas existed until the middle of the 2nd century. Today it is generally acknowledged that Gnostic ideas had already penetrated the Jewish religion before the advent of Christianity. But in his book *Pre-Christian Gnosticism*, Edwin Yamauchi has demonstrated that there is no evidence of a complete pre-Christian Gnostic system. Two older but still readable sources are Hort, *Judaistic Christianity*, p. 113ff, and Lightfoot, "Additional Notes on the Heresy Combated in the Pastoral Epistles," in *Biblical Essays*, p. 411-418.

what we find more in detail in the Pastoral Epistles."[60]   (4) More attention needs to be paid to the kind of "heresy" already introduced in Colossians (the same general geographical area where Ephesus was located). Instead of looking for affinities between the Pastorals and 2nd century Gnosticism, a more fruitful study would be the affinities between the heresy attacked in the Pastorals and that refuted in Colossians. One can make a list of the errors or tendencies that characterized the false teachers in Ephesus and Crete,[61] and then compare this list with the errors and tendencies of the Colossian heresy.[62]   There are more similarities in the Pastorals to the Colossian heresy than to 2nd century Gnosticism.

2. A second theological argument raised against Pauline authorship is the writer's method of dealing with false teachers and their doctrines. It is claimed to be different in the Pastorals than in the ten acknowledged letters of Paul. (a) Appeal is made to 1 Timothy 1:3,4, 4:3, and 6:20, wherein it is noted that Paul's attack against false teaching is somewhat generalized. (b) In the acknowledged epistles, Paul attacks false teaching step by step, giving specific refutation to each false teaching and answering objections he anticipates the readers might have.

A rebuttal of the claim of alleged differences in dealing with false teaching includes these points: (a) Consider the destination and purposes of each of the letters before declaring some to be un-Pauline. In the ten acknowledged epistles, Paul can also be very general when laying down principles that must be applied to the individual situation. (E.g., Romans 16:17, 2 Thessalonians 3:6, and the well-known passage in Philippians 3:17,18.) When the acknowledged Epistles contain the same things found in the Pastorals, they cannot be used as proof of the non-Pauline authorship. (b) The instructions in the Pastorals were not corrections of Timothy or Titus, but of the people to whom these evangelists preached. The evangelists were to apply the teaching to each situation they met. Acts 20:17ff is another example of Paul's personal communications with leaders of a church. In his address to the Ephesian elders, we see no long argumentation against false teaching. Paul simply mentions what he has already taught and expects them to recognize and withstand the error when it comes. That is exactly what we find in the Pastorals, which are also "personal" communications. (c) We would expect Paul to give general instructions in these brief Pastorals. Details

---

[60] Of course, Baur goes on to dismiss Acts 20 as having been written "post eventum."

[61] In addition to the "similarities to Gnosticism" given above, other tendencies and errors of the false teachers combated in the Pastorals include: a concern for the Law or a Jewish orientation (1 Timothy 1:7; Titus 1:10,14, 3:9); a tendency toward argument, controversy, and speculation (1 Timothy 1:4,6, 6:4,20; Titus 1;10, 3:9; 2 Timothy 2:14,16,23); immorality (1 Timothy 1:19,20; Titus 1:15,16; 2 Timothy 2:16,19, 3:6ff); deceptiveness (1 Timothy 4:1-3; Titus 1:10-13; 2 Timothy 3:6ff); and using religious teaching positions for making money (1 Timothy 6:5; Titus 1:11; 2 Timothy 3:2,4).

[62] Three elements are often identified in the Colossian heresy: A Jewish element (Colossians 2:16,17), a speculative (Gnostic?) element (Colossians 2:8), and an ascetic element (2:18-23).

concerning each false teacher or false doctrine can be accessed in the appropriate acknowledged epistle and applied to the present need. This is the same kind of application Timothy or Titus would have made to their own situations. (d) The Pastorals also contain some very specific instructions – especially in regard to the qualifications of elders and deacons, in regard to church polity, in regard to the reason women should not teach men, and in regard to the rationale for prayer.

3. A third theological argument made by negative critics is the claim that certain slight variations in theology can been ascertained when the Pastorals and Paul's acknowledged epistles are compared. (a) Attempts have been made to show certain terms are used in a non-Pauline way. (1) "*Faith*." It is asserted that "faith" is used in the Pastorals in an objective sense but is elsewhere used by Paul only in the subjective sense. Yet this assertion is inaccurate since Paul speaks of objective faith in his generally accepted epistles (e.g., Romans 12:6). Further, "faith" is used in two ways throughout Scripture: objectively – meaning a body of doctrine, and subjectively – speaking of personal trust or belief in the body of doctrine. If the word naturally has two different meanings, cannot any writer use the one the context calls for? (2) "*In Christ*." Easton raised this objection, stating the writer of the Pastorals does not "seem to use the important phrase *en Christo* ('in Christ') in the mystical way Paul does."[63] But just what is meant by "mystical way"? Being "in Christ" is rather synonymous with "being a Christian," and thus able to benefit from what Jesus did on Calvary and in His mediatorial activities. And it is difficult to see any difference between 2 Timothy 1:13 and Colossians 1:4; both speak of "faith ... in Christ Jesus." (3) "*Holy Spirit*." Easton thought the infrequent reference to the Spirit or His work in the Pastorals indicated the Holy Spirit "meant little to [the author of the Pastorals]."[64] But if "infrequent reference" is a valid criterion, we would have to reject Paul's authorship of Colossians and 2 Thessalonians (where the Spirit is mentioned but once) and Philemon (where He is not named at all). (4) "*Tradition*" ("passing the tradition on"). This objection rests on the words used in the various epistles. In the acknowledged epistles, Paul uses the verbs "received" (*paralambano*) and "delivered" (*paradidomai*) for the "traditions" he received from the Lord and handed on. In the Pastorals (1 Timothy 6:20; 2 Timothy 1:12,14), the term used is "deposit" (*paratheke*). But must this change of terms require a change of authors? Certainly not. The emphasis in the Pastorals is that the gospel (the "deposit") is to be passed on to others. And perhaps the word "deposit" is deliberately used because it agrees with the figure introduced by the word "guard"? (5) The eschatology of the Pastorals is said to be different than that of Paul's acknowledged letters. In the earlier epistles of

---

[63] Burton S. Easton, *The Pastoral Epistles* (New York: Scribners, 1948), p.12.

[64] Easton, *op. cit.*, p.22.

Paul, it is said Paul taught the "imminent return of Christ." But in the Pastorals, the writer does not expect a soon return, but is setting a pattern for a church that was to remain for centuries. One reply might be this: In 2 Thessalonians, one of the earliest of Paul's epistles, Paul does not describe an imminent return. He pointed out such things as an apostasy and the revelation of the man of lawlessness which would have to occur before the Second Coming of Christ.

(b) Another "slight variation" put forward to support the hypothesis Paul did not write the Pastorals is that supposedly many of Paul's basic theological concepts are missing from the Pastorals. (1) *The conditions of salvation.* It is asserted that instead of "faith" being the condition for justification, the Pastorals place an undue stress on "good works." Answers: i) It is true the Pastorals contain no detailed exposition of the doctrine of salvation through obedient faith in Jesus Christ, apart from works of the Law. Nevertheless, that doctrine is clearly stated in more than one passage[65] and is assumed throughout.   ii) It is difficult to identify any term or concept that is found in all of Paul's letters. For example, such a "Pauline doctrine" as familiar as "justification" is found only in five of his signed epistles (Romans, 1 Corinthians, Galatians, 1 Timothy, and Titus). iii) The truth is that the doctrine of salvation taught and presupposed in the Pastorals is clearly the same as that taught in the ten acknowledged Pauline letters:

- The redeemed (the "elect") have been chosen from eternity. 2 Timothy 2:10; Ephesians 1:4; 1 Thessalonians 1:4 ("His choice of you").
- Salvation is conditioned on faithfulness to the revelation given through Christ, not to an abrogated Jewish system. 1 Timothy 1:14, 6:11,18; 2 Timothy 1:9, 2:22; Titus 2:1-14, 3:4-8; Galatians 2:16, 3:15ff; Romans 1:5, 2:6-12, 3:21-24, 16:26.
- Christ is God. Titus 2:13; Romans 9:5; Philippians 2:6; Colossians 2:9.
- Christ is mediator between God and man. 1 Timothy 2:5; Romans 9:5; 1 Corinthians 8:4,6.
- Christ's purpose in coming into the world and assuming human nature was to save sinners. 1Timothy 1:15; 2 Corinthians 8:9; 1 Corinthians 15:9; Ephesians 3:8.
- The glory of God is the chief purpose of man. 1 Timothy 6:16; 2 Timothy 4:19; Romans 11:36, 16:27.

Where in all this is there a contrast in doctrine, a contrast supposedly so marked and definite that the author of the ten cannot have been the author of the three?

---

[65] See for example 1 Timothy 1:16 ("those who would believe on him for eternal life") in a context that says "Christ Jesus came into the world to save sinners"; or Titus 3:8 ("those who have trusted God") right after "justified by His grace" (Titus 3:7).

(2) *The "cross"* is another allegedly "missing theological concept" in the Pastorals, and this too is supposed to weigh against Paul's authorship. Yet "cross" is not found in Romans, 2 Corinthians, 1 and 2 Thessalonians, or Philemon. Does this prove they too are not written by Paul? (3) C.K Barrett lists *"words of great importance to Paul"* missing from the Pastorals. Barrett cites "evangelize (preach the gospel), give thanks, glory (boast), spiritual, wisdom, body, soul." Yet none of these seven words invariably occurs in all of Paul's letters.[66] After such lists are analyzed and their weaknesses pointed out, they are seldom repeated. Instead, a whole new list is submitted, and the analysis begins again.

4. A fourth theological argument against the Pauline authorship of the Pastorals is the allegation that many new terms are found in the Pastorals that are not found in the acknowledged epistles of Paul. (a) The recurring expression *"sound doctrine"* (Titus 1:9, 2:1; 2 Timothy 4:3) is singled out for attention as something quite different from the language found in Paul's acknowledged letters. The expression "sound doctrine" may be unique to the Pastorals, but the idea of doctrinal correctness is hardly unique to the Pastorals. The usual outline of Paul's letters is a two-point outline – doctrine and then practice. Certainly the acknowledged epistles of Paul expect Christians to hold an orthodox doctrine. (b) *"Faithful is the saying."* This expression, too, is found in the Pastorals but nowhere else in Paul's writings. Why? Is the only possibility the one that says Paul did not write the Pastorals? What of the possibility that Paul invented these "memorized summaries of Christian doctrine,"[67] taught them in his "preacher training school," and is (in these letters to young preachers) simply using the summaries to recall to their minds all he wanted to say?

The "theological arguments" alleged to prove that Paul could not have written the Pastorals have proven to be less than convincing.

---

[66] "Evangelize" is not found in Philippians, Colossians, 2 Thessalonians, or Philemon, and occurs only once in 1 Thessalonians. "Give thanks" is not found in Galatians, and occurs but once in 2 Corinthians, Philippians, and Philemon. "Glory" is not found in Colossians, 1 & 2 Thessalonians, or Philemon, and but once in Ephesians and Philippians. "Spiritual" is not found in 2 Corinthians, Philippians, 1 & 2 Thessalonians, or Philemon, and but once in Galatians. "Wisdom" is not found in Galatians, Philippians, 1 & 2 Thessalonians, or Philemon, and but once in Romans and 1 & 2 Corinthians. "Body" is not found in 2 Thessalonians or Philemon, and but once in Galatians and 1 Thessalonians. "Soul" is not found in Galatians, 2 Thessalonians, or Philemon, and but once in 1 Corinthians, Ephesians, and Colossians. It soon becomes rather evident such lists of "important words" do not prove much.

[67] Commentators give various explanations of the expression "faithful saying." The explanation one accepts influences his answer as to why (possibly) the term occurs first in the Pastorals. Also, the commentator's notion about who first coined these "summaries" (e.g., is Paul just quoting something already current in the church, and then perhaps not even of inspired origin?) will influence the answer given to "Why do we find them only in the Pastorals?" More will be said on these matters in the commentary below.

C. **Ecclesiastical Arguments** adduced against the genuineness of the
Pastoral Epistles.

1. One ecclesiastical argument is the charge that the Pastorals show a different
concept of church polity than Paul does elsewhere.   The higher critics have a
hidden agenda here.   They have accepted the evolutionary development theory
and are trying to make the doctrine of the church match what evolution says must
have happened.   We are told that, as the ages pass, people naturally have different
ideas about the church.   Liberal theologians feel it was not till about AD 100 that
the churches began to be so organized as to have elders and deacons.[68]   It is
argued that in the genuine Pauline epistles, there is found no trace of any such
official leaders of the churches.[69]   The Pastorals, we are told, reveal a marked
advance in ecclesiastical organization, far beyond the time of Paul.[70]   It is said in
Paul's day there was no official ministry, but when the Pastorals were written, on
the other hand, there was a rather complex organiza-tion, with salaried officials
whose qualifications had become standardized.[71]

The fact is that the form of church government disclosed in the Pastorals is
the simplest kind possible.   (a) The diaconate was certainly, in some shape or
other, coeval with the very early days of the church.   Jerusalem had men who
"served tables" (Acts 6:1-6) long before Paul went on any of his missionary
journeys – in fact, even before Paul was ever converted.   The functions of the
deacons at Ephesus (alluded to in 1 Timothy) were not substantively different
from the duties apparently performed by the "Seven" in Acts 6.   They assisted in
the almsgiving and the regulation of the church's charities, and also appear to have
preached and taught publicly (see comments on 1 Timothy 3).   (b) The presby-

---

[68] Some writers have tried to show that in the early days of the church it was "spiritual gifts" and not "leadership by elders and deacons" that was the norm.   Kasemann, for example (*Essays*, p.83ff) has urged that the Pauline concept of a church was based on the spiritual gifts, and it was not till the gifts began to pass (after the deaths of most of the apostles) that an organized leadership began to emerge.   But this view is incorrect.   There very possibly were "elders" ("teachers," 1 Corinthians 12:28) at Corinth at the same time there were spiritual gifts being exercised in that congregation (1 Corinthians 12:1ff).   There were "distributions of the Spirit" (Hebrews 2:4) at Jerusalem at the same time there were "elders" in the church (Acts 11:30, 15:6, 21:18).   Any contrast between the "charismatic" and the "leadership by elders" is at bottom simply false.

[69] It must be remembered that only Galatians, 1 & 2 Corinthians, and Romans were considered by the higher critics to be "genuine Pauline letters."

[70] Baur, for example, dated the Pastorals from the last half of the second century.

[71] It cannot be stated that "standard qualifications" for church leaders is something that developed after the apostolic age was past.   It is true the qualifications as given in 1 Timothy 3 and Titus 1 are in more detail than we find earlier.   But it is also true the first time men in the local church are given leadership responsibility, their qualifications were specifically stated (Acts 6:3, "men of good reputation, full of the Spirit and wisdom").   Can we assume anything other than when elders were first selected on Paul's missionary journeys (cf. Acts 14:23), that qualifications were given orally by Paul and Barnabas -- the same qualifications Paul now puts in writing in the Pastorals?

terate was almost a necessity for every congregation. No church could long subsist without leadership or oversight of some kind. From very early times the church had elders (Acts 11:30), an office which in a way was a natural outgrowth of the institution of elders in ancient Israelite communities.[72] (c) Paul talks about elders and deacons before the Pastorals were written. In Acts 14:23, on the very first missionary journey, Paul established churches and appointed elders. Paul was anxious to provide the new congregations with recognized leadership, even in the 40's AD. In Acts 20:17, elders from the Ephesian church met Paul at Miletus. Philippians 1:1 indicates the church at Philippi had both elders and deacons. (d) By the time he writes the Pastorals, Paul is coming down toward the end of his life. He realizes he will not have many more years to serve, and wishes to have these qualifications and regulations written down for all time. So in the Pastorals we have the qualifications specifically listed.

The Pastorals do not, as has been alleged, reflect a Monarchical Episcopate form of church government; such a form of government that is truly much later than Paul. "Monarchical Episcopate" equates to a "one ruler bishop" over a large geographical area. Some theologians have claimed that, by the time the Pastorals are written (c. AD 65), the Monarchical Episcopate is already in operation, and that even Timothy was a "bishop." (Remember the subscription assigned to 2 Timothy, "Written to Timothy, ordained the first bishop of the church at Ephesus."[73]) But there are substantive objections to the idea that Timothy was a "bishop": (a) Timothy is nowhere called an elder or bishop. And neither Timothy nor Titus is settled in any one location, working with one local church, as were elders in the New Testament times. We are not in sympathy with the idea that "evangelists" (such as Timothy and Titus were) are synonymous with "elders" ("bishops, pastors") in the early church. Nor are we in sympathy with those who call Timothy and Titus "sub-apostles" or "apostolic

---

[72] "The forms of the government of the Jewish synagogue, only slightly modified to suit the exigencies of the mixed Jewish and Gentile congregations of Christians, are evidently all that existed at the time when St. Paul wrote to Timothy and Titus. The presbyterate, not merely in name, but also in the matter of the functions assigned to the office, was clearly adopted from the synagogue, of course with such changes and modifications as the new and growing society required. The diaconate also, in some way, appears to have been derived from Jewish precedents. The very name 'Levites,' by which these inferior ministers of the church were often called, points to the origin of the 'order.' Thus Jerome (Ep.27) distinguishes them from the presbyters, speaking of the deacons as 'the countless number of Levites.' So, too, Salvian, AD 450, writes of the deacons, calling them 'Levites.' Frequently in the Councils the term 'Levite' is used as the peculiar title of the deacon." H.D.M. Spence, "The Pastoral Epistles of St.Paul," in *Layman's Handy Commentary on the Bible*, edited by Charles J. Ellicott (Grand Rapids: Zondervan, 1957), p.178,179.

[73] If indeed there were monarchical bishops while the apostles were still living, that would provide "apostolic precedent" for having a similar form of church government today. Some churches do indeed have "bishops" over each diocese, but the question remains, 'Is such a practice Biblical?' If we are Restoration people, striving to do things as the church did them in the first century, then this whole matter of church polity is a burning issue and demands careful attention.

delegates."[74]   Such titles and positions are not easy to find in the New Testament, whereas the designation "evangelist" is.   (b) That Timothy was a "bishop" in the sense of holding the Monarchical Episcopate at Ephesus is improbable, and seems inconsistent with the tradition of the long residence and death of the apostle John in that city.   If any one man would hold singular authority over the whole church, it would be an apostle, not an evangelist!

Further, a careful reading of Titus 1:5-9 shows that "elders" and "bishops" are interchangeable terms for the same office or function.   This agrees with Acts 20:20,27.   Thus, the Pastorals do not provide Scriptural evidence for a monarchical bishop.

The historical development of the Monarchical Episcopate form of church government likely occurred in this fashion.   (a) Monarchical Episcopacy began in Asia Minor.   The apostle John had been in this area.   The last of the apostles of Jesus to die, he died about AD 100. · The people would feel the lack of the "authoritative" man at the top, after the apostles had all died.   Gradually, the "bishop" was elevated over the "elder."   At first there were "bishops" (plural), but gradually one man (often a leader[75] in the largest church in the area) became the head bishop and the most influential man in the area.   (b) There is some indication that Monarchical Episcopacy grew up at different times in different geographical localities.   Clement of Rome (AD 96), who is claimed by some to be the "bishop of Rome," himself refused to be called "the bishop," and used the terms "elder" and "bishop" as synonymous.   After AD 100, Polycarp (at Smyrna) and Ignatius were bishops in the province of Asia, and the Episcopacy did grow up first in Asia Minor.   It was a congregational (not diocesan) episcopacy, where each congregation had one bishop, several elders, and several deacons.   Ignatius, writing about AD 115, urges the six churches to whom he writes to respect their "bishop"; but in his letter to the church at Rome, he does not even mention the bishop.   Irenaeus (AD 180) speaks of the bishop.   So by AD 180 we may assume the Monarchical Episcopacy was a regular thing among the churches.

All of this discussion about a monarchical bishop is far afield of the church polity reflected in the Pastorals.   Neither Timothy nor Titus is a "bishop," and the qualifications for "bishop" (elder) do not suggest a singular bishop in any area or even in any congregation.   So a 2nd century date for the Pastorals assigned by

---

[74] A lengthy presentation of the exact position held by Timothy and Titus will necessarily be part of the commentary on the respective letters addressed to them, at which time we shall give reasons for being hesitant to style these two men as "apostolic delegates" (if that term refers to a separate office somewhat less in authority than apostle but greater in authority than elder/bishop).

[75] Some church history books say it was an "elder" who became the "bishop."   Others suggest it was the preacher (the evangelist) who was elevated to the position of monarchical bishop.

many of the negative critics seems unrealistic.   Instead of the church polity of the Pastorals being an argument *against* the Pauline authorship, the polity reflected in the Pastorals is an argument *for* their antedating the early 2nd century development of the episcopal office in the church.   They are exactly what we would expect if they were written from Paul's time.[76]

2. The "institution of widows" is another "ecclesiastical argument" said to show a late date for the Pastorals.   The negative critics interpret 1 Timothy 5:9ff as a reference to an order of "deaconesses," and such an institution is supposed to indicate a date later than Paul.   It is true that in Ignatius' time, for example, an especial band of widows and virgins was set apart to the service of God and the church.[77]   However, remember that widows were taken care of by the church[78] (not the civil government), and that many women were active in the church (Acts 9:41 for example) without officially holding an authoritative position or office.   It is another whole matter whether or not there was a special "order of widows" in the apostolic churches such as we find in the post-apostolic age.   1 Timothy 5 may simply be speaking about being "enrolled on the list of those whom the church is responsible to care for" – not being "enrolled on the list of official deaconesses."[79]   Now it is also true that Paul deals with the care of widows only in the Pastorals.   But does this prove he cannot have written the Pastorals?   Recall that Paul deals with the Lord's Supper only in 1 Corinthians; no one on that basis discounts the Pauline authorship of that book.

Upon examination, the arguments against the Pauline authorship of the Pastorals drawn from "ecclesiastical" matters do not prove convincing.

D. **Linguistic or Literary Arguments** adduced against the genuineness of the Pastoral Epistles.

1. In vocabulary, the Pastoral Epistles are very similar to each other, but they are said to be entirely different from the other ten epistles traditionally assigned

---

[76] "Too great stress can hardly be laid on the vast difference which existed between the ecclesiastical organization presented in the Pastoral Epistles and that revealed to us in the Letters of Ignatius, written at the very commencement of the second century, even if we only admit as genuine the shorter form of the version of the Ignatian Epistles, or the still briefer recension of the three Syriac Letters edited by Dr. Cureton."   Spence, *ibid*.

[77] Ignatius, *Ad. Smyrn.* c.13.

[78] Acts 6 shows a concern for the widows in the early church at Jerusalem.   James 1:27, written about AD 62, also tells us that "pure religion" has a special concern for the widows.

[79] This important question is treated at length in the commentary which follows.   In 1 Timothy 5, Paul is emphasizing that if there are any family members or near relatives of the aged widows, it is the family member's responsibility (rather than the congregation's) to provide for the widows.   This is far different from the direction the post-apostolic church moved when it came to the care of widows.

to Paul. Therefore, say the critics, the Pastorals could not have been written by the same author as the ten. The argument is developed in this manner: (a) The Pastorals have a certain similarity in vocabulary, similar enough that all three are attributed to the same writer. (b) There is a certain difference, also, between the vocabulary of the Pastorals and that of the ten. P.N. Harrison, *The Problem of the Pastoral Epistles*, found 175 *hapax legomena* in the Pastorals. Not all writers agree with Harrison's totals. According to Lange, there are 81 *hapax legomena* in 1 Timothy, 63 in 2 Timothy, and 44 in Titus. *Pulpit Commentary* (p. xx-xxii) also gives a listing of words peculiar to the Pastorals. Also, there are 11 words in the Pastorals which are found only elsewhere in Hebrews. An additional 11 words are found elsewhere only in Hebrews, James, Peter, or in Luke-Acts. There are 44 words found only elsewhere in the LXX. Harrison, having compared Paul's writings, tells us that he finds 96 new words in 1 Timothy (15 new words per Greek page) – words "new" in the sense they occur nowhere else in Paul's ten letters. He finds 60 new words in 2 Timothy (13 new words per page). He finds 43 new words in Titus (16 new words per page). This is then compared to Romans, for example, where there are but 4 new words per page, and Philippians, where there are 6.2 new words per page. On such a basis, Harrison argued Paul could not have written the Pastorals.[80] (c) Another vocabulary feature the critics point to is the "frequent use of Latin words and idioms," which indicates, it is argued, that the author of the Pastorals cannot have been Paul, but must have been someone living in or near Rome.

Yet it is not difficult to show that the value of these linguistic arguments and of their ramifications has been greatly over-emphasized and over-estimated.[81] (a) Regarding the assertion of a certain similarity in vocabulary in all the Pastorals, to a certain extent we might say the very opposite is true. Of the "new" words ("new" in the sense they do not occur in the ten acknowledged letters of Paul), only a very few are found in all three Pastoral Epistles – only 9 out of 306! Hence, if dissimilarity in new vocabulary proves different authorship, something could be said for the proposition that a different author would have to be posited for each of the Pastoral letters. (b) Regarding the argument based on new words, note that even within the ten epistles of Paul there occur words and phrases which are not found elsewhere: i) In Philippians there are 54, in Ephesians and Colossians together, over 140 new words and phrases. ii) One fourth of the total

---

[80] Statistics such as these have impressed 20th century scholars, so much so, that this argument from vocabulary might be called the chief point of all the arguments given by the negative critics against the Pauline authorship of the Pastorals.

[81] Harrison's arguments have been carefully answered, point by point, by Donald Guthrie, "An Examination of the Linguistic Argument against the Authenticity of the Pastorals," in *The Pastoral Epistles: An Introduction and Commentary*, TNTC, revised edition (Grand Rapids: Eerdmans, 1990), p.224-240.

vocabulary of Romans is "new" in the sense that these words do not occur in the other nine acknowledged Pauline epistles. iii) There may be perfectly valid reasons for using different vocabulary words. *Subject matter*. The subject at hand determines to a great extent the language used. Note the difference between the technical wording in books of psychology or atomic energy v. aeronautical engineering. Compared with the subjects of Paul's other letters, church government and organization is a new subject. *Circumstances* create a change of vocabulary. *Destination* has a bearing on the use of words. Though the Pastorals are addressed to individuals, the church is in view, being spoken to through the individuals. The *interval of time between writings* will make a difference in the use of words. The four letters written from the first Roman imprisonment are comparable in terms of their differences and similarities to other epistles. There has been a four-year lapse of time between the Prison Epistles and the Pastoral Epistles. iv) Another way to meet the liberals' objections is to examine the evidence. What kind of words are these 175? 29 are found in the LXX. (Yet liberal theology will assert the language of the Pastorals is closer to the later apostolic fathers than to Paul!) 55 are found in special listings (i.e., lists of sins, false teachings, qualifications of elders, widows, lists of things not found in previous epistles. If such lists were not part of previous epistles, then this is no argument against the Pauline authorship of the Pastorals.) 32 are found in compounds, i.e., Paul had used the words separately before but now compounds them – which was a common Pauline and Hellenistic feature.   v) In each epistle, Paul uses the Spirit-inspired words which he needs in order to express his Spirit-intended thoughts regarding the specific subject with which he deals (cp. 1 Corinthians 2:6ff). (c) Regarding the frequent use of words and idioms derived from the Latin, this argument hangs by a very slender thread.   The critics are able to point to a total of no more than *two* Latin words in the three Pastorals: 2 Timothy 4:13, *membrana*, "parchments," and 2 Timothy 4:13, *phelonēs*, "cloak." To further reduce the value of this argument, Latin words also occur in those epistles which even the critics ascribe to Paul: 2 Corinthians 2:14, *thriambeuo*, "to lead in triumph," 1 Corinthians 10:25, *makellon*, "meat market," and Philippians 2:13, *praetorion*, "praetorian guard."

Importantly, the validity of the methodology used to create the statistical analyses is questionable.[82] (a) Statisticians indicate linguistic samples need a basis of about 10,000 words in order for the linguistic study to be meaningful and

---

[82] Bruce M. Metzger has effectively raised the question about the whole methodology in his "A Reconsideration of Certain Arguments Against the Pauline Authorship of the Pastoral Epistles," in *Expository Times* 70 (1958), p. 91-94.   Knight calls attention to two excellent critiques of the current use of the statistical methodology on the question of the authorship of the Pastorals. One is L.F. Clark, "An Investigation of Some Applications of Quantitative Methods to the Pauline Letters, with a View to the Question of Authorship" (Unpublished Thesis, University of Manchester, 1979).   The other is A.J.P. Kenny, *A Stylometric Study of the New Testament* (Oxford: Clarendon Press, 1986).

valid.[83]   Yet there are not that many words in the Pastorals. (b) Before starting an analysis of the Pastorals, should we not independently establish a norm, beyond whose parameters the number of deviations must go before they throw serious doubt on the common authorship of different works?   (c) The outcome of the analysis is greatly influenced by the way in which the variations are calculated. It has been shown that entirely different results would have been reached had Harrison calculated the percentage of *hapax legomena* in relation to the total number of different Greek words on a page rather than in relation to the number of pages of Greek text.[84]   Similar calculations have been attempted using varia-bles such as sentence length, or the grammatical category of the last words of sentences, or even the occurrence of the word *kai*.   Yet not one has been shown by itself alone to yield valid results when applied to works of known authorship.

2. Another variation on this argument from vocabulary against Paul's authorship of the Pastorals is to note words (common to the Pastorals and the other letters of Paul) that are said to carry different meanings in the Pastorals than in Paul's acknowledged letters.   Examples often adduced include: (a) The lack of "putting on Christ" in the Pastorals.   (b) "To take up," used in 1 Timothy 3:16 of Christ's ascension, is used in Ephesians 6:13,16 to refer to "taking up" spiritual weapons. (c) "Mediator" is used differently in Galatians 3:19,20 versus 1 Timothy 2:5.[85]   (d) Julicher has added, "According to the Pastoral Epistles, salvation is foreordained to the believer, but according to the Pauline Epistles, the individual is ordained to salvation."[86]   (e) "Letter" is used unfavorably by Paul when he disdainfully writes about some people needing "letters of commendation", but "letters" (writings) is used favorably in 2 Timothy 3:15 to refer to the Sacred Writings.[87]   *Answers to such examples*:   It is an argument from silence that Paul didn't emphasize elsewhere the things emphasized in the Pastorals.   Christianity does not teach one thing in one town and something else in another town; the doctrine and practice were to be uniform the world over.   Further, it is common for words to have more than one meaning.   Many words have both a figurative and a literal meaning; only the context will help decide the intended sense.

---

[83] George U. Yule, *The Statistical Study of Literary Vocabulary* (Cambridge: University Press, 1944), p. 281.   Bruce M. Metzger, after calling attention to Yule's findings, asserts that Harrison's use of this statistical method is shown to be faulty.   He didn't have enough data to work with to draw a legitimate conclusion.

[84] W. Michaelis, "Pastoralbriefe und Wortstatistik," ZNW 28 (1929), p.69-76.

[85] This commentator has never been able to see the point of this alleged discrepancy.   In both passages "mediator" simply means "go-between."   This function may be directed toward man in one case, and toward God in the other – but the "go-between" can certainly function both ways.

[86] What is the possibility that both ideas are true?

[87] Note that this comparison of "letters" is based on the translation found in the Authorized Version, rather than on the Greek text, where two different words for "letter" are used.

E. To put these critical matters into clearer focus, it is useful to study **whom the critics suggest may be the author of the Pastorals**, after they have rejected the Pauline authorship on the basis of one or more of the above critical arguments.

1. *Pseudonymity* is one suggestion. Pseudonymity means that someone else actually wrote the letters and used Paul's name. This is the majority view among those who reject the Pauline authorship (e.g., Dibellius-Conzlemann, Goodspeed, Barrett, Brox, and Hanson). Unless the name chosen is a fictitious name, to sign someone else's name is forgery. Since deliberate forgery is hardly compatible with Christian ethics, it is amazing to this commentator that anyone would even consider "forgery" to be a live option when it comes to books included in the canon of Scripture! There are other problems to be explained by those who would hold to the idea of a pseudonymous authorship for the Pastorals: (a) Signing someone else's name to a work apparently was something that some ancient people did, but it was not an acceptable practice in the church.[88] Are we to believe that an exception to this was made in the case of the Pastorals? (b) If we are to explain the personal allusions (e.g., the writer being the apostle to the Gentiles, the persecutions he suffered in Asia Minor, and the trials and imprisonment alluded to in 2 Timothy) as deliberate attempts to doctor the record so as to give it verisimilitude and make people think Paul really wrote it,[89] we have only compounded the ethics problem.[90] (c) To claim pseudonymity for a work certainly impinges on the whole possibility of the divine inspiration of the

---

[88] One explanation of 2 Thessalonians 2:2 ("a letter as if from us") is that someone had been circulating a letter that falsely had Paul's name on it. It was not to be accepted! In 2 Thessalonians 3:17, Paul notes that he regularly took up the pen from his amanuensis and personally penned the closing benediction to "all his letters" so there would be no doubt of the authenticity of any letter he wrote. Compare also 1 Corinthians 16:21, Galatians 6:11, Colossians 4:18, and Philemon 19 for more evidence of Paul's invariable practice. Furthermore, the person who first circulated the *Acts of Paul and Thecla* did so by claiming Pauline authorship for the document. When it was ascertained that this claim was not true, the man was excommunicated from the church. So how can anyone say that pseudonymity was an accepted practice in the church? Remember, there are documents in the New Testament apocrypha and pseudepigrapha that have Paul's or John's or Peter's name on them, but one of the reasons they are included in the apocrypha and pseudepigrapha (and not the canon) is that they were forgeries. Pseudonymity was not an accepted practice in the early church! (For a historical survey of the of the use and acceptance of pseudonymity in non-canonical writings, see Thomas D. Lea, "Pseudonymity and the New Testament," in *New Testament Criticism and Interpretation*, edited by David A. Black and David S. Dockery [Grand Rapids: Zondervan, 1991], p.533-557.)

[89] Paul did encourage people to imitate him as he imitated Christ. But can we, as some have attempted to do, use this exhortation to imitation as proof that Paul actually intended for people to falsely sign his name and include deceitful historical allusions in their fabricated letters? The very idea is preposterous.

[90] We reject the protestations of those writers who claim the early church had a different set of moral values than we do, and that for them pseudonymity was not an ethical problem. Protests or no, the question of ethics is precisely germane to this whole discussion. After all, is not the word of God (rather than majority opinion) the only source from which one gets any valid ethical standard?

work in question. One of the criteria by which the possibility of inspiration was attributed to a work was its authorship (i.e., was it written by an apostle, or by a close associate of an apostle who could have had spiritual gifts by the laying on of an apostle's hands). With all the internal and external evidence pointing to Paul's authorship of the Pastorals, and considering all the problems inherent in the hypothesis of a pseudonymous authorship, who would choose the latter?

2. Some *unknown editor* included some genuine "Pauline fragments," is another alternative suggestion to the Pauline authorship of the Pastorals. This is the view of Harrison,[91] Falconer, Easton, and Scott. This hypothesis, thankfully, has had fewer and fewer defenders as time goes on.[92] It certainly does make a great difference to us whether these letters were actually written by the apostle Paul or whether they are the work of a forger (whatever his motives were) who took some Pauline fragments and a larger mass of his own ideas and fabricated the "epistles" as we have them. What is ultimately involved is the difference between books that may be called "Scripture" and books that are intriguing pieces of literature, but not even as trustworthy as the writings of Ignatius, Polycarp, Irenaeus, or other second century writers.

3. Another suggestion is that *Luke exerted a great influence* on the vocabulary of the Pastorals. In recent years, several writers, including Jeremias and Moule, have suggested that Luke was the amanuensis who actually penned the Pastoral Epistles for Paul. This way, the Pauline authorship is not totally rejected, but at the same time both the differences in vocabulary and the similarities in theological outlook are supposedly explained. An evaluation of this hypothesis would include these observations: (a) True, a considerable number of significant Greek words occur both in Luke-Acts and in the Pastorals, but nowhere else in the New Testament. [93]   (b) At times, the amanuenses were given considerable responsibility in the writing of the manuscripts. (Compare what Silas did for

---

[91] In his 1921 work, *The Problem of the Pastorals*, he identified what he thought were five fragments of genuine Pauline material. In his 1964 work, *Paulines and Pastorals*, he has reduced the number of fragments to three (Titus 3:12-15; 2 Timothy 4:9-15,20,21a,22b; and 2 Timothy 1:1-18, 3:10,11, 4:12a,5b-8,16-19,22a).

[92] David Cook, "The Pastoral Fragments Reconsidered," JTS 35:1 (1984), p.120-131, argues against the mediating position which sees genuine Pauline fragments in the Pastoral Epistles while attributing the letters as a whole to a later author. He concludes that the fragment hypothesis is to be abandoned.

[93] One analysis found 37 words common to both the Pastorals and Luke-Acts but not found elsewhere in the New Testament, whereas, though the works are significantly longer than the Pastorals, only 62 words were common to Luke and Acts. In addition, another 37 words, rare elsewhere in the New Testament writings but common to the Pastorals and Luke-Acts, have been identified. The number 37 is impressive since it is nearly triple the number of words common to the Pastorals and any other New Testament author besides Paul.

Peter in the writing of 1 Peter.[94]) (c) This commentator has not been convinced that the differences in style and vocabulary are so great that we must appeal to some such "solution" as crediting a secretary with using his own words, rather than having the words of Paul himself in these Pastoral letters.[95]

Having examined the historical, theological, ecclesiastical, and linguistic arguments often adduced against the genuineness of the Pastoral Epistles, and having also looked at the alternatives to Paul's authorship suggested by the higher critics, we are more convinced than ever as to the Pauline authorship of these three letters. Moreover, to defend the Pauline authorship of the Pastorals is consistent with the conclusions of many other 19th and 20th century scholars.[96] Ralph Earle has summarized it neatly:

> In his volume on the Pastoral Epistles (in ICC, 1924), Walter Lock comes out emphatically for the genuineness of these letters. He notes many points of contact between the Pastorals and Paul's farewell address to the Ephesian elders (Acts 20:17-38): "The evidence of Church writers is the same as for the other letters of St. Paul." He also declared that the doctrinal background is essentially Pauline …
>
> Perhaps more significant is the fact that J.N.D. Kelly of Oxford, in his 1963 volume in "Harper's New Testament Commentaries," gives adequate answers to all the negative arguments we have noted. After a careful reappraisal of the whole situation, he concludes that the evidence "tips the scales perceptibly ... in favor of the traditional theory of authorship." J. Lowstuter wrote in the *Abingdon Bible Commentary* (p.1276) that, taken together, the evidence is favorable to the Pauline authorship.[97]

---

[94] The circumstances that led Silas to write the excellent Greek that we find in 1 Peter may not be reproducible in Paul's case. He was in the habit of using a secretary for the actual penning of his epistles, but there is precious little evidence that any secretary did for Paul what Silas apparently did for Peter. The usual reason assigned for the Silas-Peter matter is that Peter was not very proficient in Greek (see the rough Greek in 2 Peter); so Silas (a prophet) put Peter's ideas into his own good Greek. Paul, in contrast, had no such deficiency in language that Luke had to supply.

[95] Paul and Luke traveled together for nearly two decades. May we not suppose that the vocabulary each used reflected the vocabulary he often heard the other use? Furthermore, I. Howard Marshall has compared terms common to the Pastorals and the ten acknowledged letters of Paul, then compared the findings with the results of the Pastoral/Luke-Acts numbers, and concluded that the Pauline authorship is more in line with the data than would be a Lucan authorship. See *Journal for the Study of the New Testament* 10 (1981), p.69-74.

[96] In the 19th century, among those who affirmed the Pauline authorship of the Pastorals were Alford, Ellicott, Plummer, Lightfoot, Hort, and Godet. In the 20th century, the list includes Bernard, Weiss, White, Parry, Robertson, Lock, Zahn, Jeremias, Guthrie, Hendriksen, Kelly, and Fee. That said, we are hesitant to make such lists for and against a critical position, for the truth has never been determined by the number of "scholars" one can count per side. All such listings will do is give direction to sources for further study should the student feel it necessary to personally examine the arguments these scholars use to arrive at their studied conclusions.

[97] R. Earle, "1 Timothy," in *Expositor's Bible Commentary* (Grand Rapids: Zondervan, 1978), Vol. 11, p. 343.

IX. SURVEY OF TIMOTHY'S LIFE

The Timothy to whom two of the Pastoral Epistles were addressed is a man about whom we know a number of details.

Timothy grew up in either Derbe or Lystra (Acts 16:1ff)[98] in the middle of the land we now call Turkey. His mother and grandmother were Jewesses, while his father was a Gentile. Timothy, his mother, and grandmother evidently became Christians during Paul's visit to their town on what we call the first missionary journey (Acts 14:6; 2 Timothy 1:5, 3:15), about AD 46 or 47.[99] Because Paul calls Timothy "my son," we understand that Paul was the one who led Timothy to Christ; thus Timothy became Paul's "son" in the faith.

At the beginning of the second missionary journey (AD 51), Paul pays a return visit to these towns. It is then that Timothy, who already had a good reputation among the Christian brethren, begins to travel with Paul in a sort of apprenticeship relationship, learning from Paul how to be a good minister of Jesus Christ (Acts 16:3). Perhaps it was also at this time that Timothy was ordained to the ministry (1 Timothy 4:14; 2 Timothy 1:6).

From this time on, Timothy's life was closely associated with Paul's. Notices found in Acts after this time have Timothy serving in whatever capacity Paul needed. During the remainder of the second missionary journey (AD 52-54), Timothy was with Paul in Macedonia, for when Paul was sent away from Berea to Athens, Timothy along with Silas are said to have remained behind (Acts 17:14).[100] When Paul arrived in Athens, a message was sent to Timothy that he was to join Paul (Acts 17:15). Timothy came to Athens, and from there was sent to Thessalonica to strengthen the brethren there (1 Thessalonians 3:1,2). Paul went on from Athens to Corinth. While Paul spent the next 18 months at Corinth, Timothy had opportunity to rejoin the apostle, just before the writing of 1 Thessalonians (1 Thessalonians 1:1).[101]

---

[98] Perhaps Lystra was Timothy's hometown. In a passage where Gaius and Timothy are named together, only Gaius has the epithet "of Derbe" applied to him (Acts 20:4), as if to distinguish him from Timothy.

[99] In our "Chronology of the Apostolic Age" in *New Testament History: Acts*, we have dated the first missionary journey from AD 45-48.

[100] See comments in the author's *Acts* commentary concerning Timothy's travels at this point. It is suggested that Timothy remained for a short while with Luke at Philippi (Acts 16:40) after Paul and Silas left that town. We suppose he was not present in Thessalonica when Paul was required to leave that town, so Jason would not forfeit his "bond" (Acts 17:9) if Timothy should subsequently show up to continue the work with the infant congregation in that town.

[101] Timothy seems to have continued with Paul for some time in Corinth, since his name (along with that of Silas) is included in the salutation of both epistles to the Thessalonians.

Early in the beginning of the third missionary journey (which we have dated AD 54-58), Timothy was with Paul at Ephesus, from whence he was sent on a special mission (along with Erastus) to Macedonia and Corinth (Acts 19:22, 1 Corinthians 4:17, 16:10). Timothy was with Paul when he wrote the second Corinthian letter from Macedonia (2 Corinthians 1:1). He was with Paul in Corinth when he wrote the letter to the Romans (Romans 16:27). He was included among the representatives of the churches who carried the offering to Jerusalem at the close of the third missionary journey (Acts 20:4).

Paul was falsely accused and arrested during his visit to Jerusalem at the close of the third journey, and this began years of imprisonment: two at Caesarea and, after an eventful and dangerous voyage, two years of imprisonment at Rome (Acts 28:30).[102] During this first Roman imprisonment (AD 61-63), Timothy's name is associated with Paul in the various Prison Epistles (Colossians 1:1; Philemon 1; Philippians 1:1). How Timothy got to Rome – whether he accompanied Paul even through the shipwreck, or whether he was sent on ahead by an overland route – we are not informed.[103] Nor do we know whether Timothy ever got to fulfill the mission to Philippi suggested in Philippians 2:19ff.[104]

After Paul's release from the first Roman imprisonment (AD 63), Timothy is again his traveling companion until Paul left him at Ephesus to serve as their evangelist (1 Timothy 1:3). While serving in this capacity, Timothy received two letters from Paul (1 and 2 Timothy). If Timothy came to Rome as Paul requested (2 Timothy 4:9-13,21), it is possible he witnessed Paul's execution.

Nicephorus and the ancient martyrologies tell us that Timothy died by martyrdom under the Roman emperor Domitian some time before AD 96.[105]

---

[102] We suppose Timothy was present both at Jerusalem and Caesarea and witnessed what happened to Paul. We suppose Timothy also ministered to Paul, as far as possible, while the apostle was a prisoner.

[103] Shortly after Paul was imprisoned in Rome, the church at Philippi, having learned of his whereabouts, sent a missionary offering to help cover his expenses. How did they hear? Was it through Aristarchus (who did not change ships at Myra but instead went overland toward Thessalonica, his hometown, perhaps stopping long enough in Philippi to tell the brethren there what had happened to their offering and to Paul)? Did Timothy travel from Myra with Aristarchus and himself take the message to Philippi, and then subsequently go on to Rome to rejoin Paul there?

[104] In the Epistle to the Hebrews is an enigmatic note about "Timothy having been set at liberty" (Hebrews 13:23), that also may come from Paul's first Roman imprisonment (see introductory studies in New Testament Epistles: Hebrews). Some have suggested that the thing from which Timothy was "released" was the previous assignment to make a trip to Philippi, about which Philippians 2:19ff informs us. Others will explain that at some unknown place Timothy was actually imprisoned, and that it is freedom from this unnamed incarceration that Hebrews 13:23 announces.

[105] Baronius dates Timothy's alleged martyrdom in the reign of the Emperor Trajan, c. AD 109.

Timothy's personal characteristics have been inferred from several incidental notices in Acts and the epistles. He had a steadfast faith, a warm piety, an unflagging zeal, and a love for the churches as strong as that of the apostle Paul's (Philippians 2:19,20). Some have suggested a certain timidity about tackling difficult interpersonal situations in the churches (see notes at 2 Timothy 1:7). It has also been suggested that he had some lingering health problems (1 Timothy 5:23), perhaps aggravated by the stress and pressure of his leadership responsibilities in the congregations he served. Something of Paul's confidence in Timothy's watchfulness and fidelity is seen from the fact that it was Timothy on whom Paul depended to see to it that after Paul was dead, the necessary arrangements would be made so that the gospel would be passed on from generation to generation, just as Paul had taught it (2 Timothy 2:2).

X. SURVEY OF TITUS' LIFE

The allusions to Titus are not as numerous as those to Timothy.

The names of his Gentile parents (Galatians 2:3) and the hometown of Titus are not known, though it has often been suggested that he was a native of Antioch of Syria.

In spite of the fact that his case was the test by which the principle of gospel liberty would be demonstrated, for some unknown reason the name of Titus does not occur in the book of Acts, even though from Galatians 2 we know he was conspicuously present at the Jerusalem Conference (Acts 15), held in AD 51.[106] Since Luke omits his own name from Acts,[107] it has been suggested that Titus was a relative of Luke, or in some way was so close to Luke that Luke deliberately refrained from mentioning him by name.[108] How much before the date of the

---

[106] From the brief notice given us of what happened at that Conference, we learn that Paul deliberately introduced Titus as the test case, asking the apostles still living at Jerusalem what was to be done specifically in this man's case. He well knew that if they indeed demanded that Titus be circumcised, as some Judaizers insisted, then the freedom from the Law of Moses that we have in Christ would be seriously compromised. But, in harmony with what the apostles there had all along been teaching, not even Titus, though he was a Greek, was compelled to be circumcised (Galatians 2:3)!

[107] There is a resident at Corinth whose name is given as "Titius Justus" (Acts 18:7), but this man is not to be identified with "Titus" since the names are spelled differently.

[108] Titus, a Gentile, was a prominent leader of the churches among the Gentiles. Acts was written about AD 63, and in many areas the Judaizers still held positions of considerable influence. Therefore, one suggestion even has it that Titus' name is deliberately withheld by Luke from the history he recorded in Acts precisely so that the fierce hostility the Judaizers were capable of would not be unnecessarily stirred up.

Jerusalem Conference Titus and Paul became acquainted we have no way of knowing. We do know that Paul is the one who led Titus to become a Christian (Titus 1:4). Paul began his evangelistic work in Antioch about AD 42 or 43.[109]

Following the Jerusalem Conference, the next time Titus figures in the New Testament records is when Paul is at Ephesus during the third missionary journey, AD 54-58. Following Paul's unsuccessful intermediate trip to Corinth, Titus was sent to Corinth to deal with the tragic problem of immorality that was troubling the church. One gets the impression Titus was one of those rare individuals who today would be called a 'troubleshooter,' able to come to grips with difficult situations and help churches resolve them and get back to doing things in harmony with the Gospel. Titus had been sent to Corinth to help the church discipline the immoral man, and then reported back to Paul (who, in the meantime would be traveling away from Ephesus into Macedonia). When Titus did not meet Paul at Troas (did it take Titus longer to correct the problem than Paul anticipated?), Paul went on into Macedonia in hopes of meeting Titus the sooner.[110] We also learn from the notices about him in 2 Corinthians that Titus had special responsibilities in the organizing of the collection for the poor saints in Jerusalem (2 Corinthians 8:6,23; 12:18) that was to be delivered at the close of the third missionary journey.

The next we know of the movements of Titus we learn from the historical allusions in Paul's letter addressed to him on the island of Crete. These allusions make it evident that after Paul's release from his first Roman imprisonment,[111] Paul did missionary work on Crete,[112] and then left Titus there to see that elders were appointed in all the congregations (Titus 1:5). In his letter to Titus, Paul instructs him to come to Nicopolis as soon as he is relieved from his responsibilities by either Artemis or Tychicus (Titus 3:12). Whether these plans were carried out, we do not know.

---

[109] See notes at Acts 11:20ff. We have always supposed that Titus was one of the early converts at Antioch, and this is why he makes such a wonderful "test case" when it came time to go to Jerusalem concerning the whole question of the conditions of salvation that was agitated by the Judaizers who came from Jerusalem to Antioch, insisting that old Jewish laws had to be observed by the new converts to Christ.

[110] We learn these facts from 2 Corinthians 7:6-15. In all there are seven references to Titus in 2 Corinthians (2:13; 7:6,14; 8:6,16,23; 12:18).

[111] This dating of the time when Titus and Paul visited the island of Crete together is based on the conclusions reached earlier in these Introductory Studies concerning the time and place of the writing of the Pastoral Epistles.

[112] We suppose that Paul did more than simply make a brief stop at one of the island's seaports, before leaving Titus there to work with the churches on the island.

In the last New Testament letter that Paul ever wrote, we learn that Titus had gone to Dalmatia (2 Timothy 4:10). We know little about the planting of the church in Dalmatia, so we do not know whether Titus is involved here in evangelizing a new field or whether (like Crete), he was setting in order already existing churches.[113]

Tradition speaks of Titus as returning to Crete from Dalmatia, serving as "bishop" of Gortyna. Tradition also has Titus dying there in extreme old age.

XI. RELIGION IN AND AROUND EPHESUS

Evidence from New Testament references shows three or four major religious beliefs and practices flourishing in Asia Minor at the time when Christianity was introduced. There were Jews, worshipers of Artemis, Gnostics, and perhaps this early some were even beginning to worship the Roman emperor.

A. A Jewish Presence, Acts 19:1-20. For hundreds of years before Christ, Jewish people had migrated and settled in numerous lands, and had been scattered (either as deportees or refugees) all over the ancient world by persecution. Acts 18-19 reflects a Jewish presence in and around Ephesus. There was a synagogue at Ephesus (19:8), a fact that indicates a sizeable Jewish community. Acts 18:24-19:3 shows some Jews in Asia Minor were converts of John the Baptist. Some were "strolling Jewish exorcists" – i.e., Jews involved in the occult arts. (19:13ff. This is not totally unexpected, for the practice of magic was one of the features of rabbinical/diaspora Judaism.) The Judaism of Asia Minor was not classical Mosaism, but rather the rabbinical/diaspora Judaism of the first century AD. Rabbinical/diaspora Judaism, ever since the Jews' return from captivity, tended to assimilate local ideas. It changed and developed its faith and practices as history and local situations demanded. The Judaism of Asia Minor was similar in this respect. The Jews of Asia Minor, especially those of Phrygia, had assimilated much of the culture of their surroundings, so that there was a saying, "The baths and wines of Phrygia separated the Ten Tribes from their brethren."[114] Certain elements of Judaism, especially the biblical stories, were adopted by the larger society. At Apameia, coins minted in the reigns of three successive rulers showed Noah's ark. The legend above the box-like ark says "Noah"; but the two persons standing outside the ark indicate that the biblical account has been embel-

---

[113] This last note assumes that Titus went to Dalmatia because Paul directed him to go there, rather than that Titus (like Demas) had quit the ministry.

[114] Richard and Catherine Kroeger, *I Suffer Not a Woman: Rethinking 1 Timothy 2:11-15 in Light of Ancient Evidence* (Grand Rapids: Baker, 1992), p.55

lished, perhaps from the Greek flood story of Deucalion and Pyrrha. We shall have much more to say about the embellishment of narratives found in the Book of Genesis. In particular, we shall deal with the strange distortions of the story of Eve in which she becomes the one who gives life to Adam.[115]

B. Worship of the Mother Goddess – Artemis, Acts 19:23. For many years the area around Ephesus had been home to the worship of Artemis, a female deity (whose image "fell down from heaven," Acts 19:35).[116] In contrast to other parts of the ancient world, the primary deities of Asia Minor were female. The "great mother of the gods" was given many names in different parts of Asia Minor. But whether she was known as Mother of the Gods, Mountain Mother, Ma, Bellona, Cybele, Demeter, or Artemis, she was the mother of gods and men, the mistress of wild animals, the source from whom all life came, and to whose womb the dead were again gathered. The worship of that deity was not limited to Asia but had an impact over much of the Mediterranean region ("all of Asia and the world worship" Artemis of Ephesus, Acts 19:27). Extra-biblical literature agrees with Luke's assessment that the worship of Artemis was rather widespread. Religious conditions, the ancients maintained, were remarkably similar in Crete (the destination of the Epistle to Titus) and Ephesus.[117] Strabo (64/3 BC - AD 21) spoke of the intermingling of Cretan and Phrygian rites.[118] Tradition held that some of the tribal groups of western Asia Minor, such as the Carians, had originally migrated from Crete. On that island Artemis was worshipped using the same rites as in Ephesus and had been given the title "the Cretan Lady of Ephesus."[119] "The Cretans worship Artemis most religiously, calling her according to their language Britomart."[120] The Ephesian celebration of Artemis's birthday borrowed discernible elements from the older Cretan rituals honoring the birth of Zeus.[121] Ephesus stood as a bastion of feminine supremacy in religion. William Ramsay insists it was no coincidence that the virgin Mary was first called *theotokos*, bearer of God, at Ephesus, where Artemis herself had earlier borne the same title.[122] An elaborate system of magic developed upon

---

[115] *Ibid.*

[116] Each town was likely to have one or more tutelary deities (e.g., Apollo, Zeus, etc.) that were worshipped locally in addition to the worship of the mother goddess.

[117] Diodorus of Sicily 5.77.3-8.

[118] Strabo, *Geography* 10.3.7.

[119] A. Boeckh, *Corpus Inscriptionum Graecarum* (Berlin: G. Reimas, 1828-77), n.6797.

[120] Solinus 11.8.

[121] Kroeger, *op. cit.*, p. 54.

[122] William M. Ramsay, "The Worship of the Virgin Mary at Ephesus," *Pauline and Other Studies in Early Christian History* (London: Hodder and Stoughton, 1906), p. 125-159.

the *Ephesia Grammata*, the six mystic words written on the cult statue of the goddess. So not only was there an interest in magic among the Jews, but we find it among the worshippers of Artemis, also.

C. Gnosticism.

1. The Gnosticism in Asia Minor (including Ephesus) at the time the Pastorals were written was incipient Gnosticism, not the developed Gnosticism of the 2nd century AD. This is the same "Gnosticism" we meet in some later New Testament books.[123] Scholars have had difficulty finding a term to helpfully identify the ideas and trends that developed into 2nd century Gnosticism. Some use "incipient Gnosticism," while others differentiate between "Gnosis" and "Gnosticism."[124] Certain key emphases were found in Gnosticism throughout the years this heresy flourished. (a) *Aristocracy, based on pride of special knowledge.* The Gnostic claimed to be the elite, the wise, the philosopher, the privileged one to whom was revealed a secret knowledge which the overwhelming mass of mankind could never know. In the view of Gnostic believers, this knowledge was superior to faith. It was an "exclusive spirit" – 'We enlightened ones are better than you people who do not apprehend this secret knowledge.' (b) *Dualism.* It has recently been argued that Jewish (Essene) Gnosticism did not include a cosmological dualism,[125] though they evidently did hold to the antagonism between matter and spirit.[126] To the Gnostics the great question was not "What must I do to be saved from sin?" but "What is the origin of evil?" (Since a good god could not create matter or an evil world, where did the world come from?) Qumran Gnostics may still have held to the superiority of Jehovah the Creator, but the Gnostics at Colossae, as we shall see in a moment, taught the doctrine of creation by emanations (aeons, demiurges). (c) *Asceticism (or licentiousness) – the results of the heresy on personal living habits.* If matter is evil and spirit is good, what should be the Christian's attitude toward his body? Some practiced a rigid asceticism. "Touch not, taste not!" "Abstain from marriage, and be a vegetarian!" Others practiced a licentious lifestyle. 2 Peter

---

[123] A good starting place to learn about Gnosticism is R.M. Wilson, *Gnostic Problem: A Study in the Relations between Hellenistic Judaism and the Gnostic Heresy* (London: Mowbray, 1958), and Edwin Yamauchi, *Pre-Christian Gnosticism* (Grand Rapids: Eerdmans, 1973). The whole topic of Gnosticism has already been introduced above in "Part B: Theological Arguments" of our discussion of "Critical Problems."

[124] Since the congress on the origins of Gnosticism held at Messina, Italy, in 1966, scholars have tended to make a distinction between *gnosis* and Gnosticism. The former term is used for this movement before the middle of the 2nd century, the latter for its developed 2nd century AD form.

[125] The Dead Sea Scrolls evidently teach a belief in one God – the God of Israel – as the creator of all things and beings. The angelology and satanology of Qumran are basically that of Judaism. (LaSor, "Gnosticism," *New ISBE*, p. 486)

[126] LaSor, *op. cit.*, p. 485.

2 and Jude were written to communities where licentiousness was the lifestyle of the heretics. (d) *Keep it secret and esoteric.* An attempt was made to keep this "knowledge" limited only to those who were initiated into the group. The ancient devotees did such a good job keeping their beliefs secret that modern scholars have considerable difficulty learning many of the details. (e) *Attitude toward Scriptures*, which changed as the years passed. At first, Gnostics had an imperfect appreciation of what the Old Testament taught. Then there came a time of ignorance regarding the entire Old Testament scriptures. Then there arose a repudiation of and direct antagonism towards the Old Testament records.[127] Lightfoot, *Colossians*, p. 111, shows that the "ignorance" was the position of Cerinthus, and "repudiation and antagonism" was the position of the later Gnostic teachers. The first was the position of the Colossian false teachers.

2. **History of the development of the Gnostic heresy.** (a) *It was a Jewish heresy* to begin with.[128] It has been urged indeed by Lightfoot and others that the earlier forms of Gnostic error were of Jewish origin.[129] Harnack held that Greek philosophy and the Greek spirit generally had already had a modifying influence on Judaism before the time of Philo.[130] Others have found what they believe to be an even more comprehensive borrowing of religious ideas as Jewish "gnosticism" developed.

> Mansel (*Gnostic Heresies of the First and Second Centuries*, p.32) summed up the principal sources of Gnosticism in these three: Platonism, the Persian religion, and the Buddhism of India. To Platonism it owed much of its philosophical form and tendencies. From the dualism of the Persian religion (Zoroastrianism) it derived its speculations regarding the origin of evil, and much of what it taught about emanations. Zoroastrianism taught that there existed two original and independent powers of good and evil, of light and darkness. To Buddhism, Mansel believed,[131] it owed

---

[127] In its later developed form, Jehovah the creator is a demiurge or inferior person, the source of evil. Satan, as he tried to teach Eve in the Garden, was doing her a favor, enlightening her mind to the true God, rather than leaving her to know only the "god of darkness" (i.e., Jehovah).

[128] By the middle of the 2nd century AD, Gnosticism will be a Christian Heresy, and be violently opposed to anything Jewish, but it began as a Jewish heresy. Just when the ideas began to be taught and held among Jewish advocates is a disputed point. R.M. Grant offered the theory that Gnosticism did not arise until after the Jews were disillusioned by the fall of Jerusalem in AD 70, when they would be looking for something to replace their "discredited" religious hopes. Others, such as Lightfoot in a previous century and Dead Sea Scroll scholars since their discovery in 1948, have made a case for "incipient Gnostic ideas" already present in Judaism before AD 70, and likely as early as the first century BC. "The fact remains ... that something like Gnosticism is found in the Judaism of the 1st century BC and 1st century AD, and possibly earlier." LaSor, *New ISBE*, p. 486.

[129] J.H. Bernard, *The Pastoral Epistles* (Grand Rapids: Baker, 1979), p.lii.

[130] Adolf Harnack, *History of Dogma* (New York: Dover Publications, 1961), V.1, p.223.

[131] Mansel's view that Gnosticism owed a great deal to Buddhism has been strongly opposed in the scholarly literature. There is certainly some truth in what Mansel has said, though the idea of antagonism between matter and spirit could also be found in Greek philosophy of the time.

the doctrine of the antagonism between matter and spirit, and the unreality of derived existence – the germ of Docetism.[132]

(b) Gnosticism in its developed state was strongly anti-Jewish, yet at its outset "it seems to have *welcomed Jewish ideas and never ceased to employ Jewish material* in the construction of its myths."[133] (c) *The Essenes were adherents of Gnostic Judaism.* What the Essenes held and taught might be called "Judaic Gnosticism" or "Essene Judaism." Either way, the doctrines found in Essene thought (as documented by Josephus and Philo) are remarkably similar to what would later develop into Gnosticism.

> The Essenes were ascetic to an extraordinary degree; they conceived of themselves as a kind of spiritual aristocracy; they are said to have possessed an apocryphal literature, and to have practiced occult science; and they spoke of the immortality of the soul rather than the resurrection of the body, here standing in sharp contrast to the more conspicuous sect of the Pharisees.[134]

Did the Essenes have any of the legendary literature found in Judaism? *Jubilees* is thought by some to have originated in the Qumran community.[135] We will note in the commentary following that "endless genealogies" (1 Timothy 1:4) such as Timothy is to avoid are exactly what is found in the *Book of Jubilees*. The beliefs of the Essenes were not limited to a small community on the northwest shore of the Dead Sea. Bernard long ago put the matter in its correct light:

> We conclude therefore that the heresiarchs at Ephesus and Crete were Christians who were affected [by the same tendencies of thought and practice] that one finds among the Essenes. There is an additional circumstance which may be adduced to support this conclusion. Among the fragments of the literature of this period which have survived, not the least remarkable is the Fourth Book of the *Sibylline Oracles*, a curious collection of verses reciting the fortunes of the towns in SW Asia Minor, ascribed on all hands to a date about 10 years subsequent to the Fall of Jerusalem. This book – whether written by a Christian or not – has points of contact with Essenism which can hardly be due to chance. Here then we have independent evidence for the influence of Essene teaching about 80 AD in the very district which has been the subject of our enquiry. And it is certainly remarkable that the word used all through this poem for the elect or the faithful is a word which is characteristic in the New Testament of the Pastoral Epistles; they are called *eusebeis*, their habit of mind *eusebeia*.[136]

---

[132] A.M. Renwick, "Gnosticism," *New ISBE*, p.485.

[133] Ernest F. Scott, *The Pastoral Epistles* (New York: Harper, nd.), p. xxix.

[134] Bernard, *op. cit.*, p.lv.

[135] For example, see C.T. Fritsch, *The Qumran Community* (1956), p.70, 106-7.

[136] J.H. Bernard, *The Pastoral Epistles* (Grand Rapids: Eerdmans, reprinted 1980), p.lvi.

3. **Allusions to Incipient Gnosticism in the New Testament**, other than in the Pastorals. (a) *Paul's farewell address to the Ephesian elders (Acts 20:29ff)*. "I know that after my departure savage wolves will come among you, not sparing the flock; and from among your own selves men will arise, speaking perverse things, to draw away the disciples after them." The language and theme are so close to that of the Pastorals that some scholars have suggested the passage was inserted by the author of the Pastorals. Some suggest Luke is the amanuensis of the Pastorals, and so includes similar language in both. A better idea is this: what Paul predicted in AD 58 had come to pass by the time the Pastorals were written in AD 65. (b) *The Colossian heresy*. It is usual to suggest that there were several elements in the Colossian heresy: a Jewish element, a speculative element, and an ascetic element.[137] The Jewish element in the Colossian heresy (e.g., Paul speaks of legal ordinances, circumcision, food regulations, sabbaths, new moons, etc.) was not straightforward Judaism, but was rather a development of Phrygian Judaism, which had undergone a fusion with a philosophy of non-Jewish origin – an early and simple form of Gnosticism.[138] There was also an emphasis on angelic beings – not only elemental spirits but dominant ones as well, principalities and powers, lords of the planetary spheres, sharers in the plenitude of the divine essence – through whom the law was given. In keeping with their functions as mediators of the divine law, obeying the law was regarded as a tribute to these beings, and breaking the law incurred their displeasure and brought the lawbreaker into debt and bondage to them.[139] (c) *Ephesians*. "Ephesians" was a circular letter intended for all of Asia Minor; the doctrines taught therein were needed all over that province. It contains warnings about being blown about by every wind of doctrine (4:14, etc.). 1 Corinthians 16:9 speaks of "many adversaries" to Christianity at Ephesus. Hendriksen in his *Commentary on Colossians* has a tabular chart that compares the actual wording and phraseology of Colossians and Ephesians. "Of the 95 verses in Colossians, about two-thirds of them are clearly or rather clearly paralleled in Ephesians," he concludes. So there was likely little difference between the heresy at Colossae and what was believed and practiced at Ephesus. (d) *John's Gospel and letters*. Some regard John 19:34ff as a personal protest against Gnosticism. After describing the piercing of Christ Jesus' side by the soldier's spear, John tells us that he personally saw blood and water come out of the wound. This is thought by many to be a direct refutation of Docetism. The same is true of "The Word became flesh and dwelt among us, and we beheld His glory, glory as of the only begotten from the Father" (John1:14). 1 John is written in part to undermine the tendency among

---

[137] The best source to study about the beliefs and history of the Gnostic influences at Colossae is found in the introductory studies to Lightfoot's commentary on Colossians and Philemon.

[138] F.F. Bruce, "Colossians, Epistle to the," *New ISBE*, p.734.

[139] *Ibid.*

Gnostics to deny the incarnation (e.g., that a good God could not inhabit a material human body; see 1 John 4:2). 1 John also notes that many claimed "I know God," "I abide in Christ," "I am in the light," even when they did not love their brethren on earth, did not obey Christ, and were destitute of love. Their claims could not be true! That's not how Jesus taught it! And John may well have had the licentiousness found among some Gnostics in mind when he wrote "No one who is born of God [habitually] practices sin" (1 John 3:9, etc.).

There is the testimony from Irenaeus that John's Gospel was written to oppose a form of Gnosticism taught by Cerinthus and, before him, by the Nicolaitans.[140] Cerinthus, the earliest Gnostic known by name, was a contemporary of the apostle John. Early Christian literature tells us the two even met in a bath at Ephesus. Cerinthus was a Jew who seemed to have stood between the Ebionites and the 2nd century Gnostics. From the accounts that have been preserved of his teaching, Cerinthus taught that the world was created, not by the supreme God, but by an inferior power who was ignorant of the supreme God. Cerinthus also held a docetic theory of the incarnation; he taught that Jesus was not born of a virgin, but was the son of Joseph and Mary, born after the manner of other human children. Cerinthus taught that at Jesus' baptism, the Divine Christ descended on the human Jesus, and before His crucifixion, the Divine Christ left, leaving only the human Jesus to die. In addition, he held there would be a thousand years of unrestrained sensuality. (e) *Evidence from the Book of Revelation.* Revelation 2:12ff – Some at Pergamum held the teaching of Balaam, which included worship of idols and fornication, and they "also have some who in the same way hold the teaching of the Nicolaitans." Irenaeus tells us the Nicolaitans were a form of Gnosticism. However, this verse is difficult. The matter in dispute is this: were the Nicolaitans a separate sect, or were the terms "Balaam" and "Nicolaitans" used interchangeably? "Thus you also" may mean "just like Ephesus had Nicolaitans" (Revelation 2:6), so also did Pergamum. Or "you also" in Revelation 2:15 may mean that "the teaching of Balaam" (verse 14) and "the teaching of the Nicolaitans" are the same thing. Mansel (p. 71) and others believed the Nicolaitans were antinomian Gnostics of the licentious type.[141] Some 'secret' rewards ("hidden manna") were promised to overcomers (verse 17). Revelation 2:6 – At Ephesus was something similar to Pergamum. "You hate the deeds of the Nicolaitans," just as Christ does. Revelation 2:8,9 – Smyrna had its "synagogue of Satan," made up of people who say they are Jews and are not. Revelation 2:18ff – Thyatira had that Jezebel of a woman, a false prophetess who taught licentiousness and participation in idol feasts. People there were involved in the "deep things of Satan" (verse 24). As time went on,

---

[140] Irenaeus, *Against Heresies*, Book I, Chap.26.

[141] A.M. Renwick, "Gnosticism," *New ISBE*, p. 488.

the Gnostics made greater and greater claims for themselves. A favorite claim was that they alone "knew the depths," and the Ophites in particular claimed this. According to Jesus, the depths which they knew were not of God, but were rather "the deep things of Satan," because their works were evil.[142] Revelation 3:7 – Philadelphia is told that Jesus (not the Gnostics) has the key of David. Is this an attack on the exclusivity of the Gnostics? Again, Jewish people are called the "synagogue of Satan." Revelation 3:14ff – In the letter to Laodicea it is their pride (aristocratic attitudes?) that is attacked. One may conclude, without too much information to the contrary to be explained away, that the problems in the churches of Asia related to the same heresy. Gnosticism was one of the most subtle and dangerous heresies ever to be confronted by Christianity. By the 3rd century AD most of the congregations throughout the Roman Empire were to some degree infected by it.

4. **Gnosticism – its completed form**, as learned from the apologists and from Gnostic literature of the 2nd century. Incipient Gnosticism was Jewish religious beliefs infiltrated and modified by Gnosticism. Second century Gnosticism is Christianity perverted by learning and speculation. The rise of Gnosticism led to the composition of some of the anti-Gnostic writings of the church fathers (cp. Irenaeus, *Adv.Haer.*, Tertullian, *Adv.Marc.*, Hippolytus, *Refutation of All Heresies*, in particular). For years, our knowledge of Gnosticism came from these writings, as the church fathers characterized the false teaching they were writing against.[143]

> The letters of Ignatius, written a half a century later [than the Pastorals], contain warnings against the strange doctrines then spreading in the cities of Asia Minor, which may perhaps show us what the fruit was like of the seed which we see growing in the Pastorals.[144]

We no longer are limited to the writings of the church fathers for our knowledge of Gnosticism.

> In recent times several original Gnostic writings have been discovered such as *Pistis Sophia*, written in Coptic and discovered in Egypt. A most important find was made in 1896 when a codex containing the *Gospel of Mary*, the *Apocryphon of John*, and the *Sophia of Jesus Christ*, all of them Gnostic, were discovered in the same country. Strangely enough, [the codex] was not published until 1955.

---

[142] Renwick, *op. cit.*, p. 488.

[143] Because the apologists were writing against these heresies, some modern scholars have subtly suggested their characterizations (since they were not without "prejudice") may be overdrawn. Modern discoveries of actual Gnostic writings have shown the early Christian writers fairly presented the heresy they were trying to refute.

[144] Bernard, *op. cit.*, p.xlvi.

A more valuable discovery was made in 1945 by some peasants near the little town of Nag Hammadi in Upper Egypt. They found a large jar containing a collection of Coptic Gnostic books and documents dating from the 4th century AD. Altogether there were 48 treatises – Gnostic gospels, epistles, etc. They were found near the site of one of the monasteries founded by Pachomius ca. AD 320, at Chenoboskion, and it is suggested that instead of calling them the Nag Hammadi Library they should be called the Chenoboskion Library. This exceedingly valuable collection, with the exception of one volume, the *Gospel of Truth*, is in possession of the Coptic Museum in Cairo. The *Gospel of Truth* (tr. and ed. by K. Grobel, 1960) was the first to be published. This book is thought to be by Valentinus or one of his contemporaries. It is of great importance as it gives a clearer idea than ever before of the views of the original Valentinian Gnostics – the most erudite Gnostic sect. Hitherto only the representations of later generations of Valentinians were known among whom the views of the founder had become adulterated.[145]

Various Gnostic sects flourished by the time the 2nd century had come and gone, some more heretical than others when it came to departure from the true Christian faith. There were the Encratites, the Carpocratians, the Ophites, the Cainites, the Valentinians, the Basilideans, the Saturninians and the Marcionites, among others.[146]

D. Reflections of each of these three prevailing religious beliefs are found in the Pastoral Epistles. Once the differences between incipient Gnosticism and the full-grown Gnosticism of the 2nd century are known, it is evident the heresy reflected in the Pastorals is *not* the full-blown 2nd century kind.[147] Some passages in the Pastorals may reflect ideas learned from the worship of Artemis. Some passages in the Pastorals certainly reflect rabbinical/diaspora Judaism. And some passages in the Pastorals reflect the heretical ideas taught by incipient Gnosticism.

Passages that have been supposed to reflect some of the old religious ideas include:

---

[145] Renwick, *op. cit.*, p. 485.

[146] Each group is briefly introduced in the article on "Gnosticism" in the *New ISBE*, p.489. Also included in this article are useful summaries of the doctrines held by 2nd century Gnostics, some of which are obviously different from the doctrines held by the heresiarchs being warned about in the Pastorals.

[147] This is contrary to what many contemporary scholars attempt to demonstrate – e.g., Easton who has "Christianity ... threatened by a coherent and powerful heresy ... all the more dangerous because it claimed a revelation of divine things more profound than that set forth in the Church." His language about a "coherent and powerful heresy" is his way of saying the Pastorals are intended to combat the full-grown heresy which had not arrived on the scene of history till the 2nd century AD. See what has been said before in these notes about "incipient Gnosticism" and the "origin and development of the Gnostic heresy."

1 Timothy 1:3-7 – Timothy is warned to avoid the heterodox teachings (*heterodidaskalein*), and he is not to spend time with "myths" and "endless genealogies" which merely give rise to speculation and fruitless discussion, rather than to loving action towards other men.

There is nothing in this language beyond what could be found in Jewish Gnosticism similar to the Essene Gnosticism of Qumran and Colossae.

Gnosticism has been called a religion of rebellion. Its mythology constitutes an "upside-downing" of the Bible as we know it. The writer of 1 Timothy called for his readers to beware of "worldly and empty chatter" and "the opposing arguments of what is falsely called knowledge [*gnosis*] (1 Timothy 6:20).[148]

> What then are these 'genealogies' which the Apostle finds so unfruitful? The answer that has been most commonly given to this question of late years has been found in the peculiar tenets [i.e., the idea of emanations and the various ranks and orders of created beings, or special mystical additions to the genealogies of Genesis[149]] of the Gnostics. It has been supposed that traces of a kind of Judaistic Gnosticism may be found in the Epistle to the Colossians, that it becomes more prominent in the Pastorals, and that we see it in full vigor in the Letters of Ignatius.[150]

The mention in 1 Timothy 1:6, 6:20, and 2 Timothy 2:16 of fruitless discussions and nonsense ("worldly and empty chatter") which oppose God is interesting because Gnostic writings do indeed contain material which appears as pure nonsense. Sometimes there are long strings of repetitious nonsense syllables; sometimes there are riddles and paradoxes; and yet they conveyed significance to the initiate.[151] Many of the early Christians who engaged to refute Gnostic theology found this use of nonsense particularly

---

[148] Kroeger, *op. cit.*, p.61.

[149] See comments on the word "genealogies" in the commentary. As F.J.A. Hort (*Judaistic Christianity*, p.135ff) has pointed out, "myths and genealogies" occur in similar close connection in Polybius (IX.2.1), and that historian seems to refer to the legendary Greek mythologies, and the old world stories about the pedigree and birth of such "heroes." So, too, Philo includes under *to genealogikon* all the primitive history in the Pentateuch. We know that legends had been multiplied during the later periods of Hebrew history as to the patriarchs and the early heroes to a degree for which there is perhaps no parallel elsewhere. In the *Book of Jubilees* we have a conspicuous example of the stress laid upon genealogies as the bases upon which legends might be reared.

[150] Bernard, *op. cit.*, p. xlix. Also, see what is said above about the *Book of Jubilees* in the paragraph about the Essenes.

[151] See Patricia Miller, "In Praise of Nonsense," in *Classical Mediterranean Spirituality: Egyptian, Greek, Roman*, ed. by A. H. Armstrong, World Spirituality Series (New York: Crossroad, 1986).

exasperating.   Certainly nonsense is one of the hallmarks of Gnosticism.[152]

The charge that the false teaching involved "myths" is repeated several times in the Pastorals.   2 Timothy 4:4 is a warning that people are going to "turn away ... from the truth, and will turn aside to myths."   These "myths" are not simply pleasurable stories (like Aesop's fables); rather, they have a religious content which diverts their hearers from the truth.   In Titus 1:14 we are told they are "Jewish myths" that, if embraced, will be harmful to the soundness of a person's faith.   Likewise, 1 Timothy 1:7 seems to say the myths are presented by their teachers as being "Jewish Law," when in fact they were not, or were at best a misuse of the Torah.   These Jewish myths and stories cannot be traditional Biblical stories, for again and again the writer of the Pastorals maintains that wrong teachings like these must be combated with the use of Scripture and sound doctrine.   The norm by which truth can be discerned is the Word of God, both the Old and New Testament Scriptures.[153]

Ancient writers attest that distorted stories, including perversions of the Adam and Eve saga, were already circulating in the 1st century AD. Recent scholarship suggests that Gnostic-like myths opposed to traditional biblical values may have been afloat in Alexandria as early as the 2nd or 1st century BC.[154]   Philo, who died about AD 50, taught that Eve was the one who brings knowledge and meaningful life to Adam.[155]

1 Timothy 1:19,20 and 2 Timothy 2:17ff – Hymenaeus, Alexander and Philetus made shipwreck of the faith, and two of them taught that the resurrection was already past.

The false teachers were not "keeping faith" nor a "good conscience," but rather made "shipwreck ... of the faith."   They also were said to "blaspheme."   Blasphemy often indicates an attack on the very nature of

---

[152] Kroeger, *op. cit.*, p. 61.

[153] We are aware that some of the books of the New Testament are written after the Pastorals were written; but we have always maintained that there is nothing in the written Word other than the doctrine the apostles and New Testament prophets have been proclaiming by word of mouth before the truths ever came to be preserved in written form.   So the statement that the "New Testament Scriptures" are the norm by which truth and error is discerned is not at all misleading or an overstatement of the fact.

[154] See in particular Henry A. Green, *The Economic and Social Origins of Gnosticism*, SBL Dissertation Series 77 (Atlanta: Scholars Press, 1985).

[155] Philo, *On the Cherubim* 57-60.

God. Were the false teachers declaring that Jehovah-God is less than mighty, holy, good, or wise (as some Gnostics were wont to do)?

Their dangerous opposition to Paul and Christianity was so severe that Paul had taken action to deliver "them over to Satan, so they might be taught not to blaspheme."[156]

"Resurrection has already taken place" would be attempts to explain the "resurrection passages" according to the Gnostic philosophy/doctrine requiring the rejection of any future body in which a soul might live. After all, matter was evil. So a resurrection body for a spiritual soul was unthinkable!

1 Timothy 2:4,5 – Presenting Jesus as the "one mediator ... between God and men," might well be written to contradict the Gnostic idea of endless emanations, aeons and demiurges, etc., who stood midway between gods and men and who functioned as mediators in the Gnostic view of things.[157]

It might also be an attempt to correct the spiritual pride and contempt toward less favored individuals that one finds in Gnosticism. Jesus' religion is not limited to a favored few. He wants "all men to be saved and to come to a knowledge of the truth."

1 Timothy 4:1-5 speaks of "doctrines of demons" and specifically identifies two of these as ascetic practices, namely celibacy ("forbid marriage") and a very meager diet ("abstaining from foods").

This certainly reflects the Gnostic ideas that marriage and eating of foods were both inimical to one's higher spiritual development.

Remember, the Essenes practiced celibacy.[158] Josephus speaks of an Essene group which allowed a kind of marriage by trial, which Guthrie believes shows that celibacy was not enforced at Qumran.

---

[156] It does not seem likely that Satan is pictured as being the teacher, but rather that the delivery to Satan is the thing that would teach the false teachers a lesson, and perhaps lead them to abandon the heresy they had become enamored with.

[157] Plutarch (ca. AD 100) wrote in his *Moralia* 415A of the *daimones* and demigods who stood midway between the gods and humanity. He suggested that it may have been Phyrgian influence which first produced this system of mediators that later became so popular in Gnosticism.

[158] Pliny's *Natural History*, V.xv.

Guthrie is in error when he affirms Paul gives an answer to the matter of
"foods" but does not specifically say anything against celibacy.[159] It will
not do to affirm that Paul says nothing against celibacy because he had
ascetic tendencies as evidenced by his preferred lifestyle of celibacy. The
word "which" in verse 3 is plural and refers both to foods and marriage.
Paul is not silent on the matter of celibacy.

1 Timothy 4:7 – "Worldly fables fit only for old women" is a surprising
characterization of the false teachers.

Certainly, Paul intends no insult to older women in general. Yet is there
something about the fables that appeals to older women, or that older
women tend to believe and hand on to others?

Some English translations fail to note the Greek word *graōdeis* (pertaining
to old women). In antiquity old women had a reputation for storytelling
which sometimes put the gods in an outrageous light.[160] From earliest
times in Anatolia, female religious officials known as "old women" kept
alive the ancient myths.[161] The tales, or myths, are said to be "worldly" or
"profane" (KJV) (Greek, *bebalos*), i.e., opposed to God. Modern
translators usually give the impression that the tales were harmless, but the
writer of the Pastorals viewed them as a serious threat. The ancient power
of the "old women's" myths was pitted against the power of the Gospel.[162]

1 Timothy 5:11ff – Certain "younger widows" were not to be "put ... on the
list," for there was a strong possibility they would "set aside their previous
pledge," exhibit "disregard of Christ," and at the same time "learn to be "idle."
Then, "as they go around from house to house," they are "gossips" and
"busybodies" (workers of occult magic), "saying things they ought not to."

The word "gossip" (*phluaroi*) might also be translated "nonsense" – a term

---

[159] Donald Guthrie, *The Pastoral Epistles* (Grand Rapids: Eerdmans, 1957), p.34.

[160] For an extended list of ancient references to women as storytellers, see Dennis R.
MacDonald, *The Legend and the Apostle: The Battle for Paul in Story and Canon* (Philadelphia:
Westminster, 1983), p.13-14, 105 n.4.

[161] "The 'old woman' enacted a wide range of roles and was the most prominent magic-religious
specialist in Anatolia ... Although many of her incantations are in Hurrian and are therefore very
difficult to decipher, enough is known about their content to conclude that the 'old woman' was one
of the primary transmitters of mythic tradition in Anatolian society." Michael S. Moore, *The Balaam
Traditions: Their Character and Development*, SBL Dissertation Series 113 (Atlanta: Scholars
Press, 1990), p.21-22.

[162] Compare Kroeger, *op. cit.*, p.64.

"often used in contemporary philosophical texts to refer to 'foolishness' that is contrary to 'truth'."[163]

The word translated "busybodies" is *periergoi*, the same word translated "practiced magic" at Ephesus, Acts 19:19. "The things they ought not to be speaking might be incantations or magical curses."[164]

"Some Gnostics were heavily engaged in magic; and in the ancient world women in particular were thought to be purveyors of magic."[165]

1 Timothy 6:3-5 repeats the warning against a "different doctrine" (*heterodidaskalei*), against "controversial questions and disputes about words."

1 Timothy 6:20 warns about avoiding "worldly and empty chatter and the opposing arguments of what is falsely called 'knowledge'."

See what has been written above at 1 Timothy 1:3-7 about Gnosticism being a religion of rebellion.

The word translated "opposing arguments" is *antitheses*, a word that occurs frequently in 2nd century Gnosticism.[166]

It is true that the words "falsely called knowledge" (*pseudonumou gnoseos*) was a term used in the 2nd and 3rd centuries with reference to Gnosticism. (The orthodox of later times used the wording of 1 Timothy as a convenient missile to hurl at the Gnostic adversaries, undoubtedly because they understood that an incipient form of the heresy they faced was exactly what Paul was referring to when he wrote 6:20).

It is also true that *antitheses* ("opposing arguments") might describe the "endless contrasts of decisions, founded on endless distinctions,"[167] which one finds in the Mishna. The Mishna contains multiple examples of one rabbi making a law to walk by, only to be reversed years later another rabbi.

---

[163] Kroeger, *op. cit.*, p. 63.

[164] *Ibid.*

[165] *Ibid.*

[166] As noted in an earlier footnote, Marcion wrote a work titled "Antitheses" [or "Oppositions of the Old and New Testament"].

[167] F.J.A. Hort, *Judaistic Christianity*, p. 1440ff.

2 Timothy 2:14,16,23 – Reference is made to "wrangling about words which is useless," to "worldly and empty chatter," to "foolish and ignorant speculations," and to Hymenaeus (who has already been mentioned in 1 Timothy 1:19,20).

2 Timothy 3:5-7 – Describing the last days, Paul characterizes people who have a form of godliness but deny the power thereof. He then speaks of false teachers who "enter into households and captivate weak women weighed down with sins ..." and describes the women as "always learning and never able to come to the knowledge of the truth."

2 Timothy 3:8 – The false teachers at Ephesus incite people to withstand the truth, just as Jannes and Jambres incited people to withstand Moses.

The allusion to Jannes and Jambres is instructive. These are the traditional names of Pharaoh's magicians who produced snakes in opposition to Aaron's rod-turned-serpent (Exodus 7:9-13). Both pagan and Jewish sources characterize Jannes and Jambres as magicians par excellence.

Pliny the Elder, who died in the 1st century AD, wrote of a Jewish group which practiced magic and believed itself to have derived from Moses and Jannes.[168]

2 Timothy 3:13 – Speaks of "evil men and impostors" who "proceed from bad to worse, deceiving and being deceived."

The word translated "impostors" (*goates*, literally "wizards" who practice magical arts) harmonizes well with what we read in Acts 19:19 and elsewhere of the practice of magical arts at Ephesus.

2 Timothy 3:15 may well be written to counteract and repudiate the Gnostic rejection of many Old Testament Scriptures.

2 Timothy 4:3 – Deals with people who have itching ears and who desire teachers who will tickle their ears.

Titus 1:10 is a reference to empty talkers of the circumcision party. The heresy on Cyprus certainly had a Jewish origin or root.

---

[168] *Natural History*, 30.2.11.

Titus 1:14 – Titus is to reprove those who are not sound in the faith, and is to pay no attention to Jewish myths and commandments of men.   Paul goes on to specify "pure" and "defiled" things, which likely reflects certain ascetic distinctions.

Titus 1:14 and 1 Timothy 1:7 may well be a refutation of Gnostic allegorizing of Old Testament Scripture.

Titus 1:16 – "They profess to know God" might reflect the claimed exclusive "knowledge" prevalent among Gnostics.

Titus 3:9 – "Foolish controversies and genealogies and strife and disputes about the Law" could reflect Jewish Gnosticism (cp. 1 Timothy 1:7,8).   It is evident that on Crete some form of Jewish controversy of an entirely speculative nature had arisen.

> While there were undoubtedly minor differences between the false teaching in Ephesus
> [and Asia Minor] and Crete, the major features seem to be common, and there is strong
> justification for regarding them as separate manifestations of a general contemporary
> tendency.[169]

Certainly, more study is needed on the religious beliefs of 1st century AD Asia Minor.   A better knowledge of those peoples' religious thoughts and influences will help us to more fully appreciate what we read in the Pastorals that is in opposition to those 1st century AD beliefs.

---

[169] Guthrie, *op. cit.*, p.35.

XII. EXPANDED OUTLINE OF 1 TIMOTHY[170]

INTRODUCTORY MATTERS. 1:1,2
  A. The writer. 1:1
  B. The address. 1:2a
  C. The greeting. 1:2b

I. THE CHARGE CONCERNING SOUND DOCTRINE. 1:3-20

  A. The Danger to Sound Doctrine in Ephesus. 1:3-11
    1. The teachers who taught another doctrine. 3-7
      a. Identification of these teachers
      b. Characteristics of their teaching
        1) Different doctrine. 3
        2) Myths. 4
        3) Endless genealogies. 4
        4) Vain speaking. 6
      c. Timothy's responsibility
        1) Deliver a prohibitive charge. 3
        2) Encourage a positive response. 5
    2. Teachers who failed to use God's Law properly. 8-11
      a. The Law itself is good. 8
      b. The Law has an improper use. 9
      c. The Law has a proper use. 10-11

  B. The Outstanding Illustration of the Results of Sound Doctrine. 1:12-17
    1. Paul's former life of Law-keeping was a life of unbelief. 13a
    2. Paul's present life in the ministry was the result of mercy and grace. 12, 13b-14
    3. Paul's conversion was planned as a pattern to encourage future believers. 15-17

  C. The Responsibility of the Evangelist Toward Sound Doctrine. 1:18-20
    1. The responsibility expressed by formal charge. 18,19a
    2. The responsibility illustrated by two examples. 19b-20

---

[170] The Pastoral Epistles do not follow the usual two-point outline found in many of Paul's letters – namely, "Doctrine" and "Practice." After studying the outlines that others have offered for 1 Timothy, we have decided to follow, with some deliberate modifications, the outline offered by Homer Kent, *op. cit.*, p.69-70.

II. THE CHARGE CONCERNING PUBLIC WORSHIP. 2:1-15

   A. Prayer in Public Worship. 2:1-7
      1. The kinds of prayer. 1
         a. Entreaties
         b. Prayers
         c. Petitions
         d. Thanksgivings
      2. The objects of prayer. 1,2a
         a. All men
         b. Kings and all who are in authority
      3. The reasons for such prayer. 2b,3-4
         a. With respect to the church
         b. With respect to God
      4. The basis for such prayer. 5-7
         a. The unity of God
         b. The unity of the Mediator
         c. The availability of the ransom
         d. The commission for Gentiles

   B. Men and Women in Public Worship. 2:8-15
      1. Conduct of the men. 8
         a. Men should do the praying in public worship.
         b. This directive holds good for public worship everywhere.
         c. The prayers of the men are to be accompanied by a holy life.
         d. Men's prayers are to be accompanied by a proper attitude.

      2. Conduct of the women. 9-15
         a. Women are to dress in modest apparel
         b. Women are to learn in quietness
            This is not just a cultural instruction.
            It is founded in the creation and fall.
         c. Women are to continue in faith, love, and consecration.

III. THE CHARGE CONCERNING CHURCH OFFICERS. 3:1-16

   A. Office of Elder. 3:1-7
      1. Nature of the office
         a. An office which may rightfully be desired
         b. An office which involves oversight
         c. An office which involves work
         d. An office which is worthwhile

      2. Qualifications for the office
        a. Character
            Blameless
            Sober
            Prudent
            Orderly
            Not addicted to wine
            Not pugnacious
            Gentle
            Not contentious
            Free from the love of money
            Having a good reputation without
        b. Experience
            Desire the office
            Husband of one wife
            Able to teach
            Hospitable
            Manages own house well
            Keeps children under control
            Not a new convert

B. Office of Deacon.   3:8-13
    1. Nature of the office
    2. Qualifications for the office
      a. Personal character
      b. Spiritual life
      c. Christian experience
      d. Family qualifications
    3. Reward for Deacons who serve well

C. The Importance of this Charge to the Church.   3:14-16
    1. Paul could not be there personally to direct the church.
    2. Timothy needed instruction in Paul's absence.
    3. Both recognized the greatness of the church.
      a. It is the "household of God"
      b. It is the "church of the living God"
      c. It is the "pillar and support of Truth" (that "Truth" is further
         explained as being the "mystery of Godliness")

(The Church is the greatest thing in the world!   Therefore we must be careful whom we choose for leaders!)

IV. THE CHARGE CONCERNING FALSE TEACHERS.   4:1-16

    A. The Appearance of False Teachers Predicted.   4:1-5
        1. The time they appear
           a. It is made known by the Spirit's revelation.
           b. It occurs in the "latter seasons."
        2. The description of these false teachers
           a. They cause their victims to abandon the faith.
           b. The source of their teaching is demonic.
           c. The agents mediating this apostasy are hypocritical lie-speakers
        3. The doctrines of these false teachers
           a. Forbidding to marry
           b. Advocating abstinence from certain foods
        4. The refutation of these false teachers
           a. They challenged privileges created by God for partaking by men.
           b. They challenged privileges intended for saved people.
           c. They challenged privileges which were intrinsically good.
           d. They challenged privileges which are sanctified through the
              Word of God and prayer.

    B. The Duty of the Evangelist Toward False Teachers.   4:6-10
        1. Pass on the Spirit's warning about false teachers.   6a
        2. Be constantly nourished on words of faith and sound doctrine.   6b
        3. Avoid the worldly fables.   7a
        4. Be disciplined towards godly living.   7b-9
        5. Keep laboring and striving for the blessed promises connected to
           godliness.   10

    C. Encouraging the Evangelist Toward a Constructive Ministry. 4:11-16
        1. In Public life.   11-13
           a. Command and teach sound doctrine.   11
           b. Be an example of how believers live and thus maintain the
              respect of his people.   12
           c. Give special attention to his responsibilities to lead public
              worship.   13
        2. In Personal life.   14-16
           a. Stop neglecting the gift which was bestowed on him.   14
           b. Make steady growth in his leadership skills.   15
           c. Take heed to himself.   16
              1) Character
              2) Creed
              3) Conduct

V. THE CHARGE CONCERNING THE EVANGELIST'S CONCERNS FOR VARIOUS MEMBERS OF THE CONGREGATION. 5:1 - 6:2

    A. The Evangelist's Care for Old and Young Members. 5:1,2
        1. The persons involved
        2. The nature of the pastoral care
            a. It must not be a harsh or disrespectful rebuke.
            b. It should be a comforting, encouraging, admonishing entreaty.
        3. The manner of pastoral care
            a. It should be performed with such consideration for others as is proper in a family.
            b. It should be performed with all purity when young women are involved.

    B. The Evangelist's Concern for the Widows. 5:3-16
        1. The kinds of widows
            a. The widow who is a widow indeed (actually bereft)
            b. The widow who has a family
            c. The widow who is living in pleasure
            d. The younger widow
        2. The treatment of widows
            a. Widows who are truly helpless and meet certain qualifications (group a)
            b. Widows who have families (group b)
            c. Widows who live in pleasure (group c)
            d. Younger widows (group d)

    C. The Evangelist's Concern for Elders. 5:17-25
        1. The compensation of elders. 17,18
            a. Those to be honored are those who superintend well.
            b. Those to be honored are those toiling in preaching and teaching.
            c. Those elders are to receive double honor.
            d. This honoring has Scriptural support.
        2. The discipline of elders. 19-21
            a. Discipline must be founded on fact, not rumor.
            b. Discipline must be administered in the sight of all the church.
            c. Discipline must be administered without prejudice against or partiality toward the elder.
        3. The ordination of elders. 22-25
            a. Haste must be avoided in ordination, for those who ordain hastily are responsible for the conduct of the elders.
            b. Haste must be avoided in ordination, for their character will be revealed with the passing of time.

    D. The Evangelist's Concern for Slaves.   6:1-2b
        1. A slave should serve his unsaved master respectfully.
            a. The manner of this service
            b. The reason for this service
        2. A slave should give his Christian master even more service, and not
           look down on him.
            a. The manner of this service
            b. The reason for this service

VI. THE CHARGE CONCERNING THE EVANGELIST HIMSELF. 6:2c-21a

    A. The Charge Concerning Topics to be Preached.   6:2c

    B. The Evangelist is Charged to Avoid Improper Motives.   6:3-10
        1. Evidences of wrong motives
            a. The person who teaches different doctrine
            b. The person who does not assent to the teaching which produces
               a life of godliness
        2. Two kinds of wrong motives
            a. Pride
            b. Desire for gain
        3. The prevention of wrong motives
        4. The results of a wrong motive (the desire to be rich)
            a. It causes falling into temptation.
            b. It causes falling into a snare.
            c. It causes falling into many senseless and harmful lusts.
            d. It causes men to sink into destruction and perdition.
            e. It causes wandering from the faith.
            f. It causes many griefs.

    C. The Evangelist is Charged to Maintain a Proper Walk.   6:11-16
        1. The nature of a proper walk
            a. It is a continual fleeing from evil
            b. It is a continual pursuing of godliness
               1) Righteousness
               2) Godliness
               3) Faith
               4) Love
               5) Patience
               6) Meekness

2. The performance of a proper walk
  a. It is continual contending in the good contest of the faith.
  b. It is taking hold of eternal life.
  c. It is solemn keeping of the truth of God.
3. The incentive for a proper walk

D. The Evangelist is Charged to Perform a Faithful Ministry.   6:17-21a
  1. This is accomplished by directing men toward spiritual goals. 17-19
    a. Wealthy Christians should not be exalted in mind.
    b. Wealthy Christians should trust God, not riches.
    c. Wealthy Christians should be good stewards.
    d. Wealthy Christians should be storing up treasure for eternity.
  2. This is accomplished by guarding the deposit of the faith.   20-21a
    a. What is to be guarded?
    b. How is it to be guarded?
      1) By turning away from profane, empty talkings
      2) By turning away from falsely-named knowledge
    c. From whom is it to be guarded?

CONCLUDING BENEDICTION.   6:21b

(Note: An outline for Titus is found on page 316, while the outline for 2 Timothy is found on page 430.   These outlines are included in the two pages of orientation to each of these books, later in this commentary.)

Commentary On

1 Timothy

1 TIMOTHY

SIGNATURE, ADDRESS, AND GREETING. 1:1,2

A. The Writer.   1:1

1:1 -- Paul – The opening words of 1st century letters included three elements: the name of the sender, the name of the addressee, and a word of greeting. Our New Testament epistles follow this 1st century form, though the elements may be expanded as the Christian perspective of the letter required. This signature says Paul was the writer of this letter.[1] The "Paul" who sends this letter is then carefully identified in the following phrases. These phrases will show the author is the "Paul" we know from the book of Acts, who was once a persecutor of the church and who then became a very hard-working apostle and missionary.

An apostle of Christ Jesus – Etymologically, the word "apostle" means "one who is prepared or equipped and then sent off with a special commission." *Apostolos* is a compound word from *apo* (off, away from) and *stello* (to equip, prepare, arrange). In time, the word "apostle" became a technical term to denote one who was sent away with proper credentials to represent someone else. Paul was sent by Jesus to represent the King of Kings and to deliver a message to mankind from that King. "Of Christ Jesus" identifies what kind of apostle Paul claims to be. There were two kinds of apostles in the early church, apostles of Jesus and apostles of churches.[2] The exact position and task to which an "apostle" was called depended on who it was (i.e., Jesus or the churches) who called the person to become an "apostle." Hendriksen (*in loc.*) lists several of the characteristics of an "apostle of Jesus": (1) They were chosen, called, and sent forth by Christ himself (John 7:60, 13:18, 15:16,19; Galatians 1:6). (2) They were qualified for their tasks by Jesus and were eye and ear witnesses of His words and deeds, specifically of His resurrection from the dead (Acts 1:8,22; 1 Corinthians 9:1). (3) They were each endowed with a special measure of the Holy Spirit (Acts 1:8; Matthew 10:20; John 14: 26; 1 Corinthians 2:10-13; 1 Thessalonians 4:8). (4) God blessed their work, confirming its value by means of signs and miracles (Matthew 10:1,8; Acts 2:43, 3:2, 5:32; Romans 15:18,19; 2 Corinthians 12:12; Hebrews 2:4).   (5) Their office was not restricted to a local

---

[1] In the Introductory Studies, we have studied in detail the whole question of authorship, and have found nothing that would cause us to doubt what this signature claims as far as authorship of this letter is concerned.

[2] In Philippians 2:25 Epaphroditus is called an "apostle ("messenger" NASB) [of the church at Philippi]." He was designated to carry a missionary offering from Philippi to Paul. At 2 Corinthians 8:23 the men selected by the various local congregations to carry their portion of the offering to Jerusalem were called "apostles [messengers] of the churches." These "apostles of churches" held an entirely different position in the early church than was held by the "apostles of Jesus."

congregation (Acts 26:16-18; Romans 15:19,20).

The order in which the names "Jesus Christ" or "Christ Jesus" appear has sometimes been thought significant.[3]   "Christ" is a title; it is the Greek equivalent of the Hebrew word "Messiah."   When this title is used, there often is emphasis on the fact that He was the "promised Messiah."   "Jesus" is the name Joseph and Mary were instructed to give to the baby born in Bethlehem.   It means "Jehovah saves," emphasizing His historic human person and His reason for coming into the world.   Perhaps it is often true that whichever name occurs first does indicate the idea that was prominent in the writer's mind at the moment.   Did Paul, whose experience with the Son of God began with his vision of the glorified Christ on the Damascus Road, for that reason regularly use the order "Christ Jesus"?   Did the original twelve apostles, who became acquainted with the historic Jesus of Nazareth and then as time passed recognized more and more that He was the Messiah, for that reason often refer to Him as "Jesus Christ"?

According to the commandment of God our Savior – We have come to the phrases that tell us how Paul came to be an "apostle of Christ Jesus."   It was, he says, "according to the commandment of" (or "by order of"[4]) God and Christ.[5]   Paul traces his authority first to "God our Savior."   Since in this verse Paul's apostleship is ascribed "to the order of" both God and Jesus, it is likely that as Paul writes about the "commandment of God" he has in mind what happened at Antioch at the beginning of the first missionary journey, when the Holy Spirit said, "Set apart for Me Barnabas and Saul for the work to which I have called them" (Act 13:2).   Paul usually used the attribute "Savior" for Jesus.   That it is here used of God the Father has been thought, by some, to be un-Pauline.[6]   But this should not be surprising; even in his earlier epistles Paul ascribed the work

---

[3] The order in the KJV is "Jesus Christ," and it reflects the word order in the Textus Receptus. "Christ Jesus" is the order found in the Nestle-UBS texts.   Hendriksen, in footnote #19 on page 51, rejects the idea that the order of the names has any great significance.   Kent (*op. cit.*, p.71-2), on the other hand, thinks the order may be significant.   Paul himself could and did write it both ways (cp. Romans 1:1 and 1 Corinthians 1:1).

[4] E.K. Simpson, *The Pastoral Epistles* (Grand Rapids: Eerdmans, 1954), p.24, indicates that there are ancient inscriptions where this phrase "according to commandment of" was the recognized formula similar to "by order of" used in our official notices.

[5] Some Bible students have noted that in other places in which Paul asserts his apostleship, he ascribes it "to the will of God" (cp. Galatians 1:11,12).   There seems to be something more than an appeal to God's will in his wording of his commission here in 1 Timothy.

[6] Among Paul's signed letters, it is only in the Pastoral Epistles that we find this exact designation.   Those who tend to question the Pauline authorship of the Pastorals point to this designation for God as one evidence that Paul (who usually speaks of "Jesus our Savior") didn't write the Pastorals.   The term "Savior" does occur more frequently in the later writings of the New Testament than in the earlier, and Paul uses the title in reference both to God and to Jesus Christ in these Pastoral Epistles.   We find no evidence in this designation that is un-Pauline.

of saving men to God (1 Corinthians 1:21; Ephesians 2:4,5,8; Philippians 1:28). God the Father is the ultimate source of the salvation Paul and his readers enjoy. Nor need we suppose that the writer of 1 Timothy simply applied a word to God that many ancient kings adopted (cf. Ptolemy Soter). The term "Savior" occurs twenty times in the Septuagint, and all but two refer to God. Paul is simply using Biblical language when he calls God "our Savior." Paul uses the possessive pronoun "our" as he speaks of "God our Savior." Since 1 Timothy was written during the time Nero was emperor, and the cult of emperor worship tended to apply "savior" to Nero, perhaps there is a direct reference to the fact that for Christians "God" (not Nero) is our Savior. We who so often speak of Jesus as our Savior must not overlook the great part which the Father played in the planning and directing of mankind's deliverance from sin. To speak of God as "our Savior" should immediately call to mind all of the Father's activities.

And of Christ Jesus, *who is* our hope – In this second phrase, Paul traces his authority as an apostle to Christ Jesus. If the previous phrase about God's command looked back to Acts 13:2, then perhaps this phrase about Jesus' command looks back to what happened on the Damascus Road, when Jesus Himself appeared to Paul to call him to become an apostle (Acts 26:16-18). Lewis A. Foster (*Standard Lesson Commentary*, 1964, p.344) observed that "by paralleling Christ with God in this opening phrase" as sources of his apostolic authority, "Paul held that Jesus Christ is divine." Jesus is characterized as being "our hope." Paul balances his description of God as "Savior" with the description of Jesus Christ as "our hope."[7] Everything that is part of the Christian's hope for present and future is bound up in Jesus Christ. Our hope in Him is the anchor of the soul (Hebrews 6:18-20), and our union with Christ is the basis of our hope of glory (Colossians 1:27). It is part of the Christian's hope that we are looking for Him to return, a hope which influences behavior toward denying ungodliness and worldly desires, and positively toward living "sensibly, righteously, and godly in this present age" (Titus 2:12,13). The word "hope" used in its Biblical sense conveys an element of absolute certainty, an element that often is lacking in the modern usage of the word, where "hope" is often not much more than just "wishful thinking."[8] This strong assertion of Paul's apostolic authority was certainly not needed by Timothy. We suppose the use of such language indicates this was not just a private letter to Timothy, but was a public church document,

---

[7] The words "who is," printed in italics in our English translation, are better left out. Then the balance between the phrases is more clearly seen.

[8] Hope is a complex emotion of the human mind consisting of a desire for some known object and an expectation of receiving and enjoying it. If either the desire or the expectation is missing, it is not "hope," it is just "wishing. When the word "hope" occurs in any passage, it may refer either to the action of hoping, or it may emphasize the object hoped for. For any Christian, there are still many aspects of salvation yet to be realized. For these blessings he continues to hope.

both for Ephesus[9] and perhaps, too, for all time.

B. The Address.   1:2a

1:2 -- To Timothy – In harmony with usual 1st century letter writing practice, the addressee is named at the beginning of the letter.   In the Introductory Studies, we have had a special study about the life of Timothy.   From Acts we learn he was a native of either Derbe or Lystra; his mother (Eunice) was a pious Jewess, as was her mother also (Lois).   Barnes observed that although Timothy's father was Greek, he was not unfriendly toward the Jewish religion, for Timothy was well-trained in the Scriptures.

My true child in the faith – In delicate contrast to his formal beginning, Paul now has a word of personal warmth when he addresses Timothy.   This unusual phrase means that Timothy was one of Paul's personal converts.   "Child" cannot mean that Paul was Timothy's physical father, for Acts 16:3 tells us that Timothy's father was a Greek.   Hendriksen comments that the designation "child" (*teknon*) is a very happy one, for it combined two ideas: "I have begotten you" and "you are very dear to me."   Bruce has noted that the 'father-son' terminology was also used in the first century to express the 'teacher-pupil' relationship.   The word "child" ('little born one') means that he was "begotten" (begotten by the Gospel, 1 Corinthians 4:14-16; Philemon 10), so we can put in "my" without altering the meaning of the text.   "True" translates *gneisios*, which means "genuine."   The word used is the opposite of 'illegitimate.'   "In faith" can refer either to the body of doctrine that makes up the Christian Gospel, or it can refer to Timothy's own personal faith.   If we take it of the body of doctrine, the phase would mean there was nothing spurious about Timothy's standing "in the faith."   (We may add the definite article "the" in our translation, because the preposition "in" tends to make the noun definite.)   Alternately, if we omit the article "the" before "faith," the reference would be to Timothy's own personal faith.   This might mean the genuine nature of Timothy's conversion was proven as the years passed.   "His spiritual life was not illegitimate or abortive.   He was a genuinely born-again child of God."[10]   Or it might mean that Timothy's "faith" was equal to Paul's, as was stated in 1 Corinthians 4:17.   When Timothy taught, his message was the same as his teacher's.   Paul had no one like-minded (like Timothy was) who would care for their affairs, Paul told the Philippian church (Philippians 2:20).

---

[9] That the letter is intended for more than just Timothy, yea, for the whole church, can be seen from the benediction with its plural "you" ("grace be with you," 1 Timothy 6:21).

[10] Kent, *op. cit.*, p.74

C. The Greeting.   1:2b

Grace, mercy, and peace – There is no verb in this phrase in the Greek, so we must supply one.   It is usual to supply a verb form that makes this last half of the verse a prayer offered by Paul to God for Timothy.   "May you have grace ...."   The wording of this prayer for blessings from God to Timothy varies from the usual wording found in Paul's epistles.   Usually it reads "Grace and peace."[11]   As in 2 Timothy 1:2 and Titus 1:4, "mercy" has been added.   "Grace" may be defined as "God's unmerited favor in operation"[12] or "all that God does to save a man." The grace for which Paul prays is not the grace that operates when a man is originally being saved,[13] for Timothy is already described as "a true child in faith." It rather is some operation of grace that helps a man live the Christian life, that will sustain him constantly, that will provide forgiveness when the Christian sins and needs a covering for his sins.

What is "mercy" and how does it differ from "grace"?   Two words are translated "mercy" or "compassion" in the New Testament, and both denote sympathy, fellow-feeling with misery.   1) *Eleos*, which is the word used here, manifests itself chiefly in acts rather than words.[14]   2) *Oiktirmos*, the other word, is used of the inward feeling of compassion which abides in the heart.   A criminal might ask for *eleos*, "mercy," from his judge; but hopeless suffering may be the object of *oiktirmos*, "compassion" (Berry, *op. cit.*, p.128).   "It is difficult to distinguish between these words for grace and mercy, for their meanings overlap. Grace seems to emphasize the unworthiness of the recipients, whereas mercy brings to mind the helpless state of those receiving the blessing" (Foster, *op. cit.*, p.344).   Just why Paul adds "mercy" to his usual prayer of greeting is variously explained.   *Pulpit Commentary* explains, "The nearness of death, the weakness of old age, the ever increasing dangers which crowded around Paul, seem to have called forth from him the deeper expressions of love and tender pity."   Hendriksen suggests, "Timothy was in a difficult situation.   He faced problems which were all the more trying for a man of his disposition.   Hence, God's *tender love toward those in need* was definitely required."

---

[11] Not a few writers have noted that "grace" was the usual greeting when Greeks met, while "peace" was the usual greeting among Hebrews. Paul takes both terms, pours a new, spiritual content into them, and uses them side-by-side because in the church there is no longer distinctions between Jew and Greek – we are all one in Christ.

[12] Hendriksen, *op. cit.*, p. 54.

[13] This language is not intended to express what is sometimes called a "first work of grace."   It is intended, rather, to express what is everywhere taught in Scripture, that when the Gospel is preached, God's Spirit graciously goes to work to produce conviction and lead the person (if the person will voluntarily submit and respond to the Spirit's pleadings) to conversion.

[14] Hendriksen has a study of the word "mercy" on pages 54, 55.

Timothy will face difficult situations and people as he administers the Ephesian church, so there may be a delicate reminder that he must always be aware of his need to be merciful if he himself is to receive mercy from God (Matthew 5:7). By using this word, Paul is praying for God's sympathy and concern to be upon Timothy. The "peace" which Paul prays for Timothy may be either "peace with God" or "peace with man." Such peace is the outcome of grace and mercy experienced. It is that which keeps our hearts in confidence (Philippians 4:6,7).

From God the Father and Christ Jesus our Lord – The three blessings upon Timothy for which Paul prays must come from above. "The coupling by Paul of God the Father and Christ Jesus as co-bestowers of these divine blessings is clear indication of Paul's belief in the full deity of Christ."[15] The KJV reads "God *our* Father," reflecting the Textus Receptus which has the word "our" (*hēmōn*) in it. Whether we read "our" as the Textus Receptus, or omit it with the Nestle/UBS text, the idea of "Father" is contrasted, not with that of "Son," but with that of "Lord"; the two words express the relationship of the Persons of the Godhead, not to each other, but to the church. Christ is the mediator of all the blessings which the Father bestows.

> Paul seemed to know what Timothy needed. Timothy's task in Ephesus was the most difficult he had ever faced. He needed all the gifts of God's grace. A tradition, recorded by Eusebius, says that Timothy was later beaten to death by a mob in Ephesus because of his arraignment of the idolatrous immorality of the worship of Diana.[16] Paul's prayer for him was no mere stereotyped formula, but a fervent personal desire expressed to God on behalf of his faithful worker.[17]

I. THE CHARGE CONCERNING SOUND DOCTRINE. 1:3-20

A. The Danger to Sound Doctrine in Ephesus. 1:3-11

1. The teachers who taught another doctrine. 1:3-7

---

[15] Kent, *op. cit.*, p.75.

[16] There is some question about the historicity of the martyrdom of Timothy. A footnote on Eus. H.E. III.4.6 indicates that Nicephorus (who lived 400 years after Eusebius) records the martyrdom of Timothy during Domitian's reign, but that Nicephorus gives no authority for his claim. The footnote then goes on to discuss the probability that (after 2 Timothy is written) Timothy returned to labor at Ephesus (a town in which John the apostle also lived) in the closing quarter of the 1st century AD). Baronius, a church historian living in the 16th century, dates Timothy's martyrdom about AD 109, during the reign of Trajan, but again without giving any historical evidence.

[17] Kent, *ibid.*

1:3 – As I urged you upon my departure for Macedonia -- In the Introductory Studies, we have concluded that this language reflects the fact that after his release from his first Roman imprisonment, Paul resumed travelling among the churches he had planted on his earlier missionary journeys in the 40's and 50's AD. As he revisits the churches in the mid-60's AD, he passed through Ephesus,[18] and then was going to travel on toward Macedonia. Timothy either had been traveling with Paul up until their stop at Ephesus, or Timothy was the evangelist with the church in Ephesus before Paul arrived.[19] In any case, when Paul departed for Macedonia, Timothy was to stay behind to minister in Ephesus. Before Paul and Timothy parted, Paul gave Timothy a solemn charge concerning his ministry in Ephesus. Now, in writing, Paul repeats to Timothy the commission he had already given on that previous occasion, probably by word of mouth.

Remain on at Ephesus – There is a broken sentence in the Greek, and translators employ various expedients to make a complete sentence in their translations. (1) The NASB translates the Greek infinitive 'to remain' as though it were an imperative. (2) The KJV adds the words "so do!" in italics at the close of verse 4. (3) Others think the sentence is completed, after a long digression, at verse 18, where Paul nearly repeats the words with which the sentence began.[20] (4) Still others put a dash in the text at the close of verse 3, and leave it a broken sentence, just as it stands in our present Greek texts. However the sentence is completed, the fact that Paul had to "urge" (*parakaleō*)[21] Timothy to remain behind at Ephesus suggests Timothy had wanted instead to continue traveling with Paul. The needs of the church, however, made it imperative that Timothy stay there and serve with them as evangelist for the immediate future.

In order that you may instruct certain men – The same Greek verb (*paraggellō*) occurs several times in chapter 1. In verses 3 and 5 it is translated "instruct" or "instruction" in the NASB. At verse 18, it is translated "command."

---

[18] While the Greek does not specifically say Paul was at Ephesus with Timothy, we think that is a better interpretation of the words, rather than to think Paul was somewhere else and made the request to Timothy by messenger or letter. If Paul did come to Ephesus again after his release, then his premonition (Acts 20:38) that the Ephesians would see his face no more did not come to pass. If Paul did not personally pass through Ephesus after his release from Rome, then his premonition was correct. What is involved here is how much of an apostle's thoughts was subject to inerrant inspiration, and how much they were free to think thoughts that were not inspired. We suppose his premonition was not the subject of inspiration, but of uninspired human thinking, in light of his plans to evangelize in other places – perhaps as far west as Spain – since his work in these present areas where he has been before was done (Romans 15:19,23).

[19] The sense of the infinitive translated "to remain" may be either "to stay on" or "to abide still." The latter would imply that Timothy was already at Ephesus when Paul arrived, and then was encouraged "to abide still [longer]."

[20] The comments offered herein reflect this third option for completing the broken sentence.

[21] It is a strong expression. With difficulty Paul persuaded Timothy to remain at Ephesus.

Our titles ("The Charge Concerning ...") for the major paragraphs of this letter are derived from this term. The "instruction" Paul gives to Timothy is Timothy's "charge," his "command," his "job description" (here is what you are to do), his "orders" (like a commander to his subordinates in the army). In most of his letters, in accord with the accepted letter writing practices of the day, Paul usually includes a word of thanksgiving between the greeting and the body of the letter. But as was true of Galatians, we find no thanksgiving in either 1 Timothy or Titus. We suppose the reason is that these letters are more like mandates or official letters, which in that day did not contain a thanksgiving at the beginning.

That "certain men" need instruction implies that when Paul and Timothy came to Ephesus, they found the church there distracted and threatened by what "certain men" were teaching. Likely the dangers Paul had warned about when he addressed the Ephesian elders (Acts 20:29, 30) had come true in the years since Paul was last there. Unless these were resisted and the deadening influences removed, the faith and life of the Ephesian church was in grave danger. We wonder why Paul used an indefinite way of identifying the false teachers whom Timothy is to oppose. Does Paul purposely omit the names of these false teachers from a desire to spare them? Or does he finally get around to naming two of them in verse 20, Hymenaeus and Alexander? Commentators have suggested several plausible reasons why Paul uses the indefinite *tisin*, "some" or "certain." (1) The group includes not only some who must be named, but also several who need not be named as yet, the mild cases, who still may be won back from the errors they've been teaching. (2) Timothy, living right among these people in Ephesus, is naturally better able than is Paul (now writing back from Macedonia) to tell who belongs to the group and who does not. (3) The group of false teachers is not large, hence Paul writes "some" or "certain men" because they were not 'many.' (4) Paul uses a term that implies those who belong to this group are not as important as they think they are. They are not important leaders whose words and influence are to be deferred to, but they are merely "certain men." In the Introductory Studies, we detailed the doctrines of incipient Gnostic Judaism. These false teachers seem to have been part of this developing heresy.

Not to teach strange doctrines – Here begins a description of some of the teachings and beliefs of the false teachers that Timothy was to oppose. First, the teachings are described as "heterodoxy" (*heterodidaskalein*)[22]; it was 'different'[23] from the standard Christian doctrine already in existence and recognized. It was

---

[22] It is possible Paul coined this word, for it occurs only twice in the New Testament (both in 1 Timothy), and has not been found employed by any earlier writers (with a possible exception of the Dead Sea Scroll 1QH 4:16). It is found in later writers, e.g., Ignatius' letter to Polycarp 3:1.

[23] Two synonyms in Greek are translated "other." *Allos* is another of the same kind; *heteros* (the prefix found in the word used here in verse 3) is one of a different kind, diverse.

"strange," it was an "other doctrine" (KJV), i.e., "other" than the truth. The false teachers were teaching views and opinions contrary to that which is orthodox.[24] What the apostles had been teaching is orthodoxy, and the only valid and authoritative Christian doctrine. Whether we think of the false teachers as giving a wrong emphasis on the permanence of the Law of Moses, or whether we think of them as mixing Greek philosophy and religious speculations with Christian doctrine, in either case the result is "heterodoxy."

One wonders how Timothy went about "instructing" those "certain men" to stop teaching their different doctrines. Was it from the pulpit in public, or was it face-to-face in private, or both? The verb "instruct" ("charge") is a strong word of command. The aorist verb tense in the Greek suggests a decisive action on Timothy's part. Timothy was to make every effort to see that those "certain men" desisted at once from their hurtful teachings. Throughout the ages, the church has been plagued with false doctrine – the teachings of men who seek to supplant the truth of God. This was true in the beginning years of the church even while the apostles were still living, and it is still true. Evangelists still have a responsibility similar to Timothy's when it comes to "false doctrine."

1:4 -- Nor to pay attention to myths – The connection between verses 3 and 4 seems to be this: not only must false teachers be charged to desist from wrong *teaching* (verse 3), they must also desist from wrong *thinking*[25] (verse 4), for the former is the result of the latter. The two characteristics identified in this verse (myths, genealogies) do not encompass all that the false teachers were teaching; more will be enumerated in verses 6 and 7. We have some trouble identifying exactly what Paul was writing about. He does not describe it in detail, but simply uses a few broad terms which Timothy would understand in a moment.

"Myths" ("fables" KJV)[26] were found both in Rabbinic Judaism and in Gnosticism. Thus, there is disagreement among commentators over this term and the next, some explaining them as though they were Jewish, and some as though they were Gnostic. If we were correct in our Introductory Studies, that the problem at Ephesus was Gnostic Judaism, then either one may serve to explain to what Paul refers. Examples of Jewish myths can be found in the Talmudic fables, or perhaps in their Cabalistic lore, or in the *Book of Jubilees*. (1) Talmud-

---

[24] Paul already used *heteros* in Galatians 1:6 with reference to heretical teaching that differs from the gospel. The other place in 1 Timothy where Paul uses the compound form *heterodidaskalein* (6:3), he virtually defines its meaning in the sentence that follows – "and does not agree with sound words, those of our Lord Jesus Christ, and with the doctrine conforming to godliness."

[25] The verb *prosecho*, translated "to pay attention to" means "to turn one's mind to."

[26] The word is uniformly used in the New Testament to refer to a tale or story or fable regarded as untrue.

ic Fables.[27]   Not only was the written Law given at Mt. Sinai, but it was said in orthodox Jewish schools that an oral Law had also been given at Sinai, and that this oral Law was handed down from the time of Moses by a succession of teachers.[28]   This "Law that is upon the lip," as it was termed, was continually illustrated and enlarged by the sayings and interpretations of the more famous Jewish Rabbis.   By Jesus' time on earth, the rabbinic additions had in many cases caused the written Law to be forgotten or blatantly ignored.   That's what Jesus meant when he said "by your traditions you have made the Law [of Moses] void" (Matthew 15:6), and "you yourselves transgress the commandment of God for the sake of your tradition" (Matthew 15:3).   For centuries this supplementary oral Law was preserved by memory and handed down by word of mouth.   This strange collection of tradition and comment was finally committed to writing near the end of the 2nd century AD by Rabbi Judah the Prince, under the general name of Mishnah (repetition or teaching).[29]   (2) Cabalistic Lore.   Cabala[30] is the designation for a mystical system of philosophy which arose among the Jews during the intertestamental period (or before).[31]   In its technical sense, Cabala signifies a secret system of theology, metaphysics, and magic along the lines of pantheism.   The kernel of the cabalistic teaching is that all emanates from God. There is no creation in the common acceptance of the term, and on the other hand no eternal matter.   All nature is due to the self-development of the Deity.   God as the absolute being is also called Adam Kadmon ('the first or ideal man'). Certain esoteric doctrines are said to have first been written down by Solomon, and then passed on by word of mouth to the present.   Many of these have to do with formulas and incantations that can be used for healing purposes.   (3) *Book*

---

[27] The word "Talmud" has had several meanings through the years.   In older times it was used for the discussions of the Amoraim.   Now it means the Mishnah with the discussions thereon.   The Talmud today contains several sections: the Mishnah, the Gemara (the collection of the discussions of the Amoraim, i.e., the rabbis who lived and taught AD 100 -500), the *Halakhah* ("to walk") decisions given by Talmudists on disputed questions, and the *Haggadah* ("to toll"), which are legends, anecdotes, and sayings illustrative of the Law.   (See the article in ISBE on "Talmud.")

[28] After the Babylonian Exile, there were new conditions in society concerning which there were no instructions in the written Law.   On account of the ever-changing conditions of life, the Jews felt that new ordinances were necessary.   This is where the traditions of the elders began.   We doubt they have existed side by side with the written Law since Sinai.

[29] As time passed, these collections (and the additions made since the last writing) were committed to writing.   The *Palestinian Talmud* (sometimes called "The Jerusalem Talmud") contains the discussions of Palestinian scholars on the Mishnah from the 2nd to the middle of the 5th century. The *Babylonian Talmud* embodies the teachings of Jewish scholars in Babylonia from about AD 190 to the 7th century.

[30] The word (from the Hebrew, *kabal*, "to receive") is variously spelled: Cabala, Kabala, Cabbalah, Caballah.   The term is regularly used to denote "oral secret tradition."

[31] The currently recognized authoritative documents of cabalistic doctrine date from about AD 100.   These are the *Sepher Yetsirah* ("Book of Creation") ascribed to Rabbi Akiba, and *Sepher Hazzohar* ("Book of Brightness") ascribed to Simeon-ben-Jochai, a contemporary of Akiba. Cabalistic ideas flourished in Europe between the 12th and 16th centuries AD.

of Jubilees.   This book, also known as "The Little Genesis," is an esoteric history of the world from creation to the giving of the Law at Sinai and the entrance of Israel into Canaan.   It is a sort of *haggadic* commentary on the book of Genesis, interspersed with an abundant supply of illustrative anecdotes.   It is usually dated about the 2nd century BC.   The long stretch of time covered in *Jubilees* is divided into fifty jubilee-periods of 49 (7 x 7) years each.   In fact, the entire chronology is based on the number 7, and heavenly authority is claimed for this arrangement: the week has 7 days, the month has 4 x 7 days, the year has 52 x 7 = 364 days, the year-week has 7 years, and the jubilee has 7 x 7 = 49 years.   The separate events regarding the patriarchs et al. are pinpointed in accordance with this scheme.   The sacred narrative of the canonical book of Genesis is embellished, at times almost beyond recognition.   For example, we learn the sabbath was observed by the archangels before man ever came to observe it, that the angels also practiced circumcision, that Jacob never tricked anyone, etc.

Gnosticism also provides examples of what Paul may have had in mind as he wrote about "myths" or "fables."   The myth of Isis and Osiris is an example. In the religion of ancient Egypt, Osiris was one of the principal deities.   He represented the male productive force in nature, eventually became identified with the setting sun, and then came to be regarded as the ruler of the realm of the dead in the mysterious region below the western horizon.   Osiris was the brother and husband of Isis, goddess of the earth and moon, who represented the female productive force in nature.   According to legend, Osiris, as king of Egypt, found his people plunged in barbarism, and taught them law, agriculture, religion, and other blessings of civilization.   He was murdered by his evil brother Set, who tore the body to pieces and scattered the fragments.   Isis found his scattered remains, collected them in a casket, and when they were collected, Osiris moved his little finger (and this is supposed to be an early proof of "resurrection"!).   Osiris then lived on in the underworld as the ruler of the dead.   Horus, the son of Isis and Osiris, avenged his father's death by killing Set, and then ascended to the throne.

And endless genealogies – "Endless" (*aperantos*) is found only here in the New Testament, but the word was used in the Septuagint with the meaning 'infinite,' or 'immeasurable.'   In classical Greek it means either 'endless' or 'interminable,' or 'having no useful end or purpose.'   The genealogies, like the fables, can be explained either from Jewish or Gnostic vantage points.   The Jews meticulously kept genealogical lists (it was necessary for eligibility to priesthood, and to know who had title to family lands).   From these lists (or from those in Genesis, 1 Chronicles, Ezra, or Nehemiah) the Jews would take a name (indeed, they even invented new names) and make up a story about the person who otherwise (as far as the Biblical record is concerned) is only a name.   Such interminable allegories and embroideries on the inspired record were part of the regular bill of fare in the synagogue.   In Gnostic doctrine, there were 'emanations of aeons' responsible for creation and for guarding the entrance to the seven heavens. Irenaeus applies this passage to the Valentinians and their succession of aeons (Bythus, Nous, Logos, Anthropus, etc. – in all thirty, male and female)[32]; so does Tertullian, who speaks of the seeds of the Gnostic heresies as already budding in Paul's time.[33] There was no end to such tales, for the only restriction would be the amount of ingenuity possessed by the storyteller.

Which give rise to mere speculation – The KJV translates "which minister questions." Nuances involved in the Greek term[34] include 'disputes,' 'questions over controversial matters,' 'inquiries,' 'troublesome and angry debates.' The myths and genealogies[35] lead only to further uncertainties and the piling up of ignorance and error. If we may believe that the same heretical teachings are repudiated in 2 Timothy and Titus, then the qualifications therein found would also apply. They are "worldly" and suitable only for "old women" (1 Timothy 4:7), they are "Jewish" (Titus 1:14), and are that which people turn to when they turn away from the truth (2 Timothy 4:4). The myths and endless genealogies have little bearing on practical living. Interpretations and allegories based on the inventiveness of men can never help a man know God's will, a knowledge of which comes only by divine revelation!

Rather than *furthering* God's provision which is by faith – For "God's provision" the NASB margin offers "the administration of God." The KJV version's "godly edifying" translates an inferior reading *oikodomian theou*[36] whereas the better texts have *oikonomian theou*, which can be rendered "God's dispensation" or "God's provision." The same word (*oikonomian*) is translated "dispensation"[37] and "steward" or "manager."[38] Etymologically, the word has to do with 'ruling a house,' and speaks of God's management of the affairs of His creation and child-

---

[32] *Contr. Haer.*, lib.i., preface 1.

[33] *Advers. Valentin.*, cap. iii, and *De Praesc.*, VII.33. Some question the use made of "genealogies" by Irenaeus and Tertullian. They have been charged with applying Paul's words to a heresy current in their own day, rather than actually offering explanation of what Paul had in mind when he wrote. It is also argued that neither Irenaeus nor Tertullian actually shows the word "genealogy" was ever applied by Gnostics themselves to the series of emanations of the aeons they taught about.

[34] The manuscripts vary between *zeteseis* and *ekzeteseis*.

[35] "Which," a feminine form in the Greek, likely has been attracted to the case of its nearest antecedent ("genealogies"). Though "which" does not technically agree in gender with "myths," it would be difficult to think of "myths" as not also included as a source giving rise to "mere speculation."

[36] The spelling *oikodomian* is thought to have begun as a conjecture by Erasmus, from whose work, because of its much easier sense, it was taken into the Textus Receptus.

[37] Ephesians 1:10, 3:2, Colossians 1:25. We sometimes speak of the Patriarchal, Mosaic, and Christian *dispensations*. Verses like these (including 1 Timothy 1:4) are behind the use of the term "dispensations."

[38] Luke 16:2; 1 Corinthians 4:1; 1 Peter 4:10.

ren. God has a method for administering or managing the salvation of the world. The false teachers were not furthering the administration or management policies of God. God's provision is said to be "by faith." "Faith" comes by hearing the Word of God, not from hearing human speculations and endless genealogies. After all, the eternal purpose of God has been proclaimed by Jesus and the apostles. No human additions or added speculations are needed.[39] "Faith" here may be synonymous with 'body of doctrine.' If so, then it is in the realm of Christian faith (Christianity, not Judaism or Gnostic speculations) that God is administering the affairs of the world in this age since Calvary.

1:5 -- But the goal of our instruction – The charge to Timothy has both a negative and a positive side. Negatively, Timothy was to "instruct certain men not to teach strange doctrines" (verse 3). Positively, Timothy was to instruct about the proper lifestyle expected in the lives of Christians, a lifestyle that itself was the real "goal" (*telos*), the end, the aim, the purpose of all Christian teaching. For "instruction" the NASB translators offer an alternative in the margin, "commandment," the word chosen by the KJV at this place. Some commentators have supposed the word "commandment" here has reference to the Mosaic Law.[40] However, as noted in comments on verse 3, the root word here is the same as the word "instruct" from verse 3. Since there was no reference to the Law of Moses in verse 3, why should we suppose there is such a reference here in verse 5? Further, the noun *paraggelia* is never used elsewhere in the New Testament to refer to the Law of Moses, so it would be most unusual if that were the intended meaning here. Commentators who understand that Paul's reference is to the gospel, and to the "charge" given to Timothy about his continuing mission in Ephesus, are closer to what Paul is writing about. The only other occurrence of the word for "instruction" in Paul's writings (outside the Pastorals) is in 1 Thessalonians 4:2, which speaks of commands handed on from Christ as requirements for the Christian life. That is also the thrust of the context here in 1 Timothy.

Is love – The goal of the teacher who is working within the sphere of God's "administration" is that his pupils exhibit "love," rather than a vain show of spec-

---

[39] It has been correctly observed that a person's teaching should be judged by its fruits. Whatever fails to promote God's program of things should be rejected, even though it has no other fault. (Hendriksen)

[40] At this place, care must be taken when working through the "exposition" found in the various commentaries. Some of the writers are one-covenant theologians, who see the Law of Moses as still binding. They try to explain away what Paul writes in 1 Timothy 1, so they may continue to hold their view that the Law of Moses is still valid, despite what the Scriptures everywhere declare, that the Law was never intended to be anything but temporary, and that its validity ceased at the Cross. Other writers appeal to the old denominational distinction between "moral, ceremonial, and judicial" as they try to explain verse 5. In these works we find comments to the effect that the real purpose of the moral portion of Moses' Law (which of course is permanent) was to produce love, etc. We think all such attempts miss the mark.

ulation about myths and genealogies. The goal of Christian teaching, whether Paul's or Timothy's or ours, is love (*agape*).[41] "Love" is doing what is spiritually best for the other person.[42] This lifestyle is evident when a believer loves his fellow Christians and lost men. He does whatever is needed for their spiritual welfare. "Beloved, let us love one another, for love is from God; and everyone who loves is born of God and knows God. The one who does not love does not know God, for God is love" (1 John 4:7,8). Present-day evangelists should articulate the goal of their instruction in these words Paul has written to Timothy.

From a pure heart and a good conscience and a faith without hypocrisy – The kind of love that Christians are to exhibit has a threefold source. "Heart" is the first of these sources. "Heart" in Scripture stands for a man's mind, his thoughts, his moral affections. A "pure heart" is one whose motives and affections are noble and unselfish. Jesus one day explained to the apostles that a man's heart is cleansed through the Word (John 15:3). On that same occasion, He also indicated that sometimes impure thoughts have to be "pruned" so the heart can be cleansed. It is the "pure in heart" who shall see God, Jesus promised in the Sermon on the Mount (Matthew 5:8). "Conscience," the second of the sources from which love springs, is an innate faculty which prompts a man to do what his mind thinks is right, and criticizes him when he does what his mind thinks is wrong. It takes conversion to produce a "good conscience" in the first place (1 Peter 3:20,21). Hebrews 10:22 speaks about "having our hearts sprinkled from an evil conscience, and our bodies washed with pure water" before we attempt to draw near to God. In obedience to the truth one purifies his soul, and then he is able to love his brethren (1 Peter 1:22). Some people do loving acts once in a while, not because it has become a deliberate and habitual part of their lifestyle, but because their conscience is bothering them. What Timothy is to seek in believers' lives is a loving lifestyle that is not merely the result of a guilty conscience. Believers will continually have a "good conscience" if their acts of love match God's expectations for them as revealed in His Word. The third source of love, an "unhypocritical faith," is a faith that is something more than a few high-sounding words, something more than a pretense, performed only when people are looking. This is a faith that needs no mask to hide its insincerity or inconsistency. Some writers have offered the comment that Gnostic Judaism could never hope to produce in a man's life the sources out of which "love" would flow, for all they offered was 'ceremonial cleanness,' a 'defiled conscience' and at best a merely 'nominal Christianity.'

---

[41] Only "love" is in the nominative case (after a linking verb "is"). The other words in this verse ("heart, conscience, faith") are in the genitive case, so they are not part of the "goal."

[42] "Love" is not defined in the New Testament, but the word Paul uses is something that can be willed. It is used of Christ giving Himself for the church (Ephesians 5:25; Romans 5:8) and its characteristics are described in 1 Corinthians 13.

1:6 -- For some men – The "some men" of verse 6 are likely the same false teachers introduced as "certain men" in verse 3. "For," with which this verse begins, indicates that verse 6 is a reason for something just said, or a further explanation of it.

Straying from these things – Whenever the chief aim (i.e., love permeating the listener's lifestyles) of all preaching and of the entire work of the Christian ministry is lost sight of,[43] sad results follow, as Paul points out in verses 6 and 7. "Straying" translates *astochasantēs*, a word which means "to deviate from, to miss the mark, to swerve, to stray, to depart." These men missed the real end or goal of the gospel (love from a pure heart, etc.), and reached instead only vain and boastful talking.

Have turned aside to fruitless discussion – "Turned aside," from *ektrepō*, is a word used of a traveler who loses his bearings and turns off onto a wrong road, and then fails to reach the intended destination. These words seem to tell us that these teachers had once been on the right road, but they had not kept on it. As a result of their "straying," they have "turned aside." They were, however, still reckoned as members of the church at Ephesus, else Timothy could have exercised no possible authority over them, as Paul was exhorting him to do. "Fruitless discussion" ("vain jangling" KJV) is *mataiologia* in the Greek. The "fruitless" part of this compound word is the synonym that means "to no purpose" – with the emphasis on the result. There is also the idea of "boasting, lying" or even "windy speech." The "words" of these teachers produce no valuable spiritual result. Men's lives are not changed like the gospel can change a man and lead him to a lifestyle that exhibits "love." The wrong path which these people have taken is not even a good detour; it is more like a dead-end street beyond which lies a swamp. So the false teacher leaves the plain truths of God, and though he talks much, gives forth only empty and purposeless chatter.

1:7 -- Wanting to be teachers of the Law – This desire that motivated the false teachers[44] marks their thinking as having Jewish origin. Why had these men turned aside to strange doctrines, myths, and endless genealogies? Was it because they wanted the high reputation and honor received when one was a "teacher of the Law"? Did they covet the respect and influence which was paid

---

[43] "These things" is plural, and some have supposed the reference is to the three sources of love given in the previous verse. Others think "these things" refers to the charge about ministry and lifestyle that Paul has been giving to Timothy since verse 3. Our comments on the text reflect a choice of the latter, a choice based on the fact that "love" is the goal, not the plurals (heart, conscience, faith).

[44] The participle that begins verse 7 is related to "some men" of verse 6, so this verse is a further description of the false teachers.

to the acknowledged teachers of the Law of Moses?   In the Introductory Studies, we have offered the suggestion that the false teachers were Gnostic Judaizers. To this point, Paul's description of the false teachers fits numerous philosophical speculations in Greek wisdom that were current in the 1st century.   When, however, he characterizes these "certain men" as desiring to be "teachers of the Law," that leads us to look to some teaching that not only had philosophical speculations in it but also generous amounts of Jewish ideas, like that found in Gnostic Judaism.

Even though they do not understand either what they are saying – The most jarring accusation that can be brought against one who claims to be a scholar is to call him ignorant.   This is precisely what Paul does.   In regards to "what they are saying," some commentators have supposed the "teachers of the Law" were trying to explain that the principles valid during the Mosaic Age were still valid in the Christian age.[45]   However, to this commentator, such an interpretation does not seem to catch the flavor or emphases of 1st century Judaism,[46] nor the thrust of the preceding context.   It is much more likely that Paul charges the would-be "teachers of the Law" with not understanding the wild fables and strange doctrines which they were themselves teaching – fables, myths, and doctrines ostensibly based on the Law of Moses, but in actuality the doctrines and inventions of men. So Jesus rebuked the scribes and teachers of the Law in His day.   "You do err, not knowing the Scriptures or the power of God."   "You do greatly err." (Matthew 12:7, 22:29; Mark 12:27).

Or the matters about which they make confident assertions – "The matters" would be the "strange doctrines" alluded to in verse 3.   "Confident assertions" translates *diabebaiountai*, which means "to maintain strongly, to be positive." Such a forceful presentation is right when the minister of Christ is declaring Divine truth (Titus 3:8), but very wrong when one has "turned aside to fruitless discussion" (1 Timothy 1:6).   A wise teacher must understand what he teaches, and must, at the same time, be clear in his own mind that what he teaches is true. These would-be "teachers of Law" met neither qualification.   Paul could "read these men's minds," and know whether or not they understood what they were teaching, by the help of the Holy Spirit.   There was a spiritual gift known as "discerning of spirits."   We suppose Paul has exercised this gift before he writes this scathing rebuke of the false teachers.

---

[45] Appeal is made to the context following, namely, verses 8-10, to justify this exposition.

[46] The reader is reminded that 1st century rabbinic Judaism was a departure from the classic Mosaic religion taught in the Old Testament.   Man-made rules (called in the New Testament "works of law") based on this or that verse in the Law, were substituted for the rules God Himself had revealed to men.   1st century Judaism was not just a logical extension or outgrowth of the Law of Moses – rather, it voided what Moses taught (Matthew 15:3,6).

2. Teachers who failed to use God's Law properly. 1:8-11

1:8 -- But -- Beginning in verse 8, Paul takes up a second danger to sound teaching in Ephesus. The first danger was teachers who taught a different doctrine (verses 3-7). Verse 7 has said the false teachers at Ephesus were making wrong use of the Law of Moses. Paul hastens to add that the fault is not in the Law itself, but in the false-teachers' misuse and abuse of the Law. Verses 8 and following will show the proper use of the Law. It never was intended to be used in the way that the would-be "teachers of the Law" were using it. Their mishandling of the Law made it necessary for Paul to reaffirm what the proper use of the Law was.

We know that the Law is good -- "We know" is a strong expression of know-ledge, learned in the school of the Holy Spirit. Paul spoke with the conscious authority of an apostle of Jesus Christ, confident of the truth of what he preached and taught. "We know" may also be an appeal to the common understanding of the Christian church concerning the Law of Moses and its "goodness" if used in the manner God intended. "Good" translates *kalos* (not *agathos*), which "draws attention not only to excellence of intrinsic quality, but also to beauty of outward form" (Bruce). Paul did not condemn the Law because some of his contemporaries perverted it. The Law was God given -- we should not condemn something God has done as though it were no good! Thinking men recognize the value of the Mosaic Law (and the need of all law, for that matter). The Law's purpose, to point men to the coming Messiah and their need to be justified by faith (Galatians 3:24), was unquestionably a good thing. This affirmation that the Law is good reminds us of Romans 7:7,12. Paul is far from denigrating the Mosaic Law; his opponents are not able to blunt the apostle's thrust here by simply saying, "What else would you expect from Paul? He always has spoken against the Law!" (Compare Acts 21:20,21, or the charges against Stephen at Acts 6:13,14.) Paul says "The Law is good" to guard against any possible accusation that he was an enemy of the Law. He was not an enemy of the Law; he vindicated the true use of the Law whenever he wrote or spoke. One proper use of the Law is to make men aware of what things God calls sin (Romans 10:4; Galatians 3:24, 4:4,5).

"The Law" is the Law of Moses. Several factors indicate Paul has the Mosaic Law in view. (1) Verse 7 speaks about certain would-be Law-teachers, and identifies the false teachers as exponents of the Mosaic Law. (2) Verse 8 reads "*The* Law" (there is an article in the Greek). (3) The list of sins in verses 9 and 10 follows the same order of sins which appears in the Ten Commandments.

How do we harmonize this statement that "the Law *is* good" with the asser-tion everywhere found in the New Testament that the Law was only ever intended to be temporary,[47] and that its validity ended when Christ died (Colossians 2:14)? Whatever this passage says about a "lawful" use of the Law, verse 9 will show there is no contradiction to what the Scriptures elsewhere say about the temporary nature of the Law. In the gospel age, the Law still serves some useful purposes. There are "examples" (1 Corinthians 10:11) from which we can learn valuable lessons. 2 Timothy 3:16,17 also show a continuing usefulness in the Old Testament Scriptures. The primary purpose for which it was given by God was the restraint of evil-doing, and in that sense it may be described as "good."

If one uses it lawfully – The "one" (*tis*) here contemplated using the "Law" is any teacher or student of the Law.[48] "Lawfully" (*nomimos*) is an adverb. This verse, and 2 Timothy 2:5, are the only times this adverb is found in the New Testament. Paul will go on to describe the various classes for whom the law is especially designed. When applied to these people, it is being used "lawfully." The Law was never intended to supply materials for casuistry or idle and profitless arguments. It was never meant as a system out of which man might draw materials to justify an ascetic, rigorous lifestyle. Those are *not* "lawful" uses of the Law of Moses. "Uses it lawfully" indicates that for the Law to have its proper effect it must be used in accord with the intentions of its Giver. "As long as the Law is used as God intended for it to be used, then truth and benefits result. But when the Law is used only as a springboard into hopeless speculation, fanciful legends, and erroneous instruction, then the law is being abused to become an introducer of evil rather than the foundation of truth" (Foster, *op. cit.*, p.347).

1:9 -- Realizing the fact – This verse continues the sentence begun in verse 8. If one is going to use the Law correctly (verse 8), what is about to be said in verse 9 must be kept in mind. One must understand what follows here in verse 9 if he is to use the Law lawfully.

That law is not made for a righteous man – A "righteous man" is a Christian. He is one who has been "justified by faith" (Romans 5:1). "Justify" and "righteous" come from the same root word.[49] "Law" is likely a reference to the

---

[47] See Romans 10:4; Galatians 3:24, 4:4,5; Hebrews 7:12, 7:18, 10:9.

[48] Some have interpreted the *tis* as though it were a continued reference to the "certain ones" of verses 3 and 6. It is more likely this indefinite relative pronoun is used here as an indefinite reference to anyone who proposes to use the Law.

[49] Some think the term is used in a general, non-technical way. The verse would then say that laws are not enacted to control good men. It is to control criminals that laws are made. See Calvin, Barrett, Bernard, Ellicott, Hendriksen, and Simpson, for examples of how the passage is interpreted if *dikaios* is given an ethical (rather than theological) meaning. Not a few of these writers appeal to Romans 13:8-10 as a passage that teaches the same thing as 1 Timothy 1:9.

Law of Moses.[50]   This is evident when one realizes that the following list follows the general order of the Ten Commandments. This verse, thus, is one of many in Paul's writings that shows the Law of Moses was never intended to be anything but temporary. It was for the age before Calvary.[51] "Made" translates the verb *keitai*, whose figurative meaning in this place is 'to be given, exist, be valid.' The verb takes the dative of the person for whom the law is "given" or "valid," and all the terms following are in the dative case. The very point the false teachers at Ephesus were forgetting, in their rush to be teachers of the Law in the church, was that the Law was never intended for "a righteous man," at least never in the way they were teaching it. To bring the Law into the church at Ephesus, as the false teachers were trying to do, making it the skeleton around which speculative myths and endless genealogies and strange doctrines were woven, was to miss the very purpose of the Law.

But – Paul now begins to remind the readers about the class of people (i.e., non-Christians) for whom the Law of Moses was intended. The Law "was made centuries before Jesus of Nazareth walked on earth, as a great protest against the every-day vices which dishonored Israel in common with the rest of mankind" (Spence, *Ellicott's*, p.193). Not a few writers have found it useful to compare 1 Timothy 1:9,10 with Exodus 20:1-17. The chart on the next page is one example of such a comparison. Some have noticed, as the comparison is made, that instead of quoting one of the commandments, Paul gives an example of an aggravated form of the sin prohibited. Perhaps he does so to remind the church and the false teachers of the very specific way the Law was applied when dealing with people's sins.

---

[50] The careful student will have noted that in verse 8, in the NASB, "Law" was capitalized, while "law" in verse 9 is not.   This reflects the translators' view that in verse 9, "law in general" is the topic, and that verse 9 is a statement of principle about law in general.   It is true that there is no "the" before "law" in the Greek here at verse 9.   (The construction is called anarthrous *nomos*, and students of Romans 2:12-14 are well acquainted with the problems presented by the presence or absence of "the" before *nomos*.   The old attempt to make distinctions between "law" and "Law" on the basis of the presence or the absence of the article, an explanation that began with Origen [in *Ep. ad Rom.* on 3:7], has by examination of the evidence been shown to be incorrect.)   The absence of the article is not convincing proof that Paul is now talking about some "law" other than the Law of Moses.   For a number of reasons we think the reference is not just to law in general, but specifically to the Law of Moses which has been the topic for several verses now.

There has been much variety of interpretation offered for 1 Timothy 1:9.   (1) Clarke supposes "law" here refers to the ceremonial laws of Moses.   But the commands about to be quoted do not come from the "ceremonial" laws, so Clarke cannot be right.   (2) Some one-covenant theologians think the reference cannot be that the Law of Moses is no longer binding on Christians, since in their view the Law of Moses has never been abrogated.   But this view is hardly right in the light of Hebrews 8-10.   (3) Macknight speaks of the fact that the Law was not given for the purpose of justifying a righteous man.   But why introduce the verb "justifying" that Paul does not use?

[51] See footnote #47 above.   Also see Romans 6:14, 8:2; Galatians 2:19, 5:18, and the argument of Hebrews 8-10.

Exodus 20:1-17	**1 Timothy 1:9,10**
1. You shall have no other gods before me.	1. Lawless and rebellious
2. You shall not make for yourself an idol.	2. Ungodly and sinners
3. You shall not take the name of the Lord your God in vain.	3. Unholy and profane
4. Remember the Sabbath day, to keep it holy.	
5. Honor your father and your mother.	5. Kill their fathers or mothers
6. You shall not murder.	6. Murderers
7. You shall not commit adultery.	7. Immoral men and homosexuals
8. You shall not steal.	8. Kidnappers
9. You shall not bear false witness.	9. Liars and perjurers
10. You shall not covet.	10. Whatever else is contrary to sound teaching

For those who are lawless and rebellious – "Lawless" translates *anamos*. It refers not to those ignorant of the Law, but to those who live as if there were no law (Hendriksen). Berry defines it as contempt of Law, living contrary to the Law (*Greek-English Lexicon*, p.118). "Rebellious" translates *anupotaktos*, and means "insubordinate, resisting lawful authority."[52] Rebellious people refuse to submit to the rules God has laid down in the Law. In our chart, this term is related to the command about having "no other Gods before me." Sinners who refuse to submit to the rules God has laid down show by their refusal that, as far as they are concerned, someone or something else is more important than Jehovah.

For the ungodly and sinners – "Ungodly" represents *asebes*, "those who have no religion, who do not worship or honor God" (*Barnes'*, p.118). Berry writes of "positive, active irreligion – direct opposition to God." Those who violate the command regarding graven images have refused to give Jehovah a rightful place

---

[52] In Titus 1:10, Paul uses the same word when he writes of "rebellious men ... especially those of the circumcision."

in their hearts and affections.   "Sinners" (*hamartolos*) have "missed the mark or goal of their existence, namely, the conscious glorification of God" (*Hendriksen*, p.66).   Often in the Gospels, the disdainful term "sinners" was applied by the Pharisees to those who did not observe the traditions of the elders.   It is doubtful such is the idea here.   Instead, if our chart is correct, those who violate the prohibition of making and worshipping idols are the ones intended by "sinners."

For the unholy and profane – "Unholy" is *anosios* and refers to men who are "careless of their duties toward God" (*Hendriksen*, p.67).   Berry says this synonym for "unholy" means "they are not in harmony with the divine constitution of the moral universe, not in harmony with what men in general feel is right."[53]   In the chart comparing the lists in Exodus and Timothy, "unholy" is thought to speak about "taking the Lord's name in vain."   A "profane" (*bebalos*, from *baino*, to walk, step, tread) person is "one who does not refrain or hesitate to trample on that which is holy" (*Hendriksen*, p.67).   "The implication is not so much that the person is blasphemous in his language but that he treats religion with contempt, mockery, and scorn" (*Barnes'*, p.118).   Some observe that the chart above has no word from 1 Timothy opposite the 4th commandment (about the Sabbath).   Therefore, some defenders of Sabbatarianism have suggested "profane" is another way of saying these people "profane the Sabbath day" rather than keeping it holy.   However, there is no need in this gospel age to search for rules about keeping the Sabbath.   It is better to speak of the Lord's Day (the first day of the week) rather than the "Sabbath" (the seventh day of the week).

For those who kill their fathers or mothers – *Patroloais* and *matroloais* may not mean literally to "kill;" it may instead speak of abuse.   The allusion here is to Exodus 21:15, where the Hebrew word for "smite" is *nakah,* which sometimes means "to kill" and sometimes simply "to strike."   It does not necessarily mean "to smite to death" any more than the Greek word *aloaō* does.[54]   Perhaps Paul uses both words because the Decalog spoke of two persons when it commanded "honor your father and your mother."   Barnes (*op cit.*, p.118) speaks of the ancient world's view that the murder of mothers was a more monstrous crime than the murder of fathers.   The Biblical view does not make such a distinction; both are monstrous!   The words in the Greek speak of those persons of various ages who refuse all reverence, even all kindly treatment, to their parents.

For murderers – *Androphonos* speaks of premeditated murder, homicide.   It does not speak of those who kill accidentally (manslaughter).   Compare its use at Exodus 21:12ff.

---

[53] Berry, *op. cit.*, p.117.   In ancient Egypt, an example of something "unholy," that "men did not think was right," was for brothers and sisters to marry each other.

[54] Comments adapted from *Pulpit Commentary*.

1:10 -- And immoral men – *Pornos* speaks of sex outside of the marriage relationship. It can be illicit sexual intercourse between unmarried persons, and it can also include adultery. The root meaning also included prostitution, but in the New Testament it is used as a general word for "sexual immorality." This word and the next are both violations of the seventh commandment.

And homosexuals – *Arsenokoitēs* is found in the New Testament only here and at 1 Corinthians 6:9. Etymologically the word is made up of two parts: "male" (with a strong emphasis on "sex"[55]) and "bed" (a euphemism for sexual intercourse[56]). The word therefore seems to refer to male homosexuals, though indirectly it would speak of all homosexuals, whether male or female.[57] If our chart of comparisons between Exodus and 1 Timothy is correct, it is instructive to note that Paul's list includes this sin as prohibited by the seventh commandment.

And kidnappers – *Andrapodistis* occurs only here in the New Testament, but is very common in classical Greek. The word *andrapodon* means slave, and so the root word seems to have reference to slave dealers. This would be a gross violation of the eighth commandment. It was a crime well-known in the Roman world of Paul's day.[58] Barnes, who took a leading role in the antislavery movement of a previous century, has some good notes here on the topic. He condemns both the kidnappers and those who bought and used men as slaves after they had been kidnapped.

And liars and perjurers – In these two words, Paul is concerned with those who break the ninth commandment. *Pseustēs* may be translated "liar" or "deceiver." Among the sins which especially excited the wrath of the first inspired teachers of Christianity, "lack of truth" appears singularly prominent. One after another, in different language, the apostles expressed their deep abhorrence of this too-common sin, which in John's impassioned words will suffice to exclude one from the city of the blessed (Revelation 22:15). *Epiorkos* ("perjurer") occurs only here in the New Testament, though it is common in classical Greek and the verb

---

[55] See the article *arsen* ("male") in BAGD, p.109.

[56] See BAGD on *koite* ("marriage bed"), p.440, 441.

[57] The New Testament regularly emphasizes that homosexuality is a perversion of the God-ordained orientation of sex ever since He created male and female (Romans 1:24,26-28; 1 Corinthians 6:9-11). The eternal consequence for continued and unrepentant involvement in this, and the other sins listed here, is exclusion from the Kingdom of God. But, by the grace of God, deliverance from this and the other sins listed here is part of the Gospel message of salvation in Jesus Christ.

[58] It has been suggested that Paul's method of reducing the commands and prohibitions of the Ten Commandments to one word (or, sometimes two) may have been his way of expressing the list in contemporary terms known to the hearers. Such a use of "contemporary terms" is a continuing necessity, lest people think the sin they are about to commit is not prohibited in the Bible since they have never found the contemporary word in their (sometimes) century-old translations.

form occurs in Matthew 5:33, and twice in the LXX.   The reference may be to Leviticus 19:11,12.   A 'false-swearer' (perjurer) is guilty of solemnly (by God's name) asserting to be true that which is false, with the intention of hurting his neighbor; or is one who makes a solemn vow while not intending to keep it.

Or whatever else is contrary to sound teaching – Perhaps "whatever else" represents the tenth commandment of the Exodus' list.[59]   The Law was intended for all sinners, and no sin[60] is excluded from the list.   It was to curb all such sins that the Law was given.   "Sound" in "sound teaching" translates *hugiainousē* (compare the word "hygienic").   "Teaching" ("doctrine" KJV) is "sound" if it promotes the spiritual health and well-being of the person who learns it. "Teaching" translates *didaskalia*, which means "that which is taught."[61]   In the words "sound teaching" – an expression peculiar to the Pastoral Epistles[62] – a sharp contrast is suggested to the 'sickly and unhealthy' teaching of the false teachers, with their foolish legends and allegories.   In the Greek, there is an article before "sound teaching" – "*the* sound doctrine."   We suppose "sound teaching" is another name for the gospel.   In the Greek language, an article could either be inserted or omitted when using proper names.   Although the reference is definite, it is probably best to omit the article when making a translation into English (since English regularly omits the article before proper nouns).

1:11 -- According to the glorious gospel of the blessed God – What was it that was "according to the ... Gospel" which Paul preached?   As verse 8 explains, it is the fact that the Mosaic Law was not intended for Christians ("the righteous"), but for sinners.[63]   Paul seals this section of his argument by making this assertion that the estimate of the Law he just gave is not based on his own personal opinions

---

[59] In Romans 13:9 Paul specifically refers to the 10th commandment when he writes that he had learned from the Law that "desire (as well as the prohibited act) could be sin."   (Knight's suggestion on p.186ff that the 10th commandment is not represented within Paul's list and his page of possible reasons why Paul omitted it here are not appropriate comments for this passage.)

[60] A man's moral obligations were not exhausted when he had kept the Ten Commandments. The Scriptures elsewhere speak to this matter.   The Ten Commandments say nothing of drunkenness, polygamy, divorces on trifling accounts, retaliation, etc.

[61] *Didaskalia* becomes more commonly used in the Pastoral Epistles than it was earlier. *Didache* (that which is taught) and *paradosis* (something handed down) were the more common earlier words for Christian teaching.   One suggestion for the change of words is that by the time the Pastorals were written, the faith had been once and for all delivered to the saints, rather than being that which was just in the process of being given.

[62] See 1 Timothy 6:3; 2 Timothy 1:13, 4:3; Titus 1:9,13, 2:1,2.

[63] Scholars have not been in agreement with what "according to" is to be connected.   (a) As our notes do, some take it with "we know" of verse 8.   Just as "according to my gospel" in Romans 2:16 is connected to the thought that began that paragraph, so we connect "according to the gospel" here in 1 Timothy to the thought that begins the paragraph.   (b) Others take it with "sound teaching" of verse 10, and then write how the only thing that can be called "sound teaching" must be "in conformity with, corresponding to" the gospel Paul preached.

or conclusions, but is in truth part of the gospel which he had been commissioned to preach.[64] "Gospel," of course, is the 'good news' entrusted to Paul and preached by him, that God has provided salvation for all men in Jesus Christ.[65] But the Greek phrase in which the word "gospel" occurs, *to euaggelion tēs doxēs tou makariou theou*, cannot easily be translated as the NASB does, "the glorious gospel of the blessed God."[66]   Instead, the Greek is rightly translated "the gospel of the glory of the blessed God."   This phrase might mean any of three different things: (1) *Tēs doxēs tou theou* might simply be a periphrasis for "God," as in Romans 6:4 or Exodus 24:16,17.   (2) The "Glory of God" might be a reference to Jesus Christ, who is the brightness of God's glory, the image of the invisible God (Hebrews 1:3), in whose face the glory of God shines (2 Corinthians 4:4,6). (3) It might mean that the gospel tells about the glory of God; the gospel reveals and proclaims His glory.   If we interpret the phrase in this third way, then the "glory" of God being revealed in the gospel is one of His attributes.   In other words, the 'content' of the gospel is the glory and majesty of God.   (a) Perhaps it refers to that brilliant sphere of emerald light that one sees when he first gets a glimpse of the One on the Throne (Revelation 4:3).   (b) Perhaps it refers to His moral character and perfection.   (c) Perhaps it refers to His splendor and power. (d) Perhaps it refers to God's majesty as shown in the sufferings of Christ, or in the riches of His great mercy.   In fact, all of these aspects of God's glory are contained in and revealed in the gospel, though the fourth meaning is the one this commentator prefers.   God is here called "blessed."   This and 1 Timothy 6:15 are the only places in the New Testament where the adjective *makarios* ("blessed") is applied to God.   Usually the adjective "blessed," when applied to God, is a translation of *eulogetēs*.   Just why Paul uses *makarios* and applies it to God is not clear.   Perhaps it reminds us that God in His very being contains all happiness and bestows it upon men.   Perhaps Paul means that when people know about God's eternal and changeless perfection, and the blessed gift of forgiveness He offers to all sinners who obey the gospel, those people out of gratitude offer blessings to God.   In this sense He comes to be "blessed."

---

[64] Those who have searched the Pastoral Epistles for words and expressions that are unexampled in Paul's earlier epistles, and then think they have found proof of the non-Pauline authorship of the Pastorals, have also called attention to this passage, where the writer says that "the law was for sinners and not the righteous."   Easton has raised a question whether this approach to the Law can be reconciled with Paul's doctrine.   In fact, he even finds this statement irreconcilable with 2 Timothy 3:16,17.   Those who are familiar with Romans 6:15ff, 7:12,16 and 1 Corinthians 9:20 do not find what is said about the Law in 1 or 2 Timothy to be anything but a thoroughly Pauline statement.

[65] Those commentators who have supposed that there is some reference to the gospel we know as "According to Luke" are likely mistaken in their conclusions.   Even though Early Christian Literature tells us that the source of much of what Luke wrote was Paul's preaching, we think Paul here in Timothy refers to his preached gospel, rather than to any already written gospel.

[66] Only if we were to suppose the wording reflects a Semitic style (cp. Ephesians 1:17, "the father of glory") could we justify the translation offered in the NASB, RSV, KJV, NIV, etc.

With which I have been entrusted – The gospel is pictured as a precious deposit, a "trust" given into Paul's care.[67]   The church members at Ephesus who have been giving an ear to the false teachers, as well as those false teachers themselves, need to consider again the source of what Paul had preached to them in the first place. The gospel which they obeyed was a treasure entrusted by the Master to Paul. Before embracing any "strange doctrine" (verse 3), they would do well to carefully investigate where those doctrines came from, since they certainly were not a "precious deposit" like Paul's message was.

B. The Outstanding Illustration of the Results of Sound Doctrine. 1:12-17

1:12 --I thank Christ Jesus our Lord – The mention of the gospel (verse 11), and of the fact that it was committed to him, brings a flood of grateful memories to Paul and leads him to express his gratitude[68] to Him who called him to the work of preaching it.   One of the best ways to establish a point, to make it vivid and understandable, is to relate an experience with which all the listeners can identify. This is what Paul does in the verses in this paragraph.   First, he affirms that his present life in the ministry was the result of an empowering by Jesus (1:12). Next, Paul reminds them that his former life of Law-keeping was a life contrary to all the gospel teaches (1:13a).   When he was diligent for the Law, he was traveling a road far from the right road that God wanted him to travel.   Then, Paul explains how God's grace was greater than all his sin, and as a result he was shown mercy (1:13b,14).   Finally, he insists his own conversion was planned as a pattern to encourage would-be followers of Jesus to become believers (1:15-17). By this means he intends to impress upon his readers the difference between the Law and the Gospel, for the Law really is not intended for "righteous men (verse 9)."

Who has strengthened me – The verb *endunamaō* denotes the giving of that peculiar power which was the gift of the Holy Spirit, and which was necessary for the work of an apostle to enable him to bear witness to Christ in the face of an adverse world.   The same power Christ promised to the apostles before His ascension (Acts 1:8) Paul here claims to have received (cp. Ephesians 3:7; Philippians 4:13; 2 Timothy 2:1, 4:17).   Paul's empowering was similar to that

---

[67] Paul is not alone in the responsibility of being given a precious treasure to guard.   Any of the apostles of Jesus had the same trust.   So did the evangelist Timothy (1 Timothy 6:20).

[68] The unusual *charin echo* does have the meaning "I am grateful to," or "I give thanks to."   It is probably a virtual synonym for the verb *eucharisteo* which is the one more often used to express one's thanks.

of the other apostles.   At what point in Paul's life he was so "empowered"[69] the Scriptures do not record.   Hendriksen writes to the effect that the "enabling" and "judging" and "appointing" all took place simultaneously, on the way to Damascus (Acts 9:15,16, 22:1-21, 26:16-18).   But this does not seem to be quite right, for after what happened on the road, Ananias says to Paul that he has come to help Paul receive the Holy Spirit (Acts 9:17).   We do not know for certain to which measure of the Spirit Ananias refers (likely the indwelling gift), but if Hendriksen were right that Paul was specially empowered out on the road, would Ananias imply that Paul did not yet have the Holy Spirit?   The most reasonable conjecture is that the "empowering" took place while Paul was away in Arabia for three years after his Damascus Road experience.   In Arabia, Paul was receiving revelations from Jesus Christ (Galatians 1:12ff).   It is likely that this was the time he received the same powers (e.g., baptism of the Holy Spirit) that the original apostles received on Pentecost?

Because He considered me faithful – That for which Paul gave thanks to Jesus is here introduced.   There are two things emphasized in the closing part of verse 12:   that Christ trusted Paul, and that Christ put him into service.   A sovereign, when sending an ambassador to a foreign court, places a certain confidence in that ambassador, and would not commission him unless he had reason to believe the ambassador would be faithful.   Even when Paul was a persecutor of the church, Christ had seen in Paul the capabilities of what he later became.   Jesus' putting Paul into the ministry was an act expressive of great confidence in him.   A similar expression concerning "faithfulness" occurs in 1 Corinthians 7:25.

Putting me into service – The "service" or "ministry" (KJV) speaks of the task of being an apostle.   The word *diakonia* is expressive of the kind of "service" to which the Lord appointed Paul.   It is service rendered to the Lord in the spirit of love and personal devotion.   Barnes (*Notes on 1 Timothy*, p.120) has this thoughtful comment about Paul's thanksgiving for being put into the ministry.

> If there is anything for which a good man will be thankful, and should be thankful, it is that he has been so directed by the Spirit and providence of God as to be put into the ministry.   It is indeed a work of toil, of self-denial, and demanding many sacrifices of personal ease and comfort.   It is often identified with want, and poverty, and neglect, and persecution.   But it is an office so honorable, so excellent, so noble, and ennobling; it is attended with so many precious comforts here, and is so useful to the world, and it has such promises of blessedness and happiness in the world to come, that no matter what a man is required to give up in order to become a minister of the Gospel, he should be thankful to Christ for putting him into the office.

---

[69] There is a manuscript variation at this place. Some manuscripts read this verb form as though it were a present tense verb, expressing the fact that Paul was continuously strengthened throughout his whole ministry. Others have an aorist tense verb, pointing to one act in the past, and this is the better supported reading.

1:13 -- Even though – This verse opens with a word of concession. Paul concedes the fact that it was an unexpected thing on God's part that He should show mercy to such a one as Paul had been in his earlier days.

I was formerly a blasphemer and a persecutor and a wanton aggressor – Paul uses three strong terms as he recalls the magnitude of his wrong behavior. Paul was once where the Ephesian "teachers of the Law" would like to be! "Blasphemer" translates *blasphamos*; this noun and others from the same root mean to speak slanderously against some one or some thing.[70] The word "blasphemy" depicts the strongest type of insult against the honor of God. In Paul's case he was speaking against Jesus, the Son of God. "Persecutor" represents *dioktēs*. The root meaning of this Greek word is "to follow" or "to pursue," and as a "persecutor" that's what Paul did. He pursued Christians even to foreign cities in order to arrest them and try to make them recant their Christian faith (Acts 26:11). "Wanton aggressor" is an effort to catch the flavor of *hubristēs*, though there is no English word which exactly captures its meaning.[71] The word may well carry the connotation of "torture" or "violence." Paul acted like a "tyrant" toward those Christians whom he caught up with and arrested; he treated them with spite; he handled them roughly. In these words of bitter self-accusation, Paul sums up the characteristic features of his brilliant career as a young Pharisee leader. Can his readers see the danger at Ephesus if the church members become disciples of those would-be 'Law teachers'?

And yet I was shown mercy – Jesus did not give Paul he deserved. Rather, Jesus showed mercy in forgiving him and calling him to be an apostle.[72] Paul, his heart overflowing with love and gratitude, contrasts his Master's mercy with his own lack of it.

Because I acted ignorantly in unbelief – His plea of "ignorance" was not an excuse for his guilt; rather, it gives the reason why he received mercy. This language recalls the fact that under Moses there were two kinds of sins – sins which were forgivable, and sins which were not forgiven. The former were called

---

[70] In the Bible we observe several ways to commit blasphemy. One is to rail against (either with vile language or in eloquent language) the truth of God's nature. A second is to claim to perform tasks and make decisions that belong to God alone. A third type of blasphemy is to attack God's representatives either in word or in person.

[71] The updated NASB reads "violent aggressor." The same verb is used of the treatment Paul received at Philippi (1 Thessalonians 2:2, with its reference to what is recorded at Acts 16:22ff), and it is used of the treatment Jesus predicted He would receive while He was in custody just before His crucifixion (Luke 18:32).

[72] Most commentators think the expressions in the following verses here in 1 Timothy are all ways that "mercy" was shown to Paul.

sins of ignorance;[73] the latter were called sins of presumption (see Numbers 15:27-31).[74]   Only sins done "in ignorance" were forgivable.   Paul says what he did, bad as it was, was something that could be forgiven, and that's why God extended mercy to him.   When God acted as He did toward Paul, He was acting in harmony with what He had revealed about Himself and the kinds of sin He was willing to forgive.   It was "unbelief" in Jesus' deity and messiahship that led to his actions, not a determination to go completely against the will of God.   Had that been the cause of his actions, no mercy would have been extended to him.

1:14 -- And – The Greek is *de*, and the translation "and" makes good sense here. In contrast to the life he lived before (verse 13a), Paul is now explaining that he not only received mercy (verse 13b), but he also ("and") received abundant grace.

The grace of our Lord was more than abundant – Paul was fond of words which were superlative;[75] "super-abundant" (*huperepleonadzō*) is the word he uses here.[76]   The transition from verse 13 to verse 14 is from great sin to greater grace.   The grace of God simply overflows as a mighty river at flood stage over-flows its banks.   God's grace engulfed Paul and covered all his sins.   "Grace," here, likely has reference to God's provision to cover a man's sins (rather than, say, to his office of apostleship).   We have already talked some about "grace" when we studied the greeting at verse 2.   Paul's writing here about grace super-

---

[73] "Ignorance" should not be interpreted as though the sinner had no idea what he was doing, or was unaware that what he was doing was sin.   Every sin a man commits is the result of first being tempted by the devil, and then the man yielding to the temptation.   The man often weighs the possibilities whether or not he can do the sin without anyone whose opinion he values knowing about it.   The more likely no one will know, the more likely the man will do the thing he's been tempted to do.   There is a strange amount of deliberateness about every sin a man commits.   Perhaps we can understand that "ignorance" does not automatically imply lack of information when we recall the religious leaders knew Jesus was God's Son and Heir, and planned to kill Him anyway (Matthew 21:38).   Yet, in his second recorded sermon, Peter can say, "I know that you and your leaders did it in ignorance" (Acts 3:17).

[74] Presumptuous sins (the willful sins, i.e., "those committed with a high hand") are apparently explained at Hebrews 5:1,2.   In that passage, to sin "willfully" is explained as being in open rebellion towards God, involving an apostasy from revealed religion (closing verses of Hebrews 4).   While Paul did some monstrous things, he (in his mind) was not in rebellion to God (in fact, the very contrary is true, as "being zealous for God" at Acts 22:3,4 shows).   He thought he was doing God a service, trying to make sure men kept the Old Testament rules and religion.   His crimes against the church were not the result of a determined set of his will against God (which is what the Old Testament calls "presumptuous sin.")

[75] The use of superlative words is thoroughly Pauline (cp. *huperairomai, huperauxano, huperballo, huperekteino, huperperisseuo, huperupsoo* and other compounds with *huper*-).   It is further remarkable, as regards *huper* itself, that of the 158 times (or thereabouts) it appears in the New Testament, 106 are in Paul's signed letters, 12 in Hebrews, and only 40 in all the other NT books.   (See Hendriksen, p. 75 for all Paul's "super" words.)

[76] The word means to "be present in great abundance."   When used with a vessel, it means "to run over" or "overflow."

abounding reminds us of Romans 5:15-21 – wherever sin abounded, grace super abounds. Despite the sins of men (and they are ever increasing), God's grace is sufficient to cover all that sin.

Does "Lord" reference the Father or the Son? Does it say the Father's attitude toward sinning men is one that wants to help them out of their sins, if He can? Does this verse say Jesus' attitude toward sinning men is one that wants to help them if He can? Most often when Paul writes "Lord," Jesus is the reference.

With the faith and love which are *found* in Christ Jesus – "With" is *meta*, and means "accompanied by." Hendriksen (p.75), in Calvinistic language, says that "the faith and love" are the effect of grace in Paul's heart and life. It is true that we love Him because He first loved us, but 1 John 4:19 is certainly not saying the same thing that a Calvinist means. Calvinists believe that in salvation man is wholly passive; that salvation is monergistic, not synergistic; that there is only God's part, and not man's part. Hendriksen is incorrect in his note that makes "grace" the thing that caused "faith and love" in Paul's heart. What Paul actually wrote is that God's grace accompanied the exercise of faith and love by Paul (*Barnes'*, p.122). It was bestowed upon Paul when Paul met certain conditions or prerequisites for salvation. We are talking about Paul's conversion, not his whole earthly after-life. "Faith" therefore has reference to the 'faith that comes by hearing,' and is one of the conditions of salvation being granted. This faith is "not merely a childlike trust in Christ, but a belief which accepted Christ as the hope of an otherwise hopeless world" (*Ellicott's*, p.197). The grace was bestowed on Paul when he who had previously disbelieved in and reviled Jesus, came instead to be a believer in Him as Messiah. The "faith" that is the condition of salvation is always an obedient faith (cp. Hebrews 5:9, Romans 1:5).[77] "Love ... includes love to man as well as love to God, a strange contrast to his former cruelty and hatred" (*Pulpit Commentary*, p.14). Before his trip to Damascus, Paul had been a blasphemer; now, he came to love Jesus Christ. "In Christ Jesus" says Christ (Messiah) Jesus is the object of Paul's new faith and love. The NASB is not helpful when it adds (in italics) the word "found" at this place; this is Calvinistic bias (namely, that the "faith and love" are produced by a prior operation of "grace") being thrust at us in the text. The Greek is *en Xpristō Iēsou*, and the old ASV was correct in simply translating it as "in Christ Jesus." Verses 15-17 now take up the theme that the record of Paul's conversion was planned as a pattern for future would-be followers of Jesus.

1:15 -- It is a trustworthy statement – The KJV worded it, "This is a faithful saying." Five times this expression occurs in the New Testament, all of them in

---

[77] Obedient faith is discussed in the author's commentary *New Testament History: Acts*, in the special study on p.598ff, "The Faith That Saves."

the Pastoral Epistles (1 Timothy 1:15, 3:1, 4:9; 2 Timothy 2:11; Titus 3:8).[78] Scholars have offered several conjectures in their efforts to capture for us what this expression means.[79]   (1) In the 20th century, certain songs and choruses, whose words reflect well-loved passages of Scripture, have been sung so often that they have made a permanent impression on the consciousness of believers. Not a few scholars think the same thing happened in the 1st century, and that these 'faithful sayings' are portions of hymns that were current in the early church. Early Christians did sing hymns in their worship services, so there would be nothing inherently impossible with the conjecture that this 'faithful saying' about "Christ Jesus coming into the world to save sinners" is a portion of an early hymn. It could even be affirmed that there is some reference to a statement uttered on several occasions by Jesus Himself (Matthew 9:13; Luke 19:10).   This commentator, however, has difficulty believing that 'faithful saying' is synony-mous with 'early hymn,' especially when we look at the content of some of the other 'faithful sayings.'   Did early Christians sing about "aspiring to the office of overseer" (3:1)?   A word of caution is in order at this place.   A number of higher critics, in their quest for the alleged sources behind our canonical books, have insisted each of the passages in the New Testament writings that reflect a high Christology[80] all have their sources in some early hymn.[81]   This view is a very subtle denial of the inspiration of the Christological passages and of their truthfulness.   When critics say a passage is perhaps an early hymn, what they mean is that they doubt the Bible writers were the actual original authors of the statements: 'Since we don't know where the information originated in the first place, we have no way of knowing whether or not it is true.'   This commentator rejects this whole approach to 'explaining' the Scriptures.   If one must look for a source for this 'faithful saying,' look to the words of Jesus in Luke 19:10, "The Son of Man has come to seek and to save that which was lost."   (2) Liturgical churches have long looked for Biblical proof that the practices of the early churches were not greatly different when it comes to the use of liturgies[82] in the public worship.   In such circles, the 'faithful sayings' are suggested to be "parts

---

[78] Some have supposed that the expression, "these words are faithful and true," which occurs twice in Revelation 21:5 and 22:6, is similar.

[79] One of the better modern works is George W. Knight, *The Faithful Sayings in the Pastoral Epistles* (Nutley, NJ. : Presbyterian and Reformed, 1974 [?]).

[80] For example, 1 Timothy 3:16; Colossians 2:6ff; and 1 Peter 3:18-22.

[81] Do not miss the slight shift in wording here.   Modern songs and choruses have their source in Scripture – their words are taken from Scripture and set to music.   The higher critics are saying the verses in our Bible were taken from some humanly written song and included (perhaps uncritically) in the text of our Bibles.   What a difference!

[82] "Liturgy" is not a name often used in the Restoration Movement.   Among those churches who do, not all define "liturgy" alike.   For some, it is a prescribed form for public worship that tries to include more participation from the worshippers.   For others, "liturgy" is the order to be followed at communion (or mass), as the priest performs all the activity and the worshippers just watch.

of 1st century liturgies" that were often repeated (rehearsed) in the assemblies (much like the Lord's Prayer is repeated each Sunday in some circles). (3) Churches that hold catechism classes for their prospective converts have supposed that these 'faithful sayings' are some of the memorized answers that were expected to be given by the prospect when he was questioned to see if he was eligible for baptism or confirmation. (4) Another suggestion is that this expression 'faithful saying' was simply Paul's way of drawing attention to the importance of some truth he was about to express.[83] (5) The suggestion this commentator likes is the one which says the 'faithful sayings' were 'memorized summaries of the gospel.' Robert J. LaMonte visited the churches behind the Iron Curtain in the 1970's. He found that at times the people had no copies of the Bible at all. Other times, church members belonging to a large congregation had just one Bible between them. What they did was carefully cut the pages away from the spine of the book, and then each member could have one page of the Bible for a week. At next Sunday's service, members would exchange pages with each other. Mr. LaMonte learned that the believers might see this one page from the Bible only once in their whole lifetime. During that week when they had the page, they memorized its contents. Likewise, in the days before copies of the New Testament Scriptures were available to individual church members, they would have had to rely on memorized summaries of Christian doctrine to jog their memories as they told prospects about the gospel, and as they tried to recall what they were to believe and practice. We suppose that the apostles, prophets, and evangelists composed these 'faithful sayings' in the first place, and taught them to the Christians. What Paul would then be doing as he refers to them in these Pastoral Epistles is reminding his readers of the summaries they have already memorized. Designating this "statement" ('saying') as being "trustworthy" is Paul's commendation of the "statement" about to be quoted.

Deserving full acceptance – The KJV renders these words as if they mean "(this saying) is worthy of trust, and can be accepted by all as being fact!" *Apodoxēs* contains the idea of glad, willing acceptance, or hearty reception. This is the kind of response this 'faithful saying' should trigger. This saying about to be quoted is entitled to wholehearted and universal personal application with no reservations of any kind (with 'no strings attached').

That Christ Jesus came into the world to save sinners – This is the "saying" that summarizes the cardinal truth Paul is recalling at this place. Using this memorized statement to jog his memory, a Christian could stop on each word and explain it, as he shared the gospel to others.

---

[83] "Individuals use different phrases to call attention to the importance of certain truths. Jesus was accustomed to say, 'If any man have ears to hear, let him hear!' Paul uses this introductory phrase, 'This is a faithful saying,' to accomplish the same purpose." (Foster, *op. cit.*, p.354)

"*Christ*" – It is the promised Messiah we are talking about.   The Old Testament Messianic prophecies have been fulfilled.   He has come!

"*Jesus*" – This is the name given by God (Matthew 1:21; Luke 1:31, 2:22) when His son was about to become incarnate.   Talk about Jesus' 30+ years in human form on this earth – Bethlehem, Nazareth, at the Jordan River, in Perea, Galilee, Jerusalem, Calvary, and the empty tomb!

"*Came*" – There was a purpose in His coming.   It makes the gospel more worthy of acceptance that He had an intention, a plan, a wish, in thus coming into the world.   "Jesus came" implies there was something voluntary about what Jesus did.

"*Into the world*" – This implies an existence prior to His coming.   He left the glory He had with the Father before the world was (John 17:5; Philippians 2:5-11).   Jesus was God in the flesh while He was here (John 1:14).[84]

"*To save*" – He came not to destroy but to reveal mercy; not to denounce in judgment but to become an atoning, propitiatory sacrifice for sins.   The facts of His life, death, and resurrection cannot be explained on any other basis (1 John 4:2,3; 1 Corinthians 15:1-4).

"*Sinners*" – All have sinned and come short of the glory of God.   All (whether Jew or Gentile; all the lost, irrespective of race or time) need the salvation He offers.

He came to restore lost men to favor with God, to raise them up from their degradation, and to bring them ultimately to heaven (Ephesians 2:1-12).

Among whom I am foremost of all – Here is personal application of the truth taught in the first faithful saying.   He himself was one sinner whom Jesus' coming to earth had helped.   Paul writes "I am," not "I was."   Perhaps, this indicates that even now, years after his conversion, he deeply regrets his past.[85] Perhaps this indicates that, like other followers of Jesus, Paul is not sinless perfect. He still, on occasion, commits sins that need to be covered by the blood of Jesus. Some have accused Paul of exaggeration when he calls himself "chief" (KJV) of

---

[84] These allusions to verses in John should not be taken as evidence that we think the Pastorals contain an expression copied from John's writings.   Jesus Himself again and again referred to Himself as having "come into the world" (John simply records some of them, John 3:19, 9:39, 12:46, 16:28, 18:38).   Paul didn't get his gospel from John, he got it from Jesus (Galatians 1:12).

[85] There were other occasions when Paul expressed his great sorrow over his past in self-depreciating terms, e.g., 1 Corinthians 15:9;   Ephesians 3:18.

sinners.[86]   Be careful to observe that the word translated "chief" or "foremost" (*protos*) has no article in the Greek.   He does not say "the foremost sinner," but that he is one of many great sinners who need forgiveness.   'If anyone needs what Jesus came to provide, I do!' says Paul.   'I needed it in the past (when I was a blasphemer, a persecutor, and injurious).   I still need it.'   Nor do we see any need to limit or soften the significance of "sinner."   This is the way Paul felt about his life when he compared it to the holiness of God.

1:16 -- And yet for this reason I found mercy – In spite of what Paul once was, Jesus showed mercy to him.   "This reason" likely points to what follows: the near purpose is given in verse 16 (his example of conversion is a model that others can follow), and the ultimate purpose is given in verse 17 (so that God is honored and glorified).   "Mercy" has been explained at verse 13.

In order that in me as the foremost – See comments at verse 15 for "foremost." It does not mean Paul was the first person ever to be forgiven.   It does say that since he was "foremost (of sinners)," Jesus made him a prime or foremost example of what He can do for a sinner.   No sinner should think he is a hopeless case. Jesus forgave Paul; Jesus will forgive others like him.   "In order that" introduces a purpose clause.   There was purpose behind what Jesus did in Paul's case.

Jesus Christ might demonstrate His perfect patience – *Makrothumia*,[87] "patience" or 'longsuffering,' indicates the divine patience with respect to persons, by virtue of which wrath is withheld, the sinner is spared, and mercy is extended.   The word translated "perfect" (*hapas*) speaks of 'utmost' patience. "Demonstrate" (*endeiknumi*) means to show something publicly, for all to see. The manuscripts are not in agreement on whether it reads "Christ Jesus" or "Jesus Christ," and it is very difficult to make a decision about the likely correct reading. (On the possible significance found in the order of names, whether "Jesus Christ" or "Christ Jesus, see notes at verse 1.)   Jesus waited a long time for Paul.   Jesus was not in a hurry to punish His enemies.   Though He was provoked, He spared the sinner and gave him an opportunity to change.

As an example –*Hupotupsosis* can be translated "pattern, outline, sketch, exam-

---

[86] This phrase has been subjected to a wide variety of interpretations.   Scholars have a hard time accepting the fact that the words are to be taken literally.   Hendriksen, in a long footnote, lists more than half-a-dozen attempts at explaining this phrase.   The best way to understand the phrase is this: as Paul looks back on his life before becoming a Christian (and perhaps also on his continuing struggles with temptations), he is painfully aware of the forgiveness he needs.

[87] Berry (*op. cit.*, p.10) explains the synonyms for "patience."   *Anoche* is a forbearance that is tem-porary in nature.   *Hupomone* is patience under trials, to things.   It is not just a passive attitude toward these difficult things; it takes difficult things and turns them to something good.   ("If life hands you a lemon, make lemonade!")   *Makrothumia* is patience under provocation, and refers to persons.

ple."   The word was used of a model which was placed before someone to be copied.   It is used of the plan a workman looks at as he works.   Paul's conversion is a sketch or example of how others can experience Jesus' perfect patience and be forgiven.[88]   The dozen or more instances of conversion in Acts can be treated as examples.   As these accounts are preached, the hearers can easily ascertain what is expected of them if they too would become Christians.

For those who would believe in Him for eternal life – "Whoever believes in Him should not perish, but have eternal life" (John 3:16).   The Greek in this verse (*tōn mellontōn pisteuein*, a present tense participle followed by an infinitive) is a periphrasis for the future tense.   The NASB has caught the flavor of the original which speaks of those who in the future times would come to believe in Jesus. "Believe" followed by a prepositional phrase (like "in Him" or "on Him"[89]) is Biblical language for an obedient faith.[90]   "Faith comes from hearing ... the Word of Christ" (Romans 10:17).   Ananias preached to Paul, and Paul responded to the gospel (Acts 22:16).   When he had thus obeyed Christ, his sins were propitiated (cp. 1 Peter 1:2).   Eternal life is the result of such "faith in Him."   What is "eternal life"?   "Eternal life" is a quality of life as much as a duration.   There are times this expression refers to the blessed life of the redeemed in Heaven.   (The wicked continue to exist, too, but their wretched condition will not be a very pleasant way of living.)   The redeemed are going to share the kind of life that the Eternal Himself enjoys.   But there are also times that "eternal life" refers to a condition already experienced by the believer while still in this life (John 3:36). That's why we say "eternal life" speaks of a condition or quality of life as well as duration.   Out of the watery grave of believers' baptism they have risen to walk in newness of life (Romans 6:4ff).   What a blessed way to live!   The old slavery to sins has been broken.   The guilt of sins has been taken away.   The redeemed can respond to the leading of the Holy Spirit and bring forth fruit.   Paul's conversion has been recorded as a shining inspiration to countless souls.   In Paul's case, they would see Jesus' longsuffering, and come to expect it for themselves.   They would follow the same steps or process, come to believe in Jesus, and then share in the boon of eternal life, just as Paul did.   Like Paul, these forgiven sinners too would find in Jesus a wonderful One on whom to rest their faith.

---

[88] We do not teach that Paul was converted miraculously on the Damascus Road, and that his conversion is an example for others (i.e., that others too should look for some miraculous act of God to convert them.)   The rest of this verse explains how Paul was converted.   He was preached to and led to faith.   That's the way all the conversions in the book of Acts picture it as happening.

[89] Usually the construction is the verb *pisteuo* followed by a prepositional phrase.   Sometimes it is *en* and the dative, sometimes it is *eis* and the accusative.   Here it is *epi* and the dative, and the construction, rare in the New Testament, may be a reminiscence of Isaiah 28:16.

[90] See all this explained in paragraph 184 in Machen's *New Testament Greek For Beginners*. See also Leon Morris' *Gospel According to John*, p.335-337.

1:17 -- Now to the King eternal – Consideration of what Jesus has done for him leads Paul to break out in a wonderful doxology. *De* joins the doxology to what precedes and so "now" is a good way to translate it. To whom is this doxology addressed? The great majority of commentators think this doxology is addressed to God the Father.[91] A few think it is addressed to Jesus.[92] Perhaps it is best to think of it as addressed to the Triune God, to the Godhead.[93] The margin reads "the King of the ages."[94] "Eternal King" is also a possible translation.[95] If it is the Godhead who is addressed, then we might think about how the different ages or dispensations have been managed by the different members of the Godhead, directing everything to its predetermined goal. If it is the Godhead who is addressed, perhaps this unusual expression refers to the eternality of the Godhead. Their dominion extends over all ages and generations. Their glorious attributes are displayed in every age.

Immortal – "Imperishable" or "incorruptible" would better translate *aphthartos*.[96] His arms never become tired (Deuteronomy 32:27); He never grows weary (Isaiah 40:28); He is not subject to decay and destruction (Psalm 103:15-17); He never changes (Malachi 3:6).

Invisible – *Aoratos* means not visible to the unaided human eye (cp. 1 Timothy 6:16).

The only God – The KJV reads "the only wise God," but the best manuscripts[97] omit the word "wise" which seems to have crept in here from Romans 16:27. Erasmus conjectures the "wise" was added in the dispute against the Arians, who maintained that only the Father was God, and used this verse as one of their proof

---

[91] "King" is a title applied to God. E.g., we speak of the "kingdom of God".

[92] The title "king" is applied to Jesus (Matthew 5:35; 1 Timothy 6:15; Revelation 15:3). Further, in Hebrews 1:2, we read that Jesus is the one who "made the ages" -- He is the one who determines when one age (patriarchal, Mosaic, or Christian) ends and another begins.

[93] To insist it is addressed to only one person in the Godhead, and then to try to isolate which Person that is, gets us into trouble when we try to explain "only God."

[94] The phrase should not be given a Gnostic "twist," as though Paul describes God as "king of the aeons." Though we do find the idea of God's "imperishability" in works of Greek and later Jewish philosophers, it is certainly precarious to affirm that Paul borrowed the terms found in this doxology from speculative philosophy. The characteristics ascribed to God are all found in the Old Testament. Look no further than that, if we must have a source!

[95] Ellicott has a long note where he explains how the Hebrew construct way of writing would be typically rendered by the genitive case in Greek, just as here we have "King of the ages."

[96] The same word is used at Romans 1:23; 1 Corinthians 9:25, 15:52; I Peter 1:4,23, 3:4.

[97] "Wise" is omitted in Aleph* A D* F G H* 33, Lat., Syr^P and Copt. The word has been added by the second or third hand correctors of Aleph, D, and H. It is found regularly in the Byzantine manuscripts behind the Textus Receptus.

texts. The Arians, who deny the deity of Jesus, are answered if "King of the ages" is a reference to the Godhead, rather than to one individual personality thereof. "Jehovah our Elohim is the only Jehovah," says Deuteronomy 6:4. "Elohim" is plural, and "only" does not mean "one (numerically)."[98] The members who make up the Godhead are the only self-existent beings there are. The Godhead is unique, incomparable, glorious, "only."

Be **honor and glory forever and ever** – Our translations add the word "be" to this passage to show that this is in all likelihood a prayer on Paul's part. He is asking that such honor and glory be given to the "King of the ages." "Honor" (*timē*) may refer to respect and veneration, a respect that one is worth or has earned. "Glory" (*doxē*) here probably means "praise." If so, "Let Him be praised by all forever," is the idea. Sometimes "glory" refers to that brilliant sphere of white light that is a manifestation of God's person. Perhaps the doxology is a prayer that God's radiance may continue to be seen in all its splendor. "Forever and ever" is, literally, "unto the ages of the ages." This is the way the ancients spoke when they wanted to convey the idea of eternity. Eternity to come is made up, as it were, of ages after ages after ages. Let honor and glory be given to Him through all these ages to come!

Amen – "Amen" means "So be it!" "I agree!" "Those are my sentiments, too!" When the epistles were written as the Holy Spirit led, these "Amens" would express the human agent's agreement with what the Spirit had prompted. When the epistles were read out loud in public worship (as they regularly were), and the reader came to the end of these doxologies that were sometimes interspersed in the letters, the listeners would all respond "Amen!"

C. The Responsibility of the Evangelist Toward Sound Doctrine. 1:18-20

1:18 -- This command I entrust to you – The mention of "command" (*paraggelia*) takes us back to verses 3 and 5 where the same root word occurs. These verses are a resumption of the thought expressed in verses 3-5, and state precisely the reason for and content of Paul's charge to Timothy.[99] Hervey picks

---

[98] See all this discussed in detail in the author's comments on Matthew 22:34-46 (in *The Climax of the Earthly Ministry of Jesus*), where Jesus tried to correct the erroneous views of the Jews of His day that there was only one Person in the Godhead. He said "there is another just like it" – implying that in the Godhead, too, there can be another just like the Father. Jesus then went on to show the Jews that even David viewed Messiah as God. He reminded them that when David called Messiah "Lord" (Psalm 110:1), he was attributing deity to Messiah as much as to the Father.

[99] The "this" in "this command" could look forward to the following *hina* clause, "that ... you fight the good fight," or could look back to the charge given in verses 3-5. Our comments combine both.

up the thread of the "charge" in this way:

> Omitting the long digression in verses 5-17, the sense runs clearly thus: "As I besought you to tarry at Ephesus in order that you might instruct certain men not to teach a different doctrine, so now do I place this charge in your hands, according to the prophecies which pointed to you, that you may war the good warfare according to the tenor of those prophecies." (*Pulpit Commentary*, p.6)

Including the major idea from the "digression," the bridge from verses 3-5 to 18 is this:

> Aware of what the gospel can do for sinners (remember, what it did for Paul is an example for others!), Timothy is charged to stand for it, and to engage in warfare against any false teachers who would teach otherwise.

Used in military contexts (e.g., in Xenophon and Polybius), the word "charge" ("command") conveys a sense of urgent obligation. We suppose Paul is using this word with its military connotation to express to Timothy that the jobs of an evangelist are not trifles, but are orders from the commander-in-chief. "Entrust" or "deposit" (*paratithemi*) is a banking term when used in the middle voice.[100] Paul has deposited with Timothy the command to proclaim sound doctrine and to oppose certain men and their strange doctrines. It is a sacred trust, a solemn responsibility. Perhaps Paul, the aged, is feeling it is time to turn over the leadership of the churches to a younger generation. Whom do you trust to take over a cause for which you have given the best years of your life? Whom do you ask to face all the hardships and perils and dangers you know are connected with the ministry? It is a precious heritage, a priceless privilege, to be the one chosen to take over a ministry or a charge which represents another's life's work.

Timothy, my son – In the Introductory Studies we explained that this language indicates Timothy was one of Paul's converts, and that he was very dear to Paul. By reminding Timothy of their relationship, Paul adds weight to this charge as he conveys to Timothy his role and responsibility.

In accordance with the prophecies previously made concerning you – A prophet was a person who spoke by inspiration, and the message he delivered (whether it concerned the past, present, or future) was nothing less than a message from God, a supernatural communication from God. Such prophetic utterances

---

[100] The word here is *paratithemi*, which is a different word from the one found in 1 Timothy 1:11 (which was a form of *pisteuo*). It is instructive that the same verb (*paratithemi*) is used at 2 Timothy 2:2 of Timothy's passing on the gospel to others who will be able to teach it also.

were not infrequent in the early church.[101]   Paul's charge to Timothy was nothing new; it was entirely in agreement with the previous prophetic utterances concerning Timothy.[102]   The plural seems to suggest there was more than one prophecy concerning Timothy.   The ASV reading was "according to the prophecies which led the way to thee."   If this is the correct translation, then we learn here that one reason Paul determined to take Timothy along as a companion on the second missionary journey is because the Holy Spirit prompted some prophets to call attention to Timothy and God's plans for him.[103]   If we take the NASB reading, "prophecies previously made,"[104] perhaps 1 Timothy 4:14 gives us some guidance as we try to understand exactly what is meant.   Chapter 4 says that prophecies were uttered about Timothy at the time of his ordination.   Or perhaps the following phrase in 1 Timothy 1:18 gives some of the contents of those prophecies – namely, that Timothy is to war a good warfare.   Those prophecies appear to have been far-seeing glances into the life and work and teaching of this future Christian leader.   It is not improper to remind Timothy of the hopes which had been cherished for him; of the anticipations which had been formed of his future usefulness in the Kingdom of God; and of the expressions which the prophets had given to the message they had received from God concerning Timothy's future.

That by them you may fight the good fight – "By them" probably means "stimulated by these prophecies."   'When you remember what God Himself revealed, then you surely will be motivated to do as I am now charging you,' is the thrust of Paul's language.   "A practical consideration is seen here.   Young ministers have often found relief from occasional discouragement by recalling their own call to the ministry and the time when their spiritual gifts were recognized by the church, and the elders laid hands on them, separating them to the work of the ministry."[105]   Timothy is to "continue to fight the good fight" ("war the good warfare" KJV).   The verb tense does not indicate Timothy is now to begin such

---

[101] We read of them at Antioch (Acts 11:27, and 13:1,2), at Corinth (1 Corinthians 14), and at Caesarea (Acts 21:8-10).

[102] The KJV, "according to the prophecies which went before on thee," is certainly not too clear. This lack of precision has led some commentators to think the reference is to Old Testament prophets, and that it was their Scriptures that prepared Timothy's heart for the gospel.   However true it may be that Timothy's heart was prepared by a study of the Old Testament Scriptures, we doubt the prophecies here referred to were Old Testament.   It is more likely Paul is reminding Timothy about something said by New Testament prophets.

[103] Some appeal to Acts 13:2 where prophets called for the setting apart of Paul and Barnabas to the ministry to which God had already called them.   Did a similar event happen in Timothy's case?

[104] Not every translator is happy with the NASB handling of the present participle *proagousas*. Some try to stress the present tense, and indicate that these prophecies didn't happen years ago, but are happening right in the present as Paul writes.   This commentator has not found many lexicons that agree.   In fact, the same verb form is translated "former" at Hebrews 7:18, where it surely has reference to something that happened hundreds of years earlier.

[105] Quoted from Kent, *op. cit.*, p.92.

a fight.   Rather, it indicates he is to continue on in the fight.   In this context, as described in verses 3-11, the "fight" or the "warfare" is against false teachers and their doctrines.   Each believer's own personal life is often compared to a warfare or struggle for victory (cp. Ephesians 6:10-17; 1 Corinthians 9:7; 2 Corinthians 4:4), but that does not seem to be the point in this context.   It appears the military metaphor is continued,[106] and the work of an evangelist is likened to the activities of a soldier.   He "wars a good warfare" who is engaged in a righteous cause; who is faithful to his commander and to his post; who is unslumbering in observing the motions of the enemy, and fearless in courage in meeting them; who never forsakes his standard; and who continues faithful till the period of his enlistment has expired, or till death.   Such a soldier the Christian minister should be.[107]

1:19 -- Keeping faith – Verse 18 spoke of the "warfare" that Timothy is "charged" to wage.   Now, verse 19 tells the manner in which the "warfare" is to be carried on.   Perhaps "faith" speaks of 'the faith.'   If so, "fighting the good fight" will be a "holding on to the faith," a tenacious clinging to gospel truth.   Perhaps "faith" speaks of Timothy's own personal faith.   "As Timothy carried out this injunction to campaign as a soldier should in a good war, he must be careful in maintaining his own faith and conscience.   This is a reference to the inward state of the minister.   He must keep his own faith in good condition.   He must be uncompromising on the matter of sound doctrine."[108]

And a good conscience – The expression "good conscience" was used in verse 5.

> The religious teacher who knows the truth but teaches falsehood, or allows it to be taught under his jurisdiction, will not have a good conscience, at least not at the outset. His conscience will condemn such perversion.   However, persistence in such a course may dull the conscience so that it will fail to be a helpful guide.   Thus the minister should be very much concerned that his ministry is in accord with the standard of God's Word, in order that his conscience will be good, that it ... will have nothing to condemn.[109]

A troubled conscience would result from: (1) teaching what one knows to be false as though it were the truth;   (2) failure to teach what one knows is true;   (3) failure to correct the error one hears.

---

[106] See notes above about the military use of the word "command" or "charge."   Such metaphors were likely widely known and used in Paul's world.   In those days, enough people had been soldiers, and enough wars fought, that military expressions would become part of the common vocabulary, just like in our century.   In this commentator's opinion, it is a waste of time to search (as some other commentators have done) for the specific source from which Paul "copied" this language.

[107] Taken from Barnes' *Notes*, p.126.

[108] Kent, *op. cit.*, p.92

[109] *ibid.*

Which – "Which" (*en*) applies to the good conscience only. Deviations from the true faith, which are followed by a guilty conscience, may very well lead to a saved person needing to be disciplined, lest that person become wholly lost!

Some have rejected – Failing to heed the conscience as it prompts guilty feelings because one has failed to "keep the faith," is what "some" have done. "Rejected" is a strong word. 'Thrust it away from themselves' is the idea. It is a middle voice verb, and "is a strong expression, implying here the willful resistance to the voice of conscience" (*Pulpit Commentary*, p.7). The word used here is found in the language of sailing and ships. "The 'good conscience' represents the ballast, or cargo, of the ship. When this is put away – tossed overboard – the vessel becomes unmanageable and is tossed about, the plaything of the waves, and in the end is wrecked" (*Ellicott's*, p.201). Ellicott (*ibid.*, p.201) also thinks "some" is a quiet reference to those false teachers who seem to have been doing such evil work at Ephesus among the Christians, and against whom Timothy is so urgently warned to be on his guard at 1:3, at 1:6 and in the following verses of the chapter.

And suffered shipwreck in regard to their faith – There is a "the" in the Greek before the word "faith" (see the NASB margin). This has led to two different interpretations of this expression: (1) "The faith" is another way of saying "the gospel" – i.e., that body of doctrine that makes up the Christian faith.

> Since "faith" has the article (*tēn pistin*) it is best to understand it objectively, rather than [translate it] "their faith." The great historical and theological facts of the Gospel are settled and unchangeable, yet it is possible for heretics to wreck the message of the truth, as has been done in various ways by teachers of error in every century.[110]

If we compare what is said in 2 Timothy 2:17,18, about how doctrine concerning the resurrection was one area where Hymenaeus and Philetus had strayed from the truth, then a case might be made for "faith" here being objective faith (that which is to be believed). (2) "Their faith" (NASB) would speak of the false teacher's own personal, subjective faith (beliefs). Such a translation is possible, since the Greek may use the article ["the"] as a pronoun at times. By this understanding, certain false teachers who abandoned the true doctrine of Christ and went after falsehood caused their own personal faith to meet with catastrophe. It is by no means certain that *tēn pistin* here means "the faith" rather than " their faith" (subjective). The article might be no more than the article of previous reference – the faith here is the same faith as in verse 14 (which spoke of subjective, personal belief and appropriation of the gospel message).

The Greek for "suffered shipwreck" is *nauageo* from *naus*, "ship," and *agnu-*

---

mi, "to break." It means "to break a ship to pieces." One who has been through the harrowing experience of a shipwreck (e.g., Paul's voyage to Rome, Acts 27; plus three other occasions; also, 1 Corinthians 11:25) would vividly recollect the danger to life such a disaster can be. The man who willfully resists the prompting of his conscience, when his mind knew what was right (as found in the Gospel), was deliberately courting a danger as serious as "shipwreck." Afloat in the deep, you may perish or you may be rescued. But whichever it is, it was no trifling matter to be adrift in the deep! Both defenders and opponents of the doctrine of the unconditional security of the saints have misused this verse as they try to make their comments match the position espoused. Some other passage will have to be used to demonstrate whether or not a person once saved may ever be finally lost. A person who has been shipwrecked may be rescued, or he may perish. The fact of "shipwreck" alone does not decide the ultimate fate, though it certainly implies dangers! Even the next verse, using the example of Hymenaeus and Alexander, gives hope that, because of the discipline adminis-tered, they will learn to stop blaspheming; if they do, they may be rescued. They have not become irrevocably "lost" yet, though they are in grave circumstances.

1:20 -- Among these are Hymenaeus and Alexander – Two persons are cited as examples of the "some" who made shipwreck of the faith (1:19). So that Timothy can't possibly miss the point of this charge, his responsibility toward sound doctrine is illustrated by two specific examples. "Among these" indicates that Hymenaeus and Alexander are not the only individuals in this category. "Hymenaeus" is perhaps referred to again in 2 Timothy 2:17,18 as holding a heretical doctrine concerning the resurrection,[111] thus overthrowing the faith of some. (*Hymenaeus* was not a common 1st century name, so perhaps both Timothy passages speak of the same person.) "Alexander" was a common name among the Greeks since the time of Alexander the Great. Therefore we are hesitant to say this "Alexander" is or is not the same as some "Alexander" in another passage.[112] Nevertheless, not a few writers are of the opinion this Alexander is the same as "Alexander the coppersmith" of 2 Timothy 4:14. Kent rejects the identification on the grounds that "the coppersmith" is so called precisely to differentiate him from the Alexander of 1 Timothy 1:20. An Alexander is mentioned in Acts 19:23 in connection with the events in the theater at the silversmiths' riot (which occurred ~10 years before 1 Timothy was written).

---

[111] Hymenaeus taught that the resurrection is already past. Greek philosophy (spirit is good, matter is evil) would not square with the Christian doctrine of a future resurrection of men's bodies, so numerous expedients were adopted by those who wanted to hold on to their philosophy. One was to say that all there is to "resurrection" is what happens at conversion, when a person "rises to walk in newness of life." Perhaps Hymenaeus thus spiritualized the doctrine of the resurrection, related it to conversion, and thus denied any future bodily resurrection.

[112] We've found no commentator who believes the "Alexander" of Acts 4:6, who was a Jew of the high-priestly family, is to be identified with the Alexander named here in 1 Timothy.

That was at Ephesus, the same place (presumably) where the Alexander of 1 Timothy 1 lived. That Alexander seems to have been a Jew opposed to Christianity. This one (now delivered to Satan) had before been a Christian. Unless we assume the one-time persecutor became a convert and then regressed so as to need discipline, it is doubtful the two are to be identified. An Alexander is also named in Mark 15:21. If tradition is correct about Mark being written in Rome, then the inference is that "Alexander and Rufus" are living in Rome at the time Mark is written. We hope the Alexander of 1 Timothy 1 is not the same fellow.

Whom I have delivered over to Satan -- Where did Alexander and Hymenaeus live? Likely at Ephesus; they thus would they be known to the church there and could serve as an illustration of what Paul is trying to teach Timothy and the church in Ephesus. What is signified in "delivered to Satan" is disputed since there is no clear Scriptural explanation of this expression. (1) The same language occurs in 1 Corinthians 5:5. There it likely refers to expulsion (excommunication) from the church, a sentence to be carried out there by the congregation (probably under the direction of the elders). *Note*: In 1 Corinthians, the church did the excommunicating. Here the apostle says he did it. The different agents involved in doing the excommunicating may indicate that we have two different types of church discipline involved.[113] (2) Excommunication from the church places the offender back in the world which is Satan's domain (1 John 5:19).[114] In the church, there is afforded to the believer a divine protection from Satan.[115] That protection is removed when one is disciplined. (See the passage about "binding and loosing," Matthew 18:16-18.) (3) Whether such a sentence includes more than simply losing one's "protection" is debated; perhaps it also includes bodily suffering or disease of some kind. Lenski denies that physical suffering is involved in "delivered to Satan." Others point to Job 2:6,7; 1 Corinthians 5:5; 11:30; Revelation 2:22; and Acts 5:1-11, 13:11, as Scriptural evidence that the devil does have the ability to inflict, within limits, certain bodily sufferings, sickness, and even death, on men.

So that they may be taught not to blaspheme – This *hina* clause indicates Paul's purpose for delivering Hymenaeus and Alexander to Satan. The discipline was to be remedial or corrective. Reclamation, not damnation, was the object. The verb "taught" is *paideuō*, "to train, to discipline, to instruct as one does a child."

---

[113] See the author's special study on "Church Discipline" in *New Testament History: Acts*, p.230ff.

[114] Both Jesus (e.g., John 8:44) and Paul distinguish between the "kingdom [domain] of darkness" and the "kingdom of God's Son" (Colossians 1:13).

[115] The petition in the Model Prayer, "Deliver us from the Evil One" (i.e., put some limits on Satan so he cannot tempt and hurt us), would no longer be a valid prayer for the excommunicated person. Romans 8:1-3, which speaks of limits put on the devil, are true for those who continue to be among the justified, and might not be true for the excommunicated.

"Blaspheme" was used at 1:13. False teachers allowed to continue their evil practices unhindered would not only lead others astray, they would delude themselves into a false sense of spiritual security. Removal to Satan's realm might cause the offenders to face the issues and hopefully lead them to amend their ways.

If someone is returned to Satan's power/realm, how would that contribute to his learning not to blaspheme? If there is physical suffering involved in the delivery to Satan, it is easier to see how they might be led to come to their senses. That God can use Satan and his works to His own end and for the good of His people can be seen in Paul's description of his "thorn in the flesh." It was a "messenger of Satan sent to buffet him," and it had a good purpose, "to keep him from exalting himself" (2 Corinthians 12:7). Perhaps the shock of being rejected by the church community would lead the person to finally see how displeasing to God his actions have been, thus leading him to repent (cp. 2 Thessalonians 3:14).

If the purpose of restoration is ignored when discipline is administered today by a local church, the discipline can be harsh and prove a barrier to progress. Churches today are to practice discipline, though it is not certain all discipline practiced by a local congregation carries with it the same awesome powers that discipline by an apostle did (1 Corinthians 5:5, "for the destruction of the flesh", would need to be studied concerning this matter). Apostles possessed this awesome power to inflict bodily suffering, but we presume they did not act with a vindictive spirit. Their aim was always eventually to win the offender. In passing, in the light of this last phrase in verse 20, it perhaps should be observed again that "shipwreck" of verse 19 does not mean completely and irrevocably lost.

II. THE CHARGE CONCERNING PUBLIC WORSHIP. 2:1-15

A. Prayer in Public Worship. 2:1-7

2:1 -- First of all, then – "Then" (*oun*) indicates there is some connection between the topic begun in chapter 2 and the preceding discussion. We think that it continues Timothy's "orders," i.e., the "charge" Paul is giving to Timothy to guide him as he does the work of an evangelist with the church at Ephesus. "First of all" indicates either that this is the first in a series of subjects which will follow one after the other in this letter, or else of all the subjects dealt with, this one, dealing with his leadership of public worship, is the one of primary importance to the evangelist.[1] It is generally inferred that all of chapter two deals with public

---

[1] It has sometimes been taken as an exhortation that public worship meetings should be opened first with prayer.

worship and how Timothy is to take the lead in seeing that worship is conducted in a proper manner.[2]   It is quite important in the exegesis and application of this chapter to inquire about the place to which the instruction given by Paul in this chapter applies; that is, is that place the public assembly for worship, or is it in private devotions at home, or where?   Zahn gives a number of reasons for adopting the conclusion that public worship is the subject.[3]   He argues that (a) the reference to prayers "being made" in the original implies public prayer;   (b) the reference to prayers for kings and rulers refers to an old controversy among Jews about prayers in public worship for heathen rulers;   (c) on any other interpretation, Paul would be limiting (by verse 8) who may pray only to men even in the home.   Others have added additional reasons for thinking Paul is writing about public worship (as we have indicated in our title for this section):   (a) It is affirmed that the posture of praying with uplifted hands was customary in public prayers, not private.   (b) Some believe the section that begins in 2:1ff extends to 3:15, so the whole section involves how one ought to behave in the house of God (i.e., the public assembly).   (c) What is written in verses 9 and 12 can hardly be applied to private devotions.   Hence, the topic must be public worship.

I urge that entreaties *and* prayers, petitions and thanksgivings – "Urge" translates the same Greek word used in 1 Timothy 1:3.   Again we note Paul refrained from commanding his young friend, choosing rather to "urge" as a brother.   Paul is calling Timothy aside to give him this earnest exhortation, namely, that whenever God's people in Ephesus gather to worship, Timothy (their evangelist) is to see to it that certain prayers are included as part of the worship. Four synonyms for "prayer" are employed.[4]   (1) "Entreaties" ("supplications," KJV) is *deēsis* in the Greek.   The word speaks of a request to God that certain keenly-felt definite needs be met.   "Fully aware of his complete dependence on God, the Christian asks that this particular illness may be removed, or that these disturbing tidings be overruled for good, etc." (*Hendriksen*, p.91).   (2) "Prayers" translates *proseuchas*.   This word speaks of prayers to God for needs always present (in contrast to "entreaties" which are specific situations).   This is a general word for prayer.   E.g., requests for more wisdom, greater consecration, progress in the administration of justice.   Think of words of adoration, confession,

---

[2] As the evangelist opposes false doctrine and false teachers, his responsibility to lead public worship will give him opportunity to limit how much exposure those teachers would get for their message.

[3] Zahn, *Introduction to the New Testament*, V.2, p.40.

[4] Students of grammar have tried to distinguish between these terms for prayer.   Two useful examples are R.C. Trench, *Synonyms of the New Testament*, p. 188ff, and Geo. R. Berry, *New Testament Synonyms*, #6.   We think Paul had a distinct meaning in mind when he used each word, and was not just accumulating synonyms to add force as is sometimes done in legal documents.

or a recital of God's mercies. It would include vows made to God. Even when thus interpreted, the meaning of "prayers" is still very broad. (3) "Petitions" ("intercessions" KJV) is how *enteuxis* is translated. This word speaks of "pleading" on behalf of others, either for or against them.[5] The word picture is that of coming to a king and appealing for the king's favorable response to whatever request is made. In one ancient piece of literature, this word occurs in the prayer, "O thou who understands the petitions even of those who are silent ...." These silent prayers are often "appeals" to God, made with urgency and boldness. Perhaps the term implies that even at public worship, there are private prayers addressed to God; as it were, each worshipper seeking a private audience or a personal interview with Deity. (4) "Thanksgivings" is the familiar word *eucharistias*. This word may be an expression to God of gratitude for the blessings that have come from Him. Some of the blessings recently received may well be answers to previously asked entreaties and petitions. No matter what his immediate condition, every Christian enjoys numerous blessings from God. Unthankfulness is a great sin (Romans 1:21; 2 Timothy 3:2). Trench gives us the thought that thanksgiving will persist even in Heaven (Revelation 4:9, 7:12), when all the other forms of prayer have ceased because of the fruition of things prayed for.[6]

The evangelist who leads public worship needs to carefully plan the "prayer" part of the service. Several helps have been suggested by experienced preachers: (1) The evangelist usually leads at least one prayer during public worship. Spend one hour each week planning the morning prayer. Don't spend all your preparation time on just the sermon, or coordinating the song service with the theme of the message. Put quality time into the planning the morning prayer, too. (2) Dick Eastman, *The Hour That Changes the World*, offers practical ideas for different ways to pray. (3) This exhortation to Timothy gives a picture about how worship was conducted in the first century. This exhortation about prayer is inconsistent with the supposition that a *liturgy* was then in use, or with the supposition that there ever would be a liturgy, since in that case the objects to be prayed for would be prescribed. If the prayer were prescribed (as in a liturgy), there would be no need for such instructions as Paul gives here. The four words for prayer are all plural, suggesting both a number of prayers at the public worship service and also the involvement of a number of people offering these prayers. More will be said about this in the following verses.

Be made on behalf of all men – Here begins the "people" for whom, or on whose

[5] See Acts 25:24; Romans 11:2, 8:27,28,34; Hebrews 7:25, in which God is asked both to take action *against* and *in favor* of some third party.

[6] Trench, *op. cit.*, p. 191.

behalf, prayers are to be made in public worship.   That prayers were to be made for "all men" (*anthropos*, i.e., all human beings) is probably a conscious contrast to the Jewish attitude toward Gentiles which led to a refusal on the part of the Jews to pray for Gentiles or for government officials who were Gentiles.   "All men" is an unlimited expression.[7]   We are not talking about praying just for believers or, in the next verse, just for Christian kings.   It is difficult for us always to love all men, to think of all men as equally dear to God, or to regard all men as equally capable of being blessed.   And what is the content of these prayers on behalf of all men?   (1) Not a few writers comment here about "the duty of praying for the salvation of the whole world," as they offer exposition on these verses.   What about praying for the salvation of the lost?   Are there any Biblical examples of such prayers?   Perhaps Romans 10:1 is Paul's prayer for the Jews' salvation.   We don't just pray that God will save them (as though man is wholly passive in the hands of God).   If the lost are saved, it will be by hearing and obeying the gospel.   It might be better to pray that God would guide us to make efforts to reach and minister to those who need His special help and forgiveness.   In our comments on verse 4, below, more will need to be said on this important matter.   (2) Others would insist that the "content" of the prayers and supplications is not specified in this context.   Not even the "that we may lead a quiet and tranquil life," is a "content" statement, since it begins with *hina* rather than *hoti*.   *Hoti* is the way indirect discourse is introduced.

2:2 -- For kings and all who are in authority – We are continuing the list of people for whom prayers are to be offered as part of the public worship service.   "Kings" was the term was used for the Roman emperors.   It was also used for the highest government official in some of the provinces, even though they were answerable to the Emperor – e.g., "Herod the king" or "Aretas the king."   Jeremiah (19:7) and Ezra (6:10) had commanded the Jewish people to pray for their conquering heathen rulers.   These commands had been later disregarded by many, especially the zealots who taught that God's people should not yield any

---

[7] At this place, commentaries will very likely reflect the theological beliefs of the commentator concerning whether or not the Bible teaches limited atonement or universal atonement.   The former will somehow try to limit the "all" (in "all men"), while the latter take it as unlimited.   This commentator takes the position that Christ's death was potentially for all, if only each and every one would respond to the invitation.   It is in light of this view of the atonement that we have offered our comments.

Hendriksen (p.94), who defends the Calvinistic doctrine of limited atonement, writes about how "all" must be limited to *groups* or *classes* of men (like "kings" and "those in high position," or groups like "Gentiles" and "Jews").   "He is urging Timothy to see to it that in public worship not a single group is omitted."   Hendriksen is adamant that "all" must not be interpreted *individually*, as though the exhortation were to pray for all individuals.   Per Calvinist theology, many individuals are among the non-elect; the "limited atonement" doesn't apply to them, so it would do no good to pray for them.

Barnes, though of Calvinistic background, urges over and over again a "universal, unlimited atonement."   (In the same volume, Robert Frew, his English editor, contradicts the notes Barnes has offered, and in extensive footnotes – especially at 2 Corinthians 5:14, p.118ff, to which reference is repeatedly made – defends the doctrine of limited atonement.)

obedience to idolatrous rulers.[8]   Paul repeated the admonition of those Old Testament leaders, in spite of the sorry record of the kings he knew – Herod the Tetrarch, Herod Agrippa I and II, and Nero under whose reign he now lived and would eventually die.   The expression "all who are in authority" would cover the lesser officials appointed by the emperor or the senate to govern various areas, including proconsuls, Asiarchs, politarchs, town clerks, lictors, tax collectors, judges, etc.   It is still true that the powers that be are ordained of God (Romans 13:1), so prayers for them, that God will so intervene as to make their government conducive to the church performing her task in the world, are certainly in order.

In order that we may lead a tranquil and quiet life – This clause gives one reason for offering prayers especially for government officials.   The lives of all Christians, in their concern to worship God as He has directed, to proclaim the gospel wherever there are lost men, and to live a godly life, are affected by what the civil authorities do.   A "tranquil" (*ēremos*) life is one that is free from outward disturbance.   Freedom from persecution or molestation as one goes about his Christian walk is what is involved.   Pray that the civil officials so govern that there is no persecution or molestation, either from government officials or unbelievers.   A "quiet" (*hēsuchios*) life is one that is free from inner turmoil and worry.   What a blessing to live in a land whose government secures freedom from fear of what unprincipled and unruly men might do to thwart what the church members have been commissioned by God to do.   If churches are to flourish spiritually, public worship is highly desirable, to say the least.   But such public worship cannot be conducted to the best advantage (quietly, without disturbance), unless the church does its duty with respect for the state (prays for the civil authorities), and unless the state scrupulously guards the church's God-given rights and privileges.   While all men should be the subjects of prayer, those who are in authority should be particularly remembered before the throne of grace. So much depends on their character and plans, and the security of life, liberty, and property depends so much on them.   God has the power to influence their hearts, and to incline them to do what is just and equal; hence, Christians should pray that a divine influence may descend upon such rulers and authorities.

In all godliness and dignity – "Godliness" (*eusebeia*) speaks of one's conduct or attitude toward God.   Involved would be religious devotion.   The prayer is that government officials will do nothing to interfere with the people's free exercise of devotion to God.   "Dignity" ("honesty" KJV) translates *semnotēs*, which speaks

---

[8] Josephus mentions how a refusal on the part of the Jews to pray for the Roman magistrates led to the great war with the empire which ended in the fall of Jerusalem and their destruction as a separate nation.

of conduct or attitude toward men. It is a quality of life that earns respect.[9]
Christianity teaches that its followers have certain responsibilities towards their
fellow men. The prayer is that government officials will do nothing to interfere
with the Christians' attempts to minister to the spiritual and physical needs of their
fellow men. Let it be emphasized again – the duty of government is to protect
men's God-given rights! It is not the government's prerogative to determine by
vote what is right. God has already settled that! There is evidence from Early
Christian Literature that the instructions to Timothy about the prayers at public
worship were being observed in many parts of the ancient world. In a well-
known passage in Tertullian's *Apology*, written about a century and a half after
Paul wrote this letter to Timothy, we have this statement which shows how the
church in Carthage was doing just as Timothy was to lead the church at Ephesus
to do. Christians on trial for their lives replied to Roman magistrates that they
were unwilling to pray *to* the Caesar, but instead they did something better, they
prayed *for* him.

> We Christians ... do intercede for all the emperors, that their lives may be
> prolonged, their government be secured to them, that their families may be
> preserved in safety, their senates faithful to them, their armies brave, their
> people honest, and that the whole empire may be at peace, and for whatever
> other things are desired by the people or the Caesar.[10]

Early in the second century, Polycarp of Smyrna bears a similar testimony to this
practice of praying publicly for the non-Christian rulers:

> Pray for all the saints; pray, too, for all kings and powers and rulers, and for
> your persecutors, and those that hate you, and for your cruel enemies.[11]

2:3 -- This is good and acceptable – In the sentence that begins here and ends in
verse 4, we are given a second reason for offering prayers for all, and especially
for government officials.[12] The first reason (verse 2) had to do with the church's
life in the world. The second reason has to do with God's will concerning the
salvation of lost men (verses 3,4). Two things are said about such universal
prayers: (1) Such prayer is "good." *Kalos* means "attractive, winsome." Per-

---

[9] The word "honesty" found in the KJV should be understood in the sense of "honorableness,"
the kind of lifestyle that wins respect among men.

[10] Tertullian, *Apology*, chap.30.

[11] Polycarp, *Ad Philippians*, chap.12.

[12] The verse in the KJV begins with "for," but it is questionable whether the word belongs in the
text since the manuscript evidence supporting it is late. With its omission the connection of thought
with the preceding verses is less clear, though "this" appears to refer to the thrust of verses 1 and 2,
namely universal prayer.

haps it is in God's eyes[13] that such prayers are "attractive," or perhaps it is in the eyes of men[14] who are watching the Christians looking for something to criticize. (2) Such prayer is "acceptable." *Apodekton* comes from the family of words that means "to receive gladly." There are some prayers that are not acceptable to God. Either the heart of the one doing the asking is wrong, or the things being asked for are not in harmony with God's will.

> There was a practical reason that the prayers of the church for rulers should be pleasing to God. They would show that the church was not like the Jewish community with its narrow bigotry, and they would help to offset the resentment felt by pagan rulers when they observed that the Christians did not indulge in the social customs and nationalistic worship practiced in the empire. Thus such prayers would serve to protect the church as well as to advance the divinely arranged program of civic order.[15]

In the sight of God our Savior – "In the sight of God" probably means "in His opinion or judgment." We usually think of Christ as our "Savior" because He died for us, but since God sent His Son and Christ was doing the will of the Father perfectly, it is proper to speak of either Christ or God as Savior. Here, as in 1 Timothy 1:1, the title of "Savior" is given to the Father, and it is in this place singularly applicable, as it immediately precedes the famous statement of the next verse, respecting God's desires for all to be saved.

2:4 -- Who desires all men to be saved – Prayer for all men is acceptable to God, for God's attitude towards men is positive and favorable. Even though they are not yet converted, God is "pulling" for them. The logic is that since God desires all men to be saved, it must be good and acceptable to him that we pray for all. We can surely use God as our model for concern in this area. "All men" echoes the "all men" of 2:1, and we interpret it the same way.[16] "Desires" translates *thelo*, and this word has become a storm center among the theologians. Those who view God's sovereignty and His predestination of men either to salvation or damnation to be the controlling motifs of Scripture will likely struggle with this verse. The KJV reads that God "will" have all men to be saved.[17] Commentators spend much paper and ink telling us that "will" here cannot be taken in an

---

[13] If the second part of the verse, "in the sight of God," goes with both adjectives, then it is in God's sight that such universal prayers are attractive.

[14] This suggested interpretation takes the words "in God's sight" only with the second adjective.

[15] Ed Hayden, *Standard Lesson Commentary*, 1953.

[16] As was true of that verse, so here – those who believe in "limited atonement" must somehow explain this verse so that it does not contradict their cherished doctrine.

[17] Those teachers who hold to a doctrine of universalism, namely that God will ultimately save everyone, find this verse in the KJV a very useful proof-text.

absolute sense, as though it denoted a decree like that by which God willed the creation of the world, for then it would certainly be done. If it were certainly done, how should we harmonize those passages that indicate the great majority of men are lost? (1) Defenders of "limited atonement" are accustomed to call attention to the fact that two different words are translated "will" – *thelo* and *boulomai*. The former word denotes a desire springing out of the emotions, while the latter one refers to a determination springing out of deliberation.[18] Thus God can "wish" or "desire" (*thelo*) something and it doesn't necessarily have to happen; but if God "wills" (*boulomai*) something, that is absolutely decreed to happen. (2) Theologians who tend to be Arminian in their leanings do not find any great need to do theological hair-splitting over the two words for "will." They do not teach that if God "wills" something He is bound therefore to do it.

God desires or wills or wants all men to be saved, but He does not force it on men against their wills. He has so limited Himself with respect to human freedom that he makes the accomplishment of His purpose dependent upon the individual's own acceptance of the proffered salvation. God certainly does not desire people to sin, but they do! Consequently, if men are lost, it is because they opposed God's will; they were not interested in His "wishes" for them. "To be saved"[19] in this verse seems to have its regular meaning of 'saved from sin.' It is the same idea Peter expresses when he writes that "the Lord ... is not wishing for any to perish, but for all to come to repentance" (2 Peter 3:9). Certain Calvinists, still struggling in their efforts to make this verse harmonize with some of their key doctrines, suggest that "save" should be understood in a weaker sense – such as "preserve" or "protect." They can then speak of God's providential protection for all men during this life, without giving up the idea that certain are predestined to be saved or lost eternally, no matter what they do with Jesus.

And come to the knowledge of the truth – In the process of "to be saved," men are not passive. On the contrary, they become active. They must "come" to the knowledge of truth. "Truth" here is another word for 'the good news about salvation, and God's desire for all men to be saved.'[20] There may even be a reference to Jesus who said "I am the truth" (John 14:6). If so, "knowledge of

---

[18] J.H. Thayer, *A Greek English Lexicon of the New Testament*, p. 286, and Sanday and Headlam in the *ICC* on "Romans," p.182. The exact distinction between *thelo* and *boulomai* is difficult to fix, and Cremer and Berry do not agree with Thayer and Sanday/Headlam.

[19] The infinitive is in the passive voice in the Greek. Someone else does the acting on the person, as the person is being led to salvation. 1 Corinthians 12:13a tells us that one of the agents who helps lead a person to salvation "in the body of Christ" is the Holy Spirit. Some human messenger must preach the gospel to the prospect, for faith which leads to salvation comes by hearing the Word of God.

[20] "Truth" is used in Paul's letters for the gospel at 2 Corinthians 4:2; Galatians 5:7; Colossians 1:5; 2 Thessalonians 2:10-12.

the truth" is not merely a correct understanding of 'things,' but is a knowledge of Christ (John 8:31,32). God grants us His salvation when we recognize Jesus as the Christ, surrender our lives to Him, and make Him king of all our being. Is "knowledge of the truth" equal to conversion, or is it a knowledge that follows conversion? Certainly, once a man has become a Christian, his knowledge about Jesus grows every day. Paul describes this growth in knowledge in Ephesians 4:13-15, and Matthew 28:20 ("teaching them to observe all that I commanded you") alludes to this continued growth in knowledge of revealed truth. However, we are not convinced that "knowledge" here is a knowledge that follows conversion. We think Spain is correct when he says that, in the Pastorals, "knowledge" (*epignōsis*) is almost a technical term for conversion.[21] The Gnostics were fond of the word "knowledge" (*gnōsis*). Paul says that when a man comes to Christ he already has not only *gnōsis*, he also has *epignōsis*, "full knowledge" or "full realization" of the truth. Implied in this language is a tacit suggestion that one does not have to become a Gnostic to get "full knowledge." We already have that when we give our lives to Christ.

Since we have been studying Paul's words about prayers for all men, and how God wishes all men to be saved, we once more must address the question of "prayer for the lost." J. Herbert Kane has given us a brief history of the idea that prayers for the salvation of the lost are a duty of all Christians. He notes that in the early 1700's in England, interest in missions was beginning to stir.

> In 1723 Robert Millar of Paisley wrote *A History of the Propagation of Christianity and the Overthrow of Paganism*, in which he advocated intercession as the primary means of converting the heathen. The idea soon caught on. Twenty years later prayer groups were to be found all over the British Isles. Their chief petition was for the conversion of the heathen world.
>
> In 1746 a memorial was sent to Boston inviting the Christians of the New World to enter into a seven-year "Concert of Prayer" for missionary work. The memorial evoked a ready response in Jonathan Edwards, who the following year issued a call to all believers to engage in intercessory prayer for the spread of the gospel throughout the world.
>
> Almost forty years later, in 1783, Edward's pamphlet was introduced to the churches in England by John Sutcliff of the Northamptonshire Ministerial Association. Following the reading of the pamphlet, he made a motion that all Baptist churches and ministers set aside the first Monday of each month for united intercession for the heathen world.[22]

---

[21] Carl Spain, *The Letters to Timothy and Titus* (Austin, Tx.: Sweet, 1975), p.41.

[22] J.H. Kane, *A Concise History of the Christian World Mission* (Grand Rapids: Baker, 1978), p. 83,84.

Curtiss Mitchell has written a provocative article, "Don't Pray for the Unsaved!"[23] He opens his article with these words, "How should we pray for an unsaved friend or loved one? Prayer relating to evangelism has been more misunderstood and more subject to 'malpractice,' I believe, than any other." He calls attention to the fact that it is difficult to find verses of Scripture that teach Christians to pray for the lost,[24] or any for that matter that contain actual prayers by Jesus or the apostles themselves for the lost. He reminds us of what the Scriptures do say: (1) Christians are to pray for the Lord of the harvest to send harvesters (Matthew 9:38). (2) Paul asked for prayers that he might be bold when he had opportunity to witness (Ephesians 6:19,20). (3) Paul prayed God would open for him a door of opportunity for the Word (Colossians 4:3). (4) There is certainly nothing out of place in voicing your concern for unsaved loved ones, but also entreat God to send a messenger of the gospel across the path of that loved one.

How do we go about praying for lost countries, for example, that God will open the land of China to the gospel? Do we pray that God will change the government by raising up rulers who will not oppose the coming of missionaries, or do we pray that God will prepare the harvesters who will go as soon as they are permitted to do so? What about prayers by a mother for the alcoholic son or daughter, or for the prodigal son? We are not saying that all such expressions of concern should be abandoned. Rather, we are saying that we should examine the content of our prayers in the light of Biblical examples. Think through what we are asking God to do, and why we are asking. As we offer these prayers for God's intervention in men's lives, we must remember that man is not wholly passive in salvation. God doesn't just save men by unilaterally bestowing salvation on them whenever He gets around to it. God uses human messengers who carry the ·gospel to those lost people. Our prayers should not be worded as though we expect God to act in ways other than He has revealed that He acts.

2:5 -- For there is one God – "For" tells us that we are now being given a reason for something just said. The affirmation that "God ... desires all men to be saved and to come to the knowledge of the truth" is true, and now four reasons why it is true are given. Or perhaps there is a connection to the topic of prayer for all men at public worship. If so, in addition to God's desire that all be saved, verses 5 and 6 give four additional grounds for offering such prayers – the unity of God, the unity of the Mediator, the availability of the ransom, and the commission for Gentiles. In the Greek, "one" is first in the sentence, for emphasis. "There is one God," not many. If there were many gods, some men could be left out of any salvation one of the other gods offered. But if there is only one God, then He is

---

[23] *Christianity Today*, Sept. 16, 1983, p.28,29.

[24] He suggests that Matthew 5:44; 1 Timothy 2:1,2; and Romans 10:1 are the only passages that might be construed as prayers that God would save the lost.

the God of all men and all men are of interest to Him.   There is not one God for this nation and one for another, one God for slaves and one for free men, one God for rulers and another for subjects.   There is just one God, and His wishes cover all creatures!   His plan of salvation is the same for all,[25] whether they are aware of the fact or not.   Care must be exercised as we contemplate the meaning of these words, lest we get the mistaken idea that there is only one person in the Godhead.[26]   And even more discernment is needed when source and redaction critics offer comments to the effect that this verse is a quotation of some unknown source.[27]

And **one mediator also between God and men,** *the* **man Christ Jesus** – There is "one mediator," not many.   If there were many mediators, say one for each nation or group of nations, some people who needed a mediator could be left out.   If there is one mediator, his activities are available to all men.[28]   "The man Christ Jesus" was not a human who became God.   He is God who became a man (Philippians 2:5-8).   Why is attention focused on Jesus' humanity?   (1) Note the manner in which the identity of this Mediator is revealed: "one Mediator also between God and *men*, the *man* Christ Jesus."   Had salvation been intended for one particular group – e.g., only for the Jews – the apostle would have written, "the *Jew* Christ Jesus."   The way it is written shows that the gospel is for all men, whether Jew or Gentile.[29]   (2) The human nature of our Lord is insisted upon, to show how fit he is to mediate for man, as his Godhead fits him to mediate with God.[30]   We are reminded of the theme that occurs several times in Hebrews; namely, that by taking on our human nature, being tempted in all points like as we, having become a perfect sacrifice for sin, having offered his own blood in the Heavenly Holy of Holies, and ever living to make intercession for the saints, Jesus is perfectly qualified to be our Man in Heaven.   (3) This designation of Jesus as a "man" – with emphasis on his true humanity – may be a deliberate refutation of

---

[25] God's interest in all men was expressed in the words of the Abrahamic covenant, "In you all the nations of the earth shall be blessed" (Genesis 12:3).   That covenantal promise came to fruition in Christ (Acts 3:25; Galatians 3:8-29).

[26] This matter has already been introduced in comments on 1 Timothy 1:17 under the expression "only God."

[27] Both Moffatt and Easton treat this verse as a quotation, and not as being Paul's own words spoken by inspiration.

[28] It may be added also that the doctrine of the Roman Catholic Church, that the saints or the Virgin Mary may act as mediators to procure blessings for men, is false in the light of the fact that there is "one" mediator between God and man.   That church's attempt to make this phrase mean something like "Christ is 'one' among many," so they can include angels, saints, and the Virgin Mary as other mediators, is exegetically impossible.

[29] Paraphrased from Hendriksen, *op. cit.*, p.97.

[30] Suggested by Spence, *op. cit.*, p.206.

the docetic errors of some of the Gnostic false teachers. These false teachers taught that the Jesus who was nailed to the cross was no man, but simply a phantom.[31] Jesus is elsewhere in the New Testament designated as "mediator" (Hebrews 8:6, 9:15, 12:24). The incarnation of the Son of God answered the plea of Job 9:32,33. A "mediator" is a 'go-between.' The position of Jesus as mediator, or a 'go-between' relating man to God and God to man, is a topic worthy of much study. On the one hand we have the infinite, holy, eternal God. On the other hand we have human creatures, limited, and separated from God because of their own personal acts of sin. How shall the two ever be brought together? A mediator is needed. As mediator, Jesus makes God known to man (John 1:18). Jesus is mediator also because He has offered himself as a sacrifice to cleanse us of our sins (Hebrews 9:28) and to bring us back to God (John 3:14-17). Jesus is our high priest, who intercedes on our behalf before God; thus we find God's mercy and receive help in our need (Romans 8:34; Hebrews 4:14-16, 7:25).

2:6 -- Who gave Himself a ransom for all – This verse is related to the expression "the man Christ Jesus" in verse 5. The train of thought depends on how we understand the "for" in verse 5. (1) Verse 6 may explain why the man Christ Jesus can function as a mediator. He's earned the right by giving up His life for all those for whom He would mediate.

> The declaration (v.5) that there was but one God for fallen man would have been scarcely a joyful proclamation had it not been immediately followed by the announcement that between the one God and sinning man there was a mediator. Now (v.6) we have in a few words the inspired description of the manner in which the Mediator performed His office and work; of His own free sovereign will, He yielded up Himself to death as the price of the redemption of all mankind – His life in exchange for their forfeited lives.[32]

(2) Or, if verse 5 is connected with the idea of "prayer being made for all" at the public service, verse 6 is stated as a reason why prayer should be offered for all, and as a proof that God desires the salvation of all. Prayer must be made on behalf of all men (verses 1,2) because: (a) Salvation was intended for all, verses 3,4. (b) There is but one God and one Mediator for all, not one for each group, verse 5.   (c) There is but one ransom for all, verse 6.[33] Regarding "gave Himself," the Bible writers all insist repeatedly that Christ's sacrifice was made willingly by Himself (John 10:18; Matthew 20:28; Galatians 1:4). "Ransom" translates *antilutron*, the only place this compound word appears in the New Testament. This verse strongly echoes the words of Jesus, "The Son of man came

---

[31] Against such Gnostic errors John wrote most positively some 30 years later (1 John 4:2,3).

[32] Spence, *ibid.*

[33] This is the way Hendriksen constructs the train of thought in these verses.

... to give his life a ransom for many" (*lutron anti pollon*, Matthew 20:28; Mark 10:45).[34]   The prefixing of *anti-* emphasizes the idea of substitution and its usual translation is "instead of."[35]   This is confirmed by the findings in the papyri.[36] The word "ransom" in ancient times was common; it referred to the buying back of people who had been sold as slaves or captured in war.[37]   This is the meaning of the term here.   We were lost and enslaved to sin.   Christ died on the cross to set us free and to make us children of God (Foster, *op. cit.*, p.356).   The addition of the preposition *anti*, 'instead of,' is significant in view of the preposition *huper*, 'on behalf of,' used after it, in the phrase "for all" (*huper panton*).   Christ is conceived of as an 'exchange price' on behalf of and in place of all.[38]   Paul's teaching here is very definite, and utterly irreconcilable with much of the popular theology of the present day, which rejects the great Christian doctrine of the vicarious sacrifice and substitutionary atoning death of Christ.   The language "for all" leads this commentator to agree with those who urge an unlimited atonement as the doctrine taught in the Bible.   Potentially, Christ's death is for all.[39]   It is not limited by nationality or position.   Its only limitation is that occasioned by the unwillingness of any to receive the gift and accept the redemption.

The testimony *borne* at the proper time – Christ's death as a ransom *had to be proclaimed.*[40]   It was the intention of God that when 'the appropriate seasons' or 'favorable opportunities' arrived, the fact that God "desires all men to be saved and come to the knowledge of the truth" (verse 4) had to be published.   As the italics show, there is no verb in the Greek at this place.   Though this phrase is somewhat obscure and is differently explained, the context ("for this I was appointed a preacher," etc.) suggests the NASB's insertion of the verb "borne" may be on the right track.   A rather satisfactory explanation is this: the mediation and redemption of Jesus Christ is the subject matter of the testimony

---

[34] Some note that Jesus said "for many" and Paul writes "for all."   The terms are interchangeable.   We presume that Jesus said "for many" because He was making conscious reference to one of the Suffering Servant poems (Isaiah 52:13-53:12) in which the prophet's words were "for many." See the author's comments on Matthew 20:20 (and Mark 10:45) in his commentary on the Gospels, *The Climax of the Earthly Ministry of Jesus, in loc.*, for details about this expression "for many."

[35] Dana and Mantey, *Grammar*, p.100.

[36] Moulton and Milligan, *Vocabulary of the Greek New Testament*, p.46.

[37] See a careful discussion of the term "ransom" ("redemption") in the author's commentary on Romans 3:24.

[38] Donald Guthrie, *The Pastoral Epistles*, p.72.

[39] Recall the attempts by some commentators to limit "all men" in verses 1 and 4 because of a preconceived notion about a "limited atonement."   Any such idea of limitation is to be jettisoned.

[40] As the following comments will show, we think the suggestion of some, that the giving of Christ Himself as the testimony, is not the point in this passage.

(witness) which Paul and the other apostles of Jesus were appointed to bear at the proper time. The "proper time" ('due season') is the beginning of the Christian dispensation. It is the 'due season' because it corresponds with God's eternal plan with respect to when the mystery should be made known (cp. Romans 16:25-27). "It was in the fullness of time that God sent forth His son (Galatians 4:4), and it was only through the accomplishment of His task that, at the appointed time, the gospel could be proclaimed in its fullness. That appointed time had come, and the apostles now lived in the days of proclaiming that full gospel to all men."[41]   Before Jesus ascended back to the Father, He commissioned His followers to evangelize and make disciples. He gave this commission because "the proper time" had arrived. The proclamation of the ransom could not be made before the price had been paid on the cross, so Jesus forbade premature announcement of the gospel (Matthew 17:9; Luke 9:20,31). The "due time" for the testimony lies between the coming of the Spirit which empowered the witnesses (Acts 1:8) and the second coming of the Lord (2 Thessalonians 1:10).

2:7 -- And for this I was appointed a preacher and an apostle – The antecedent of "this" is "testimony" in the previous verse. It was exactly for this purpose, namely, that he could be one of the ones to 'bear testimony in due time,' that Jesus had called Paul to be an apostle. In Paul's final argument that prayer should be offered for "all men" because God desires the salvation of all men, he calls attention to his own commission to the Gentiles. The word "I" is emphatic in the Greek. Whatever may be said about others, Paul was sure that he had been appointed a preacher and apostle! Where the NASB has "appointed," the KJV has "ordained." The word "ordain" has now acquired a technical significance (meaning 'to set apart to a sacred office by the laying on hands') that the word did not have in the 1600s. *Tithemi*, the word used here, is not the usual word used when "ordination," or laying on of hands, was meant. For that, such words as *kathistemi*, *cheirotoneo*, and *epitithemi* were used. Paul has already used this same word at 1 Timothy 1:12, "putting me into service." If God put Paul into this ministry to the Gentiles, then it must be true that God is interested in "all men." The Greek for "preacher" is *kērux*, a "herald." In the ancient world, a "herald" was the person who by order of a superior made a loud, public announcement of the exact message the superior wanted made known. Perhaps when the "proclaimer" heralded the good news, he had in view an evangelistic purpose or thrust. "Apostle" has already been explained at 1 Timothy 1:1.

(I am telling the truth and not lying) – At times this matter of Paul's having been divinely appointed to be an apostle had been called into question by his enemies (cp. Romans 9:1; 2 Corinthians 11:31; Galatians 1:20). Surely, Timothy

---

[41] Foster, *op. cit.*, p.356.

needed no reminder of Paul's apostleship.   So it is only natural to surmise that the reason for this strong asseveration about his office of apostle is that at Ephesus the teachers of false doctrine had begun to raise questions about Paul's authority. Remembering that 1 Timothy was as much for the benefit of the Ephesian church as it was for Timothy's, then this asseveration is understandable.   Don't let the church ever forget the divine character of Paul's appointment to apostleship!

As a teacher of the Gentiles – This is not a third "office" to which Paul was called, but rather is an explanation of what was involved in his being a preacher and apostle.[42]   He was called to go to the Gentiles and teach them (Romans 11:13; Galatians 2:7.)   Here is further evidence that God is interested in the salvation of all men.   Paul had specifically been commissioned to go to the Gentiles with the good news.

In faith and truth – These words mean that Paul was appointed to instruct the Gentiles about faith and truth.[43]   Perhaps "faith" speaks of a body of doctrine, the faith once-for-all delivered to the saints.   Perhaps it speaks of the kind of response God expects of men who would be forgiven – faithfulness to the revelation that has been granted to them.   "Truth" refers to the truth of Christianity, the well-known facts of the gospel story.   Hearers of the message heralded are to respond in faith to the message of truth.

B. Men and Women in Public Worship.   2:8-15

1. Conduct of the men at public worship.   2:8

2:8 -- Therefore – "Therefore" connects this paragraph with the preceding.[44] Having made clear that public worship service prayers are to be offered for all men, now Paul provides instruction to both the men and the women about their lifestyles and everyday conduct if they expect their prayers and their worship to

---

[42] At 2 Timothy 1:11 he does use all three terms and connects them each time by "and."   We suppose that the function of apostle sometimes demanded Paul be a herald, sometimes a teacher, sometimes a shepherd, etc.   The higher office often includes functions of lower offices.

[43] The KJV reads in such a way that the phrase could be taken as a boast by Paul that he taught faithfully and truly.   While there is no doubt that he did that, this is not, we think, the meaning that should be assigned to these words.

[44] Scholars do not agree about the paragraphing of the text at this place.   Some place verse 8 with verses 1-7, and begin a new paragraph with verse 9.   Others opt to begin a new paragraph with verse 8, noting that, without verse 8 to introduce it, verse 9 has no main verb.   For example, the paragraphing in the UBS[3] text includes verse 8 with what follows, as does the NASB.   Others, noting links to both what precedes and what follows, treat verse 8 as a transitional link between the two paragraphs.   See, for example, how NA[26] has breaks both before and after verse 8.

be acceptable to God.[45]   A word about what the public services were like in the early church may be in order.   Several New Testament verses give a glimpse into their assemblies: (1) Acts 2:42 has been explained as picturing some things that were part of the public worship services – teaching or preaching, fellowship such as offerings or meals, observance of the Lord's Supper, and prayers (note the plural).   (2) 1 Corinthians 11:2-16 pictures women taking part, with instructions about how their heads should be covered as they pray or prophesy.[46]   Men are to have their heads uncovered as they pray or prophesy.   (3) At 1 Corinthians 11:17ff we learn that a meal, called the love feast, often was served at these public assemblies, followed by the celebration of the Lord's Supper.   (4) 1 Corinthians 14:12-19 indicates any spiritually gifted person at Corinth was given opportunity to exercise that gift for the benefit of the whole congregation.   Included are prayers, songs, offering "blessings" (i.e., giving thanks), and (1 Corinthians14:26) psalms, teachings, revelations, tongues, and interpretation of tongues.   A few verses later we have instructions about the use of the gift of tongues and of prophecy at the public services (1 Corinthians 14:26-33).

I want the men in every place to pray – "I want" is *boulomai*.[47]   Having just declared his apostolic authority, this verb may be regarded almost as a command from the Lord.   "Men" is *tous andras*, and denotes men as distinguished from women.   (This is something the *anthropos* of verse 1 does not do.).   Before this paragraph is finished, the topic will, we believe, change from men and women to husbands and wives.   But to begin with, we suppose, Paul is speaking about males.   In fact, if this verse were translated "husbands" rather than "men," then we would find the commentaries suggesting that only married men should offer prayers in the public worship services.   In the notes below it will be shown that such a conclusion would be out of harmony with what we find elsewhere in Scripture about prayers at the public services.   "Every place" means every place where congregations assemble to worship.[48]   Prayer is to be an important and

---

[45] Hendriksen's (*op. cit.*, p.102) comment, "having made clear that prayers must be offered for all men, the apostle proceeds to indicate who should offer these prayers and in what spirit they should be offered," reflects his choice to treat verse 8 as the conclusion of verses 1-7.   If his paragraphing is wrong, then his comment (i.e., males only may so pray in public) may be in error, too.

[46] 1 Corinthians 14:34-36 does say that the women in public assemblies are not to speak habitually or all the time.   "To speak" in these verses is a present tense infinitive.   If it were an aorist tense, it would say women are *never* to speak, but that is not the case.

[47] See notes above at 1 Timothy 2:4 on the possible connotation of this verb.

[48] Several explanations have been offered for the words "in every place."   (1) Many early congregations met in members' homes.   1 Corinthians 16:19 speaks of Ephesus and the surrounding area.   Perhaps "in every place" implies the "church at Ephesus" was made up of several house churches, each of which had their own public worship service.   (2) Perhaps "in every place" means what Paul says concerning the conduct of public worship at Ephesus is no different than he teaches in every other place.   This is not just a local rule for Ephesus.   It is true of churches all over the empire.   (3) Perhaps "every place" stands in sharp contrast to Jewish (1 Kings 8:29) and pagan

continual feature of Christian worship. "To pray" is a present tense infinitive. It indicates continuous, habitual, or customary action. Perhaps there is some connection to what was said about prayer in verse 1 ff. (1) Those who treat verse 8 as the close of the first paragraph of chapter 2 comment on this fashion: Paul is likely continuing his instructions about prayer in public worship, after the digression occasioned by the direction that such prayers were to be for "all men." (2) Those who treat verse 8 as the beginning of a new paragraph think that Paul here begins a second point which he wished to stress; namely, the spirit and behavior expected of men and women as they share in the public worship.[49]

In harmony with what we can learn about worship in the early church, we understand the "praying" here in Paul's mind to be the kind of individual and free participation by the worshippers in the numerous public prayers offered during the time of worship. But just what Paul's emphasis is at this place is not entirely clear. (1) Perhaps Paul is saying it is the "males" who are to be the ones who regularly offer the public prayers.[50] Those who think the emphasis is that men are the ones to regularly[51] lead in the public prayers should observe that there evidently are times when women may lead in prayer. More will be said on this in comments on verse 9 below. Suffice it here to say that this commentator disagrees with those who adamantly insist that if a woman should pray while the public worship service[52] is being conducted, let her prayer be as Hannah's: "She spoke in her heart; only her lips moved, but her voice was not heard" (1 Samuel 1:13). Plummer traces the historical development of restrictions on who may offer prayers in public worship as men later and gradually changed what was done at such services.[53] (a) In apostolic times, it was, Plummer infers, "all men" (1 Timothy 2:8). (b) By about AD 120 extemporaneous prayer was limited to "the prophets" (*Didache*). (c) By about AD 150, the "president," i.e., the one who presided at the service, offered the prayers (Justin Martyr). (d) Shortly thereafter

---

ideas that only in temples could specially-efficacious prayers be offered. God can be worshipped in spirit and truth in any place, not just a temple (John 4:20-24). Any or all of these may be true.

[49] Note our paragraph title and subtitles, "Conduct of the men at public worship," and "Conduct of the women at public worship."

[50] No real evidence has ever been produced to show this general rule was only true at Ephesus, and that only there was it adopted, and only temporarily and in just that one locality, as a compromise with the Jewish adversaries whose synagogue and temple services were exclusively led by males.

[51] "Regularly" does not mean "on every occasion, without exception." It does mean "most of the time."

[52] One difficult matter to settle is just what constitutes a "public worship service"? Is only the service that convenes at 10 AM on Sunday morning a "worship" service? Would a prayer and praise service, conducted on Sunday or Wednesday evenings not be a "worship" service, and would women be permitted to pray in public at these, if they are not "worship" services?

[53] A. Plummer, "The Pastoral Epistles," in *The Expositor's Bible*, ed. by W. Robertson Nicoll (Grand Rapids: Eerdmans, reprinted 1943), V.6, p. 410-411.

free prayer was abolished altogether.   (2) Perhaps Paul is saying that only those males whose "hands are holy" should be invited to lead out in the public prayers.

The titles and subtitles in our outline are intended to show how we propose to treat the paragraph.   It must be understood from the standpoint of what first century worship services were like, not what contemporary services are like. Paul is dealing with men and women in public worship.   He points out the proper conduct of the men and the women.   Both the men and the women are welcome at the worship services, and are expected to take part in the worship.   Both are to make a deliberate effort to see that their lives are in harmony with their profession as they worship.   Some of the things, specifically, that the men are to do and that the women are to do will be highlighted in the verses following.

Lifting up holy hands – Many see a reference here to one of the common bodily postures assumed by early Christians while they were praying.   Wherever the meetings for worship were held and prayer was offered, the man who prayed customarily stood with outstretched arms and hands with the palm raised upward, symbolic of awaiting a gift from above.[54]   Perhaps the key emphasis is not so much the posture but what the posture signifies, in this case, a holy life.[55]   It is very likely that these instructions about public worship are given in this letter to Timothy, the evangelist, because the evangelist is the one who guides and leads the public service.   Now Timothy has some guidelines to help him choose who offers public prayer.   If it is true that it is not just the posture of prayer, but what the posture signifies, then not every "male" would be asked to lead a public prayer; it would be only those whose lives are "holy."[56]   "Only men whose lives manifest practical righteousness should pray in public.   This is objective and can be observed by the church.   Persons living openly in sin have no business offering public prayer and should not be called upon to do so.   'If I regard iniquity in my

---

[54] On occasion we read about other postures assumed during prayers.   Kneeling, in token of submission, was a Jewish practice (cf. Psalm 95:6; Daniel 6:10; Luke 22:41; Acts 9:40).   Sometimes we see the person prostrating himself as he prays (Matthew 26:39, 17:6; Revelation 11:16). Hendriksen, *op. cit.*, p.103,104, has an excellent discussion of possible postures that may be assumed while praying, and the spiritual significance of each.

[55] The word translated "holy" here is *hosios.* *Hosios* speaks of being in harmony with the divine constitution of the universe.   In other words, the "males" who lead in prayer are Christians, in harmony with what God is doing in his world in this Christian age.   There were several Greek synonyms for "holy," each with a slightly different connotation.   *Hieros* meant sacred, holy, because it was used at the temple.   *Hagios* meant separated from the world and dedicated to God's service, separated from evil and defilement.   *Hagnos* meant pure, morally or ceremonially clean.   *Semnos* speaks of reverence, awe, magnificent, grand, venerable.

[56] Clement of Rome, I Clement 29, may allude to this verse when he wrote, "Let us then draw near to Him with holiness [*hosiotetoi*] of spirit, lifting up pure [*hagnos*] and undefiled [*amiantos*] hands unto Him, loving our gracious and merciful Father, who has made us partakers of the blessings of His elect."

heart, the Lord will not hear me' (Psalm 66:18)."[57]

Without wrath and dissension – A "holy life" is a condition of "praying" (i.e., offering acceptable public worship), and so are proper attitudes. "Wrath" is a settled indignation against a brother. It is the attitude of the unmerciful debtor of the parable (Matthew 18:21-35), and it makes prayer unacceptable to God (Matthew 6:14,15; Ephesians 4:31,32; Colossians 3:8; James 1:19,20). Barnes (*in loc.*) has a delightful quote of Jeremy Taylor's work on prayer, showing how anger is an attitude that is in alienation to prayer. Another writer wonders if the excesses of evil rulers against the Christians had resulted in lingering wrong attitudes towards the rulers that would preclude their praying for "kings and all in authority." The Greek word translated "dissension" is *dialogismos*. (1) Some writers opt for the meaning "evil deliberation," which results from malice against a brother. Luke 5:21,22 would be an example of such "evil deliberation." A person who harbors such an argumentative attitude toward another, or irritation or resentment, can hardly be one to offer a sincere prayer. Angry feelings can have no place in the heart of one who really prays, whether in public or in private. (2) Some writers opt for the meaning "questionings" or "doubting" (KJV).[58] This is then explained in various ways: (a) If the person who is praying "doubts" that he will receive what he is praying for, he might as well not pray at all. He is not praying as Jesus taught, "do not doubt" (Matthew 21:21). (b) The person praying (a prayer for "all men", 2:1ff) has doubts about the goodness and power of God (James 1:6-8), and perhaps even doubts about His interest in "all men." Such persons might as well not pray at all, because their hearts are not in tune with the One to whom their prayers are addressed.

Let us summarize the point Paul has made. Wherever they assemble to worship, men are to offer public prayers. Men who wish their "prayers" to be answered, and their worship to be acceptable, are to have lifestyles that match their profession. God looks for a life that is characterized by holy living, and attitudes towards one's fellow men that exclude any anger or resentment.

2. Conduct of the women at public worship. 2:9-15

2:9 -- Likewise – "Likewise" (*hōsautōs*, meaning "in the same way, similarly") links this paragraph with the preceding discussion which began at 2:1, showing that public worship is still being considered. In verses 11ff, Paul is certainly dis-

---

[57] Kent, *op. cit.*, p.104. What about lifting up our hands as we sing in public worship? If the words are a prayer, we have Scriptural precedent.

[58] Liddell and Scott do not admit this as a possible meaning for *dialogismos*. Nor can any New Testament passage, other than this one in 1 Timothy 2, be adduced as one where *dialogismos* might clearly mean "doubting."

cussing matters that pertain to public worship. It is hard to conceive that here in verses 9-10 the topic temporarily begins with something not related to worship. We suppose the suppressed connection is on this order: just as the **men** are to make necessary preparations before coming to worship (2:8), so the **women** are to give evidence of the same spirit of holiness as they make preparations to come to worship. Just as men's lives are important to their worship and offering prayers, so women's lives are important to their worship. It would be a misunderstanding to think that only when a woman is at worship is her behavior to be as herein instructed.

I *want* – The italics indicate that there is no verb in the Greek. When this occurs, we usually supply one from the context. The NASB translators have done what is normal in such cases by repeating the verb "want" from verse 8. In addition to supplying "want," it is also possible to repeat the infinitive "to pray" from verse 8, thus making verse 9 an injunction or directive by Paul to women concerning their dress and demeanor as they offer prayer in public worship. Since "likewise" forbids the supposition that the apostle has now closed the subject of public prayer in order to give a general rule as to the dress and attire of the women, some form for "pray" (perhaps the participial form *proseuchomenas*, not the infinitive form *proseuchesthai*) may certainly be supplied after *gunaikas*.[59] If we supply a form of "pray," then Paul is giving instructions to both men and women who are engaged in the same activity, i.e., "prayer" at public worship. In favor of supplying the word "pray" is that it provides an easy way to follow the thread of thought through these verses about public worship. In reply, various arguments have been advanced why *only* the verb "want" should be supplied from verse 8. (1) Just as the verb "want" is completed by an infinitive "to pray" in verse 8, so "likewise" is completed by the infinitive "to adorn" here in verse 9. It would be clumsy to translate if a second infinitive ("to pray") is implied. (Though it would not be clumsy if we supply a participle, so that the verse reads "praying women.") (2) Others argue that supplying some form of "pray" results in women offering public prayer in the worship assemblies, making this verse contradict what the New Testament elsewhere teaches on this subject. Those making this argument are of the conviction that the New Testament elsewhere demands that women not lead in public worship (e.g., 1 Corinthians 14:34; 1 Timothy 2:11,12).[60] Those who argue against women leading in public are of the conviction that the correctives in 1 Corinthians 11:5,13 concerning women having a proper covering on the head when praying in public are really an *ad hominem* argument, and that Paul later implies that not only was their lack of covering improper, but even their

[59] Van Oosterzee, "1 Timothy," in *Lange's Commentary*, p.33.

[60] Such an interpretation, in this commentator's opinion, does not do justice to what those passages teach about the role of women in public worship. 1 Corinthians 11:5,13 indicate that women were in fact offering prayer in public services.

praying in public at all was out of place (1 Corinthians 14:34).

Whether or not women may offer public prayers in the worship services is a point to be proven.[61] At this stage of our discussion, one conclusion or another should not be assumed, and that assumption then be used as an argument for or against the supplying of "to pray" as well as "I want" here at the beginning of verse 9. Whatever verb forms we supply to complete the sense, do not forget that the context apparently is not just "prayers" but public worship in general.

Women – *Gunaikas* may be translated either "women" or "wives."[62] The manuscripts are evenly divided on whether or not there is a "the" in the Greek before "women" like there was an article earlier before "men." This being true, no interpretation of the passage should be made to depend on what the original may or may not have read.

To adorn themselves with proper clothing – "Adorn" thus speaks of women's dress as they are attending public worship. "Proper clothing" is an attempt to translate *katastolē kosmiō*. *Kosmios* means well-ordered, decorous, becoming. It does not mean "modest" in the sense of being opposed to that which is immodest – i.e., that which tends to excite improper passions and desires.[63] *Kosmios* is cognate to the verb *kosmeō*, translated "to adorn" or "to arrange." Thus the apparel (if that is what the next word means) of the Christian woman is to be "well arranged," or we might say, it should be "in good taste."[64] *Katastolē* may refer to behavior as well as to dress. Paul was shrewd enough to know that a woman's dress is a mirror of her mind.[65] There is some doubt as to the exact meaning of *katastolē* here. Alford argues strongly in favor of the meaning "apparel," but it may also refer to an attitude, "steadiness" or "quietness" of demeanor. If so, this phrase would exactly parallel 1 Peter 3:5, "the incorruptible apparel of a meek and quiet spirit."[66] Thus the meaning is, "Let Christian women adorn themselves with a decent and well-ordered quietness of demeanor, in strict accordance with [or, 'together with'] shamefastness and sobriety [*kata*, 'in strict accord with' or

---

[61] The fact of a contrast between "males" and "women" in verses 8 and 9 does not prove women are excluded from praying in worship services. Would we argue that the emphasis on women dressing modestly and discreetly means that men are not to be concerned about this? If not, then why take the verse about men offering public prayers as excluding women from praying?

[62] Just as "men" (verse 8) can be either "men" or "husbands," and we tentatively opted for "men," so we think the reference here is still general, "women" rather than "wives" in particular. Apparently it is not until verse 11 that the topic narrows from women in general to wives in particular.

[63] Barnes, *op. cit.*, p.135.

[64] Kent, *op. cit.*, p.105.

[65] Guthrie, *op. cit.*, p.74.

[66] Hervey, *op. cit.*, p.35

'together with'], not with braided hair, etc."[67]   A woman's true ornament is not the finery which she gets from the milliner, but the chaste discretion which she has from the Spirit of God.

Modestly and discreetly – The Greek phrase begins with *meta*, "accompanied by," and so these words denote a state of mind necessary for one who is concerned with "adorning themselves with proper clothing." "Modestly" translates *aidōs*, a word denoting reverence, respect, modesty (Kent, *The Pastoral Epistles*, p.105). *Aidōs* is a sense of shame, a shrinking from trespassing the boundaries of propriety; hence a proper reserve.[68] (Bashfulness, shamefastness was the word used in the 1611 KJV. "Shamefacedness" in the later editions of the KJV is therefore a corruption.).   R.C. Trench compared "steadfast," "soothfast," "rootfast," "masterfast," "footfast," "bedfast," with their substantives to help us understand the meaning of "shamefast."[69]   The word signifies the 'innate shrinking from anything unbecoming.' *Sōphrosunē*, "discreetly," denotes good sense, good judgment, self-control, self-restraint. "Women, when getting dressed for church, must practice sanity. Dress in sensible attire. They must not try to show off, wearing flashy apparel so as to make others jealous of them."[70] Berry gives us this help with the synonyms for "modest" and "discreet":

> *Aidōs* is an innate moral repugnance to doing a dishonorable act. It is the fear of doing a shameful thing.
>
> *Aischunē* is disgrace in the eyes of others, after one has done a disgraceful act. It is fear of being found out. ("*Aidōs* always will restrain a good man from an unworthy act. *Aischunē* might sometimes restrain a bad man." [Trench])
>
> *Sōphrosunē* is self-command. It expresses positively what *aidōs* expresses negatively.[71]

Sōphrosunē represents an inner self-government, a constant living by proper spiritual desires. "One's attire is the expression of tastes, interests, and even character. Consequently, the manner in which a woman dresses indicates a great deal about what sort of woman she is."[72] These two words indicate the inward feelings with which the apostle desires the Christian women to come to worship.

---

[67] Hervey, *ibid.*

[68] Hendriksen, *op. cit.*, p.106.

[69] Trench, *Synonyms*, p.71.

[70] Hendriksen, *ibid.*

[71] Berry, *New Testament Synonyms*, p. 119.

[72] Kent, *op. cit.*, p.105.

Not with braided hair – Beginning with this particular, Paul names certain practices which would violate the norm he has just enunciated in the previous phrases. We doubt that his list is exhaustive of the practices that would violate the norm. We also tend to believe that the practices named are intrinsically inappropriate to the lifestyle of Christian women, both in that culture and in ours. *Plegmasin* occurs only here in the New Testament. In classical Greek the word indicated anything entwined, not just hair – whether tendrils of the vine, wickerwork, chaplets, a twined garland. Compare 1 Peter 3:3.

> Paul has been criticized severely for these words, as if he did not want [women] to look their loveliest ... But the combination of words here -- "braided hair, gold, costly clothing" -- should have sufficed to help the critics see that it is the sin of extravagance in outward adornment that is to be rejected. ... Braids in the first century often represented *fortunes*.[73]

For pictures of braided hair on first century women, see *Good News* (a New Testament with over 500 illustrations, published by the American Bible Society), 1 Timothy, p. G19, and *Everyday Life in Bible Times* (published by National Geographic), p.244,245.

And gold or pearls or costly garments – Was the "gold" entwined in the plaits of the hair, or is it speaking of gold jewelry (elaborate ornaments to catch the attention)? Pearls were obtained at that time from the Persian Gulf or from the Indian Ocean. These were often fabulously priced and thus far beyond the purchasing power of average people. "Earrings, necklaces, and bracelets are included here. These costly ornaments were worn by the ladies of the luxurious age in which Paul lived, in great profusion."[74] "'Costly array' [very expensive splendid garments] includes that which can be ill-afforded, and that which is inconsistent with the feeling that the principal ornament is that of the heart."[75]

> It may be a difficult question to settle how *much* ornament is allowable for the Christian woman, and when the true line is passed. But though this cannot be settled by any exact rules, since much must depend on age, on the relative rank in life, and the means which one may possess, yet there is one general rule which is applicable to all, and which might regulate all. It is, that the true line is passed when more thought is given to this external adorning than to the ornament of the heart. Any external decoration which occupies the mind more than the virtues of the heart, and which engrosses the time and attention more, we may be certain is wrong.[76]

---

[73] Hendriksen, *op. cit.*, p.107.

[74] Ellicott's *Commentary*, p.209.

[75] Barnes' *Notes*, p.136. "Array" translates *himatismon*, the regular word for the outer garments worn in the ancient world.

[76] Barnes' *Notes*, p. 135.

2:10 -- But rather by means of good works – Verse 10 carries the discussion about the women's inner preparation for worship to its conclusion. Rather than depending on what she herself simply wears outwardly, the ultimate adornment is a life of good works and loving service. We must repeat the first part of verse 9 in order to get the complete statement: "I want women to adorn themselves (not with ..., but) by means of good works." Men's lives, as indicated by "holy hands", are an important part of their preparation for worship. So also women's lives, as indicated by their "good works", are important to their preparation. "Good works" are acts of loving service to others. Scripture provides examples of Christian women who did such deeds: Phoebe was a "helper of many" (Romans 16:1,2); Lydia's good works involved hospitality to missionaries (Acts 16:14,15); Dorcas made garments so the needy would not be ill-clothed (Acts 9:36,39). Paul's instructions remind us of 1 Peter 3:3,4, "let not your adornment be external only – braiding the hair, and wearing gold jewelry, and putting on dresses; but let it be the hidden person of the heart, with the imperishable quality of a gentle and quiet spirit, which is precious in the sight of God."[77] Every Christian woman should prize more highly a testimony to her loving deeds of service than a reputation as the best-dressed woman in the congregation.

As befits women making a claim to godliness – In other passages where the word for "making a claim to" occurs in the New Testament, *epaggellō* means "to promise" or "to profess." In the middle voice it speaks of an announcement or proclamation made about oneself. A woman who wants to proclaim loudly and clearly that she is a Christian does so by her deeds of loving service, not by the clothes and jewelry she can put on. "Godliness" translates *theosebeia*. A word from the same family is found in John 9:31, and is translated "God-fearing" (i.e., a "worshiper of God"). The word speaks of reverence for God. If we profess to be followers of Him who "went about doing good," then the performance of good works is especially becoming. If anyone says she loves God, and does not love her brother, her profession about loving God is a lie (1 John 4:20). "Whoever has the world's goods, and beholds his brother in need and closes his heart against him, how does the love of God abide in him?" (1 John 3:17)

2:11 -- Let a woman quietly receive instruction – What is the connection with the context? We are still in the portion of the epistle that we've titled "Charge

---

[77] It should be obvious that neither Peter nor Paul is forbidding all jewelry and hair styling and dress clothes. The word Peter uses for "apparel" (KJV) is the regular word for ordinary garments. If all these items were totally forbidden, the women would have no clothes on at all! Paul is concerned with braided hair and jewelry and costly garments that violate the principle of "proper and modest and discreet," not with the items in and of themselves. Women may wear Rebecca's jewelry (Genesis 24:53) if they have Rebecca's modesty.

Concerning Public Worship" which began at 2:1. The directives Paul is about to give still concern women's behavior in public worship. "Wife" rather than "woman" would appear to be the better translation. The term here is singular, rather than plural as in verses 9 and 10. Did Paul change number because there has been a slight narrowing of his topic from "women" in general to "wife" in particular? The verses that immediately follow seem to suggest the topic has narrowed to "wife" instead of still being "woman" in general.[78] "Quietly" ("in silence" KJV) translates *hēsuchia*, which refers not to a complete absence of speaking, but to an attitude, a spirit, a disposition, and is more properly translated "quietness" as in the ASV.[79] This same word is used in 1 Timothy 2:2 to describe the tranquil and quiet life, and in 2 Thessalonians 3:12 to urge Christians to walk in "quiet fashion." This is not the same word rendered "keep silent" in 1 Corinthians 14:34 (*sigaō*). There are places in the New Testament that *hēsuchia* has the meaning of "keep silent" in the sense that one has stopped arguing (Luke 14:4; Acts 11:18, 22:2). Thayer[80] has a study on synonyms:

Hēsuchiadzein -- Describes a quiet condition in general, inclusive of silence.

Sigan – Describes a mental condition and its manifestation, especially in speechlessness (silence from fear, grief, awe, etc.).

Siōpan -- The more external and physical term, denotes abstinence from speech, especially as antithetic to loquacity.

If all of chapter 2 deals with the charge concerning public worship, then "receive instruction" (*manthanō*) suggests one activity involved in 1st century public worship. The word means to learn, to be informed, to understand, to learn through instruction. As a present tense verb, it implies a continual learning.

With entire submissiveness – The "quietness" will exhibit itself in "submissiveness." "Submissiveness" translates *hupotagē*, to range oneself under someone else.[81] But who is that someone else here? (a) Is it under God's authority and

---

[78] In the special study at the close of chapter 2, we show that interpreting 1 Timothy 2 and 1 Corinthians 14:34-36 as references to "wives" submitting to their husbands, rather than "women" submitting to "men," helps to effectively harmonize all the passages that deal with the role of women in the public assemblies of believers.

[79] Vine, *An Expository Dictionary of New Testament Words*, p. 242.

[80] Thayer's *Greek-English Lexicon*, p. 281.

[81] Subordination or submissiveness, voluntarily done, is neither degrading nor dishonoring. There is no suggestion that a wife is the husband's toy or slave. As the church is not dishonored by being subject to Christ, as Christ is not dishonored by being subject to the Father, so neither is a wife dishonored by being submissive. In fact, the opposite is true. One who submits finds in it a place of ultimate fulfillment.

law for her life? Cp. Hebrews 12:9; James 4:7; and 2 Corinthians 9:13, which are examples of such a use.[82] (b) Is it the appropriate response to those in authority? Cp. 1 Corinthians 16:16; 1 Peter 5:5; Romans 13:1,5. (c) Is it under her husband's authority? Cp. Ephesians 5:22; Colossians 3:18; Titus 2:5; 1 Peter 3:1. It would seem in this context which speaks of "husbands" that this is precisely the one under whom the wife is to range herself. The use of the word "entire" to modify "submissiveness" is at first surprising. Why did Paul add this word? Perhaps Paul is thinking that while it might be possible to receive instruction quietly, it could also be done with a rebellious attitude of heart. This last phrase ("entire submissiveness") would rule out such an attitude while a wife is assuming the attitude of a student (learner, disciple). Perhaps the degree of submissiveness a Christian wife could offer to a Christian husband differs from the submissiveness a Christian wife could give to a non-believing husband. In 1 Peter 3:1, Christian wives are instructed to be submissive to their non-believing husbands so that the wife's behavior would be winsome and perhaps make it easier to lead the husband to Christ. (Of course, if the non-Christian husband asked the Christian wife to disobey Christ, the Christian would obey God rather than man.) Here in 1 Timothy in its public worship setting, it is implied that both husband and wife are Christians. A Christian husband's expectations would be such that the Christian wife could be "entirely" submissive. Paul's expression "entire submissiveness" shows he was averse to anything which would mar the quiet solemnity of their public meetings for prayer and praise and instruction.

2:12 -- But – In contrast to the Christian directive that women are to be taught the Christian religion (verse 11), Paul here says he does not allow a wife to teach.

I do not allow a woman to teach – "I do not allow" is *epitrepein*. Some versions read "permit," some "suffer," others "allow." It is doubtful the present tense means no more than "I am not at present allowing it" (implying that 'I might allow it at other times and places').[83] We suppose Paul's position on this matter was more than local and temporary, and he has not changed views from those written in earlier letters. It misunderstands the authoritativeness of *epitrepō* as used by Paul to interpret this as simply a note of personal disinclination which may or may not be in harmony with God's revelation on such matters. Paul's appeal to the creation and fall (verse 13) indicates this is not just personal disinclination.

---

[82] Hendriksen (*New Testament Commentary* on 1 Timothy, p.109), who is very conservative in his comments, wrote, "She should *range herself under* God's law for her life. Her full spiritual equality with men as a sharer in all the blessings of salvation (Gal. 3:28, 'there can be neither male nor female') does not imply any basic change in her nature as a *woman* or in the corresponding task which she *as a woman* is called upon to perform." In an earlier comment he observes, "Though these words may sound a trifle unfriendly, in reality they are the very opposite. In fact they are expressive of a feeling of tender sympathy and basic understanding."

[83] Knight, *The Pastoral Epistles*, p.140.

"Woman" carries the same sense it had in verse 11. We think there are special instructions to the "wife" in this passage. "To teach" translates the present infinitive *didaskein*. Evidently the word "man" at the close of the verse (though in the genitive case after *authentein*) is also the object of this infinitive. If so, the first directive to wives reads, "In the public assembly, I do not permit a wife to teach a husband." While Paul does not allow wives to teach their husbands in the public assembly, he does instruct women to teach other women and children (2 Timothy 3:14; Titus 2:3). If we have understood this verse correctly, "wives" have some limitations on their teaching that single women (e.g., Philip's virgin daughters, Acts 21:9) do not. The verb *didaskō* and its cognates are the most common terms for "teaching" in the New Testament. The word refers almost exclusively to public instruction or teaching of groups.[84] In the New Testament, a teacher is one who systematically teaches or expounds the Word of God and gives instruction based on the Old Testament and the apostles' teaching (1 Corinthians 4:17; 2 Timothy 2:2).[85] Teachers were able to grasp revelation that had already been given and communicate this truth effectively to others. Teaching was an activity Paul engaged in as "a teacher of the nations" (1 Timothy 2:7; cf. 2 Timothy 1:11). His disciple Timothy is encouraged to "command and teach" (1 Timothy 4:11, 6:2; 2 Timothy 4:1). Paul instructs Timothy, "the things which you have heard from me in the presence of many witnesses, these entrust to faithful men, who will be able to teach others" (2 Timothy 2:2). Elders were to be "able to teach" (1 Timothy 3:2; Titus 1:9; Ephesians 4:11).

Not many women were teachers in the 1st century world. In the Hellenistic period, the specified activity of teaching was barred to women. As Sigountos and Shrank write in their study of Greek standards for women in public, "It is in fact quite difficult to find Hellenistic women who could be termed teachers ... The Greek view of teachers prevented 'respectable' women from occupying that role."[86] In the LXX, the term "teach" became "a specialized term for the translation of the Torah into concrete directions for the life of the individual."[87] In Judaism women were barred from the study of the Torah, so it would be impossible for them to take part in any "teaching."

---

[84] Roy B. Zuck, "Greek Words for Teach," *Bibliotheca Sacra* 122 (April-June 1965), p. 159-60. He notes that in only three of nearly 100 occurrences does the word refer to the teaching of individuals – John 8:28; Romans 2:21; Revelation 2:14.

[85] Harold Mare, "Prophet and Teacher in the New Testament Period," *Bulletin of the Evangelical Theological Society* 9 (Summer 1966), p. 146.

[86] "Public Roles for Women in the Pauline Church: A Reappraisal of the Evidence," JETS 26, 1983, p.189.

[87] Rengstorf, *Didaskein*, TDNT, Kittel, V.2, p.138.

"Teach" is a present tense infinitive – what Paul prohibits is continual, habitual, customary, repeated, action.[88]   The present tense infinitive does not prohibit occasional teaching; an aorist tense infinitive would be required to do that.   The present tense infinitive does not prohibit all acts of teaching even when "men" are present.   That, too, would require the use of an aorist tense infinitive. What is prohibited is continual, repeated, or customary teaching by the wives.

Failure to observe the present tense infinitive – and then treating this prohibition as though it were an absolute prohibition of women teaching in public – has led to a deluge of books and scholarly articles written in an attempt to harmonize this 'prohibition' with those New Testament passages that indicate women did teach men and did pray and did prophesy in public.   (1) One teacher emphasized the distinction between the office and function of teacher, in a way similar to the distinction in the Old Testament between the office and function of prophet.   He then concluded the *office* of teacher was prohibited to women, but not the occasional *function*.[89]   (2) Religious groups that equate leadership (teacher, preacher) in the church with a special priesthood, or with the eldership, traditionally have tended to say this prohibition against women teaching or exercising authority means that any attempt to ordain women is hereby proscribed as against the will of God.   (3) The modern feminist movement, taking the prohibition to be absolute, sees 1 Timothy 2:12 as demeaning to women. Feminists have characterized Paul as being a woman hater, or have suggested the Timothy passage is cultural and temporal, rather than an abiding rule from God. Or they have denied the Pauline authorship of the Pastorals, so that Paul is not speaking, but some disciple of Paul.   Most feminists tend to make Galatians 3:28

---

[88] Note the difference between present and aorist tense infinitives.   Outside the indicative mood, tense in a Greek verb denotes only kind of action.   Whenever you see a present tense (and it is not in the indicative mood – and an infinitive is not an indicative mood), stop and ask why it is there.   The writer used it deliberately – he uses the aorist tense unless he has some reason for using the present.   **Present** tense indicates the action is on-going, repeated, habitual, or customary. **Aorist** tense indicates the action is unitary in some sense, a single event.   When translated into English, the present and aorist tense infinitives are often translated just alike (though some grammars suggest using a phrase such as "to be in the process of" or "to perform the act of" as a means of distinguishing between the two tenses).

Dana and Mantey in their *Manual Grammar of the Greek New Testament* (p.109) have this to say on the subject: "The aorist infinitive denotes that which is eventual or particular, while the present infinitive indicates a condition or a process.   Thus *pisteusai* (aorist) is the exercise of faith on a given occasion, while *pisteuein* (present) is to be a believer; *douleusai* (aorist) is to render a service, while *douleuein* (present) is to be a slave; *hamartein* (aorist) is to commit a sin, while *hamartanein* (present) is to be a sinner."   By parity of reasoning, *didaxai* (aorist) would be a single act of teaching, while *didaskein* (present) would be to act habitually as a teacher.

[89] Geo. Mark Elliott, Unpublished Class Notes on 1 Corinthians, 1953.   Professor Elliott thought such a distinction between the office and function of prophet would explain why the Old Testament book of Daniel is included among the collection of books called "holy writings," rather than among the "prophets."   (Another possible explanation sometimes offered to explain this phenomenon is that the collection of the prophets was completed before Daniel was written, so Daniel had to be included with the last collection made, the one called "holy writings.")

normative as they assert the rights of any and all women to hold any leadership position in the church.   (4) Another proposes that "teach" – the verb is *didaskō* – prohibits not the act of teaching (that, it is alleged, would require the word *didaskalia*) but the content (i.e., false doctrine) of the thing taught.[90]   (5) Still others make a distinction between "worship" (church services) and home Bible studies; in one case the woman was not to teach, but in the other she could indeed teach as occasion required.[91]   For a closely reasoned and sweetly worded presentation of the pros and cons of other interpretations suggested for this passage, plus a defense of the position that women are excluded from preaching to or teaching the whole congregation, from the pulpit or elsewhere, see Jack W. Cottrell's books and articles.[92]   (6) There are those who suggest a woman is not to teach, but it is permissible for her to prophesy if she is suddenly inspired by the Holy Spirit to deliver a message, as Philip's daughters (Acts 21) or the women at Corinth (1 Corinthians 11) were.

See the special study, "What Did Wives and Women Do in the New Testament Church Assemblies?" at the close of this chapter. In that study we make note that if we read this passage as "*wives*" not teaching or "exercising authority" over their "*husbands*," we ease many of the problems that create challenges to harmonizing the passages about women in the public services. Of course, such a prohibition, not being absolute, would not preclude the Christian

---

[90] This is the hypothesis put forward by Joseph M. Webb, "Women as Christian Leaders: [Part] 1. Searching for Meaning of 1 Timothy 2," (Published by the Center for the Study of Christian Communication, Malibu, Calif., [1985]) Vol.4, #9. It has been shown that Webb has the words exactly backwards if one were to rely on the distinction between *didaskō* and *didaskalia*, to denote either the action or the content of teaching. "Where is the Command to Silence? -- 1 Timothy 2:11-15," *Christian Standard*, May 21, 1989, p.460, 477.

[91] Kent (*op. cit.*, p.108) writes, "The role of teacher in New Testament days was an authoritative office. The teacher was the declarer of doctrine. Another name for 'teacher' was 'rabbi' (John 1:38). Christ Himself as a man was recognized as one who held this office (John 3:2). Consequently, teachers were among the early officials of the church, exercising their function of declaring the Word of God (Acts 13:1; Ephesians 4:11). Such a responsibility is denied to women. Nowhere in the New Testament is a woman presented as a teacher in the church. Priscilla is no exception, for she was with her husband in the home and both of them instructed Apollos (Acts 18:26)."

While limited in her authority to teach, the Christian religion does greatly enlarge the role of women as compared to the Jewish religion of the 1st century. "Rabbinic prohibitions were much more severe than Christian, since a woman, although theoretically permitted to read the Torah in public, was in practice not allowed to teach even small children (cf. Strack-Billerbeck, III, p.467). The teaching of Christian doctrine, nevertheless, is confined by Paul to the male sex, and this has been the almost invariable practice in the subsequent history of the Church." (Guthrie, p. 76).

[92] Jack Cottrell's series of four articles: "1 Timothy and the Role of Women," "1 Timothy 2:12 ...: Were the Ephesian Women Uneducated?" "1 Timothy 2:12 ...: Women and Authority," and "1 Timothy 2:12 ...: The Meaning of Galatians 3:28," appeared in *Christian Standard*, 128 (Jan. 10, 17, 24, 31, 1993), p.20ff, 44ff, 64ff, 84ff. This was followed by a three-part series, "1 Timothy 2:12...: Response to My Critics," *Christian Standard* 128 (Nov.21, 28, Dec. 5, 1993), p.997ff, 1020ff, and 1036ff. Dr. Cottrell has also published a longer work on this topic, *Gender Roles and the Bible: Creation, Fall, and Redemption* (Joplin, MO: College Press, 1994).

wife from teaching an unconverted husband how to become a Christian. This context, which talks about husbands lifting up holy hands as they pray, and the wife's likewise chaste behavior, assumes both husband and wife are Christians.

Or (I do not allow a woman to) exercise authority over a man – "Man" is *anēr*, the same root word used in verse 8, but with this difference – it is singular at this place. In this context "husband" (as distinguished from wives) would be the ideal translation.[93] "Or" translates *oude*. The force of this negative particle which joins two infinitives ("teach" and "exercise authority") has been debated. Does Paul give one prohibition, or two? If one, the two infinitives form a hendiadys whose meaning would be either "to teach authoritatively" or "to teach a man in a domineering way" (depending on the meaning assigned to *authentein*). However, an analysis of the instances in the New Testament in which *oude* joins two infinitives shows that two separate, albeit closely related, ideas are meant.[94] A wife is not to habitually teach at public meetings when her husband is present. A wife is not to habitually "exercise authority" at public meetings when her husband is present.

Next, it should be observed that the Greek *authentein*, translated "to exercise authority over," is a word whose meaning is the center of a raging dispute. (a) The word occurs nowhere else in the New Testament, and it does not occur often elsewhere in extant Greek literature. The usual word for "authority" is *exousia*, so one surely should pause to reflect why Paul used the unusual word *authentein* in this place. (b) In the Latin versions over the years, the word used to translate the Greek has changed. In the Old Latin we have both *praepositam esse viro* and *principari in viro* ("to be placed over, to be set before a man" and "rule or have first rank over a man"). In the Vulgate, the Latin is *neque dominari in virum* ("nor dominate a man"). But by the time of Erasmus and Beza, one finds the readings *neque auctoritatem usurpare in virum* ("nor usurp authority over a man"). It was from these later Latin versions that the KJV translation "usurp authority" entered our English Bibles. That may be too strong a rendering, and it certainly can leave the reader with a wrong idea about what the woman/wife is prohibited from doing.[95] (c) What do the lexicons and the word studies say on

---

[93] If we translate it as "man" (in general, rather than "husband"), we immediately find ourselves thrown into the very thorny issue of how to harmonize this passage with all the other passages that grant women much more involvement in the public assembly.

[94] Ann L. Bowman, "Women in Ministry: An Exegetical Study of 1 Timothy 2:11-15," *Bibliotheca Sacra* 149:594 (April-June, 1992), p.202.

[95] For example, some argue a woman could preach or teach on a regular basis if she were authorized to do so by the elders of the congregation. In such a situation, she might not be guilty of "usurping" authority, though she still would be in a position where she would be "exercising authority" of some kind. Others have supposed that it was permissible for a woman to preach or teach in the public service as long as she did not do it in a domineering way (this view depends on taking the two infinitives connected by "or" as a hendiadys).

authenteō? Thayer notes it is a compound word – from *autos* (self) and *entea* (arms); hence, in earlier usage, the Greek word spoke of one who with his own hand kills either himself or others. In later Greek, it was used of one who does a thing himself, i.e., the author, one who acts on his own authority, autocratic (absolute master); to govern another, exercise dominion over another.[96] Arndt and Gingrich give "to have authority over, or domineer over another."[97] While some modern translations use the term "domineer" – a term that today has a negative connotation – George W. Knight III concluded that the Greek word does not necessarily have such a negative connotation.[98] Since the second fascicle of the 9th edition of Liddell and Scott was published in 1926, it has been commonly known that the verb occurs in a Berlin papyrus fragment from the 1st century BC with the unmistakable meaning "to exercise authority over someone." The one appearance of the noun *authentēs* in the Apocrypha (Wisdom of Solomon 12:6) speaks of parents "killing" their own helpless children as part of a pagan sacrifice, strongly suggesting how feeble the accepted English translations of the verb *authentein* really are. The word is the source of the Turkish *effendi* (master). The usual Greek word for "authority" or "power" or "rights" is *exousia*. (d) Perhaps Paul used the unusual verb *authentein* here in Timothy because it has a connotation of something "selfish" or "personal" (*autos*) about it. In addition, the word may imply that there is something "bad" or "criminal" about the action that results from the self-interest or self-will.[99] *Authentein* clearly bears the nuance of using one's power in a hurtful or destructive manner, describing the activity of a person who acts for his or her own advantage apart from any consideration of the needs or interests of anyone else. It speaks of someone who "takes the lead" in an action that is improper to do, a perpetuator or instigator of an action. From this context (1 Timothy 2:14), we would suppose that what Eve did when she encouraged Adam to eat of the forbidden fruit is a classic Biblical example of the kind of "taking the lead" that Paul here prohibits.

---

[96] *Greek English Lexicon of the New Testament*, p.84.

[97] *Greek English Lexicon of the New Testament and Other Early Christian Literature*, p. 120.

[98] George W. Knight III, "ΑΥΘΕΝΤΕΩ in Reference to Women in 1 Timothy 2:12," *New Testament Studies* 30 (January, 1984), p. 143-157. This examination of secular and religious usages of the verb *authenteō* in texts, dating from the 1st century BC to the 15th century AD, gives justification for taking its meaning in 1 Timothy in the neutral or positive sense of "to have authority over," rather than in the more negative sense of "to domineer."

[99] See Leland E. Wilshire, "1 Timothy 2:12 Revisited: A Reply to Paul W. Barnett and Timothy J. Harris," EQ 65:1 (1993), p.43-55. There is a new *Thesaurus Linguae Graecae* computer database (Univ. of California) which contains ~63 million words from ~3000 Greek authors spanning a thousand years beginning from the time of Homer 600 BC. This database makes it possible to do a word study (or write a lexicon) in rather quick fashion. Wilshire used the TLG database to challenge three of the conclusions reached by Knight (who did not have access to the TLG data): (1) The paucity of the occurrences of the term *authenteō* [Wilshire finds 31 instances of the use of the word and its cognates]; (2) The idea of "murder" is not integral to the basic meaning of the word; and (3) The recognized meaning for the 1st century BC and AD documents is "to have authority over."

Wives are prohibited from "taking the lead" (rather than letting their husbands "take the lead") in the public worship services. What Paul is objecting to is the idea of role reversal where the wife leads and the husband submits. (Scripture everywhere has it the other way, the wife submits to the husband.) Paul's point is that role reversal caused great devastation at the beginning. Such must not be repeated in the church! Just what might have prompted the wives to "take the lead" is not specifically stated by Paul. Gnostic treatment of the Genesis 3 account is opposite Christian doctrine. In Gnostic thinking Eve pre-existed Adam. The Serpent was trying to do something good. And Eve, in taking the lead, was trying to do something good. Were the Gnostic false teachers telling wives it was their prerogative and the right thing to do to "take the lead" just like the Gnostics doctrine affirmed Eve was not in error when she "took the lead" at the time of the fall. Perhaps there is some truth to this suggestion, since Paul immediately affirms that the Biblical account of Eve's actions were not right – but were the result of being deceived by the Devil.

"To exercise authority over" is a present tense infinitive – what Paul here prohibits is the continual, habitual, customary, repeated exercise of authority over men (husbands). It would take an aorist tense infinitive to deny "exercising authority" on any occasion whatsoever. Those who have missed the *present* tense of the infinitive, and thus treat Paul's words as an absolute prohibition of women ever exercising authority over a man, have struggled to explain this verse so as to make it harmonize with what Scripture seems to teach elsewhere. (1) One suggested that *authenteō* meant to offer sexual favors to one's students.[100] (2) The KJV translators have used the words "usurp authority," as though it were permissible to teach if the women did not "usurp authority." (3) Still another view is that the prohibition was temporary and locally conditioned – by something then happening in Ephesus. (4) Still another has suggested 1 Timothy 2:12 prohibits but one thing – teaching when one would be domineering over a man (rather than prohibiting two things, teaching men, or exercising authority over men). It was often interpreted to mean that the woman was not *ever* to teach in the case where she would have authority over men, or where men were present in the class or the assembly. Since we have two infinitives ("to teach" and "to exercise authority") connected by *oude*,[101] followed by one object ("man") in the genitive case (genitive because the nearer infinitive takes the genitive), Greek grammar would suggest we have two activities, neither of which is to be habitually done by women when men are present. (6) Another suggests that the

---

[100] Catherine Kroeger, "Ancient Heresies and a Strange Greek Verb," *Reformed Journal* 29 (1979), p.12-15, suggested that the verb should be rendered "to engage in fertility practices." Carrol Osburn, "*Authenteo* (1 Timothy 2:12)," *Restoration Quarterly* 25:1 (1st Quarter, 1982), has satisfactorily answered this far-out view.

[101] We have a similar construction at Acts 8:21.

hierarchical viewpoint – God, Christ, Man, Woman – where woman is submissive to man – is something that resulted from the fall, and furthermore, it has been reversed when men and women become "new creatures" in Christ. It is not unusual to see higher critical views intrude here. Higher criticism has "discovered" two different accounts of creation in Genesis 1-3. The first account (Genesis 1), the higher critics affirm, has "God creating *them*." Then they allege that it is the second account of creation that has man created first, and it is affirmed we ought not base our theology on just one creation account! Higher critical views of the Old Testament never did help us understand God's will for our lives! (7) Still others suggest 1 Timothy 2 has nothing to do with public worship, but that instead the verses are an outline of "the apostolic value of a Christian community in a minority situation." What Paul is writing about is a genuine Christian life style in a pagan environment.[102]

How much simpler, and how much more believable, is the explanation of this difficult passage which affirms that wives are not to take the lead in the public services when their husbands are present, and would thus be deprived of their God-given leadership roles. Christianity does emancipate women. They enjoy new freedoms and opportunities not available to women in the 1st century world. But women must be careful! Their new status does not permit them to ignore the God-given revelation about the submissive role expected of wives to their husbands. God's expectation in this matter is still a controlling and overarching guideline to women in any situation where they might otherwise have freedom to teach or prophesy or to lead out.

But to remain quiet – "But" indicates a contrast. Instead of regularly "teaching" or "exercising authority," wives are regularly (it is a present tense infinitive) to 'be in quietness.' The KJV translates this phrase as "but to be in silence." The Greek is *hēsuchia*, the same term used at 1 Timothy 2:2 and translated "quiet," and the same term used at 1 Timothy 2:11 and translated "quietly" (NASB) or "in silence" (KJV). Whatever the term meant in those two previous instances, it also means here. By way of reminder, at 2:2 we spoke of an inward tranquility or calmness that keeps a person from doing something rash. At 2:11 we observed that Thayer's treatment of the synonyms *hēsuchiadzein* (a mental condition [willingness to receive instruction]), *sigan* (speechlessness), and *siopan* (abstinence from speech, the antithesis of loquacity) show that total and absolute silence is not necessarily what the first term implies. The Kroegers catch well the flavor of "quietness" – they speak of "willingness to heed and obey instruction."

---

[102] See Jerome Murphy-O'Connor, "Community and the Apostolate," *The Bible Today* 11 (1973), p. 1260-66.

[Paul] turns from the prayer life of women to their study of the Word of God, "Let a woman learn in silence with all submission" [1 Tim. 2:11]. The women are to be well taught in the Word. This was not ordinarily the practice in Jewish tradition. Although Beruiah, a second-century woman was famed for her erudition in the Torah, her case is somewhat unusual. In view of typical rabbinic reluctance to teach women the Torah, Paul's decree that they should learn is an enlightened one.

Indeed, the rabbinic scholar himself was required to learn in silence. This was how one gained a knowledge of God. The people of Israel were told to keep silence before the Lord [Isa. 41:1; Hab. 2:20; Zech. 2:13]; and they were instructed, "Be still, and know that I am God" [Psm. 46:10 NIV]. Silence was a wall around wisdom, and Rabbi Isaac asked, "What should be a man's pursuit in this world? He should be silent. Perhaps he should be so with regard to the words of the Torah?" [B. Hullin 89a]. Silence, then, was the duty of the learner. The phrase *silence and submission* is a Near Eastern formula implying willingness to heed and obey instruction – in this case that contained in the Word of God.

The Greek-speaking Jews who prepared a Greek version of the Hebrew Bible (the Septuagint) saw a remarkable correlation between "silence" and "submission." There are three places in the Psalms where the Hebrew text speaks of being silent unto God (Ps. 37:7; 62:1,5). In each case, the Septuagintal translators rendered this by the Greek verb meaning "to submit oneself." The original implication is certainly one of attentiveness and receptivity to God.[103]

The true type of the womanly attitude is that of Mary, who "sat at Jesus' feet, and heard his Word" (Luke 10:30).

2:13 -- For – "For" indicates that Paul is now giving a reason (in fact, he will give two) for what he has just written in the previous verses about a wife's submission and about not habitually teaching her husband or "taking the lead."

It was Adam who was first created – The first reason for the instructions to the wife is based in the order of creation. Man was created first.[104] "Adam" is a transliteration of the Hebrew word for "man" used in Genesis 1:26 and 2:16 (cp. also 1 Corinthians 15:45). "Adam" the "man" is distinct from Eve; so the quotation exactly fits the point being made here about "husband" and "wife." "Created" (margin, "formed") translates *eplasthē* (from *plassō*, compare "plastic"), and means to form, shape, mold. It is the verb the LXX uses at Genesis

[103] Richard and Catherine Kroeger, *I Suffer Not a Woman: Rethinking 1 Timothy 2:11-15 in Light of Ancient Evidence* (Grand Rapids: Baker, 1992), p.75,76.

[104] Paul is not the only one to refer to the original creation of man and woman in order to ascertain what God's intentions for them are. Jesus, too, referred to the original creation of man and woman as he taught His contemporaries about God's intention for marriage (Matthew 19:3-6).

2:7, "The Lord God *formed* man out of the dust of the ground."   "First" is *prōtos* in the Greek.   Kent offers the suggestion that *prōtos* indicates rank in this passage, and if so, the argument is even clearer: "For Adam, as chief one, was formed, then Eve."[105]   This verse is a terse statement of the same argument Paul uses in 1 Corinthians 11:3, where some measure of hierarchical arrangement is affirmed – God, Christ, husband, wife.[106]

And then Eve – Paul's argument here is very similar to the one in 1 Corinthians 11:8,9.   There he argues from the order of creation that woman was created "for" the man.   Hence, for a wife to habitually teach or exercise authority over her husband is out of place with her created role of being a "helper"[107] (not the man's master).   Lest someone attempt to evade the force of this argument by saying what we read in the Old Testament was nailed to the cross, let it be remembered that when we say the Old Testament was temporary and is no longer binding on us in this church age, it is the Law of Moses (Exodus 20-24, and following) in particular that was temporary.   What one reads in the early chapters of Genesis, things which antedate the revelation on Sinai, is still true today.

2:14 -- And – Here is Paul's second reason for what he has earlier written about the wife's submission and not habitually teaching or taking the lead over her husband.   "And" joins this verse to the preceding.   It basically says that as long as it is true that woman was first in the fall, that's how long it will be true that the wife is to be submissive, and not habitually exercise authority over her husband.

It *was* not Adam *who* was deceived – Adam and Eve both sinned, but even the account in Genesis 3:12,13 does not say that Adam was "deceived."[108]   Both transgressed, but only Eve was thoroughly tricked or seduced by the devil.   When Adam sinned, he did it deliberately, knowing full well what he was doing.[109]

---

[105] Kent, *op. cit.*, p.109.

[106] The NASB reads "man" and "woman" at 1 Corinthians 11:3.   The translation "husband" and "wife" is defended in the *Special Study* at the close of comments on 1 Timothy 2.

[107] Genesis 2:18 is the verse that says the woman was "a helper suitable for man."   See the *Special Study* at the close of this chapter for more detailed information about this word "helper."

[108] Some have suggested that Paul is basing his argument on the *silence* of the account in Genesis about any deception happening to Adam.   Such "silence" (in Genesis 14) about Melchizedek's family pedigree and about his death is used as an argument in Hebrews 7.   In Hebrews we are told that the Old Testament record was "silent" by design of the One who inspired it.   As God led Moses in writing Genesis, the record about Melchizedek was "made like" the Son of God (i.e., so he could serve as a type of Christ).   If God did that at Genesis 14, perhaps the record at Genesis 3 was deliberate, too.

[109] This comment is true only if the previous footnote is not.   If God, as He inspired Moses to write Genesis 3, deliberately omitted the fact that Adam, too, was deceived, then we could not say for sure that Adam was not deceived.   All we can say is that there is no record of that deception, as there is of Eve's deception.

But the woman being quite deceived – Paul uses the same word "deceived" found at Genesis 3:13, where the woman replies to God's question by saying, "The serpent *beguiled* me." Paul perhaps writes "the woman" (instead of "Eve") because that is the way Genesis reads, and because "woman" connects this thought with the whole instruction to wives about their conduct in public worship.

Fell into transgression – "Fell into transgression" *first* seems to be the idea. After she transgressed, she then "took the lead" in encouraging her husband Adam to transgress, too. It is precisely the kind of wrong-headed "taking the lead" that *authenteō* denotes (verse 12). "Transgression" translates *parabasis*, which means to overstep set limits. God had set some limits regarding the trees from which they might eat, and which one was to be avoided. As long as it is true that woman was second in the creation and first to transgress, that's how long Paul's directions to wives about submission and not exercising authority over their husbands in public worship will be true.

If this commentator's suggestion that we mentally supply the word "first" (thus understanding this verse as a Biblical illustration of what happens when the wife steps out of her submissive role and "takes the lead") is correct, there are several comments made by others on these verses that we would be slow to accept. Most needlessly offend women. One has written, "This is a second reason why the woman should occupy a subordinate rank in all things. It is, that in the most important situation in which she was ever placed, she had shown that she was not qualified to take the lead."[110] This is needless. The argument that a woman should not teach men because what happened to Eve proves woman is mentally, morally, and spiritually inferior to man is hardly acceptable. It goes far beyond anything Scriptures actually do say. Admittedly, there were dire consequences when Eve was first deceived by the devil, and then took the lead. But let it not be forgotten that men, too, can be deceived. And the consequences to home and church when they lead after being deceived can be just as dire! Nor do we accept the idea that women should be excluded from teaching men because Eve's example proves women are easier to fool into wrong doctrine and behavior than men. If the woman were teaching women (something the Scriptures do countenance), would it somehow be less a catastrophe or tragedy if she were fooled and taught wrong doctrine than if she taught the same wrong thing to men? If in case some married women may object that what Eve did is no reason they should be required to be submissive to men, let it also be remembered men too have been hurt and still suffer dire and lasting consequences because of Adam's part in the transgression. In fact, his part in the sin has brought declining health and ultimately physical death on every member of the whole race (Romans 5:19).

---

[110] Barnes' *Notes*, p.136.

2:15 -- But – For many commentators, this verse has proven to be very difficult to explain. The difficulty lies in trying to find some logical connection between what this verse says and what the previous verses have been saying. Some commentators, hurrying over the passage, excuse their haste by saying "no proposal is without difficulties." Those who have seen the current paragraph as dealing with "women" in general (rather than "wives") have struggled to explain the reference to "childbearing." Some have supposed it says that unless women have children they will not go to heaven. When this idea proved unacceptable to many, some other approach was made to explain the verse (e.g., ladies should aim at being homemakers rather than church leaders). But how would this type of explanation be squared with Paul's explicit statement that, for some, the single lifestyle is an acceptable way to serve the Lord without distraction (1 Corinthians 7:25-35)? So it is almost a given that commentators, in attempting to explain how this passage is related to the context, will hurry over this verse as though it really has no special bearing on the whole topic Paul is writing about. We think this is unfair to Paul and the Holy Spirit.

The *de* with which this verse begins can be translated either "but" or "and." (1) If we translate it "but," there is a contrast to something just said. Lest the statements that the wife is to be submissive and willing to heed and obey instruction, and is not to be the one who habitually teaches or exercises authority over the husband, be taken as though woman had no place in the life of the church, Paul opens this verse with "but," showing a strong adversative reaction to any such interpretation being put on his words. (2) If we translate it "and," then verse 15 continues the thought of verse 14.[111] Verse 14 has reminded us how Eve was deceived and fell into transgression. "And" the narrative of Genesis 3 does not end there. It also contains the protevangelium, the promise that the "Seed" would come and undo the temporary victory Satan had won. It is likely the first part of verse 15 refers back to this protevangelium from Genesis 3.

She shall be preserved – Whereas the first edition of the NASB reads "she shall be ..." the second edition of the NASB reads "women shall be ..." (making it plural, though the Greek in the first part of the verse is singular). The second edition of the NASB may obscure the transition from the personal "Eve" (the singular person in the first part of the verse) to the generic "women" (the plural) in the last part of the verse. The transition from the singular to the plural is clearly denoted in the

---

[111] This close relationship believed to exist between verse 14 and 15 is indicated by Alford who puts a comma between the verses, and by the scholars who produced Nestle's Greek text by the semicolon they put between the verses. The ASV has a colon between the verses. (The reader is reminded that the oldest manuscripts of the Bible have no punctuation marks in them at all, and that all these marks are added by men. We can examine the same evidence and probabilities that were relied on to do the punctuating in the first place, and we are free to agree or disagree if the evidence warrants, without being accused of denying the Bible.)

NASB's original edition. We think the ASV treated the Greek text with more care. It reads, "But she shall be saved ...." The NASB uses "preserved" to translate *sōdzō*, the same Greek word translated "to save" in the faithful saying at 1 Timothy 1:15. In fact, the word "save" has several different connotations: (1) It may speak of deliverance from danger, Matthew 8:25, 14:30 (e.g., *save* a drowning man). (2) It may speak of deliverance from disease, Matthew 9:21,22; Luke 17:19. (3) It may speak of deliverance from the condemnation of God and the resulting second death, Matthew 10:22, 18:11, 24:13. (4) It may speak of deliverance from the power of sin, Matthew 1:21. (5) It may speak of preserving something in good condition (e.g., he *saves* stamps).[112] Each time the translator comes to *sōdzō*, he must decide from the context which meaning to give the term. How we render *sōdzō* at this place will depend on what we decide about the meaning of "childbearing." The verb *sōdzō* is in the passive voice. This "deliverance" is wrought for her by someone else. It is future tense, and points forward from Eve to the promised future deliverance "through the childbearing."

Through the bearing of children – A variety of interpretations has been assigned to the expression *dia tēs teknogonias* (rendered in the NASB, "through the bearing of children"). It should be carefully noted that the Greek for "childbearing" is singular.[113] Kent has very succinctly summarized the leading interpretations.[114]

> (1) *A promise of physical preservation when giving birth to children.* This view is held by Ironside, Simpson, and others. There are several weaknesses with this interpretation: (a) Many godly women have died while giving birth. When we read what the remainder of verse 15 says, to hold this view would compel us to say those women who died were deficient in faith or love or sobriety. This is cruel and baseless. Scripture no more promises physical safety for every faithful woman in childbirth than it promises good health to every Christian man. (b) A spiritual catastrophe ("fell into transgression," verse 14) is the topic immediately before verse 15. To explain verse 15 as though it were promising physical safety is out of keeping with the spiritual topic under discussion. (c) Why do writers talk about "children" (plural) when the Greek is singular? (d) What would be the connection to the topic

---

[112] This meaning can be documented from extra-biblical sources, but in not one of the thirty-one times the verb occurs in the New Testament can the meaning "preserved" be indisputably assigned to the verb *sōdzō,* unless it be here at 1 Timothy 2:15.

[113] The KJV reads "saved in childbearing." The ASV reads "saved through her childbearing." The RSV (for some reason, like the NASB, renders the singular in Greek as though it were plural) offers "saved through bearing children." The RSV's marginal note has "by the birth of the child."

[114] The following notes are excerpted from Kent, *op. cit.*, p.112-114. We have not included any interpretations offered by those who attribute this text to non-Pauline sources. In fact, some of these critics do not feel any obligation to further pursue the meaning of the text once they have decided it is not from Paul's pen.

in 1 Timothy 2, namely, conduct at the public worship service?   Are we prepared to say that the thrust of Paul's words are that "women" are to be "giving birth to children" rather than "leading public worship"?

(2) *A promise of forgiveness of sins because they have given birth to children.* Why women should "give birth" has been explained in several ways: (a) Some Roman Catholic writers teach that motherhood is one means of grace. If the woman dies while giving birth, her soul will be saved. (b) One writer has suggested recently that this verse has an anti-Gnostic thrust, and Paul says "bearing children" will not cause one to be condemned like the Gnostics teach.[115] There are several weaknesses in this "forgiven for giving birth" interpretation: (i) The words at the end of this verse refute the idea that it speaks of a woman who dies while giving birth to a child, since those words indicate the woman is to continue on in faith and love and sanctity if she expects to be saved. (ii) If giving birth to children is a condition of salvation, what about the women who have never had children. Will this cause them to miss salvation? (iii) It is difficult to see any connection between such an interpretation and the topic of the whole chapter, conduct in public worship.

(3) *A promise of forgiveness of sins if the woman fulfills her God-given job of being a homemaker.*   Calvin, Barnes, Alford, Scott, Bernard, Hendriksen and others hold that what Paul is doing is explaining the proper role of the woman – that her role is more private in the home rather than being one who regularly speaks or exercises authority at the public services.   There are weaknesses in this interpretation, too. (a) It does not give a satisfying explanation to the preposition *dia*, which after passive verbs often indicates agent.[116] (b) Paul says "childbearing," not "homemaking." By what means do we make this shift of emphasis?[117]   (c) Had Paul's focus been on "motherhood," would

---

[115] David R. Kimberley, "1 Timothy 2:15: A Possible Understanding of a Difficult Text," *JETS* 35:4 (Dec. 1992), p.481-486. Kimberley's thesis – that much of what we find in 1 Timothy is anti-Gnostic – is not objectionable, and his explanation of the Gnostic attitude towards the sexes is correct. But he fails to do justice to the meaning of the word "saved." Paul did not write "not condemned;" he wrote "saved." Further, Paul used a genitive of agent construction ("through the childbearing"), a construction Kimberley simply ignores in giving his "possible understanding."

[116] A passive voice verb can be followed by *hupo* and the genitive, indicating the direct personal agent who acts on the subject of the passive verb, or it can be followed by *en* and the dative, indicating the impersonal agent who does the acting, or it can be followed by *dia* and the genitive, indicating the intermediate personal agent who does the acting upon the subject.

[117] This writer is not opposed to the idea that women make a profound impact on society when they remain at home, giving personal guidance to the children as they grow up. He has lived through World War II, and has seen the devastating effect on society that has resulted from women abandoning the home for lucrative jobs in the factory or workplace. While mother (and dad) is away, the children are cared for by impersonal child-care centers, or fend for hours by themselves without any adult supervision, and the result to society has been a tragedy. This writer believes woman's best place of service is in the home, but he is not prepared to use 1 Timothy 2:15 as proof.

not a term from the *teknotropheō* word group (see 1 Timothy 5:10) have expressed this idea better than the word Paul uses here?

(4) *A promise of forgiveness of sins through the incarnation of Jesus, as promised to Eve* (Genesis 3:15[118]).   Jesus is "the Child" who provides salvation not only for Eve but for other women, too.[119]   There are several things which can be said in support of this interpretation: (a) The context has had Eve under discussion, and to suppose that the singular ("she shall be saved") is still a reference to Eve, has much to commend it.   (b) The singular "the childbearing" does not have to be treated as some of the other views require as though it were plural (i.e., "bearing of children").   If it is a reference to the one "Seed" in particular, the singular can be taken at face value.   (c) This interpretation allows us to take the preposition *dia* in its usual significance.[120]   The "child" is the agent who provided God's salvation to Eve (and to other women, too).   (d) The definite article "the" ("through *the* childbearing") can be easily explained as pointing to "the Child."   It is not easy to explain the presence of the article if the topic is childbearing in general.   If we adopt this view, and this commentator thinks we should, then the verb *sōdzō* is to be understood as talking about salvation from sin and the condemnation of God.   It should be translated "saved" (rather than as the NASB, "preserved").

We have arrived at the conclusion that Paul is saying the wives are to be submissive to their husbands.   They do have a special role to play.   But fulfilling this role does not mean they are somehow less eligible for the salvation wrought by Christ, the "Child" promised to the woman when she led Adam into sin.   Just as Galatians 3:28 says males and females are equally eligible for the salvation offered in Christ, so Paul here says women are "saved" if they prove faithful to the revelation God has given them.

If *the women* continue – Note the change to the plural.   The NASB has added "the women" in italics to make it clear there has been a change in subjects in the middle of this verse.   The Greek says "If they continue," and some have wrongly understood this plural to speak of the children.   If that interpretation is adopted, the passage says the mother must have so taught the children that the children will

---

[118] As God speaks to Eve, He says "He [the seed] shall bruise you [the serpent = Satan] on the head."   God was announcing salvation in terms of a child to be born by the woman.

[119] While this clause is true of men as well as women, Paul's topic in these verses is specifically the women.

[120] In the New Testament, there are seven occurrences of the verb *sōdzō* followed by *dia*.   In the majority of them, *dia* indicates the means (or agent) through whom salvation from sins is wrought or accomplished.

remain faithful, else the mother will be lost.   This is hardly acceptable, for since when did the salvation of one person depend on the faithfulness of another person?   Earlier in our comments, we offered the explanation that now that Paul has finished his allusion to what is recorded in Genesis 3, he here begins to make application to the women in the church at Ephesus.   This is a conditional clause, and it signifies that the previous statement is true only when the following condition s are met.   Paul is telling the women that continuing in faithful service to the Savior is the condition of salvation for them.[121]   The conditions which follow help us to see that *sōdzō* (at the beginning of this verse) refers to spiritual salvation.   The reading the NASB relegated to the margin ("she shall be saved") is preferred to the one chosen by those translators.

In faith and love and sanctity with self restraint – The women whose conduct is being discussed are already believers and part of the church.   Now Paul reminds them of the need for "faithfulness" until death.   Observe how both God's part (the allusion to the Child's birth that had soteric significance) and woman's part (the qualities about to be enumerated) in salvation are made plain in this verse.   "Faith" translates *pistis*.   Perhaps it refers to faith in the Redeemer and in divine truth.   Perhaps it refers to a life of faithfulness in the service of God. "Love" is *agapē* in the Greek.   We suppose this is intended to recall what was said in 1 Timothy 1:5 about "love" being the goal of our instruction.   "Sanctity" represents the Greek word *hagiasmos*, the word sometimes translated "holiness" and sometimes "sanctification."   We could even use "consecration" to catch the idea.   It speaks of spiritual growth.   "Without sanctification no man shall see God" (Hebrews 12:14).   Hendriksen defines it as "the daily dying unto sin and being renewed unto holiness."   "With self-restraint" is *metasōphrosunēs* in the original.   We had the same word in verse 9, where it was translated "discreetly." We explained it there as meaning self-control, good judgment, constantly living by proper and spiritual desires.   This Greek phrase begins with *meta*, "accompanied by," and so "self-restraint or good judgment" is the state of mind necessary for one who is concerned with "continuing in faith and love and sanctity."

---

[121] The conditions Paul reiterates here are no different from what Scripture teaches elsewhere, namely, that God looks for "deeds" – He judges the tenor of a man's life – as He pronounces "justified."   Jesus taught the need for continual good deeds as a condition of salvation when he said no one would enter the Kingdom of Heaven except the one who "habitually does the will of My Father who is in Heaven" (Matthew 7:21).   Paul taught the same thing in Romans 2:6,7 as he tells how it will be in the final judgment.   He wrote that God "renders to every man according to his deeds," and grants salvation to those who seek it "by perseverance in doing good."   Of course, it is never taught that these deeds merit salvation.   They are simply the conditions (according to the plan of God) that individuals are to meet if they would participate in the free salvation He offers.

Special Study #1

WHAT DID WIVES AND WOMEN DO IN THE NEW TESTAMENT CHURCH ASSEMBLIES?

INTRODUCTION

This writer's formative years were in churches where women were not permitted to take the lead in any public assembly. They might teach the children in Sunday School and Vacation Bible School. They were welcome to teach classes at church camp and in the Sunday evening youth groups. But on Sunday morning, it was unthinkable to ever invite a lady to lead the congregational singing, though ladies were asked to accompany the singing at the piano and organ. While a lady might be asked to sing a special number immediately before it was time for the preaching, certainly no lady was permitted to fill the pulpit during the "preaching" part of the morning worship service, even if she were a visiting missionary and not "preaching" but simply reporting about what had been done on the field during the 5 years prior to this current furlough. The reason given was that the Bible clearly states that ladies are not to speak in the public worship, nor teach, nor usurp authority over men. The churches neatly distinguished between "morning worship" and "evening evangelistic services." It was at "worship" where the ladies were not to take the lead.

Next came the years at Bible college, as a student and then as a teacher. In his student days, his teachers offered both some traditional and some innovative ways to explain the verses that deal with what wives and women did in the public assemblies. Philip's daughters who prophesied must have been speaking to women only, since (according to 1 Timothy 2:12) women were not permitted to teach men. When it was noted that Priscilla evidently was the one who taught and corrected a male's deficient theology (Acts 18:26), one explanation was that a woman might teach privately one-on-one, but not in the public assembly. Another explanation offered was that there was a difference between the function of teacher and the office of teacher, much like there was a difference between the function of prophet and the office of prophet in the Old Testament (e.g., the book of Daniel is in the collection of books called the Holy Writings, rather than in the Prophets, because he held the function but not the office). It was taught that the offices of elder and deacon were open only to men, and Phoebe was a "servant" of some kind (Romans 16:1) but not a deaconess. Young women who enrolled in Bible college all had the noble intention of marrying a preacher and serving the Lord by fulfilling the demanding task of being a preacher's wife and helpmeet.

Because the Scriptures were interpreted to mean that the woman's place was in the home, and that women are to be submissive to men, there was a question of whether or not women who came to Bible college should be encouraged to pursue a career outside the home. Perhaps such tasks as church secretaries or choir directors or even Christian education directors were permissible; so, one-by-one, training for these church-related occupations began to be offered in our schools, especially when it became evident that not every young woman would become a preacher's wife. After all, what were the young women who chose the single life as an acceptable way to serve the Lord to do with their lives?

Of course, what women may actually do in church has not always been as this writer found it taught and practiced in mid-western America in the 20th century.

I. A BRIEF HISTORICAL OVERVIEW

The first book published in English *(Women's Speaking Justified, Proved and Allowed by the Scriptures ...)* defending full and equal participation of women in ministry was written in 1666 by a Quaker, Margaret Fell, and published in London. Fell argued that 1 Timothy 2:11-12 was directed only against the deviating women described in 1 Timothy 5:11-15. Some three dozen books appeared in the 18th century advocating that it is in harmony with Scripture to allow women to share in much of the public ministry of the church.

The writings of Alexander Campbell (*The Christian System*), Barton W. Stone (*The Gospel Restored*) and Robert Milligan (*The Scheme of Redemption*), tended to crystallize Restoration Movement thinking on the permissibility of women in positions of church leadership. Each was negative to it.

> The Restoration Movement has not been without controversy on the subject. See Mary E. Lantzer's thesis, *An Examination of the 1892-93 Christian Standard Controversy Concerning Women's Preaching* (Johnson City, TN.: Emmanuel School of Religions, 1990). See also Gary Selby, "'Your Daughters Shall Prophesy': Rhetorical Strategy in the 19th Century Debate over Women's Right to Preach," *Restoration Quarterly* 34/3 (1982), p.151-166. This essay examines four examples of 19th century rhetoric arguing for the right of women to preach. Unlike some feminist movements, these debaters tried to move within the framework of traditional Protestant doctrine which was controlled by Scripture texts deemed to be inspired and therefore authoritative. Most would re-interpret one passage or another that traditionally had been used to argue against the idea of women preachers in order to show that a favorable view of women preachers was "doctrinally correct." They would show the practical benefits that would accrue from women being permitted to fill the pulpits.

From about 1900 to 1960, women were not ordained to the ministry, save in Pentecostal and Holiness circles. But several things were happening in our culture that would eventually impact the thinking of people in the churches.

One of these was a combination of changing life spans and the social changes precipitated by World War II. (1) *Changing life spans.* In 1900, American women had an average life expectancy of about 45 years. By 1986, women could expect to live past the age of 80. If a woman adopts the traditional role of wife and mother in the home, she will find herself extremely busy for perhaps 20 years. When the last child has left home, she still has 30 or 40 years of life expectancy remaining. What then does she do with her time and energy? (2) *World War II* was the greatest agent of social change the world has seen. Women began working outside the home. Many women never marry. Others remain childless in spite of a desire to have or adopt a child. Working outside the home may not be a choice but an urgent necessity. Approximately 50 percent of all American women are gainfully employed. Only 21 percent of American women consider themselves full-time homemakers. As churches have recognized this, they have had to reconsider their traditional approach to women's ministries. (3) Women are better educated than in any previous age. Perhaps it was true of an earlier time that women were not highly educated so as to have the credentials many positions require, but it is no longer true. Since 1982, the number of women in college has exceeded the number of men.

Another change occurred in the 1960's when the feminist movement began to affect society's thinking and practices. An article in *Christianity Today* ("Women in Leadership: Finding Ways to Serve the Church", October 3, 1986, p.3-I) has summarized the changes experienced in our culture since then.

> When Betty Friedan asked "Who knows what women can be when they are finally free to become themselves?" in *The Feminine Mystique*, scarcely half of the American population seemed to care about an answer. But the questions raised by Friedan and her colleagues in 1963 would not go away. In 1964, Congress passed Title VII of the Civil Rights Act, banning sex discrimination in employment. In 1965, the President's Commission on the Status of Women concluded that women were indeed victims of discrimination in the market place. And by 1966, Friedan founded the National Organization of Women (NOW), and a movement that would change the nature of American society had begun.

> Like most movements, the struggle spilled over into the church. Within a year of the publication of Friedan's book the Presbyterian Church in the U.S. voted to ordain women, an action that caused considerable alarm among the more conservative members (as well as among onlookers from other denominations) ...

> Evangelicals were divided on the extent to which women should participate in the leadership of the church. Most agreed that women represented a valuable resource for ministry for the kingdom, and that the task of spreading the gospel belonged to all believers. Many believed women should be given greater opportunities for service within the church, but should not be ordained. Others felt ordination offered women but another avenue for expressing their unique brand of spiritual leadership.

Well-known scholars began to publish articles and books supportive of roles for women broader than generally were permitted in the first half of the 20th century. Two works by writers who might be called evangelicals were influential. One was Paul Jewett's *Man as Male and Female: A Study of Sexual Relationships from a Theological Point of View*,[1] published in 1975. It was controversial in its hermeneutical approach to Paul, yet it stirred up further inquiry. A second book was Letha Scanzoni and Nancy Hardesty's *All We're Meant to Be*,[2] published in 1974.

Not all those who wrote have held an evangelical view of Scripture. In 1966, Krister Stendahl, who likely would not be viewed as "evangelical," published his influential book, *The Bible and the Role of Women*. In it he called Galatians 3:28 Paul's "Emancipation Proclamation for Women" which legitimized the ministry and place especially of *single* women in Christ.[3] In fact, some defenders of the feminist position have held a very low view of Scripture. A.Y. Collins edited a book entitled *Feminist Perspectives on Biblical Scholarship* (Missoula, MT: Scholars, 1985) which is representative of a non-evangelical egalitarian approach. Contributors to that volume reject the Bible as an absolute, timeless revelation. They view Biblical texts as sexist and thoroughly androcentric, requiring a "hermeneutics of suspicion." The androcentric texts are 'theological interpretations, argumentations, projections, and selections rooted in a patriarchal culture.' Therefore, such texts must be read critically, evaluated historically, and a total reassessment made of the role of women in Judaism and early Christianity. "While the non-evangelical egalitarian approach continues to regard the Bible as a religious document, it often does not uphold the Bible as the only infallible rule of faith and practice. It employs the historical-critical method for adjudicating which texts are acceptable for developing a theology of women and which texts are unacceptable. In the final analysis, contemporary feminism serves as a judge of the Bible; the Bible cannot serve as a judge of contemporary feminism." (Hoch, *Grace Theological Journal*, 1987, p.243).

---

[1] Jewett stresses the equality of the sexes from a pro-Barthian theological position, and blames rabbinic tradition for the social roles that became part of our Western heritage. Scriptures teaching a position different from that adopted by Jewett are dismissed as "culturally conditioned," and Galatians 3:28 is wrongly construed as abolishing subordination (rather than referring to the privileges of all to become believers).

[2] Scanzoni and Hardesty argue that Paul's texts that seem to prohibit women preaching and teaching were cultural limitations of a temporary nature.

[3] Stendahl offered the suggestion that it took some years for the full consequences of the new life in Christ to be applied to church and society. "Neither slave nor free" took time to work itself into social practice. So also, he supposed, "neither male nor female" was a long time working itself out. Because the church was slow to realize the implications of this emancipation, the actual descriptions of 1st century church life became the normative "biblical" viewpoint instead of what Paul had actually written. (Readers will recognize in this the neo-liberal idea of three levels of information in our New Testaments – what Jesus said and did [of which we have little], what the apostles taught [of which we also have little], and the early church's beliefs [which form the majority of our Biblical writings].)

The Charismatic Movement of the 1960's also changed beliefs about the accepted role of women in the church. In some Charismatic and Pentecostal circles, it is assumed[4] that supernatural spiritual gifts are still available to all Christians, and women receive "spiritual gifts" as well as men. The question is then asked, Are we to deny to women the opportunity to exercise the gifts they so obviously have been given by God?

As the years passed, women became more visible in positions of church leadership. The home Bible-study movement was led primarily by women (the Women's Aglow Fellowship, for example). Evangelical seminaries witnessed the enrollment of more women. Between 1956 and 1977, five of the largest major denominations – Methodists, Presbyterians, National Baptists, Lutherans, and Episcopalians – reversed their stand and began ordaining women. Dozens of smaller denominations, such as the Reformed Church of America and the Evangelical Covenant Church, likewise changed their constitutions and bylaws to allow the ordination of women as elders and preachers. A controversial vote in 1977 by the General Convention of the Episcopal Church to ordain women opened the door to women as priests in the Episcopal Church. By 1985, over 1,000 women had been ordained in the United Presbyterian Church.

Women became prominent in executive positions in the church. 1986, for example, saw a woman leader (commander) for the Salvation Army. One study suggested that 80% of protestant denominations (including the African Methodist Episcopal Church, American Baptist Churches, Christian Church (Disciples of Christ), the Free Methodist Church, the Lutheran Church in America, and the Assemblies of God, among others) encourage women into the ministry.

Christian Churches were not insulated from the profound cultural shifts taking place. Appeals to broaden our position on women's role in the churches began to be made from the pulpit and in writing. In some of the debates in Christian Church periodicals, appeal was made to successes women had as preachers. There were hundreds of baptisms, and the churches served by women were well-pleased with their ministries. With such a shortage of preachers, why should we settle for an empty pulpit, or with a male denominational preacher, when we could have a Christian woman teaching us the Word of God?

For decades, Christian churches supported single women as missionaries. Those women went on preaching tours, planted churches, started Bible colleges,

---

[4] This commentator holds the studied conclusion that supernatural spiritual gifts were temporary and intended for the infancy of the church. With the passing of the last apostle, such gifts would gradually cease since there were no more apostles to lay on hands and pass on the supernatural spiritual gifts. He would question the appeal to personal experience, rather than Scripture, as a valid evidence for or against women in positions of leadership.

and trained preachers – in short, all that a man would do were he in the same situation. Why were we not consistent? Why would we support on a foreign field what we would not allow at home, namely, a woman serving as evangelist?

II. BACK TO THE BIBLE*!* or, BACK TO THE BIBLE*?*

Conservatives in the Restoration Movement still advocate that we must be faithful to what the Scriptures teach. It is important to such faithfulness to the Scriptures that we restore every part of the ancient apostolic order that we can. Just what do the New Testament Scriptures, our rule of faith and practice, have to say concerning the wives' and women's tasks in the church? Whatever we find there, we may do, and by so doing continue to be faithful to our Lord.

Because the Bible is so central to the life and practice of members of the Restoration Movement, they are happy to restudy the Scriptures to be certain they are thinking God's thoughts after Him. At one time in the Movement, all students would have approached Scripture intending to use the same hermeneutical method – the grammatical-historical method. However, because of the inroads of various kinds of theological liberalism, issues about how the Bible is to be interpreted have become matters of critical importance for those wrestling with women's issues, as well as every other area of faith and polity.

Presently for some, restudy of the Scriptures is likely to be hampered by the "assured conclusions of higher criticism"; for others, by a shift in the way "hermeneutics" is done; and for still others, by the attempts to apply certain sociological tools to the interpretation of the New Testament. At least three different methods of interpreting Scripture are used among modern-day Bible scholars. One will take us back to the Bible; it is this writer's conviction that the other two will not take us back to the Bible. Yet each has been used in the last half of the 20th century to explain to us what the Bible says on women's issues.

A brief orientation to these methods of interpreting Scripture is needful, if for only to help students who are studying the journal articles and learned books to be better able to sort through what they are reading. The three methods are the traditional approach, the new hermeneutic, and the critical approach.

1) The **traditional approach** maintains that there are culturally transcendent and normative principles taught in Scripture – including with regard to the roles of husband and wife.

> Using the grammatical-historical method, each word is carefully studied, as is the historic background out of which or to which the particular work is written. Then, in the 20th century, when problems or questions arise

that are similar to those in the 1st century, the teachings and commands given then are still good today.

For most issues this method has achieved very satisfactory results, and the life and practice of the church has been the same through the centuries. However, when it comes to wives and women's issues, the traditional approach has been unable to suggest a way to harmonize the apparently discrepant passages, at least in a way that appeals to or will be agreeable to all evangelicals. Furthermore, beyond being unable to harmonize all the verses, the traditional view seems to hold to the subordination of wives to husbands – a view unacceptable to many in the 20th century.

2) The **"new hermeneutic" approach** asserts that recent generally accepted hermeneutical principles indicate certain passages (especially the prohibition passages about women's public ministries) were either circumstantial or cultural (specific for Paul's culture) and therefore are not normative for the 20th century. Closely akin to the new hermeneutic would be socio-critical methods of Bible study. The "new hermeneutic" is a stepchild of neo-liberalism's attempts to make the Bible match the currently popular philosophy of existentialism. Socio-critical hermeneutics, a stepchild of attempting to use the social sciences to help understand the Bible, have resulted in still another set of "principles." Both these approaches accept the assured conclusions of higher criticism, with the result that men sit in judgment of the Scriptures. Higher criticism's preconceptions do not permit the use of the hermeneutical rules that have been used for centuries and which conservative Bible believers affirm are correct. The "new hermeneutic" approach works in this fashion:

First, a decision is made that a certain view is the Biblical view. In the present study, the view accepted is the currently and culturally popular egalitarian view of men and women. Once a view is chosen, verses are then marshaled to prove it is the Biblical view. When it comes to the topic of this study, certain egalitarian advocates appeal to one or two passages (Galatians 3:28, and perhaps Genesis 1:26-27) as teaching societal equality. They insist these are normative, that all other passages must be interpreted to match the equality emphasized in these passages.

Once the Biblical view has been established to the scholar's satisfaction, verses that seemingly do not agree must be explained. It is not unusual to find a surprising twist given to certain passages in order to make them "support" the chosen view. Here's where currently popular "hermeneutical rules" are employed.

Sometimes, advocates of the "new hermeneutic" solution attempt to identify a peculiarity in the church situation addressed in the specific letter, be it Corinth or Ephesus (in 1 Timothy). The claim is that, since those circumstances have changed, the commands based on them are no longer relevant or binding.

> One serious objection to assigning a cultural or temporary flavor to certain passages is that the advocates of this approach do not follow a consistent pattern across the New Testament. What's "cultural" and what is not too often becomes simply a subjective decision.

> Further, the advocates of making certain prohibitions about wives and women to be simply "cultural and temporary" seldom deal with Paul's appeal to the way God created things, and the fact that certain things were to be done in "all the churches", not just locally in a certain problem situation.

Other advocates of a hermeneutical solution attempt to find the social context of 1 Timothy. Once that is "found" and it becomes obvious that the social context in the 20th century is different, the prohibitions on women in leadership positions are said to be irrelevant to the modern situation. A variation of this theme is to suggest Paul is merely repeating the [alleged] opinion of the day, namely that women were intellectually inferior. Paul's views are now known to be anachronistic and should be dispensed with.

Still another modern hermeneutical approach is to divide the texts of the New Testament into three broad categories: 1) normative, 2) descriptive, and 3) problematic. The "normative" texts are those which declare "the way things are to be" in the New Covenant (i.e., now) without reference to any particular problem or misunderstanding within the Christian community. The "descriptive" texts are those which report the activities of Christian people without any comment for or against these activities. The "problematic" texts are those dealing with special problems within the Christian communities, and often are texts which seem to contradict what the normative texts say. Of course, the first two are the most useful when attempting to decide the Bible's teaching on any current issue.[5]

3) The **critical approach** may take us down any one of several paths. One says that over the years Paul changed his theology of women. Another questions the Pauline authorship of one or more texts and assigns those texts to a deutero-Pauline authorship in order to save Paul from the charge of "male chauvinism."

---

[5] This is the modern hermeneutical method used by S. Scott Bartchy, in his "Power, Submission, and Sexual Identity Among the Early Christians," in *Essays on New Testament Christianity*, edited by C. Robert Wetzel (Cincinnati, OH: Standard, 1978).

There is even a critical approach that says the Bible contains "paradox," and that the truth really lies somewhere between otherwise conflicting statements.

How did Paul's theology change, it might be asked?   One answer has Paul's theology developing in this order – he was first an egalitarian (like Jesus is alleged to have been), but later changed his views to the hierarchical position.   Another answer has Paul changed in the other direction, moving from old Jewish hierarchical beliefs held early in his ministry to egalitarian views taught late in his ministry.

Views that have Paul's theology changing and developing tacitly deny any inspiration to what he writes.   That is hardly acceptable when Paul himself claims inspiration for his writings.   To this writer, it appears that the developmental approach wrongly attempts to apply the theory of evolution to the Scriptures, so that Scripture is made to match evolution's assured conclusions.

The critical approach that denies the Pauline authorship to letters that contain his signature (Ephesians, 1 Timothy, and even certain verses in 1 Corinthians) constructs a "Paul" who, ever so conveniently, is a feminist.

It is very difficult, however, to deny the Pauline authorship of all the passages involved, both those that deal with husband-wife relationships and those that deal with what men and women may and did do in the public assemblies.

A slight variation on this theme finds higher critics identifying two different accounts of creation in Genesis – an "equal" male and female presentation in chapter 1 versus a subordinate female presentation in chapters 2 and 3.   Then the critic opts for one or the other as being the true story, and rejects the other as a spurious piece of editorializing.

Neo-orthodoxy, which finds paradox in the Bible, really leaves us with no test for truth.   Consistency is the test for truth.   However, if a man must hold in his mind two conflicting views at the same time, he ends up with all "truth" being relative.

Having carefully and deliberately chosen the historical-grammatical approach to interpreting the Scripture, it is now necessary to turn to the Scriptures themselves, and see what they say about the role of wives and husbands and what wives and women did in public worship.

III. ANOTHER LOOK AT THE DISPUTED PASSAGES

A. The problem:

There are New Testament verses that seem to have women speaking and praying in public. There are also New Testament verses that seem to prohibit women speaking or teaching in public.

There seems, at least on the surface, to be a tension or contradiction in the Bible on the position and role of women – in fact, even between 11:2-16 and 14:34 within the same letter (1 Corinthians)! May a woman speak and teach in the public assemblies or not? Can the apparently discrepant verses be harmonized?

B. Our goal:

There must be some underlying idea that permits us to harmonize all the verses on the topic of women "speaking."[6] Perhaps we misunderstand 1 Timothy 2:12. Perhaps we have taken 1 Corinthians 14:34 out of context. Perhaps the choice of words used in our English translations has led us to miss the underlying principle that would help reconcile the apparently contradictory verses. So let's try again.

A key working hypothesis is this: *If we must give any verse a "peculiar meaning" (one that is not rather obvious to the average reader) in order to make it harmonize with what we've judged the Scripture to say elsewhere on the topic being studied, we may well be on the wrong track.*

At stake is the ministry of women in the church, i.e., what, if any, ministry should be encouraged? Every effort, therefore, should be expended as we grapple with the issues, as we attempt to reach a position that neither vitiates the authority of Scripture nor robs women of a vital, Biblical place in the body of Christ. If the Scriptures permit women a larger role in ministry functions than has been traditionally allowed, they should not be forbidden to function. If the Scriptures do not permit women to teach or lead or speak in public, then the Biblical view should be carefully and lovingly and firmly presented.

C. **A study of the verses concerning the roles of men and women,** in order to refresh our minds about what God says.

---

[6] As a conservative evangelical, this writer holds that the Scriptures are inspired and therefore without error in the original manuscripts. This teaching implies that the Bible is consistent within itself, and that no two statements of Scripture contradict each other. "Consistency" is the recognized test for truth.

1. Old Testament passages

Genesis 1:27 – Care must be taken in reading Genesis 1:26-28. "And God created man (Hebrew '*adam*[7]) in His own image, in the image of God He created he him; male (Heb: *zakur*; LXX: *arsen*) and female (Heb: *neqebah*; LXX: *thelu*) He created them." Does 1 Corinthians 11:7,8 help us understand what Genesis says? Paul writes in verse 7, "... he [man] is the image and glory of God; but the woman is the glory of man." And in verse 8, "For man does not originate from woman, but woman from man." In verse 7, there seems to be a reflection of what is recorded in Genesis 1:27. Does 1 Corinthians lead us to understand that Genesis means that Adam (the male) is created in the image of God? Paul does not repeat the words "the image" when he writes of the woman. Is this significant? In verse 8, which gives a reason for saying that "woman is the glory of man," there seems to be a reflection of what is recorded in Genesis 2:21-23. Because men and women share in a special creation (Genesis 1), women are personally and spiritually equal with men. Because of their derivative creation (Genesis 2), women are societally subordinate to their husbands.

Genesis 2:18-23 – God makes for Adam "a help meet." Genesis 2 gives in detail what Genesis 1 has given in broad strokes.[8] The "help meet" is of the same kind as Adam – human, not animal. Since both male and female are of the same kind, both are equally capable of a personal relationship with their Creator. Both can worship and pray and serve. Likewise, both can rebel against God, and both must bear personal responsibility for their own sins. She is a "helper." The Hebrew word for "helper" ('*ezer*) does not imply a mere servant status for woman. Woman was not just another animal to be ruled over by man. Perhaps our understanding of '*ezer* ("helper") can be aided when we note that the word is used 16 times in the Old Testament of God in his salvific activity on behalf of humans. Men needed something. The "helper" provided it. Perhaps we get some aid to our understanding from 1 Corinthians 11:9, where we are told "man was not created for the woman's sake, but woman for the man's sake." She was to benefit Adam, to help him, to complement him.[9] According to Genesis 2:21-23, Adam was created before Eve. As Adam names the animals, he becomes

---

[7] The Hebrew word is translated both "Adam" and "mankind." Each time the translator comes to this word, he must decide whether the reference is to the first man Adam, or to mankind in general.

[8] Are there two (perhaps even conflicting?) accounts of creation in Genesis – one in chapter 1 and another in chapter 2? Source and Form Critics claim to have found two different sources for these chapters. These same critics then tend to dismiss one or the other of the accounts because they are allegedly not in agreement. The conservative evangelical explanation rejects this approach to Genesis. The accounts are not conflicting, but supplementary. Genesis 2 & 3 unfold in more detail how some of the things introduced in chapter 1 were actually accomplished by God.

[9] Egalitarians interpret "helper suitable" for Adam (Gen. 2:18) as meaning "an equal partner." In the light of its use for God, and in light of 1 Corinthians 11:9, that may be saying too much!

aware that there is no suitable helper like himself to be found among the animals. So God takes a rib and from it forms the suitable helper, Eve. Woman was created second. Or as 1 Corinthians 11:8 words it, "man does not originate from woman, but woman from man."

Genesis 3:16 – "Your desire shall be for your husband, and he shall rule over you." It is Genesis 3 that gives a very explicit statement of woman's subjection to her husband. The husband's "rule" over woman is part of the woman's punishment. According to the writer of Genesis, this is not the ideal relation of the sexes, just as thorns and thistles in the ground, enmity between human beings and the animal world, and woman's pain in bearing children are not God's created ideal. The phrase "rule over" need not connote tyranny of power, but it does reflect a subordinate position for the woman.

Proverbs 31 – The ideal woman. The managerial ability of a good woman is praised in Proverbs 31:10-31. She is not one who constantly stays in the house, caring only for the children, and doing nothing outside the home. She enhances her husband's reputation when he sits in the gates of the city.

2. New Testament Verses about the Husband-Wife Relationship

1 Corinthians 11:2-16 – Verse 3, with its repeated "the head of," sets the tone for everything written in verses 2-16.[10] "God is the head of Christ, Christ is the head of man, the man is the head of a woman." There are descending levels of authority – God, Christ, man, woman. The word translated "man" in the NASB is *andros* (one of the declensional forms of *anēr*), a word that quite often means "husband", as contrasted to *anthrōpos*, the generic word for "man" or "mankind". Likewise, *gunē* can be translated either "woman" or "wife." Since the context (verses 7-9) alludes to the creation of Adam and Eve (the first husband and wife), we think it possible to use "husband" and "wife" as we translate verse 3. "Head" in verse 3 indicates some kind of order and subordination. *Kephalē*, "head", does not indicate simply "source" with no connotation of "subordination" – cp. Ephesians 5:22-24 and 1:22, where "put all things in subjection under"[11] in the first part of the verse corresponds to "head over all things" in the next clause.

---

[10] As he writes Corinthians, and tries to help people sort out the right way to do things when problems have intruded, Paul regularly states some principle or principles which will help the readers solve not only the immediate problem, but others like them when they arise. The principles are always true; the immediate rulings based on the principles sometimes have abiding validity, and sometimes may be true only of that time and place.

[11] See Wayne Grudem, "Appendix One: Does *kephale* Mean 'Source' or "Authority Over' in Greek Literature? A Survey of 2,336 Examples," in G.W. Knight III, *The Role Relationship of Men and Women* (Chicago: Moody, 1985), p.68. Grudem's research has failed to turn up any clear examples from the classical or Hellenistic periods where the word means merely "source." Only when *kephalē* occurs in the plural might the idea of "source" be maintained. The most influential

A reading of the places where *kephalē* occurs in the New Testament, especially in Ephesians and Colossians, certainly suggests a "preeminence" – the top, the crowning place, a superior position – is involved in the word. Such subordination is voluntary, not forced, and such subordination is not necessarily degrading. It certainly was not and is not for Christ! As noted above, verses 7-9 reflect what we read in Genesis 1 and 2. Verse 9, which reads "indeed man (husband) was not created for the woman's (wife's) sake, but woman for the man's sake", reminds us of God's words, "I will make him a helper suitable for him" (Genesis 2:18).

3. A number of New Testament verses speak to the matter of the wife's **submissiveness** to her husband.

Ephesians 5:22-24 – It is a voluntary submissiveness that verses 22 and 24 call for. Verses 23,24 speak of the husband as "head" of the wife as Christ is "head" of the church. Verse 24 shows that "headship" certainly involves submission, at least it does in the case of the church to her head, Christ. The traditional explanation suggests that 5:23 means the husband is to assume the role of *leader* in the family. It does not mean that the wife simply fades into the background, meek and mute, and takes orders. It means that she *allows* her husband to take the lead while she assists and contributes in every way possible (Cottrell, *Tough Questions – Biblical Answers*, p.56). The husband's role as head of the wife does not give him the right to boss or browbeat, to be domineering or abusive. This is specifically forbidden in the comparison with Jesus' headship over the church in Ephesians 5. Christ's lordship is tempered by love. The husband likewise must love, nourish, and cherish his wife (Ephesians. 5:25-29).

Colossians 3:18 – "Wives be subject to your husbands (*andrasin*), as is fitting in the Lord." A plain-sense reading of this passage certainly teaches a voluntary submission, a role to be filled, if she will do so.

1 Timothy 2:11 – "Let a woman (wife) quietly receive instruction with entire submissiveness."

Titus 2:1-5 –Paul clearly says that women's roles are part of sound doctrine. Wives are to habitually obey ("being subject to") their own husbands (verse 5).

paper in recent years to suggest that *kephalē* means "source" was S. Bedale, "The Meaning of *kephale* in the Pauline Epistles," JTS n.s. 5 (1984), p. 211-215.

Berkley and Alvera Mickelsen, "What does *Kephale* mean in the New Testament," in *Women, Authority & the Bible* (Downers Grove, IL: Inter-Varsity, 1986), p.97ff, make the most coherent attempt to explain that *kephalē* means "source", not authority. They quote Liddell and Scott's lexicon which never gives "authority" as a possible meaning for the word, and they quote places in ancient Greek literature where, for example, a father is called the "head" of the son – in a context which speaks of the father being the "source of life" to the son. Perhaps their argument proves too much. If *kephalē* in 1 Corinthians 11:3 means "source," then 1 Corinthians 11:3 would also be saying that Christ is a "created being", for God is called the "head" of Christ. This will hardly do!

1 Peter 3:1 – "In the same way, you wives, be submissive to your own husbands." Such submission is expected even if the husband has not yet become a Christian. The verb tense indicates habitual and voluntary submission. In 3:6, the Old Testament example of Sarah, who habitually obeyed Abraham and called him "lord" (*kurios*), is held out as an example to be emulated by Christian wives.

4. What is the specific principle that stands out in all these verses?

It is the wife's submission to the husband's authority and headship! That is the thrust of 1 Corinthians 11:3, 14:34 ("even the Law says" – Genesis 3:16); 1 Timothy 2:11; Ephesians 1:22 (compare the use of "head" and "put all things in subjection under") and 5:22-24; Colossians 3:18,19, and 1 Peter 3:1-6.

It is the wife's responsibility to be in submission; it is not the man's to put her in submission. She does so because this is part of her obedience to God.

D. A study of the verses where we find **women at work in the public assemblies** of the churches.

1. Several verses seem to present women as speaking and praying and teaching in public and in mixed assemblies of both men and women.

(a) There are passages about women prophesying and being prophetesses. "Prophecy" is Holy Spirit-inspired speaking in the local language of the people.[12] Acts 2:17ff indicates women shall prophesy in early days and years of the church age, as was predicted by Joel, after the Holy Spirit was poured out on them. Certainly the Holy Spirit would not inspire women to do something that the Spirit later (in 1 Corinthians 14 and 1 Timothy 2) will say it is improper for women to do. If God has poured out his Spirit on both the sons and daughters so that both could and did prophesy, it will not do for us to erect a modern-day "court of the women" for our churches. Before whom did Philip's virgin daughters prophesy in Acts 21:9? Women only? In public assemblies, or in home Bible studies? The New Testament nowhere tells us. 1 Corinthians 11:5 indicates women were praying vocally and prophesying in the public meetings of the church at Corinth. Paul does object to the manner (e.g., the improper dress) in which they were doing it (11:5-16). Did Paul also object (14:34) to their doing it at all?

(b) Priscilla evidently taught a man, Apollos, at Acts 18:26. She took him aside and corrected a male's deficient theology. How can this behavior be reconciled to 1 Timothy 2:12 where Paul does not permit a woman to teach a man? Shall we say that she may teach at home, but not in the public meeting? Is there another way to reconcile these apparently contradictory verses?

---

[12] See Acts 11:28 where we are told Agabus, a prophet, spoke as the Holy Spirit prompted.

(c) In two passages, women are called "fellow laborers in the Gospel." (1) In Philippians 4:2-4, Paul names two women who "labored [side by side] with me in the Gospel, with Clement also, and with other my fellow-laborers" (KJV). How did the women labor? Only as hostesses, secretaries, laundresses, cooks, and waitresses? In many places we no longer have the "house churches" that were found in numerous 1st century towns. Do women lose a significant part of ministry in the modern church where they no longer need serve as hostesses for the gathering of the saints? When Paul uses this term "fellow worker," he is often referring to someone – usually a male – who was a minister or evangelist.[13] Do women lose a significant part of ministry in the modern church where they are not permitted to serve as ministers or evangelists? (2) Is the Junia of Romans 16:7, (KJV; "Junias" NASB) a woman, and what does it mean when she/he is called "outstanding among the apostles"? Did the apostles hold her/him in high regard, or did she/he not only hold the office of an apostle of Jesus, but also did an outstanding job in the office? The verse is ambiguous enough to keep any interpreter from being dogmatic for or against equality of women even to holding the office of apostle. If it can be shown "Junia" was a woman, and that she held the office of apostle, what are the implications of this for church order today? Are there apostles today? Are there similar leadership positions open to women? What are the implications in light of the "hierarchy of authority" where apostle is a higher position[14] than evangelist or elder? If in Junias we have a woman apostle, would we have a woman in a position of authority over male evangelists or elders? Would that be prohibited by 1 Timothy 2:12?

So, there are in fact verses that have women leading and speaking and praying in public.

2. There are some verses that have traditionally been used to prove a woman should not do things in public.

1 Corinthians 14:34 – "Let the women keep silent in the churches; for they are not permitted to speak, but let them subject themselves just as the Law also says ...." The traditional view takes "women" generically, and sees in this command a blanket prohibition of any public speaking by women.

1 Timothy 2:12 – "I do not allow a woman to teach or exercise authority over a man, but to remain quiet." The traditional view takes "woman" generically, and sees in this verse a blanket prohibition of any woman ever teaching a

---

[13] Philemon is called a "fellow worker" (Philemon 1) and it is doubtful he was a preacher/evangelist. In Romans 16:3, Priscilla and Aquila are called "fellow-workers."

[14] The order in which apostles, prophets, evangelists, pastors and teachers (better, "pastoring-teachers" [i.e., elders]) are named in Ephesians 4:11, is probably an order of descending authority.

man in the public assemblies.   Evangelicals who oppose or limit the participation of women in preaching, teaching or exercising authority in the church consider 1 Timothy 2:11-12 the clearest and strongest Biblical text supporting their position.

These verses do restrict, in some degree, women's participation in the "ministries" of the church.   But what is that degree?

E. **An Attempt to harmonize the passages.**

The passages that have women speaking and the passages that appear to prohibit women speaking seem to contradict.   Is there a way to reconcile them?[15]

It is the thesis of this study that the key to reconciling all the verses is to recognize the verses that contain prohibitions are really addressed to *wives* (rather than to "women" in general), and that the prohibitions are related to the Biblical mandate of **submission of wives to their husbands**!

Can "wives and husbands" be what the verses are really about, and not "women and men" in general?   Let's take a second look at three of the passages, to demonstrate this thesis.

1 Corinthians 11:2-16 – The traditional view, that this paragraph is an original Pauline pericope, has been rejected by several scholars recently.[16]   This writer holds that the paragraph enjoys integrity[17] and genuineness[18] (i.e., Paul wrote it!).   The paragraph may be outlined as follows:

---

[15] In the past half century, almost every word in each of these difficult passages has been the subject of scholarly papers as writers have attempted to find the key to reconciling these passages. Some have looked at "head." Some have looked at "exercise authority." Some have looked at "silence." Some have looked at "prophecy." Some have looked at "teach." This writer, in recent years, even called attention to the tenses of the Greek verb forms used in the "prohibition passages," and emphasized that those present tenses do not prohibit all teaching or speaking. A prohibition on all teaching would require an aorist tense verb form. So he concluded women could speak or teach on occasion, just so it didn't become something expected all the time. However, none of the proposed solutions looking at these words has carried conviction, or solved all the difficulties.

[16] Documentation of the denial (and the alleged reasons for it) of the Pauline authorship may be studied in H. Wayne House, "Should a Woman Prophesy or Preach before Men?" *Bibliotheca Sacra* (April-June 1988), p.142,143, footnote #1. Of course, if Paul did not write it, then perhaps it does not belong in the letter to the Corinthians, and thus we can dismiss its thrust as far as the matter of what a woman may do in public services is concerned.

[17] "Integrity" is a technical word meaning "wholesome preservation of the text in substantially the same form as it proceeded from the pen of the writer." If 1 Corinthians 11:2-16 enjoys integrity, it means it was originally in the letter when Paul wrote it.

[18] "Genuineness" is a technical term relating to authorship. A work is "genuine" if the one whose name it bears actually penned the letter. In this instance, 1 Corinthians 11:2-16 is genuine only if Paul wrote it.

1) The principle stated, verse 3.

The principle is that there is a "headship" – God is the head of Christ, Christ is the head of the husband, the husband is the head of the wife.[19]

2) The principle applied, verses 4-6

This principle of "headship" gives guidance to both husbands and wives when it comes to their participation (e.g., praying or prophesying) in the public worship.

Praying – means to speak vocal and audible public prayers in the worship assembly.[20]

Prophesying – means to speak by the Holy Spirit's inspiration in the language of the people. 1 Corinthians 14:3,5,12,26,31 give us some idea as to what "prophecy" was. It was inspired speaking which could strengthen, or encourage, or comfort, or convict, or edify, or instruct (people could "learn"[21] from prophecy).

Though some prophets likely "preached" their message, we should probably not equate "prophecy" with what we in the 20th century call "preaching."[22]

Men praying or prophesying with their heads *covered* dishonor their head (Christ), says verse 4. Women praying or prophesying with their heads *uncovered* dishonor their head (husband), says verse 5.

Note, it was not the praying or prophesying *per se* that dishonored, but doing it in such a manner (covered or uncovered) as to violate the principle of headship that is condemned.

---

[19] See notes above on the meaning of "head" in 1 Corinthians 11:3.

[20] Though "prophesying" was by definition something done by the power of the Holy Spirit, it is not at all certain that we should think of the "praying" as something done "in the Spirit."

[21] If people could learn from a prophet, can we say that prophecy included teaching? And if prophecy included teaching, how shall we square this with 1 Timothy 2:11ff if 2:12 prohibits all women from all teaching? Does Paul contradict himself? We think it unlikely.

[22] "Prophecy" and "preaching" likely are not exactly synonymous in the New Testament. "Prophecy" depends upon an immediate revelation flowing from God (cp. 1 Corinthians 14:30); preaching and teaching do not seem to depend on or flow from such an immediate revelation. A person could preach without having immediately before the message received special revelation from God. A prophet, however, would not be speaking or preaching unless he had first received such an immediate revelation.

3) <u>The principle defended</u>, verses 7-10.

Verses 7-10 deal with the Biblical view of **husbands** and **wives** – not "men" and "women" in general. The conclusion reached about head coverings when worshiping reflects what is written in Genesis 2:21-23. The wife's dress as she participated in the public worship was to demonstrate the fact that she was the "glory" of her husband, whereas the husband's dress as he participated in the public worship was to reflect that he was the image and glory of God.

The conclusion reached about head coverings when worshiping also reflects what Genesis 2:18-20 says about the woman being a "help-meet." Verse 10 says a woman ought to have a "symbol" on her head that she is "somebody" (an honored wife), not just a tramp!

4) <u>The principle clarified</u>, verses 11,12

Under the rule of Christ – where women's rights are realized as nowhere in Judaism or heathenism – both husbands and wives have their God-given roles. All things, including the roles of husbands and wives, originate from God.

Verses 7-12 show that customs that symbolize and/or reflect the facts of creation are not to be arbitrarily changed just because one has become a Christian.

5) <u>The principle agreed to</u>, verses 13-16.

The reader's own personal sentiments agree with Paul's position.
"Nature" teaches the same thing.
The universal practice of all the churches teaches the same thing.

In 1 Corinthians 11:2-16, Paul makes sure that the behavior of the worshipers as they pray and prophesy in the public service does not impinge on the Biblical place of husbands and wives.

1 Corinthians 14:33-36 – These verses fall within the section (chapters 12-14) of 1 Corinthians that concerns the abuse of spiritual gifts in the public worship assembly. As far as authorship is concerned, the verses are Paul's[23] and

---

[23] Some have denied the Pauline authorship of these few verses. Some egalitarians have used this denial to explain away the difference in the point of view taken by the true Paul (Galatians 3:28) and this "problem passage." If 1 Corinthians 14:34-36 are not Pauline, then of course they would not have to be harmonized with Paul's views on equality as expressed in Galatians 3:28.

enjoy integrity.[24]   The chapters may be outlined as follows:

1) <u>Principles</u>
  a) Test by which the Holy Spirit's leading may be discerned, 12:1-3.
  b) Diversity of gifts is necessary, 12:4-31. (Includes a 3-part argument
     to show the need for diversity, not uniformity.)
  c) The necessity of allowing love for the other person to control one's
     use of his gift(s), 13:1-13.

2) <u>Applications of the principles to correct the abuse of spiritual gifts,</u>
   14:1-40

  a) The principle of **edification**, 14:1-5.
     This principle encourages spiritually gifted people to major in sharing
     the Word of God so the church will be strengthened and grow.
  b) The principle of **understanding**.   14:6-25.
     By this criterion, prophecy is better for edifying believers, 6-19.
     By this criterion, prophecy is better for convicting unbelievers, 20-25.
     (Both of these mean *"prophecy is better than tongues [given the way
     the Corinthians were using tongues]."*)
  c) The principle of **order**.   14:26-40
     Restatement of the principle that should govern the use of spiritual gifts,
     26
     Guidelines for tongues and interpretation of tongues, so that order is
     maintained, 27-28
     Guidelines for prophecy and discernment of prophecy, so that order is
     maintained, 29-31
     Dehortation concerning "confusion", 32-33
     Prohibition of women speaking in the public service (a prohibition of
     speaking that would disrupt the "orderliness" Paul seeks), 34-35
     Final appeal to "orderliness", 36-40
     *Do you contend that of all the churches in the brotherhood, you alone
     have the right to adopt practices that are irregular?*

Now for some details out of verses 33b-35:

"As in all the churches of the saints", verse 33b.   This phrase can conclude the

---

[24] Some scholars have argued, because of the displacement of this passage to a later point in some early texts, that 1 Corinthians 14:34-35 was not originally part of Paul's letter to Corinth.   See the Nestle-Aland textual apparatus for the relevant data as to the placement.   Earle E. Ellis, "The Silenced Wives of Corinth," in *New Testament Textual Criticism*, edited by E.J. Epp and G.D. Fee (Oxford: Clarendon, 1981), pp.213-220, supposes that this passage was originally a marginal gloss that eventually was included in the text of the next manuscript copied.   This commentator finds inadequate support for either of these suggestions.

previous paragraph, or introduce the following one.[25]   If it introduces the following one, then what Paul asks of the wives[26] at Corinth is the same behavior he teaches and expects in all other Christian congregations.[27]   Wives are to be "silent," they are not to "speak," they are to "submit themselves."   Verses 34 and 35 seem to be Paul's statement of how things are, not a quotation by Paul of a legalistic slogan used by the teachers who were agitating the church at Corinth.[28]

"Let the women keep silent in the churches."   As in the earlier place in Corinthians, we would suggest rendering the Greek word as "wives" rather than "women".   Notice, the very next verse speaks of "asking their husbands at home."   This confirms our rendering of the word as "wives."   "Silent" is the same word used at 14:28 and 14:30, and should be understood the same way as it was there.   There, it does not mean "unqualified silence" or "absolute silence", and it should not be so interpreted here.[29]   In the context, the "silence" demanded is a "silence" necessary for the sake of orderliness.   Orderliness is the topic of the paragraph (14:26-40) in which these verses occur.

"For they are not permitted to speak."   "To speak" is a present tense infinitive, indicating continual, habitual, customary, or repeated action.   What "speaking" is the topic of this passage?   The immediate preceding context (verses 30-33a) has to do with how many prophets should speak at any one public meeting of the church.   Perhaps this prohibition says that wives are not permitted to [habitually] speak *among the prophets* in the public gathering of the whole church.[30]   The immediate following context has to do with asking questions of their husbands at home rather than in the public service.   Perhaps this prohibition says wives are not to habitually ask their husbands questions in the middle of the public service.

---

[25] In cases like this, when a phrase can look either way, it is perfectly proper to teach both emphases. We would reject one of the possible emphases only if it makes the verse contradict what Scriptures say elsewhere. Taking this phrase both ways tells us two things: (1) God wants peace rather than confusion in all the churches. (2) God wants women to be silent in all the churches.

[26] See below where this change from "women" as the NASB reads to "wives" is defended.

[27] To think that the prohibitions Paul gives apply only to the Corinthians is out of harmony with Paul's appeal that they conform to the rest of the Christian church.

[28] The adversative with which verse 36 begins in the Greek has been used by some to argue that verses 34 and 35 are not Paul's teaching, but an opinion he wishes to refute. Of course, if the passage is not Paul's own view, then one of the "contradictory passages" has been disposed of.

[29] If "silence" were absolute, then ladies would not be permitted to join in the congregational singing, or voice an "amen" when someone finished offering a public prayer. Earlier in chapter 14 (see verse 26 for example), "each member" is participating in the public service, whether by praying, singing, instructing, etc. When Paul uses the words "each member," it would be hard to exclude women from such activities. And if they cannot be excluded, then "silence" is not absolute silence!

[30] The suggestion that the prohibited "speaking" was of a particular kind – i.e., critically evaluating another prophet's words (14:29) – is hard to accept. 14:29 seems too far removed to be what would present itself to the average reader as he reads the prohibition about speaking in 14:34.

"But let them subject themselves, just as the Law also says." The prohibited "speaking" is that which is out of harmony with the submission God requires of wives to husbands. "The Law" likely references Genesis 3:16 ("your desire shall be for your husband, and he shall rule over you"). Some might disagree, recalling that the "Law was temporary, and nailed to the cross." How then can appeal be made to Genesis 3 as the Scriptural reason for "not speaking but being in subjection"? We remind such thinkers that it was only the Mosaic Law which was temporary. Genesis 3 is not part of the now-abrogated Mosaic Covenant, since the Mosaic Covenant was not given till Exodus 19-23. Paul was not parroting Jewish tradition when he gives this limitation on the wives' participation in the public service. He appeals to the Law. Later, he will appeal to the fact that what he has written is a "command" of the Lord (1 Corinthians 14:37).

"If they desire to learn anything, let them ask their own husbands at home." A wife's request for knowledge is not to be denied; she has as much right to know the truth of Christianity as does her husband. Her questions are to be answered at home, not by asking her husband in the public service and so possibly disturbing the assembly's orderliness by talking when someone else is preaching, etc.

"For it is improper for a woman to speak in the church." It may mean "improper" in light of God's revelation of His will. "Improper" may refer to the way the Corinthian women were doing it, and destroying the orderliness of the public service. It may mean her behavior is "shameful" (ASV) to her husband.

"Or was it from you that the word of God first went forth?" What Paul negates by his use of the adversative Greek particle (ἤ, "or") is *not* the *command* in verses 34-35 but the assumed *disobedience* of the command, just as in the structurally similar passage in 1 Corinthians 6:18-19. How do we harmonize 14:34 ("silence, not speaking") with 11:5 ("praying and prophesying in public")? If we recognize that it is a "wife's" silence that is enjoined (and not silence of all "women"), we have immediately arrived at a plausible harmonization of these apparently discrepant verses. *Wives* have a responsibility not to pray or prophesy publicly when they have husbands present in the assembly.[31] Those who do not have *husbands* present (virgins, widows, Christian wives whose unbelieving husbands are absent, etc.) have no such limitation on public speaking.

1 Timothy 2:8-15 – We shall include here but a summary of the key points already made in the comments on these verses in this book. The passage is Pauline. Those who deny the Pauline authorship of the Pastorals, or of this pas-

---

[31] According to 1 Corinthians 14:32, even after a prophet had received a revelation from on High, he could still control when and where and even whether or not he ever delivered it to a human audience. So even if a prophetess has received a revelation from God, she could still control whether or not she spoke the message in the assembly.

sage in particular, are in error.   Chapter 2 deals with the public worship service. Paul's words "I permit" are not just Paul's private practice in this one instance. He has written about how things are to be done in "every place" (every congregation), 1 Timothy 2:8.   Again we propose that the Greek words used (verses 11-14) should be translated "wife" and "husband" (rather than using the generic "woman" and "man").   "Submission" and "childbearing" in the context fit the topic "wife."   According to verse 11, wives are to "quietly receive instruction (in the Christian religion) with entire submissiveness."   The imperative that a woman "must learn" or "be allowed to learn" was revolutionary in the first century world!   Quietness and submissiveness give the guidelines within which the woman may learn.   "Submissiveness" (verse 11) is voluntarily subordinating oneself to someone else.   It is the very instructions we have seen all through Scripture concerning the *wife's* relationship to her *husband*. *Hēsuchia* ("quietly" in verse 11 and "quiet" in verse 12) is the "willingness to heed and obey instruction."[32]   In verse 12, we propose that in this context it should be translated "I do not allow a *wife* to teach or exercise authority[33] over a *husband*". The very next verse, which gives a reason why the wife should not teach or exercise authority, calls attention to the first husband and wife, Adam and Eve. Both of the verbs "teach" and "exercise authority" (verse 12) are present tense infinitives.   What Paul prohibits is the continual, habitual, customary, repeated teaching and exercising of authority.   Wives are not to be in roles of general leadership in the church if the exercise of that role would have them habitually teaching or exercising authority over their husbands.   Leadership roles in the church do not annul or supersede the Biblical doctrine of submission of the wife to the husband.   Again, let it be observed that *andros* in this context very likely refers to not just any man, but to a "husband."   If so, then this passage says the wife is not to teach or exercise authority over her husband.   If she is in a place where her husband is not, then she may teach or prophesy, etc.[34]

The very simple key suggested above for reconciling Paul's statements about "women" not speaking or teaching and his statements about such public ministries being performed by "women", can be applied to this Timothy passage as well as 1 Corinthians 14:34-36.   The *wife* does not function in the public service if her speaking or teaching would put her in a position over her *husband*,

---

[32] Though the word is translated "silence" in the KJV, it is not the same word rendered "silence" at 1 Corinthians 14:34.

[33] *Authenteō* simply denotes "exercise authority over."   See this documented in the notes above at 1 Timothy 2:12.   Both the KJV's rendering "usurp authority" as well as the English word "domineer" may be too strong an English word for this Greek word.   Bauer's lexicon, in English translation, does give "domineer" as a possible meaning for *authenteō*, but the translator may have not exactly rendered the German in this instance.

[34] Again, the widow or the unmarried woman could function as a "prophet" or a "teacher" in the public service and not have any problem of violating this matter of submissiveness to one's husband.

rather than being in her God-appointed submissive position. If it is true that the principle that governs the "woman's" behavior is the submission of wives to husbands, then when Paul writes 2:12, he is not saying a woman may not teach at all, but only that she may not teach when her husband is in the audience. If it is true that the principle governing a "woman's" behavior is the submission of wives to husbands, then Paul does not say she may not exercise authority at all, but only that she may not exercise authority over her husband. In 1 Timothy 2:13-15, Paul gives the reason for the prohibition on wives teaching or exercising authority over their husbands. He grounds his argument in the first three chapters of Genesis, not in Jewish or Greco-Roman cultural practices. As long as it is true that Adam was created first, that is how long this prohibition on wives continually teaching or exercising authority over husbands is true. As long as it is true that Eve sinned first, that is how long the prohibition stands. Verse 15 then says that while she may not be "teacher" or an "authority" over her husband, she certainly may avail herself of equal opportunity to salvation provided by "the child (Jesus)." Women are not less eligible for salvation in God's sight than men.

SUMMARY STATEMENTS

We started with verses that, as translated in our English versions, appear contradictory. Through the years, a number of attempts have been made to find a way to reconcile them without doing anything "unusual" with the verses. None of these attempts has proven very satisfactory.

Now we offer this suggestion – each of the passages that put limitations on what "women" may do in the public assembly are in a context where the "women" are really "**wives**" and the "men" are really "**husbands**." Once this fact is noted, we have a key to reconciling the apparently contradictory passages.

Women may serve in a number of capacities in the public service – praying, prophesying, teaching, singing, etc. The one thing the married women must be careful of is that they do not step outside or flaunt the Biblical mandate of submission to their husbands. Any public activity that would put the wife over the husband is an activity the married woman should refrain from doing.

By this criteria, women would be welcome to serve as evangelists, servant-helpers, teachers, and (in the early church, when the gifts were still available) perhaps even as apostles and prophets. The two *offices* women would not be qualified for are "elder" and "deacon" – since, to be qualified for either office, one must be male (i.e., the husband of one wife).

SELECTED BIBLIOGRAPHY

First, some general articles to serve as an introduction to the whole dispute:

Bowman, Ann, "Women in Ministry: An Exegetical Study of 1 Timothy 2:11-15," *Bibliotheca Sacra* (Apr-June 1992), p.193-213.

House, H. Wayne, "A Biblical View of Women in the Ministry" (5 part series), *Bibliotheca Sacra* (Jan-March, 1988, and issues following), p.47-56, etc.

Second, some articles that contain the usual arguments, pro and con, concerning the ordination of women to the ministry.

"Women as Preachers: Evangelical Precedents." *Christianity Today* 19 (May 23, 1975), p.822.
  Churches and theologians who, through history, have recognized the rights of women to be preachers.

"Why I Favor the Ordination of Women," *Christianity Today* 19 (June 6, '75), p.873.
  Neither the arguments about "the nature of woman," or the "nature of the ministerial office," or "the nature of God himself" – restrict the office of minister to men only!

"Why I Oppose the Ordination of Women," *Christianity Today* 19 (June 6, 1975), p. 878.
  The only question that matters is "Has God spoken?"

Perspectives on Evangelical Theology, edited by Kantzer and Gundry. Grand Rapids: Baker, 1979.
  E. Margaret Howe, "The Positive Case for the Ordination of Women," p. 267ff.
  Robert L. Saucy, "The Negative Case Against the Ordination of Women," p. 277ff.

John Reumann, "What in Scripture Speaks to the Ordination of Women?" *Concordia Theological Monthly* 45:1   (Jan. 1973), p. 5ff.
  There is no such thing in the Bible as what today is called "ordination" – with the idea of apostolic succession and the prerogative of administering the sacraments officially.

Christianity Today Institute, "Women in Leadership: Finding Ways to Serve the Church," *Christianity Today* 30:14 (October 3, 1986), p. I-1 to I-16.

Lown, W. F., "Women in Roles of Leadership," *The Lookout* 92:36 (September 7, 1980), p. 2, and later issues.

Cottrell, Jack, *Feminism and the Bible* (Joplin, Mo.: College Press, 1992).
  Readers will find in greater detail much of what was included in the four-part series ("1 Timothy 2:12 and the Role of Women") printed in the 1993 *Christian Standard*.

Cottrell, Jack, *Gender Roles and the Bible: Creation, Fall, and Redemption* (Joplin, MO.: College Press, 1994).
  A very readable response to standard egalitarian handling of Scripture verses about the role of women.

Finally, sources to see the way the contemporary "winds of doctrine" are blowing:

John T. Bristow, *What Paul Really Said About Women*, San Francisco: Harper & Row, 1988.
  A Disciples of Christ preacher defends his views that encourage women into the preaching ministry.

Richard and Catherine Kroeger, *I Suffer Not a Woman: Rethinking 1 Timothy 2:11-15 in the Light of Ancient Evidence*. Grand Rapids: Baker, 1992.
  Certain trial balloons are launched in an effort to "explain" 1 Timothy 2 in a way that does not contradict the egalitarian view of women's Scriptural roles.   What is prohibited is a woman teaching false doctrine (Gnostic doctrines, an Earth Mother as the source of all life, etc.), not all teaching by a woman.

III. THE CHARGE CONCERNING CHURCH OFFICERS. 3:1-16

A. Office of Elder. 3:1-7

3:1 -- It is a trustworthy statement – As explained at 1 Timothy 1:15, this formula introduces a memorized summary of Christian doctrine. Most commentaries find the words of this "statement" in the rest of verse 1 that follows.[1] However, beginning with Chrysostom, some have tried to make the words of 2:15 the "faithful saying."[2] The object of chapter 3 is to give directions respecting the qualifications of the officers or leaders[3] of the local congregation, in order to help the local churches pick the caliber of men needed for such an important task in Christ's church. It is evident that Timothy was to be partly involved in the selection and appointment of suitable officers for the Ephesian church. Since these kinds of officers were to be permanent in the church, it was important that a full statement should be on record, under the influence of inspiration, regarding their qualifications. Titus, on Crete, had similar responsibilities concerning leadership for the local congregations on that island (Titus 1:5ff).

The passages in Timothy and Titus that deal with the qualifications for men who would be church leaders are important. From an early time, the offices of elder and deacon are found occupying a place in the church. There were also spiritually gifted men (prophets, teachers, etc.) who functioned as leaders. As time went on, the offices associated with the special miraculous gifts of the Holy Spirit gradually passed from the scene. The offices of elder, deacon, and evangelist became more and more important (see comments at 1 Timothy 3:15,16).

If any man aspires to the office of an overseer – "Office of an overseer" is one word in the Greek, *episkopos*. The "function" of overseeing is emphasized by this word. The "overseer" (*episkopos*) or "bishop" (KJV) is the same official

---

[1] Admittedly, there is no fixed pattern for these "faithful sayings." Of the four other uses of this phrase in the Pastoral Epistles, in two the saying follows the formula (1 Timothy 11:15; 2 Timothy 2:11), in one the saying precedes the formula (Titus 3:8), and one is ambiguous (1 Timothy 4:9).

[2] The argument most often heard to prove that the words preceding the formula are the saying is the one which says that formula elsewhere is always concerned with salvation. 2:15 speaks of salvation, not 3:1b. The problem with this argument is that it assumes the very point to be proved. Only a few modern Greek texts (Westcott and Hort, NA[26]) and English translations put "This is a faithful saying" at the close of chapter 2.

[3] It is difficult to find a satisfactory word to call these leadership functions. "Office," at the present time, has a connotation of a position of authority from which one rules. Since such a connotation is not in harmony with Jesus' view of leadership (Matthew 20:25-28; Luke 22:24-24), some have preferred the word "function." This word stresses that leadership positions are jobs to do, not just offices to be filled. We shall use "office" quite regularly in these comments; but we keep in mind that we are speaking of a service to perform, a work to do, when we use this word "office".

designated "elder" (*presbuteros*) in other passages.[4]   While the apostles were still living, these two terms designated the same office.[5]   A comparison of Acts 20:17,28 will show this, where the leaders from the church at Ephesus, in their meeting at Miletus with Paul, were called both "elders" and "overseers."   Likewise, at Titus 1:5-7, we find both terms used for the same "officers" whom Titus was to see were selected in each city's congregation.   It was in post-apostolic times that men made "bishop" an office of higher rank than "elder."   Some have labeled this elevation of one man to be a "bishop" the first departure from the way Jesus left the church.   By the time of Ignatius, AD 115, there is not much doubt that the position of "bishop" was already recognized in the churches.[6]   When the term "overseer" or "bishop" appears in the New Testament, do not identify those men with modern "bishops" who exercise authority over many churches in a given geographical area.   Rather, the "overseeing" concerned only the members of the congregation who selected the overseer.   There were, in apostolic times, no lower orders of "clergy" in a whole "diocese" over whom the "bishop" ruled.

Each of the names for this office is somewhat descriptive of the man who holds the job, or of one of the responsibilities that goes with the job.   (1) "Elder" says the man is "older."   Jewish synagogues had chief officials who bore this title.   In their hands was the leadership of the religious life, and in many cases, even the responsibility to ensure wholesome everyday behavior of the worshipers who assembled at the synagogue.   Because of their age, these officials

---

[4] Not every time the noun or verb for "oversee" occurs in the New Testament is it a reference to the office of elder.   In Hebrews 12:15, believers in general are directed to "*look diligently* lest any should fail of the grace of God."   Judas, chosen as one of the apostles, became the traitor and fell from an "office" he once held (Acts 1:20).   Jesus is called "the Shepherd and Bishop of your souls" (1 Peter 2:25).   However, the use of "bishop" at Philippians 1:1 likely does refer to the office of elder.

[5] See J. B. Lightfoot, "The synonyms 'bishop' and 'presbyter'." in his *Commentary on the Epistle to the Philippians*, p. 95-99.   Lightfoot also has a long dissertation on "The Christian Ministry," on pages 181-269 of that same work.   In that, he documents the rise of the monarchical episcopate. In this dissertation, Lightfoot reacts to presbyterian Professor Rothe who had set out to document the thesis that "immediately after the fall of Jerusalem, a council of the surviving apostles and first teachers of the gospel was held to deliberate on the crisis, and to frame measures for the well-being of the Church.   The center of the system thus organized was episcopacy, which at once secured the compact and harmonious working of each individual congregation, and, as the link of communication between the separate brotherhoods, formed the whole into one undivided catholic Church."

[6] The letters to the seven churches, Revelation 2-3, are addressed to the "angel" (the word could also be translated "messenger") of each of the churches.   Some have tried to show that before the apostle John died, these "messengers" were really what we know as "bishops."   If they were, then we cannot call a monarchical bishop a departure from the way Christ intended the church to be, for they would have arisen under John's ministry and during the lifetime of the apostles.   This commentator, having looked at the evidence available, has concluded that it was the death of the last apostle that led to influential men in the cities being looked to for someone to fill the void the death of the apostles made.   So the local evangelist in the bigger churches became the "bishop." (*Note*:   Some books on church history say it was an "elder" who was elevated to the office of "bishop."   We think a more likely candidate is the "evangelist.")

were respected, and their judgments sought. They presided over the worship services at the synagogue; they administered rebuke and discipline where these were necessary; they settled disputes and petty cases that in other nations would have been taken to the law-courts. The Jews were not alone in having "elders." The presiding body of the Spartans was called the *gerousia*, which means "the board of the older men." The law-making body of the Roman government was called the "senate," a word whose root is in "old men." In England, the men who looked after the affairs of the community were called the "aldermen," which means "older men." In Egypt, in New Testament times, each village had village elders who looked after the community's affairs. We presume that, given the widespread familiarity with the idea of "elders" being important community leaders, the same attitude toward "older" men was quickly understood in the churches which selected them. This word describes the leaders as being the older and respected members of the community. (2) "Overseer" indicates a duty or function the leader had. The word, in common 1st century use, implied two things: (a) It implied an oversight or management or superintending task;   (b) It implied responsibility to some higher power and authority. In the church, this higher authority is none other than the Lord Jesus Christ. This word describes one of the functions or tasks of the leaders, which was to oversee or superintend the life and work of the congregations.

It must not be thought that Paul is here calling for the initial organization of the church at Ephesus. According to Acts 20, the church at Ephesus had elders eight or more years before 1 Timothy was written. Instead, Paul is instructing the church that only qualified men are to fill this office whenever vacancies or new needs occur. For more detailed information about the function and qualifications of elders and deacons, see the special studies at the close of comments on chapter 3.

"Aspires to" (or "seeks" ASV) translates *oregetai*, "to reach after" or "desire something" (Thayer). There is no need to think this might be sinful ambition, even though the verb is in the middle voice in the Greek (i.e., the subject is acting for his own benefit). It has always been true that willingness to serve as an elder includes sacrifice, persecution sometimes, or long hours trying to help people with physical and spiritual problems. No one should be chosen an elder against his own wishes. In this commentator's experience, churches which impose the eldership on men who did not really seek it find out (to their sorrow) that it was a mistake to 'talk the man into it.' On the other hand, young men can study the qualifications, and begin now preparing their lives to serve in this capacity.

It is a fine work he desires to do – Surely, when so much is asked of the man who would be elder, and so many extra responsibilities are being undertaken, a word of praise for the man who indicates a willingness to serve in this high office is not out of place.   "Good" is *kalos*, something that is attractive to the beholders, something that is winsome.   "Desire" is another strong verb used to depict the yearning for the office.   Once more, note that eldership is a "work" to be done, not just an office or position of honor to be filled.

3:2 -- An overseer, then, must be – "Then" translates *oun*, a word often translated "therefore."   Because of the nature of the task (verse 1), these qualifications are necessary.   Paul wrote "must be."   How shall we view these qualifications?   (1) Shall we agree with those interpreters who view them as ideals – to come as close as we can, but not expecting each Christian man to exhibit them all?[7]   Yet are these merely ideals when, with but a few exceptions (e.g., not a new convert, the husband of one wife, and [perhaps] able to teach), every Christian could be expected to exhibit these qualities?   If Jesus died for the church, if He wants to present the church spotless and without blemish, if leadership is so important to the future ongoing and welfare of the church (1 Timothy 3:15,16), dare we pick men as leaders who meet only a few of the qualifications?   (2) Shall we ignore the qualifications and choose whom we please?   But this presumes the Holy Spirit meant nothing when He prompted Paul to write "must".   (3) We should treat these as "musts", as necessities!   The Greek word is *dei*, "It is necessary."   If young men were encouraged to develop these necessary qualities in their lives, by the time they were old enough to be "elders," we would have men who met the qualifications.   Admittedly, we are not absolutely certain what some of the qualifications require or prohibit.   Yet we can treat each with full respect for God's commands, seeking to do all of His will, not seeking to avoid any of it.   We apply these qualifications to potential elders, not with the aim of getting rid of all elders, but with the aim of raising up good elders.   (If we interpret them so rigidly and arbitrarily that there are no men who seek to be elders, we do not follow the New Testament example.)   Notice, also, the list of qualifications in Titus 1:6-9 has some additional qualifications not found in Timothy's list, and Timothy has some not found in Titus'.   We must put both lists together to get a comprehensive view of the qualifications to look for in a prospective elder.

Bible students have attempted to arrange the various qualifications under orderly classifications.   Kent (*op. cit.*, p.121-130) offers these:

1) *General* – blameless ("above reproach," NASB).
2) *Moral* – husband of one wife.

---

[7] More will be said on this matter later, but those who treat "elder" and "preacher" as being the same office tend to uphold this "ideals" view. After all, a young man, just graduated from preacher training school and beginning his first ministry, may not be married, or if married may not have children who believe. Hence, we may not expect our preacher (elder, pastor) to meet *all* the qualifications. On the other hand, those who view "elder" and "evangelist" as two different offices have no problem thinking of the qualifications as something more than just "ideals."

3) *Mental* – temperate, prudent, respectable, able to teach.
4) *Personality* – hospitality, not addicted to wine, not pugnacious, gentle, not contentious, free from the love of money.
5) *Domestic* – manages his own household well, children under control.
6) *Christian experience* – not a new covert.
7) *Reputation* – having a good reputation with those outside the church.

J. W. McGarvey[8] offered five categories:

1) *Experience* – not a new convert, able to teach.
2) *Reputation* – having a good reputation to those without.
3) *Domestic* – husband of one wife, ruling his own house well, children under control.
4) *Character* – blameless, not covetous, not greedy of filthy lucre, not self-willed, not a striker, not a brawler, sober, a lover of hospitality.
5) *Habits* – vigilance, not given to much wine.

Seth Wilson for years taught classes on elders and deacons, using just two classifications. He thinks the qualifications can all be subsumed either under *Christian Character* (personal self-discipline and maturity), or under *Christian Experience* (especially how he relates to others). Men whose character and experience warrant are the ones to be selected as leaders by the churches.[9]

Above reproach – *Anepilēmptos* occurs only three times in the New Testament, all in 1 Timothy (at 3:2, 5:7 and 6:14). In classical Greek, the word had the sense of "not open to attack." Some suppose the figure of speech behind the word is that of a wrestler or boxer who leaves no part of his body exposed to the attack of his adversary. "Blameless" (KJV) does not mean the person is never accused, even if falsely. It speaks instead of "one against whom no charge can be sustained" when fair methods of investigation are applied. "Above reproach" does not mean a man must be sinless perfect to be an elder. It does say he should be a man against whom no charge of immorality, or of holding false doctrine, or of habitually practicing any sin, can be sustained. His conduct is such that no one is given a handle by which to injure his reputation. Since verse 7 speaks of the man's reputation outside the church, we suppose "above reproach" speaks of his reputation among the church members who know him best from their day-in and day-out relationships with him. Also note, we look at the man's life since his conversion. What he was is not so important as what in Christ he now is.

---

[8] J.W. McGarvey, *A Treatise on the Eldership* (Murfreesboro, TN: DeHoff Publications, 1956 reprint of 1870 edition), p.53ff.

[9] In fact, keeping the two categories of *Character* and *Experience* in mind as we explain what each qualification means may keep us from making the kind of legalistic and strict interpretations that have sometimes characterized discussions on qualifications for elders and deacons.

The husband of one wife – It is clear from this statement (and from all the others in this passage since every adjective used in this list is masculine) that the overseer, or elder, must be male.   The New Testament record shows no women elders (i.e., bishops) in its church polity.   If we do things as they were done in the New Testament, we will not contemplate selecting women to be elders since they cannot meet this qualification, and the qualifications are "musts."   The Greek could be translated "a man of one woman" or "husband of one wife."[10] Whichever way we render it, it speaks of a man who is true and faithful to one woman.   The actual meaning of this expression has been disputed from earliest times, and has been the occasion of much research and scholarly writing.   Among the views recently advocated are: (1) The "wife" is the church, and the "elder" is married to the church.   This is the view of some Roman Catholics,[11] and is alluded to by Van Oosterzee.[12]   Kent characterizes this as a rather clumsy attempt to protect the Romish doctrine of celibacy for their priests (elders).   (2) Another view is that the thing being prohibited is bigamy or polygamy.   Students of the Old Testament are aware that even some of God's heroes practiced polygamy.   It might be assumed, on the surface, that the practice continued in the Roman Empire, so Paul must show that for leaders this is no longer permitted by God as it once was.   However, there are objections to this view: (a) Kent in his commentary urged that "Polygamy at this time was forbidden in the empire, although some of the Jews are known to have practiced it,[13] and even many Romans found ways to circumvent the Law."[14]   (b) Polygamy is forbidden to all believers, not just those who are church leaders (1 Corinthians 7:2; Hebrews 13:4).   (c) In 1 Timothy 5:9, in the list of qualifications for widows to be cared for by the church, we find the same kind of construction, "a one-man woman." If 3:2 prohibits polygamy, then 5:9 must be a prohibition of polyandry.   Is there any reason to suppose polyandry was a prevailing sexual sin in Ephesus?   Were polyandrous women so plentiful that this qualification had to be considered? While "husband of one wife" may indeed include a prohibition of polygamy, we

---

[10] We've already seen in notes on 1 Timothy 2:14-16, that *gunē* can be translated either "woman" or "wife," and that *anēr* can equally be rendered as "man" (male) or "husband."

[11] Some Catholic writers admit that celibacy for the priesthood was an ecclesiastical law enacted long after Paul was dead, and that 1 Timothy 3:2 must refer to some other qualification than "marriage to the church."

[12] J.J. Van Oosterzee, "1 Timothy" in *Lange's Commentary*, V.8 of the New Testament Series, p.38.

[13] Josephus, *Antiquities* XVII.14, and *Wars* I.477, has been appealed to as proof of polygamy among the Jews.   In AD 212, the *lex Antoniana de civitate* made monogamy the law for Romans, but Jews were excepted.   In AD 393, the Roman emperor Theodosius enacted a special law against polygamy among Jews, since they persisted in the practice.

[14] Kent, *op. cit.*, p.122-3.   In a personal correspondence, Mr. Kent was asked to document his statement that "poly-gamy was forbidden in the empire."   In his reply, Mr. Kent expressed dismay that it was not documented in the book.   He could not recall the source, he wrote.

doubt that such an explanation exhausts the meaning of the apostle's words. (3) Another view, more common in Europe than in America, is that this requirement prohibits remarried widowers from serving as elders. This view holds that a man may marry a new wife after the death of his first one, but that such remarriage disqualifies him from the eldership. There are objections, too, to this view: (a) It cannot be harmonized with what the New Testament says elsewhere on the subject of remarriage. Nowhere do Scriptures suggest that remarriage after the death of a mate is forbidden or even morally objectionable.[15] Exactly the opposite, in fact, is true of younger widows (1 Timothy 5:14). They are to marry and let the husband take care of their needs, rather than being a burden on the church's finances. (b) Again apply the argument about 3:2 and 5:9. If 3:2 forbids remarried men from serving, then 5:9 would have to forbid remarried women from the possibility of aid in their later years. That hardly seems likely. (c) This is the only qualification in the area of sexual morals. Is "remarriage for a widower" the greatest sexual sin, so that it needs to be specifically listed? We think not. (4) Another view, related rather closely to the one just studied, is that this qualification prohibits divorced men from being eligible for the eldership. This was a rather common interpretation in the 20th century. There are several variations in this view: (a) One thinks no record of divorce is to be found in the man's life, either before or after his conversion. (b) Another limits it to no record of divorce or marital infidelity since becoming a Christian. (c) Another thinks that there are legitimate grounds for divorce given by both Jesus and Paul, so this qualification says those with divorces for other than Scriptural reasons are disqualified from the eldership. Objections have been voiced to interpreting this qualification simply as excluding divorce. Again, since this is the only moral qualification in the list, is "divorce" the greatest sexual sin?

(5) "Husband of one wife" says that to be qualified to be an elder, a man must be married, and implies that his marriage is to be exemplary.[16] In favor of this view are: (a) It includes the strong points of several of the other options, but is not limited to those single points.[17] The candidate for eldership must be mar-

---

[15] To cast suspicion on the holiness of the marriage bond, be it first or second marriages, reflects the spirit of asceticism rather than the Spirit of the Lord. Asceticism never was recognized in New Testament times as an acceptable or desirable lifestyle.

[16] Knight (*Commentary on the Pastoral Epistles*, p.158) writes that this qualification "affirms marital and sexual fidelity in monogamous terms."

[17] It would treat any violation of God's will for marriage (one man and one women married for life) as serious. The potential bishop must not have a reputation for extra-marital affairs. This commentator is slow to recommend a man for elder who has been divorced and remarried since becoming a Christian. In countries where polygamy is practiced, he would teach those who wish to become married what God's standards for marriage are. He would discourage newlyweds from thinking in polygamous possibilities. The real problem arises when men were polygamous before their conversion. As they become Christians, are they expected to get rid of all their plural wives but one, so they can measure up to the Biblical standards? What happens to the discarded wives?

ried. It clearly forbids having less than one wife as clearly as it forbids having more than one wife.[18] (b) It treats this qualification as an experience qualification.[19] Elders will surely be called on to counsel couples who are experiencing marital difficulties. If his own marriage is stable, he can speak from experience about what is needed to work through the difficulties, rather than getting a divorce. (c) The fact that this qualification would disqualify Paul and perhaps Timothy from the eldership is irrelevant. Those men held different offices (apostle, evangelist, not elders).[20] (d) It would appear that only a married man would qualify to be an elder, in view of the further instruction (1 Timothy 3:6,7; Titus 1:6) concerning children and managing his household. (e) The idea of holding up the elder's marriage as exemplary would exactly suit the 1st century need for a strong ethic in this matter. In the Roman world, a great and general indisposition towards marriage at all, and the orderly restraints of home and family life, had become so marked a feature in Roman society, that we find Augustus positively enacting laws against celibacy. Divorce was rampant in the 1st century world. A married man who remained faithful to his spouse is just what the world needed to see, in addition to being an example to the flock. The most common objections to this view come from those writers whose church polity does not quite require their "pastors" (elders) to be married, or from those whose church polity requires celibacy of their leaders. It would seem to be a case of special pleading when they opt against this view. The marital relations of one who would be an elder should be such as to cause no offense.

Temperate ("vigilant," KJV) – This and the next two words may be grouped together. They denote a quality of mind. *Nēphalion* is found in the Pastorals and in classical Greek. Etymologically, the term can mean "abstinent, especially in respect to wine."[21] It was used of a trustworthy guard who did not drink on the job. Figuratively, the word denotes a state of mind that in order to keep watchful and alert is careful in the use of meat and drink. The opposite state of

---

[18] Barnes (*op. cit.*, p.143) has this rather pointed comment: "One thing is clear from this passage, that the views of the Papists in regard to the celibacy of the clergy are directly at variance with the Bible."

[19] Under this view, a widower, after long years of marriage, is qualified to be an elder, even after his wife has died. He has had the experience needed to help him do one facet of his function.

[20] A reference to 2 or 3 John, where the apostle John styles himself as "elder," has been advanced as a reason to reject the idea there is a difference between the office of apostle and the office of elder. The use of the passages from John proves more than is desired. In the Greek, those verses read "the elder." Did John's churches have only one elder rather than the plurality everywhere else found in the New Testament? A better explanation of John's title "the elder" is to take it in its literal sense, "the old man." See 1 Peter 5:1 for a similar usage, where the term is a term of affectionate endearment, rather than an official title. We think Paul's designation of himself as "the aged" (*presbutes*, Philemon 1:9) is also a term of endearment.

[21] Some doubt that this qualification speaks of abstinence from wine since that is the topic of another qualification in a later verse (verse 3).

mind is described in Luke 21:34. Some think the English word that comes closest to the meaning of the Greek is "sober" – i.e., sober in judgment, in order to be able to think problems through carefully, in order to make good decisions concerning the physical and spiritual matters the elder faces.

Prudent ("sober," KJV) – *Sōphrona* refers to 'common sense'. One with this trait is not swayed by sudden impulses; he is level-headed. 'Sensible' is the way one version translates it. Another thinks the prospective elder must not have the reputation of being a 'clown.' Another has offered the word 'thoughtful' (of others' sensibilities and needs) as a possible English word to convey the meaning.

Respectable ("of good behavior," KJV) – This word refers to another character quality required of those who would be elders. The word *kosmion* (related to *kosmos*, 'order') is defined in the lexicons as "well-arranged, orderly." The eldership is no place for a man who is known for unfinished plans and unorganized activity. The NASB rendering takes the metaphorical meaning of this word – courteous, good manners, polite, not uncouth or rough. The elder should be a gentleman, not slovenly in his appearance, not of rough and boorish manners, because he has set his mind to so relate to people.

Hospitable – This might be either an attitude qualification or an experience qualification. The inns along the road were scenes of brawls and vice. In a day when there were not many suitable accommodations for Christian travelers, whether missionaries or refugees, or for those on business trips, church members would have to open their homes to afford travelers a safe place to stay. A potential elder cannot expect others to extend all the hospitality; how much better if he sets the example in this virtue.[22] It will take wisdom and practice to know what kind of hospitality, and how much, to extend to visitors, homeless, etc.

Able to teach ("apt to teach," KJV) – *Didaktikon* does not mean the prospective elder is teachable. Rather, it says that he possesses a degree of knowledge that enables him to encourage believers and those who would become believers, and to convict false teachers (cp. Titus 1:9, 2 Timothy 2:25). A man must be a good Bible teacher to be qualified to be an elder.[23] There were not Sunday morning Bible schools in New Testament times, so this does not say that the man has to be a Sunday school teacher before he can be an elder. There are many places where a man can communicate the gospel to another person – in the living room, across the fence, at the grocery store, in the hunting lodge, across the dinner table at the factory. Men can teach others what they know. People with little formal edu-

---

[22] "Hospitality" is a virtue expected of all Christians (Romans 12:13; Hebrews 13:2; 3 John 5ff.)

[23] The KJV rendering "apt to teach" has facetiously been explained as "he doesn't have to do any teaching; if he is apt to teach sometimes, that is all that is required." Hardly!

cation can take others and show them how to fix machinery, or shoe a horse, or plant a garden, or how to drive a car. Anyone ought to be able to tell the less-instructed what they have learned. What the elders have received from apostles, prophets, evangelists, etc., they can certainly repeat to others. The implication is that "teaching" is one of the elders' important tasks. "How to teach" is a skill that can be acquired. It doesn't have to be a native ability. There is also an implication that the prospective elder is to have a "knowledge of the Word of God" if he is going to have something to teach.

3:3 -- Not addicted to wine – The "must be" main verb found in verse 2 is carried on through verse 6. The KJV reads "not given to wine," while the ASV reads "no brawler." The Greek is *mē paroinon*, a word occurring only here and at Titus 1:7 in the New Testament, but a word which (along with *paroinios*) was common in classical Greek in the sense of 'quarrelsome over wine.' The original meaning of the word is of one who sits long beside his wine, and then it came to mean one who becomes quarrelsome after drinking (Kent *op. cit.*, p.128). While the NASB rendering "not addicted to wine" would not absolutely prohibit all drinking (as if to be qualified to be an elder, a man must be a teetotaler), it is not unusual to find rather strong wording at this place. Barnes, for example, has "It means that one who is in the *habit* of drinking wine, or who is accustomed to sit with those who indulge in it, should not be eligible for the eldership." (*Barnes'*, p.144) "'Not given to wine' means not a drunkard ... The prohibition is against imbibing wine to the place where one becomes argumentative, noisy, or unreasonable."[24] "Not under the influence of wine, not violent because of it. Bearing in mind the prevalence of wine drinking in the average Greek and Roman home, and the evils associated with it, we would expect the great apostle to bar from the eldership one addicted to the habit of strong drink. The prohibition holds good today, and for the same reasons."[25] Before someone would affirm that drinking alcoholic beverages in moderation is perfectly compatible with being qualified to be a leader and example in the church, it should be remembered that "temperate" (earlier in this list of the qualifications) does mean abstinence from wine.

Or pugnacious – *Mē plēktēn* also occurs only here and at Titus 1:7, but is used in classical Greek for "striker, brawler." It is a quick-tempered person, ready to use his fists when annoyed, willing to use physical force to attempt to achieve his own ends. "The next words, *no striker*, warn against the same pattern of a quarrelsome, contentious person. This attitude may be present in some people, even without drink; but no contentious person is to be chosen as bishop."[26]

---

[24] W. Carl Ketcherside, *Standard Lesson Commentary*, 1975-76, p.355.

[25] Frank H. Marshall, *Standard Lesson Commentary*, 1958, p.35.

[26] Foster, *op. cit.*, p.362.

("Not greedy of filthy lucre"[27]) – This qualification for elder found in the KJV is not included in most older Greek manuscripts of 1 Timothy 3; it evidently was a later addition to the text.   But this phrase does enjoy integrity at Titus 1:7.   The manuscript authority for the reading of the Textus Receptus, *mē aischrokerdē*, is weak.   Nevertheless, Hervey (*Pulpit Commentary*, p.51) defends of its inclusion at 1 Timothy 3:   "The internal evidence, however, is in its favor, as something is wanted to correspond to *aphilarguron*, just as *paroinon* and *plēktēn* correspond to *epieikē* and *amachon* respectively."   An elder is to be honest and kind in his dealings; his occupation should be above reproach.   It denotes a man free from selfish lust for materialistic gain.   Elders who engaged in preaching and teaching were supported by the other saints (1 Timothy 5:17,18), and Peter declared to them, "Feed the flock of God ... not for what you will get out of it, but because you are eager to serve the Lord" (1 Peter 5:2, LB).

But gentle – *Epieikēs* is very common in classical Greek in the sense of "fair," "fit," "suitable" of things; and of "fair," "kind," "gentle" of persons.   "The ideas of patience, forbearance, and yielding are to be understood in this word.   This sort of personal disposition will avoid much contention and will make the overseer's work more effective.   People do not enjoy being domineered."[28] "Though he never compromises with respect to the truth of the gospel, he is willing to yield when it comes to his own rights, in the spirit of 1 Corinthians 6:7 ... The qualities of yieldedness, fairness, sweet reasonableness, gentleness, helpfulness, and generosity are combined in this word. "[29]   A bishop must be able to control himself when provoked.   He must be considerate toward the feelings and needs of others.   "The word for 'patient' is a very difficult word to translate from the Greek.   A deep significance of the word is the constant awareness of one person for the feelings and needs of others.   Even though the elder may have authority to command, this commanding can be done in such a way that people will not feel they have a domineering person over them."[30]

Uncontentious – Some versions read "not a brawler."   The Greek here is *amachon*, and the adjective denotes one who is not offensively aggressive, who does not always insist on his own rights.   A quick-tempered, arrogant, assertive disposition will create problems, but never settle them.   The bishop is not to be

---

[27] Literally, the Greek says, "not desirous of sordid gain."   The KJV translation "filthy lucre" is used not to indicate that wealth itself is "filthy" or "unrighteous" or "shameful" or "sordid," but because it so often is unrighteously obtained and used.   Jesus, by His parables, encouraged men to prosper. Consecrated Christians with great possessions are an asset of good proportion in the church.   Such are both honest and generous.   The man who is "desirous of sordid gain" is neither.

[28] Kent, *Pastoral Epistles*, p.133.

[29] Hendriksen, *New Testament Commentary on 1 Timothy*, p.125.

[30] Foster, *op. cit.*, p.362

one who insists upon his own way in an obnoxious manner. He keeps his temper and tongue in check at all times, conducting himself in a loving and kind way.

Free from the love of money – The KJV reads "not covetous," though the word here is not the usual word translated "covetous." This word is *aphilarguron*, literally meaning 'not a lover of money.' The word is a compound made up of an alpha-privative, a form of *phileo* ('to love'), and the word for 'silver' (*arguros*). The meaning of the word can be ascertained by comparing the contrasting words used in Hebrews 13:5, "being content with what you have." The man who would be qualified to be an elder must be far removed from making the acquisition of earthly treasure his chief goal in life; one who worships money will be deterred from worshiping God with all his heart. Congregations have often suffered in reputation as well as in spiritual growth through the covetousness of some of her leaders. This qualification, if heeded, can save churches from considerable grief.

3:4 -- *He must be* – In the original, this is a continuation of the sentence begun in verse 2, so the verb "must be" is repeated.

One who manages his own household well – Since the elder is going to be an "overseer" – a manager, superintendent, protector, etc. – of the church members ("the house of God" in verse 5), it would be a good barometer of his ability to "manage" to observe how he does with his own household.[31] "Well" may be explained in the last half of the verse, "having his children under control."

> The way in which a man controls his home reveals his capacity for leadership and government. This ability is most obvious when there are children in the home ... The administrative ability required to cause a home to function smoothly will also be necessary if one is to superintend a church. Deficiency in these matters at home disqualifies a man from serving in a ruling capacity in the church.[32]

"Manages" translates *proistēmi*. Thayer gives these meanings: "to set before, place before, set over; to be over, to superintend, preside over; to be a protector or guardian; to give aid; to rule, to care for, give attention to." The word "emphasizes the leadership role of one who has been placed at the head of the family or church and who is therefore responsible to 'rule, direct and lead' ... The word also has a secondary meaning, i.e., 'to be concerned about' or 'care for'."[33]

Paul turns to the vein of thought first struck in verse 2: the life of the officer

---

[31] It is significant that the same verb (*prohistēmi*) is used here for fathers ruling their children as later for elders ruling the church (1 Timothy 5:17).

[32] Kent, *op. cit.*, p.134.

[33] Knight, *op. cit.*, p.161.

> in the church must be a pattern life for those without and for those within the
> Church's fold, to copy and imitate ... His high standard must be imitatable;
> the example must be one all honest men may follow and copy, if they will.[34]

The man who has learned to so live that his children copy him will know how to be an example that the flock of God can follow.

Keeping his children under control – Must there be children? It seems preferable. The testimony given in this passage for a married eldership is clear. If we make an exception on this qualification by saying, "This statement doesn't require one to have children; Paul is simply stating what is true in most situations", we open the doors to making exceptions on all of them. If children are not required, what then does the word "must" (3:2) mean? The "children" may be his own, or adopted. Must the elder's children be believers, i.e., Christians? That is what it says in Titus 1:6![35] This would lead us to infer that a man must be upwards of 40 years of age before he has enough experience and is old enough to be qualified to be an "elder." Paul used the word "control" (*hupotagē*) at 1 Timothy 2:11, translated there as "submissiveness". An oft-raised question deals with the continued faithfulness of the children after they have grown, moved away from home, and then no longer show a real interest in spiritual things. Does this failure on the part of grown children disqualify a man from being an elder? This commentator's opinion is that the children are no longer part of the potential elder's own "household" at this point. It is while they are in his household that his ability to "lead" so they are submissive believers is one of the qualifications to be looked for. It must be remembered, too, that the children are responsible to God for their own conduct when they are grown. The father's 'child-rearing methods' may have contributed to their later rejection of the church, but that is not always the case. (If it were the case, we might want to think twice about asking that man to serve as elder.)

With all dignity – The meaning of the word "dignity" was explained in notes at 1 Timothy 2:2. "With" is *meta*, meaning "together with", as in 1 Timothy 1:14. It is difficult to decide whether "with all dignity" refers to the children, or to the fathers.[36] Compare Titus 1:6, which leads some commentators to apply the words "with all dignity" (*semnotētos*, the contrary to "dissipation," *asōtia*), to the children. The children of the elder are to exhibit that seriousness and sobriety of conduct which is in accordance with their father's office. Barnes and Kent think it is the *father* who displays the dignity. "The kind of father who cuffs his child-

---

[34] Spence, *op. cit.*, p.216.

[35] The use of *teknon* does not prove the "children" in view are all still just little children. The word *teknon* can be used of adults. See 1 Timothy 1:2,18, 5:4.

[36] This may be one of those cases in the New Testament where both ideas are right.

ren around will usually treat church members in similar fashion. Even in the close association which exists among members of a family, there must be a dignified and respectful relationship maintained."[37] This last phrase would tell how the father keeps his children under control. He uses "dignity" to do it.

3:5 -- (But if a man does not know how to manage his own household – This whole verse is in parentheses. It is not a separate qualification for elders; it explains the reason for the qualification given in verse 4. "Manage" and "house-hold" are the same words used in verse 4. "Household" includes the wife and children and, in some cases, servants. There is a 'how-to-do-it' the man needs to know by experience before he is asked to take a leadership role in the church.

How will he take care of the church of God?) – "Take care of" translates *epimelomai*. The only other place in the New Testament where this verb occurs is in the parable of the Good Samaritan. The personal and thorough care given by the Samaritan is a pattern for the kind of care church members may need. The word speaks of having a tender care for the church. It is not an arbitrary authority the elder practices. The "church" is that local congregation which the elder was chosen by to serve as their "overseer." "Church of God" reflects the truth that the "church" (congregation, assembly) belongs to God.[38] "The way a man conducts himself and leads his household will be an indication of the way he would act in a responsible position in the church. Likewise, the results that he obtains within his own family will be an indication of the results that may be expected in the household of God."[39] The argument is that inability to manage the home indicates a likely inability to lead the church as she needs to be led.

3:6 -- *And* not a new convert – "New convert" ("novice" KJV) translates *neophutos*, a word used of "planting" a tree. A new convert is newly planted in the faith. This word does not refer to age. A man of 80 years can be a "neophyte" if he was just recently converted to Christ. It takes time to learn the will of God through His Word, and to develop the requisite spiritual characteristics required of an elder; and it takes time to gain experience in the work of the Lord.[40] Men who have just recently been baptized are not yet ready

---

[37] Kent, *op. cit.*, p.129.

[38] The word *ekklēsia* could be used for assemblies other than the church, so it regularly must be specified what "assembly" we are talking about.

[39] Foster, *op. cit.*, p.362.

[40] In Acts 14:23 we find Paul and Barnabas appointing elders in congregations that at most were 2 or 3 years old. Hence, the converts had not been Christians longer than that. Weren't they "novices"? Was Paul there doing something that he writes against in 1 Timothy? Not necessarily. Converts from Jewish backgrounds, especially the mature leaders of the synagogues, might not take as long to grow the requisite qualifications for elders as perhaps a convert from paganism might.

to be an elder.   The reason why this is so is given in the rest of the verse.

Lest he become conceited – The root of "conceited" is *tuphos*, 'smoke.' Whether the idea is that his real position and the needs of the congregation are 'obscured in smoke,' or whether his own ideas about himself are like living in a 'cloudland' (a land of delusion), is not easy to determine.

And fall into the condemnation incurred by the devil – "Fall into" is a verb used with reference to sin and its consequences.   The old arch-enemy of God is identified by several names in the Scriptures.   He is called the "devil"; the Greek word *diabolos* means 'accuser'.   He is known as "Satan", the transliteration of a Hebrew word that means 'adversary' – i.e., he is opposed to all that God is trying to do in His world and in His people.   He is known as "the serpent" because that is how he appeared to Eve in the Garden.   As the NASB marginal note on "incurred" shows, all the Greek says is "fall into the condemnation of the devil." It is not certain what this phrase means: (a) Perhaps "of the devil" is an objective genitive.   If so, it means that the proud novice falls into the same condemnation which the devil receives because of his pride.[41]   It has often been taught that the sin that led the devil to rebel and then led to his expulsion from the courts of heaven (Revelation 12:7-9) was pride.   Not only did his "condemnation" include expulsion from heaven, ultimately the devil will be cast into the lake of fire.   Care must be exercised before making the assertion that it was "pride" that caused the devil to fall.   It is not proper to use Isaiah 14 or Ezekiel 28 as passages from which to learn about the origin of the devil, and the reason for his fall.   And that his sin was pride is only one possible interpretation of 1 Timothy 3:6.   (b) Perhaps it means that the proud novice is easier prey for the devil's temptations – a condemnation to a life of being subject to the intrigues and lures the devil uses for bait.   (c) Perhaps "of the devil" is a subjective genitive.   If so, it means the condemnation or accusation which the devil ("the accuser of the brethren") makes against the novice.   If we accept this interpretation, then *krima* would be used in the same sense that *krisis* is used in Jude 9.   The devil still makes accusations against the brethren before the throne of God (Revelation 12:10) just as he did in the case of Job (Job 1:9).   A new convert who has succumbed to the sin of pride

---

We've noted that some qualifications given in Titus are not included in this list in 1 Timothy, and vice versa.   We do not think it is because different qualifications hold true for different congregations.   It is not likely that the reason "not a new covert" is omitted from the list in Titus is that Crete was a new work, and so this qualification could not yet be insisted upon.

As new congregations are planted, they can go for a time without elders.   All the men who show promise of future leadership can be trained, and called upon for input concerning matters that affect the life of the congregation.   Only when they meet the qualifications are they formally chosen and installed into office.

[41] This interpretation was the one accepted by the NASB translators, and is why they supplied the word "incurred."

would give the devil a real opening for making accusations. Since we cannot tell whether the genitive case ("of the Devil") is objective or subjective, perhaps interpretations (a) and (c) are both true.

3:7 -- And he must have a good reputation with those outside *the church* – This qualification is a "must" – as are all the qualifications listed beginning with verse 2 – and refers, of course, to the prospective elder's life since his conversion. To be qualified to become an elder, the man should possess a stainless reputation for integrity and honor with the world outside the church. Non-church members will often judge a church by the lives of its leaders. If their lives are not above reproach, the careless living might become a stumbling block potential converts could appeal to in an effort to excuse their lack of interest in becoming a Christian. The KJV reads "good report", an attempt to translate *maturian kalēn*. *Maturian* is sometimes translated "testimony," meaning the witness a man gives to others by word and deed. (It is seldom, if ever, used of the kinds of "testimonies" sometimes heard in modern "testimony meetings.") The NASB has rightly added "the church" to the expression "those outside", for the phrase obviously refers to those who are not members of the church. "There is something blame-worthy in a man's character if the consensus of outside opinion is unfavorable to him, no matter how much he may be admired and respected by his own party."[42]

So that he may not fall into reproach and the snare of the devil – Both these expressions are a bit ambiguous, but "snare" seems to be a further explanation of "reproach" (we would translate *kai* in this place as "even" rather than "and"). If this is true, then the "snare" is the trap laid by the devil into which a careless living Christian will easily fall when he is among outsiders. This appears to be a more satisfactory explanation than to think "snare" refers to the devil's sin of pride that the previous verse had reference to. "Reproach" would then speak of the accusations the non-church members would make as they mocked him to his face about being chosen as a church leader. "We can imagine how, on the morning after this undeserving person's election to office, the men who work with him will greet him with the mocking exclamation, 'What do we hear now? Have they actually made *you* an elder ... *you*?' And the devil will rejoice."[43] Another suggestion is that "reproach" refers to the sneers non-church people would direct at a church which would choose such an unsavory character (as they know the man to be) for a prominent position of leadership. To defy public opinion and select unqualified men for leadership will only bring discredit on the church. The teaching here (verses 6,7) about the devil is deserving of some comment:[44]

---

[42] Kent, *op. cit.*, p.131. Kent is quoting Newport J.D. White's commentary.

[43] Hendriksen, *New Testament Commentary on 1 Timothy*, p.129.

[44] Partially excerpted from Spence's comments on "1 Timothy" in *Ellicott's Commentary*, p.218.

(1) The personality of the devil is distinctly affirmed.   (2) That unhappy being has fallen and has been condemned, and is now able to lay snares for and to tempt men.   (3) An over-weening pride seems to have been the cause which led to this once mighty one's fall.   (4) All ideas of dualism – the old Persian belief of two equally and eternally opposed powers presiding respectively over the realms of light and darkness – are distinctly here repudiated by Paul.   (5) Paul, in the course of his presentation of the qualifications of elders, casually introduces the devil – as the enemy of man; as one who at some remote period rebelled, was crushed, and condemned; but to whom, in the supreme providence of God, some terrible power over man was left.   Paul could hardly have introduced these statements so casually unless they already were accepted doctrines within the church.   (6) What was true of the devil at Ephesus, should they choose men with poor outside reputations as their leaders, was evidently (in the mind and will of the Holy Spirit who inspired these words) something true of the devil's activity in all time and places where leaders might be selected.

SPECIAL STUDY #2

THREE STUDIES ON THE ELDERSHIP

THE NEW TESTAMENT PICTURE OF ELDERS OF THE CHURCH
by Seth Wilson.

INTRODUCTION:

We do not own the church. We do not govern it. Christ bought it with His blood, and He is absolute Head over everything pertaining to the church. It is His body and His Kingdom (Ephesians 1:21-23; Colossians 1:13, 16-18; Romans 14:17). The people who make up the body are subject to Him as a King. He is not merely Head of an institution's corporate business. He is Lord of all (Acts 2:36; 10:36). All authority in heaven and on earth is His (Matthew 28:18).

No majority can ever be large enough to set aside His will on anything, or *to establish any other rule over His people.* Any vote by any member or officer of the church does not express our right to decide or rule. It expresses the consent each of us gives to a person or a policy as being what Christ wants for His church.

We do not have a right to vote in the church as in a democracy; but we have a duty to God to express our understanding of His will for us and to work for agreement with others concerning His will. A "vote" may not settle what is the Lord's will; it may only begin a devoted study and effort to clarify it for all the members. If Christ's will can be found in the Bible, we should find it, clarify it and accept it without voting.

Of course, the whole church can agree that other matters (not settled by scripture) may be done according to the decision of a certain number of members, or by some responsible representatives of the congregation. But a vote never gives any majority any right to disregard any minority (Matthew 18:6-10).

Christ Himself gave to the church ministers of His word to teach His will: apostles, prophets, evangelists, pastors and teachers (Ephesians 4:10,11). These pastors are shepherds, also called elders or bishops (overseers). The Holy Spirit, said Paul, made them overseers (Acts 20:28). And the Holy Spirit, speaking through Peter and Paul, commanded them to do the shepherding (Acts 20:28-35; 1 Peter 5:1-4). "They watch in behalf of your souls, as they that give account" unto the Lord (Hebrews 13:17). They are to be esteemed exceeding highly in love for their work's sake (1 Thessalonians 5:12,13), and they are to receive the additional honor of financial support (1 Timothy 5:17,18).

WHAT IS AN ELDER?

The New Testament gives a fuller picture of the elder and his work than most people realize. Please read each passage.

1. *An older man.* The Greek word *presbyteros* gives us the English derivatives "presbyter" and "presbytery" (1 Timothy 4:14). He is a man of maturity, looked up to for his experience, wisdom and leadership ability.

2. *An overseer.* Our English word "bishop" is derived from *episkopos*, which means overseer (Acts 20:28; Titus 1:5,7).

3. *A shepherd* of God's flock (Acts 20:28; 1 Peter 5:1-4). "Pastors" in Ephesians 4:11 is used to translate the *poimen*, which everywhere else is translated shepherd.

4. *A steward, manager of God's business* (Titus 1:7). This passage does not say that he is to be blameless in living; but he is to be a man with nothing laid to his charge, because he is God's manager of the household of God on earth.

5. *A teacher.* (1 Timothy 3:2; 5:17; Ephesians 4:11-16; Titus 1:9-11).

6. *A superintendent, caretaker*, one presiding or taking the lead (1 Timothy 3:5; 5:17; 1 Thessalonians 5:12). In these passages *prohistēmi* is sometimes translated "rule" or "are over you"; but it means to stand before, lead, attend to. Jesus told the apostles they must not exercise authority as rulers do (Matthew 20:25-27). Peter taught the elders they must not be lords over the flock (1 Peter 5:1-4).

7. *A leader.* In Hebrews 13:7,17,24 some versions say "them that have the rule over you"; but it is a form of *hegeomai* and is better translated "your leaders" in at least forty distinct versions I have checked. These include four by preachers of our Restoration Movement, and at least two Roman Catholic versions done by large committees. The four best English versions made before the King James Version all said: "them that have the oversight."

The point is this: there is no Bible passage which clearly makes elders *rulers* of the church! They have responsibility to lead, teach, oversee, help, serve and show the way; but they have no authority to coerce anyone.

Members are indeed taught to obey (*peithomai*, be persuaded, trust, rely upon) them, and to submit (*hupeiko*, yield) to them (Hebrews 13:17); but these are milder verbs than ones used in teaching Christians to serve (*douleuo*, be a slave) and be subject to and in reverence for Christ.

Summary: Elders are men of faith, understanding, commitment, exemplary life and character, experience, teaching ability, and loving concern for every member.   They are leaders, whether elected or not, and not made such by being appointed an elder.

WHAT SHOULD ELDERS DO?

Read these passages which state what elders in the early church were doing or were told to do.   The pictures are in them, not in my remarks.   I only list them with brief notes of what I see there.   Am I seeing something that is not there?   Is there something there which you have not seen before?

1. *Acts 11:19-30*.   Elders may handle money for the church and oversee benevolence.   Didn't Barnabas know about Acts 6:1-6?

2. *Acts 15:2,4,5,22,23; 16:4*.   Elders are obligated to help settle doctrinal disputes.   Their most constant responsibility is to find out what God has really revealed and to teach it.

3. *Acts 20:28*.   Elders shepherd all the members of God's flock.   They are overseers of the church by God's appointment.

4. *Acts 20:29-32*.   Elders protect Christ's church from false teachers, whether members or outsiders.   They use God's Word for this, and with it build up the members.   Elders *feed, lead*, and *guard* members of the household of faith.

5. *Acts 20:33-35*.   Elders work to meet the needs of each Christian and "help the weak" even at their own expense and when it involves hard work, after Paul's example.   (Cf. 1 Thessalonians 2:3-12; 2 Corinthians 11:28,29; 12:14-18).

6. *Acts 21:17-24*.   Elders lead in planning strategy and over-coming obstacles.   They give advice to all, even to an apostle.

7. *Ephesians 4:11-16*.   Elders use the Word of God to develop all the members to maturity, understanding of Christ, unity of faith, and ability of each one to do his or her part in the body of Christ.   They promote effective use of each member.   What a big job!   Memorize this *key* description; repeat it often.

8. *1 Thessalonians 5:12,13*.   Elders work among the believers, lead, attend to, counsel and admonish all of them.

9. *Galatians 6:1-3*.   Elders surely are among those "who are spiritual" and who restore gently any who fall into sin.

10. *1 Timothy 3:2,4.* Elders are expected to teach. At home too.

11. *1 Timothy 3:5.* Elders take care of the church.

12. *1 Timothy 5:17.* Elders lead and maintain the church, especially by laboring in the word and teaching.

13. *Titus 1:7.* They are God's stewards, managers of God's affairs, superintendents of His business. They do not do all the work of the church, but they lead, assist and oversee it all.

14. *Titus 1:9-11.* Elders persuade Christians to accept sound doctrine; they correct, refute and silence false teachers.

15. *Titus 3:10.* Elders lead in admonishing the makers of division again and again. They lead the church in refusing the influence of such folk, if they do not change.

16. *Hebrews 13:17.* Elders watch out for the spiritual welfare and security in Christ of each Christian. They lead and teach so that persons obedient to Christ rightly submit to their teaching and care. They do not rule as Christ taught the apostles not to rule (Matthew 20:25-28); they teach and uphold the rule of Christ in every part of every heart.

17. *James 5:14-20.* They pray for the sick, including counseling and aiding in confession of sin, restoring sinners.

18. *1 Peter 5:1-4.* Elders do not "run the church" or exercise authority; they are shepherds who set an effective example for all and who lead members in a holy and mature walk with Christ. Their reward is from the Chief Shepherd.

Elders have responsibility for every kind of action and program by which all the members are built up in the faith, matured spiritually, completely filled with Christ, and used in the service of the Lord. The key word is responsibility:

1. *Responsibility for INSTRUCTION* of all in divine truth,

2. *Responsibility for PROTECTION* from being led astray,

3. *Responsibility for CORRECTION* of ideas and actions which are contrary to Christ's rule in each of us.

4. *Responsibility for DIRECTION* of every member in a life that works to contribute to the growth and good of all the rest.

Each of these applies until we all attain unto *PERFECTION* in the likeness and activity of Christ in each one (Ephesians 4:11-16; Colossians 1:27-29). Read the descriptions of the life to be lived (Ephesians 4:17; 6:19) and think of the great changes that had to be made in each of thousands of people.

The responsibility of the elders is not to do what the people want, but to serve and lead the people in the will of Christ, even when resisted or persecuted.

Elders are not merely board members like directors of a corporation, meeting to hear reports and make decisions for others to carry out. They are much more than of officer figures to stand at worship stations for part of the Sunday ceremonies.

Elders are not bosses, but servants of servants in a serving brotherhood of love. They do not make rules for the church. Christ had done that. In their responsible work they do make decisions, and it cannot be completed in board meetings.

Their task is difficult and not always welcomed; it is to *change people's minds*! But who can do that? We cannot, but the Word of God can – not simply as words undigested, but the Word of God realized as controlling conviction and actualized in real lives, full of hope and love. Acts 20:32.

Yes, elders have to make decisions and form judgments – a just as other Christians do. Theirs have more influence, and may lead and assist in the judging we all have to do. They certainly do not make all the decisions and judgments and hand them down as binding on others because of authority. What they really are to do is teach and show the will of Christ.

If elders do their work with real submission to Christ and with enduring love for His people, they will have effective influence – enough to look like authority! They will not need authority. When men with the Word of God in their hands and love of Christ in their hearts come to minister God's truth and grace with humble and gracious persistence they are more irresistible than they would be if they used authority.

The work is not done by human skills and institutional devices. It is the work of Christ by the transforming power of His Word and His Holy Spirit. We cannot make Christians by hand, or by any other kind of manipulation. We can offer our hearts and lives to God, for Him to work through us as carriers of His Word, examples of His work, expressions of His love.[45]

---

[45] Seth Wilson, *Elders and Deacons According to the Bible,* Dallas, Tx: Bible Bookstore, 1965.

THE MUST OF A SPIRITUALLY QUALIFIED ELDERSHIP
by Russell E. Boatman

In 1 Timothy 3:1-7 and Titus 1:6-9 Paul states the qualifications we must look for in the men whom we would appoint to be elders. Twenty qualifications are given, thirteen of them stated positively and seven negatively.

WHAT AN ELDER MUST BE

1. *Blameless, without reproach.* The term is metaphorical, used to describe a fighter who keeps himself so well guarded his adversary cannot get at him. Elders must do this in respect to the spiritual warfare in which they are engaged. Paul declared they "must have a good report from them that are without"!

2. *The husband of one wife.* The special emphasis in this phrase should be upon the word one, rather than upon the "husband"; polygamy and adultery, not bachelorhood, are the things condemned. Still, if elders are to be indeed pastors of the flock, according to the duty assigned to them by the New Testament Scriptures, common sense would prescribe that elders be men who are married, and happily married at that. Moreover, a man is better fitted to cope with situations which arise if his own relationships in life are normal. (See next item.)

3. *Having children that believe, who are not accused of riot or unruly.* The reason stated is that "if a man know not how to rule his own house, how shall he take care of the church of God?" Again we see that ideal family relationships help to qualify a man for leadership in the household of the faith. I have a growing conviction that God meant that the eldership should be limited to married men with families which show evidence of their ability to lead others in the way of the Lord. Couples not privileged to bring children into the world could well adopt children. The hospitality that the Scriptures require of elders could certainly include that act of grace.

4. *Given to hospitality.* This is fast becoming a lost virtue among the elders of the churches of Christ, as any evangelist or other visitor among the churches can testify. It is becoming an unwritten rule in our churches that the preacher must house and feed the special guests; and oft-times the casual visitors, the strangers in the Lord's House, are not greeted by the elders, the elders in many cases arriving too late and leaving too early to meet the visitors in the house of God.

5. *A lover of good.* This may be contrasted with the injunction against being a lover of filthy lucre, but it need not be limited to just that. This is a phrase that best profits us when we meditate upon it instead of being satisfied when we have simply interpreted it.

6. *Sober-minded*. Literally, of a sound, steady mind. An elder should be a man you can count on, from whom you know what to expect. A man "turned about by every wind of doctrine" or swayed by "smooth speech and flattering tongues" or capable of being intimidated or "used" by pressure groups, is no man for the eldership.

7. *Just*. A natural sense of justice, of fairness, is essential to the eldership, since as overseers they are often called upon to exercise judgment.

8. *Holy*. The doctrine of sanctification is not popular among people. Yet "without sanctification (or holiness, KJV) no man shall see the Lord" (Hebrews 12:14). Worldly elders make a worldly church. Holiness in the eldership is an imperative if we are to have a restored church of Christ-restored in its fruits and manner of life as well as in its ordinances and names.

9. *Self-controlled*. Many an elder is but the mouthpiece of his wife. One knows oft-times how a certain elder will vote on a given issue because his wife has freely "spoken her piece" before the issue comes to a vote. Other men are controlled by habits – habits of thinking and doing. They do not have the smoking habit, the smoking habit has them, to mention only one prevalent habit in particular.

10. *Holding to the faithful word which is according to the Scripture*. Here is another phrase that needs to be meditated upon and acted upon rather than merely interpreted. (Surely it demands an accurate knowledge of the faith according to the New Testament).

11. *Apt to teach, able to exhort*. One who is really able to teach is "apt" to do so. The Lord gave elders to be "pastors and teachers." We call the preacher "the pastor," which he is not, and then scold the elders because they do little or no pastoring. The preacher may be a pastor, but not *the* pastor. My judgment is that preachers should be satisfied with the titles the scriptures give to them (preacher, minister, and evangelist), and not appropriate also the titles which belong to the elders (pastors, bishops, and elders) and the titles which belong to God (Reverend and Father).

12. *Able to convict the gainsayers*. "But sanctify the Lord God in your hearts; and be ready always to give an answer to every man that asketh you a reason for the Hope that is in you, with meekness and fear; having a good conscience, that, whereas they speak evil of you, as of evil-doers, they may be ashamed that falsely accuse your good conversation (meaning manner of life) in Christ" (1 Peter 3:15,16). This was not spoken only to preachers. It is a shame when men who can learn a trade in a few months, after years of membership in the church have

to "ask the preacher" before they can refute a false doctrine with the truth that is contained in the Word.

13. *Orderly*. "Let everything be done in decency and in order," is an apostolic injunction. It takes "orderly" to carry it out.

WHAT AN ELDER MUST NOT BE

1. *Self-willed*. The self-willed man is a carnal man. He will look after his own interests, but cannot be depended upon to serve the interests of God's kingdom.

2. *Soon angry*. It is nowhere said that any elder cannot become angry. Even our Lord was known to manifest the fury of righteous indignation. But an elder must not be "hot-headed". He must be self-controlled.

3. *A brawler*. The task of an elder calls for men who are to accomplish by the process of teaching and patient guidance the end to which they are appointed.

4. *A striker*. A striker, literally a pugnacious person. The eldership is no place for a person who "loves to scrap." His love for scrapping will precipitate crises that patient teaching would prevent.

5. *Greedy*. Paul calls covetousness idolatry in Colossians 3:5. A covetous man will never lead the church into a program of advancement. Someone has said that no man who does not love the Lord enough to give at least a tithe has a right to vote against expenditures for which other men are willing to pay, or to vote for expenditures of which he is not willing to pay his rightful share.

6. *Contentious*. A man who "wears his feelings on his sleeve" or "carries a chip on his shoulder" should not be appointed to the eldership under any circumstances.

7. *A novice*. If it is necessary for candidates for the deaconship to "first be proved," how much more is this true of those who would be elders. It is easier to get men into "church offices" than it is to get them out if they prove unworthy.

"BUT WE BESEECH YOU, BRETHREN, TO KNOW THEM THAT LABOR AMONG YOU, AND ARE OVER YOU IN THE LORD, AND ADMONISH YOU: AND TO ESTEEM THEM EXCEEDING HIGHLY IN LOVE FOR THEIR WORK'S SAKE." –   1 Thessalonians 5:12,13.[46]

---

[46] From Russell E. Boatman, "The Must of a Spiritually Qualified Eldership, " *Christian Standard*, 83:6 (Feb. 8, 1947), p.93ff.

THE WORK OF THE ELDERS IN THE NINTH STREET CHURCH OF ELDON, MISSOURI
by Roy Weece

INTRODUCTION -- Initial suggestions to Elders and Deacons

1. Remember Qualifications – You're now being watched more than ever!

2. We are to be Peace-makers – not trouble makers.

3. Speak your feelings here – Don't speak against each other elsewhere. Don't conspire or plot against one another.

4. Listen to others' opinions. Respect them! Go with Majority Vote. Don't always insist on selling only your own idea.

5. Constantly look for Growth ideas.

6. Keep "What's BEST for the Congregation" in mind.

7. Present a "united front" to the church – You'll be a personality as a group, both Elders and Deacons.

8. Problems will increase as family grows. Don't be frustrated by them.

THE ELDERS' WORK

1. SHEPHERDING PROGRAM. We divided the church into six groups. Each Elder is assigned a group for one year. He is to call on every family at least once within the year. This can best be done by appointment with one family each week. When someone is sick, the Elder over that group calls immediately. When someone is absent, the Elder over that group calls immediately to check why.

2. RECLAIMING DELINQUENT CHURCH MEMBERS. We checked the membership list to find who presently showed no signs of love for Christ. We prayed about them and our responsibilities toward them. We contacted them by letter and asked them to meet with us for thirty minutes at the church building. We talked with them about their earlier interest in Christ. We questioned them about their delinquency. We encouraged them to return to Christ and meet with us again. Two of those we talked with stated their desire to "go the world's way." We announced this to the congregation.

3. COUNSELING WITH YOUTH AND ADULTS. We have called in youth

Page 134   Special Study #2

five at a time and talked with them about their relationship to Christ. We have talked with married couples who were contemplating separation. Also disputes among members who asked that we do so. (Elders must build these "bridges" and people will come.)

4. APPOINTMENT OF TEACHERS IN THE CHURCH. Each July, the Elders meet to appoint all the teachers for Sunday morning classes, Sunday evening classes, Wednesday evening classes, and any special classes to be taught that year. (The Elders also appoint annually money counters, a Bible School preside, music leaders, Bible School secretary, organist, pianist, song leader for Bible School, church dinner sponsors, church recorder, financial recorder, floral arranger, etc.)

5. MISSIONS. We are presently supporting two Bible Colleges and one foreign missionary with a percent of our offering. We are supporting one man in Canada and two children's homes on a part-time basis. We have sent four young men to other countries for summer work (i.e., one each year for the past four). We are presently paying the salary of one man in another country. Our missions giving for this year will be about 35 to 40 percent of total income.

6. WOMENS' WORKS. The ladies of the church who are willing are assigned tasks related to the church life. Twenty different ladies are capably filling jobs related to the church office. Others work in other areas.

7. ASSIGNMENTS FOR DEACONS. Realizing that the Deacons are a special group of servants in the church, the Elders assign each of the eight Deacons a major task in the church life. These assignments release the Elders and the evangelist for their responsibilities before God. The Deacons' tasks presently are: Lord's table, widows, supply room, buildings, utilities, literature, ushering, grounds, treasurer.

8. FACILITIES. The Elders have determined the needs of the church in the area of building expansion. We have built three times in the past ten years. We are presently in a building program.

9. RELATIONSHIP TO LOCAL EVANGELIST. The Elders have released him for teaching and evangelization throughout the United States. They have recognized the value of his being "itinerant" as well as "located." They have felt free to discuss his work with him and have been specific in work assignments.

10. NEW CONVERTS. When a person gives his or her life to Christ and is baptized immediately, he is then introduced to the Elders and his relationship to them is explained. One Elder then takes three pages of instruction to the home of the new convert. The pages are: "What the Church Teaches." "What You,

as a New Christian, can expect from the Elders and Evangelist."   "What God Expects of You as a New Child."

11. LETTERS TO NON-RESIDENT MEMBERS.   When a member moves to another city, a letter is sent encouraging him to identify himself with the Christians there.   A letter is sent to the church telling them of the arrival of the Christian.

12. ENCOURAGING YOUNG MEN TO QUALIFY FOR THE ELDERSHIP. The Elders have summoned other men to special meetings in order to encourage them to prepare themselves to be Elders.   This has also been done in private talk.

13. YOUNG PREACHER INTERNSHIP.   In two recent summers, a young Bible college student was employed by the church with hopes that he might help us and we might help him.   We have talked of employing a young preacher after he graduates from Bible College and giving him some "on the field" training for six months or a year before he moves on to another work.

14. NEW CHURCH.   Property on the lake was offered with the understanding that a new church be started.   The Elders investigated the possibility of doing so by a scheduled meeting with interested people in that area.   If such a project continues, the Elders will guide it until such a time that it can continue on its own strength of local leadership.

15. TEACHING OF ELDERS.   Some of the Elders are presently teaching three classes each week.   All are teaching.   They have taught special courses for 6-8 periods in addition to the regular teaching.

16. INVITING CHURCH to bring grievances to them by setting definite time when members could come in.[47]

---

[47] Roy Weece, A Session of the *Elders and Deacon's Training Workshop*, held in Moberly, Mo., at Union Avenue Christian Church, Feb. 1970.

B. Office of Deacon.   3:8-13

3:8 -- Deacons – The word translated "deacon" means "servant, assistant, minister."[48]   It is probable that in this context of church offices, "deacon" is used in its specialized sense to designate an office.[49]   Besides this passage in 1 Timothy, there are a few isolated references to the office of deacon in the New Testament.[50]   Though the noun "deacon" is not used in Acts 6:2-6, most Bible scholars conclude that the seven men chosen to assist the apostles were the first deacons to be chosen.   The verb translated "to serve [tables]," *diakoneō*, is from the same family of words as "deacon," *diakonos*.   The letter to the Philippians is addressed to the "overseers and deacons," Philippians 1:1.   Certain passages in the epistles are thought to refer to the office of deacon, though our English translations sometimes mask that possibility from our view.   Deacons may be alluded to under the term *antilēpsis*, "helps" (1 Corinthians 12:28).   Others appeal to 1 Corinthians 12:5, "varieties of ministries."   Deacons may be alluded to in Romans 12:7 ("serving").   Deacons may be alluded to in 1 Peter 4:11 ("whoever serves").   The plural here in 1 Timothy may indicate that several men from each congregation will be functioning in this office at the same time.   The exact nature and duties of this office are nowhere set forth in any systematic way.   Some have suggested that the absence of two requirements given for elders ("able to teach" and "take care of the church of God") indicates that these two tasks are not part of the necessary duties of deacons.   For some possible duties, see the special study at the close of comments on chapter 3 for a special study on "The Deacons."

Likewise *must be* – As the italics indicate, there is no verb specifically stated in the Greek.   But the adverb "likewise" makes it clear which verb is to be supplied, namely, the same verb that has controlled the list of qualifications since verse 2.

Men of dignity – This same term (*semnos*) was found in the list of qualifications for elder (verse 4).   The ones considered to become deacons are males (*anēr*).[51] (Whether or not there was an office of "deaconess" for women will be studied at

---

[48] Care must be exercised here.   In the contemporary world, "minister" is a title often given to the man who does the work of an evangelist.   In the New Testament, "deacon" was an office separate from "evangelist."

[49] Any one (apostles, evangelists, etc.) who serves may be styled a *diakonos*, a minister, a servant, and there is no reference to the office of "deacon" at all in such passages.   It is a rather common designation of "Christian leaders" (1 Corinthians 3:5; 2 Corinthians 3:6, 6:4; Ephesians 3:7, 6:21; Colossians 1:7,23, 25, 4:7, etc.), likely because Jesus taught his leadership trainees they were to be servants, just like He was.

[50] There are enough references to justify the conclusion that there is no need to suppose that the office of deacon was a late development, and therefore, since they are named in 1 Timothy, this letter is to be dated much later than the traditional date assigned to it.

[51] See comments on the difference between *anēr* and *anthropos* at 1 Timothy 2:8 on page 58.

1 Timothy 3:11.)   Men who would become deacons are to manifest a quiet dignity that inspires respect.

Not double-tongued – *Dilogos*, from *dis* ("twice") and *lego* ("to speak"), denotes a person who says one thing to one person and something different to another. Or the term may include gossip in general.   The office of deacon (an intermediate position, dealing with the elders on the one hand, and with the people on the other) would give special temptation along this line.   If he were double-tongued in reporting the attitudes and conduct of the one to the other, havoc and dissension in the church would result in short order.   Likewise, in his role of visitation, delivery of food, and assistance in general, he meets and talks to the various families who make up the congregation.   How easy to spread gossip, unless he is very watchful.   The church cannot afford double-tongued members, for they bring misery and trouble upon the people.   In the words of James, the deacon must know how to bridle his tongue.

Or addicted to much wine – The Greek phrase is different from that given as the elder's qualification, "not addicted to wine."   This does not necessarily mean that since much wine is prohibited, then a little wine is allowed.   Before such a conclusion is drawn, one must understand the time and place to which this letter was addressed.   In Paul's time, Ephesian society did not have modern means of water purification.   In such a situation, diluted wine became the common beverage.   It was a way to avoid the diseases and sicknesses that can be picked up by drinking contaminated water.   The one who would become a deacon must be careful not to abuse this usage.   Wine can become addictive; if one is not careful, even what is drunk at the table can be the beginning of a life of addiction. Some men, in some cases wishing to justify questionable behavior when it comes to alcoholic beverages, will say that the fact the man who would qualify to be a deacon does not have to be a total abstainer means that Christians today can use alcoholic beverages in moderate amounts.   Before one uses this to justify drinking in moderation, he should consider that present-day wines are considerably higher in alcoholic content.[52]   (Distillation, which makes possible a higher alcohol content than simple fermentation, was not invented until c. AD 600.)   One's decision about total abstinence must also take into account the warnings of 1 Corinthians 10 about our responsibility of example to others.

Or fond of sordid gain ("not greedy of filthy lucre" KJV) – When "lucre" is the price for doing wrong, it is "filthy."   When lucre is sought on occasions where none is due, it is "filthy."   Balaam, Gehazi, Achan (Joshua 7:21), and Judas Iscariot (John 12:6) are prominent examples of professed servants of God

---

[52] William Patton, *Bible Wines: Or the Laws of Fermentation and Wines of the Ancients* (Forth Worth, TX.: Star Bible and Tract Corp., 1976).   First issued in 1874, and reprinted many times since.

who got in trouble because of this sin.   We infer from this qualification that the office of deacon may give the holder a temptation and an opportunity to yield to this impulse.   If one of the tasks of the deacon was to distribute alms to the needy, unless he had this qualification, what would keep him from pocketing some of the alms he was supposed to distribute to others?   This qualification can be checked in the life of another.   One could tell if a person were "greedy for money" if the most important thing in his life is money and the things it will buy.

3:9 -- *But* – After a list of negative qualifications, we now turn to the positive qualities expected in a man who would become a deacon.   Paul lists characteristics concerning how a prospective deacon relates to others, and also highlights the matter of a prospective deacon's grasp of the Christian faith; both must be considered before a man is appointed to office by a congregation.   How a man holds the faith and how he relates the faith to everyday life are important qualifications.

Holding to the mystery of the faith – "The faith" is synonymous with the body of doctrine we call the gospel, "and the sense is that the deacon should have a good understanding of the great doctrines of the Christian religion, which had so long been concealed from men but are now [since Calvary and Pentecost] revealed" (*Barnes'*, p.148).   "Of the faith," a genitive construction, goes with "mystery" and describes or defines or explains that which the "mystery" is about. What does "mystery" mean?   The Roman Catholic Church came to think of the word "mystery" as a reference to the sacraments, and so found herein one of the tasks of deacons.   But this is an improper use of the word "mystery," not found in New Testament times.   Throughout the New Testament, a "mystery" was something which having been long hidden is now revealed.[53]   Christianity was dimly foreshadowed and predicted in the Old Testament Law and Prophets, but it is now clearly made known to men through the New Testament apostles and prophets.   "Holding the mystery" says that although a prospective deacon does not have to meet the qualification "able to teach" that is required of prospective elders, a deacon needs to be a man who is settled in his faith.   If the church selects a man to become a deacon, and when that man begins to share his beliefs, there should not be any danger that his beliefs will one day be found to be different from the faith once for all delivered to the saints.   When Paul could have written simply "the faith" and have conveyed the idea that a prospective deacon must have a good understanding of the gospel, there must have been a reason for writing the

---

[53] "Mystery" does not have to be given the connotation 'incomprehensible, hard to understand' in order to understand verse 9.   It is an unwarranted use of this verse to prove certain modern philosophical views about how men accept the gospel; for example, "It is assumed that although men cannot understand the gospel, they must accept it with implicit faith."   The Bible has never taught that even though two statements are contradictory, one must somehow hold on to both in order to "grasp" the truth.   Nor does the Bible teach the "blind faith" one finds expected by the neo-orthodoxy school of interpretation.   The rest of verse 9 should cause us to pause when we read neo-orthodox explanations.   How can one hold with a "pure conscience" what he fails to understand?

expression "the mystery of the faith." Recall that there were certain "Jewish" elements to the doctrine the false teachers at Ephesus were proclaiming. A man who understood the "mystery of the faith" would know that the Mosaic Law was temporary, and that it had been abrogated at Calvary, being replaced with a new priesthood (that of Jesus), and a new covenant. If the prospective deacon is not clear on this doctrinal matter, he should not be appointed to office.

With a clear conscience ("pure conscience" KJV) – The conscience is an innate faculty that prompts you to do what your mind thinks is right, and condemns you when you do what your mind thinks is wrong (see notes at 1 Timothy 1:5). A clear conscience results when one's actions match his beliefs, when the conscience does not bother or condemn a person for actions inconsistent with the "faith." Before a person is chosen to be a deacon, he should be careful to show he lives in harmony with what the gospel teaches.

3:10 -- And let these also first be tested – There is an ambiguity in the English word "also" not found in the Greek. One might think it means "deacons also (in addition to others, i.e., the elders) are to be tested." So Knight (*op. cit.*, p.169) explains it: "These are compared ('also') with the elders." Or one might think the evidence (or lack thereof) of the presence of the required qualifications for deacon is something that is "tested" over a period of time. Instead, what the Greek truly says is that in addition to the qualifications already named, deacons are "also" to be "tested." How this "testing" is done is not specified. (1) Some believe the church authorities should conduct a formal investigation, either in public before the whole congregation or in a meeting with the evangelist and elders. The Church of England, for example, acts upon these directions by requiring written testimonials, by personal enquiries made by the bishop, by the *Si quis*,[54] and by the appeal to the congregation during the ordination service, "Brethren, if there be any of you who knoweth any impediment, or notable crime, in any of these persons presented to be ordained deacons, for the which he ought not to be admitted to that office, let him come forth in the name of God, and show what the crime or impediment is," as well as by the careful examination of the candidates. Missouri Synod Lutherans require a multi-day ordination investigation (quiz, examination). (2) Some have prospective deacons serve a trial period first, during which church members can carefully evaluate their qualifications. "This verse seems to mean that men should be given tasks related to the office before being appointed to it. If they show themselves capable, they can be trusted with the function."[55] (3) Others believe a formal test is not required, but instead a constant observation by the church members, so that when members are

---

[54] The Latin denotes a notice posted in public that a candidate seeks ordination, and that if anyone knows of any impediment to this ordination, they should come forward.

[55] Ketcherside, *op. cit.*, p.356.

asked (as the Jerusalem church was, Acts 6:3) to consider thoughtfully and carefully the qualifications, the members will have a good idea how well each candidate meets the required qualifications.[56]   If a time of testing is required "first," it would be difficult to see how a recent convert could be appointed as deacon.[57]

Then let them serve as deacons if they are beyond reproach -- The Greek has a circumstantial participle here, which can be translated as though it were conditional ("if they are beyond reproach" or "found blameless" KJV), specifies the outcome of the "testing."   *Anegklētos* is a synonym of the word for "above reproach" used in 1 Timothy 3:2.   While the word in 3:2 has the idea of "nothing upon which an adversary might seize, in order to make a charge against him," the word here in verse 10 designates "one against whom there is no accusation, implying not acquittal of a charge, but that no charge has been made."[58]   Let this truth be highlighted and its solemnity impressed on our minds: the whole passage, from verse 3 through 13, shows the supreme importance of a holy and blameless lifestyle in those who would be elders and deacons.   The church would do well to heed Paul's instructions here!   "Let them serve as deacons," that is, let them be appointed to the office, and fulfill its duties.[59]   Since it has been determined they are qualified, let them serve as deacons.   The other side of this statement is also true – if they are not qualified, then do not put them into office.

3:11 -- Women – Which "women" does Paul have in mind?   In a context dealing with offices in the church, it is not a reference to women in general.   Since the term can be translated either "women" or "wives," four views have been offered:

- the wives of deacons (e.g., see the KJV's, "Even so must their wives ...")
- the wives of elders and deacons
- women who were to be ordained into the office of deaconess (an office distinguished from, but comparable to that of deacon)
- they are female assistants to the deacons

---

[56] Some of the qualifications given for elder (3:4-7) were also things that could be observed over a period of time, as one was looking for men who meet the qualifications for the job.   Paul will return to the matter of testing of prospective elders in 1 Timothy 5:22-25, as he warns Timothy not to be hasty about laying hands on men to ordain them to office.

[57] For some time, the Disciples of Christ in Missouri appointed every newly baptized person (male or female) as "junior deacons."   The rationale was, 'If you want to keep a person in church, give him or her a job to do.'   While we strongly encourage training classes for prospective elders and deacons, putting a new convert on the church board and giving him (or her) a vote of equal weight with the elders on decisions affecting the life and teaching of the church, seems fraught with peril and wholly at variance with what Paul here writes.

[58] Berry, *New Testament Synonyms*, p.121.

[59] The Greek is a present active imperative verb, "let them serve!"   It reminds us that the work of a deacon is "service."

For the first view, "wives of deacons," it is argued that: (1) The evidence for the existence of an order of deaconesses at this early date is far from clear. The language here in verse 11 is too general to postulate with certainty a distinct order of deaconesses. (2) The mention of these "women" in the midst of – not after – the qualifications for the office of deacon, seems to point to the deacons' wives, whose character would be material to their husbands' fitness, rather than to deaconesses unconnected with them. (3) It is probable that the wives of deacons, whose office contained a larger lay element than the bishops' does, would be more associated with them in their work, assisting them especially in the distribution of alms. Other areas where a deacon's wife would be of great assistance would be the visitation of women, and in administering baptism to women converts. (4) If it becomes the accepted explanation that a class of female ministers (deaconesses) is indicated by the "Catalog of Widows" (1 Timothy 5:9),[60] it becomes at least probable that "women" here is to be understood as a different group, i.e., the wives of deacons. (5) If Paul wished to designate an office of deaconess, he had a word to use that would have been less ambiguous (i.e., he could have used a feminine form of the word "deacon"). (6) The use of *gunē* (which can be either "wife" or "woman") in chapter 2:14 and 3:2 as "wife" might make it likely that the term is used a third time with the same sense in the same context.

For the second view, that "wives of elders and deacons" are intended, it is argued that there is no pronoun used with "women" to relate them to the deacons alone, nor is there even any article which might serve as a possessive pronoun.

For the third view, that "deaconesses" are intended, it is argued that: (1) It is not likely that Paul, in his directions to Timothy, would omit all mention of an order[61] which, in the case of Phoebe, appears to have existed at least at Cenchrea (Romans 16:1). (2) The same expression in verse 8, "must likewise be," introduced the qualifications of a new office. (3) That the qualifications required include no special reference to domestic duties is *prima facie* evidence the "women" were to be engaged in church work, rather than homemaking. (4) In the case of elders, the qualifications of their wives were not alluded to. Why, then, would we think that the qualifications for deacons would concern their wives?

For the fourth view, "female assistants to the deacons," it is argued that the way verse 11 is sandwiched between two verses that discuss the qualifications for po-

---

[60] Anticipating the conclusions reached in chapter 5, we do not think widows were being "enrolled" into a class of deaconesses, whose time was spent in church-related activities especially suited to women. We think "enrolled" means 'put on the official roll of widows who, having none else to care for them and provide their daily sustenance, the church accepts responsibility for.'

[61] The argument's wording assumes the thing to be proven, namely that there was an "order" of deaconesses in the early church. As already noted, just because some form of *diakonos* occurs, it does not necessarily reference the office. Phoebe may have been a "female servant" of the church, without holding any ecclesiastical position at all.

tential male deacons, and the introductory word "likewise," indicates that the task these women are called on to perform is in some way related to the work of the deacons. The comments about to be given on the qualifications listed in this verse will assume that "wives of deacons" is the correct interpretation.[62]

Must likewise be – This same word was used without a verb in the Greek at verse 8. What was true there, about supplying a verb ("must") from verse 2, is true here. The qualifications for wives of deacons are as obligatory as the qualifications for elder.

Dignified – The same "dignity" required of the deacons is required of their wives. In comments on this word at 1 Timothy 2:2, it was noticed that Christianity teaches its followers they have certain responsibilities towards their fellow men. A person who is "dignified" ("grave" KJV) is willing to recognize the seriousness of the Christian walk and to pursue it regardless of cost.

Not malicious gossips ("not slanderers," KJV) – The adjective used here *diabolous* is the same one that when used substantively (in the singular, *ho diabolos*) is translated "the devil." The deacon's wife must not partake in this characteristic of the devil, being a 'false accuser.' One who engages in malicious gossip or destructive secret criticism is working for the devil. Nothing is as likely to create turmoil as the whispering and backbiting indulged in by thoughtless persons who are in positions of trust. It is easily understood why Paul emphasizes that wives who support their deacon husbands, performing loving ministries, must not be gossipers or scandal mongers.

But temperate – The word in the Greek is *nephalios*, which was already explained in notes at 1 Timothy 3:2. Literally it means to be a total abstainer from wine. Metaphorically, it means to be "sober minded in judgment."

Faithful in all things – It may say that a deacon's wife is to be a faithful Christian. If she is not, he is not qualified for the office. Or it may mean that the deacon's wife is to be faithful to her husband, to her family, to Christ, and to the church. "Absolutely trustworthy" is how one translator renders it.

3:12 -- Let deacons be the husbands of *only* one wife – Paul continues his list of qualifications for the office of deacon. "Husband of one wife" is the same qualification given for elders (see 3:2). Like the elders, prospective deacons must not have a record of divorce or marital unfaithfulness behind them.

---

[62] Too many assumptions have to be made to make it "deaconess" (including the assumption there was such an office separate from the deacons). The idea of "female assistants" who traveled with the deacons is an idea from later church history (Pliny's letter to Trajan) when single women traveled with and ministered alongside the deacons. As the centuries passed, the post-apostolic order of "female assistants" eventually retired to the cloister.

And **good managers of** *their* **children** – What was said about prospective elders being "managers" is also true for prospective deacons (see 3:4). Both "managers" and "children" are plural. This is usually understood to mean deacons should have at least one child, i.e. at least one per deacon. Nothing is said about the children of deacons being "believers," as is said about the children of elders (Titus 1:6). In the case of prospective elders, it takes time for their children to grow up and reach the age of accountability before they make any response to the gospel. The omission in the list for deacons of the qualification about children being believers is usually interpreted to mean a man may become a deacon at a younger age than could an elder.

And their own households – We've explained the word "household" in comments at verse 5. It is "their own" in contrast to "God's house." How deacons do at home offers a barometer of how they will do in positions of responsibility for the church. For example, proper administration of finances at home will enable them to assist in handling the same kind of responsibility in the church.

3:13 -- For – Paul offers encouragement to men to aspire to the offices of church leadership. His word of encouragement to those who would be elders is found in 1 Timothy 3:1 ("It's a fine work," a beautiful work!) As he closes the list of qualifications for prospective deacons, two encouraging promises are held out: (1) They obtain a "high standing." (2) They obtain "great confidence in the faith." This is not only an incentive to men considering becoming deacons. It is also an incentive to those who are already deacons as they labor faithfully.

Those who have served well as deacons – Just as in verse 10, there is simply the verb "to serve" (*diakoneō*), but we translate it the same, to "serve as deacons." It is not a perfunctory doing of a deacon's duties, but serving "well" that promises the good outcome called to our attention in the rest of the verse.

Obtain for themselves a high standing – The margin reads "good standing," and the word *bathmos* has the following meanings: a step, a rung, a base, degree in rank or standing. It is the latter one that commentators usually pick as fitting the thought here. "Obtain for themselves" translates *peripoieō*, a word which means to gain or acquire and which suggests the idea of advancement.

But just what is the "high(er) standing" a deacon obtains? (1) Is it an advanced church office? (a) Are there higher offices? In some sense, yes. Elders lead and shepherd, something apparently not included in the deacon's task. And evangelists have an administrative role, sometimes even over elders (see comments on 1 Timothy 5:17ff). (b) But how does a deacon advance? Is he promoted by some church authority? Is he selected by the congregation to be an elder or evangelist? (c) Objections have been offered to this view since it does not harmonize well with the latter part of the verse (which offers spiritual blessing, not promotion in church office), and it is an unusual inducement for a man to become a deacon: 'You can move up, son!' (2) Is it "good standing" (ASV) in the eyes of God and men? (a) It is true a man who serves for some length of time as a deacon, and does his job well, will achieve a respected reputation in the church, and we think in God's eyes, too. (b) On the other hand, if "good standing" in the eyes of men is the incentive to become a deacon, what is the point of the previous qualification which stressed the man's having good standing in the eyes of his fellow believers *before* he is even ordained to the office? (3) Is the "high(er) standing" somehow related to degrees of reward in Heaven? The Bible apparently teaches degrees of reward (1 Corinthians 3:14-15; Matthew 5:12). Looking forward to a greater reward is not at all sinful if one plans to use this reward for the glory of God and for even greater service in His kingdom. Let no deacon be misled by the fact that it is the deacon's job to serve, or that it is a "lower office" than elder or evangelist, so that he thus begins to think lightly of the role. Deacons who serve well acquire for themselves a high(er) standing.

And great confidence in the faith that is in Christ Jesus – "Confidence" ("boldness," KJV) translates *parrēsian*, a word often used of boldness or freedom in speaking. Consciousness of a job well done will give greater confidence and boldness in imparting to others the faith that is in Jesus Christ. Perhaps Paul is contemplating "preaching" as one of the tasks a deacon gets to do. We think of Stephen, one of the seven men chosen to serve tables, who spoke the word of God with great boldness in the synagogues and before his judges (Acts 6:8-10, 7:2ff). We think of Philip, another of the seven, who became "Philip the evangelist" (Acts 21:8), laboring in Samaria, on the road to Gaza, and all through the plains of Philistia and Sharon (Acts 8:6ff). Deacons of today can become this, too!

Shall we explain "in the faith" as a reference to a deacon's personal exercise of faith, or is this another place where "the faith" stands for a body of doctrine? The meaning of the phrase "the faith that is in Christ Jesus" has been much discussed. (1) Some use this phrase to cast doubt on Paul's authorship of the Pastorals, by comparing what Paul wrote in these letters to those categorized as "the undoubted letters of Paul." In his "undoubted letters" the words "in Christ Jesus" are applied to persons, not qualities. Here it is "faith" (not a person) that is said to be "in Christ Jesus." But even if we admit this phraseology is a bit unusual for Paul, it is not beyond belief that he could use one of his favorite expressions, "in Christ Jesus", to describe the "faith." There would be no "faith" were it not for Christ Jesus and His mission to seek and save the lost. (2) Some explain this phrase to mean that deacons who perform well have as a consequence a real confidence in the sphere of their own personal Christian faith. They have boldness confessing their faith in Jesus Christ both in word and deed. The faith in which they already stand (Romans 5:1) continues to grow. (3) Others explain it to mean that deacons can become bold proclaimers of the faith (the gospel) which rests on (*en*) Jesus Christ. This last interpretation is the easiest to see.

C. The Importance of this Charge to the Church. 3:14-16

3:14 -- I am writing these things to you -- The charge to Timothy was important, and Paul could not wait until he could make a personal visit before these instructions were shared and acted upon. How much of what has been written already in this letter are included in the words "these things"? Some think everything since 3:1 concerning the qualifications for church leaders is what Paul has specially in mind.[63] Some affirm that everything since 2:1 concerning both the conduct of worship and the selection of leaders is in view.[64] Others wonder if all the charges since 1:3 are not included in "these things."[65] Instruction on "these things" is something that cannot be delayed, because it concerns 'behavior' in "God's household" (i.e., the church, verse 15). The singular "you" used here has reference to Timothy, but we have already noted that the letter was intended for a wider audience than just the young evangelist himself.

Hoping to come to you before long – Timothy is in Ephesus. Paul hopes to visit him there. Whether or not this visit ever came to pass we have no way of knowing for sure. (See the matter of Paul's travels at this period in his life discussed in the Introductory Studies.) The participle "hoping" may have a concessive force here – "though I hope." "Before long" is how our NASB renders the Greek, which might be rendered "more quickly."[66] More quickly than what? Perhaps Paul hoped to visit Timothy "more quickly" than circumstances might allow. Perhaps it means "more quickly" than you can initiate the selection of elders and deacons. Perhaps it means "more quickly" or 'sooner' than such detailed instructions might suppose.

3:15 -- But in case I am delayed, *I write* - Verse 14 has indicated Paul's 'hope' that he would 'shortly' be able to return to Ephesus for a personal visit to Timothy. But in case of delay, when this letter is read out loud in the worship service, the congregation will know how the household of God is to "behave." Paul's travels

---

[63] So Kent (*op. cit.*, p.139) and Ellicott (*op. cit.*, p.223) interpret it.

[64] So Hendriksen (*op. cit.*, p.136) explains it.

[65] Foster, *op. cit.*, p.369.

[66] "More quickly" translates the comparative form *tachion* found in Aleph D[2] F G and the Byzantine text, and Nestle-Aland 25. It has been replaced in UBSGNT[3] and Nestle-Aland 26 by the reading *en tachei ("in haste, quickly")* found in A C D* P ψ 33 81. To get the sense of *en tachei*, see how it is used at Acts 12:7, 22:18, where it expresses a sense of urgency and immediacy.

were always subject to the will of God and the direction of the Holy Spirit; Paul has long ago learned that his own wishes were sometimes overruled.[67] "*I write*" (supplied from verse 14) has reference to this very letter we call 1 Timothy. In case Paul's plans do not turn out as he anticipates, he writes this letter so that Timothy and the Ephesians may have certain knowledge of the course they should be following in their work for the Lord. After all, the matter being discussed – i.e., the need for and the importance of well-qualified church leaders – is so crucial, it can't wait. It needs to be implemented before Paul has any opportunity to arrive on the scene personally.

So that you may know how one ought to conduct himself -- The verb "you may know" is second person singular. Timothy is particularly in Paul's mind, since it is his responsibility as the evangelist to help the church conduct itself in a proper manner. The Greek simply reads "how it is necessary to conduct oneself." There is no word in the accusative case,[68] which hinders us from knowing just "whose" conduct Paul has in mind.[69] It might be Timothy;[70] it might be the entire congregation;[71] it might be both.[72]

> In view of the context which discusses the organization of the church, plus the fact that the infinitive is not limited by any subject and thus must be understood in its widest sense, we refer the notice to a general statement regarding general church conduct. However, the singular subject of *eidēs* (know) indicates that Timothy must know these regulations in order to effect them. (Kent, *op. cit.*, p.139)

"To behave" is the way the KJV renders *anastrephesthai*, a present middle infinitive. The word is variously rendered in our English versions – "to have one's conversation," "to live," "to pass (one's time)." It literally means "to go up and down" a given place, "backwards and forwards," hence, "to dwell in it." It then comes to refer to one's "manner of living" or "behavior." The middle voice indicates the congregation is to so "behave" for its own benefit.   "Ought

---

[67] The verb *braduno* is present subjunctive, and is active in voice. It may be that Paul himself is the one doing the "delaying", rather than being delayed by someone else (as the NASB suggests).

[68] The subject of the infinitive "to conduct" would be in the accusative case.

[69] In the Greek text, except for a few Western authorities, the subject of "to conduct" is omitted. In fact, the NASB translators have here added the words "one" and "himself" without even putting them in italics to warn the reader that there is no corresponding word in the original.

[70] It is rightly pointed out that Timothy is the subject of the main verb "know," so it is certainly proper to assume he is the subject of this relative clause also.

[71] The idea that the whole church at Ephesus is intended is in harmony with the thrust of this whole letter, which was intended as much for the church as it was for Timothy's benefit.

[72] In a situation where the original is capable of different interpretations, any one may be true as long as it does not contradict what the Bible clearly says elsewhere.

to" translates *dei*, a word we met at 1 Timothy 3:2.   It is a "must"![73]

In the household of God, which is the church of the living God – The second phrase explains exactly what Paul means when he speaks of the "household of God."   The older versions read "the house of God".   Since some buildings in the Old Testament were denoted as being the "house" of God, some have mistakenly supposed that the reference here was to a "building" also.   There were no "church buildings" this early in the history of the church.   At this early date, congregations did not meet in buildings constructed for that exclusive purpose. Congregations usually met in the homes of individual Christians.   Hence it was clear that when the word "church" was used, it had reference to the people, not the building.   Likewise, it is the people (not the building) who are here called the "household" of God.   The idea of the local congregation (the church) being something like a "household" has been introduced in 1 Timothy 3:5. A similar idea is found elsewhere in Scripture, e.g., Hebrews 3:6 and 12:22,23; 1 Peter 2:5; 1 Corinthians 3:16; 2 Corinthians 6:16.   The Old Testament used "house of God" for both the temple building and for the covenant-people.   The latter is the idea here – God's new covenant people are His "household."   Let it not for a moment be forgotten that this household belongs to "God, yea, the living God"!   Both Timothy and the Ephesian Christians must know how to defend and propagate the truth (against false doctrine), how to conduct public worship, and how to select proper leaders, because what they have been entrusted with is not a private business – it is *God's household!*

Why is attention focused on the fact that God is the "living" God?[74]   It seems unlikely that the only reason is that 1 Timothy was addressed to people living in a town where the temple and *lifeless* image of Diana were located.   The phrase seems to be a reminder that one day each of us will stand before the living God to give an account of the deeds done in the body, whether good or bad. Since we will one day answer for our behavior, it would be wise to act in the way God has revealed is pleasing to Him.

The pillar and support of the truth – This chapter closes with a statement which seems to have been intended to impress Timothy's mind with the importance of the duties in which he was engaged.   Perhaps the imagery is changed.   In the previous phrase, the church was pictured as a vast congregation of people ("household") with the living God dwelling in the midst.   Now the congrega-

---

[73] These are not simply rules of etiquette that may change over the years, and so may be safely ignored.   These are directions, given by an apostle speaking for his Lord Jesus Christ, intended to be the standards regularly subscribed to by any group who calls itself "*God's* house."

[74] The designation "the living God" occurs quite often in Paul's writings (11 times, if we may count the four times in Hebrews as being Paul's).   It occurs much less frequently in other New Testament writings: 3 times in the gospels, and once each in Acts and Revelation.

tion[75] is pictured as a massive pillar, holding up "the truth" and displaying that "truth" before men and angels.   Or perhaps the figure behind "pillar" here is this: just as a pillar supports the span of ancient buildings (there were no large, clear span buildings; instead, the ceiling and roof were supported at regular intervals by pillars), so the church is something that holds up the glorious truth of the gospel.   If the church doesn't do this task in the world, who will?   The word "support" (*hedraiōma*) is also used, perhaps alluding to the massive "footing" that must be present to support the pillar.   Hendriksen explains it in another fashion: "As the pillar supports the roof, even better (note the climax!) as the foundation supports the entire superstructure, so the church supports the glorious truth of the gospel."[76]   It is important to note that neither "pillar" nor "support" has an article in the Greek.   It is not "*the* pillar and *the* support," but rather "*a* pillar and *a* support."   F.J.A. Hort was right in supposing that each congregation of Christians is "a pillar and support," but not the only one.[77]   "The truth" has reference to the truth of the gospel, some of whose key points will be enumerated in verse 16. The meaning is that the witness to the truth on earth is dependent on the church. Given this fact, it becomes clear why the selection of leaders is a matter of such serious concern.   Churches who ignore the qualifications when selecting leaders just do not know "how to behave" in the household of God!

3:16 -- And by common confession ("without controversy" KJV) – The "truth" referred to in verse 15 is expanded here.   It is even possible that the *kai* at the beginning of the verse should be rendered "indeed."   *Homologoumenōs* is an adverb found only here in the New Testament, but used in the same sense in the LXX and in classical Greek.   Here it modifies the adjective "great."   As far as the household of God is concerned, every one admits ('confesses') that the mystery of godliness is Great!   There can be no denying the fact.

---

[75] It is "household" and not "Timothy" that is the antecedent of "pillar and support." We think that some of the early church fathers were mistaken when they applied this phrase to Timothy, after the analogy of Galatians 2:9 where James, Peter and John are said to be "pillars" in the church.

[76] Care must be exercised here lest the church be given greater eminence than the truth of the Gospel.   One running debate among conservative and liberal theologians has been "which came first, the church or the Scriptures?"   Liberals answer that the church came before the New Testament books were written, therefore the church can sit in judgment of the Bible.   Some conservatives have tried to say "the Scriptures, first in oral form, then written, produced the church."   A better answer to the question is, "Neither!   The Holy Spirit produced both the church and the Scriptures."
Having missed this better answer, conservatives have scrambled to avoid giving the appearance that the local congregation (the church) is more important than the Word of God.   Their attempts have usually followed one of three lines: (1) The whole phrase "pillar and ground of truth" refers to Timothy, not the church.   (2) The word *hedraiōma* should be rendered "bulwark" or "support" instead of "ground" (KJV).   Then the writers can speak about how the church has been to a greater or lesser degree the custodian of the truth of the gospel.   (3) The last phrase in verse 15 should be attached to verse 16, and thus be regarded as a description of "the mystery of godliness." (This third view has against it the fact that it would be an awkward construction in the Greek.)

[77] *Christian Ecclesia*, p. 174.

Many scholarly pages have been written about these next phrases in verse 16. (1) The phrases that follow are so measured[78] and cover so neatly the panorama of God's revealed truth in the person of Jesus Christ, that some suggest they may have been a customary creedal confession made by Christians as part of their weekly worship services. If indeed such a creed was used regularly as part of their worship, that would explain why Paul wrote of a "common confession"[79] and why the lines begin with "who" (a word that has no apparent antecedent[80]). (2) Others suggest these phrases are part of a hymn that was sung frequently in the services of the church.[81] (3) The view that Paul coined these phrases for the first time as he wrote to Timothy must certainly be considered a live possibility. "Paul was of sufficient literary ability to compose such phrases at this particular time in his correspondence with Timothy, and the guidance of the Spirit supplies adequate explanation of both the beauty and the truth."[82] Numerous analyses have been made of these phrases in an attempt to arrange them in some kind of order. Some divide them into two strophes of three lines each;[83] others offer three couplets, with each line in the first trilogy matching its respective member in the second.[84] Still another offers the idea that the six lines were arranged by Paul in chronological order, covering Jesus' stay on earth from Bethlehem to the ascension.[85] Gundry suggests the "hymn" (lines 2-5) is framed by lines 1 and 6.

---

[78] Each of the six lines are almost identical in form. Each has an aorist passive third person singular verb. All but one line have *en* and all end with a dative noun.

[79] One flaw with this view is that it takes the phrases as the content of the confession, whereas *Great* is the mystery of godliness" seems to be what Paul and the church were commonly confessing.

[80] If the lines of this verse come from a creed or a hymn, it may well be supposed that the creed had an antecedent to which "He who" relates. Paul just didn't begin the quotation with a relative pronoun.

[81] Source critics think they have found the source of this hymn in the enthronement ceremony for kings in ancient Egypt. The disturbing thing about the suggestion that these phrases were a "creedal confession" or a "hymn," is the implied corollary that their origin is in doubt, and if their origin is in doubt, so also may be the "truth" of what they say. The suggestion that they were part of an early hymn would not be so difficult to accept if the suggestion also included the idea that some apostle or prophet (or other inspired person) first wrote the words and music, and then introduced it into use in the churches.

[82] Foster, *op. cit.*, p.369-70.

[83] According to Knight (*op. cit.*, p.183), Lock and Scott are examples of this arrangement. Both strophes are thought to be chronologically arranged. The first deals with Christ's life on earth. The second with the ministry of the church making that life known. The third line in each may be a refrain. (This is one way to keep the sixth line from being "out of chronological order.")

[84] The first three of the couplets presents Christ's work accomplished, the second His work made known, and the third His work acknowledged. Knight, Kelly, Jeremias, Foster, and others have followed this arrangement.

[85] Henry Alford, *Alford's Greek Testament* (London: Rivingtons, 1871), p.333 and Barrett opt for the chronological progression idea, though they do not agree on the meaning of the six lines.

Great is the mystery of godliness – "Godliness" was used at 1 Timothy 2:2, and was explained as having to do with one's conduct or attitude towards God. The "mystery of godliness" is all the truth which "in ages past was not made as fully known unto the sons of men, as it is now revealed unto us by his holy apostles and prophets by the Spirit" (Ephesians 3:5). The "mystery of godliness" is another name for "the Christian faith." At 1 Timothy 3:9, it was called "the mystery of the faith." At 1 Timothy 6:3, it is called "sound words of our Lord Jesus Christ, ... the doctrine conforming to godliness." At Titus 1:1, "the truth which is according to godliness."[86] True godliness is seen and known only in Jesus Christ. "Great" says other religions are insignificant compared to Christianity. This is our "common confession"! Nothing is more sublime or more important than the Christian faith![87] Having exalted the "mystery of godliness," Paul now lists some of the contents of that "mystery." Each point recalls a high point of Jesus' earthly ministry, and the continuing results of that ministry.

He who was revealed in the flesh – Where the NASB reads "He who," the KJV reads "God was manifest in the flesh ..." "He who" (*hos*) is now generally adopted by textual critics as the true reading, instead of "God" (*theos*). Where did the manuscript difference come from? It was a common thing to write the earliest manuscripts in all capital letters. It also was a common thing to abbreviate or contract certain "theological" words. That an abbreviation or contraction had occurred was indicated by placing a faint line or dash over the letters. Thus the word ΠΑΤΕΡ ("father") was abbreviated $\overline{\text{ΠΡ}}$. The word ΚΥΡΙΟΣ ("lord") was abbreviated $\overline{\text{ΚΣ}}$. The word ΘΕΟΣ was abbreviated $\overline{\text{ΘΣ}}$. Now when the words "He who" (ΟΣ) and "God" ($\overline{\text{ΘΣ}}$) are written in capital letters, there is not much difference in their looks. Unless a scribe was very careful, he could easily confuse one for the other. There is no agreement among the critics as to whether the original reading was "God" or "He who." Ellicott satisfied himself that the original reading of Codex Alexandrinus was ΟΣ, and that it had been altered by a later hand to $\overline{\text{ΘΣ}}$. The same thing is true of Codex Sinaiticus. Most of the older versions read "He who."[88]

---

[86] The reader should observe that our comments have treated "of the truth" (verse 15) and "of godliness" (verse 16) as though they were objective genitives. Ellicott tries to make them both subjective, and then tries to show how each person's subjective faith and godliness are somehow mysterious. His attempt to take them as subjective is against the regular way "mystery" is understood in passages where it occurs. It is always mysteries (or mystery) of the kingdom of God, of Christ, of God, of the gospel, etc. The "of" is always objective. Furthermore, there are several passages where "the faith" must refer to a body of doctrine, rather than just one's personal beliefs. In the following passages the objective sense of "the faith" is either necessary or by far the most natural: Acts 3:7, 13:8, 14:22, 16:5; Galatians 1:23; Ephesians 4:5; Philippians 1:27; Colossians 1:23, 2:7; 1 Timothy 1:19, 5:8, 6:10,11; 2 Timothy 4:7; Titus 1:13; James 2:1; Jude 3.

[87] One wonders whether there may be a tacit allusion to the pagan confession often heard at Ephesus, "Great is Artemis of the Ephesians" (Acts 19:28).

[88] The Latin Vulgate is an exception. It reads *quod*, agreeing with *sacramentum* (the Latin

What is the meaning of the accepted reading, "He who"? *Hos*, "who," is a relative pronoun in the masculine gender, and must, therefore, have an antecedent in the masculine gender. But there is no expressed antecedent in the masculine gender with which it should agree. The antecedent, therefore, must be understood, and gathered from the preceding words "the mystery of godliness." If we do this, the implied antecedent can only be "Jesus Christ."

> The mystery of the whole Old Testament, that which was wrapped in types and hidden under veils, was Christ (Col. 1:27). Moses spoke of Him, the Psalms speak of Him, the prophets speak of Him; but all of them spake darkly. But in the gospel "the mystery of Christ" (Col. 4:3) is revealed. Christ is the Mystery of Christianity. It is, therefore, no difficult step to pass from "the mystery" to "Christ," and to supply the word "Christ" as the antecedent of "who."[89]

If we accept the reading of the Textus Receptus as represented by the KJV, the meaning is the same. Jesus Christ was God incarnate.

"Revealed in the flesh." "Veiled in flesh the Godhead see," the familiar carol says. While we may not see all three persons of the Godhead, we do see Jesus as God in the flesh (John 1:14).[90] "Revealed" means 'to become visible to human eyes.' It is a verb frequently applied to Jesus (John 1:31; 1 John 1:2, 3:5,8). God is the implied agent of this passive verb. God is the one who "revealed" Jesus. The phrase necessarily presupposes Jesus' pre-existence. He existed before becoming visible in human form at Bethlehem's stable.

Was vindicated in the Spirit -- *Diakaioō* is rendered "justified" in the KJV, where the NASB has "vindicated." It can also mean 'to show to be righteous,' 'to pronounce or treat as righteous,' 'to hold guiltless.' There is disagreement over how to translate *en pneumati*. (1) The KJV, RSV, and NASB read "in the Spirit," making it a reference to the Holy Spirit.[91] So understood, the vindication is related to Jesus' claim to be the promised Messiah and the Son of God. When this vindication took place depends on how one outlines these verses (couplets, strophes, chronologically). Perhaps it was during Jesus' earthly ministry (Luke

---

word for "mystery"), and *quod* would represent a Greek text that read *ho* rather than *hos* or *theos*.

[89] A.C. Hervey, "1 Timothy," in *The Pulpit Commentary*, p.55.

[90] *Sarx* here, as often, refers to the body of flesh and blood and bones that Jesus shared in common with us other humans.

[91] This interpretation requires that we take "in the Spirit" as a dative of agent, rather than a dative of means. "By the Spirit" would be the translation. Compare Footnote 96 below. In five of the six lines, the construction is *en* and the dative. Should they all be taken as a dative of place, or a dative of agent, or a dative of means? Or are we free to pick and choose whichever one gives the right sense? A case could be made that because of the nearly identical format, each occurrence of *en* and the dative should be construed the same way.

4:14; Matthew 12:28).   At Jesus' baptism the Spirit's coming on Him vindicated who He was to John (Matthew 3:16; John 1:33,34) and anointed Him with power (Acts 10:38).   The "eternal Spirit" helped Jesus offer Himself as a sacrifice to God (Hebrews 9:14).   Perhaps it was after Jesus' resurrection from the dead that this vindication took place (cp. John 14:17, 16:13,14).   (2) The ASV reads, "in the spirit, "making it a reference to Christ's inner man, his human spirit.   Thus, the verses would the same contrast between Jesus' divine and human natures that we find in 1 Peter 3:18 and Romans 1:3,4.   Jesus was "shown to be righteous" in that no one, not even His enemies, let alone God, ever accused Him of sin.   (3) Another thinks we should read "in the spirit," but instead of understanding it of His "human spirit," we should think of that inner spirit which included His "divine nature."[92]   The whole verse then would mean that although His divine nature was often veiled during His stay on earth, there were times when the veil was lifted and witnesses saw the "glory of God" (John 1:14; Matthew 17:5; cp. 2 Peter 1:16-18).   Attempts to translate this rather obscure expression include: "He was pronounced righteous in spirit"; "He was proved spotless and pure in His Spirit"; "He was proved righteous by the Spirit."

Beheld by angels – *Aggelos* can be translated "angel" or "messenger."   It can refer either to angelic beings or human messengers.   Some would translate it "messengers," and immediately call to mind the post-resurrection appearances which the vindicated Jesus made to the apostles.   In a number of those appearances, the same verb *ōphthē* is used.   Some would translate it "angels." An angelic host was present at Bethlehem and welcomed the birth of the Babe. They would have seen the new-born Babe just as the shepherds did, "wrapped in cloths and lying in a manger."   Angels ministered to Jesus after the temptation in the wilderness (Mark 1:13), and after the agony in the garden of Gethsemane (Matthew 22:43, where the same word *ōphthē*, "beheld," is used).   Angels also were present at the empty tomb (Matthew 28:2) and became God's messengers to tell the visitors to the tomb the significance of the fact it was empty.   The special interest of angels in the "great mystery" is alluded to in 1 Peter 1:12, Hebrews 1:6.

Proclaimed among the nations – The KJV reads "preached unto the Gentiles."[93]

---

[92] At this time and place, this commentator has no inclination to dig into the thorny problem much discussed in earlier generations.   Trichotomists teach that man is made up of three parts, body, soul, and spirit.   Now the theologians got to wondering whether the incarnate Jesus was made up of three parts (body, soul, and the "divine nature" taking the place of "spirit"), or whether Jesus was four parts (body, soul, spirit, and the "divine nature") much as a converted man is not only body, soul, and spirit, but also has the indwelling Holy Spirit.   The decisions made and conclusions held by the commentators on this matter are likely to be reflected in their comments on "in spirit" ASV (or "in Spirit" NASB) at this place in 1 Timothy 3:16.

[93] Those who treat these six lines as three couplets, tell how the contrast between line 3 and line 4 is between the witness of the angels, and the proclamation of the good news (not to angels, but) to the nations of the world.

It may have been better to keep the wording "Gentiles" so the identity of thought with Ephesians 3:6 and 3:8 might come more quickly to mind. In Ephesians, Paul's thought that the preaching of the gospel to the Gentiles, that they might be fellow-heirs with the Jews of the promises of God, is one main feature of the "mystery." Elsewhere, the universality of the gospel is called a "mystery" (Ephesians 6:19; Colossians 1:26,27, 4:3). It was the risen Christ who, before His Ascension, issued the Great Commission, "Go therefore and make disciples of all the nations" (Matthew 28:18-20). This proclamation began a few days later on Pentecost and, by the time 1 Timothy was written, had been preached to Gentiles for over 20 years.

Believed on in the world – After the good news is preached to the nations, the next step is the hearers' acceptance of Christ as their Savior.[94] The claim made here in 1 Timothy is comparable to the claim of Colossians 1:5,6, "The word of the truth, the gospel, which has come to you, just as in all the world also it is constantly bearing fruit." At the time 1 Timothy was written, "the world" would have been the Roman Empire. Five years before Paul wrote 1 Timothy, he wrote Colossians, in which (1:23) he tells us that the gospel has been preached "in all creation under heaven." Different from Buddhism, or even from Islam, Christianity has found acceptance among widely different nationalities. Alone among religions, the religion of the Crucified has a fair claim to the title of a world-religion. No modifications to it are needed to make it applicable to whatever nation it enters.

Taken up in glory – "Received up into glory" is the way the KJV words it. What event is in Paul's mind? Not a few would assert that "taken up" refers to the ascension of Jesus into heaven (Acts 1:9; Luke 24:50,51). Barrett, however, refers this phrase to the second coming.[95] (1) If the verse speaks of the ascension, how shall we understand *en doxē*? Shall we read "in glory" as though, at His ascension, the risen Lord's body was "glorified" just as it was at the Transfiguration (Matthew 17:2)? Shall we read "by glory,"[96] as though the "glory" (i.e., the Shekinah cloud) was Jesus' chariot that carried Him home to His Father's house at the time of the ascension? Shall we read "into glory," as though Paul's statement here is similar to what we read in Mark's gospel, "He was received up into heaven   and [there] sat down at the right   hand of God" (Mark

---

[94] Those who see three couplets in these six lines, make the contrast in the third couplet to be between the world and glory. The triumphant Christ and the salvation He brought to earth were accepted by men. And triumphantly He returned in a glorious manner to the Father in glory.

[95] It is evident that if one opts for a "chronological progression through the earthly ministry of Jesus," then he cannot explain "taken up in glory" to be a reference to the ascension, for the ascension happened before Jesus was "preached among the nations, or believed on in the world."

[96] *En* and the dative, after a passive voice verb, can express the "means" by which something is done to the subject of the verb.

16:19)?   His session "in glory" right beside the Heavenly Father would fulfill his prayer about being glorified "with the glory that [He] ever had with [the Father] before the world was" (John 17:5).   (2) If the verse speaks of the Second Coming, how shall we understand *en doxē*?   Perhaps just as Jesus comes on clouds with great glory, once the redeemed have been caught up to meet Him, all are taken with Him "in glory" to the New Jerusalem.

When we look at these six statements that give us some of the contents of the "mystery of godliness," we can begin to see how great the task of the church is.   The church is the pillar and support of the truth.   It is her task to tell the world about such an exalted Head.   Let Timothy (and 20th century evangelists, too) remember this as he goes about his task of supervision, and in particular, leading out in the selection of qualified men to be local elders and deacons.   Such a "great" message deserves our very best!

SPECIAL STUDY #3

The Deacons

"Now these were more noble minded ... for they received the word with great eagerness, examining the Scriptures daily, to see whether these things were so."   Acts 17:11

> "The first and almost the only book deserving of universal attention is the Bible.   I speak as a man of the world to men of the world, and I say to you, 'Search the Scriptures' ... The earlier my children begin to read it the more confident will be my hopes that they will prove useful citizens of their country and respectable members of society."-- *John Quincy Adams*

To finish the quotation Mr. Adams made: "Search the Scriptures for in them ye think, ye shall find salvation."   Let us work carefully since knowledge of salvation and of Christ are obtained by searching the Scriptures.   The Bible does not say, "Let someone else search the Scriptures for you."   It is a personal matter, open to every Christian.

Read carefully these references: Matthew 20:26, 25:34-40; Mark 9:35; John 12:26; Acts 6:1-6; Romans 15:8; 1 Corinthians 3:5; Ephesians 6:21; Philippians 1:11; Colossians 1:7; 4:7; 1 Thessalonians 3:2; 1 Timothy 3:8-13.

Fill In The Blanks

1. The term "deacon" means _____

2. There are several persons to whom this term is applied.   Name two of them?

    a. _____   b. _____

3. Name two qualifications of the person who is to become a deacon.

    a. _____   b. _____

4. Name a few places (geographically speaking) where deacons were present.

    a. _____   b. _____

5. Name two specific tasks that you feel a deacon could perform.

    a. _____   b. _____

Why do you suggest these?

LESSON DISCUSSION

All the offices of the church need to be so carefully understood that a person wanting to serve in any of them would know just what the Lord expects of him – as an evangelist, as an elder, or as a deacon.

Another introductory word needs to be said: None of these offices, either by way of qualifications or duties, are too lofty for present-day attainment. The difficulty in this area has to do with human interpretation and application of these qualifications and duties. Some men (and perhaps some who are now in office) are very obviously not at all qualified. On the other hand, in the eyes of some, no one could ever measure up to their estimate of the application of these terms. But, thanks be to God, the decision of who is or is not qualified, is not left in the hands of such men.

1. The name, its meaning and use.

A. **General.** The word "deacon" is from a Greek word that means "a waiter, attendant, servant, or minister;" and this is taken from the verb "to wait upon, to serve, to minister;" and this verb is derived from a root word meaning "to run, to hasten." The essential idea is **active service.**

In this sense it was applied to:
(1) Christ. Romans 15:8; Galatians 2:17.
(2) To the Apostles. Matthew 20:26, 23:11; Mark 9:35; 1 Corinthians 3:5.
(3) To evangelists. Ephesians 6:21; Colossians 1:7, 4:7; 1 Thessalonians 3:2.
(4) To all faithful servants of Christ. John 12:26.
(5) To civil magistrates. Romans 13:4.

B. **Specific.** The word is used to denote a particular class of "servants," servants in an official sense. Note:

(1) "Paul and Timothy, bond-servants of Christ Jesus, to all the saints in Christ Jesus who are in Philippi, with the overseers and **deacons."** Philippians 1:1.
(2) **"Deacons** in like manner must be . . . And let these also first be proved; then let them **serve as deacons** ... for those who have **served well as deacons** obtain for themselves a high standing, and great confidence in the faith that is in Christ Jesus." 1 Timothy 3:8-13.

From a careful reading of these verses, it seems that there is a distinct office in the church. This office of deacon ought to be occupied and fulfilled by men.

2. The deacons mentioned in the New Testament.

A. Those of Jerusalem.

> "Now in those days, when the number of the disciples was multiplying, there arose a murmuring of the Grecian Jews against the Hebrews, because their widows were neglected in the daily ministration. And the twelve called the multitude of the disciples unto them, and said, It is not fit that we should forsake the Word of God and serve tables. Look ye out therefore, brethren, from among you seven of good report, full of the spirit and of wisdom, whom we may appoint over this business. But we will continue steadfastly in prayer, and in the ministry of the word. And the saying pleased the whole multitude: and they chose Stephen, a man full of faith and of the Holy Spirit, and Philip, and Prochorus, and Nicanor, and Timon, and Parmenas, and Nicolaus a proselyte of Antioch; whom they set before the apostles: and when they had prayed, they laid their hands upon them." Acts 6:1-6 ASV.

Note that whereas these men are not called deacons in the noun form, they are so called in the use of the verb. Their appointed task was "to serve tables." The word from which we have the two English words "to serve" is the same Greek term that is translated "deacon" in the noun form.

If a foreman hired a man to dig a ditch he would be a ditch-digger. If the church in Jerusalem appointed these seven men to serve the church, they were then servants or "deacons" of the Jerusalem church, a capacity in which none of the other members of the church served.

B. **Those of Philippi**. They are only mentioned. No record is given as to what they did as servants of the Philippian church, Philippians 1:1.

C. **Those of Ephesus**. Since it is thought that Timothy was in Ephesus when Paul wrote to him, the instructions here were probably applicable to the deacons at Ephesus, 1 Timothy 3:8-13.

3. The Qualifications of a deacon.

A. **Must be of good report**. He should have a life above all honest reproach in the eyes of the congregation, the community, and his immediate neighborhood. (Acts 6:3a, ASV).

B. **Must be full of the Holy Spirit**. This means that a deacon's life will be empty of self and full of God's Word and of prayer. Then the Holy Spirit, who dwells in the heart of every Christian, will be able to direct him. (Acts 6:3b)

C. **Must be full of wisdom.** He must be one who acts wisely in all his contacts and dealings with his fellow man. (Acts 6:3c)

D. **Must be grave or serious.** The meaning of the Greek word "grave" is "august, venerable, reverend; to be venerated for character, honorable." (1 Timothy 3:8a, KJV)

E. **Not double-tongued.** He must not be a person who speaks one thing before Christians and something else before the world. (1 Timothy 3:8a.)

F. **Not given to much wine.** The word "much" seems to be for the sole purpose of forbidding drunkenness and does not in any way indicate that a little wine is permissible. (1 Timothy 3:8c.)

G. **Not greedy of filthy lucre.** "Not greedy of base gain" (1 Timothy 3:8d KJV). "The love of money is a root of all kinds of evil" (1 Timothy 6:10a ASV).

H. **He must hold the faith in a pure conscience.** James McKnight has this comment to make: "He must hold fast the doctrines of the gospel with a pure conscience; he must not, from fear or self-interest either conceal or disguise these doctrines." (1 Timothy 3:9)

I. **He must first be proved** (KJV) or "tested" NASB). The word "prove" in the Greek means also: "To test, examine, scrutinize (to see whether a thing be genuine or not); to recognize as genuine after examination, to approve, deem worthy." The names of the deacons should be made known to the congregation before they are set aside to the office. The word "also" in verse ten would seem to indicate that the elders were also given this period of examination or proving (1 Timothy 3:10a).

J. **The husband of one wife.** He must not be an adulterer either by act or by thought. (1 Timothy 3:12a KJV)

K. **He must rule well his own children.** The deacon is to exercise Christian rule over his own children. (1 Timothy 3:12b)

4. The work of the deacons.

In Acts 6:1-3 we read the first account concerning the work of a deacon. The following quotation is very much to the point on this subject:

> To wait on the secular concerns of the church was, therefore, the limit of [the deacons'] **official** duties. Their office comprehended nothing less, and it

certainly embraced nothing more. It conferred no authority whatever, either to teach or to preach, in either the public or the private assembly. The Elders must all be **apt to teach**, and every Evangelist is required **to preach the Word**. But, in all that is said of the deacons in the New Testament, there is not given a single intimation that either teaching or preaching is any part of their office.

They may, indeed, in a certain sense, preach the Word **unofficially**. This is, to a certain extent, the duty and privilege of every disciple, Revelation 22:17. And certainly there is no better time to administer to the wants of the soul than when we are feeding and clothing the body. Every deacon should, therefore, 'know his opportunity' and improve it. He should ever be ready to speak a word of comfort and consolation to the weary soul while he is laboring to supply the wants of its clay tabernacle. But, in doing so, it is well to remember that he acts simply as a Christian, and not as an officer of the church.   *-R. Milligan, Scheme of Redemption, page 341-342.*

Following W. L. Hayden's outline (*Church Polity*, p.66ff), we could say that the task of the deacon has to do with **waiting on tables** today as it did in the past:

A. **The Table of the Lord**:   Or, the care and the preparation of the emblems of the Lord's Supper. These duties could and should include the care of the entire building. This is no small task and should not be treated as such. Those who prepare the emblems and keep the meeting house clean are as truly serving the Lord as any and every other servant of Christ. The efficient cleaning of the house of worship is something of a problem in a number of places. Let the deacons take upon their hearts the responsibility of doing this job as "unto the Lord." Someone has truly said that the only man more important than the preacher in a public service is the janitor.

B. **The table of the minister**. Having help in this particular field would be a marvelous boon to the average minister. What a joy to have someone who could help in the thousand little tasks that need to be done in the efficient management of the administration of an average size church.

Someone will doubtless think this refers to the job of a church secretary ... and **they are exactly right**. This is, indeed, a field where a deacon can serve, that of secretary to the minister or to the church. The business matters of the Lord's work should be managed with no less efficiency than that of any other work.

C. **The table of the poor**. When will the church awaken to her heaven-sent responsibility in this area? The benevolent agencies in the world today are here because the church has failed to fulfill the desire of the Lord. Hear His words:

Then shall the King say unto them on his right hand, Come, ye blessed of My Father, inherit the kingdom prepared for you from the foundation of the world: for I was hungry, and gave me to eat; I was thirsty, and ye gave me drink; I was a stranger, and ye took me in; naked, and ye clothed me; I was sick, and ye visited me; I was in prison, and ye came unto me. Then shall the righteous answer Him, saying, Lord, when saw we thee hungry, and fed thee? or athirst, and gave thee drink? And when saw we thee a stranger, and took thee in? or naked, and clothed thee? And when saw we thee sick, or in prison, and came unto thee? And the King shall answer and say unto them, Verily I say unto you, inasmuch as ye did it unto one of these my brethren, even these least, ye did it unto me." Matt. 25:34-40 ASV.

It is the major task of the church to give the bread of life, but it is rather difficult to feed the soul while the body is crying for physical nourishment.

BIBLIOGRAPHY ON ELDERS' AND DEACONS' QUALIFICATIONS

Hayden, W. L., *Church Polity*. Kansas City, MO: Old Paths Book Club, Reprint.

Phillips, H. E., *Church Officers and Organization*. Clearwater, FL: Cypress Press, 1948.

Walker, W. R., *A Functioning Eldership*. Cincinnati: Standard, 1942

McGarvey, J. W., *A Treatise on the Eldership*. Murfreesboro, TN: DeHoff Publications, 1956 (reprint).

Wright, Noble, *Notes Concerning the Eldership*. Petersburg, IN: Published by the author, 1977.

DeWelt, Don, *The Church in the Bible*. Joplin, MO: College Press, 1958.

Milligan, Robert, *The Scheme of Redemption*. St. Louis: Christian Board of Publication, nd.

Boatman, Russell, *What the Bible Says About the Church*. Joplin, MO: College Press, 1985.

Wilson, Seth, *Elders and Deacons*. Dallas, TX: Bible Book Store, 1965.

Willis, Pearl A., *Elders' and Deacons' Manual*. Cincinnati: Christian Restoration Association, 196?

Ketcherside, W. Carl, "That They All May Be One" [a study of the qualifications], *Mission Messenger* 19:9 (Sept. 1957), p.7ff.

Ketcherside, W. Carl, "Must Elders be Married?" *Mission Messenger* 19:10 (Oct. 1957), p.1ff. and 19:11 (Nov. 1957), p.1ff.

-- This special study on Deacons is abridged from D. Dewelt, *The Church in the Bible,* p.115-120.

IV. THE CHARGE CONCERNING FALSE TEACHERS. 4:1-16

A. The Appearance of False Teachers Predicted.   4:1-5

4:1 -- But the Spirit explicitly says – "But" is in contrast to the sublime elements that are part of the mystery of godliness (4:16).   With such wonderful truths to occupy their minds and fill their hearts, one would think that men would not busy themselves with other and very different things.   Without the influence of the devil on them, perhaps they wouldn't.   "The Spirit explicitly says" is a present tense in the Greek, indicating continuous action.   Perhaps it means that for a long time now, over and over again, the Holy Spirit has been warning Paul about false teachers in Ephesus (see Acts 20:29,30; Colossians 2:8).[1]   Perhaps it means that at the very moment Paul gets to this place as he writes this letter, the Holy Spirit in an act of sudden revelation[2] calls this warning to mind.   Whether the Spirit spoke directly to Paul (leading him, as he did in Acts 16:6,7), or whether the Spirit spoke to one of the prophets near Paul and who in turn revealed to Paul what had been said (as in the case of Agabus, Acts 21:11), it cannot be certainly determined.   Certainly, the Spirit could have spoken directly to Paul.   It would not be greatly different in his case than it was for the Old Testament prophets, who tell us the source of their message in the words "The Word of the Lord came [to me]."   "Explicitly" translates *hrētōs*, an adverb, which occurs only here in the New Testament, and is very rare in classical Greek.   But the adjective *hrētos*, meaning "something laid down, definite, expressly mentioned," is common.   The Holy Spirit was not using symbols or shadowy images of the future.   The revelation was given in a plain manner, in spoken words.

That in later times – This *hoti* clause contains the message the Spirit is speaking.   "Later times" (*en husterois kairois*) is a different expression than "last days" (*eschatais hēmerais*).   "Last days" is Old Testament prophetic language for the whole church age between the first and second comings of Jesus Christ (see notes at 2 Timothy 3:1).   "Later times" says this church age is made up of seasons or

---

[1] It is true that the Holy Spirit "speaks" to us through Scriptures written years earlier.   Could Paul then be referring to Old Testament Scriptures as the place where he can still hear the Spirit speaking?   Whether or not one would appeal to prophecies like Daniel 7:25, 8:23; 2 Thessalonians 2:3-12; and 2 Peter 3:3, as places where the Spirit "explicitly" says something to Paul about false teachers coming, depends on our identification of the false teachers in those passages and here in 1 Timothy 4.   If, as seems probable, those prophecies have something to do with the end of the age, while 1 Timothy 4 relates to the beginning of the age (called "the last days" in Bible language), then they would be two different 'fallings away' and two different groups of false teachers.

[2] "Revelation," rather than "inspiration," is the right word here.   "Revelation" is the act of the Holy Spirit making known to the Bible writers truths they cannot discover by personal investigation.   "Inspiration" is the act of the Holy Spirit helping the Bible writers to write down in God-chosen words the truths they have learned by revelation.

eras or short segments of time.   The plural says these 'seasons' will recur from time to time.   How much later are these times when false teachers are coming? After Paul writes?   After Paul is dead?   Certainly not too much later, or Timothy would not be around to counteract them, as Paul here instructs him to do.

Some will fall away from the faith – Those who follow the false teachers are denoted by "some."   Not all will be affected, but some will.   "Faith" here is used in its objective sense, a body of doctrine, the redemptive truth, the Christian religion.   "Fall away" is *aphistēmi*, a word that means depart, apostatize from, to move away from one's original position.   One can 'depart' by denying what is true.   One can 'depart' by adding what is false.   We are talking about a departure from the great doctrines which constitute the Christian faith.   Are the same teachers in view in chapter 4 that were in view in chapter 1 of 1 Timothy?[3]   (1) Are these different false teachers?   Protestant interpreters for years have viewed 1 Timothy 4 as a prediction of the rise of the Roman Catholic Church ("forbidding to marry, and commanding to abstain from meats [on Fridays]" KJV). Protestants then brand Romanism with the same strong words of condemnation they find in these verses.   It is difficult to accept the standard Protestant interpretation, for Timothy who is instructed to help the church deal with these teachers will hardly be around to counteract Gregory I, AD 550, who was the first pope.   (2) Is it the same group of false teachers?   Supposing the same Gnostic Judaizers are in view in chapter 4 as were in view in chapter 1, each phrase in chapter 4 (taken as being in opposition to that incipient heresy) makes beautiful sense.

Paying attention to deceitful spirits and doctrines of demons – The circumstantial participle "paying attention" indicates what will influence the "some" to depart from the faith.   It is because of who and what they listen to.   "Deceitful" in "deceitful spirits" translates *planos*, "causing to wander, misleading, deceiver."[4] "Spirits" here seems to be a reference to human teachers, similar to what we find in 1 John 4:1.   Implied in the expression is the idea that these human teachers are getting their information, not from the Holy Spirit, but from demonic spirits.   It is staggering to contemplate how many religious groups have begun because their founders were dabbling in the occult.   The tragic thing is these 'teachers' lead their followers away from God's revealed truth.   "Of demons" in "doctrines of demons" probably should be understood as a subjective genitive, so it speaks of 'teachings inspired by (or suggested by) demons,' rather than 'teachings about

---

[3] This topic has been discussed at some length in the Introductory Study entitled "Religion In and Around Ephesus."

[4] The ancients noticed that some of the bodies in the heavens appeared to follow rather constant orbits through the heavens, while others appeared to wander.   The former they called "stars" while they assigned the name "planets" (see the Greek *planos*) to the wanderers.

demons.'[5]   There are several passages that indicate the continuing activity of demons all through the church age, Ephesians 6:10ff, esp. v.12; 1 Timothy 4:1.[6] Doctrines often emphasized by demonic sources are: (1) an impersonal God, (2) Jesus is a created being, (3) dualism, (4) auto-salvation, and (5) reincarnation.

4:2 -- By means of – Verse 1 spoke of the source of the false teaching – namely, demons.   Verse 2 introduces the human agents who mediate the demonic teachings.

The hypocrisy of liars – The Greek words here should be translated 'through the hypocrisy of men who speak lies.'   The KJV translates the word *pseudologōn* as though it were a participle modifying "demons."   However, there are difficulties with this view, not the least of which is the fact that Scripture does not seem to attribute conscience to demons.   Yet these *pseudologōn* have a conscience, as verse 2 goes on to say.   It is better to take *pseudologōn* as though it were a noun; "liars" or 'men who speak lies' (so ERV, ASV, RSV, NASB).   That these false teachers were "liars" is the apostle's judgment.   The doctrines they were teaching were hardly the truth; the doctrines were all *lies*!   Did the false teachers themselves know they were telling lies?   The answer to this question depends on what is done with "in hypocrisy" (Greek) and "seared in their own conscience." If, as we have proposed to do, we make "liars" a noun, then we must rethink what "in hypocrisy" means.   Ellicott suggests that the dative *en hupokrisei* explains the means by which the demons get the men to listen to the seductive doctrines.   The demons use pretense and masks to cover the real import of their devilish doctrines. Men are tricked, and then become followers of the doctrines of demons.   Others suggest "hypocrisy" describes the false teachers' pretenses as they speak the lies. Their hypocrisy consisted in their assumption of a mask of holiness, a holiness they considered to be derived from their false asceticism and their abstinence from the things which the Paul proceeds to show were lawful.

Seared in their own conscience as with a branding iron – "Seared ... with a branding iron."   The Greek word is a medical term for "branded" or "cauterized." The ASV and NASB take it as "cauterized."   A cauterized wound would leave a

---

[5] Barnes argues for "doctrines *about* demons."   He even offers what he believes are good examples: (1) Teachings in accordance with Jewish views respecting demon possession, and the power of exorcising them.   (If Barnes is right, it is sobering to think of the 20th century emphasis on demonic activity in the light of this verse.)   (2) Teachings in accordance with heathen views respecting the departed spirits (demons) of the good and the great, who were exalted to the rank of demi-gods, and who, though invisible, were supposed still to exert an important influence in favor of mankind.   Barnes (typical of Protestants a century ago) goes on to find both of these in the Roman Catholic Church – he points to their emphasis on exorcism, and the influence of the virgin and the saints so that they are prayed to.

[6] It appears not to be in harmony with the thrust of the New Testament to say demonic activity ceased with the passing of the spiritual gifts (including the ability to exorcise demons, Mark 16:17).

person with no feeling in the burned spot. KJV takes it as "branded." It might be translated 'branded on their own conscience' or 'their consciences having been seared.' "Conscience" is an innate faculty that prompts a man to do what his mind thinks is right, and criticizes him when he does what his mind thinks is wrong. Kent (*op. cit.*, p.145-6) lists four interpretations for this phrase from sources he studied: (1) The conscience is made callous from constant violation. The idea is that the conscience no longer works, it no longer prompts or criticizes, because it is past feeling, and callous from constant violation. "By constantly arguing with conscience, stifling its warnings, and muffling its bell, they at last have reached the point where conscience no longer bothers them" (*Hendriksen*, p.146). (2) Ownership marks of Satan. First century slaves were branded with a capital "D" (for *doulos*, "slave") on their foreheads.   This view says the false teachers belong to the devil; he has branded them with his own mark of ownership. (3) Self-condemnation. This view treats the participle "seared" as middle voice (i.e., the subject acts upon itself). "The false teachers felt the brand they bore, and yet with a show of outward sanctity (cp. *hupokrisei*) they strove to beguile and seduce others, to make them as bad as themselves" (*Ellicott*, p.228). (4) Radical act of perversion. The conscience has been made insensitive to right and wrong by some radical act of perverting the truth. "Seared" is supposed to reflect something "radical and violent." At first, the men who are now the demons' mouthpieces knew better. Their consciences bothered them when they first began to listen and spread the 'seducing spirit's doctrines.' But no longer.

> These men tried to teach the efficacy of a substitution of certain counsels of perfection [e.g., abstaining from marriage or certain foods] in place of a faithful loving life. They based their teaching on wild Oriental specula- tions about the evil nature of all matter. They were often themselves evil- livers, who, conscious of their own stained, scarred lives, strove with a show of outward sanctity and hypocritical self-denial to beguile and lead astray others, and in the end to make them as vile as themselves.[7]

4:3 -- *men* who forbid marriage – Verse 3 identifies two of the doctrines taught by the false teachers, and indicates why the doctrines are wrong. Some sort of ascetic thinking is evidently behind this forbidding of marriage. Behind the ascetic views was the Greek philosophy of dualism, which held that spirit is good, but matter is evil. Anything material is therefore the enemy, be it the world, the human body, or anything non-spirit. The enemy must be conquered, but how to do so was debated. Some said, "Avoid it!" Some said, "Indulge it, because what you do with the body won't affect the soul!"[8] The ascetic practice of avoid- ing any sexual relationships, even in marriage, first appeared among the Jews

---

[7] Spence, *op. cit.*, p.228.

[8] In 1 Timothy, Paul warns against the former "solution." John (in Revelation 2:15,20,24; 1 John 3:4-10), Peter (in 2 Peter 2:12-19), and Jude (Jude 4,6,11,19), warn against the latter "solution."

in the groups known as Essenes and Therapeuetai.[9]   When it had finally flowered into its completed form, Gnosticism also forbade marriage as one of the necessities for the person who would be holy.[10]   God instituted marriage in the Garden of Eden, and says marriage is honorable for all men (Hebrews 13:4). What the false teachers were doing is casting aspersions at God's own assessment of matters.   According to the teaching of Jesus, there are some men who may choose the single life (Matthew 19:11,12).   The false teachers at Ephesus were not making marriage optional just for those who chose to serve God this way. They were demanding "no marriage" of all of their followers.

***And advocate* abstaining from foods** – The NASB supplies the verb "advocate" from the previous *kōlountōn*, "forbid."[11]   The KJV reads "abstain from meats." The word "meat" has changed meaning since its use in the KJV.   Then it meant 'foods of all kinds'; now it means 'flesh of animals.'   When it meant 'foods of all kinds,' it exactly represented the Greek *brōma*, which also means 'food of all kinds', whether animal, fruit, vegetables, or bread.   Apparently, the ascetics at Ephesus demanded adherence to certain dietary rules relating to all foods, not just those relating to "meat" (flesh).[12]   If this had been clearly understood, perhaps Protestants would not have incorrectly used this passage against Catholics. Catholics fasted on Friday, abstaining from eating flesh.   Protestants, when reading this verse in 1 Timothy 4, thought they had found another Biblical proof text showing the Roman church to be in error.[13]   Care should be exercised here! It is not just the old Levitical distinction between clean and unclean meats (all of

---

[9] "None of the Essenes marry," wrote Philo, *Fragm.*, p.633.   "A people without a single woman, for they renounce marriage," said Pliny, *Natural History* V.15).   See also Josephus, *Wars* II.7.2, and *Antiquities* XVIII. 1.5.   See "Religion in and Around Ephesus" in the Introductory Studies for details about the Essenes.   The Therapeuetai were an ascetic sect, mentioned in the *De Vita Contemplativa* (doubtfully ascribed to Philo) as living chiefly on Lake Mareotis, near Alexandria, Egypt.   Their discipline resembled the Essenes.   Throughout the week each lived in his lonely dwelling, but on the Sabbath they assembled for worship.   They held that salvation is achieved through mystical knowledge of God.

[10] Clement of Alexandria, *Stromata* III.6; Irenaeus, *Haer.* I.22.   Years after Timothy was dead, the Roman church demanded celibacy for its priests.   A more recent example of forbidding marriage would be the Shakers in the 18th and 19th centuries.

[11] The grammatical construction is an example of zeugma, and is legitimate.

[12] *Brōma* is also used in Romans 14:20,21 and 1 Corinthians 8:13.   In both passages, *brōma* ("food of any kind") is illustrated by some specific kinds of food, including *krea* ("flesh").   A completely different word, *lachana*, meaning "herbs, vegetables," occurs at Romans 14:2.

[13] This commentator is hesitant to make application of 1 Timothy to the Roman Church.   It is usual in Protestant circles to date the Roman Church from the time of Gregory the Great, AD 590. While what Gregory took over as the first "pope" had been slowly departing from the New Testament practices for years, we doubt that the "false teachers" here identified by Paul, whom Timothy was to personally oppose, would be called "Roman Catholics" by any Protestant interpreter.   It's just too early for "Roman Catholics" to be on the scene while Timothy is still alive.

which pertained to which animals were edible and which were not), that is the thing advocated by the false teachers. The false teachers' dietary restrictions were stricter than the Levitical rules had been. Worded another way, the false teachers were not asking for a 'meatless' diet, permitting a diet of vegetables only. They were demanding their followers to 'hold away from all foods' – they were demanding them to exist on an extremely meager diet. If ascetic notions (ideas of a rigorous denial and avoidance of anything material) are in the background of the dietary rules imposed by the false teachers, we can see why they would call for almost no food intake at all. The diet of the Essenes may give us an example. As regards their food, Lightfoot (*Colossians*, p.86) said, "The Essene drank no wine; he did not touch animal food. His meal consisted of a piece of bread and a single mess of vegetables." According to the words of Jesus, there are times to fast (Matthew 9:15), and it is to be done without ostentation (Matthew 6:16-18). While there is a place in the Christian's life for fasting on appropriate occasions, what the false teachers at Ephesus were asking their followers to do is something completely different than simple fasting. Neither meat nor vegetables will make a man better or worse spiritually. No matter what diet the false teachers insisted upon would help a man to know God.

Which God has created to be gratefully shared in – Here Paul begins a brief refutation of the doctrines advocated by the false teachers. "Which" in the Greek is plural, and indicates that both of their ascetic doctrines (forbidding marriage, abstaining from foods) were wrong.[14] God created food (Genesis 1:29, 9:3), and God instituted marriage (Genesis 1:28). The fact that God had created them[15] was proof they were not to be regarded as evil. When the false teachers forbade them, either deliberately or unconsciously they were disputing God's wisdom and morality. When one has to dispute God to justify his doctrine, something is wrong with the doctrine! "To be gratefully shared in" is the Greek 'for partaking with thanksgiving.' 'Partaking' is *metalēpsin*, a classical word found only here in the New Testament, and not used in the LXX. The instruction about 'giving thanks', for food and marriage and for everything created by God, is repeated with greater emphasis in verse 4. The appropriate personal response to what God has created is for men to receive them with thanksgiving, rather than avoiding or abstaining from them for some supposed religious reason.

---

[14] *Ha* ("which") is neuter plural, and agrees with the nearest antecedent "foods" which is also neuter plural. However, it also can and probably does include "forbidding to marry," since what Paul writes in the following verses applies to marriage as much as to foods. (Spence, in *Ellicott's Commentary*, p.229, took "which" as a reference to "foods" alone, and explained that Paul says nothing more about marriage because that was a point easily proved, whereas the matter about foods needed the presentation he gives it in verses 3b and 4.)

[15] This is a refutation of Gnostic doctrine. Gnostics held that some lesser aeons, generations removed from God, did the creating. In their view, that's how a good God would have to make a material world. He couldn't do it himself. So one of his underlings must have made matter. "No!" says Paul. "God created!"

By those who believe and know the truth – People who "believe and know the truth" in this context are Christians.[16] "Believe" is *pistois*, an adjective that means 'trustworthy, faithful.' "Know" is *epegnōkosi*, a perfect tense participle, indicating past completed action with present continuing results. There is a refutation of Gnostic doctrine! You don't have to keep listening to the false teachers in order to eventually "know" the "truth." Christians have access to all the "knowledge" and "truth" there is, without ever having to give a thought to the false doctrines of demons.[17] "Truth" is either 'Christian doctrine' or a reference to Christ himself (who said, "I am the ... truth"). Paul says, in effect, 'What God created for all men must surely be legitimate for Christians.' Satan and the demons are completely wrong when they say that marriage and food are not for believers.

4:4 -- For everything created by God is good – "Everything created" represents *ktisma*, and emphasizes the result of the act of creating.[18] "Good" reminds us of God's own estimation of his creative work, "God saw that it was good," Genesis 1:12,18,31, etc.[19] This is the first of two reasons why "marriage" and "food" (verse 3) may be gratefully shared in by Christians. God created them (verse 4), and God consecrated them (verse 5). The person who teaches that there is something morally or spiritually wrong with marriage or eating is calling something evil that God has pronounced good.

And nothing is to be rejected – "Rejected" is an attempt to translate *apoblēton*, a word which occurs only here in the New Testament, though it is quite common in the LXX, in the sense of 'unclean' or 'abominable.' The word represents the preposition 'away' and the verb 'to throw,' so nothing is to be 'thrown away' as though there were something wrong with it, when God has declared it good. Moffatt used the word "tabooed" to catch the force of this passage. Nothing that God has made, for the purposes for which He has made it, is to be treated as "taboo" by the people of God.[20] Paul is repudiating the actions and doctrines

---

[16] The use of only one article with the two nouns ("believe" and "know") in the same case, shows that just one group of people is meant.

[17] A similar phrase "know the truth" was used at 1 Timothy 2:4.

[18] Greek forms that end in *-ma* all emphasize the result of the action signified by the rest of the word. Paul also, in other contexts, uses *ktisis* for "creation" – a word ending in *-sis*, and like all such nouns emphasizes the act signified by the rest of the word; *ktisis* it puts emphasis on the act of creating. (Compare *brōma*, 'food' and *brōsis*, 'the act of eating.')

[19] Care must be taken lest this statement about "every created thing being good" is used to justify something it was never intended to cover. For example, some who are looking for ways to defend drinking alcohol use this verse, "everything created by God is good." Barnes replies that it cannot be inferred that what God has made is necessarily good *after* it has been perverted by man. It is not talking about what man has 'created' but about things that resulted from God's creation.

[20] This statement is in a context where Paul corrects the doctrine of certain false teachers who

of the false teachers.   They have been "rejecting" marriage and certain foods, but the Christian does not need to.

If it is received with gratitude – "Gratitude" ("thanksgiving" KJV) likely has reference to giving thanks to God in prayer (see next verse which specifically names "prayer").   Christians have numerous encouragements to offer "thanks" to God for the "good things" He provides.   Verses 3-5 of this very passage emphasize this idea.   Compare also Romans 14:6.   In addition, take our Lord's action at the Last Supper (Luke 22:17,19), at the multiplication of the loaves and fishes (Luke 9:16), and Paul's actions on the voyage to Rome (Acts 27:35).   The repeated emphasis on gratitude and thanks in this passage reminds us that the point Paul is defending is thankful acceptance of God's good gifts.   He is not advocating an autonomous attitude that thinks anything that satisfies or gives pleasure is perfectly acceptable behavior.

4:5 -- For – Verse 5 is giving the second of two reasons why "food" and "marriage" may be gratefully received by the Christians (verse 3).   God has declared them fit, or acceptable, for the Christian to use and enjoy.

It is sanctified – The verb *hagiadzetai* is present passive, and means 'continually being set apart for a holy purpose.'   Some difference of opinion has prevailed over how to explain this present tense idea of 'continually' or 'repeatedly' being sanctified.   Some think that on every occasion when prayers are offered or the Word of God is read, God again declares "everything" acceptable.   Some think verse 5 is just a summary of what has already been said in verses 3 and 4.   Once the truths there emphasized are known, it is obvious that "everything" is 'acceptable' (sanctified).   The antecedent of "it" is "everything created by God" (verse 4).   We probably should not limit our discussion in this verse simply to "foods."   Anything the ascetic false teachers rejected (including marriage) may well be in view here.

By means of the word of God – While the reference to the "word of God" may recall the text from Genesis where everything was pronounced "good," there is every reason to suppose Paul may have been thinking of a more recent revelation than the Genesis record (the verb "sanctified" is present tense).   The Word of God does speak on the sanctity of marriage.   We already have noted some of the verses in our comments on "marriage" in verse 3.   It should be repeated that it was ascetic notions about marriage being taboo that Paul here says are not in harmony with God's view of things.   The Word of God does speak on the matter

---

were insisting that 'marriage' and certain 'foods' were taboo.   What Paul writes must not be taken out of its context.   What he says has nothing to do with marijuana or heroin or cocaine, or perhaps even tobacco.

of food.[21]   Jesus expressed the "Word of God" for his people when "He declared all foods clean" (Mark 7:18,19).   Peter, too, learned this truth via the vision of the sheet full of animals he was commanded by God to kill and eat, just before he went to preach to Cornelius (Acts 10:13,15,28).   Since the "Word of God"[22] declares that Christians may eat any food, the ascetic prohibitions against certain foods, as though such abstinence would make a man more holy, are clearly false!

And prayer – We have had the word 'thanksgiving' ("gratitude" NASB) in verse 4, which might also be a reference to prayers of thanks at mealtime.   How then does this verse differ from what was already said in verse 4?   The word here is *enteuxis*, a word already explained at 2:1 as indicating 'to approach someone in a confident, familiar manner,' or 'boldness and freedom' in approaching God. (After all, a Christian does have this kind of close and personal relationship with his Father in heaven.)   Perhaps, too, we should think of the possibility that such a "prayer" would keep a man from misusing his privileges, as though he could do just as he sees fit, with no thought of what God might wish or expect.

B. The Duty of the Evangelist Toward False Teachers.   4:6-10

4:6 -- In pointing out these things to the brethren – "The brethren" is one of the Biblical names for the members of Christ's church.   Though the words are addressed to Timothy, the instructions contained in the letter are intended to be heard by the whole church.   "These things" which Timothy was to point out to the brethren certainly include the foolish, false ascetic practices just alluded to in the previous verses.[23]   Having passed on the Spirit's express warning about the coming of false teachers, and having given a rebuttal concerning some of their false doctrines, Paul now gives direct admonition to Timothy, the evangelist, con-

---

[21] Not a few commentaries have treated chapter 4 as though the false teachers were Judaizers (rather than ascetics, as we have determined should be done).   As a result, a large number of the comments offered at this place explain that the point of verse 5 is that the old Mosaic distinction between clean and unclean meats has been abolished.   A typical example would be, "Before the Law of Moses was given, God's word allowed all kinds of food to be eaten (Genesis 1:12, 9:3,4). The Mosaic laws about meats and drinks were 'carnal ordinances' imposed only 'until the time of reformation' (Hebrews 9:10), i.e., till Christ came."

[22] Some have offered different explanations for the "Word of God" than we have offered in the text.   Bernard, for example, reached the conclusion that this verse teaches the inclusion of verses of Scripture in our "grace" at mealtime.   Another thinks it refers to "the blessing of God" given in answer to the prayer of thanks for the food.   Still another opines that Paul refers to a reading of Scripture preceding the eating of the meal.

[23] Many commentators on 1 Timothy also include all the things covered in this letter so far: the strange doctrines with their myths and endless genealogies (chapter 1), the proper way to prepare for public worship (chapter 2), and how much of a church's healthiness is affected the choice of good elders and deacons (chapter 3).

cerning his responsibility in this matter. Paul's directives to Timothy also serve as instructions for all evangelists. These are some proper "things" to preach and teach about: that God created things "good," that the Word of God says foods are not taboo, and that prayer and gratitude are important. "Pointing out" ("put in remembrance of" KJV) gives *hupotithēmi* its metaphorical meaning. Literally, the word means to 'lay down something' as a principle on which conduct is based, or to 'lay down something' like stepping stones over treacherous ground. 'Hypothesis,' the assumed basis from which you start, is from the same root. Most writers suggest that the term is a mild one, with a meaning like 'advise' or 'counsel' or 'suggest' or 'teach.' As Timothy presents the truths which the brethren need to know if they are to put up a good defense against error and deceitfulness, he is instructed to do it kindly but forcefully. The participle "pointing out" is present tense, indicating continuous or repeated action. It requires teaching, repeated teaching, of the fundamental truths basic to the Christian religion.[24] Timothy's primary task in Ephesus was to put a stop to false teaching (1 Timothy 1:3,4), which involves putting something in the place of what he roots out. Paul tells Timothy to fill people's lives with the truths of Christianity.

You will be a good servant of Christ Jesus – This is high praise from Paul to the young preacher. It is a title of honor that every evangelist should aspire to deserve. "Servant" is the word translated "deacon" in chapter 3. However, in this the context it is clear that that office is not the topic, but rather the word is used in its general meaning, "servant" or 'minister.'[25] The way Timothy will continue to be a good servant (minister) of Christ Jesus is by pointing out the proper truths on which Christian people are to base their lives. Continued proclamation of the word of truth was Paul's test for being a good minister of Jesus Christ. An 'excellent minister' is one who, in loving devotion to his task, to his people, and above all to his Lord and Savior, warns against departures from the truth and shows his listeners how to deal with error.

Constantly **nourished** – Who is it who is "nourished" by the words of faith? At first, one might think it is the "brethren" who are to be nurtured and sustained by a steady diet of the words of faith. But the Greek seems to show that it is Timothy, the preacher, who is to be so nourished, before he attempts to nourish others. Here is what a man, who would deserve the appellation "good servant of Christ Jesus," must do as part of his preparation for "pointing out these things to the brethren." The NASB translators have properly added "constantly" to render

[24] Before the chapter we are now studying ends, we will see that Timothy was not only to tell the Christians how to live; he was also to show them how to live.

[25] One controversy that should never have made the rounds in the Christian Churches is whether or not it is Scriptural to call our preacher "minister." Evangelists, such as Timothy and others, are called "servants" or "ministers" in a number of places in Scripture, e.g., Colossians 4:17. It certainly is a Biblical term.

the present tense participle "nourished." It marks a continuous process of self-education.[26] If Timothy is going to instruct the brethren in the truth, he himself must be nourished on the truths he is about to teach.[27] The preacher must first fill his heart and mind with the Word of God before he will havenourishment to offer to his listeners. Men today, who would serve as evangelists as Timothy did, must never relax their efforts for self-improvement in their knowledge of the Word. The education of a good minister of Jesus Christ is never finished. We regularly counsel preachers to spend an hour or two each day in the preparation of a verse-by-verse commentary on the different books of the New Testament.[28] We have suggested that, before a preacher preaches a series of sermons through one of the New Testament books, he make his own verse-by-verse commentary on that book – and have it finished 6 months before he begins the sermon series. When it comes time to prepare the actual messages, the preparation will be quicker, and the content of the messages more nourishing to his hearers.

On the words of the faith and of the sound doctrine – The "words" that will nourish Timothy are those which embody "the faith" and "the excellent teaching"[29] of the church, i.e., true Christian doctrine.[30] "Words of the faith" is another name for the body of Christian doctrine. In 1 Timothy 6:3, the "sound words" are "those of our Lord Jesus Christ." In 2 Timothy 1:13, the "words" are those which Timothy has heard from Paul. "Words of ... the sound doctrine" is another name for the body of Christian doctrine, perhaps specifically those doctrines which would be in direct opposition to "doctrines of demons" (4:1). Paul uses different descriptive phrases for this body of true Christian doctrine. Here he styles it 'the good doctrine' (*hē kalē*). In 1 Timothy 1:10 and Titus 1:9, he writes of "sound teaching" (*hē hugiainousa*). In Titus 2:10 he writes "doctrine of God." In 1 Timothy 6:3 he wrote "doctrine conforming to godliness" (*hē kat' eusebeian didaskalia*). Exactly why Paul used two different names for Christian doctrine at this place has been variously explained: (1) Some suppose Paul has in mind those summaries of doctrine which he elsewhere calls "faithful sayings" ("trustworthy statements" NASB). (2) Other suppose Paul has reference to the oral and written parts of the New Testament already published.

---

[26] The Greek verb rendered "nourished" occurs only here in the whole Greek Bible, but it is common in classical Greek. There it has the meaning 'brought up in,' 'trained in from childhood.' This helps us to capture the 'growing' and 'continuing in' sense found in the word.

[27] The following verses give additional prerequisites to being able to 'nourish others.'

[28] Bible students acquainted with Barnes' Notes have seen the completed results of his daily study of the Word. That's the kind of "set of notes" or "comments" we have in mind that each preacher should do for himself, as part of his preparation to preach.

[29] Note the NASB marginal reading.   Literally the Greek here is "good doctrine."

[30] The noun "words" is followed by two genitive phrases, both of which explain which "words" are in Paul's mind.   They are "words of the faith" and "words of the sound (good) doctrine."

Which you have been following – The verb *parakoloutheō* can mean either 'which you have closely investigated,' or 'which you have followed as a standard.' Implied is the idea that Timothy has wanted to know it perfectly so as to be able to teach it identically. Timothy's doctrine (learned from the apostle) does not need any modification. He's been teaching it aright. He simply needs to advance in his study yet further, to gain an ever deeper facility in pointing out to the brethren the things that will help them in their Christian walk.

4:7 -- But have nothing to do – Timothy must see that he constantly nourishes himself on "words of the faith and the sound doctrine." On the other hand, there are some 'junk foods' (perhaps we should say 'poisonous foods') he must avoid. *Paraiteomai* is a word that speaks of 'strong refusal, decline to receive, avoid, shun.' Some have interpreted this prohibition as though it said 'don't even take any time to find out what it is (fables) the false teachers are teaching.' Certainly, if one were going to avoid such fables himself, and teach others to do likewise, the evangelist will have to make some effort to get acquainted with the false doctrines. The prohibition says, 'don't try to nourish yourself on worldly fables.' And if the evangelist is to avoid these fables, then the Ephesian church members ought to get the idea that they too should avoid these "worldly fables." If such fables won't nourish the ministry, they certainly won't nourish them, either.

With worldly fables fit only for old women – "Worldly" translates the same word rendered "profane" in 1 Timothy 1:9. These "fables" treat Christianity with contempt. We've already seen how the false teachers attacked the very nature of God as the maker of every good thing and the giver of a reasonable revelation of His will. "Fables" is the same word translated "myths" at 1 Timothy 1:4. We suppose the same "myths" are in view here, as were warned against in chapter 1. "Fit only for old women" translates *graōdēs*, which means 'characteristic of old women,' 'pertaining to old women,' or 'told by old women.' As "fit only for old women" is explained, we must be careful lest we needlessly offend today's elderly women, such as might happen were we to make an implica-tion that all old women are silly or frivolous or afflicted with limitless credulity. We must also be careful lest we leave the impression that these 'tales' were 'harmless.' Paul certainly did not view them that way. In this part of the ancient world, old women had a reputation for storytelling which sometimes put the gods in an outrageous light.[31] From earliest times in Anatolia, female religious officials known as "old women" kept alive the ancient myths.[32] We wonder if behind this characterization is Paul's

---

[31] For an extended list of ancient references to women as storytellers, see D.R. MacDonald, *The Legend and the Apostle: The Battle for Paul in Story and Canon* (Philadelphia: Westminster, 1983), p. 13-14.

[32] "The 'old woman' enacted a wide range of roles and was the most prominent magic-religious specialist in Anatolia ... Although many of her incantations are in Hurrian and are therefore very difficult to decipher, enough is known about their content to conclude that the 'old woman' was one

knowledge that in times past these "fables" were kept alive and passed on by elderly female religious officials.[33]

On the other hand – Paul quickly balances the negative with a positive. The false teachers' ascetic practices will do nothing to help promote a holy life; yet there are things a Christian is to do to promote godliness in this life. The two imperatives in this verse, "have nothing to do with" and "discipline yourself," are contrasting thoughts, but perhaps there is also an underlying connecting thought. As the punctuation in the NASB shows, this part of the verse begins a new section that runs through verse 8. The thread running through the next several phrases is the need for "godliness." Could it be that the false teachers tried to tell their students that their "fables" (perhaps dealing with certain rules about eating and drinking, and other "bodily exercises"?) would be a help towards "godliness"?

Discipline yourself for the purpose of godliness – The concept of "godliness" (*eusebeia*) has already been introduced and explained at 1 Timothy 2:2. There are a number of very close synonyms translated "godliness;" a comparison of some of these will help us understand the Paul's thrust:

> *Theosebēs* (not the word used here), according to derivation and usage, means "worship of God" (or the gods), a fulfillment of one's duty towards God.

> *Eusebēs*, a cognate to the word used here, is distinguished from *theosebēs* in two ways. (1) It is used to include the fulfillment of obligations of all kinds, both towards God and man. It is applied to the fulfillment of the duties involved in human relations, e.g., towards one's parents. (2) When used in the higher sense, it means not any kind of worship, but, as the etymology indicates, the worshiping of God *aright*.[34]

Eusebeia (which at Acts 3:12 is translated "piety"), "godliness," describes the man who is careful lest he fail either in his duties to God, or his duties to man. There is a lifestyle the Christian is to live, but it is not arrived at by ascetic practices like the false teachers at Ephesus were teaching. How is it arrived at? Paul goes on to explain. As the verb *gumnadzō* suggests, "discipline yourself" or 'exercise yourself' towards godliness is a metaphor taken from training for gymnastic exercises. The present imperative means 'keep on exercising.' "Godliness" is

---

of the primary transmitters of mythic tradition in Anatolian society." Michael S. Moore, *The Balaam Traditions: Their Character and Development* (Atlanta: Scholars, 1990), p. 21-22.

[33] Perhaps it is of some significance that certain religions today that embrace some of the old fables were introduced to the western world by women. Madam Blavatsky, Annie Besant, Ellen G. White, and Mary Baker Eddy are well-known examples.

[34] Berry, *New Testament Synonyms*, p. 124.

a progressive state, something arrived at only by sustained effort and rigid discipline.[35]   Once one has rejected the ascetic practices (as Paul here insists must be done), does that mean he does nothing?   No!   He must strive to live in a godly manner himself.   He must "discipline himself" habitually to do his duties both to God and man.   Timothy is charged to train himself towards a lifestyle characterized by "godliness" with the same intensity that a gymnast trains to physical perfection in his chosen exercise.   Paul calls Timothy and each of us to make vigorous effort to build up our "godliness."[36]

4:8 -- For – It seems likely that verse 8 is intended to give a reason for what was just said about 'exercising yourself unto godliness.'   The reason for such exercise is that it is beneficial both for this life and the one to come.

Bodily discipline is only of little profit – Can we specify some particular "bodily discipline" (or 'exercise,' *hē somatikē gumnasia*) that Paul may have had in mind? (1) Some suppose that by 'bodily exercise' Paul refers to the ascetic practices of forbidding marriages and certain foods, just repudiated in 4:1-5.[37]   Others object that Paul would not refer to these practices as profiting even a little.   (2) Some suppose Paul refers to certain ascetic practices (other than those mentioned in 4:2) which are a useful discipline toward godliness.[38]   Objection to this explanation revolves around whether or not the expression 'bodily exercise' is a suitable figure to describe the self-control that is necessary to curb the physical appetites lest they become more important than godliness.   (3) Still others suppose Paul refers to ordinary physical exercise that results in physical fitness.[39]   The ruins of a great stadium, scene of athletic contests at Ephesus when Timothy lived there, have remained to modern times.   The Greeks gave great emphasis to the attainment of physical strength, grace, and skill.   Paul does not deny a certain value to physical development, but he insists its worth is limited in time and nature.   It is not out of reason that Paul could use athletic imagery to encourage the proper kind of Christian living.   Even though the asceticism just described in 4:1-5 is repudiated, there is a 'discipline' (an "exercise") that is necessary for the Christian who would grow to wards godliness.   What does "of little" ("for a little" ASV)

---

[35] In the list of qualities that Peter urges a Christian to develop, "godliness" is near the summit of the list, 2 Peter 1:6,7.

[36] Most of us admit that godliness is an excellent thing for attaining to a peaceful death, but we show little evidence that we are convinced of its being necessary for spending a happy life. Plummer, *Exposition of the Bible*, The Pastoral Epistles (Hartford: S.S. Scranton, 1908), p.421-3.

[37] See this view developed in Bernard, Calvin, Easton, Ellicott, Hiebert, Lenski.

[38] Passages such as Romans 13:14; 1 Corinthians 8:13, and 9:27 do teach a commendable self-restraint.   But it is doubtful that this self-restraint should be called "asceticism."   Nor can we understand how the profit of such commendable self-restraint would be categorized as "a little."

[39] See this view developed in Alford, Bengel, Fairbairn, Guthrie, Hendriksen, and Kent.

mean? Note the ASV margin "for little." (1) If we translate *pros oligon* "for little," the statement means that bodily exercise is not worth much at all. Those who adopt explanation (1) above for "bodily discipline" are quick to explain that such ascetic practices as the false teachers advocated were actually not worth much at all! (2) If we translate "for a little" ("of little profit") perhaps the passage says there is some benefit to physical exercise and physical fitness – it profits 'for a little while.' So understood, Paul is comparing the limited benefit of bodily exercise with the unlimited benefit of godliness. Physical exercise helps a person to be healthier and happier and more capable if we get enough to keep ourselves in good condition. But its benefit is physical and mental, not spiritual, and it lasts only as long as we live on earth. This is "little" in comparison with the eternal benefits of well-developed godliness.[40] (3) If we translate it "for a little," perhaps we should explain that "little" is the opposite of the "all things" that godli-ness is profitable for. It benefits only the person doing the exercising.

But godliness is profitable for all things – "Godliness" has been explained in verse 7. *Eusebeia* describes the man who is careful lest he fail either in his duties to God or his duties to man. When we compare the two parts of this verse, we see the wording is almost identical. It would make the phrases match word for word if we were to supply "exercise" before "godliness" – so that it reads "but exercise in godliness is ..." "Profitable for all things" shows the vast difference between gymnastic exercises and godly exercises. Gymnastic exercise affects chiefly the physical part of man; it doesn't do much to benefit the exerciser's neighbors and friends; and it lasts only a little while when compared with the far-reaching effects of godliness. "The influence of 'godliness is worldwide' ... [It] transfigures and illumines with its divine radiance all busy, active life – every condition, every rank, all ages" (*Ellicott's*, p.233).

Since it holds promise for the present life and *also* for the *life* to come – "The *promise of life* is not an equivalent for worldly prosperity, but sums up the blessedness of godliness. Irrespective of his present earthly circumstances, a Christian may fairly be said to have the best of both worlds."[41] The genitive here is the genitive of the thing promised, and the thing promised is 'the life that now is.' Hendriksen's explanation of "eternal life" at John 1:4 and 3:15 as being "the abundant life" is the right concept. Such "life" is the highest blessedness which the creature can enjoy (*Ellicott's*, p.233). "The present life" indicates that whatever is really necessary for this life is promised to the godly: food and clothing (Matthew 6:25-33); comfort in affliction (Hebrews 13:5); support in old age and death (Psalm 23:4; Isaiah 66:4); a good reputation and an honored name

[40] Orrin Root, *Standard Lesson Commentary*, 1985-86., p.85

[41] Guthrie, *Pastoral Epistles*, p.95.

when we are dead (Psalm 37:1-6). False asceticism crushes out all the joy and gladness God intends for a man to enjoy in this present life. On the other hand, every worthwhile experience of this life is enriched by godliness. In this, Paul agrees with the promise given by Jesus to those who would "seek ... first the kingdom of God" (Matthew 6:33 KJV), and again to those who would leave possessions and loved ones for His sake (Matthew 19:29). The "life to come" is blessed eternal living with God in heaven hereafter. Godliness is the only lifestyle that promises such a life to come. False asceticism is an unreal preparation for that future life. Infidelity makes no promise of future happiness. Vice promises pleasure for the present life, and disappoints both here and hereafter. Let it be emphasized that *godliness* – giving what is due both to God and men – is the way to the abundant life, both here and hereafter.

4:9 -- It is a trustworthy statement – On the meaning of this formula, see notes at 1 Timothy 1:15. Whether the actual words of the saying are found in verses 7b-8 or in verse 10 is a matter of debate among the commentators. In favor of verse 10: (1) In the two previous occurrences of this formula (1:15 and 3:1), the statements which followed were the actual words of the formula. Might we not expect the same here? Perhaps it was this thinking that led the translators of the NIV, by their paragraphing and punctuation, to emphatically treat verse 10 as the faithful saying. (2) One writer opines that the subject matter of verse 10 is more theologically weighty than that of verse 8, and therefore would be more admirably suited to be a "faithful saying."[42] (3) Some suggest that the words of the faithful saying begin in verse 10 with "because we have fixed our hope ...."[43] In favor of verses 7b-8: (1) Verse 8, with its matching wording in both parts of the verse sound more like a "proverbial saying" than do the words of verse 10. (2) The fact that verse 10 begins with "for" seems to indicate that the words that follow are intended to give a reason for something just said, rather than the contents of a "faithful saying."[44] We suppose the words of this "faithful saying" are found in verses 7b-8, and include these words: "Discipline yourself for the purpose of godliness, for bodily discipline is only a little profit, but godliness is profitable for all things, since it holds promise for the present life and also for the life to come."[45]

---

[42] The idea of "theologically weighty" is that, if verse 10 were the faithful saying, then this faithful saying would be saying something about "salvation." This appeals to writers who have asserted that all the faithful sayings have some statement in them about "salvation." However, careful examination shows that those who make such a claim about "salvation" in each of the faithful sayings are not able to defend their assertion (see 1 Timothy 3:1, and 2 Timothy 2:11-13).

[43] This introduces the difficulty of why (in this instance only) the words of the saying are removed from the introductory formula by some intervening words.

[44] Before too much weight is given to this argument, it should be noted that the same conjunction "for" forms part of the faithful saying in 2 Timothy 2:11.

[45] Some limit the words of the saying to what is found in verse 8. We have followed the suggestion of the punctuation in the NASB, which makes 7b and 8 all part of one sentence.

Deserving of full acceptance – Because the truth expressed in this trustworthy statement is the heart and soul of the gospel message about how believers are to live, it is something every Christian is to embrace. "Deserving full acceptance" calls for a personal response to the 'saying.' If these "faithful sayings" were short memorized summaries of Christian doctrine which expressed the emphases or thrusts of Christian doctrine and life in the first century, one wonders if present-day Christians understand the importance of "exercising godliness" so that they could make this 'saying' theirs, too. Does it still have "full acceptance"?

4:10 -- For it is for this we labor and strive – We are still in a section where Timothy's responsibility toward false teachers is being clearly spelled out. Timothy's responsibility is not just to repudiate the ascetic practices the false teachers advocate. He must teach something positive in its place. What they are teaching isn't right, but there is something that is, namely, the importance of 'disciplining oneself toward godliness.' Verse 10 begins with "for," and it probably offers a reason why one can give whole-hearted acceptance to the faithful saying about the importance of developing "godliness" in one's character. "We" likely includes Timothy along with Paul in this statement.[46] Both the apostle and the evangelist have been laboring and striving for godliness now for a good while. "For this" means 'to obtain the glorious promise of the highest blessedness here, and the endless life with God hereafter, that godliness entails.' If Paul and Timothy were not deeply convinced about the reliability of that saying about godliness, they would not be working so hard! The word "labor" (*kopioō*) is the synonym for work that points to the weariness and exhaustion which results from the strenuous toil.[47] It takes work, mental and spiritual as well as physical exertion, to become more godly in attitude, character, and life. "Strive" (*agōnidzomai*) is a word from the world of athletics. It pictures the strain an athlete exerts to win. (The KJV reading "suffer reproach" represents an inferior reading, *oneididzomai*.[48]) "The extent to which an athlete throws his whole being being into striving for the prize in no way excels the extent to which Paul throws himself into the service of the Lord."[49] Many of us have 'trained' and spent long and painful effort to get into shape for some athletic team. Have any of us modern athletes given as much effort to excel at godliness as we did to win some fleeting game or championship? Both verbs are present tense and speak of continuous action.

---

[46] Others suppose the "we" is simply an editorial "we" and that Paul is talking about himself and his own commitment to the truth of his message.

[47] Berry, *New Testament Synonyms*, p.135.

[48] Commentaries based on the KJV will call attention to the bitter reproaches and persecutions Paul endured in order to continue preaching, and referred to at 2 Timothy 3:11; 1 Corinthians 4:9-13; 2 Corinthians 11:23-27.

[49] Foster, *op. cit.*, p.371.

Because we have fixed our hope on the living God – Paul here explains the motive behind his "labor and striving." He says, 'We know that any promise the Living God has made will be fulfilled.' The verb *ēlpikamen* is a perfect tense, a past action with present continuing results. It implies a continuous state of hope, "we have fixed our hope." The ground of hope (*epi* with the dative) is given as "the living God who is the savior of all men." Perhaps attention is called to His being a "living" God, to strongly contrast Him to those dumb and lifeless idols enshrined in the well-known Ephesian temples. Perhaps there is emphasis on the fact that He is the source and giver of life, and is able to fulfill any promise He makes about "life", either in this age or the one to come. Such energy and striving are not pointless, for Paul's confidence rests on the right foundation.

Who is the Savior of all men – This seems to be offered as a reason why one can confidently "hope" in the living God. He after all is the Savior! The argument is similar to the one offered at 1 Timothy 2:4, namely, that there are not many gods, one of whom is interested in this ethnic group, and another of whom is interested in that group. If there were numerous gods, then it might not matter whether one who was not your god was really pleased with your "godliness." But if all men have to answer to the "living God," then it does matter whether or not He is pleased with men's "godliness." These words, like those in 1 Timothy 2:4, have been given a variety of interpretations. (1) *The universalist school of interpretation*. The statement that "God ... is the savior of all men" has been pressed into service by the universalists as a proof text that all men will actually be saved. These kindly, but mistaken, interpreters ignore, or explain away, the plain doctrine of the Holy Spirit which tells us there are those whose destruction from the presence of the Lord shall be everlasting, whose portion shall be the "second death" (2 Thessalonians 1:9; Revelation 21:8). God wills that all men come to repentance (2 Peter 3:9), but there are many who will not repent. If they don't repent, they perish (Luke 13:3). If everyone is going to be saved ultimately as the universalists teach, what would be the point of the laboring and striving for godliness which this passage inculcates as of eternal importance? If universalism is true, wouldn't men be saved whether or not they 'labored and strove for godliness'? (2) *The providential school of interpretation*. These interpreters give the term "Savior" its possible sense of "preserver" or "deliverer." The verse that tells about God sending the rain on the just and the unjust, would be a parallel idea. The part of this verse that says there is something 'especially for believers' becomes one of the proof texts for special providence – that God does things for the redeemed He does not do for the unredeemed. While the doctrine of the providence of God is a Biblical idea, it is difficult to see how that emphasis can be made to fit this context. The verse we are studying is intended to be a reason why the faithful saying about the importance of 'exercising unto godliness' is to be accepted by all, since it holds promise both for this life and the one to come.   While providence is something operative in this life, it is hard to see how it can be applied to "the life to come."   (3) *The potential-actual school of interpretation.*   This view holds that God potentially is the Savior of all men (just as in 2:4 He potentially wills the salvation of all), but not all actually will be saved from sins.   This view does not easily explain the adverb "especially."   Its ordinary meaning demands that all men must enjoy to some degree what believers enjoy to the highest degree.   (4) *The double-salvation (or temporal-eternal) school of interpretation.*   This view shows that there is a double salvation available from God.   There is salvation (or safety) in this life, for God saves (or else preserves) all men.   But He is also the Savior (or preserver) of believers especially in the life to come.[50]   "Especially of believers" would say that God does something for the believers in the life to come that He does not do for unbelievers.   Since this double salvation is available, how important it is to strive for godliness, which has promise both for this life and the life to come!

Especially of believers -- The ordinary meaning, as noted above, is that believers (Christians) enjoy 'salvation' to a greater extent than non-believers.   Some, however, try to show that the word *malista* can be used to provide further defini-tion or identification of whatever precedes it.   If we give "especially" its usual meaning, this final phrase may be an indication that the term "Savior" is to be given a two-fold application.[51]   Of all men God is the Preserver, but of some men (i.e., believers), He is the Savior in a deeper, more glorious sense.   If we give *malista* its function of 'further definition or identification,' then "all men" is specifically limited to believers.   "Savior" would be given its usual sense (i.e., forgiveness from sin), and the close of verse 10 would teach what is everywhere else made clear in Scripture, namely, that salvation is granted only to believers.

---

[50] Bengel, *Gnomon of the New Testament*, V.4, p. 270.   Hendriksen studies the term translated "savior" as it is used elsewhere in the OT and NT and in archaeology, to show that it has a meaning that we today do not immediately attach to it.   That meaning is 'deliverer' or 'preserver.'

[51] That idea that "Savior" must be given a double meaning at this place to satisfy "especially" rests on an unspoken presupposition.   That is that only "believers" (i.e., Christians) are going to be saved (in the sense of having their sins forgiven and being granted eternal life with God).   But that presupposition is only one of three possible answers given in the long-running debate concerning the fate of the unevangelized.   Are the unevangelized eternally lost?   (1) The least satisfactory of the three oft-given answers is that the unevangelized will be offered a second chance after death to hear and believe the gospel.   It is difficult to find any Scriptures to substantiate such a claim of a second chance.   (2) Many would appeal to verses like Acts 4:12; John 14:6; and Mark 16:16 ("he who disbelieves shall be lost") to insist only believers in Jesus will be saved.   (3) Others hold out a greater hope to the unevangelized (who have never even had any opportunity of hearing or believing the gospel).   They ask, is there not the possibility that some of the unevangelized may be living up to the available light they have, and so be saved?   Men, after all, have always been saved on the basis of available light (Romans 2:12-15).   Now if the man who is faithful to the revelation he has may be saved, it would just be possible to give 1 Timothy 4:10 an interpretation not offered in the notes above.   It is this – God is the Savior of all men (who are faithful to their available light), but especially is He the Savior of believers (i.e., Christians), precisely because such 'belief of the gospel' is more likely to be achieved than faithfulness to Patriarchal or Mosaic revelations.

C. The Encouragement of the Evangelist Toward a Constructive Ministry. 4:11-16

1. In public life. 4:11-13

4:11 -- These things – Verse 11 can be taken either as the conclusion of what precedes (verses 6-10), or as the beginning of the next section (verses 12-16). (1) Since verse 11 repeats the note with which verse 6 began, perhaps "these things" looks back at the material in chapter 4 concerning false teachers and their errors, and gives one final exhortation to teach what is correct and most needed.[52]

> Referring to the former verses, the writer directs Timothy to command the believers to remain faithful to the revealed truth, to avoid captious questions and fables, and to exercise themselves unto godliness. He is to teach that God is the provider of all good things, and that all are to be received thankfully; that godliness is universally and eternally profitable; and that God through Christ offers salvation to all men. These matters are still of primary importance.[53]

(2) Since verse 11 repeats the note with which verse 6 began, perhaps Paul repeats the idea to tie together the material about refuting the false teachers with correct doctrine and the fact that Timothy is to exemplify the correct doctrine he teaches. Either way we take verse 11, we are suggesting that a new paragraph begins either at verse 11 or at verse 12. We are still in "The charge to Timothy concerning False Teachers" (4:1-16). First, Paul singled out and repudiated their doctrines that spring from an ascetic mindset. Then he emphasized to Timothy the positive exercise to godliness that should be taught in place of those ascetic ideas. Now, as he closes this topic, Paul adds these few words to Timothy to help him know how to make his ministry more effective. Paul offers advice both for the evangelist's public life (verses 11-13), and for his personal life (verses 14-16).

Prescribe and teach – If Timothy wants to be effective in his ministry, both against error, and in building up the church in spiritual health, he will need to 'continue prescribing and teaching.' Both verbs are present tense imperatives; what is commanded is to be continual, habitual, repeated, or customary action. "Prescribe" translated *paraggelle*, a word meaning 'command, to give orders.'

---

[52] "In the natural realm God has provided food to sustain the physical body, and in the spiritual realm He has given us a balanced diet calculated to make us strong and capable. Nutritional experts point out that Americans suffer from malnutrition in a land of plenty. The food is here, but pampered tastes demand exotic substitutes that please the palate but do not provide energy. In a land where the Bible is the best-seller many are spiritually illiterate. Our task is not to provide these hungry people the sensational or exciting, but to expound the truth as it is revealed. The bread of life does not always taste like cream puffs." (Ketcherside, *op. cit.*, p.434)

[53] Ed Hayden, *Standard Lesson Commentary*, 1953.

This word was used at 1 Timothy 1:3, and it will occur again at 5:7 and 6:13,17.[54] There is to be a note of authority in Timothy's preaching. There will be public commands and charges given to the congregation.[55] The authority of the evangelist comes from the Word he is delivering,[56] but any messenger can display firmness as he delivers the authoritative Word. Using the Word of God as his authority, the evangelist, as he would lead the people spiritually, is to prescribe certain behavior on the part of the congregation. "Teach" is *didaske*. Not only was Timothy himself to follow the instruction given to him by Paul, he was to teach the same spiritual truth to others.[57] Some have supposed the "teaching" is private, whereas the "prescribing" was public, but there is no way to demonstrate this proposed distinction. The teaching could be public as well as private. Continual teaching of the Word of God is the way an evangelist can safeguard his audience from false teachers and their doctrine, and in the place of what is refuted give the people something solid to stand on. We are not to suppose Timothy has been neglecting to preach and teach these things. Rather, Paul is giving him encouragement to continue what he has been doing, and at the same time letting the congregation know that what Timothy is doing is exactly what the apostle wants the evangelist to do.

4:12 -- Let no one look down on your youthfulness – The admonition and teaching demanded by verse 11 may evoke resistance. If Timothy will but exemplify in his own life the truths about exercising oneself to godliness that he teaches publicly, he will remove any barrier to the message his "youthfulness" might cause. At the time Paul writes this letter to Timothy, Timothy was about 35 years old, as calculated from the following bits of information. Timothy began to travel with Paul about AD 51, just as Paul began his second missionary journey (Acts 16:1-3). Timothy was certainly in his late teens or early twenties

---

[54] The word is used very frequently in the Gospels of our Lord's commands to the apostles and others, and by Paul of his own apostolic directions to the churches (1 Thessalonians 4:11, 2 Thessalonians 3:4,6).

[55] Hendriksen (*op. cit.*, p.156-7) goes back through chapter 4 highlighting certain "commands" he thinks Timothy is to habitually emphasize as he preaches. "Avoid worldly fables fit only for old women" (verse 7). "Never reject what God has intended for use" (verses 3,4). "Train yourself for godly living" (verse 7). "Nurture yourself on the words of faith and sound doctrine" (verse 6). "Rely on the living God and on His promise to all who live the godly life" (verses 8,10).

[56] By this note we have carefully and deliberately avoided saying that Timothy's authority rested in some delegation of authority from Paul to Timothy.

[57] Just as Hendriksen (*ibid.*) found certain "commands" in the previous verses, so he identifies certain topics that Timothy is to "teach." "Apostasy from the faith in favor of asceticism is coming" (verses 1-3). "The doctrines emphasized by ascetics are an insult to God and to His work of creation" (verses 4,5). "The benefit which accrues from godly living transcends that which results from physical exercise" (verse 8).

when he began his travels with Paul. We have dated 1 Timothy in the middle 60's AD, so it has been at least 15 years since Timothy began to travel with Paul. Twenty and fifteen would make Timothy about 35 years old when he is serving as evangelist at Ephesus and Paul writes this first letter to him.[58] Timothy must have been younger than most of the Ephesian elders whom he would have to "command and teach."[59] He had not, therefore, the authority of superior age. But there remained to him the authority of Christian character and example. "Look down on" (*kataphroneō*) means to 'think down upon,' and indicates an inferior estimation. Many of the Ephesian Christians were as old as Timothy. They had been evangelized by and served under the veteran missionary Paul. Now they had this "young man" preaching to them. He would have to be very careful that he doesn't lose the respect of the people to whom he is trying to minister. If Timothy desired that his teaching should be listened to with respectful, earnest attention, if he hoped to use a holy influence over the flock, there was something he could do to win their ear – he could live in a manner that was above reproach. In this way he would win their respect in a way that the mere issuing of orders would never do.

But *rather* in speech, conduct, love, faith *and* purity – Paul lists five areas[60] of life where the evangelist can be an example to his people. (1) *Speech*. Here we are talking about Timothy's personal conversation. ("Preaching" – public speech – is included in the next verse.) "Speech" includes everything said in public or private.[61] Men can lose other people's respect by the language they use in everyday communication. (2) *Conduct*. The word *anastrophē* talks of public life, general behavior, ways of dealing with people.[62] The word covers a multitude of practical matters involving such things as work habits and business

---

[58] According to Irenaeus, *Against Heresies*, II.22.5, in the ancient world, a person was considered a "young man" until he reached the age of 40. When Paul speaks about Timothy's "youthfulness," therefore, it is implied he is under 40 years of age.

[59] If being a young man (in his thirties) might prove to be a handicap in Timothy's day, perhaps the young evangelist today (fresh out of preacher training school) ought to carefully consider the possibility that his "youth" too may prove to be a handicap, unless he, like Timothy, is an example of what believers are to be.

[60] The KJV has an additional area, "in spirit," but the words apparently do not enjoy integrity since they are absent from the best ancient manuscripts. Those commentaries based on the KJV explain "spirit" to mean "a fine Christian spirit, a cheerful, kind, generous, helpful attitude."

[61] Knight (*op. cit.*, p.206) appeals to Ephesians and Colossians to find examples of speaking to be avoided (falsehood, anger, bitterness, slander, malice, abusive speech, filthy talk) and speaking to be practiced (truth, edification, admonition, tenderness, forgiveness, and thanks).

[62] Knight (*ibid.*) appeals to Ephesians 4:22-24 to explain the radical change that is expected in the Christian's behavior. "He has laid aside ... your old self, and put on the new self ..." (Goodspeed's translation).

dealings as well as morals and leadership in public worship. (3) *Love. Agapē* is an intelligent, unselfish and deliberate good will towards another. It is seeking to do what is spiritually best for the other person. "Charity" is how the word is rendered in the KJV, and it tries to catch the idea of personal attachment and genuine concern for others that seeks to promote their welfare. (4) *Faith*. Perhaps it speaks of being 'faithful' to God's revelation, of being an example of whole-hearted commitment to the revealed truth. Perhaps it speaks of being a man of your word, dependable. (5) *Purity*. The word *agneia* occurs also at 1 Timothy 5:2. It denotes complete conformity, both in thought and act, with God's moral law. Purity is clean thinking and talking and living, unstained by anything bad. Moral purity or chastity is the thing indicated.[63] How careful the evangelist must be in this area of human relationships! There should be nothing in his relationships with the other sex that would give rise to scandal.

Show yourself an example of those who believe – The statement does not imply that before he receives this letter that Timothy had been careless in his conduct. The present imperative ('continue being an example') simply denotes a continuance in a course of activity. The Greek word translated "example" (*tupos*) speaks of a 'pattern' or 'model' after which anything is made or fashioned or copied. Being an example is a valid and basic requirement for any leader. "Of those who believe" in the Greek is *ton piston*, in the genitive case. Perhaps it says Timothy should be a model *of* what believers (Christians) are. Perhaps it says that Timothy is to be a model *to* believers, i.e., a model they can follow.[64] A similar exhortation to Titus about his example is found in Titus 2:1,7. Every young man called to be an evangelist, with its responsibilities towards the congregation and its elders, would do well to heed Paul's fivefold admonition.

4:13 -- Until I come – Paul expected to return to Ephesus for a visit in the near future. (Compare 1 Timothy 3:14.) This is the third in a series of encouragements to Timothy regarding how he can have a constructive ministry in the face of the false teaching he is charged to confront. He is to command and teach sound doctrine (verse 11), he is to be an example of how believers live so as to maintain the respect of his listeners (verse 12), and he is to give careful attention to his public worship leadership responsibilities (verse 13). Paul specifies three tasks in this verse to which Timothy is to give special attention, all related to the evangelist's public life, i.e., to his responsibility to lead public worship. (Though Timothy is to "give attention" to what he does in public, implied also in the verb

---

[63] Of course, this is not to be interpreted as meaning a command to celibacy for the evangelist.

[64] The NASB is not consistent when it translates the genitive case after the word "example." Here the preposition "of" is used, but in a similar construction at 1 Peter 5:3, the NASB uses the preposition "to."

"give attention to" is prior preparation in private.)   Some suppose that Paul intended to give Timothy some new mission once he arrived in Ephesus.   In the meantime, Timothy was to give special attention to his leadership of the public services.   Others suppose that when Paul himself arrived, Paul would do the preaching, and could give New Testament emphases that Timothy, not being an apostle or a prophet, might not be able to give.

Give attention to – The three things about to be listed do not give an exhaustive summary of the essentials of public worship.   For example, "prayer" is not named but it has already been covered in detail in chapter 3.   Further, it is an interpretation that these terms deal with the public worship service.   But it is the well-nigh universal explanation given to these terms.   "The three terms, reading, exhortation, and teaching, are all used with the definite article [in the Greek], and it is most likely that these are all *public* functions."[65]

The *public* reading of *Scripture* – "Public" is added in the NASB because the Greek word "reading" is the word used of reading out loud in public. "Scriptures" were what was read in the assemblies.   Likely it is the Old Testament Scriptures to which reference is made.   The Law and the Prophets had been read for years in the synagogues of the Jews.[66]   Some of the New Testament writings were in existence in the mid-60's AD – Matthew, Luke, Thessalonians, Corinthians, Romans, Galatians, and from the early 60's the Prison Epistles -- and could be read in the public services.   We can see the beginning of reading the New Testament in the Christian assemblies in Ephesians 3:4, Colossians 4:16, and 1 Thessalonians 5:27 (and remember that 1 Thessalonians was one of the first New Testament letters to be written).   That the reading of the "Gospels" very soon became a part of the regular public service in the congregations of Christians is evident from the words of Justin Martyr, *Apologia* 1.67, written about AD 150. By the third and fourth centuries, the 'reader' or 'lector' was a regular order of ministry in the churches.   The language of Revelation 2 and 3 ("He who has an ear, let him hear what the Spirit says to the churches") and 1:3 ("blessed is he who reads [out loud in public] ... the words of this prophecy") indicate that Revelation (written about AD 96) was intended to be read in the public services of the churches of Asia Minor.   In the early church, when few individuals owned private copies of the sacred writings and all such material had to be copied by hand, one can imagine how important was the public reading of Scripture.[67] Perhaps it is not less necessary today when not private ownership but private reading of the Word is all too rare.

---

[65] Kent, *op. cit.*, p.156.

[66] Luke 4:16;   Acts 13:27,   15:21;   2 Corinthians 3:15.

[67] Hendriksen, *1 Timothy*, p. 159.

The art of reading Scripture effectively during the services is greatly neglected in our day. To cultivate the art, here are some helps on public reading:

> Andrew Blackwood, *The Fine Art of Public Worship*. Chapter 7, "The Public Reading of Scripture," p. 128-141. Note especially the excellent suggestions on p. 140,141.

> Ron Willingham, *Men's Leadership Training Course*. Section 4, "How to Read Scripture so the Audience will Understand it."

> J.B. Rotherham's *Emphasized New Testament*.

"All who treasure the Scripture as God's revelation to man should give the reading of it a prominent place in public worship."[68]

To exhortation – This Greek word *paraklēsis* includes warning (for example, against error in doctrine and morals), calling for (something to be done), advice, and encouragement. Perhaps we should think of encouragement of the listeners to carry out the injunctions of the Scripture just read. Such a custom was carried out in the synagogues (Acts 13:15), and perhaps was carried over into the church. See Acts 11:23 and 14:22 for good examples of "exhortation."

And teaching – The word *didaskalia* is almost always rendered "doctrine" in the KJV. But here, where *the act of teaching* – like the *act* of reading and the *act* of exhorting, in the two preceding clauses – is intended, "teaching" is the better translation. We suppose the word would cover both what we call "techniques of teaching" and the content taught. "It does make a difference what one believes! The attitude of the heart is not everything. There are certain facts with respect to doctrine and morals that must be taught, and which one must accept and embrace, so that one's life is founded upon them."[69] The word speaks of formal instruction of the people based on the word of God. Teaching is directed primarily to the intellect, whereas the exhortation is aimed at the will. The church at Ephesus may have had some of the New Testament books to read (see above), but certainly it did not have all of them. But Timothy and others had heard the apostles teach, and they could give by word of mouth the teaching that we can now read in the New Testament Scriptures. Part of public worship, which is the evangelist's responsibility, is to see that instruction in the great truths of the Christian faith is given to the whole audience.

---

[68] Kent, *ibid.*

[69] Hendriksen, *ibid.*

2. In personal life. 4:14-16

4:14 -- Do not neglect the spiritual gift within you – At 4:11 began the paragraph of encouragement of the evangelist toward a constructive ministry, both in his public life (4:11-13) and in his personal life (4:14-16). "Do not neglect" is a present imperative with *me*. This construction prohibits the continuance of an action already going on.[70] We get the impression that Timothy has been neglecting his "gift," but such neglect is to stop! The exact nature of the "gift" (*charisma*) is nowhere explained for us, so there is no way to know exactly what Paul was talking about, though Timothy would have known. Yet various conjectures have been offered in an effort to give modern readers a possible understanding of what is here referred to. (1) Some suppose it refers to some natural endowment. At 1 Corinthians 7:7, the same word is used to designate how it was that Paul was able to live the single life without having constantly to master powerful temptations of lust. It is difficult to see how some "natural endowment" could be thought of as having been received by Timothy at the time of his ordination service. (2) Some suppose it refers to the blessings resulting from redemption we enjoy in Christ. At Romans 5:15,16 and 6:23, the word "gift" is used to refer to the result of Christ's redemptive act. At Romans 11:29, the word "gift" is used to refer likely to those supernatural blessings already enumerated in Romans 9:4,5. It is difficult to see how this gives us much guidance in trying to ascertain what it was that Timothy received at his ordination but was now neglecting. (3) Some suppose it refers to that by which Timothy was qualified to do his work as an evangelist. 1 Timothy 4:14; 2 Timothy 1:6; and 1 Peter 4:10 are all looked at as being verses that speak of the same "qualification."[71] In those early years of the church, did evangelists (in addition to apostles, prophets, and teachers) need special inspiration from the Holy Spirit, so as to know what to preach?[72] Is this what Timothy has been neglecting to listen to as he prepares his public messages? (4) Some suppose it was a supernatural spiritual gift. In 1 Corinthians 12-14 and in Romans 12:6-8, we read about special "spiritual gifts," special endowments produced by the Holy Spirit as he worked in the lives of certain individual believers. These spiritual gifts were given for the benefit of the whole congregation. If someone "neglected his gift," the church would not be receiving the benefit God intended. Did Timothy receive

---

[70] Wm. G. MacDonald, *Greek Enchiridion: A Concise Handbook of Grammar for Translation and Exegesis* (Peabody, Mass: Hendrickson Publishers, 1986), p.50.

[71] The exact relationship between 1 Timothy 4:14 and 2 Timothy 1:6 cannot be affirmed with certainty. Did Paul lay his hands on Timothy at the same time the body of elders did? Did Timothy get some special miraculous gift when Paul laid his hands on the young preacher? Was this gift an enabling, or empowering gift, to assist Timothy in fulfilling his function as evangelist?

[72] Did Timothy the evangelist have some "miraculous power" that evangelists today do not receive? If he and other evangelists like Titus and Philip received such miraculous powers, is it proper to suggest today's preacher and the "evangelist" in the New Testament are the same office?

a special endowment to enable him to do a certain special ministry? Might one of the three tasks named in verse 13 be the "spiritual gift" he was given at his ordination? Some have appealed to 1 Timothy 6:10 (where Timothy is called "a man of God") to show that Timothy had received a special gift of "prophecy." Such spiritual gifts were ordinarily given either at conversion or when an apostle laid his hands on a person. Are we to assume this is a third way such gifts might be received, namely, at an ordination service? (Or perhaps Timothy's ordination was different, in that not only did elders lay hands on him, but so did the apostle Paul.) (5) Some suppose he received a special ecclesiastical power at the time of his ordination. Proponents of the doctrine of apostolic succession suppose that there is a special grace from the Holy Spirit given to those who are separated for the office and work of a leader in the church of God. (6) Perhaps all that can be said is that the "gift" which Timothy was neglecting was something that would have helped him in his own personal spiritual life. His "personal spiritual life" seems to be the topic of verses 14-16.

Which was bestowed upon you through prophetic utterance – At 1 Timothy 1:18, we've called attention to the "prophecies" that were uttered at the time of Timothy's call or ordination.[73] This phrase does not mean the gift was bestowed by means of a prophecy, but rather that it was made known to Timothy by an inspired prophet[74] what the gift was.

With the laying on of the hands of the presbytery – "Presbytery" is a group of elders.[75] We may suppose the elders of Timothy's home church[76] laid their hands on him to ordain him to his ministry as an evangelist.[77] In all probability this happened just before Timothy began to travel with Paul (Acts 16:1-3). At

---

[73] The reader should review the comments made at that previous place.

[74] The word "prophecies" at 1:18 was plural. It is possible that the Greek word here in 4:14 is accusative plural, rather than genitive singular (both forms look exactly alike in the Greek).

[75] It is a "presbyterian" ordination, not an episcopal ordination. This is not apostolic succession! "Presbytery" occurs two other places in the New Testament, at Luke 22:66 and Acts 22:5, and in both it refers to the Jewish Sanhedrin. This passage in Timothy certainly does not refer to that body of "Jewish elders." It must refer to a body of elders of a Christian church.

[76] Each congregation in New Testament times had a plurality of elders, a body of elders. See information about "elders" given in comments at 1 Timothy 3:1. (It is to be expected that those who hold to a presbyterian form of church government [rather than congregational], think that each "district" would have had a body of elders, and that this body from the district of Lystra, or the body from the district of Ephesus, were the ones who ordained Timothy.)

[77] The idea sometimes offered that the genitive "of the presbytery" really means that Timothy was being ordained "to the presbyterate" appears to be a case of special pleading by men whose church polity is different than the polity that existed in apostolic times. "Elder" and "evangelist" are different offices. Timothy was not old enough, nor did he meet a number of the other qualifications for elder (1 Timothy 3), when on about his 20th birthday, hands were laid on him. He was not being ordained "*to* the presbyterate." It was "*by* the presbytery" that Timothy was ordained to the office of evangelist.

the very time the elders were laying their hands on Timothy is when this prophecy was made that revealed the nature of Timothy's gift.[78] The laying on of hands was an ancient custom with symbolic connotations. In Old Testament times, hands were laid on the sacrificial animal to symbolize the transfer of guilt from the sinner to the animal (Leviticus 16:21). Hands were laid on when imparting a blessing (Genesis 48:14,20). Hands were laid on when installing someone into office (Numbers 8:10, where Levites are consecrated, and Deuteronomy 34:9, the ceremony of the dedication of Joshua).

It probably is incorrect to say that laying on of hands was the *means* by which the authority to do something was publicly delegated. No authority was delegated in Acts 13:1-3 when Paul and Barnabas were set apart for the ministry to which the Holy Spirit had already called them. We might say that in their case authority to do something was thereby recognized, but it was not the people who laid on hands who had any authority to delegate. Sympathetic support for what Paul and Barnabas were about to do was perhaps implied, but not a delegation of authority.

4:15 -- Take pains with these things – The older translations read "Meditate upon these things," but Paul is not asking just for "meditation" alone. He is asking Timothy to make these things his business. He is to practice them over and over.[79] It is the opposite of "do not neglect" with which the previous verse begins. "These things" certainly includes all the commands given since verse 12. In fact, Paul may be thinking of the entire contents of chapter 4. Timothy must refute the false teachers. He must encourage exercise in godliness. He must be an active and industrious public teacher. He must pay attention to his own spiritual life so as to be an example to his fellow-believers.

Be *absorbed* in them – "Absorbed" is added by the NASB translators to catch the meaning of the Greek verb. Robertson paraphrases this to mean that Timothy is to "be up to his ears" in these things.[80] Let the matters of exemplary life and effective public ministry be the special subjects of his thought and care. Be completely wrapped up in these things. Devote your life wholly to these. Have no other grand aim of living. Your time, attention, talents, are to be absorbed in the proper duties of the work of ministry. It is the evangelist's 'magnificent obsession,' the one thing he does.

---

[78] "With" (*meta*) denotes not agency, but accompaniment. The prophecy accompanied the laying on of hands.

[79] The verb *meletaō* can mean 'practice,' so some think Paul is still continuing his athletic metaphor.

[80] A.T. Robertson, *Word Pictures in the Greek New Testament*, V.4, p. 582.

So that your progress may be evident to all – "Progress, advance, growth" are ideas included in *prokopē*. A minister of the gospel ought to make steady improvement in all that pertains to his office. No man ought to be satisfied with his present attainments. This progress should be evident "to all."[81] "It should be apparent to all persons who attend on the preaching of the minister, that he is making steady advances in knowledge, wisdom, piety, and in all things that pertain to the proper performance of his office."[82] When the whole community can observe the steady spiritual growth of the Christian leader, there will be little tendency to despise his youth, no matter how few his years. It is by wholehearted commitment to the spiritual, moral, and practical phases of Christian activity that such visible growth is attained.

4:16 -- Pay close attention to yourself and to your teaching – We are still in the paragraph where encouragement is being given to Timothy concerning his personal life, all with a view to helping him have a constructive ministry. Paul advises Timothy to take heed to his character, to his creed, and to his conduct. And he closes this section by reminding Timothy why perseverance in these is so important – namely, because it has as its outcome salvation for Timothy and his hearers. "Pay close attention to yourself" concerns Timothy's own personal character. "This may be understood as relating to anything of a personal nature that would qualify him for his work. It may be applied to personal piety; to health; to manners; to habits of living; to temper; to ruling purposes; to the relationship with others."[83] Preachers have even been known to develop mannerisms that reflect against their character and bring their message into disrepute. "Pay(ing) close attention to yourself" is the first care of the Christian leader, for he can hardly lead others to be something that he himself is not. This charge to Timothy becomes more impressive when it is compared with the complimentary notices concerning him in Philippians 2:19-23. Even such a one as he needed constantly to take heed lest he fall from his own steadfastness (cp. 2 Peter 3:17,18). "Pay close attention ... to your teaching" concerns Timothy's creed. *Didaskalia* is the same word used at verse 13. The use of this word in 1 Timothy 6:1,3, and Titus 2:10 strongly supports the sense of "doctrine," i.e., the thing taught. Evangelists must keep a strict eye on their own doctrines, their own beliefs, the things they will soon be teaching in public. If others' salvation depends on presenting God's message aright, then the evangelist had better have

---

[81] There is a manuscript variation here. The Greek Text behind the KJV reads "in all" (*en pasin*), so that it speaks about 'all things' with which a minister is concerned. The better attested Greek text behind the NASB reads "to all" (*pasin*), so that it speaks about 'all people.'

[82] Barnes *Notes*, p.171.

[83] Barnes, *ibid*.

his own doctrine right![84]

> One places his soul in jeopardy when he tampers with revealed truth,
> watering it down and adjusting it to the prejudices and weaknesses of men.
> In all ages faithful prophets and teachers have endured persecution from
> those whom they have attempted to help, and there is no indication it will
> be any different now.   Yet the only hope for God's teacher and the taught
> is to be faithful to God's purpose.[85]

Persevere in these things – Earlier in this verse Paul has spoken about Timothy's
character and creed.   This phrase begins the instructions we refer to as Timothy's
conduct.   It is not entirely possible to answer satisfactorily the question, To what
does "these things" refer?   Perhaps it refers to what immediately precedes, the
evangelist's own conduct and the quality and character of his teaching.   Perhaps
it refers to what was said in verse 15.   Perhaps it refers to all the things
enumerated from verse 12 onward.

For as you do this – That is, paying close attention and persevering in these
things.   The fact that perseverance is essential to salvation is taught not only here,
but also in Romans 11:22 ("if you continue in His kindness; otherwise you will
be cut off") and Colossians 1:22,23 ("If indeed you continue in the faith ...").

You will save both yourself and those who hear you (NASB mg.) – The NASB
text reads "you will insure salvation ..." and the addition is theologically
motivated.   Some theologians have hesitated to interpret "save" in this passage
in its usual sense of 'spiritual salvation.'   Those who think salvation is
monergistic – something God does to a wholly passive man – must somehow
make this verse match their doctrine.   This is the doctrine the NASB translators
were defending.   One commentator suggests it means "preservation from
difficulties."[86]   Another suggests it means "preservation from demonic teaching",
the topic with which this charge began (4:1-3).[87]   Those who understand that
salvation is synergistic – that there is both God's part and man's part in salvation
– have no trouble explaining this in harmony with the conditions men are expected
to meet if they would continue to be treated as saved by God.   God has always
looked for "faithfulness" to His revealed will, for that is the condition men must

---

[84] In the present age, when preachers "borrow" other speaker's sermons, and preach them
(almost verbatim), this warning needs to be sounded loud and clear!   It is inexcusable for a Christian
Church preacher to mouth denominational doctrines that are flat-out unscriptural, and to present
them as though they are what the Bible says.   It is heartbreaking to hear our people "speaking half
the language of Ashdod" because they have learned it from our own preachers.

[85] Ketcherside, *op. cit.*, p.436.

[86] H.A. Ironside, *Timothy, Titus and Philemon*, p.110.

[87] K.S. Wuest, *The Pastoral Epistles in the Greek New Testament*, p.76.

meet if they would be saved! Eternal happiness for the evangelist is vitally connected with how faithfully he carries out his God-given responsibilities. The warning here is equivalent to saying that an unfaithful minister of the gospel is likely to forfeit his salvation. "The Christian leader needs always to remember that he has a soul of his own to be saved, and that his position as a Christian leader does not assure his salvation. Quite the contrary, it brings upon him greater responsibility and more severe judgment (Romans 2:1-3,21-24; James 3:1; cp. 1 Corinthians 9:27)."[88] Eternal happiness for the evangelist's audience is vitally connected with how well they learn God's will, and how faithfully they put it into practice in their lives.[89] Unfaithfulness or carelessness on the part of the evangelist can be ruinous to the church. If he lives and teaches according to the Scriptures, he will lead many to life eternal; if not, he will lead them to condemnation, and their blood will be upon his hands (Ezekiel 3:17-21; Acts 20:26,27).

---

[88] Ed Hayden, *Standard Lesson Commentary*, 1953.

[89] "Those who hear" is a natural way to refer to those who hear and obey the Gospel, which in those days was communicated orally.

SPECIAL STUDY #4

EVANGELIST

INTRODUCTION

A. Absence of detail

The absence of a detailed account of the organization and practical working of the Church of the first century leaves some uncertainty as to the functions and position of evangelists, elders, deacons, etc. On the other hand, there is enough information given specifically and by implication that we are caused to question some of our old established beliefs and practices. This is certainly true when it comes to a study of the word "evangelist" in the New Testament.

B. The name Evangelist – Its Meaning.

"Evangelist" occurs three times in the New Testament (Acts 21:8; Ephesians 4:11; 2 Timothy 4:5), but does not occur in the LXX or other Greek versions, in the Apostolic Fathers, or in the *Didache*, and not in classical Greek usage. It is a translation of *euaggelistēs*, and it is from the same root as the words translated "gospel" (Grk. *euaggelion*) and "to preach" (Grk. *euaggelidzō*).

> If *angelos* signifies *a bearer of a message*, then *euaggelistēs* means a bearer of a good message ... The word is not to be understood of a person who occasionally bears a good message, but **one whose business, or work, is to deliver good messages** ... If John, the Baptist, means John whose business it was to baptize; then Philip the Evangelist means that Philip whose work it was to evangelize, or publish a good message.[1]

General meaning of the word – The term simply means "a proclaimer of good news" and has general application to all Christians. Each Christian is held responsible to "let [his] light shine," to be the "salt of the earth" (Matthew 5:13-16) and should realize that God has given him the task of reflecting the light of the Christ; of permeating the earth with the teachings of the Lord. Per Acts 8:4, the early Christians who were scattered went everywhere preaching.

Specific meaning of the word in the New Testament – In a specific sense, the term "evangelist" has reference to one of the offices in the church of Christ. "And on the morrow we departed, and came unto Caesarea: and entering the house of **Philip the evangelist**, who was one of the seven, we stayed with him" (Acts 21:8). "He gave some as apostles, and some as prophets, **and some as evangelists**, and some as pastors and teachers" (Ephesians 4:11). "But you (Timothy), be sober in all things,

---

[1] A. Campbell, *Millennial Harbinger*, 1855, p.376,377.

endure hardship, **do the work of an evangelist**, fulfill your ministry" (2 Timothy 4:5). In this verse, "evangelist" is not preceded by an article in the Greek. "When that is the case, character, quality, or nature is stressed. The idea is, Let your work be evangelistic in character. Always be a bringer of good news. Be ever reaching out for lost souls in your teaching and preaching" (Wuest, *op. cit.*, p.159). In Romans 10:14-15 the term "preacher" (*kērux*, or *kerusso*) is used in a sense that this commentator conceives to be synonymous with the word "evangelist." And there are times the word "minister" ("servant") seems to be used of the same office or task in the church (Archippus, Colossians 4:17; Timothy, at 2 Timothy 4:5; Tychicus, Colossians 4:7; etc.).

For the specific meaning of "evangelist" in post-apostolic writings, two quotations from Eusebius' *Church History* are significant because of the way he refers to "evangelist". The first quote talks about evangelists being present in the period immediately following the close of the apostolic age, i.e., early second century, as well as being used as a title for the "writers of the four Gospels."

> Among those that were celebrated at that time was Quadratus, who, reports say, was renowned along with the daughters of Philip for his prophetical gifts. And there were many others besides these who were known in those days, and who occupied the first place among the successors of the apostles. And they also, being illustrious disciples of such great men, built up the foundations of the churches which had been laid by the apostles in every place, and preached the Gospel more and more widely and scattered the saving seeds of the kingdom of heaven far and near through the whole world. For indeed most of the disciples of that time, animated by the divine word with a more ardent love for philosophy, had already fulfilled the command of the Savior, and had distributed their goods to the needy. Then starting out upon long journeys they performed the office of evange-lists, being filled with the desire to preach Christ to those who had not yet heard the word of faith, and to deliver to them the divine Gospels. And when they had only laid the foundations of the faith in foreign places, they appointed others as pastors, and entrusted them with the nurture of those recently brought in, while they themselves went on again to other countries and nations, with the grace and the co-operation of God. For a great many wonderful works were done through them by the power of the divine Spirit, so that at the first hearing whole multitudes of men eagerly embraced the religion of the Creator of the universe. But since it is impossible for us to enumerate the names of all that became shepherds or evangelists in the churches throughout the world in the age immediately succeeding the apostles, we have recorded, as was fitting, the names of those only who have transmitted the apostolic doctrine to us in writings still extant.[2]

In another place, Eusebius makes reference to Pantaenus (fl. AD 180-190).

---

[2] Eusebius, H.E. iii.37.

> About that time, Pantaenus, a man highly distinguished for his learning, had charge of the school of the faithful in Alexandria. A school of sacred learning, which continues to our day, was established there in ancient times, and as we have been informed, was managed by men of great ability and zeal for divine things. Among these it is reported that Pantaenus was especially conspicuous, as he had been educated in the philosophical system of those called Stoics. They say that he displayed such zeal for the divine Word that he was appointed as a herald of the Gospel of Christ to the nations in the East, and was sent as far as India. For indeed there were still many evangelists of the Word who sought earnestly to use their inspired zeal, after the examples of the apostles, for the increase and building up of the Divine Word. Pantaenus was one of these, and is said to have gone to India. It is reported that among persons there who knew of Christ, he found the Gospel according to Matthew, which had anticipated his own arrival. For Bartholomew, one of the apostles, had preached to them the writing of Matthew in the Hebrew language, which they had preserved till that time.[3]

Theodoret, AD 393-458, was the first to restrict the term to itinerant preachers.[4] Ecumenius was the first to use the term "evangelist" for one of the writers of the four gospels. At a later time, the name of "evangelist" was given to the writers of the four gospels because they tell the story of the gospel and because the effect of their promulgation at the beginning was very much like the work of a preaching evangelist (*ISBE, Vol. II*, p.1040). In later liturgical language, "evangelist" was the name given to the reader of the gospel for the day. The evangelist became an appellation of the *anagnōstēs* (i.e., the reader of the gospel) who also had to be *diēgētikos*, capable of explaining it. We may further recall that Philip explained the prophet Isaiah to the eunuch (*Hastings Dictionary of the Bible*, New York: Scribner's, 1908, p.796).

I. EVANGELISTS OF THE CHURCH

A. Philip, Acts 21:8. Philip was one of the seven chosen to care for the widows of Grecian Jews (Acts 6:1-6). What did he do as an evangelist? Acts 8:4-13 and 26-40 note the following: (1) Upon being scattered with other Chris-tians he went to Samaria and proclaimed unto them the Christ, Acts 8:4,5. (2) He confirmed his word by signs, Acts 8:6,7. (3) He baptized believers, including Simon the sorcerer, Acts 8:9-13. (4) Following the instructions of an angel and the Holy Spirit, he met, taught, and baptized the treasurer of the queen of Ethiopia, Acts 8:26-39. (5) He preached in all the villages of the Philistine plain until he came to Caesarea, where he remained for 10 years or more, Acts 8:40 and 21:8.

B. Timothy, 2 Timothy 4:5. Timothy was a young man converted to Christianity through Paul's ministry during the first missionary journey, ca. AD 45. Timothy was

---

[3] Eusebius, H.E. v.10.

[4] *Schaff Herzog Religious Encyclopedia*, V.4, p.225.

likely in his late teens at the time.   When Paul came to Lystra and Iconium on the second missionary journey, he found that Timothy had a good reputation among the churches.   Paul wanted Timothy to join the travelling group of missionaries.   This was about AD 51, and Timothy is in his early twenties.   Evidently at this time the elders from the churches of Lystra and Iconium laid their hands upon Timothy and ordained him to the office of evangelist.   Paul probably gave him spiritual gifts at the same time (Acts 16:1-3; 2 Timothy 1:6; 1 Timothy 4:14).   Timothy accompanied Paul on the rest of the second missionary journey, to Philippi, Thessalonica, Berea, Athens, and Corinth.   Paul sent Timothy to work with the newly planted church at Thessalonica (1 Thessalonians 3:2).   Timothy accompanied Paul on the third missionary journey, AD 54-58.   When Paul was in Ephesus in the midst of this tour, he sent Timothy and Erastus on missionary business to Macedonia and Corinth (Acts 19:22; 1 Corinthians 4:17, 16:10).   Timothy was with Paul a short time later, and joined with him in sending greetings to Corinth (2 Corinthians 1:1).   Timothy sends greetings to the church at Rome from Corinth (Romans 16:21).   From Corinth, Timothy accompanied Paul to Jerusalem with the offering for the saints (Acts 20: 4).   Timothy was with Paul when Paul was a prisoner during the first Roman imprisonment (Philippians 2:19; Colossians 1:1).   Timothy was left behind at Ephesus after he and Paul visited the church subsequent to Paul's was release from that first Roman imprisonment (1 Timothy 1:3).   He will stay at Ephesus for 3-4 years, until the instructions given to him in 2 Timothy reach him, then he will depart for Rome to visit Paul during Paul's second Roman imprisonment.

What did Timothy do as an evangelist?   The answer depends on what time in his life one is talking about.   His duties on the second missionary journey seem less weighty with responsibility compared with the duties later at Ephesus.   Ephesus, where Timothy was evangelist, was a church that had elders *before* Timothy was sent there (Acts 20:20,28 and 1 Timothy 5:19ff).   Also observe that Timothy's evangelistic work on a permanent basis with a local congregation like Ephesus (as contrasted with his activities during the second missionary tour) is undertaken by a man who is in his mid-30's chronologically.   (He is still considered a "young man" - for by the mid 60's AD, some twenty years after his conversion, he would be in his mid to upper thirties.)   Alexander Campbell, *Millennial Harbinger*, 1855, p.378,379, has succinctly summarized Timothy's duties as specified in 1 and 2 Timothy:

1. Let it be noted that Timothy is recognized by Paul as an evangelist.
2. He was to have the charge of inexperienced and subordinate teachers, and to see that they taught the same doctrine which the apostles taught.   "I besought thee to abide still in Ephesus ... that thou mightest charge some that they teach no other doctrine" 1 Timothy 1:3.
3. He was to direct that prayers be made for all men, for the reasons assigned, and for the object proposed; to teach where the men should pray and teach, and the relative position of women.   chap.2
4. He was instructed whom to appoint as superintendents (*episkopoi*) or overseers, and (*diakonoi*) ministers, ch.3:1-15.   To the end that he might discharge these

duties, the apostle told him to "give attendance to reading, to exhortation, to (*didaskalia*) teaching, ch.4:13, and to connect therewith meditation, v.15. He was to take heed to himself, and to the teaching -- to continue in this that he might save himself and his hearers, v.16.

5. It was his business to reprove, under proper circumstances, although but a youth. It was not the privilege of his *age*, but a duty of his office.

6. He was to see that the widows were properly cared for, and that the elders were properly compensated, ch.5:1-18.

7. He was to hear accusations against elders under proper circumstances, and rebuke them publicly when they sinned, that "others might fear." This was to be done impartially, 5:19-21.

8. He was to teach the servants ... how to esteem their masters.

9. He was to charge the rich to do as required in 5:17-19.

10. He was to hold fast the *form of sound* words, and keep the good which had been committed to him.

11. He was to make other evangelists; and not entangle himself with the affairs of life, 2 Timothy 2:2-4.

12. He was to put the brethren and all others in remembrance of the cardinal proof of the Messiahship of Jesus Christ the Son of David; namely, that he was "raised from the dead," v.8, and that if we suffer with him, we shall also reign with him.

13. He was to make it the business of his life, "rightly to divide the word of truth" to show himself a workman who need not be ashamed, but approved of God, v.15.

14. He was to shun profane and vain babblings, and to "deprecate (*paraitou*) the dull (*moros*) and (*apaideutous*) silly (*zeteseis*) enquirers," knowing they beget strifes, v.23

15. He was to continue in the things which he had learned, and been assured of, knowing who had been his great teacher, ch. 3:14.

16. He was to "announce the word" (*keruxon ton logon*) - "to be on hand (*epistethi*), conveniently [and] inconveniently (*eukairos akairos*), ready to reprove, rebuke, and exhort, (*en pase makrothumia*) in all patience and (*didaske*) instruction."

17. In order to sum up the whole the Apostle says to Timothy, "be sober (*nephe*) in all respects - endure afflictions - accomplish an evangelist's work ... - carry out fully the ministry."

C. Titus, Titus 1:5-9. Titus likely was a convert of Paul (Titus 1:4), and perhaps a native of Antioch. Evidently he was another of the young men whom Paul constantly challenged to travel with him and serve in the gospel of Christ. We first meet him at the Jerusalem Conference, when he is used as a "test case" of how Gentile converts should be treated (Galatians 2:3). Next we see him sent to Corinth in an attempt to correct some of the problems that congregation was having (2 Corinthians 7,8). Then, we see him left on the island of Crete, after he and Paul had visited it. The epistle to Titus was addressed to him, giving him instructions about his task while on the island. Finally, we see him sent to Dalmatia (2 Timothy 4). Tradition has it that after his ministry to Dalmatia, he returned to Crete, where he served as evangelist until his death at age 94.[5]	What did Titus do as an evangelist?	We know about a few of his activities at Corinth and on Crete.	We presume his duties are the same as those given to Timothy at Ephesus.	(May we say that Titus' area of service was a whole island, while Timothy's was but one church, or one city?)	Each was to appoint elders, each was to reprove, rebuke and exhort, each was to see that none taught anything contrary to sound doctrine.	Special attention should be paid to Titus 1:5 where some of Titus' duties are specified.	"For this reason I left you in Crete, that you might set in order what remains, and appoint elders in every city as I directed you."	The epistle begins by reminding Titus of his commission which had been given by word of mouth before Paul departed from Crete, leaving Titus behind.	Who started the churches on Crete?	Paul and Titus together, after Paul's release from his first Roman imprisonment?	If so, Titus' responsibilities would seem to be similar to what was done at the close of the first missionary tour when elders were first selected in the new, recently planted churches (Acts 14:23).	Someone else, at some time before Paul and Titus visited the island?	If to be qualified for elder, a man is not to be a novice Christian, perhaps the churches are older than 1 or 2 years.

What are the "things lacking" that need to be "set in order"?	The compound "set in order" implies that it has been done up to a certain point before Paul left, but more was needed.	Titus is to supply and give a finishing touch to these things.	We surely may suppose that what is included in the remainder of Titus specifically names some of the things high on the agenda.	(1) Appoint elders in every city, *katastēsēs kata polin presburterous*.	'Ordain' is too strong a translation, and has a technical meaning.	What Titus is to do is arrange for the selection and see that it is properly carried out.	Per Titus 1:6ff, when Paul was on Crete, he had stated the qualification of elders.	He now repeats them.	There is no satisfactory evidence that the elders were imposed on the churches without the consent of the individual congregations (Huther, *Meyer's Commentary on the New Testatment*, p.292).	The work was city by city, and elders (plural) were to be appointed in every city (singular).	There were 100 cities on the island.	It seems Christianity has spread widely on the island.	These 'shepherds, guardians, overseers' were needed because of the presence of false teachers in the area, whose doctrines would ruin the churches if not opposed.	If we may add what is learned in Ephesians 4:11ff about the need for such offices in the church, it is that the saints may be equipped for service.	(2) Conduct among church members, chapter 2.	Another thing needing attention was the conduct of older men, younger men, older women, younger women, slaves.	Titus was also to emphasize the basis of all Christian conduct (verses 11-15).	(3) Conduct of church members in the world, chapter 3.	The nature, reason, and encouragement of proper conduct are stressed.	This is part of an evangelist's job.

**D.	Luke.**[6]	Luke was a traveling companion of Paul on the second missionary jour-

---

[5] Eusebius, H.E., iii.4.	*Apost.Constit.*, vii.46.

[6] Luke is not specifically called "evangelist" in the New Testament, but he is in early Christian literature.

ney (Acts 16). He is the one designated as 'Famous for the gospel' (2 Corinthians 8:18), i.e., a good preacher of the gospel, and this before he began traveling with Paul on the second missionary journey. He was present with Paul during both of Paul's Roman imprisonments (Colossians 4:11; 2 Timothy 4:11). What did Luke do as an evangelist? He was the preacher with the newly established congregation at Philippi for 5 years, as demonstrated by the "we" passages in Acts 16:40 and 20:6. He not only wrote a history of the early church (Acts), but he also wrote the third Gospel. Tradition has it that Luke wrote what Paul had been preaching. Luke 1:1-4 tells us Luke made historical inquiry as to the factuality of what he recorded.

E. 'St. Paul's Bible College' or **the school of the evangelists**. Who were the students? A number of young men are named in the epistles. They would seem to be doing activities similar to those specifically recorded of Timothy and Titus. These young men are likely "evangelists" in training. Lucius, Jason, and Sosipater are named in Romans 16:21. Tychicus is named in Ephesians 6:21. He evidently came to Rome from the province of Asia and was being sent back to fill the Asians in on how things were going with Paul. He is also named in Colossians 4:7, with the information that people at Colossae, too, will learn more about Paul from the lips of this man. Tychicus will be sent to Crete (or perhaps it will be Artemas) to relieve Titus, and then Titus is instructed to report to Paul at Nicopolis (Titus 3:12). A "true comrade" and "Clement" are named in Philippians 4:3. Aristarchus, Mark, Jesus Justus, Luke, and Demas are present with Paul when he writes Colossians (4:10ff) and the letter to Philemon (verse 24). So is Epaphras, a native Colossian. From Colossians 1:5-8, we learn Epaphras has recently come to Rome from Colossae, and that he was the evangelist from whom that town had heard the gospel. In his absence, Archippus has been carrying on the ministry in Colossae (Colossians 4:17). Philemon 2 indicates that Archippus is a fellow-soldier (preacher?), and that he is involved with the church that meets in Philemon's home. In the letter to Philemon (verse 23), Epaphras also sends greetings back to the congregation where he had been preaching. Erastus is again at Corinth (2 Timothy 4:20) while Trophimus was left behind at Miletus because he was too sick to travel (2 Timothy 4:20). What did they do? This writer has always had the impression these young men were 'interns' or 'apprentices' – learning from Paul how to be preachers – until their age and experience warranted them being sent out on their own, with less and less supervision from the apostle. During Paul's second imprisonment, we read that one of the young men (Demas) apparently quit the ministry. But the others were still faithfully at it, 2 Timothy 4:10-12. "Crescens has gone to Galatia (France?), Titus to Dalmatia (Yugoslavia), Tychicus I have sent to Ephesus (if this is an epistolary aorist, then Tychicus has been sent to replace Timothy as evangelist in that place)." Luke is with Paul. Mark is somewhere between Ephesus and Rome, and Timothy is to bring him along when Timothy himself comes to Rome.

II. LESSONS AND APPLICATIONS LEARNED

A. Evangelist is a permanent office in the church.

Arguments that the office was temporary for the early church: (1). Evangelists were "personal agents or representatives" of the apostles. When apostles ceased, there would be no more such personal agents. (But is this is true, whose agent was Philip?) (2) They were charismatically endowed. (Philip in Acts 8; Timothy in 1 Timothy 4:4 and 2 Timothy 1:6.)

> True, the first evangelists were thus gifted; and so were the first deacons, the first elders, the first teachers. In this sense elders and teachers were as much given (supernaturally endowed) as were evangelists. Yet teachers we must have, so long as it is needful to learn; pastors [elders] we must have, so long as there is a flock to feed; evangelists we must have, so long as there are sinners to whom it is needful to preach the gospel. It is nowhere implied that fitness to preach, baptize, teach, and set in order churches cannot be obtained otherwise than by supernatural bestowments; nor is it ever hinted, that, obtaining the required fitness by miraculous agency was a pre-requisite to the work and designation.[7]

It might be well to give some reasons for concluding that there is such an office in the church today. The following are taken from Robert Milligan, *Scheme of Redemption*, p.313-314).

1. The nature of the work assigned to the evangelist makes the office a perpetual one. Their job was to convert sinners, to feed the flock of God, to teach the ignorant. While time endures this will be necessary. Therefore the job must be perpetual.

2. Evangelists from the beginning received their commission from churches, and not directly from Christ (as did the apostles), or from apostles.[8] This can be shown in the case of Timothy in which the hands of the eldership were laid on him (Acts 14:1-3; 1 Timothy 4:14). The imposition of the hands of the eldership (probably of Lystra and Iconium) was for the purpose of setting him aside for the work upon which he was embarking. Paul laid his hands upon Timothy (2 Timothy 1:6) to impart to him those miraculous gifts which in that age were necessary in order to enable him to fulfill the commission. Since we still have local churches after the order of those of that day, we have the prerogative of setting aside evangelists.

---

[7] D. King, *Memoir of D.King*, p.272.

[8] A possible exception to this statement might be the 500 brethren who were given the Great Commission as recorded in Matthew 28:16-20.

3. Paul told Timothy to choose certain faithful men and commit to them what Paul had committed to Timothy (2 Timothy 2:2). This hardly needs comment; it is only necessary to ask, What was the work of Timothy? and then realize that he was to commit that work to others, and then they in turn were urged to commit the work to others. If this admonition was followed by Timothy and those who succeeded him, we have the permanence of the office assured.

4. The office has actually been continued from the beginning to the present day. That evangelist was the name by which these servants of the church were usually designated in primitive times seems evident from the testimony of several of the Christian fathers. Eusebius, for instance, the learned Bishop of Caesarea, AD 315-340, thus speaks of evangelists who lived and labored during the reign of Trajan, AD 98-117.[9] "Bishop" in the Christian literature from the second to the fourth centuries was none other than the "evangelist."[10]

B. **Evangelist is similar to today's preacher**, and is not the same as the office of elder.

J.W. McGarvey has made a contribution to the Restoration Movement's church polity. Before McGarvey's time, "evangelist" was an itinerant preacher, a circuit rider, who did not work with any one congregation for any extended period of time. Alexander Campbell wrote, "Evangelists constitute the living itinerant ministry of the church, sent abroad into the world and sustained in their labors by the church. They preach the word of life. They convert the world. They institute churches and set them in order."[11] Influenced by Presbyterian polity – with its ruling elders and teaching elders – early Restoration Movement preachers had the idea that preaching and teaching for the settled congregation should be the work of the elders. McGarvey defended the permanent service of an evangelist within a local congregation. He maintained that "preachers" were better identified with the New Testament evangelists than with New Testament elders. See Special Study #5, "J.W. McGarvey's Concept of the Ministry."

C. **Duties of the Office of Evangelist**

1. PREACHING

---

[9] Eusebius, *H.E.* III.37

[10] Kim Mallette, *The Evangelist,* A thesis presented to Central Christian College of the Bible, Moberly, Mo., 1977.

[11] Alexander Campbell, *Millennial Harbinger*, 1853, p.481.

Where New Testament evangelists did their preaching. (1) Unevangelized places, e.g., Gaul and Dalmatia. In this, the evangelist who serves as a 'state evangelist' for an area men's fellowship, would serve in a similar capacity. (2) In towns where there already was a church with elders, e.g., Timothy at Ephesus, Titus at Corinth, the "true yoke-fellow" at Philippi. The Christians are encouraged and urged to do all things necessary for the maintenance of their spiritual life. "Exhort" is an action word. It is one thing to tell a person what he must do, it is quite another to so speak as to create a desire on his part to do as he has been told. (3) In towns where churches had no elders yet, e.g., Philip? or Titus on Crete?. The Christians must be made aware of the need and the qualifications for such servants. (4) To crowds of people, e.g., Philip in the city of Samaria, or to a few individuals, e.g., Philip and the Ethiopian. (5) Some evangelists were itinerant, e.g., Philip, and some were 'located' ministers, e.g., Luke at Philippi, Philip at Caesarea, Timothy at Ephesus. (6) Sometimes multiple churches constitute an evangelist's field of service, e.g., Titus had responsibility for a number of churches on Crete, Archippus served three congregations in the Lycus River valley, namely Colossae, Laodicea, Hierapolis. However, care must be exercised here. Paul's instructions to Titus hardly constitute "the germ of the episcopal office" as *Pulpit Commentary* suggests. Titus is evidently *not* the bishop over a number of other evangelists already on the island. Nor is he the bishop over a number of congregations, who must submit to his authority even in the matter of selecting local elders. Like any evangelist whose field of service is not limited to one local congregation, Titus may go into any of those towns and preach for any of the congregations, and by presenting the Word and will of God, lead the people in the right paths.

The message, the content, of their preaching. The gospel or good news was the sole message. The "gospel" has been outlined as facts to be believed, commands to be obeyed, warnings to be heeded, and promises to be enjoyed. As one preaches he charges, reproves, and rebukes. The evangelist is to refute, counteract, and correct false and vain teaching (1 Timothy 1:3; 2 Timothy 2:14; Titus 1:13,14). Listeners to the gospel who trusted in riches were urged to transfer their faith to God (1 Timothy 6:17). Admonishing and warning are also a part of gospel preaching. Christians are notified of their faults and of approaching or possible dangers.

The purpose or the aim of their preaching. The ultimate purpose was the salvation of mankind, thus the preaching was to the unevangelized. Some intermediate steps toward that ultimate goal are to inform, instruct, move to action, confirm, convince, and set right.

2. TEACHING.[12]

Sinners are informed of their sinful and lost condition and instructed regarding

---

[12] "Teaching" is implicit in the allusions to "sound doctrine" in the letters to Timothy.

salvation and what they must do to be saved, e.g., Philip. The Christians are given a knowledge of their relationship to God and of the things that He expects of them as His children. The backslider learns of his condition and what he must do to be restored again to the divine family, e.g., Simon the sorcerer. Those who suffer are comforted through the hearing of God's word and promises.

3. SEE THAT ELDERS ARE APPOINTED IN EACH CHURCH. Titus 1:5.

Before there were evangelists, this is something the apostles themselves did (Acts 14:23; 1 Timothy 5:22). It likely will require working with the newly-converted men, training them to do the task they will one day be selected to do.

4. SET THE CONGREGATIONS IN ORDER. Titus 1:5.

Evangelists help troubled churches. See Titus' work at Corinth, where there was a lack of discipline toward a habitual and unrepentant sinner.

5. EQUIP THE SAINTS FOR THE WORK OF MINISTRY. Ephesians 4:11ff.

The evangelist, by reason of his office, must of necessity do some of the same tasks that constitute the work of elder, of deacon, and of teacher. Leaders "equip the saints for the work of ministry" (Ephesians 4:11ff). The higher office includes the lower. He will therefore often find himself doing jobs the lower (later) offices do, as well as teaching those newer workers how to do the job they have been set apart to do. Especially is this true in a new congregation where there are no Christians qualified to be elders or deacons.

6. REPRODUCE HIMSELF IN OTHER EVANGELISTS. 2 Timothy 2:2

The evangelist has the privilege of looking out for and training other men to be evangelists (2 Timothy 2:2). This might be done through internships. It might be done as an older evangelist in a given area has a 'fatherly' oversight of a number of younger, learning, evangelists.

D. Qualifications and Ordination of the Evangelist

There is no list of qualifications in one passage of Scripture, like those given for elder and deacon in 1 Timothy 3 and Titus 1. DeWelt has given a 15-point list (*The Church in the Bible*, p.94,95), divided into two categories, stated and implied.

    a.   Stated qualifications

        1. He must be a man of righteousness, godliness, faith, love, patience, meekness, and peace. 1 Timothy 6:11; 2 Timothy 2:22

2. He must be a man of purity.   1 Timothy 4:12c; 5:22b.
3. He must be a diligent student of God's Word.   2 Timothy 2:15
4. He must be gentle and apt to teach.   2 Timothy 2:24
5. He must be a man of contentment.   1 Timothy 6:6-10.
6. He must be one who avoids foolish questions.   2 Timothy 2:16,23; Titus 3:9,10; 1 Timothy 6:3-5.
7. He must be one who will conscientiously fulfill all his duties.   1 Timothy 4:15,16; 6:12,14,20;   2 Timothy 4:5.
8. He must not be ashamed of the testimony of the Lord.   2 Timothy 1:18.
9. He must be willing to suffer hardship. 2 Timothy 2:3; 4:5.
10. He must be an example in all things.   1 Timothy 4:12; Titus 2:7,8.

b.   Implied qualifications

1. He must first of all be a Christian of the highest type.
2. He must be a speaker who is capable of delivering in a clear, forcible and becoming manner the whole counsel of God.
3. He must have strong convictions regarding his message.   Titus 3:8.
4. He must be as wise as a serpent and harmless as a dove.   Matthew 10:16.
5. He must meet all the character qualifications of an elder.   The duties of an evangelist and elder are similar and overlap each other to some extent; it therefore seems logical that his qualifications should exceed or at least be equal to those of an elder.

It might be possible to summarize this list under two or three points.   The would-be evangelist should be of good report in the church that ordains him, as was Timothy.   He should have a good knowledge of the Scriptures, the Gospel, again like Timothy who knew the Scriptures from childhood.   2 Timothy 2:2 tells Timothy what kind of men to look for – faithful men to whom he may teach and entrust the gospel message heard from Paul, who themselves will be able to teach others also. There are some common sense skills that could be studied and developed while the young men are interns or apprentices: management skills (Timothy is the example); people motivation skills (Titus); personal evangelism skills (Philip).

What about ordination?

The call and ordination of Timothy furnishes an instructive example ... Paul found him in Lystra, and learned of the faith of his mother and grandmother, and that from a child he had known the Holy Scriptures.   He learned also that he was well-reported of by the brethren at Lystra and Iconium.   He would have him to go forth with him, Acts 16:1-3.   Paul gave him an evangelical education, and taught him all the details of the important work to which he had been called (all this followed his ordination service). There was an ordination service, 1 Timothy 4:4; 2 Timothy 1:6.   (There was a prophecy that suggested to Paul that Timothy be set aside for the ministry.) Evidently, elders from two local congregations united in this installation service. They represented the churches in a special service of official recognition. (Common sense suggests that all the churches ... who become obligated [by ordaining a man to the office of evangelist] for his support, should have some voice in his selection and ordination.) All Christian communities on earth, however numerous, constitute but one church of Christ. ... [I]n all cases where public officers are to be chosen, and especially evangelists who are to be regarded as officers of the whole body, a concurrence of a plurality of churches ... should be regarded as necessary. Ordination involves the proving of the fitness of the candidate by competent testimony, or by a personal examination, to the satisfaction of a fairly representative body of men in the church, and the formal approval of him by prayer, fasting, and the imposition of hands by such a body. Then from this formal and real induction into office, there flow certain natural and important consequences. Of course, the main facts of such an ordination will be recorded and the record should be carefully preserved. A certified copy of this record is the evangelist's credential to the churches ... In case of an ordained man's falling into sin, a similar representative body will be the proper authority to inquire into his standing, and, if found unworthy, to withdraw the church's approval from him as an evangelist.[13]

E. Elder-Evangelist relationships

Younger evangelists likely are still under the supervision of the one who encouraged the churches to ordain them. Older evangelists are given greater responsibility over churches and areas. Perhaps evangelists rule until the congregation is established with duly chosen elders, then turn the congregation over to the authority of the elders.

What about an evangelist also being selected to serve as an elder? This commentator has no objection if he meets the qualifications given in Scripture for elder. But this also limits his field of service to the congregation that selected him as elder. The evangelist also must be careful lest he wants to become an elder just so he has more "voice" in the affairs of the congregation to which he ministers. Until recently, this commentator had never once heard of an "evangelist" desiring to be selected to the office of "deacon." Why? What is there about "elder" that is so desirable, and "deacon" that is seemingly less desirable?

What about the subordination of elders to the evangelist? No! said McGarvey in Missouri Christian Lectures, 1889, p.202ff.

One reason given to Titus why elders ought to be able to convict the gainsayers is that "there are many unruly men, vain talkers and deceivers, specially they of the circumcision, whose mouths must be stopped; men who overthrow whole

---

[13] Hayden, *Church Polity*, p.41-43.

houses, teaching things which they ought not for filthy lucre's sake." These were unruly evangelists, and the only way to stop their wide mouths was to convict them as gainsayers – not *convince* them; for such fellows can never be convinced; but to *convict* them, which means to convince the brethren as to who they are, and thus stop their mouths by depriving them of hearers.

Again, the elders of the church at Ephesus were put on the watch of all evangelists who might visit their flock, and required to stand guard against any who were unworthy (Acts 20:29-31). And Revelation 2:2 says they did it: "they tried those who claimed to be apostles and were not ...."

The first innovation on this apostolic order of church government, which is traceable in history, consisted not in the displacement of the eldership, or in a change of its character and functions, but in subordinating it to the resident evangelist, making him the chief ruler, and ascribing to him alone the title *episkopos*, "bishop," which had hitherto belonged to every elder. The certain existence of this order is first found in the writings of Irenaeus, who wrote in the last quarter of the second century; unless we admit the genuineness of the Ignatian epistles, which were written, if genuine, in the first or second decade of that century. In three of the fourteen Ignatian epistles, we find that Ignatius may be regarded as the first advocate of this innovation, if not the originator of it. He presses the subject of obedience to the bishop with vehemence, often dragging it in without regard to the connection of thought, and thus he betrays the untempered zeal of a convert to an innovation. Doubtless the other eleven epistles, if genuine, in which are still more allusions to this subject, were written in great part for the purpose of emphasizing an order of government which at the time of their date, had become common, but which still seemed to need the support of authoritative names. As such names were not found among the apostles, or among men like Clement of Rome, Polycarp and Justin Martyr, all of whose writings indicate the continuance of the apostolic order, Ignatius was seized upon as the single man of the first half of the second century whose authority could be plausibly claimed for separating the bishopric from the eldership.

No! says DeWelt, *1 and 2 Timothy and Titus*, p.279-283.

As in the case of apostles and elders and their relationship, there is a relationship between elders and preachers that must be observed strictly if both are to do their work properly and scripturally. The work of elders and preachers is different, although one might be an elder and a preacher at the same time. He can do things as a preacher that he cannot do as an elder, or do things as an elder that he cannot do as a preacher. E.g., he may preach for several congregations but he cannot exercise oversight of an overseer in any congregation. Or he may exercise the oversight as an elder in a certain congregation, but he cannot exercise the oversight of several congregations at the same time.

Preachers sometimes try to dominate elders. Preachers often ignore the eldership. Young preachers sometimes try to do their work without elders, thinking that they can better carry out their ideas and plans without the restraint of the eldership to check them. Many think they know more than the elders; sometimes they do, but this does not authorize preachers to usurp control of the oversight ... Most men who have been made elders get little encouragement for the efforts they make. They are looked upon by some preachers and many members as sort of a necessary useless sort of men. Some of us will accept the advice of a man who was never chosen by anyone to oversee, rather than follow the counsel of a properly selected and appointed eldership.

Many preachers act as sole judges of who is and who is not qualified to be elders in a certain place, disregarding the Bible qualifications. We can all go to the Bible and determine who is and who is not a qualified elder. But when preachers say, "That is not necessary to be an elder," when speaking of some qualification, "so I'll just appoint him anyway," that is going too far. Sometimes a preacher refuses to appoint, or allow to be appointed (as if he were the only judge), a qualified man to the eldership by giving some point of qualification that the Bible does not give.

Preachers claiming the position and authority of elders when they begin regular work at a place. A few preachers are so careless in the Scriptures as to claim to be an "Automatic Elder" when they move to a certain place to begin regular work there. They argue this way: The elders labor in word and doctrine (1 Tim. 5:17); the preacher also labors in word and doctrine, and since the preacher always labors in this field, and it is the work of elders, it follows that the preacher is automatically an elder where ever he labors ... There are some things wrong with this idea. It completely disregards the qualifications for an elder given in the Scriptures.

Preachers exercising oversight in the place of the eldership. Some preachers follow the practice of denominationalism to make themselves THE PASTOR of the congregation where they preach. Why do they do this? (1) Sometimes the elders are irresponsible and do not perform their work. This necessarily leaves the duties upon the shoulders of someone else, usually the preacher. He begins little by little to assume their work until finally he is acting as the elder-ship, even though he did not seek it from the beginning. (2) In some places there are no men qualified to become elders, and either the membership places all responsibility and authority upon the preacher, or the preacher thinks he must assume the oversight in order for the work to go forward. (3) In some places the elders insist that the preacher take the leading part and make most of the decisions for them.

Preachers exercising oversight over the elders. This is the most extreme claim toward popery we have found to date in the church of Christ. It is contended that preachers are not only EQUAL to the elders in the oversight, but are ABOVE them! ... Imagine a preacher claiming oversight over several bishops ... it makes him sort of an ARCHBISHOP! ... The Bible teaches that elders have the OVERSIGHT of the flock which is among them. If the evan-gelist is among the flock he is under the oversight of the elders ... Titus was told to "rebuke with all authority" (Titus 2:15), but that is a far cry from "oversee with all authority." The authority of an evangelist is toward the preaching of the word.

Elders exercising too much authority over preachers. Many times elders keep placing their own responsibilities upon the preacher until he is actually trying to do all the work of the eldership. Christ did not give elders authority to delegate their responsibilities to others. They may assign certain work to others to do, but the OVERSIGHT and responsibilities for such can never be assigned to another ... Then some elders try to control a preacher when he is beyond the bounds of their authority. Some ask, "Do the elders of one congregation have oversight of a preacher who regularly works with them but goes away for a meeting in another locality? Are the elders still over him while he works there?" The answer is, NO. The simple reason is that the elders cannot oversee ANY WORK beyond the local church of which they are elders. A congregation may send a preacher into a new field of labor and support him, but they do not exercise the oversight over him or those converts where he is preaching in that work. They may discipline him for an unchristian conduct while away in a meeting after he returns, or they may withdraw their support from him, and mark him as a false teacher if he does not continue true to the word while at some other place preaching, but this is the extent of their authority over an evangelist whom they may be supporting when he is not laboring among them.

No, the evangelist is not over the elders! say others. Will you let a young man, still in his twenties, give directions to elders when it comes to church administration? (Yet if the evangelist is 50-60 years old, may he then give direction and leadership?)

Yes! say others, appealing to 1 Timothy 5:19,20, where the evangelist is to discipline the elder who has been accused of sin by two or three witnesses. (However, note that it is possible that it is not the elder who is rebuked, but the sinning people who brought accusation against the elder. Note that "them" is plural, whereas "elder" is singular.) I.C. Nance in the *Gospel Broadcast* of Feb. 24, 1949, p.141, wrote:

Whereas it cannot be shown that either Titus or Timothy, evangelists, were *ever under* any eldership *after* they began their work of evangelism, it can be definitely shown that both of them were *over* the eldership of at least one (and that's enough). Timothy was placed over the eldership at Ephesus by apostolic authority. And Ephesus was an old, large, and established church which had had elders for years *when* this happened. Titus, on the other hand, just a plain evangelist, was placed by apostolic authority over all the churches in Crete ... Since an evangelist is given power to exercise "all authority" over a number of churches and, whereas, an elder has only partial authority in only *one* congregation, it follows that the authority of the evangelist supersedes that of the elder or the eldership. Hence, Titus was over any eldership you might name in Crete. If not, why not?

The elder's area of responsibility or field of service is limited to the local congregation, whereas the evangelist's is not so limited. The evangelist's position is best described as an outside advisor to the elder. That is Timothy's position at Ephesus.

CONCLUSION

An "evangelist" is one who is well acquainted with the good news and makes it his business to share it. He encourages men to regulate their lives so they are in harmony with the Gospel. He recognizes and refutes wrong "doctrine" by how it harmonizes or fails to harmonize with the gospel. The writers of the Gospels are called "evangelists" because they did what evangelists do – they were telling the story (oral tradition). "Tell me the story of Jesus!" is our appeal to those who would be evangelists. Do the work of an evangelist! Set the churches in order with your great preaching! Reproduce yourselves as you recruit young men for the office of evangelist!

Fulfill your ministry!   Don't quit the ministry!   Keep on!

SPECIAL STUDY #5

J. W. McGarvey's Concept of the Ministry[1]

WELDON BENNETT
Abilene Christian University: Dallas

No leader in the Restoration Movement in America had a higher view of the gospel ministry nor did any promote the training of preachers more than John William McGarvey (1829-1911). Being unusually gifted as a preacher, scholar, debater, author, commentator, Bible instructor, organizer, and counselor in almost every aspect of church life, McGarvey "came to the kingdom" when his talents were needed the most.

At the time of his graduation with high honors from Bethany College at the age of twenty-one, McGarvey had decided to devote his life to preaching the gospel of Christ, but he felt that his preparation was not yet adequate. He moved to Fayette, Missouri, and opened a school for boys. Almost all of his leisure time was used to further his knowledge of Latin and Greek and, with the aid of commentaries, to become well acquainted with the entire Bible. After two years in Fayette, having spoken often at the Lord's Day church services, McGarvey accepted the church's invitation to become its minister, and he was ordained by two Disciples ministers through the laying on of hands.

The work for which McGarvey is best known is as Professor of Sacred History in the College of the Bible at Kentucky University, Lexington, Kentucky. In the April 1865 *Lard's Quarterly,* McGarvey published an essay which clearly and concisely set forth his ideas concerning the need among the Disciples for a special program of education. He was convinced that the existing Christian colleges supported by the Disciples did not properly prepare men *to preach.* Five months later his plan became a reality as the first class of students enrolled in the College of the Bible. The Lexington professor recognized that the New Testament term *diakonos* carries different meanings, depending on the context. In the King James Version it is rendered minister, servant, and deacon. McGarvey stated that although the word "minister" in modern usage refers "to the public speakers of the church," the original word has no such limitation.[2] He employed the term in the current usage, however, as he wrote articles on "an edu-

---

[1] *Restoration Quarterly*, Third Quarter 1981, p. 167ff.

[2] *A New Commentary on Acts of Apostles* (Cincinnati: The Standard Publishing Co., 1892. First pub. in 1863). pp. 106f.

cated ministry" and "ministerial education."[3]   "The duty of preaching the gospel is laid ... on every member of the church," he wrote, "by example, by private admonition and exhortation."   The Scriptures, nevertheless, appropriate the term *preaching* in a special way to the "public and formal proclamation of the word of God."   Such was Paul's meaning when he wrote, "they who preach the gospel shall live by the gospel," which shows that those who preach shall be supported by those who do not preach.[4]

Before McGarvey, the Disciples understood an evangelist to be one who was of necessity a traveling preacher, who could not work with a local congregation for any extended period of time.   To McGarvey this was an erroneous concept.   In an 1875 editorial in the *Apostolic Times,* he confidently declared:

> Let us make the affirmation, and let it challenge denial, that a preacher who spends a year preaching exclusively to one congregation, is doing the work of an evangelist as certainly as he who spends a year preaching from place to place. The apostles knew nothing of the distinction we have created ... by which a man is said to evangelize when he is traveling, and to do pastoral work when he is located.   On the contrary, it was while Timothy was located for a term of years in Ephesus, doing what is now improperly called pastoral work, that Paul said to him, with special reference to that work, "Do the work of an evangelist, make full proof of thy ministry" (2 Tim. 4:5).   The work which an evangelist does then, when located with a congregation, is *the work of an evangelist,* and his proper designation is not "pastor," but evangelist and preacher.[5]

McGarvey consistently affirmed that the *elders* of the local church are the pastors, not the *preachers.*   Only when the preacher is appointed as one of the elders may he be styled a pastor.[6]

As to the preacher's call to the ministry, the Lexington professor, like Campbell and other leaders of the Restoration Movement, believed that "good order" demanded the endorsement of the congregation.   Any Christian, however, might find himself in a community where there is no congregation, and should he "feel constrained to preach the gospel to his neighbors, there is no impropriety in

---

[3] "Ministerial Education," *Lard's Quarterly, 11* (1864-65). 239.

[4] "Review of 'W.' on Missionary Societies," *LQ,* V (April 1868). 195f.

[5] *Apostolic Times,* VII (March 4, 1875), 79.   McGarvey recognized the distinction between "preaching" and "teaching," but he believed the settled preacher was engaged in both.   *AT,* VI (November 19. 1874), 4.

[6] *AT,* VII (July 1. 1975), 283.

his doing so, provided he can obtain a hearing and accomplish good by his efforts."[7]   Men are thus called to the ministry of the word "by the church, some by other preachers, and some by their own sense of duty."[8]

No trait is more important to a successful ministry, McGarvey often exhorted, than a holy, exemplary life.   "The people are not very hard to please in preaching," he wrote in an 1872 editorial titled "Preaching."   "If the preacher is a good man, faithful and energetic, the people do their best to like his preaching. If a man is acceptable in other respects, his preaching has to be extremely poor, and continuously poor, in order to create dissatisfaction."[9]   The professor could not tolerate indolence.   How sad he must have been when he wrote: "If there is one sin characteristic of preachers it is laziness."[10]   In an editorial on "Straggling Preachers," he said: "Let us beg our church officer ... to receive no man, though he have the eloquence of an angel, until he accredits himself properly."[11]

The eminent Bible professor considered the neglect to prepare their sermons properly a primary reason for some preachers not being sought by churches.   "It is the absence of thought which makes a sermon dull," he wrote in 1872.   "And if thought is absent, it is because the preacher, in his preparation, has done no thinking."[12]

For McGarvey the most important consideration in sermon preparation was filling the heart with Scriptural truth.   Speaking at the 1883 Missouri Christian Lectures on "Preachers' Methods," he underscored "the neglect of the word of God" as the greatest defect in the lives of preachers.   People who listen to the preacher have a right to demand of him, "after he shall have spent some years in his calling, that he be well acquainted with all of God's word, and that he be able to give an intelligent answer to the questions commonly arising on every point."[13] The professor's own studies exemplified this basic task of the minister.   Probably no man of his time was better equipped in a knowledge of the Scriptures than he, and his forty-five years of teaching in the College of the Bible demonstrated the earnestness of his appeal to preachers to "know the Book."

---

[7] *AT,* III (February 15, 1872), p.355.

[8] *AT,* VIII (August 17, 1876), p.513.

[9] *AT,* IV (July 25, 1872), 4.

[10] *AT,* VII (February 4. 1875). 31

[11] *AT,* V (February 5, 1974). 4.

[12] *AT,* IV (June 6, 1872), 4.

[13] *The Missouri Christian Lectures* (St.   Louis: John Burns, Publisher, 1883). pp. 84f.

McGarvey recommended the reading of scholarly books on the Bible but such reading should come only after one has a good knowledge of the text. "Read introductions after you have studied the books and not before," he advised. "Thus read, they may correct or modify your own conclusions, but read in advance they may mislead you."[14]   Taking issue with some previous Disciples leaders, the Lexington professor believed the judicious use of recognized commentaries can be helpful. "The man who attempts to gain a knowledge of the Bible by his own unaided powers," he declared, "while the aid furnished by a multitude of learned and devout predecessors is at hand, seems to declare himself the equal in exegetical power of all who have gone before him."[15]

Addressing himself to the method of locating proper sermon illustrations, McGarvey declared the Bible itself "the richest and the most profitable" source accessible to any preacher. He gave three reasons that ministers should prefer Bible illustrations above others: First, searching the Scriptures for illustrations makes the preacher more intimate with the word of God; secondly, an illustration drawn from the Scriptures carries with it an intrinsic force and authority; and, thirdly, while making his audience acquainted with an illustrating incident, the speaker is imparting to them additional knowledge of the word of God.[16]   Such an emphasis on giving the Bible priority in one's study and preaching does not mean McGarvey eschewed acquaintance with secular literature. On the contrary, he once wrote: "There is no department of knowledge which the preacher cannot make subservient to his high calling." But he thought the preacher's "knowledge of general literature is confined chiefly to what he acquires before he enters fully upon his life work," because, in the active ministry, the preacher finds that demands for study in his special field are so great as to occupy almost all of his time.[17]

The inimitable McGarvey encouraged each preacher to adapt his style of preaching "to the class of persons from whom his converts must chiefly come; and what class is this but the children?" Subject matter that is well chosen for adults, he considered to be equally well chosen for children. For the latter to comprehend, the preacher must speak with simplicity. He then added:

> While thus aiming at the children, we will most successfully reach those of maturer years. It is astonishing how much of our preaching overshoots the heads

---

[14] *Ibid.*, pp. 85, 98.

[15] *Ibid.*, pp. 93f.

[16] *AT,* VI (September 17, 1874), 5.

[17] *Missouri Christian Lectures: 1883,* pp. 104f.

of our congregation.   Aim lower; aim at the heads of our children and you will strike much nearer to the hearts and also the heads of their parents.[18]

The aim of every sermon, McGarvey stressed, "is always a change for the better in the life of the hearer.   It is the reformation of the sinful and the more complete sanctification of the righteous."   Instruction is merely a means to an end.[19]   "We teach," he reminded, "that we may have a basis for exhortation, and we exhort that we may move to proper action."[20]

About 1875, Dwight L. Moody had gained fame as a successful lay evangelist.   McGarvey wrote an article that year evaluating Moody and another evangelist, Whittle.   He attributed their popularity and success to the earnest-ness, simplicity, and pointedness of their preaching, and more especially to the undenominational character of their meetings.   He was very critical, however, of the predominantly emotional nature which characterized their style.   "Ours is not an age of thought," he said.   "The people demand entertainment rather than instruction.   They have little taste for either books or sermons which call for mental effort on their part."[21]   Such a criticism is reminiscent of that which Campbell made of the revivalists in the early nineteenth century.   The Lexington preacher and professor believed, as Campbell, that an appeal to the emotions is proper after the hearers had been sufficiently instructed.   His criticism of the Moody-type revivalism seems to have been shared by the majority of Disciples preachers.   They believed the revivalists were in error in equating the emotional excitements of the audiences with "the workings of the Spirit."   But they all recognized that more is involved in conversion than the mere belief of testimony. An appeal had to be made to the will and the emotions.   McGarvey felt that a lack of ability to make such appeals was the chief weakness in his own preaching. As an octogenarian, he told the students of the College of the Bible:

> When preaching was my work, I thought to myself many times, and I think I said it many a time to others, that of all the gifts which I crave, if I had my wish, the first would be that I might have the power to bring men to repentance ... I have been perhaps unusually successful in convincing my hearers of the truth of what I had to present to them, but I have made a failure in trying to bring them to repentance.[22]

---

[18] *AT,* VI (November 26, 1874). 4.

[19] *AT,* VI (December 3, 1874). 4.

[20] *Missouri Christian Lectures: 1883,* p. 105.

[21] *AT,* VII (April 22, 1875). 163.

[22] J.W. McGarvey, *Chapel Talks* (Lufkin, Texas: Gospel Guardian Co., 1956), pp. 72,74.

On the matter of ministerial support, the Bible professor held that "the amount should vary not with the talent and the success of the preacher, but with the size of his family and the expensiveness of living where he resides."[23] He often urged the churches to support their preachers adequately, and, at the same time, he called upon those interested in preaching never to make financial support a major consideration. If the brethren do not contribute sufficiently to the preacher's needs, "let him add tent-making like Paul," McGarvey advised.[24] In his advanced years, speaking to students of the College of the Bible he declared that any young man who declines to prepare himself for the ministry because of the prospect of poverty is "not fit to enter upon it."[25]

Disciples leaders who preceded McGarvey maintained that the preaching and teaching for a settled congregation should be the work of the elders (bishops). One of the significant contributions which McGarvey made to the Restoration Movement was to defend, on the basis of New Testament teaching, the permanent services of an evangelist within the local church. He understood the term *poimaino,* rendered "shepherd" and "feed" in the English New Testament, to mean rule and to be correctly so translated. Thus the elders' principal duty in the congregation is to rule rather than to teach.[26] In an 1865 article in *Lard's Quarterly,* McGarvey declared the translators of the Authorized Version were mistaken in rendering *poimainein* in Acts 20:28 "to feed." "Taking the custom of the cold climate of England and Scotland for their guide," he wrote, "instead of that which prevailed in Judea, they assumed that feeding was [the shepherds'] principal labor ... It would have been far nearer the truth to have rendered it 'rule the flock. ' This rendering, indeed, is found necessary in several places in the New Testament, as in Revelation 2:27, 12:5, 19:15 ... In only one instance is it properly rendered feed, which is Jude 12."[27] It is not necessary, therefore, that the elders do the preaching for a congregation, he maintained. They may engage the services of an evangelist for that purpose. In the 1889 Missouri Christian Lectures, McGarvey referred to Paul's instructions to Timothy in 1 and 2 Timothy, saying: "Every duty is laid on Timothy that was laid on the elders, with the single exception of that of ruling.   With this exception his work was coordinate

---

[23] *AT,* VI (July 16. 1874), 4.

[24] *AT,* VII (September 9, 1975), 403.

[25] *Chapel Talks,* p. 62.

[26] *Lard's Quarterly,* II (April 1865). 313f.

[27] *Ibid.*, 315.

with theirs."[28]   Such a service does not make the evangelist a pastor, for the "pastoring" – ruling – remains the prerogative of the elders, the Lexington professor affirmed.

It is not the purpose of the present article to deal with all aspects of the eldership ministry, although McGarvey wrote much on the subject, but only with the problem of how elders relate to the evangelist's work.   Since, as has been noted above, the elders are the rulers in the congregation, the local preacher "is one of the flock, and the pastors have the rule over him."[29]   McGarvey reasoned that it is not wise to have men who depend on the financial support of the church bear the responsibility of disciplining the members.   "Salaried preachers, as a class, dare not attempt to enforce scriptural discipline alone," he stated, "and if they do, the attempt recoils upon their own Heads."[30]   He spoke out strongly against preachers "taking charge of the church," an expression which was often heard in his time.[31]   McGarvey held that the first innovation against apostolic order of church government was the subordination of the eldership to the resident evangelist, "making him the chief ruler, and ascribing to him alone the title *episcopos,* 'bishop'."[32]

McGarvey possessed the ability of uniting biblical principles of the ministry with the practical needs of his time.   He discovered that the churches which had "the constant services of preachers ... possess more of the elements of church life" than churches without a regular minister.   His position, unique at the time, was destined to become the practice of most churches of Christ by the middle of the 20th century.

Concerning the Lexington professor's contribution to ministerial education, his biographer, William C. Morro, wrote:

---

[28] "Church Government," *Missouri Christian Lectures: 1889,* pp. 199f.

[29] *Ibid.,* pp.199-201.

[30] *Octographic Review,* Daniel Sommer, ed. (Richwood, Ohio, 1887-1906), XXXIV (October 1, 1891), p. 2.

[31] *Ecclesiastical Observer,* David King, ed. (Birmingham, England), XLII (April 1, 1889), 47. McGarvey did agree with Isaac Errett, founding editor of the *Christian Standard,* that the evangelist has ruling authority over the church in the formative period of that congregation, but that such authority is relinquished when elders are appointed.   He disagreed strongly with Daniel Sommer, editor of the *American Christian Review,* who interpreted 1 Timothy 5:19 to mean the evangelist may "sit in on the merits of the case" when an elder is charged with misconduct.   McGarvey insisted that an elder accused of misconduct or of teaching error is subject to the other elders or the entire congregation.

[32] *Missouri Christian Lectures: 1889,* pp.201, 203.

In the College of the Bible he did a type of work and showed a concentration of spirit that elevated the work of the ministry throughout all the adjacent region ... In his teaching he planned a type of instruction that had not been attempted in other colleges. The College of the Bible sent out ministers equipped with a knowledge of the Bible and inspired them with confidence that they could correctly interpret the Scriptures.[33]

For many years, pulpits of most churches of the "Disciples" were supplied by men who had been trained by McGarvey and his associates at Lexington. Young men of various intellectual levels were enrolled. McGarvey's method "fitted the day." He did not intend to produce scholars; he wanted rather an army of men filled with a knowledge of the Lord Jesus Christ. Many came with poor academic backgrounds who became preachers of great power, and their debt to J.W. McGarvey was incalculable.[34]

---

[33] William C. Morrow, *Brother McGarvey: The Life of President J. W. McGarvey of the College of the Bible, Lexington, Kentucky* (St. Louis: The Bethany Press, 1940), p. 82.

[34] *Ibid.*, p.233.

V. THE CHARGE CONCERNING THE EVANGEL-IST'S CONCERNS FOR VARIOUS MEMBERS OF THE CONGREGATION. 5:1 - 6:2

A. The Evangelist's Care of Old and Young Members. 5:1,2

5:1 -- Do not sharply rebuke an older man – Up to this point in this letter, Paul has been giving instructions on matters that touched Timothy's relationship with the whole congregation. Almost the whole of the remainder of the letter is concerned with specific directions to Timothy to assist him in dealing with various groups and individuals within the congregation. For the evangelist, there is not only the administrative needs of the whole congregation, there is also the daily, private relations with individual members to which someone in Timothy's position must give careful attention. We have the same command with respect to persons to be admonished in Titus 2:1-6, where, however, we have the forms *presbutas* and *presbutidas* for "older men" and "older women," and *neas* and *neōterous* for "young women" and "younger men." The verb *epiplēsso* ("sharply rebuke") occurs only here in the New Testament (the usual words are *epitimaō*, as at 2 Timothy 4:2, and frequently in the Gospels, and *elegchō*, as at Titus 1:13, 2:15 and Revelation 3:19), but in classical Greek expresses a sharp castigation with words. The word literally speaks of "striking with blows." Figuratively, as it no doubt is used here, it means to 'smite with words' (rather than with fists). In this context, with the other people grouped by age, *presbuteros* ("elder") has reference to age rather than to office.[1]   Timothy was still a young man, under 40 years of age per 1 Timothy 4:12, when Paul wrote this letter to him.   There would be many men in the congregation who would be "older men" to Timothy.   It is Timothy's behavior towards men old enough to be his father and grandfather with whom Paul is here concerned.   Admonition and correction are needed by all; but a disrespectful, roughshod assault upon an older man by a young evangelist is out of place, and in fact lays the preacher open to rebuke for his methods.

But rather **appeal to him as a father** – If correction is needed, Timothy is to "appeal" or "entreat" or "exhort."   The word is *parakaleō*, and "exhort" or "encourage" is a good translation.[2]   What Timothy is not to do is to let people

---

[1] We have observed in chapter 3, during the study of the qualifications for "elder," that in the 1st century church, "elder" and "bishop" were interchangeable terms. The word translated "elder" is the same term here translated "old man."

[2] The verb used in the original means "to call alongside." Instead of dealing harshly with those who need correction, and instead of doing it in public, Timothy is to "call them alongside" for the purpose of giving a personal and private word of encouragement, appeal, or admonition.

just go on in their sins. The word "appeal" actually goes with all four following groups – older men, younger men, older women, younger women. How would you talk to your own father if he needed correction? That is the way the evangelist is to talk to older men, as he endeavors to persuade them to lead more holy lives.[3] In the Old Testament and here, as the understood reason behind the instructions to Timothy, the Bible teaches God's people to respect older people.

The younger men as brothers – The verb "appeal to" should be understood, so as to complete the thought. "Appeal to the younger men as brothers." Some members of the church at Ephesus would be Timothy's age and younger. How was he to deal with them when they needed correction? Well, how would you talk to your own brother, if he were habitually sinning and needed to be directed aright? Use that same tone of voice and that same kind of appeal to the younger members of the church. Implied in this instruction is the idea that the evangelist really does have an "authority", not in himself personally, but in the message he delivers, that could be taken advantage of when it comes time to "admonish." Nevertheless, the evangelist's relations with the younger members was to be one of a brother and friend, rather than that of a superior in rank and dignity.

5:2 -- [Appeal to] the older women as mothers – It seems proper to supply the verb "appeal to" (*parakaleō*, from verse 1) in order to understand Paul's instructions to Timothy with reference to his personal relationships with various members of the congregation. It also seems likely that the prohibition against harsh rebukes when people need correction carries into verse 2. If so, then the instructions to Timothy are concerned with how to counsel those members who sin and who need help toward repentance. Timothy was not to let people stay in their sins. When the brethren needed rebuke, entreaty, admonishing, or encouraging, Timothy was not to shun and avoid the sinner. But he was also to have watchful care over his approach to people who need correcting, lest there be some assumption of superiority as he tries to correct. That the evangelist has a responsibility to "appeal to" the "older women" tells us that the "female members of the congregation must not be excluded from the sphere of private pastoral counseling with respect to sin. Though this talk may at times prove delicate, it must not be shunned."[4] No son who has proper feelings would rebuke his own mother with severity. So when Timothy admonishes the older women, he must deal with them as a loving adult son would deal with his own mother were she erring. To correct one's own mother requires a deep humility, genuine searching

---

[3] Old men do not have a liberty to do anything they please, merely because they are old. Old men can succumb to the allures and temptations of the devil just as younger people can. When this happens, there will be occasions when correction is needed. This is when the evangelist gets personally involved in the lives of the people to whom he preaches.

[4] Hendriksen, *op. cit.*, p.166.

of the heart, tender language, and wrestling at the throne of grace for wisdom.

And **the younger women as sisters** – Since Timothy is in his mid-thirties when Paul writes this instruction, "younger women" would be those his own age and younger. He is to treat them as he would his own sister. Those readers who have tried to correct a brother or sister who has erred know immediately the tone of voice needed, the loving approach, the expressions of concern that must accompany the correction, if the person being appealed to is ever to consider a meaningful change of behavior for the better.

In all purity – Likely this phrase is to be taken with the preceding clause, and tells Timothy something else about which he must be concerned when he deals with the younger women. On "purity" see the notes at 4:12. See how jealously the apostle guards against any possibility of abuse of the familiar relationships between a minister and the women of the congregation. They are his sisters, and *hagneia* (purity) is to be the constant condition of his heart and character.

> This is not a warning only against acts of immorality (such would of course be understood), but against any breach of propriety. Even if immorality is not involved, thoughtlessness or indiscretion will ruin the ministry of any pastor, regardless of his eloquence. When his pastoral duties require him to deal with young women, he should behave as he would want other men to act toward his own sister, or as he would act toward his sister. This warning is most significant, for at this very point many young men on the threshold of long and fruitful service have lost their usefulness.[5]

> Paul ... knew the danger which would beset a youthful minister of the Gospel when it was his duty to admonish and entreat a youthful female; he knew too the scandal to which he might be exposed if, in the performance of the necessary duties of his office, there should be the slightest departure from purity and propriety. He was therefore to guard his heart with more than common vigilance in such circumstances, and was to indulge in no word or look or action which could possibly be construed as manifesting an improper state of feeling ... A youthful minister who fails here, can never recover the perfect purity of an unsullied reputation, and never in subsequent life be wholly free from suspicion.[6]

B. The Evangelist's Concern for the Care of Widows.   5:3-16

5:3 -- Honor widows – "Honor" certainly includes the idea of providing financial assistance to meet the everyday needs of those who are "widows indeed".   The

---

[5] Kent, *op. cit.*, p.169.

[6] Barnes, *op. cit.*, p.174.

instruction concerning the care of widows covers a rather long paragraph. The need for special care and provision for the widows[7] in the church was something the early church recognized from the beginning (Acts 6), and is one of the evidences that a person's Christianity is genuine (James 1:27). The evangelist with the congregation at Ephesus is to see that the widows are properly provided for. It does not instruct him to personally do it all, but he is to see that it is done. Evidently, the care of widows by the whole body, which began at Jerusalem in the very early days of the church, was continued in the churches planted by Paul.

Who are widows indeed – In this and the verses following there are several categories of widows. (1) There is the widow who is a widow indeed. Her husband has died, and there are no living family members or even relatives on whom she may depend (verses 3,5,16).[8] (2) There is the widow who, though her husband has died, has a family or relatives who can care for her (verse 4). (3) There are widows who give themselves to wanton pleasure (verse 6). (4) There are the "younger widows" (verses 11,14). In these verses, the evangelist Timothy is directed to treat each category differently. Again, we assume the evangelist is to ensure that the church also knows how to treat each of these categories, and that it actually does get involved where women are "widows indeed."

5:4 -- But if any widow has children or grandchildren – As noted in verse 3, the widow who has living relatives is a different category of widow than the widow who is a "widow indeed." Not all widows fall into the category of those who are to be provided for by the congregation. "Children" (*tekna*) is a reference to her own children, now old enough to provide a place for their widowed mother. "Grandchildren" (*ekgona*) is a general word which means both "grandchildren" and "close family relatives." The KJV reads "nephews," but this word had a meaning 300 years ago which has now disappeared. (In Latin *nepotes*, "descendants;" in French, *nos neveux*, "our descendants." The English word "nephews", derived from *nepos*, through the French *neveu*, properly means "descendant" to the second and third generations. In fact, one English dictionary gives this example: "their nephews, or sons' sons, which reigned in the third place.") While the word *ekgona* may not actually cover nephews or close relatives, still we know of exemplary cases where such more distant relatives have taken care of a widowed saint. We think this is as Jesus would want it.

---

[7] In the 1st century world, women did not ordinarily work at a job outside of the home in order to support themselves. No such jobs of an honorable kind were even available. Thus when a woman was widowed, if there were no relatives to see to her needs, she would soon become destitute. Christ never intended that Christian widows should be left in such dire straits. The New Testament Scriptures are full of precepts and examples which teach the church how to meet the needs of her own.

[8] Per verse 4, a widow is not a "widow indeed" if she has living "children or grandchildren."

Let them first learn to practice piety in regard to their own family – Clearly, it is the children or grandchildren who are to "learn piety." Sometimes children and grandchildren are not inclined to provide for their needy parents.[9] In such cases, the evangelist will have to help them learn this lesson, including the especial blessing promised to those who faithfully carry out this too-often-forgotten duty (Ephesians 6:2,3). Notice, responsibility for one's forebears is carried over to the second and third generations. Christian children and grandchildren have a divinely given responsibility to care for their elderly progenitors. "Piety" (*eusebein*) is reverent action, giving God and man each their due. It is not something that can be treated lightly. "Their own family" shows that a widowed mother or grandmother is included in "family." The force of "their own family" lies in the implied contrast with the congregation of Christians. As long as a widow has members of her own family who are able to support her, the church ought not to carry the responsibility. Of course, no congregation would allow a widow to sink into destitution and hopelessness should her own family members, who ought to be taking care of her, fail their God-given responsibility.

And to make some return to their parents – "Parents" (*progonoi*) speaks of "parents," "grandparents," and "ancestors." Here is a statement that the church is not to be burdened with caring for elderly people when those people have living children or grandchildren who are Christians.[10] Instead, the younger members of the family are to show appreciation for the sacrifice and care their parents and grandparents extended to them when they were too little and weak to care for themselves. "Some return" translates *amoibas*, a plural noun that may suggest intensity. The children are to make a "real return"! Literally, the word means "to give back the return or exchange due." Do something more for those who brought you up than occasionally offering some small gift. Remember, old age comes upon us all. Eventually those who are now children and grandchildren will become old and may be dependent on their offspring for care.[11]

For this is acceptable in the sight of God – "Acceptable" (*apodekton*) is used

---

[9] Hendriksen calls attention to an old Dutch proverb which indicates it frequently seems easier for one poor father to bring up *ten* children than for ten rich children to provide for one poor father.

[10] We've added "who are Christians" for several reasons. First, it likely is not to be expected that the evangelist could "admonish" any widow's non-Christian relatives about a "duty" they had toward their destitute relatives. Second, the New Testament frequently appears to distinguish between benevolence owed to those who are of the faith versus those who are not part of the body (Matthew 25:40, James 2:15, 1 Timothy 5:16).

[11] It is frequently true that what we have done to others will eventually be done to us. "Ironside records the Jewish tale of the young Jew who had housed his aged father until his young wife finally demanded that he be sent to the poorhouse. After fruitless discussion, he took his father on the way. At last he had to begin dragging his protesting father. When they reached a certain tree, the father refused to be dragged farther, and cried, 'You can't drag me past this tree, because this is as far as I dragged my father!'" (Kent, *op. cit.*, p.169-70)

only here in the New Testatment or LXX, and is rarely found even in classical Greek.   The same idea, however, is expressed in 1 Timothy 1:15 by *pasēs apodochēs axios*, and in 1 Peter 2:19 by *charis* (as in *touto charis para theo*, "this is acceptable with God").   Most writers call attention to the Fifth Commandment, about "Honor(ing) your father and mother" (Exodus 20:12; Ephesians 6:2a).   They also remind us that in the Old Testament, Joseph's concern for the welfare of his father should serve as a lesson for all time (Genesis 45:3).   We might also remember Jesus' teaching on this subject (Mark 7:9-12), and His own care for His mother as He hangs on the cross (John 19:26,27).

5:5 -- Now she who is a widow indeed – We have in verse 5 a further description of the desperate situation of the widow who fits the category of being a "widow indeed."   The word connecting this verse to the preceding is *de*.   In the KJV, ASV, and NASB it is rendered "now", though it can also be rendered "but."   Paul is contrasting the condition of the "widow indeed" with the widow who has children and grandchildren (verse 4).   The expression "widow indeed" was explained in comments on verse 3.

And who has been left alone – That is, she has no family or descendants who might provide her support.   "Left alone" (*memonōmenē*) occurs only here in the New Testament, is rare in the Greek versions of the Old Testament, but is frequent in classical Greek.   The word means "left alone," or "made solitary."   The KJV translates it "desolate," a word derived from the Latin *solus*, alone.

Has fixed her hope on God – The verb is a perfect tense verb.   She has fixed her hope on God in the past, and still does.   The "widow indeed" to whom Paul is urging Timothy to pay special attention is a Christian woman.   Only to them does the church bear the special responsibility taught in this chapter.[12]   There may also be involved the idea that without love of friend or child, they must cast themselves on the support of the everlasting arms of God.   The "real widow" has nowhere else to go for help.

And continues in entreaties and prayers night and day – These are two terms for different kinds of prayer.   As explained at 1 Timothy 2:1, the first speaks of requests about specific situations and definite needs which are keenly felt, while the second is the general word for prayer about needs that are always present.   A "widow indeed" would regularly have the second, while the first would arise from time to time.   Perhaps "*by* night and by day" would express the genitive better (cp. Matthew 2:14; Luke 18:7), indicating the time "when" rather than the time

---

[12] Non-Christian widows may, from time to time, be given care by individual Christians, but it is hardly the responsibility of the church to care for all non-Christian widows.   The "social gospel," which urged that justice and care for the poor is the *major* thrust of Christianity, is not quite correct in its attempted distillation of the heart of the gospel.

"how long."[13]   The words describe the desolate one casting all her care on the Lord, and telling Him, as her only friend, of all her thoughts and actions and needs.

5:6 -- But – This verse contrasts with what was just said in verse 5.   Verse 5 spoke of one who was desolate.   Verse 6 speaks of one who has "plenty" to live on.   Verse 5 spoke of one who continues to hope in God.   Verse 6 speaks of one who is "dead" to things spiritual.

She who gives herself to wanton pleasure – The present tense participle (*spatalōsa*) denotes a continuance or course of life.   But just what is "wanton pleasure"?   The root meaning of the word is prodigality, riotous and luxurious living.   In the world of Paul's day, many widows were tempted to resort to prostitution as a means of support, and Paul may be alluding to this fact, and at the same time suggesting what happens to a person spiritually who was once a Christian and then resorts to such a lifestyle.

Is dead even while she lives – She may be living physically, but she is "dead" spiritually.   What Romans 8:13 warns the Christian about has happened to the "merry widow."   "For if you are living (habitually) according to the flesh, you must die," he wrote.   Romans 6:16, 23 also underline the same truth.   Compare also Jude's expression, "twice dead" (Jude 12 KJV).[14]   A widow who is wanton, and who therefore is no longer a Christian (i.e., spiritually alive), certainly has no further claim on any church-provided food, clothing, or shelter.[15]

5:7 -- Prescribe these things as well – The margin reads "Keep commanding."

---

[13] The genitive expresses "time within which," while the accusative is used for extent of time. In Luke 2:37, Anna the prophetess is said to worship "with fastings and supplications night and day" (*nukta kai hemeran*), where the accusative conveys rather more the notion of vigils prolonged through the night.   If the form here were accusative, we might be more inclined to include the comment found in many commentaries, that this "characteristic" of the real widow is intended to be descriptive of a holy life.   We, instead, reading the genitive, are inclined to see it as no more than another statement of the woman's destitution.   If it were not for God's answers to her persistent prayers, there would be no one to care or provide.   As regards the order of words, "day and night," or "night and day," there seems to be no rule.   Mark always has "night and day," Luke uses both, Paul always uses "night and day," and John always uses "day and night."

[14] The expression in Revelation 3:1 ("you have a name that you are alive") does not have quite the same meaning.   That expression means "though nominally alive as a Christian."

[15] When habitual sinners are first disciplined by the church, there is the possibility they will be brought to repentance (cp. 1 Corinthians 5:5).   While there is still the remotest possibility they can be won away from their wicked ways, the church makes an effort to woo and reach them ("let him be to you as a Gentile and a tax-gatherer," i.e., as needing to be rescued from being lost, Matthew 18:17).   But the time may come when their spirit has died a second time (although this is something that is very difficult for mere men to determine has actually happened).   When that occurs, there seems to be nothing more that can be done for the ex-Christian; this seems to be the thrust of "death" in the "wages of sin is death" in Romans 6:23.   Neither is the church responsible to provide for the person's physical needs, nor can it do anything to win that person back to Christ.

Paul is in the midst of giving Timothy some personal instructions concerning the evangelist's concern for widows. Now he is told to teach these same things to the Ephesian church, lest they be guilty and blameworthy of acting in a different spirit. But what is included in "these things"? (1) Is verse 7 to be connected with verse 6? If so, then pleasure-loving widows are to be warned of the grave consequences of their conduct before they become spiritually dead, lest that very thing happen to them and those who were once saved become lost. (2) Perhaps verse 7 refers to the entire paragraph (verses 3-16) concerning widows. Timothy must see to it that the church honors those really dependent and deserving widows; that children and grandchildren do their duty to their parents; and that everyone knows how to distinguish between the widow who should be honored (supported) by the church and the widow who should not be so honored.

So that they may be above reproach – Who is "they"? Is it the widows, or is it the church at Ephesus? Perhaps Timothy is to keep commanding widows about the absolute and eternal necessity of an irreproachable Christian life. Perhaps Timothy is to keep commanding the church to carry out her sympathetic and helpful responsibility toward godly widows. And who does the "reproaching"?[16] (1) Is the "blame" (reproach) something God does? Christians have been informed ahead of time that some are likely to be found blameworthy at the final judgment, unless their lives are in harmony with what God has shown men He expects. (2) Is the "blame" something the community does, as it watches the "Christians" ignore their helpless widows? If they did not care for the widows, they would be liable to the terrible reproach mentioned in verse 8, that Christians were in their conduct worse than unbelievers.

5:8 -- But if any one does not provide for his own – This is how Christianity prescribes that widows who have "children and grandchildren" (verse 4) are to be cared for. "What Paul has stated positively in verse 4 is now stated negatively, more inclusively, and with greater force. The sin here censured is present in every community and in every age."[17] This speaks of providing the needs of widowed relatives who may have need, not just immediate family members.[18] The Greek word "provide" (*pronoei*) means to "think beforehand" of the probable needs of his own family and relatives, and to make arrangements to meet them.

---

[16] At 1 Timothy 3:2 the word "reproach" was explained. It means 'not open to attack,' 'one against whom no charge can be sustained,' 'one whose conduct is such that his reputation is not besmirched.'

[17] Hendriksen, *op. cit.*, p.171.

[18] Hendriksen (*ibid.*) asks, Does the expression "his own" as here used mean "his own close relatives," for example, a widowed mother or grandmother, an aged or infirm father or grandfather, a physically or mentally ill cousin, an uncle or aunt on the verge of collapse? Are *friends* included or only *relatives*? No doubt, indefiniteness is here a virtue. The next phrase seems to show that "his own" is a wider circle than just one's own immediate family members.

What is the responsibility of the church toward widows whose families do not support them? Paul does not discuss the possibility. He rather emphasizes what should be the proper thing, that families should care for their own, and not shift responsibility to the congregation. However, it should be obvious that the church could not stand idly by if a Christian widow were in material need.[19]

And especially for those of his household – LaSor observes that in the New Testament, the word "family" or "household" included the lord or master of the family (the 'father' figure), his wife, children, slaves, plus servants, employees, and even clients who formed an association with the household for mutual benefit. Spence (*Ellicott's*, p.242) comments that the circle of those for whose support and sustenance a Christian is responsible is here enlarged. Not only is the man who professes to love Christ bound to do his best for his nearest relations such as his mother and grandmother, but Paul says "he must assist those of his own house," a term which includes much more distant relatives, and even dependents connected with the family who have fallen into poverty and distress. Even if the widow is not living in the house of her son or grandson, filial duty would prompt a proper provision for her needs.

He has denied the faith – Is this objective faith?   To shirk this filial responsibility is to deny one of the articles of the Christian faith. Such passages as Ephesians 6:2 and Mark 7:9-12 are where care for widows is plainly included as part and parcel of the Christian religion. Is this subjective faith? Lack of positive action, the sin of omission, gives the lie to his profession of faith. Either way we take "faith," to refuse to take care of one's relatives is sinful negligence, a deliberate repudiation of the teachings and life expected of the Christian.

And is worse than an unbeliever – "Worse" for at least two reasons. First, to claim to possess true teaching and then flagrantly deny it is worse than making no such claim. Though professing to be Christian, he lacks the most precious of all the fruits – love. Second, even unbelievers assent to this filial obligation (Matthew 5:46,47 suggest sinners feel a family devotion and responsibility).[20]

Most unbelievers have never heard about the specific precept of John 13:34, 15:12, and Galatians 6:2. But the Christian has been instructed in it. Most unbelievers are strangers to Christ's glorious example of love for his own. But the Christian has heard about it. Unbelievers, in general, know nothing about the promise of an enabling power – the Holy Spirit – operating in the heart. But the Christian has heard about it. Yet in spite of this threefold lack, "unbelievers" often show affection toward those who belong to their family.[21]

[19] Kent, *op. cit.*, p.170.

[20] Kent, *ibid.*

[21] Hendriksen, *op. cit.*, p.171.

Unbelievers acknowledged the obligation to provide for their own relatives. Galgacus, in Tacitus, says, "Nature dictates that to everyone, his own children and relatives should be most dear." Cicero says, "Every man should take care of his own family." Likewise, Apuleius, Plutarch, Homer, Terence, Virgil, etc. When pagan moralists in contemporary society acknowledged their obligation to their parents, it is unthinkable that Christian morality should lag behind general non-Christian standards.

5:9 -- Let a widow not be put on the list – "Put on the list" (*katalegesthō*) occurs only here in the New Testament or, in this sense, in the LXX, but it is the regular classical word for enrolling or enlisting of soldiers, etc. Hence our word "catalog." The KJV reads "taken into the number." The ASV reads "enrolled." Alford and others take "widow" as the predicate rather than the subject, and render it "Let a woman be enrolled as a widow not under sixty years old, etc." Since the thrust of the paragraph has to do with certain widows (the "widows indeed") whom Timothy is to see are properly "honored" (i.e., supported, verse 3), we suppose the "list" onto which certain widows were to be enrolled is the "list of those eligible for church support."[22] Some believe the word "pledge" found in 5:12 indicates that those being enrolled were required to take some kind of pledge. In our comments at verse 12 we will opt for another meaning entirely than "pledge." Because we know so little about the church institutions of the apostolic age, we are not able to speak with certainty about the status or functions (if any) this "order of widows" held.[23]

---

[22] If we take "put on the list" literally, and there is little reason not to, it appears there was a regular roll kept by the church of those who were "widows indeed," and with whom therefore the church had entered into an official arrangement of support and care as long as the need for such support continued. Whether or not there was a literal list of "widows whom we support," this language about a "list" cannot be equivalent to a "church membership roll," for it is hardly likely that a Christian widow under 60 years of age would be denied "church membership" simply because of her age. In fact, it is another question altogether whether or not early congregations had anything comparable to our "membership rolls." Civil law now makes such membership rolls a useful expedient, almost a necessity, since if the church's business ever gets into a civil court, one of the first things the judge will ask is how membership in this society is determined.

[23] Bonnie B. Thurston's *The Widows: A Women's Ministry in the Early Church* (Minneapolis: Fortress, 1989), is the first scholarly work devoted to the study of widows in the first three centuries of the church. Thurston uses both Biblical sources and the literature of the Early Church Fathers. In brief, the author points out a rapid development in the status and function of women, from providing for the needs of widows in the apostolic age, to the raising of women to the status of a "clerical order" by the 2nd century AD. Thurston finds three groups of widows in 1 Timothy 5:3-16, and contends that one of these groups was already a developing "clerical order." The elderly widows in the "order" were to meet certain qualifications, and in return for support (she affirms) they were to pray and live a contemplative life. (While verses in Timothy can be found which specifically talk of the qualifications, we do not find any that speak of duties or functions. The paragraph in 1 Timothy has to do with what the church should do for the widow, not what the widow should do for the church.) Moving on to the 3rd century AD, Thurston calls attention to Tertullian's writings where widows are a distinct group, a definite order, and listed along with bishops, presbyters and deacons. For example, the widows sat unveiled in the assemblies in a separate place near where the elders

If she is less than sixty years old – Here begins a brief list of qualifications a widow was to meet if her support was to become the regular responsibility of the congregation.[24]   Because this first qualification sets a rather high age limit (could not widows be destitute and need help before reaching 60 years of age?), many commentators believe this list onto which certain widows is to be enrolled is something other than a list of those who are to receive material help from the church.[25]   (1) Some suppose it is an ecclesiastical order of deaconess into which the widows are not to be enrolled if they are younger than 60. "Deaconesses" has been discussed in our comments at 1 Timothy 3:11. If it were to be granted that there was an ecclesiastical order of deaconess somewhat analogous to the order of elder and deacon, there still is considerable doubt that the same group of women is being talked about here at 5:9. The suggestion that the 60-year-age limit is set because Paul (allegedly because of his belief that the single life was more holy) did not approve of the widows marrying again after they had embraced this life of widowhood, will hardly satisfy the requirements of the text either.[26]   Nor will it harmonize with what Paul wrote in 1 Corinthians 7.[27]   (2) It is also rather common for commentators to suppose that those widows who possessed the necessary qualifications to be "put on the list" were also expected to perform certain spiritual and charitable functions on behalf of the church.[28]   One writer summarizes their duties as: giving counsel to the younger women, praying and fasting, visiting the sick, preparing women for baptism, taking them communion, giving guidance and direction to widows and orphans who were supported by the

---

sat; they received a special ordination by laying on of hands. Thurston also examines "the most instructive text" on widows from the 3rd century, the *Didascalia Apostolorum*, which shows work and support as being regulated and controlled by the bishop, and their duties as praying in homes, laying on of hands and ministering to the sick, and working at wool. They now must be 50 years of age (a change has been made from Paul's instructions for Ephesus) to be enrolled in the order. Thurston then concludes that by a century later, according to the *Apostolic Constitutions*, the order of widows has gone into decline and their work has been passed on to the deaconesses.

[24] While the church might and would supply the needs of widows who did not meet all the qualifications about to be listed, it was only those widows indeed, who did meet the qualifications, with whom the church entered into an official arrangement ('enrolled them on the list').

[25] Would the church refuse to support widows under age 60 who had small children? Indeed, 1 Timothy 5:11 will give Paul's instructions for "younger widows" who are still able to bear children (verse 14). But what about those between 40 and 60 years of age? Do they get no support? Or were families larger than they are now, so that until a person reached about 60 years of age, there would still be living relatives who could care for them?

[26] Where is anything said about "embracing the life of widowhood"? Certainly not in the word "pledge" found in verse 12. Nor, in our opinion, is it found in the word "enrolled" ("put on the list").

[27] 1 Corinthians 7:39 grants permission to Christian widows to remarry as long as their new mate is a Christian. A widow at Ephesus who remarried, even if she were over 60 years of age, would no longer be a "widow indeed," since she now would have someone to care for her needs, thus relieving the congregation from further responsibility in her case.

[28] See Ellicott, Robertson, Hendriksen, Barnes, and Bernard.

church.[29] There is some evidence that by Tertullian's time (AD 200)[30] there was an order of widows with definite functions to perform in exchange for the church support they received, but it is far from certain that the group Paul talks about "enrolling" had any such functions assigned.[31] "There is no proper evidence whatever to show that such widows as those here mentioned by the apostle were invested with any sort of office, or were called to do anything but such pious and free-will service as their own hearts might prompt, and their limited opportunities might enable them to perform" (Fairbairn, *Commentary on the Pastoral Epistles*, p. 202). (3) We suppose there was something in the society of the 1st century that made 60 years of age the age at which "widows" were most likely to be "widows indeed," and therefore in special need of care by the congregation.[32]

***Has been*[33] the wife of one man** – To be qualified for being enrolled on the list of those supported by the church, the widow must have had a blameless married life. Whatever "a one-woman man" meant in the list of qualifications for elder (1 Timothy 3:2), this qualification ('a one-man woman') for the widow means the same thing.[34] The woman was already a widow when she was enrolled on the

---

[29] See paragraph IV.5 in the article on "Woman" in *International Standard Bible Encyclopedia*, edited by James Orr (Grand Rapids: Eerdmans, 1939), V.5, p.3103. It is not difficult to offer hypotheses about how these functions came to be the "duties" of the widows. Jesus taught that the poor, the needy, and the sick should be succored, the helpless should be helped, and the comfortless comforted. Then we see certain ladies like Dorcas held up as an admirable example. It would not be long before the evangelist, leading out in the support of the "widows indeed," would also recognize that he had in these ladies an untapped resource of service and ministry to the poor and sick and helpless. What one evangelist might encourage, a generation or so later another evangelist would make an institution.

[30] *On the Veiling of Virgins* IX. The institution of widows in the 3rd century is of somewhat different character than in the apostolic age. Widowhood, as well as virginity, became a religious profession. Widows were admitted with certain ceremonies, including placing on their heads a veil consecrated by the bishop.

[31] It might be possible to show how the later office (order) of widows gradually developed from what Paul here wrote about the support of widows. But the 2nd and 3rd century functions and duties assigned to the order of widows cannot be found in 1 Timothy without reading much additional material into the text. We have already seen, for example, that "continues in entreaties and prayers (by) night and day" (verse 5) was not some act of piety the widows devoted themselves to, but rather were the results of their destitution and the need to call on God for help, since there was no one else they could turn to.

[32] Of course, this age limit would not bar a younger widow from receiving temporary assistance in a time of need, on the basis of verse 3.

[33] Some word must be supplied, since we took the participle *gegonuia* ("being") with the preceding clause. When such verb forms need to be supplied, we get them from the context, so we repeat "being" ("has been," NASB).

[34] If it meant "no divorce" for the prospective elder, it means no divorce for the widow. If it means "no remarried man" is qualified to be an elder, then it means that "no woman who has been married a second time" is qualified for enrollment as a widow. If it means "no polygamy" for the prospective elder, then it must mean "no polyandry" for the widow. If it meant "no marital unfaithfulness" for the prospective elder, then it means "no marital unfaithfulness" for the widow.

list, so this qualification must refer to her past life and conduct rather than her present situation. The NIV translators chose "has been faithful to her husband" in an effort to express the idea suggested by the Greek. Perhaps we must speak a further word about the interpretation that is placed on these words by some, namely, "a woman who has had only one husband." We are aware that the Roman world paid honor to the *univirae* ("a one-man woman"). Certain poets extolled the woman who did not remarry after her husband had died.[35] The title *univirae*, engraved on certain Roman tombs, shows that this devotion was practiced and esteemed. We doubt, however, that Paul, writing under the inspiration of the Holy Spirit, got his ideas from Roman or Jewish ideals. We adopt for this clause the same interpretation we adopted for the qualification for elder, namely, that in order to be considered for enrollment on the list of church-supported widows, the Christian woman must have been faithful to her marriage vows, so as to set an example for others of what God's intentions for marriage are (one man and one woman for life, see Matthew 19:1-10).

5:10 -- Has a reputation for good works – This verse continues the qualifications a widow was to meet if she was to be "put on the list" of those cared for by the church. "Reputation" translates *marturoumenē*, a word that occurs in 3:7, and also frequently in Hebrews (7:8, 11:2,4,5,39), and also 3 John 6,12. The idea is that others "testify" to the woman's good works. It does not suggest that before the widow is enrolled, there must be a time when such "testimonies" are heard and collected by the church or by the evangelist. The expression "good works" occurs frequently in the Pastoral Epistles, both in the singular and in the plural. Jesus used the phrase, and taught how "good works" were to be one of the distinctive marks of His disciples (Matthew 5:16). He Himself set the example during His own mission on earth (John 10:32,33). The phrase denotes good *actions* as distinguished from *sentiments*. Love, for example, is not a good "work." Feeding the hungry and clothing the naked and visiting the sick are good works (Matthew 25:35). Since the expression "good works" occurs both here and at the end of the verse, we are probably to understand that the five "if" phrases that are in between are examples of the kind of good works Paul has in mind that would qualify a widow to be "put on the list." Each of these "good works" are the kinds of things one would do for others. We probably should not call these qualifications "extraordinary." They are the kinds of good works that might be expected of any follower of Jesus.

***And* if she has brought up children** – Some have thought the use of "if" to intro-

---

[35] Dido, *Aen.* iv.28. Statius, *Sylv.* v., *in Proemio*, "To love a wife when living is a pleasure; to love her when dead is an act of religion." Compare too, the examples of the wives of Lucan, Drusus, and Pompey, who on the death of their husbands, devoted the remainder of their lives to retirement and to the memory of the dead. Writers also have pointed to Jewish writings such as Judith 16:22 where remaining celibate after the death of her only husband is extolled as a virtue.

duce this and the next four clauses may be examples of what are called indirect questions, and are thus indicative of the kind of questions asked of the widow at a formal hearing where her "enrollment" was being considered. However, there is no real evidence that such a formal hearing is envisioned by Paul. An informal but careful study of the widow's "good works" would satisfy this instruction to see that she meets certain qualifications before she is "put on the list." "Brought up children" translates *teknotropheō*, a word occurring only here in the New Testament or the LXX. One lexicon explains that it means to "care for them physically and spiritually." Whether the children were her own or orphans is not said. One writer insists they are her own. "The compound word includes *teknon* which emphasizes the relation to the parent from whom the child descends. We must, therefore, understand that Paul means 'if she has brought up her own children well and carefully, and been a good mother to them.'" (*Pulpit Commentary*, p.97) Another writer observes that all the other examples of good works are oriented primarily to those outside the woman's own family, so the children could well also be other than her own family members. (Knight, *op. cit.*, p.224)

If she has shown hospitality to strangers – Hospitality (i.e., a readiness to feed and shelter strangers) towards Christian brothers is a virtue greatly commended in the Scriptures (cp. comments at 1 Timothy 3:2). Jesus taught that hospitality ("I was a stranger, and you invited Me in") was one of the things which will be taken note of in the final judgment (Matthew 25:35ff). 3 John 5 also teaches the practice of hospitality. In our society perhaps more than in the oriental society, "the lodging of guests is largely the responsibility of the woman in the home. It is she who usually expresses the geniality and simple kindnesses which are true indications of hospitality" (Kent, *op. cit.*, p.167).

If she has washed the saints' feet – For "saints" the margin offers an alternate rendering, "holy ones." *Hagiōn* is an adjective, plural in form. When we find such adjectives by themselves, we must supply the noun. It is regularly rendered "saints" rather than "holy (ones)." It would be a great mistake to think that the plural "holy ones" implies that there were certain people in the church who were considered to be dignitaries, and whose feet it would be a special act of piety to wash. In the ancient world, whenever a guest entered your house, it was customary to provide a towel and basin, and wash the dust and dirt of travel off the guest's feet. Servants sometimes provided this courtesy. The woman of the house also often did this task. It is not easy to decide whether the phrase should be taken literally or figuratively. Taken figuratively, this is a picturesque reference to humble and menial service of any kind. Taken literally, was there an "ordinance of footwashing" observed in the early church, or is this merely a reference to another kind of hospitality? (1) *Footwashing*. Some hold that at John 13:5-14, Jesus was *not* introducing a third ordinance (baptism and the Lord's Supper being

the other two) to be practiced religiously by His followers.[36]   Others disagree,
believing that footwashing is an ordinance instituted by Jesus.   They believe the
widows have been participating in the ordinance of footwashing, and thereby
showing both their devotion to Christ and a desire to obey His commands.
"Perhaps this one ordinance was picked by the apostle because it most clearly
demonstrates the individual's willingness to follow unreservedly the Lord's
commands, even to the point of personal inconvenience, and thus reveals [the
widow's] spiritual nature" (Kent, *op. cit.*, p.168).   (2) *Another kind of hospitality*.
If we take footwashing as a general reference to hospitality, what is the difference
between this phrase and the preceding one?   The difference would be found in
the word "strangers."   Not only was she hospitable to strangers, she also
"welcomed" friends and neighbors as guests into her home.   Among those who
believe that Paul was referring to another kind of hospitality, it is not uncommon
to find the commentator pointing to the fact that none of the other "good works"
(such as bringing up children) were religious rites or ordinances; so why should
we think "footwashing" is a reference to an ordinance here in 1 Timothy 5:10?

If she has assisted those in distress – "Assisted" translates *epērkesen*, a word
used only here and twice in verse 16 in the New Testament, but common in
classical Greek.   It means to 'ward off' or 'drive away' anything for another's
advantage, 'to aid, give assistance, relieve.'   "Distress," *thlipsis*, speaks of any
kind of trouble or affliction.   The attitude behind such helpful actions is one of
friendship, willing to reach out to try to help people who were in trouble.

And **if she has devoted herself to every good work** – This statement is usually
thought of as a summary reiteration of the expression with which this verse began.
Notice, several additions are made to what was written earlier.   One new word is
"every."   'Every kind of,' or 'anything in the class of' good works is what is
looked for in the widow as a qualification for being "put on the list."   Another
new word is "devoted," or 'diligently followed,' which is an effort to translate
epakolutheō.   The word literally means 'to follow (closely) upon, follow after,'
i.e., to tread in one's footsteps, or imitate his example.   We get the idea that this

---

[36] Christian Church people have posited two tests for something to be treated as an "ordinance
of Christ":   it must have been commanded by Jesus and also practiced by the early church.   Take
the Lord's Supper, for example, to illustrate this.   It was instituted by Jesus with the words "(Continue
to) do this in remembrance of me" (Luke 22:19).   Then we find the early church actually doing what
Jesus commanded (Acts 2:42, Acts 20:7; 1 Corinthians 11:23ff).   So, without hesitation, the Lord's
Supper is called an "ordinance of Christ."   The same two tests could be demonstrated with reference
to immersion.   What has made most Christian Church people hesitant to call "footwashing" an
"ordinance" is the fact that we have no example (unless it be 1 Timothy 5:10) of its being practiced
as part of a worship service by the early church.   In fact, there is some well-founded reason to doubt
that Jesus actually was commanding his followers (John 13:4ff) to literally wash another's feet; He
may simply have been urging the practice of humble service so well illustrated by footwashing.   So,
since they could find no clear command, nor any example of practice by the early church, Christian
Church people have not been wont to call footwashing an "ordinance of Christ."

qualification infers the widow has followed the good actions the Master Himself performed, and which He wants His followers to imitate. We are reminded of Dorcas (Acts 9:36-39) who was noted for her good works as a seamstress, to whom the widows bore testimony. The qualifications taken together picture a widow who is past the time when one usually remarries and past the age where she is likely to be able to care for herself. At the same time, she is a woman whom everyone in the church can look to as an example of how Christian women should have lived. After such a life of loving service, no one in the congregation will be tempted to think the church is wasting money to provide for such a one regularly, the rest of her life.

5:11 -- But refuse *to put* younger widows *on the list* – "Younger widows" would be those who were "widows indeed," yet who were less than 60 years old; Paul even indicates many were still in their "child bearing" years (verse 14). The words added in italics correctly catch the point Paul is making since the context deals with which widows are to be "put on the list" and those who are not. These "younger widows" are not to be "put on the list." This direction by no means shuts younger widows out from receiving occasional help from the church, but it does direct the church not to take over permanent financial obligations for the needs of the younger widows. Does the use of the word "refuse" imply that the "widows indeed" had to apply to be "put on the list," or does it imply that someone in the congregation has suggested to the leadership that this needy widow should be put on the list, and then a decision must be made?

For when they feel sensual desires in disregard to Christ – "Sensual desires" (KJV, "wax wanton") is from the verb is *katastrēniadzō*, a compound form that occurs only here in the New Testament, though the simple form *strēniaō* is found in Revelation 18:7-9. The older lexicons and word studies on synonyms compare *strēniaō*, *truphaō*, and *spatalaō*. Berry (*op. cit.*, p.91) writes, "The fundamental thought of *strēniaō* is of insolence and voluptuousness which spring from abundance; of *truphaō*, effeminate self-indulgence; of *spatalaō*, effeminacy and wasteful extravagance." Those commentators who believe being "put on the list" implies an official inauguration into an office where church duties are required in return for financial support explain this metaphor by alluding to young oxen who try to escape the yoke. The younger widows, it is explained, are likely to become restive and will then want to be released from their "pledge" (verse 12) concerning church duties whenever opportunity of getting another husband presented itself. Certainly, a number of assumptions must be made by those offering such an explanation. We have already commented on the matter of whether or not being "put on the list" included the assumption of certain church duties. The word "restive" implies certain restraints have been placed on the widow, or voluntarily assumed by the widow. Where has anything been said about a vow of celibacy or any other restraints other than being a "widow indeed" (i.e., with no family or relatives to help supply her needs)?   What, in the context, would cause us to limit the "yoke" (if such be the figure of speech) to the duties a "yoke of service" might impose?   If there is another plausible explanation for the words translated "waxed wanton" and "pledge,"[37] we should be very slow to embrace the view that being "put on the list" obligated the widow to perform offices and duties of a humble and self-denying kind.

The NASB has pointed the way in the right direction by suggesting Paul had in mind the "feeling of the impulse of sexual desire" by the younger widows, a desire that can preoccupy the mind and even result in people denying their faith in Jesus[38] in order to find a husband.   "In disregard to Christ," if the latter suggestion is the correct one, refers either to disregard of Christ's wishes concerning whom one should marry,[39] or disregard of their own earlier relationship to Jesus after they had taken Jesus' "yoke" upon them (Matthew 11:29).

They want to get married – Of course, Paul finds no fault whatever with the idea that the younger widows should wish to get married.   In fact, he wants them to do just that (verse 14).   Do not forget, the topic being discussed is those who are eligible to be "put on the list."   People whose names were added to that "list" become the obligation of the church to care for, because there is no one else to whom they can turn.   However, a younger widow, who remarries, now has someone to provide for her, so she would not need perpetual subsidies by the church.   If, as has been suggested, the enrollment indicated full and permanent support, then to include in this group women who may be only temporarily widowed, and who might at any time remarry, would not provide a practical grouping.   Paul is not finding fault with remarriage.   He is simply arguing for the enrollment of those who (because of age and circumstances) are not likely to have any further opportunity to find other means of support.

5:12 -- Thus incurring condemnation – The Greek reads *krima*, "having judgment."   "Having" ["incurring" NASB] is a circumstantial participle, from which the NASB translators derived the word "thus" used to introduce it.   The circumstances named in verses 11 and 12   (i.e., disregard of Christ to get married and

[37] As comments on verse 12 will show, an explanation for "pledge" other than some kind of religious "vow" (i.e., such as a "vow" of perpetual seclusion from the world, or a "vow" of celibacy) is certainly available.

[38] This can most easily be understood if we think of the Christian widow marrying a pagan.   In that age, the husband often decided the religious preference the family would embrace.   And not only might the pagan insist on continuing to worship the old idols, he might expect behavior from the wife that would be out of harmony and character for a person who would profess faith in Christ.

[39] Elsewhere, Christians who seek to marry are encouraged to marry "in the Lord," i.e., to marry people who also are Christians.   We assume Paul learned this principle from the teachings of Jesus.

setting aside their previous pledge) are the reasons they incur judgment, or condemnation. What is meant by *krima* ("condemnation" NASB; "damnation," KJV; "sentence," Rheims; "judgment," Alford) depends on the context. The Greek word *krima* does not necessarily mean condemnation, though it is often unhappily thus translated in the KJV. The context of the passage must decide the nature of the "judgment," whether favorable or the contrary (*Ellicott's*, p.247). "[*Krima*] means a 'judgment,' 'decision,' or 'sentence,' ... and this was the meaning of the English word 'damnation' in 1611. It has only recently acquired the signification of 'eternal damnation'."[40] What the "sentence" or "judgment" is thought to be often depends on a number of factors other than what the word itself means. One of those factors is the commentator's views on the matter of "once saved, always saved." Not a few explanations at this place tend to reflect a bias on the disputed question of eternal security. For example, according to many Calvinistic authors, if the young widows were once saved, there is no way this verse can be saying that they, because of their actions in getting married and repudiating Christ, are thereby liable to eternal damnation. This commentator, who has elsewhere written a special study[41] showing that "conditional eternal security" is the doctrine presented by the Scriptures, would not hesitate to offer the comment that the younger widows, by quitting Christ just to get married, thereby incur for themselves condemnation from Christ Himself. Another factor is the commentators' views on what "put on the list" involves – i.e., whether or not it involves a devotion to a life of prayer and special service for the church on the part of the widow. Writers who write from within this viewpoint tend to speak of the condemnation one should feel when she gives up her religious vocation to return to the ordinary pleasures and avocations of the world. The guilt that is incurred, or the condemnation that is incurred, results from the injury done (to the church or to the widow herself) when widows who had been "put on the list" began to disregard Christ and left their faith, because the sensual desires for marriage were thought more important than continued faithfulness to Christ.

Because they have set aside their previous pledge – The word "set aside," *ēthetēsan*, is often used of disregarding or breaking an oath, a treaty, a promise or the like. In the KJV, the word is variously rendered "reject," "despise," "bring to nothing," "frustrate," "disannul," "cast off."[42] "Previous pledge" has a marginal reading, "lit. previous faith." The Greek is *tēn prōtēn pistin*, which simply means "the(ir) first faith." The explanation that most easily fits is that the young widow, her behavior motivated by sexual desires, has disregarded the desires of Christ and married a pagan. In the first century world, this new union would regularly

---

[40] Hervey, *op. cit.*, p.98.

[41] See the author's special study on "Once Saved, Am I Always Saved?" in *New Testament Epistles: Romans* (Moberly, Mo.: Scripture Exposition Books, 1987), p.348ff.

[42] Hervey, *ibid.*

necessitate that the woman give up the church and the cause of Christ since the woman was expected to embrace the religion of her husband. *The young widow had to give up her faith in Christ* – she abandoned her previous *faith* – in order to marry the pagan, and this in turn results in her condemnation.

Other explanations offered are these:

(1) The Roman Catholic Church uses this verse to justify asking people to make a *pledge* to the single life – i.e., vows of celibacy. It is this "vow" that is disregarded when the young widow decides to marry a new mate. Further, there was a certain condemnation to be felt by those who gave up the more devoted life -- the life of self-sacrifice and self-abnegation -- for the ordinary joys and cares of domestic life, because they thus were an example of backsliding that could not fail to harm the cause of Christ. We remind those writers who speak of the single life as somehow being more holy and more devoted that Hebrews 13:4 indicates there is nothing intrinsically less holy about the married life. The instructions found in 1 Corinthians 7:25ff are somehow related to what Paul calls "the present distress". A married person may be 'divided' or 'distracted' as he tries to fulfill his responsibilities to both mate and to the Lord (verses 32-35), but Paul does not say there is something inherently less spiritual about being married!

> It is clear from this that the apostle did not contemplate any vows which would prevent their marrying again; nor does he say that it would be absolutely wrong for them to marry, even if they were admitted into that rank; or as if there were any vows to restrain them from doing it. This passage, therefore, can never be adduced in favor of that practice of taking the veil in nunneries, or of a vow of perpetual seclusion from the world.[43]

(2) Hendriksen, typical of many Protestant writers, thinks *pledge* refers to an important spiritual ministry the widows were enrolled to do. The "condemnation" is the feelings of guilt when they stopped doing the special work to take up housekeeping again. Rather than putting the young widow in a position where she might not keep her word, Paul advises against putting young widows on the list in the first place. Observe that Hendriksen must take both *pistis* (faith) and *krima* (guilt) in their secondary senses to make his interpretation stand. Also note that Hendriksen does not envision the widow marrying a non-Christian – he simply speaks of remarriage. The only way there could be anything wrong with the widow's remarriage, assuming she marries "in the Lord", is if the qualification "wife of one husband" prohibits all remarriage, a view that is difficult to sustain. In this commentator's opinion, the hidden problem that causes Hendriksen's real difficulty is his Calvinistic belief in "once saved, always saved." He must explain this verse in some way so as not to impinge on or contradict that doctrine.

---

[43] Barnes, *op. cit.*, p.179.

It is difficult to see how a pledge to celibacy or a pledge to do a special work could be called a "first faith" – since *tēn prōtēn pistin* would lead one to suppose the original faith in Christ was the thing being repudiated. In the light of instructions given elsewhere (e.g., 1 Corinthians 7:39, that Christian widows are to marry Christians), for a young widow to reject the "first faith" and marry outside the Lord would indeed incur condemnation. Unless one is faithful to Christ till death, she forfeits salvation. Interpreting the verse as we have permits us to take both *pistis* and *krima* in their primary senses, which in our view seems exactly what the context requires (see verses 11, 14, 15). "It appears more likely to this writer, that the judgment (*krima*) resting upon a widow who marries without regard to Christ, is a judgment which she incurs because she has set aside the very principle of godliness and separation from sin which she professed to accept when she became a Christian."[44]

5:13 -- And at the same time they also learn to be idle ... and not merely idle – This seems to give a second reason why the younger widows should not be "put on the list." "Idle" translates *argai* (an *a*-privative + *ergon*, "to work") which means "free from labor, at leisure, lazy, shunning labor which one ought to perform, idle."[45] "They learn to be idle" says that they get into a new habit, idleness.[46] Since the church has assumed responsibility for the enrolled widow's support, the widow now has free time. What she does with it can become a great curse. Not only was the idleness a blameworthy fault, but younger widows could be susceptible to other blameworthy behavior were they to be "put on the list."

As they go around from house to house – Are they making rounds doing church duties? So hold Hendriksen and Spence, who comment, "the going about to the various dwellings was for the object of consoling, instructing, assisting." (*Ellicott's*, p.248) Instead of doing the duties they came to perform, they soon begin to spend the time socializing, wasting precious hours, enjoying tea parties and coffees. (*Hendriksen*, p.177) But the idea that widows who were "put on the list" were then obligated to engage in some important spiritual ministry on behalf

---

[44] Kent, *op. cit.*, p.173.

[45] Thayer lists two synonyms of "idle" that help us to fix in our minds the meaning of the word used here. He writes, "SYN. *argos, bradus, nothros*: *argos* [means] 'idle,' involving blameworthiness; *bradus*, 'slow' (tardy), having a purely temporal reference and no necessary bad sense; *nothros*, 'sluggish,' descriptive of constitutional qualities and suggestive of censure."

[46] The Greek here is an unusual construction, and there may perhaps be no similar construction elsewhere. The word translated "idle" is in the nominative case, yet our translation makes it the object of the verb "learn." Several hypotheses have been advanced to ease this seeming anomaly. Some, including the Latin Vulgate, put "learn" with the verb that follows, so that it reads "they learn to go about." Another proposes to take "learn" as a separate area of faulty life style, such as "they are inquisitive, or curious," but this can hardly be justified since *manthanao* regularly has an accusative case or an infinitive mood after it. None of the explanations offered are entirely without problem, but the one offered by the KJV, ASV, and NASB, is perhaps the right idea.

of the church has been shown to be reading considerably more into this paragraph than it allows. Then why are they going from house to house? We suggest that they were going from house to house because that is part of what being "put on the list" obligated the church to do for the widows – different families in the church would take turns providing a place for the "widows indeed" to live.

But also gossips and busybodies – "Gossip" or "tattler" (KJV) is an attempt to express what *phluareō* means. Literally, the word means "to overflow," "to throw up bubbles" (of water). It then came to speak of an "uttering or doing silly things," and then "to make empty charges" against someone. As the widows lived first with one family and then another, they would become acquainted with the secrets of each. After moving in with the next family with whom they stayed, they would indulge in idle and improper conversation, blabbing what they knew. "Busybody" (*periergoi*) is usually defined as someone who meddles in what does not concern them. People with little or nothing to do on their own commonly fill their time by interesting themselves in the affairs of neighbors. And there may be more here. This same Greek word is used at Acts 19:19 for "magic" (i.e., dabbling in the occult). It is interesting to compare what is said in 2 Timothy 3:13. The "busybodies" at Ephesus – remember the religious emphases that abounded in that city! – could well be dabbling in the occult.

Talking about things not proper *to mention* – Whether it was the secrets they learned concerning previous host families, or whether it was "magnifying trifles" or "dabbling in the occult," those things certainly were not proper topics to be spoken about every time a widow moved to a new home.

5:14 -- Therefore – Because of the "dangers" of "setting aside their first faith (previous pledge)," and of "learn(ing) to be idle," verse 14 is Paul's counsel for the "care" of the younger widows.

I want younger *widows* to get married – "Want" ("will" KJV; *boulomai*, Greek) expresses Paul's opinion, his counsel. It is a general rule, not an absolute and universal command, that young widows must remarry. Paul, of course, cannot command the younger widows to get married, since the widow is not the only one involved in a marriage. But remarriage for such young widows is the better solution to the problems of being a "widow indeed." Paul specifically encourages remarriage of "younger widows"[47] with no hint of disapproval.[48] The same

---

[47] Since the whole paragraph is about widows, and in particular about those who are "widows indeed," it is certainly better with the NASB to supply "widows" as the understood noun agreeing with "younger" than the word "women" used in the KJV. Further, in verse 11 we have had the word for "widow" in the Greek, and verse 14 certainly ("therefore") is a continuation of the same topic.

[48] The difference between verses 11 and 12, on the one hand, and verses 13 and 14 on the other, lies in *who* it is the younger widow is marrying – or, more specifically, on the *effect* the

endorsement was given by Paul to the Corinthians (1 Corinthians 7:39), along with the stipulation, specifically stated,[49] that the she must marry a Christian. Again, recognize that Paul certainly does not regard asceticism or celibacy as the higher or more holy form of the Christian life.[50]

Bear children – One of woman's functions is to bear children (cp. 1 Timothy 2:15). "The woman for whom it is possible should look forward in the will of God to marriage, children, and managing a household" (Kent, *op. cit.*, p.173).

Keep house – The other versions read "rule the house," or "guide the house," or "manage the home." She is the mistress (*oikodespotēs*) of the household, or family. Compare what was given as a qualification for elders and for deacons ("manages his own household") at 1 Timothy 3:5 and 3:12.

And give the enemy no occasion for reproach – The "enemy" (*ho antikeimenos*, "the adversary," "the opponent") here is probably not Satan as would at first appear to be the case from the direct reference to him in the next verse. Rather, the "enemy" is any human enemy of Christ, any sneering worldly man, who delights to find flaws in the character of Christ's followers.[51] "Occasion" translates *aphormē*, "the starting point or base of operations for an expedition." In this case, it denotes a starting point from which the enemy can carry out his desire to revile the people of God. "No" translates *mēdemian*, "not even one." The adversary, the opponent of Christianity, was always seeking some occasion to speak reproachfully of Christians and revile them. Any misconduct on the part of Christian widows would give him the occasion for which he was looking. It is clearly evident that Paul is seeking to promote the welfare of Christ, His church, and these young widows all at the same time. He would give the enemies of the church no occasion to dishonor any of them. "For reproach" translates *loidorias charin*. The noun *loidorias* means "rail at, revile, heap abuse upon." The other

---

proposed marriage will have on the ability of the widow to continue living a consistent Christian life. Paul's topic is not merely remarriage, whether *before* or *after* being "put on the list."

[49] Here in Timothy, with its condemnation of "feel(ing) sensual desires in disregard of Christ," and "set(ting) aside the first faith (previous pledge)," the same stipulation is necessarily implied. Christian widows (and by parity of reasoning, Christian widowers) should hear and heed the words of the apostle in any new choices they make for marriage companions.

[50] Spence's lengthy note (*Ellicott's*, p.248) may be more of a reflection against certain Romish practices than a comment on the actual words of this passage, when he writes, "Here the Apostle deliberately expresses his *will* that in these Christian communities the younger widows should not, in the first fervor of their zeal, when borne down by sorrow, attempt anything like an ascetic life ... Paul's practical mind, guided by the Spirit of God, has left us no impossible rules of perfection, no exaggerated praises of asceticism, or lofty self-denial, no passionate exhortings to a life made up entirely of self-sacrifice and self-surrender."

[51] New Testament passages where other human beings (rather than the devil) do the "reviling" include James 2:7; 1 Peter 2:12, 4:4,14, and 15. Were we to identify the devil as the "enemy", we immediately find it difficult to explain where and when and to whom he does his "reproaching."

word, *charin*, is a preposition meaning "in favor of, for this cause." If the first three things are done – marry, bear children, and manage the home – the Christian widow will be greatly limiting the enemy's opportunity for reproach.

5:15 -- For some have already turned aside – The "some" are generally understood to be "some widows." Spence (*Pulpit Commentary*, p.99) suggests Paul has in mind certain contemporary examples of such reproachful behavior, and that these examples were the immediate occasion of these directions to Timothy about "younger widows." "Turned aside" says the widows have turned aside from the right path (cp. 1 Timothy 1:6) of being faithful to Jesus Christ. They have left their "first faith" and married "in disregard of Christ" (verses 11,12).

To follow Satan – The widows were obeying Satan's leading[52] instead of obeying Christ's commands. Satan beguiled them into quitting Christ in order to get married. The suggestion by some that "turned aside to follow Satan" involves immoral conduct may not be easy to substantiate. It would satisfy the language if it were simply a mixed marriage – a Christian marrying a non-Christian, and abandoning Christianity to do it – that the Christian widow has entered into.

5:16 -- If any woman who is a believer – Are we still speaking of the "younger "widows" since the immediate context preceding this injunction has been dealing with younger widows? The woman would be specifically delegated this responsibility since she was the person who had the management of the house (verse 13). Young widows, having remarried and established a home, would then be in a favorable position to help the older widows who had no one to help them – those who were widows indeed. Since the Greek simply says "believing woman," perhaps it could include even a single woman who takes it as her responsibility to care for another family member who has become a "widow indeed." There is a manuscript variation at this place. Some read as does the NASB;[53] some read "If any believing man ..."[54] and still others read "if any believing man or woman has widows."[55] Guthrie has written, "...the alternative reading any

---

[52] Another interpretation of this verse has been offered. "Some" are the enemies of Christ, and they are following the example of Satan, "the accuser of the brethren," as they have begun to revile Christianity, using the conduct of certain people who were called Christians, but were not consistent in their living. We have rejected this interpretation since it is not easy to explain "turned aside." Ellicott thinks the revilers are not just unbelievers in general, but apostate Christians, since the same verb "turned aside" is used of such people in 1 Timothy 1:6 and 2 Timothy 4:4.

[53] The United Bible Society critical apparatus assigns the letters A, B, C, D to any given variant reading to indicate the relative degree of certainty for the reading adopted in the text. The apparatus gives the reading "woman who is a believer" a "C" rating. The major manuscripts that support it are Sinaiticus, Alexandrinus, and Ephraemi.

[54] It is mainly some Old Latin version manuscripts that support this reading.

[55] This reading is found in Codex Beza, in certain Old Latin Manuscripts, and in the Peshito and Harkleian Syriac Versions. It is the way the Textus Receptus reads, and so does the KJV. Alford,

man or woman would seem to accord better with the sense, for it is difficult to believe that the exhortation to relieve the Church of its responsibility to care for widows would be confined to women."[56]   If the KJV reading ("man or woman") be adopted, then the precept here would be an extension of the one given in verse 4, where children and grandchildren were given a command to care for any relatives who were widows, so the church did not have any unnecessary care placed on it.   Now the "children and grandchildren" on whom the responsibility of care for their relatives falls are identified as being either man or woman.

Has *dependent* **widows** – This "widow" does not appear to be limited, as were the widows spoken about in verses 4 and 8, to those who happen to be relatives of the members of the church at Ephesus.   These widows might be servants, or friends, as well as relatives.   Now any believing woman (or perhaps it says "man or woman") may have a servant, or a friend, or a relative who happens to be a widow.   "Dependent," added by the NASB translators, is likely intended to carry the idea that these widows are what earlier were called "widows indeed."   They have no one else on whom they can depend for help.

Let her assist them – The Christian brother or sister can provide a home for the widow, or even for more than one widow.   The same word translated "assist" was used in verse 10 of the widow's activities back in happier days before she became a "widow indeed."   Needy widows are first of all the responsibility of those who are nearest of kin to them.   Let a widow's own family members support her before the church is called on to assume the support.   Next, let a widow's own friends take on the blessed privilege of supporting her before the church is called on to provide all the support.

And let not the church be burdened – It is implied that the church (the whole congregation), out of compassion and mercy, would likely assume the cost and effort of providing for the widow's needs, even though it shouldn't be expected to. "Burdened" says it is possible for the whole congregation church to be "weighed down with too heavy a load," whether it be financially or by additional work. That ought not be allowed to happen by any individual member who by personally taking care of their dependent widows could help keep it from happening.

So that it may assist those who are widows indeed -- To require or expect the church to support those whom we ourselves (men or women who are believers) ought to support, is, in fact, to rob the poor and friendless whom the church could

---

Ellicott, and other New Testament scholars who have also had facility working with the Greek text, adopt the reading even though in their day the preponderance of manuscript evidence favored "if any believing woman ...."

[56] *Op. cit.*, p.104.

otherwise support (*Barnes' Notes*, p.181).   Among the members of the congregation, there would be just so many homes which could assume the burden of taking in and caring for those who were "widows indeed."   If these spaces are taken up by widows whose families should be caring for them, then those with no families at all would really begin to suffer.

C. The Evangelist's Concern for Elders.   5:17-25

1. The compensation of elders.   5:17,18

5:17 -- Let the elders who rule well – The "elders" here discussed, as the context makes obvious, are the church leaders,[57] not merely the older men.   (See 5:1 for the instructions concerning the evangelist's care for older men.)   In Bible times, each congregation of Christians had "elders" (plural).[58]   The qualifications for "elders" were given in chapter 3.   Now Timothy is being instructed concerning the way these elders were to be treated by Timothy and the congregation.   It was the evangelist's responsibility to see that these instructions were carried out by the congregation.   We also, in this paragraph, have a hint at some of the work an elder was expected to perform.   One of the tasks of an elder was to "rule."   The word rendered "rule" is *proistēmi*, which means to be over, to preside over, to be concerned for and care for.[59]   It seems that in the congregations of Christians we find an organization similar to what had been found in the synagogues, with a group of elders who presided or cared for the congregation.   These elders at Ephesus,[60] when Paul spoke his farewell address to them (Acts 20:18ff), were admonished to "shepherd the church of God" and "be on guard yourselves and for all the flock among which the Holy Spirit has made you overseers."   Elders, according to this Acts address, certainly did have a responsibility for and over the congregation in such matters as seeing that only sound doctrine is taught to the church members, and caring lest "sheep" stray from the flock, and in helping the weak by ministering to their needs.   "Well" does not require us to make a critical comparison of one elder against another, to determine if he is doing well.   All it means is that each man's performance in ruling, or preaching, or teaching is to be evaluated by itself, to see if he is doing well.

---

[57] It earlier has been shown that in the apostolic age, the terms "elder" and "bishop" were interchangeable terms.   Compare Acts 20:20-28 and Titus 1:5-7.

[58] See, for example, Acts 14:23, where it reads "elders" (plural) in each church (singular).

[59] The same word is used at Romans 12:8; 1 Thessalonians 5:12, and earlier in this epistle to Timothy at 3:4,5.

[60] The farewell address was given in the Spring of AD 58.   It was less than ten years later that 1 Timothy was addressed to Ephesus.   We would suppose that some of the same men who heard Paul's farewell address are still serving as elders in the church at Ephesus.

Be considered worthy of a double honor – If "honor" for the widows (verse 3) meant that the congregation provided for their material needs, then it certainly involves that here for the elders, also. "Honor" shown to the elders means the congregation provides for their material needs. It seems rather obvious that the eldership in the early church was a paid position. The following verse seems to show that "pay" is certainly involved in the "honor" the elder is to receive. When men gave their time to the needs of the church, they had little time to earn their own livelihood. Therefore, the church was to provide their needs. Further, we suggest that "double honor" means the elder should receive twice as much "honor" as the widows.[61] The warnings about not getting into the eldership simply for "filthy lucre's sake" (1 Peter 5:2) and about "not coveting silver or gold" (Acts 20:33 and following) certainly are meaningful only if the position were a paid position. And since the one who "rules well" or who "works hard" is to get the double honor, perhaps we are to understand that those who have "served with distinction" are the ones who get a double honor. Those who served without undue exertion or without ruling well are still to be honored, but not with a "double honor." Adequate respect and appreciation for all the elders certainly includes adequate remuneration. Anything less would not be "honor".

Not all agree that "honor" means material reward or pay, or that "double honor" means double pay. A number of other suggestions have been offered, some rather curious. Melanchthon spoke of "victuals and reverence" to explain the term "double honor." Others write of "honor and honorarium" – that is, they should receive both honor and material reward. Expositor's Greek Testament suggests Paul's meaning of "double honor" is that they are to get better remuneration than they are now getting, i.e., they are to get twice the salary they now receive. In the 3rd century, believers put a double portion of food before the elders at love feasts.[62] Another suggestion is that they are to get a double honor – one for their age (i.e., old men) and another for the office they held (eldership).[63]

It also seems obvious Paul did not mean for "double" to be taken with strict arithmetical exactness. We say "twice as good" or "twice as much", expressions that contain a certain indefiniteness. The same is true for "double" in Scripture (Matthew 23:15; Revelation 18:6; Isaiah 40:2; and Jeremiah 16:18 in the LXX).

---

[61] The "honor" to be given to the widows certainly included material support (1 Timothy 5:3,4). The "honor" to the elders can hardly include less. We therefore would reject commentaries which affirm that "honor" in the New Testament never means "wages" or "salary" or "material support." The word certainly carried that meaning in Classical Greek, and we would urge the context requires a similar meaning here in 1 Timothy 5.

[62] Conybeare and Howson, *Life and Epistles of St. Paul* (London: Longman and Greens, 1873), p.755.

[63] This suggestion requires us to give an ambiguous sense (i.e., both old man and elder) to the term *presbuteroi* in verse 17, instead of taking it of the "office" as the context rather demands.

Especially those who work hard at their preaching and teaching – Here are two more tasks that at least some of the elders may be expected to do. (1) Some elders may preach.[64] This is not to be interpreted to mean that there should be no paid evangelist working with any congregation that already has elders or that instead of the evangelist doing the preaching, the elders should do all the preaching.[65] Certainly Timothy himself is an example of an evangelist continuing to preach in a community that already had elders. In the 20th century, with a shortage of preachers for the smaller rural churches, it has not been uncommon for elders from the city to fill the pulpit of the area churches, lest those churches have no preaching at all. Perhaps something similar was taking place in and around Ephesus.[66] In the early 20th century, in Missouri, it was not uncommon for the elders to get up and "exhort" the congregation after the preacher had finished his message. In this exhortation, they made personal application of the message to the people in the audience who had just heard it. "In word" just might picture the elders at Ephesus as exhorting and applying the message the evangelist delivered; it might not refer to "preaching" at all. (2) Some elders may teach. Such things as "Sunday Schools" did not exist in the 1st century. Where then did this teaching take place? Perhaps they were teaching from house to house. Someone must see to it that the second half of the Great Commission is fulfilled, "teaching them to observe all that I commanded you." Both new converts and believers who are older in the faith still need teaching in sound doctrine and the concomitant duties of the Christian life.[67] These elders are said to "work hard" at their preaching and teaching. The word used here for "work" is *kopiaō*, and it emphasizes the fatigue one experiences after a prolonged

[64] The Greek is simply *en logo*, "in word." It likely carries the idea of "speaking" in this place, and because of its use in a context where "teaching" also appears, most modern translations render it as "preaching."

[65] Daniel Sommers, an Illinois preacher of a former generation, advocated the abolition of the "paid minister" system. LeRoy Garrett of Texas also taught this doctrine in the middle of the 20th century, trying to show that there is no such thing as a "located minister" in any of the churches in the New Testament. As a result of these men's influence, Restoration Movement churches have had to wrestle with this question, and not a few congregations, tragically, have become so agitated over this question that the Movement has tended to polarize and divide over this very issue. Luke's 5 year ministry at Philippi, Philip's 20 year ministry at Caesarea, and Archippus at Colossae (Colossians 4:17) are but a few Scriptural examples of a long "located ministry" and demonstrate that a "located ministry" is wholly warranted as one of several ways a church may function.

[66] Admittedly, at first reading, we probably should understand that the elders who "work hard at preaching" and who were therefore worthy of double honor, were preaching to the very people who were expected to honor them, rather than to a neighboring congregation in need of pulpit supply.

[67] This commentator advocates that evangelists (until the congregation becomes so large that such personal visitation would be prohibitive) and elders visit regularly in the homes of the members, and that, as they visit, they have a definite agenda of "doctrinal emphases" that each home is expected to know and practice. In this way (and probably only in this way), over a period of time, the whole congregation will have a good grasp of the "sound doctrine." Failure to do such teaching can lead to grief down the road, as church members who are untaught and who do not see eye-to-eye with the Word of God begin to pull for programs and teachings other than what the Word teaches.

period of toil. The work that conscientious elders do can leave them weary and exhausted, but the close of a day of such toil brings a feeling of satisfaction and joy to the worker who has been doing it for Jesus!

Does this phrase about "preaching and teaching" suggest there were some "preaching elders" as distinguished from say, "ruling elders" (first part of this verse)? "Especially" (*malista*, Greek) might indicate that those elders who preach and teach are a subgroup of elders, a subgroup differentiated from those who rule.[68] But it is also true that *malista* can be used to introduce a further description of something already said.[69] If that is how it is used here, then "rule well" is simply being defined by the terms "working hard at preaching and teaching." Verse 17 does not give sufficient warrant for the view that there were two classes of elders, preaching elders and ruling elders.

What about a paid eldership today? Indeed, why not! New Testament polity does not support the idea that "preacher" and "elder" are interchangeable terms.[70] Nevertheless, there are several 20th century religious bodies who do teach that "elder" and "pastor" (i.e., preacher) are the same function. In the larger churches in those fellowships it is not uncommon to find a plurality of paid "pastors." A case could be made that those churches who have a plurality of paid pastors have come close to having "elders" (plural) who receive "honor" (or double honor). But we do not see that as being exactly a reproduction of the polity reflected here in Timothy, where the evangelist has separate responsibilities from those of the elders. What we would advocate is that both the preacher (evangelist) and the elders should be on the payroll of the church. Should be, that is, if the job that needs to be done is to get done adequately! It may be something that could be introduced gradually, as a congregation grows. As a

---

[68] Certain Presbyterian groups, who have "preaching elders" working with different congregations, but who do not have anyone apart from the preaching elders called an "evangelist," do not seem to be doing things the way Timothy and the elders were doing them at Ephesus.

At the time of the Reformation, Calvin taught there were four "orders or offices" which Christ had instituted for the government of the church: elders, pastors (or bishops), doctors (teachers), and deacons. Note that he made a distinction between "elders" and "pastors," and both offices were responsible for discipline in the church. "Elders" and "pastors" were both "presbyters," but on the basis of 1 Timothy 5:17 a distinction was made between a "teaching elder" (minister, preacher) and "ruling elder" (pastor or bishop). In Scotland the "elder" was ordained for life, without the laying on of hands, and was given the duty of examining communicants and visiting the sick. Presbyterians elsewhere laid hands on both "elders" and "bishops" when either were being ordained.

[69] When Paul says (2 Timothy 4:13), "Bring the books, *especially* the parchments," we suppose he is carefully defining which books he meant, rather than that he wants two groups of writings to be brought.

[70] The special study at the close of chapter 4 (on "Evangelist") has led to the conclusion that the modern "preacher" is a position like "evangelist" in the New Testament. This verse, which has the elder working hard at his preaching, does not mean the elder is the same as evangelist. It is possible for the elder to preach from time to time, without thereby holding the office of evangelist.

congregation grows, first one, then another of the elders, could begin receiving a living wage from the congregation among whom he ministers.

5:18 -- For the Scripture says – Such "honor" or support or compensation[71] for workers as is taught in verse 17 has Scriptural support. "For," with which this verse begins, shows this verse is a reason for what was just said about "honor." Paul will make reference to two different passages of Scripture[72] to clinch his point. God has spoken on the subject, and that settles the matter!

"You shall not muzzle the ox while he is threshing" – This first Scripture quotation comes from Deuteronomy 25:4. To fully appreciate the thrust of this verse, one must recall the ancient method of threshing. The threshing floor was a piece of level ground, often the flat top of a rock hill, and of necessity exposed to the wind. The stalks of grain were bound into sheaves as they were cut, and the sheaves were brought to the threshing floor, and then unbound. Oxen, often pulling a heavy wooden beam, or a rough sledge on which the driver stood, were driven round and round over the stalks. Their hoofs would trample (*aloaō*, "to thresh," i.e., by trampling over) the stalks and the beam would further crush them till the ripened grain was shaken out of the heads. Once the grain had been separated from the heads, the task of winnowing would follow, throwing the chaff and grain up into the air, which allowed the wind to blow the chaff aside while the heavier kernels of grain fell back to the threshing floor. Cruel men would at times muzzle the oxen so they could eat nothing while they were being driven round and round. God distinctly forbade Israel to thus muzzle their oxen.[73] This same verse is quoted in 1 Corinthians 9:9, where Paul drives home the point he has learned from this passage. This rule about not muzzling the ox does not mean that God's only concern is that animals be treated humanely.[74] Any worker – be he an ox, a common laborer, a preacher of the gospel, or an elder – has a God-given right to partake of the fruits of his work!

And, "The laborer is worthy of his wages" – This verse is an exact quotation

---

[71] The Scriptural quotations which follow certainly lead us, even more than what was written above, to assume that the word "honor" had some reference to financial support or maintenance.

[72] Paul always uses "Scripture" (*graphē*) to designate the Sacred Writings. It was a technical term; the inspired writings were (to a Jew) the only thing worthy of the name "writings." Holy Scripture was regarded as "God speaking," both in its origin and in its abiding authority, so it is not surprising that we find the present tense verb ("says") here. "God is speaking to us" in these verses!

[73] "You shall not muzzle" is a future indicative used as an imperative and expressing a prohibition.

[74] Indeed, God certainly intends that his people should treat animals humanely. But that is not all the passage is intended to teach.

of Jesus' words as recorded in Luke 10:7.[75]   Paul is thus putting Luke's Gospel
on a par with "Scripture."[76]   This quotation of Luke's Gospel also has some
bearing on the date of Luke's Gospel.   Paul wrote 1 Timothy in AD 65.[77]   Luke's
Gospel would have to be dated before this.   Taking into account both this
information from 1 Timothy, and the fact that "Acts" (written about AD 63) is
volume two of Luke's history, we date Luke's Gospel about AD 60.   It is worthy
of notice that this quotation of Luke's Gospel as "Scripture" certainly shows that
the writings we call the New Testament were recognized as being Scripture at the
very time they were written and received.   It was not a process that took decades
or centuries to determine.   "Worthy" is similar to saying that the laborer is
"entitled" to his wages.   That is as true of elders who "rule well" as it is of those
who preach the gospel (1 Corinthians 9:9-14).   Paul thus has shown from the Old
and New Testament Scriptures that the idea that elders should be properly paid
for their work is a Scriptural principle.   Verses 17 and 18 have indicated it to be
one of the evangelist's responsibilities to see to it that elders are paid.   Of course,
it may not be the plan of wisdom for an evangelist to attempt to impose bluntly
this teaching upon a congregation which has never had the practice of having full-
time elders who are paid.   He likely will need to lay adequate foundational
instruction before the congregation even begins to think about paying elders for
their work.   Part of that foundational instruction would be to see that visiting
preachers and missionaries who fill the pulpit or who work with the congregation
for a period of time are properly compensated.   This will help drive home to the
congregation the principle that this passage is teaching.

2. The discipline of elders.   5:19-21

5:19 -- Do not receive an accusation against an elder – The evangelist's
responsibility toward the elders includes more than seeing to it that they are
"honored" (verse 17).   The evangelist has another responsibility: he must be
very careful about listening to criticisms of and accusations against the elders of

---

[75] Matthew also records this statement by Jesus, but the wording in Matthew is slightly different than the wording found in Luke. Matthew has *tes trophēs* (his meat) where Luke has *tou misthou* (his wages). But in Luke 10:7 the words are identical with those used here in 1 Timothy, even to the omission (cf. Nestle text) of the linking verb *estin*. The conclusion is inevitable that the writer of 1 Timothy was acquainted with and was quoting from Luke's Gospel.

[76] Paul joins both statements by *kai* ("and"). That can only mean both quotations are placed on the same level. New Testament writers commonly connect quotations of different portions of Scripture by the use of *kai*. Paul calls both quotations "Scripture." The Gospel of Luke is equal with the Old Testament Scriptures in regard to inspiration. Of course, the New Testament has taken the place of the Old Testament as the covenant for God's people to live by, and so likewise the writings of the New Testament are our rule of faith and practice in this Messianic Age.

[77] See the discussion concerning the date of 1 Timothy in the Introductory Studies to this volume, p.xxvi.

the congregation. "Accusation" (*categoria*) is a charge against. The person is being accused of some sin. (The next verse makes it plain that the charge is something more than that the elder was not "ruling well.") "Elder" here is a reference to the church leader, as the context demonstrates. It would seem from this verse that an evangelist like Timothy would be called upon to hear charges against elders. Are they formal, or just in the course of daily interactions, that the evangelist hears such charges? The evangelist is also pictured as having to express his judgment upon such charges. Here is Paul's advice on how to handle such "charges." He is not to "receive" or "acknowledge as correct" such accusations without first having adequate witnesses who can substantiate the charges. The instructions in verses 19ff have some bearing on a question that agitates Christian churches from time to time – namely, the relationship between evangelist and elders. Is the evangelist under the elders (i.e., the elders are thought of as being "rulers" over the congregation, including the preacher)? Is he over the elders? Or is he an outside advisor to the elders? If he "receives charges" against an elder, and sees to it that sinning elders are disciplined (verse 20), it implies something other than the idea that the evangelist is "under" the elders.

Except on the basis of two or three witnesses – Any discipline must be founded on fact, not on rumor or innuendo. An accusation against an elder must be "on the basis of" (*epi*, "upon"), that is, it must be based "upon" the oral testimony of, two or three witnesses. Of old, any Israelite was safeguarded against indictment and sentencing unless two or three reliable witnesses testified against him. Here, elders are safeguarded even against having to answer a charge unless it is at once supported by two or three witnesses. Permit no man to accuse an elder unless he is accompanied by two or three witnesses who are ready to back up the accusation.[78] "Lacking such support, the accusation must not even be taken up or entertained. The reputation of the elder must not be unnecessarily damaged, and his work must not suffer unnecessary interruption."[79]

> It is of utmost importance to safeguard innocent men from false accusation, and as Jewish law required the agreement of two witnesses before a man might be called upon to answer a charge (cf. Deut. 19:15), so it must be in the Church (cf. Matt. 18:16; 2 Cor. 13:1), especially when an elder is implicated. He must be protected against malicious intent; but if there are real grounds for accusation then disciplinary action should be taken before the whole Church (unless "all"

---

[78] Here is another view of "on the basis of two or three witnesses." Timothy was not to encourage *delatorēs*, secret accusers and defamers; but if anyone had a charge to make against an elder, it was to be done *in the presence of* witnesses (*epi* with the genitive). A doubt arises whether "the witnesses" here spoken of were to be witnesses able to support the accusation, or merely witnesses in whose presence the accusation must be made. The close juxtaposition of the legal terms "accusation" and "upon witnesses" favors the strict meaning of "witnesses" as being witnesses able to support the "accusation." (Hervey, *op. cit.*, p.100)

[79] Hendriksen, *op. cit.*, p.182.

[verse 20] means "all the elders").[80]

Just as Paul referred to Jesus' teachings about "honor," so Paul refers to Jesus' teaching about the proper process of discipline (Matthew 18:15-18). Timothy is instructed to follow the procedure taught by Jesus before he accepts or acknowledges as correct any accusation against an elder. No charge against an elder which would involve a public rebuke or other disciplinary measures must be even entertained unless there are several witnesses on which to base this accusation. This follows the Mosaic command (Deuteronomy 17:6), which Jesus reiterated (Matthew 18:16). The witnesses are not thought of as appearing at the trial, but rather at the time when the disciplinary process is first contemplated. Unless the evidence is sufficient and practically certain, no action should be initiated against an elder.

> This safeguard of the elder is a wise one. No person is more subject to Satan's attack in the form of gossip and slander than God's servant. If every accusation necessitated full investigation, the evangelist and the elder would have time for little else. Therefore, no elder should be brought to trial on the accusation of one person, for even charges of which an elder is acquitted can damage his work. How often has a godly elder been remembered as "that man who was in some sort of trouble," even though he may have been exonerated![81]

An accusation against an elder is a serious thing. The character of an elder is of value, not only to the man himself, but is of special value to the church and to the cause of Christianity.

> Charges – owing, possibly, to jealousy, party feeling, suspected doctrinal error -- will not infrequently be brought against an elder. Timothy is not even to listen, unless the evidence is perfectly clear. Every possible precaution against simply vexatious charges brought against the one occupying the hard and difficult position of elder, must be taken by the evangelist.[82]

At the same time, however, the wicked, even if in the eldership, must not be shielded from any punishment or correction they deserve.

5:20 -- Those who continue to sin – There may be times when the charge against an elder is true (i.e., the elder is, in fact, guilty of habitual sin), and the elder refuses to hear either the original accuser or the two or three witnesses, and repent. When the previous steps have failed and there is still refusal to repent, according to Jesus' own instructions concerning discipline, the next step is to "tell it to the church" (Matthew 18:17). "Continue to sin" indicates it is habitual sin, not sim-

---

[80] Guthrie, *op. cit.*, p.106.

[81] Kent, *op. cit.*, p.178

[82] Spence, *op. cit.*, p.251.

ply a one-time act, about which the elder is "accused" and for which he is being disciplined.[83]

Rebuke in the presence of all – "Rebuke" here translates *elegche*, not *epiplēxēs* as in 5:1. There, the fault being a private one, the rebuke was to be administered in private. But in the case of the habitually sinning elder, where he has been proven guilty by adequate witnesses and where the case has become public, the rebuke[84] is more severe. It is a public censure of the offender, including a public call to repentance, done with a broken heart that the offender has not already repented, and done with the full anticipation that the offender will by the rebuke be led to repent. Such a loving but firm rebuke is the way the church expresses its strong and decided disapproval of the wrong being habitually done. Habitual sin among the eldership (or the ministry) is not to be shielded or hidden. It is to be publicly rebuked. There is no power of inflicting any corporal punishment, or fine, or imprisonment. There certainly is implied the possibility of excommunication, until the offender repents (at which time he would be publicly reinstated into the fellowship of Christian brethren). "In the presence of all" could be taken either with "sinning" or with "rebuke." Since the rest of the verse deals with others being warned by the rebuke, most writers understand we should take "in the presence of all" with the verb "rebuke." A public rebuke[85] is most appropriate where the habitual sin has been of a public nature. In this day of litigation, extreme care must be taken by those responsible for church discipline, lest their actions be unfeeling and open them up to a lawsuit in court by those who refuse to repent but would rather attack the ones trying to help them be more Christ-like. The evangelist, Timothy, is here given the responsibility of seeing that discipline is practiced by the church. If Timothy is an example for preachers today, then present-day preachers should learn from this exhortation another of their responsibilities as they serve the various congregations. "When faced with sinning elders, a spineless attitude is deplorable," writes Guthrie (*op. cit.*, p.106). Sometimes, sadly, the ones responsible for administering the discipline have done

---

[83] The present tense likely indicates the sin is being continued into the present moment. Such a person would be dealt with in a way different from the person who "sinned" in the past, but is not at the moment habitually engaged in his old sins.

   Not all translations add some word like "continue" or persist" in this phrase about sinning. Those translators thereby have expressed their opinion that the present tense denotes that *guilt* is presently established beyond doubt, rather than that the offender is at present continuing to sin. We doubt that *guilt* concerning only past sins is the topic intended by this present tense.

[84] BAGD lexicon uses "rebuke, reprove," or "correct" to translate the word used here. It has the sense of showing someone his sin and summoning him to repentance.

[85] We have already indicated our belief that Paul, as he gives these directions to Timothy is following Jesus' instructions concerning discipline. Jesus said "tell it to the church" (Matthew 18:17). Thus the comment by Hendriksen that "before all" means "in the presence of the entire consistory" likely misses the point. (A consistory, in Reformed and Presbyterian churches, is the body governing the local congregation, consisting of the minister and ruling elders.)

so in a harsh and intolerant spirit. Care must always be exercised, lest the discipline be done with a wrong spirit or a wrong motive. But neglect of discipline is just as great a sin, perhaps greater, as going about it with a wrong attitude.

So that the rest also may be fearful *of sinning* – "So that" indicates one of the purposes for making the rebuke in public. Church discipline not only is intended to save the sinner. It also is intended to fill the whole church with a godly fear of wrong doing, and of what will happen to a church member if he embraces habitual sin as his lifestyle.[86] The goal of the discipline is not the gratification of the private feelings of the one who administers it. The goal is to prevent more such sins in the lives of the other Christians, who might at first be tempted to follow the example of their leaders. When church members see that even leaders are not exempt when discipline is needed, they will have more respect for the church and her attempts to save them when they are the ones needing discipline.

5:21 -- I solemnly charge you – This is a strong word, *diamarturomai*, not *paraggello* as at 6:13. The strict meaning of *diamarturomai* is "I call heaven and earth to witness the truth of what I am saying"; and then, by a slight metonymy, "I declare a thing," or "I ask a thing," as in the presence of those witnesses who are either named or understood. In the following phrases, the witnesses are named. The use of the strong word implies that the subject is of great importance. The use of this strong word implies Timothy must have been tempted to shrink from publicly disciplining those men who should have been disciplined. Perhaps Timothy tended to be timid about such matters, so needed stiffening up. Perhaps Timothy was no different from the rest of us in this matter of being too hesitant to begin administering discipline when it is needed.

In the presence of God – The reference is to God the Father, who is ever present and all-seeing. This is the first in a list of ever present witnesses who are watching Timothy as he goes about doing the work of an evangelist. Instead of worrying what men will think, Timothy, like us, was to remember that there were some beings watching him whose approval was vastly more important than what mere men may think.

And of Christ Jesus – Not only is Timothy to remember that Jesus, at the right hand of the Father, is watching His servants on earth, but there also may be an allusion to the future judgment, where Jesus will do the judging (2 Timothy 4:1). It certainly would be a matter of wisdom to so act now as to not cause the Judge to find fault with how we lived and ministered. Some writers, in addition to

---

[86] The NASB adds "of sinning" to express the translators' opinion concerning what is the object of the word "fear." Others suppose fear of a similar public rebuke is the thing in Paul's mind. Interpreted either way, one of the purposes of this discipline of leaders is to discourage similar behavior on the part of others. "Fear" of the consequences is one motive that can lead to the proper lifestyle.

making an allusion to the final judgment, call attention to the fact that Jesus faithfully carried out difficult tasks and, thus, has given us an example.

And of *His* chosen angels – The "chosen angels" are the good angels, in distinction from those who rebelled and did not keep their proper position (Jude 6). This is the only passage where angels are said to be "chosen." "Chosen" (or "elect" KJV) probably implies there was a time when the angels were on probation, just as it implies such a time for the saints. Only the fact of their "election" or "choosing" is here stated. The reasons which led to this choice, or the conditions involved in the choice, are not stated. There is repeated mention in the Scriptures of the "fallen angels" (Matthew 25:41; 1 Corinthians 6:3; 2 Peter 2:4; Jude 6; Revelation 12:7-9). So the obvious suggestion to explain the word "chosen" is that the reference is to the "holy angels," the "angels of God," the ones who did not rebel and fall. Some have suggested that Paul alludes to "chosen" angels in view of the fact that the false teachers at Ephesus held faulty opinions about angels. In contradistinction to what the Gnostics were saying, there were some angels whose observation of Timothy's ministry was of vital importance.

Just why Paul calls attention to the fact that the "chosen angels" are watching Timothy has been variously explained. (1) "His" chosen angels may suggest these good angels are at the beck and call of Jesus. The day will come when He will send them to separate wicked men from the righteous, and gather them for the judgment (see Matthew 16:27, 25:31; Mark 8:48; Luke 9:26, 12:8,9; 2 Thessalonians 1:7). (2) Some call attention to the phrase in the model prayer about "Thy will be(ing) done on earth as it is in heaven." If this idea is in the background, then Paul wants Timothy's obedience to resemble that of the angels of heaven who cheerfully and fully carry out God's will. (3) Some call attention to Ephesians 3:10, where we learn that angels are spectators of what goes on in the church and are learning about God's eternal plans and purposes by watching the church. Timothy must not be lax about needed discipline and thereby give the angels a faulty lesson! Timothy stands in an awesome presence – the God of the universe, the Messiah at His right hand, and the angels as His chosen attendants and ministers, gathered around the throne – as he goes about doing the work of an evangelist in Ephesus. Evangelists today have the same audience!

To maintain these *principles* without bias – "Principles" has been added by the NASB translators to complete the sense of the sentence since the word "these" (a neuter plural) occurs in the Greek without any noun. The context would lead us to suppose that the "things" Paul has in mind are those having to do with the receiving of an accusation and the public rebuke of sinning elders.[87] When it

---

[87] Barnes thinks the "things" intended include the whole of the epistle previous. It is better to make "these" refer to the imperative tense verbs in the previous verses.

comes to the discipline of elders (yea, the discipline of any church member), one must be careful not to be influenced by purely subjective considerations. The words rendered "without bias" are *chōris prokrimatos*, an expression found only here in the New Testament and not found in the LXX or classical Greek, although the verb *prokrinō* is found in both. The ASV renders it "without prejudice," and when the ASV was first translated this was an apt rendering. However, the word has changed meaning; to us "prejudice" means "to form a judgment before making any examination, pre-judging a case." Such a prejudgment would prevent coming to a right or fair conclusion in the matter being considered. What the Greek (and the Latin *praejudicium* from which "prejudice" comes) means is "to prefer" some person or thing to others. The better English words would be "preference" or "partiality," or as the KJV reads "without preferring one before another." When two sides present their "positions," how prone their listeners are to decide which is right or wrong by "siding with their friends," rather than listening to the evidence and letting it decide. This is the very thing that Timothy is to be careful not to do!

Doing nothing in *a spirit of* **partiality** – "In ... partiality" translates *kata prosklisin*, another *hapax legomena* as far as the Old and New Testaments are concerned. It means literally to "incline" the scales to one side or the other, and hence a "bias" of the mind to one party or the other. The balance of justice in Timothy's hands was to be equal. When it came to public discipline, Timothy was to act without being inclined to favor one party or person more than another. There should be no purpose to find one guilty and another innocent, no inclination of heart which would lead to a resolve to find one innocent, and no aversion from another which would lead to a resolve to find him guilty. Before all the facts are heard, Timothy must not lean either toward the accuser or toward the accused.

3. The ordination of elders. 5:22-25

5:22 -- Do not lay hands upon any one *too* **hastily** – An appropriate time span should be allowed (not "too hastily") before Timothy takes part in the laying on of hands on individuals. Much trouble can be avoided, including having to be involved in difficult disciplinary situations, if, in the matter of laying hands upon men, Timothy will exercise the necessary precaution of not acting in haste. But for what purpose is Timothy "laying his hands" on others? Upon whom is Timothy the evangelist laying hands? The ancient view sees a reference to an ordination service, with the evangelist laying hands on the elders. The immediately preceding verses (5:17ff) spoke of Timothy's relationship to "elders", so it is reasonable to suppose that topic is continued here. If we may be guided by Paul's own use of the phrase "laying on of hands" in the only two places in his

74547844

writings where it occurs (1 Timothy 4:14 and 2 Timothy 1:6), we should abide by the ancient interpretation of these words, that they mean the laying on of hands in ordination.[88] Elsewhere we are told that a new convert is not qualified to be an elder. One would be acting "hastily" were he to ordain a new convert. Also, to be qualified to be an elder, a man must be "above reproach." This takes time to ascertain, and one would be acting "hastily" if he did not take time to learn the reputation of the man about to be ordained. If indeed the topic is the ordination of elders, this verse has some bearing on the question of the evangelist's part in the selection of elders.[89] We seem to find several "methods" of selection depicted in the New Testament. In some passages, the congregation does the selecting, as in the case of the men to serve tables (Acts 6:1-6). In some cases, the evangelist may do the selecting (Titus 1:5). Does this verse have the evangelist doing the ordaining of elders by himself, or does he do the ordaining after the congregation has done the selection? If the evangelist is taking the lead, and presiding as he and the elders ordain others, then Timothy – and by parity of reasoning, the evangelist today – still has a responsibility to exercise restraint on the proceedings, lest someone be ordained too hastily.

Not all commentators agree that "ordination" is referred to in "laying on of hands." Other explanations for this verse include: (1) It is the way penitent elders were restored to their former position after they had been disciplined.

> Many modern expositors, because of the immediate context, decide for the latter interpretation. However, the earliest exposition (Chrysostom) explains it as original ordination. Furthermore, there is no evidence at all that the laying on of hands was employed to restore elders in the apostolic age. Inasmuch as the laying on of hands is known with certainty to have been used in the ordination of elders (Acts), and the other two uses of laying on of hands in the Pastorals refer to ordination, this writer adopts the viewpoint that the reference is to original ordination, and sees no lack of harmony with the context.[90]

(2) Perhaps Timothy the Evangelist is participating in the ordination of men to the office/function of evangelist. Having entrusted the gospel to faithful men, and having shown them how to teach others, these men are now being ordained after completing their period of training (2 Timothy 2:2). (3) Another alternative suggestion is that Timothy is laying hands on the sick to heal them.

---

[88] Some writers have objected to interpreting this as an ordination service on the grounds that Timothy would not alone be responsible for such an ordination (cp. 1 Timothy 4:14). But if Timothy took the lead in arranging for such an ordination service, taught the church how to do it, and then presided at the service, this admonition about exercising restraint would not be out of place.

[89] It has been a disputed point in Christian Church polity whether or not the evangelist ever takes the responsibility upon himself to appoint elders (as Titus 1:5 seems to require), or whether the congregation must always have a voice in the choice.

[90] Kent, *op. cit.*, p.180.

And thus share responsibility for the sins of others – "Ordination without a preceding thorough investigation would render Timothy co-responsible for the wrongs which such elders might subsequently commit."[91]

> If we ordain a man to the office of elder who is known to be living in sin, or to cherish dangerous error, we become the patrons of his sin and of the heresy. We lend to it the sanction of our approval and give it "support" from whatever reputation we may have. Hence, the importance of caution in investing anyone into the office of elder.[92]

(Of course, if the laying on of hands refers to the restoration of penitent elders, then the sins here spoken about would be sins committed by those elders after they were restored. Timothy is pictured as having restored the "penitent" on insufficient evidence of repentance. The harmful consequences upon the church of the elder's relapse into the old sins is something for which Timothy would be partially held responsible.)

Haste must be avoided in ordaining men to leadership positions, for those who ordain hastily are responsible to God for the conduct of those whom they ordain.

> Paul seems to mean that failure to exercise this caution implicates those responsible for hasty ordination in the sinful effects of their unwise choice. Of course, even after careful examination, those who ordain may find that they have been deceived. Certainly, if they have used every reasonable precaution available to them, they are not held responsible by God for the sinful lapse [and their effects on others] of an erring elder.[93]

A present-day application: Those who ordain men to positions of leadership in the church have a continuing obligation to the brotherhood. After recommending a man to the brotherhood – or, in the case of elders, to the local church – if the person ordained so lives or teaches that he no longer warrants the original recommendation, we think the ordaining body has an obligation to withdraw the ordination recommendation. By exercising care when an elder is selected, the possibility of future need for disciplining is greatly reduced.

Keep yourself free from sin – Observe that the stress is on "yourself." A preacher cannot always prevent others from sinning, but he certainly has a responsibility when it comes to his own sins. If Timothy has unadvisedly ordained certain men, he will find it more difficult to discipline them. Timothy

---

[91] Hendriksen, *op. cit.*, p.185.

[92] Barnes, *op. cit.*, p.186.

[93] Kent, *op. cit.*, p.180.

must keep himself "pure" (KJV, i.e., in full conformity with God's commands), or "free from sin" (NASB)[94] with respect to this and all other matters. "If they [evangelists], out of partiality or haste, born of failure to take seriously the nature of the eldership, have ordained hastily, then guilt to some extent must rest upon [the ones who did the ordaining]. Timothy is to keep himself spiritually pure from blame on this score."[95] This seems to say that participation in hasty or unadvised ordination is the "sin" that Timothy is to avoid. Hear it -- it is *sin* to choose an unqualified man to be elder. "The rather abrupt personal charge to Timothy, keep thyself pure, must primarily be understood in the general sense of honorable and upright behavior. It is as if the apostle had said -- make sure you appoint 'pure' men and keep yourself 'pure' in the process."[96]

5:23 -- No longer drink water *exclusively* – The command with which verse 22 closed, to "keep yourself free from sin," was of a personal nature. That leads Paul to offer another remark which is also personal.[97] Most writers make the connection between the verses on this fashion: A command like "Keep yourself pure" may have been interpreted (by some people in the early church) too rigidly as an exhortation to ascetic practices.[98] By adding what he does in verse 23, Paul makes it very clear that "purity" was not synonymous with total abstention. Keeping oneself "pure" at the expense of one's health is carrying "purity" too far! However, there may be no connection between verses 22 and 23 except as we have indicated – it is simply another personal admonition to Timothy. The NASB rightly adds the word "exclusively."[99] We learn from this verse that Timothy was a total abstainer.[100] We learn from this verse that Timothy had

---

[94] The marginal note shows that the words "from sin" are not actually in the text. They certainly are implied by the context.

[95] Kent, *op. cit.*, p.180.

[96] Guthrie, *op. cit.*, p.107-108.

[97] Commentators have felt a difficulty in regard to the connection of verse 23 with the context. Not a few have thought verse 23 to be so different from the verses about the evangelist's responsibility toward the elders, that they have supposed the verse has been misplaced, and that it was originally located in some other place than here in 1 Timothy 5.

[98] Total abstinence from wine was a well-known characteristic feature of the Essene and other Jewish ascetic sects. Since 1 Timothy is a warning against such false doctrine, we can easily understand why Paul makes perfectly clear his stand on the matter of "purity."

[99] The Greek verb *hudropoteō*, found only here in the New Testament, but once in the LXX (Daniel 1:12), and regularly in classical Greek means "drink *only* water." Paul is not telling Timothy to stop drinking water altogether (that would require *hudor pinein*).

[100] Barnes, who advocated total abstinence as being the Biblical standard for Christians, has this paragraph: "This whole passage is one of great value to the cause of temperance. Timothy was undoubtedly in the habit of abstaining wholly from the use of wine. Paul knew this, and he did not reprove him for it. He manifestly favored the general habit, and only asked Timothy to depart from it in some small degree, in order that he might restore and preserve his health."

some health problems. We also learn from this verse that, in Paul's judgment, total abstinence did not need to be adhered to if injurious to a person's health.

But use a little wine – In the ancient world, the water was far from safe for drinking purposes. If one insists on drinking nothing but water (unboiled), attacks of dysentery regularly result. One way of offsetting such attacks was to drink a "little wine." Water, diluted with a small amount of wine, was a common method of drinking wine in the eastern world. "Wine" usually indicates the fermented grape juice (though any fermented juice would be called "wine"). Readers of 1 Timothy should not overlook the epithet "a little." Was Doctor Luke with Paul when he wrote this prescription? Timothy was to use some wine.[101] "Little" in terms of quantity. This will help his health problems.

For the sake of your stomach and your frequent ailments – This phrase shows that Paul is speaking of wine as a medicine, not as a beverage to be regularly consumed.[102] This passage has some bearing on the matter of "doctors versus faith healing." Paul's instructions about a little wine as a medical remedy for illness certainly refutes the doctrine, often heard in the late 20th century, that the Biblical means of curing disease or illnesses is through faith healing or the prayer of faith. Paul certainly recognized "medicines" as useful for curing illnesses. Besides problems with dysentery (stomach), there is another possibility for the source of Timothy's ailments. The labors of the ministry are such as to demand much time and effort, and there is not a little stress as one deals with people problems in the local church – people problems like accusations against elders, and the need to rebuke some who continue sinning. Stress and anxiety can lead to health problems. In such a situation, medicine[103] to sustain the health is surely proper.

---

[101] Ellicott has a thoughtful note at this place. He calls attention to the difficulty those who think 1 Timothy is a forgery written in the 2nd century have accounting for the presence of this verse. Would anyone writing from an age when asceticism was becoming the common practice have written a verse like this? "No ecclesiastical forger of the 2nd or 3rd century would have dreamed, or, had he dreamed, would have dared to weave into the complicated tapestry of such an epistle a charge such as 'Drink no longer water, but use a little wine ....'" This verse can in fact be explained only on the supposition that the letter was, in truth, written by Paul to Timothy in all freedom and in all love.

[102] It is almost surprising to learn that this is one of the verses people use when they want to quiet their consciences about drinking alcoholic beverages. Timothy's weak stomach is no argument for drinking alcoholic beverages today. Before passages such as this, or Jesus' turning the water to wine at the wedding at Cana, are appealed to as "proof" that it is acceptable for a Christian to consume alcoholic beverages, it would be well to consult Farrar Fenton's *The Bible and Wine* or William Patton's *Bible Wines* to get a better idea of the vast difference in alcoholic content between fermented beverages of the ancient world and the distilled spirits the world has used since the Arabs introduced distillation in the 6th century AD.

[103] In the days before science produced modern medical drugs, wine was regularly used as a medicinal agent for many ailments. In the 20th century, medicines may be more useful for many ailments than a "little wine."

5:24 -- The sins of some men are quite evident – We presume that the subject of caution or lack of haste in ordaining men to the eldership is here continued.[104] About all one could rely on if he acts in haste is first impressions, and first impressions can be deceptive. But, if one avoids hasty action, with the passing of time the character of the men being considered for the job will become evident. It will become evident that some are not fit for the office because of their sins. Likewise, the passing of time will permit those whose deeds are good to become well known. The men whose lifestyle makes them unfit for the eldership are divided into two groups: those whose sins are clearly evident, and those whose sins are not so clearly evident. "Sins" translates *hamartia*, a word that means "to miss the mark"; it refers to any departure from God's standard of righteousness. "Evident" is used to translate *prodēloi*, a word found in the New Testament only in 1 Timothy 5:24,25 and Hebrews 7:14. The *pro* may indicate "beforehand" or "before the eyes of all." A few writers think it means "before the eyes of all." The word is thought to mean "open" or "obvious." The very idea of nominating such men for eldership, when their evil doing is out in the open and can be seen by anyone who has eyes to see, is preposterous. Most writers urge that in compound verbs like this, the *pro* indicates "before" in point of time. When it is asked what "time" we are talking about, the usual answer is "before it comes time to make a formal examination[105] of the man's qualifications." Some men's sins are so well known that no careful inquiry in order to find them out is required.[106] Instead of setting such men aside to a position of leadership, there needs to be discipline so they repent and quit their sinning!

Going before them to judgment – There is little agreement in the commentaries concerning what "judgment" Paul has in mind. One thinks it is the formal inquiry, or perhaps the decision reached by the inquiry set up to ascertain a potential elder's qualifications for the office. Some men's sins are so notorious that they of themselves go before the sinner to the attention of the ones doing the

---

[104] The style of writing known as "Pauline digressions" is well known. Verse 23 may or may not have a close-knit relationship to the whole paragraph's theme of "the evangelist's responsibility concerning the elders." Even if there is no close connection such as suggested in notes above on that verse, there would be nothing out of line with such "Pauline digressions" to have Paul come back in verse 24 to the topic (the selection and ordination of elders) that occupied the verses before 23.

[105] We are at a loss to know what expression to use when speaking of this "examination" or "inquiry" into a potential elder's qualifications. Some writers confidently speak of a "public inquiry into a man's conduct and teaching," as though Timothy the evangelist was to oversee a formal public hearing. We are not at all confident such a formal examination is necessarily implied in the language of this verse (though this decision rests somewhat on how the word "judgment" in the next phrase is explained). Other writers speak just as confidently of a private and personal investigation of each candidate's qualifications. We wonder if the actual practice was somewhere between these two extremes?

[106] The "men" in view are certainly already converts, members of the congregation, but men whose self-control and mortification of sin in their bodies (Romans 6:12ff) needs special attention.

examination.[107]   Another thinks the reference is to the final judgment. Christians may live in notorious sin, a sin that disqualifies them for the office of elder.   Not only that, there is another judgment where such unrepented sins will lead to further disqualification – disqualification from spending eternity in heaven.   Another thinks the judgment here mentioned is that of Timothy, and that his judgment will be shown in the careful selection he makes of candidates for ordination.   Still another thinks the reference is to the "judgment" rendered by those who are involved in the church-administered discipline which is intended to get the sinner to stop his sinning.

For others, their *sins* follow after – The others, it is implied, are those whose sins[108] are not so evident as to be common knowledge.   The sinner has carefully covered his tracks, so that his sins are not immediately nor easily discovered. These sins are not found out until "after" some close inquiry.   To the average person, their lives look innocent enough.   Before any careful examination is made, these men look like possible candidates for the eldership.   As the examination is made, sins are uncovered, and it becomes obvious that the man is unfit for the office.   Now we see why Timothy should be anything but hasty in laying on hands.   It will take him some time to be able to make an informed decision about potential elders' lifestyles.   When the inquiry or examination one must make of potential elders discloses such hidden (and habitual) sin(s), such men are thereby disqualified from present consideration for the eldership.[109] Timothy's only possible course of action is to refuse to lay hands on such men, lest he share in the blame for the harm that regularly results from putting such men into office.   Furthermore, by taking some time to get to know his men, Timothy may avoid the necessity of having to publicly rebuke one he has helped ordain as an elder (cp. verse 20).

5:25 -- Likewise also – What is true of sins is "likewise also" true of a man's good deeds.   Just as some sins are clearly evident, and some do not come to light for a long time, so men's good actions may be clearly evident or they may not have been done in such a way that everyone knows about them.   Verses 24 and 25 make parallel observations about men's sins and about their "good deeds," and we are hereby introduced to the complexities involved in selecting suitable candidates

---

[107] While we may agree that the judgment in Paul's mind is some judgment made by humans (that is about the only idea that is meaningful in the context), we are not in agreement that it is a "*formal* inquiry."   Nor are we at all certain that a plurality of humans are sitting in judgment.   It may be no more than the evangelist Timothy's judgment that is in Paul's mind.

[108] "Sins" (taken from the earlier part of this contrast between "some" and "others") is the understood subject of the plural verb "follow after."

[109] This is not to say the person is by his present sins forever disbarred from consideration for the eldership.   If he repents and his life changes, he may be considered at a later date for the office/ function.

for the eldership. Ascertaining a man's true qualifications takes time. There can be no haste in the laying on of hands! Unworthy men, whose "sins" lie below the surface, should not be ordained. On the other hand, worthy men, whose good qualities are not at first obvious, are not to be overlooked.

Deeds that are good are quite evident – The KJV translators have understood that the words "of some" found at the beginning of verse 24 also are to be taken with verse 25, so that version reads "likewise also the good works of some are manifest beforehand." "Good deeds" would be those deeds in accordance with God's standards. Such "deeds" may be explained by the qualities commended in verses like Matthew 25:35ff and James 1:27. Or, if "good deeds" are the opposite of "sins" in the previous verse, then this verse at least speaks of growth in Christian character and living or "holiness" (Hebrews 12:14; Romans 6:22). Self-sacrifice, generosity, stern principle, and a steady contending for the faith are not always known by those who have not benefited personally from the potential elder's sacrifice or generosity. "Evident" would be explained the same way the same word was in verse 24. If it is Timothy whose "judgment" is involved, and to whom either sins or "good deeds" are "evident beforehand," then this verse says that if Timothy will take a little time to get to know the men – rather than laying hands on some hastily – he need have no fear that men's good qualities will be missed. In some cases he will know about these good qualities even before he begins to make his careful investigation into the candidates' qualifications.

And those which are otherwise cannot be concealed – "Those which are otherwise" would be those good works which are not at first sight evident.[110] The good works have been done without fanfare. The growth is there; it is just not common knowledge to the casual observer. "Cannot be concealed" indicates that those hidden qualities which are not at once evident will not long remain hidden. A little investigation by Timothy, and he will know about those actions and characteristics which at once say this man is qualified to be ordained to the office of eldership. Just as the previous verse warned Timothy against any tendency toward hasty approval, this verse warns against any tendency to hasty condemnation. If Timothy would just exercise a little caution, and not be hasty in ordaining men to office, he would end up with good elders in the church at Ephesus. Likewise, if evangelists today will get to know their men, and only lay hands on those Christian men whom investigation shows to be doers of good, then the churches today will have good elders.

---

[110] While it is possible to understand "otherwise" to be a contrast to "good deeds," and so actually refer to "bad deeds or sins," such an interpretation would break the parallelism between the two verses. We therefore choose to understand "otherwise" as a contrast to "evident."

What an awesome privilege and responsibility it is for the evangelist to be on the lookout for good men to call into the Master's service as elders! Not only this, but it seems proper to reflect on the "authority" of the evangelist in the light of 1 Timothy 5. He is a supervisor over (or at least a promoter of) congregational activities, such as the care of widows and the financial support of the elders. He has a watch care over the lives of the individual members of the congregation. Sinning members are to be gently rebuked and appealed to. Those who fail to take care of their relatives are to be encouraged to do so, so the church is not burdened. He has a responsibility concerning elders who sin, to see that public rebuke is administered. His, too, is a leading responsibility to see to it that only qualified men are selected for the eldership, and then he has the right of ordaining them to their job of service. Add to these the responsibilities delineated earlier in the epistle: (1) He has a responsibility to grow in his own knowledge of the Word of God, so that he can impart sound doctrine as he preaches and teaches. He gets to read the Scriptures publicly, and then encourage and teach, so the listeners will put the truths from God into practice in their everyday lives. (2) He has the wonderful privilege to lead public worship, and to help his congregation prepare themselves to worship. (3) He is to teach people how to behave in the household of God.

D. The Evangelist's Concern for Slaves.   6:1-2b

6:1 -- Let all who are under the yoke as slaves – Chapter 6:1-2b continues Paul's admonitions with respect to how Timothy the evangelist should relate to various groups in the congregation.   These two verses are addressed to Christians who are slaves.   While the word "slaves" (*douloi*) can be used in several senses, here Paul is talking about literal slaves, as is clear from the fact that he also speaks of them as being "under the yoke."   "Under the yoke" calls attention to the fact that in the 1st century world, men and women slaves were regarded as little more than cattle; the power of the master over the slave was almost absolute, like that over his yoke-animals.   That slaves formed a considerable portion of the membership of the first Christian churches may be inferred from the frequency with which their duties are pressed upon them (see 1 Corinthians 7:21-24, 12:13; Ephesians 6:5-8; Colossians 3:11,12; 1 Peter 2:18 [*oi oiketai*], and 1 Corinthians 1:27-29).

Regard their own masters as worthy of all honor – "Masters" is *despotas*, the technical correlative of "slave."   Even an unsaved despot (master) was to be given honor by the Christian slave.   "Whenever it is at all possible thus to respect the master, let the slave do so."[1]   A Christian slave who has found freedom in Christ might be tempted to maintain less respect for his pagan master than he ought, particularly if the master were harsh and tyrannical.   Yet in such circumstances the cause of Christ is best served by an attitude of respect on the part of the Christian slave.   Slaves were to manifest the right spirit themselves, whatever their masters did; they were not to do anything that would dishonor Christ.   The slaves' new-found liberty in Christ gave them no warrant for less faithful service.   Hendriksen has a good survey of the life of the slave in the 1st century world, and how the gospel preachers met the issue.   His sentence that Paul "advocated neither outright revolt by the slaves nor the continuation of the status quo" is succinct.   His emphasis on the idea that Christianity would change the hearts both of master and slave, and thus change the institution, is in harmony with the idea that social betterment is a natural by-product of Christianity being put into practice.   Most writers feel the need to address the matter of slavery and why, if slavery is an evil, the apostles (and Jesus) did not attack this evil head-on.   Most attempts to answer to this question read in this way: The institution of slavery was well entrenched in the 1st century.   A problem any Christian faced was how to speak and act when Christian doctrine and the current social system came into conflict, as they were bound to do.   Paul did not handle the matter of slavery on the basis of theory, but with regard to the individual's responsibility for Christian conduct in whatever state he chanced to be.   Paul did not preach revolution.   By proclaiming the Gospel of Christ, which issues in a life of godliness, he accomplished much toward eventually ridding much of the world of the evil of slavery.

---

[1] Hendriksen, *op. cit.*, p.193.

Slavery was perhaps the most perplexing of all the questions Christianity had to face. It entered into all grades and ranks. It was common to all peoples and nations. The very fabric of society seemed knotted and bound together by this miserable institution. War and commerce were equally responsible for slavery in the Old World. To attempt to uproot it – to preach against it – to represent it in public teaching as hateful to God, shameful to man – would have been to preach and to teach rebellion and revolution in its darkest and most violent form. It was indeed the curse of the world; but the Master and His chosen servants took their own course and their own time to clear it away. Jesus and His disciples, such as Paul and John, left society as they found it, uprooting no ancient landmarks, alarming no ancient prejudices, content to live in the world as it was, and to do its work as they found it – trusting, by a new and lovely example, slowly and surely to raise men to a higher level, knowing that at last, by force of unselfishness, loving self-denial, brave patience, the old curses – such as slavery – would be driven from the world. Surely the result, so far, has not disappointed the hopes of the first teachers of Christianity.[2]

So that the name of God and our doctrine may not be spoken against – This is the reason the Christian slave was to show his pagan master "honor." "Our doctrine" is equivalent to Christianity as taught by the apostles and the New Testament prophets. (See the frequent use of the word "the doctrine" in the Pastoral Epistles, though with differing shades of meaning. 1 Timothy 1:10, 4:6,13,16, 5:17; 2 Timothy 3:10, 4:3; Titus 1:9, 2:10). "The slave ought to show the Christian spirit towards his master who was not a Christian; he ought to conduct himself so that Christianity would not be dishonored; he ought not to give his master occasion to say that the only effect of the Christian religion on the mind of a slave was to make him restless, discontented, dissatisfied, and disobedient."[3] If Christian slaves withheld the honor and respect due to their master, it would be as sure to bring reproach upon the Christian doctrine as if it taught insubordination and rebellion. The offending slave likely would be beaten, and the gospel and the Lord would be blamed by the unconverted for causing the rebellious or morose conduct. "Spoken against" ("blasphemed" KJV) is not necessarily "blaspheme" in its restricted sense. It often means "to speak evil of," "to defame," and the like. "God's redemptive revelation in Christ, in other words God's name, and also his instruction, the teaching of the gospel, would become contemptible in the eyes of the pagan masters if the Christian slaves treated them with disdain and the spirit of rebellion. And nothing is more important than God's name and His doctrine. These must not be exposed to ridicule and abuse."[4] An act, or course of action, on the part of professed servants of God, which gives occasion to the enemies of the Lord to blaspheme, is reckoned in Holy Scripture as a sin of the deepest dye.

---

[2] Spence, *op. cit.*, p.256,57.

[3] Barnes, *op. cit.*, p.191.

[4] Hendriksen, *op. cit.*, p.193.

Compare Nathan's words to King David (2 Samuel 12:14), or Paul's reproach to the Jews (Romans 2:24).

6:2 -- And let those who have believers as their masters – Paul now addresses Christian slaves who had Christian masters. A Christian slave with a Christian master might be inclined to think, "If my master is really a Christian, how can he keep me a *slave*? His religion must not amount to much. How can I be equal to my master in opportunities for salvation (Galatians 3:28), and yet be inferior to him at home?" Barnes, who wrote in the midst of a movement for the abolition of slavery, urged that the slave owner *became* a Christian, not that the man became a Christian and then purchased slaves. However, this might read more into the text than is warranted.

Not be disrespectful to them because they are brethren – The word translated "disrespectful" is composed of *phroneō*, 'to think,' and *kata*, 'down.' It means to think less of, to look down on someone. A Christian slave might begin to think, "Shall I remain my brother's slave? If he were truly Christian, he would not expect me to continue serving him." Such thoughts would poison relationships. A Christian slave might soon come to despise a Christian master who did not grant him freedom. Yet it appears that Christian slave owners were not compelled to free their slaves. They might be encouraged to do so, but were not compelled. (Compare Philemon in the matter of his slave, Onesimus.)

But let them serve them all the more – This phrase says something more about the manner in which Christian slaves serve their Christian masters. If a slave is in the exceptionally privileged position of having a Christian master – as compared to his lot when he had a pagan master – then let the slave render exceptional service! Serve with more cheerfulness and alacrity than they did before the master was converted. *Mallon* is not to be regarded as corrective ("rather"), but as intensive ("the more"). This does not mean that the slave of an unsaved master may render half-hearted service, but it does indicate that the slave of a Christian master has even more reason to render service. The reasons assigned for rendering such extra-special service follow in the next phrase.

Because those who partake of the benefit are believers and beloved – The KJV makes "partakers of the benefit" part of the predicate, rather than part of the subject as does the NASB. The KJV translators rendered it, "because they are faithful and beloved, partakers of the benefit." There is a good deal of obscurity in the sentence, but it seems that "partakers of the benefit" is the subject, not the predicate.[5] The difference in interpretation is this. If "partakers of the benefit"

---

[5] *Pulpit Commentary* gives two reasons for taking "partakers of the benefit" as being the subject, rather than the predicate. (1) The nearest antecedent for "the ones partaking" is "brothers," i.e., the Christian masters. (2) The construction of the two clauses (verses 2a and 2b) makes it likely that

is part of the predicate, then it is the Christian slave who benefits. If "partakers of the benefit" is the subject, then it is the Christian master who benefits. The "benefit" seems to have reference to who receives the "benefit of the labors of the slave." The slave's work did result in "benefit" or "profit" for the master. The Christian slave delights to see his brother in Christ receive "benefit."[6]

Barnes thinks "benefit" speaks of the "benefit of the gospel." (Such an interpretation would assist an abolitionist argument more than would a statement that the master gets "benefits" from the slave's work.) This is rather far-fetched. *Euergesia* means 'well-doing,' or 'a good deed done.' The meaning of *antilambanomen*, rendered "partakers," is also difficult to explain. The word occurs in only two other places in the New Testament (Luke 1:54, Acts 20:35), though it is used frequently in the LXX, and it has the meaning of "help." In the middle voice it means "to lay hold of." You may "lay hold of" for the purpose of helping, supporting, clinging to, laying claim to, holding in check, etc. (see Liddell and Scott). Thus, 1 Timothy 6:2 has the masters laying hold of the benefit for the purpose of enjoying it or using it. There does not seem to be any sense of reciprocity, as some think, in the use of the preposition *anti*. Neverthe-less, Hendriksen believes it should be rendered "reciprocate," suggesting that Christian masters are the ones who reciprocate exceptional service. He thinks Christian masters might take it upon themselves to give a "return" to the slave who gives ready and enthusiastic efforts on behalf of his master.[7]

Guthrie notes a certain ambiguity in the Greek grammar at this place (both "benefit" and "partakers" are ambiguous), so that the benefit may be either to the master or to the slave. The master gains a certain advantage from the slave's goodwill and extra work. The Christian master had a responsibility to his slave, to see that the slave benefits – especially if the "faithfulness and love" was mutual, as could be expected between Christian brothers. The word *pistoi* ("faithful," "believers") means the masters are Christians, too, just like the slaves. Since masters and slaves share a common faith, a relationship exists between Christian master and slave that does not exist if the master is unconverted. "Beloved" probably means the masters are "beloved by God," for so the word is often used. It is also true that the word "beloved" can speak of brother's love for brother. If that is the idea here, then Paul is reminding the Christian slave that he has an obli-

---

the subject in this clause ("those who partake of the benefits") are the same as the "masters" in the preceding sentence, since it would be indicated in the two clauses that the masters are "faithful" (2a) and "faithful and beloved" (2b) – expressions which are convertible terms.

[6] The "benefit" spoken of would be that special *service* – that service of love and good will running ahead of necessary duty – which the Christian slave gives to the Christian master.

[7] This sounds like "the reason you should work harder is so that you will get something extra in return". Is pay or hope of reward a proper motive to hold out for slaves to work harder?

gation in Christ to love his master, who is also a brother in Christ. Every good work the Christian does, be he slave or master, is, after all, done with the same spirit he would exhibit if he were personally serving Jesus Himself, rather than another human being. Slavery does not now exist in America, but the responsibility of conduct is the same for employees and employers.

VI. THE CHARGE CONCERNING THE EVANGE-LIST HIMSELF. 6:2c-21A

A. The Charge Concerning Topics to be Preached. 6:2c

6:2c -- Teach and preach these *principles* – Where does the new paragraph begin? (1) The paragraphing of the NASB has this sentence as a summary of what precedes. "These *principles*" would have reference to something already written.[8] Guthrie concludes that the "principles" intended are probably all the subjects mentioned thus far in the whole epistle. Some think everything from 5:1ff is included in "these principles" (i.e., the evangelist's responsibility to old and young members, to the care of widows, to the care of elders, and to the care of slaves and masters, 5:1ff). Others write that what Paul has been saying with reference to slaves (6:1,2) must be continually repeated in the ears of people. Timothy must keep on teaching, and keep on urging, because folk would not easily change their social customs with reference to the institution of slavery. (2) The paragraphing of the RSV and the Nestle-Aland Greek text takes this sentence as introductory for the paragraph that follows. When read together with verse 3, this sentence says that Timothy is to stand in obvious contrast to those who "teach otherwise." It seems better to begin the new paragraph ("The Charge Concerning the Evangelist Himself") with this phrase.[9] Thus, verse 2c becomes the first of several imperatives that together make up this "charge" to the evangelist.[10] Paul actually uses the word "charge" for the first time in verse 13.

---

[8] The usual meaning for the Greek word *tauta* is to point to something already said, though this is not its invariable use in the New Testament. (*Hode* was the word regularly used to refer to what follows, at least in classical Greek.) *Tauta* at times in the New Testament refers to what follows.

[9] If we take this phrase about teaching and preaching "these principles" (*tauta*) as the beginning of a new point, we must still decide to what "these *principles*" has reference to. The topics Timothy is to preach and teach could well include all that has been said thus far in this epistle.

[10] If we let the imperatives found in chapter 6 become the main points of this "Charge Concerning the Evangelist Himself," we find a certain relief from one of the problems many authors have confessed as they begin comments on this last chapter of 1 Timothy, namely, that "the concluding portion of the Epistle contains no clear sequence of thought" (Bruce) or "the fact that Paul is speaking more personally to Timothy accounts for the rather loose grouping of thoughts in this final chapter" (Kent, *op. cit.*, p.184).

"Teach" and "preach" are present tense imperatives.   One part of the charge Paul gives to Timothy is a command to "continue to preach and teach these things!"   Certain topics are to be constantly emphasized – sound doctrine, prayer in public worship, the importance of good church leaders, how to recognize false teachers and teaching, how to relate to other people in the church.   Note how this pertains to the subject of whether or not there are absolutes in the realm of ethics.

> What is especially important in this connection is that, wholly contrary to certain present-day trends, the apostle is definitely NOT of the opinion that all propositions touching religion and ethics are necessarily subjective and relative, and that the only justifiable method of arriving at some measure of truth is that of asking questions, such as, 'Brother Brown, what do you think about this?' and "Brother Smith, what is our opinion about that?' *Paul has accepted certain definite propositions which he considers to be the truth of God! He wants these taught! And he requests that Timothy urge their acceptance and application to life!* See also 4:11 and 5:7.[11]

B. The Charge to Avoid Improper Motives. 6:3-10

1. Evidences of improper motives.   6:3

6:3 -- If anyone advocates a different doctrine – In the following phrases, Paul explains the "different doctrine" he has in mind. It is a doctrine that "does not agree with sound words" and which does not encourage "conforming to godliness." Who is intended by the general designation "anyone" is not at all certain. "Who the teachers were who taught otherwise is not known nor is it known what arguments they employed."[12]   Barnes also supposed that the "different doctrine" the false teachers were urging was that slaves should at once assert their freedom, that they should refuse obedience to their masters. If the "different doctrine" is not just limited to one specific topic (e.g., the relation of slaves to masters), then "anyone" could include any teacher, Timothy himself included. "Modern indifference to Christian doctrine is not an apostolic trait. Paul exhibits no toleration whatever toward those who would deviate from the well-defined standard for truth, the Gospel message (cp. 1:3-20)."[13]

And does not agree with sound words – On the adjective "sound," see comments at 1 Timothy 1:10. "Sound words" would be those which supply spiritual life and health to the believer. The word translated "agree" (*proserchetai*) means 'come over to, join, fall in with.'   "Proselyte" (i.e., a convert to Judaism) comes

---

[11] Hendriksen, *op. cit.*, p. 194.

[12] Barnes, *op. cit.*, p.193.

[13] Kent, *op. cit.*, p.185.

from the same root. *Proserchetai* is very common in the New Testament in the literal sense of 'coming to' or 'approaching,' but perhaps only here does it have its metaphorical sense of 'assenting to' ("agree" NASB). "The steps seem to be, first, approaching a subject with the mind with a view of considering it; and *then* consenting to it – coming over to it."[14] The verb is a little stronger than 'consent' or 'agree with.' A mere listener may eventually agree with the words of a speaker. An enthusiastic listener will 'come over to' or join the speaker.[15]

Those of our Lord Jesus Christ – What Paul means by "sound words" is here further described and identified. The genitive may be understood in either of two ways. (1) It may refer to words Jesus Himself said. (2) It may indicate words about Jesus (i.e., in harmony with what He taught and lived). Those who opt for the first explanation offer the following elucidations: Paul could be referring to such well-known sayings as, "Render to Caesar the things that are Caesar's"; or, "Blessed are the meek, for they shall inherit the earth"; or, "If any man will come after me, let him take up his cross daily and follow me"; "But I say unto you, Resist not evil"; "Love your enemies, pray for them which despitefully use you." Acts 20:35 might be an illuminating parallel. The words the apostles and evangelists used as they taught were the very words that came from Christ's mouth, and were exemplified in His life and death. This expression may refer to the oral tradition (which antedates our gospel narratives) about the ministry and message of Jesus. It was fixed at an early date, and repeated exactly time after time.[16] Those who opt for the second explanation offer these suggestions: Spicq thinks Paul has Luke's Gospel in mind. Others say Paul has both Matthew and Luke in view since both were circulating by the time Paul wrote 1 Timothy.

And with the doctrine conforming to godliness – "Godliness" was explained at 1 Timothy 2:2, 3:16, and 4:7,8. The people who "advocate a different doctrine" are here characterized by a second trait. Not only will these self-willed men refuse to acquiesce to "sound words, those of our Lord Jesus Christ," they will also fail to insist upon a holy life. Sooner or later, the lives of the false teachers will show how far from Christian truth they really are, for Christian truth is inseparable from purity, single-heartedness, self-forgetfulness, and patience. The wrong motives that frequently lead men to advocate a "different doctrine" are identified in the following verses: pride and the desire for financial gain.

---

[14] Hervey, *op. cit.*, p.120.

[15] Hendriksen, *op. cit.*, p.195.

[16] See the delightful presentation of how informal controlled oral tradition still is handed on in K.E. Bailey, "Middle Eastern Oral Tradition and the Synoptic Gospels," *Expository Times* 106:12 (Sept. 1995), p.363-367. A longer article by Bailey, "Informal Controlled Oral Tradition and the Synoptic Gospels" appeared in *The Asia Journal of Theology* 5:1 (1995), p. 34-54.

2. Two kinds of wrong motives.   6:4,5

6:4 -- He is conceited – The verb *tuphroō*, as explained at 1 Timothy 3:6, means to inflate, puff up (with pride).

And **understands nothing** – The "and" added by the NASB may be misleading. The Greek word is a circumstantial participle, and it could be translated "because he knows nothing." So rendered,[17] the rest of verses 4-5 give the reasons the false teacher is "puffed up." We say the "rest of verses 4-5" because several circumstantial participles follow the verb "puffed up" –"understanding nothing, being diseased (doting, has a morbid interest), being corrupted and deprived, and supposing (godliness is a means of gain)."[18] The conceit grows first from the fact that the false teacher does not understand the nature of Christianity like he thinks he does. Christianity, in fact, everywhere condemns pride.

But he has a morbid interest in controversial questions and disputes about words – The KJV read "doting." The margin of the NASB offers "is sick about" as a way to translate *nosōn*. In classical Greek, this verb had the idea of "being in an unsound state" in mind or body. So here it could mean "going mad about" or "having a morbid love of." It obviously is chosen in order to make a pointed contrast with "healthy words" by which sound doctrine was described in verse 3. "Controversial questions" translates *dzētēseis* (seekings, questions, controversies), while "disputes about words" translates *logomachias* (word fights). Ketcherside and Barnes, among others, note that Jews abounded in disputes of this sort, and it would seem probable that such persons here referred to were the same Jewish-Gnostic false teachers met in chapter 1. Hendriksen, agreeing that there is something Jewish in the background, offers the following illustration as an example of battles over words and questions.

> When a person rejects sound or healthy words, sickness results. This sickness reveals itself in a "morbid craving for controversies and word-battles." Somewhat after the fashion exhibited in the Talmud, he will get excited about questions like this one, "Is it permissible on the Sabbath to throw away the pits of dates?" One person might answer, "The pits of dates to which some of the meat adheres may be thrown away. Other pits must not be thrown away." Another person would disagree in no uncertain terms. Again, the question

---

[17] Circumstantial participles may be rendered by the helping words "while" (used with present tense participles), "after" (used with aorist tense participles), "since," "if," "although," "because," etc. Any helper that makes sense is a possible translation.

[18] Whereas the first two participles are nominative singular (thus agreeing with the "he" in "he is puffed up"), the last three participles are genitive plural, having been (as is likely the case) attracted to the case of their nearest antecedent ("men"), which was in the genitive case. Nevertheless, we suppose the "men" are not a different group than was earlier designated as "anyone who teaches a different doctrine," the same persons who are "puffed up."

might be asked, "If it be permissible to throw them away, where and how should they be thrown?" And the answer might be, "They are to be thrown outside." To which another might reply, "No, indeed, they should be thrown under the bed." Or he might say, "The person confronted on the Sabbath with the problem of what to do with date pits should turn his face toward the back of the bed and throw out the pits with his tongue."[19]

The question that immediately suggests itself to present-day evangelists and church leaders is whether or not we are ever involved in such controversies and word battles. Commentators have offered some sobering examples of what they believe are present-day "word battles." Spence writes about "verbal disputes, barren and idle controversies about words rather than things; such wild war as has raged, not only in the days of Paul and Timothy, but all through the Christian ages, on such words as Predestination, Election, Faith, Inspiration, Person, Regeneration, etc." Hendriksen urges that the largely futile controversies in his own Reformed church circles, as, for example between Infralapsarians and Supralapsarians, or the "hot" debate about the age of the earth, are examples of modern day word battles. In the Restoration Movement, some would classify as word battles the on-going debates about the meaning of the word "sing" (a capella, or not?), and the eschatological questions (pre-, post-, or a-millennialism). These attempts to apply this Timothy passage to contemporary matters in the church may or may not be legitimate examples of what Paul writes about when he condemns "controversial questions and disputes about words." There is also something to be said about legitimate "debates" and controversies; for when one "contends earnestly for the faith once for all delivered to the saints" (Jude 3), that would not be condemned as a debate about useless topics. Of course, it is a real tragedy when profitless debates tear apart congregations, break up old friendships, and sow the seeds of bitter irreconcilable hatred. The cause of Christ is hurt.

Out of which arise envy – Quibblings and word-battles produce bitter fruits, several of which are named, beginning with "envy." "Envy" (*phthonos*) is to be filled with malignant ill will or spite against someone who has defeated us. It is the uneasiness, pain, mortification, and discontent produced by the perceived prosperity or superior knowledge the other disputant showed, given that he won the argument!

Strife, abusive language, evil suspicions – "Strife" is *epis*, "bitter discord, constant wranglings." The person who has lost the argument, smarting under defeat, attempts to get even. Such contention, resulting from holding different opinions, results from dogmatism, which seeks to bind opinions as law. "Strife" is sin, one of the works of the flesh (Galatians 5:20). Out of the envy and strife comes "abusive language" (*blasphēmiai*), "blasphemies" or "insults." Bitter ac-

---

[19] Hendriksen, *op. cit.*, p.196.

cusations, made in harsh and abusive language, are directed towards those who will not change their minds and agree with the one speaking the abusive words. This is a common effect of disputes, and more commonly of disputes about small and unimportant matters. And the disputants are filled with mistrust and evil suspicions about each other. "Suspicions" (*huponoiai*) occurs only here in the New Testament. In classical Greek it means "suspicion," or any under-thought. It has reference to those surmisings, those uncharitable insinuations in which angry controversialists indulge toward one another. They suspect the opponent's every action, word, and gesture as being "evil." "Evil" is *ponerai*, which has the connotation that the actions are not only bad in themselves, but they are trying to get others to be evil. Suspicions arise that our opponents are led to hold their views, not by the love of the truth but from sordid or worldly motives. It is always hard to do justice to the motives of one who seems to us to be living in sin, or to believe it possible that he acts from right motives. Frequently, when someone differs with us, we suspect him of being dishonest and unscrupulous, and accuse him of holding his views because of some unworthy or sordid reason.

6:5 -- And constant friction – "Constant friction" is the last of a list of the bitter fruits resulting from a "morbid interest in controversial questions and disputes about words" (verse 4). The KJV reads "perverse disputings," which reflects the Greek word *paradiatribai*, the reading found in the Textus Receptus. The noun *diatribai* (English, "diatribe") means, among other things, a "discussion" or "argument." The addition of *para-* gives the sense of "perverse discussion" or "disputing." The NASB translates a different word, *diaparatribai*, a noun that means (in Polybius, in its uncompounded form) "collision," or "friction" or "provocation" and the like. This is the reading of the manuscripts older than the Textus Receptus. Think of mutual altercations and incessant frictions, and mutual irritations. Each opponent 'boils' underneath. Each rubs the other the wrong way (note the root idea of the original). Their religious discussions frequently assume the nature of diatribes – full of scurrilous abuse, stinging insult, heated invective, and thinly veiled disdain. The addition of the preposition *dia-* suggests these disputes would be no mere temporary difficulties, but the false teachers would indefinitely prolong their weary story. They were "constant" and continued wranglings. With this word Paul ends the list of spoiled fruit that is produced from the teaching of the false teachers who reject the wholesome doctrine of the gospel just as Jesus and the apostles gave it.

Between men of depraved mind and deprived of the truth – Where does "between" come from that we find in the NASB? The Greek simply has a genitive case, and says that all the fruits just listed are characteristic "of (or result from) men of corrupt mind and deprived of the truth" – this is their not unexpected lifestyle. "Depraved mind," *diephtharmenōn*, is a perfect tense participle, and "mind" is the area or specification in which the corruption has occurred. The participle is passive in voice, which implies someone else, or something else, as the agent who did the "corrupting" or "changing for the worse." Was it the false teaching they embraced that did it, or was it the pride that did it? "The language used seems to imply that for these unhappy men a time had existed when corruption had not done its fatal work."[20] The change for the worse was a gradual thing,[21] but by now for the errorists at Ephesus the action has proceeded so far that they have now entered an abiding state (perfect tense) of being "depraved (in) mind." The "truth" – ultimately, the truth that God has revealed – of which they are now deprived may be taken either objectively or subjectively. If subjective, it speaks of a personal appropriation of the truth, from which they have fallen away. If objective, it speaks of objective revelation in the Word, from which they are separated. "Deprived" (*apesterēmenōn*) is rendered "destitute" in the KJV and "bereft" in the ASV. The latter implies they once had possession of the truth, but had lost it by their own fault. They had fallen away from the truth they once had. The form used here is a perfect tense. It indicates a now permanent state resulting from past continuing actions.

Their situation is one of complete and permanent separation from the truth. This participle is also passive in voice. Someone else or something else is the agent who has "deprived them" of the truth. Again, did the devil blind their minds (2 Corinthians 4:14), or was it the "pride and doting" that did it, or is a judicial action on God's part in response to their own initial wrong behavior also in view? The whole thrust of this expression now depends on how "truth" was taken. If subjective, it says the false teachers once had personally appropriated the truth of the gospel, they had been truly converted, but now have lost it. This would be in harmony with what the Scriptures elsewhere teach, of the possibility of once being saved, and then again being lost because of lack of faithfulness. If objective, it says they had at some former time been in contact with the truth (is this "gospel truth"[22] or "truth" as it was known through the Old Testament Scriptures), but now no longer possess it. This latter would be in harmony with what was learned in our special study about the Gnostic-Judaizers, who started with the Jewish Scriptures, then added human speculations and doctrines of demons, till the original revelation is no longer important and even becomes totally repudiated and forgotten.[23]

---

[20] Spence, *op. cit.*, p.260.

[21] Don't miss the negative impact of this verse on the doctrine of total depravity inherited from parents.

[22] "Truth" has regularly, in 1 Timothy, been a reference to the truth of the gospel. See 1 Timothy 2:4,7, 3:15, and 4:3.

[23] As earlier documented, 2nd century Gnosticism was a Christian heresy, that it grew from certain Christian starting points. It was also documented that Gnosticism, in its infancy, was a Jewish

Who suppose that godliness is a means of gain[24] – "Suppose" is a present tense participle, and being in the genitive plural agrees with "men." We could use "while" or "because" to help translate it. Either way, it suggests a second motive that led men to become false teachers, and thus introduces a second wrong motive (along with pride) against which Paul is warning Timothy. "Godliness is a means of gain" is much to be preferred to the KJV, "gain is godliness."[25] The KJV utterly confused the subject[26] with the predicate, and in so doing destroyed the connection between this clause and what follows in verse 6. The Greek brings out that these men are supposing all along that the practice of their religious profession will be lucrative and will serve their worldly interests. Their thinking is that "religion is gain!" In Titus 1:11, similar warning is given concerning those who subvert whole households, "teaching things they should not teach, for the sake of sordid gain." The false teachers looked at their 'religion' as a "means of making money."[27] They pretend to be religious: they make an outward show of "godliness," just for the sake of becoming rich. "Whether these false teachers charged high fees for their specious teachings, or used their garrulous religious profession as a cloak for material advancement is not clear."[28] Being devoid of the truth, the false teachers measure everything by financial considerations and practice their religion in hopes of prospering materially. Such persons are more concerned about finding out what's in it for them than they are in the temporal and eternal spiritual needs of their audiences.

---

heresy, that it grew from certain Jewish starting points. So in verse 5, the question is whether the incipient Gnosticism, against which Paul is warning the Ephesian church, has departed from, or is deprived of Christian "truth" (the truth of the gospel) or Jewish "truth" (the truth as taught in the Hebrew Scriptures). It is not possible to determine the meaning of "truth" with absolute certainty.

[24] The Textus Receptus, and thus also the KJV, has another clause in verse 5, "from such withdraw thyself." If we were to accept it as genuine, Timothy is instructed to have no communion or fellowship with the false teachers.

[25] If we were to paraphrase the KJV as "making money is their religion," it would be necessary to render the participle by some word like 'thinking' rather than 'supposing.' Something else of a technical nature also must be considered. If we treat "gain" as the subject (as does the KJV), then we must be cognizant of Colwell's Rule of Grammar (E.J. Colwell, *Journal of Biblical Literature*, 1933, p.lii), which reads, "A definite predicate nominative has the article when it follows the linking verb; it does not have the article when it precedes the linking verb." "Gain" would be definite, and the word order would put some emphasis on the word. "GAIN is their religion!"

[26] The presence of the article "the" before "godliness" in the Greek makes it clear that "godliness" is the subject. Common sense also confirms this understanding. It is doubtful if anyone ever thought that gain was godliness, but the reverse is often inferred. (Kent, *op. cit.*, p.186)

[27] Kent (*op. cit.*, p.186-7) observes, "How often the Christian church has been plagued by [preachers and leaders who held] this sordid, materialistic view, that their profession of Christianity (i.e., their godliness) was to be a source of personal gain. Tetzel and the papacy, with their sale of indulgences, is a noted example ... And how many religious workers of recent times have capitalized on the financial!" One is broken hearted by the movie "Elmer Gantry," which has, all too sadly, rather clearly depicted the character of too many modern evangelists. Contrast this with the spirit of Paul, who refused at times to take his daily bread from his converts (2 Thessalonians 3:8).

[28] Guthrie, *op. cit.*, p.112.

3. The prevention of wrong motives.   6:6-8

6:6 -- But – The opening word "but" tells us that what we are reading is in contrast with something written just before this. He has been writing about the wrong motives that led to men embracing and then promulgating false teaching. "But" Timothy is to avoid these! Paul is now (verses 6-8) going to give Timothy some help so he may avoid the wrong motive of "money." Because the accumulation of earthly riches was one of the chief concerns that motivated the false teachers, Paul proceeds to deal with some of its dangers, and lays down principles of universal significance. If Timothy – or any evangelist or any Christian – lets these principles fill his heart, he will be greatly protected and guarded against the possibility that "desire for gain" will become one of his driving motives.

Godliness *actually* is a means of great gain – One of the "faithful sayings" (see 1 Timothy 4:8) has said that "Godliness is profitable for all things." Paul now shows that that faithful saying is true, when understood in the correct sense, not the sense just condemned. "Great gain" confirms that the godly man is rich indeed. He wants nothing in this world but what God has given him, and has acquired riches which, unlike the riches of this world, he can take away with him (cp. Luke 12:33). One might say that there was a sense in which the false teachers' thoughts were true – "godliness is a means of great gain." The error in their thinking was their notion that the best and most desirable "gain" was only earthly riches. Laying up riches in heaven is where real gain is to be found, not just in amassing this world's goods.

When accompanied by contentment – The word *autarkeia* (from *autos*, "self," and *arkeo*, "be satisfied or content") occurs elsewhere in the New Testament only in 2 Corinthians 9:8 where it is rendered "sufficiency." It means 'sufficient in or of itself' or 'needing no external aid.' In this context, where desire for worldly riches is the thing being opposed, "contentment" would speak of needing or desiring no more worldly riches than has already been provided by God. Paul says a man's satisfaction or sufficiency should not be connected with his outward circumstances. The godly man's satisfaction is independent of poverty or wealth. Paul does not praise poverty, nor does he declare that possessing a large amount of worldly riches is a crime. He is declaring that in contrast with the mercenary attitude of the false teachers, "godliness accompanied by contentment" is greater riches than all the offerings collected by the false teachers. Paul himself had learned such contentment (Philippians 4:11-13), and he recommends it to us. Foster has commented, "Godliness of the right kind, with no mercenary thought of its being used as a steppingstone to wealth or worldly acclaim, but coupled with a pure conscience and peace of soul, will furnish satisfaction far beyond anything this world offers. This is 'great gain'." (Foster, *op. cit.*, p.377)

6:7 -- For – Verse 7, beginning with "for," gives a reason for what was just said in verses 5 and 6 about the relative unimportance of gaining this world's goods, as compared to the weighty importance of "godliness with contentment" (KJV).

We have brought nothing into the world – Paul is perhaps thinking of Job's famous saying, "Naked I came from my mother's womb, and naked I shall return" (Job.1:21). See also Ecclesiastes 5:15. But there is a difference between what Paul writes and those Old Testament passages. Those passages carry a sense of resignation; they see only the earthly side of the grave, and it seems futile. Paul speaks of contentment growing out of things eternal. Paul is not thinking of present futility, but of eternal joy. "We bring no property with us into the world – no clothing, no jewels, no gold – and it is equally clear that we can take nothing with us when we leave earth ... This is an obvious reason why we should be contented if our actual needs are supplied."[29] Thus the gaining of material acquisitions can be only of temporary significance. Since God provides for His righteous ones the few things they actually need while on earth (Matthew 6:33), the possession or lack of material riches should not unduly disturb the minds of godly people. The material things of this life are subject to loss, damage, destruction by use (Colossians 2:22), or such changes of circumstances as may render them worthless (1 Timothy 6:17). But treasures laid up in heaven never waste away. They are eternal. No wonder Paul was content. "Every earthly possession is only meant for this life – for the period between the hour of birth and the hour of death. We enter this world with nothing, we shall leave the world with nothing."[30] Orrin Root (*Standard Lesson Commentary*, 1985-86, p.91) comments, "We can't take our money beyond the grave; and if we could, what would it be worth in a city where gold is used like blacktop to pave the street? Why give top priority to getting rich when our riches must soon be left behind?"

So we cannot take anything out of it either – For "so," there is a marginal note in the NASB to the effect that "later manuscripts read, 'it is clear then'." Indeed, there is a problem with the grammar in the last part of this verse: the beginning word (*hoti*) is regularly translated "because," but such a meaning here is not easy to explain.[31] One interesting suggestion is that the correct reading shows that the controlling factor is exit rather than entry into this life. We have no control over the circumstances into which we were born, but we can exercise considerable control over our circumstances while we are here; any emphasis on simply acquiring the transitory riches of this world, while at the same time ignoring godliness, will make the exit a sad time indeed. Verse 7 is still giving a reason

---

[29] Barnes, *op. cit.*, p.198.

[30] Spence, *op. cit.*, p.261.

[31] Hendriksen, in a footnote #96, offers half-a-dozen proposed attempts at supplying the suppressed idea, but none is entirely satisfactory.

why "godliness with contentment" (verse 6) is such an abidingly important desire each man should cultivate.   The truly pious person has peace with God, spiritual joy, assurance of salvation, the conviction that "God causes all things to work together for good to those who love [Him]" (Romans 8:28).   Hence, he feels no need of ample earthly goods stored up for many years, for they never really satisfy the soul.   He is content with what he has.   "If we could take anything with us when death parts soul and body there would at once be an end to the 'contentment' (verse 6), for the future then would in some way be dependent on the present."[32] "If we die as we are born, without material possessions, then the only thing that has been gained during this life which will remain for the life to come is godliness, which has laid up treasures in heaven."[33]   Verse 7 is quoted by Polycarp (AD 115) in his letter to the Philippians.   Such a reference shows that this letter we call 1 Timothy was known and used in the Church even at that early date.

6:8 -- And if we have food and covering – "Food" (*diatrophas*) is found only here in the New Testament.   "Covering" (*skepasmata*)[34] is plural in the Greek – "coverings" – and in all probability includes the dwelling in which a man resides as well as the clothing he wears.   Paul emphasizes again that contentment should come into the heart of the Christian who has the basic things of life.   "When we have all we really need (and our Father knows and provides), why fret about the attractive things we do not need?   Our happy relationship with God is worth more than all the unneeded riches of the world.   Let us give top priority to that happy relationship." (Root, *op. cit.*, p.91)

With these we shall be content – Perhaps verse 8 gives a definition of Christian contentment.   If the Christian has the basic necessities in this life, he has enough! Though the Greek is a simple future tense, some writers (following the KJV) think it is used as an exhortation: "Let us be content."   There is no contradiction between this verse and 1 Timothy 4:1-5.   There Paul warns the church against a false, unreal asceticism, which was teaching men to look upon the rich gifts of this world, its beauties and its delights, as of themselves sinful, forgetting that these things were God's creations and were given for man's use and enjoyment. Here Paul is pressing home the truth that the highest good on earth is godliness accompanied by contentment, which neither rejects nor deems evil the fair things of this life, but which also never covets or longs for them.   It is one thing to be rich; it is another to wish to be rich.   In God's providence, a man may have riches without those riches necessarily being sin.   But coveting and longing for wealth expose a person to many grave dangers, as Paul will show in the following verses.

---

[32] Spence, *ibid.*

[33] Kent, *op. cit.*, p.188.

[34] This form is found only here in the New Testament.   Two kindred words, *skepē* and *skepas* are used of the covering or shelter of clothes, or tents, or houses.

4. The results of a wrong motive. 6:9-10

6:9 -- But -- To further enforce the exhortation to "contentment" (verses 6,8), Paul refers to some of the evils which necessarily attend an insatiable desire to be rich. While what is said about the "desire to get rich" is true for all men, it must be remembered that in the context Paul is warning Timothy the evangelist against falling victim to this evil motive. Preachers sometimes are not well paid compared with men and women in secular vocations,[35] and they may be tempted to think that their lot in life should be somewhat better off financially than it is.

Those who want to get rich -- It is not those already rich, but those who are ever grasping to become so. It is those who desire, or intend to become wealthy. It is those whose minds are set on becoming rich(er). The KJV reads "They that will be rich." "Will be rich" is not just a simple future tense, meaning that some are going to be rich out in the future. Paul is writing of those who *wish* to be rich, who *set their will* on getting rich, who mistakenly give top priority to riches. Paul is no Stoic. It is not "desire" as such that is condemned. In this passage, it is "desire to be rich." Such people fall into "temptation, etc." Six hurtful and deleterious things which accompany a "desire to be rich" are now listed.

Fall into temptation -- The present tense verb, "fall," suggests a continual falling, not just a one-time thing, but over and over again. The desire to be rich leads them to over and over again find themselves being tempted. They fall time after time into temptation. The preposition "into" seems to introduce not only the word "temptation," which immediately follows, but also the next several words -- "snare and desires." Some modern translations therefore render it "into a temptation and a snare ...," so that all the nouns that are dependent on the preposition "into" are treated alike. The word translated "temptation" can mean either "trial" or "temptation" (cp. James 1:2,12). "Temptation to sin" is evidently the idea here, as the context would suggest. "Those longing to be rich fall into the temptation to increase their worldly goods, even at the sacrifice of principle. Some unlawful method of gratifying their passion for gain will present itself; conscientious scruples will be thrown to the winds, and they who wish to be rich will fall into the temptation."[36] Those desiring to be rich are "tempted to do wicked things in order to accomplish their purposes. It is extremely difficult to cherish the desire to be rich, as the leading purpose of the soul, and to be an honest

---

[35] We have regularly taught that a preacher's support from the church to which he preaches should at least be comparable to the average earned by the people to whom he is preaching. Some rural churches find it difficult to pay the preacher as they would like to -- we are not speaking against this. But churches that tend to "starve" their preachers surely will have to answer in the Judgment for putting their preachers in a more easily temptable position because of being strapped financially.

[36] Spence, *op. cit.*, p.262.

man."[37]   A person with worldly gain as top priority will necessarily find his motives and worldly ambition leading him into predicaments that bring temptation to sin.   It becomes tempting to compromise one's integrity of character in order to get ahead.   When top priority is given to amassing riches, "honesty, generosity, and helpfulness have to take second place, or third or fourth place. Those engrossed in the pursuit of riches are snared in temptations to disregard others, to become cruel and grasping and friendless" (Root, *op. cit.*, p.91).

The context suggests there is something about "fall(ing) into temptation" that is blameworthy.   On the one hand, in a world in which the devil is active, men cannot help it if they are tempted from time to time.   The Bible also teaches that men who endure temptation are pronounced blessed.   But it is not implied that they are tempted through their own actions; they do not invite the temptation. Jesus was tempted – more than once and in all points like as we -- but He surely did not go looking for the temptation, like a man does whose driving desire is to be rich!   The desire to be rich(er) opens the door for temptations.   Some write along the lines that what is wrong is that the man has fallen into the sin to which he was tempted.   The falling or entering into temptation indicates also a yielding under the test.   Others explain that what is wrong is that a man ought not to put himself into the position where he invites the devil to tempt him the more.   What is blameworthy is inviting the temptations, or taking no precautions against the possibility of being tempted when they know such a possibility exists.   To the one whose supreme purpose is to acquire wealth, there are always opportunities of a questionable nature that are presented to his mind whereby he can take advantage and acquire still more wealth.   There is something incongruous when a man prays, "Do not permit us to be tempted," and at the same time harbors a desire for more, a desire that his earthly goods may be increased or his position bettered.   Do we not realize that our longing for an increase of riches will hinder the Lord from answering our request for limitations on the temptations?

And a snare – The illustration is carried a step farther and pictures the victim who fell as now caught in a trap.   As a snare (see the word explained at 1 Timothy 3:7) keeps an animal imprisoned, so the unchecked desire for wealth will cause a man to find he has fallen into a "trap."   "The net was sprung upon him, and he cannot escape.   The idea is that those who have this desire [to become rich] become so *entangled*, that they cannot easily escape ... In their efforts to make more money, they are no longer free men.   They become so involved in these things that they cannot break away from them if they would."[38]   Snares are everywhere around the person whose chief motive is "to get richer."   They find

---

[37] Barnes, *op. cit.*, p.198

[38] *ibid.*

themselves entrapped in temptation to lie, cheat, steal, to sell products they know to be harmful rather than helpful, to cover up wrongs in order to make some gain. Further, when a person faces in the wrong direction, one sin can lead to another. Questionable business transactions lead to dishonesty of various kinds. Lust for power and importance may lead to disregard for moral laws as well as disregard for the rights and liberties of man. When it comes to riches, no one will go to heaven simply because he is poor, and no one will go to hell simply because he is rich. It is the attitude a person has toward riches, and the use he makes of them, that matters. Now it is very possible for a person to "will" to be rich who has very little and may never have much. If that is his driving ambition, temptation will be increased for him upon every hand; he will find himself constantly seeking to extricate himself from some scheme that traps him as a snare.

And many foolish and harmful desires – The desire to be rich never walks alone. One kind of craving leads to another. The person who craves riches generally also yearns for honor, popularity, power, ease, the satisfaction of the desires of the flesh, etc. Some of these "desires" are "foolish." They are not such as intelligent and immortal beings should pursue. These new desires into which men fall (all stemming from a desire to be rich) are "senseless" (*anoētous*), "for they cannot be logically defended, nor do they bring real satisfaction."[39] Spence (*op. cit.*, p.262) explains, "The desires ... are well named 'foolish,' because in so many instances they are passionate desires for things utterly undesirable, the possession of which can afford neither pleasure nor advantage." The desires are foolish because one sacrifices what is better to gratify them. Others of these new desires into which men fall are "harmful" or "hurtful" (*blaberas*); that is, they are injurious to morals, to health, and to the soul, not only of the one desiring to get rich, but often to others who are affected by the "greedy" person's actions. "They do great damage to one's character and spiritual life, and they dissipate one's energies and call away one's interest from spiritual activity."[40] The desires are hurtful because they destroy relationships that are rich and full.

Which plunge men into ruin and destruction – The nearest antecedent of "which" is "foolish and harmful desires." Those are the things which lead to ruin and destruction. The word translated "plunge" (*buthidzō*) is used elsewhere in the New Testament only at Luke 5:7, to describe the sinking of a boat overloaded with fish. Here in Timothy, the sinking is caused by the excessive load of riches, temptations, and sins. "Plunge" ("drown" KJV) is the image not just of a person drowning, but of a wreck, where the ship and all that is in it go down together.[41]

---

[39] Kent, *op. cit.*, p.189.

[40] Kent, *ibid*.

[41] Barnes, *op. cit.*, p.199.

Can any distinction in meaning be understood in the words "ruin" and "destruction"? Both words, *olethros* and *apōleia*, refer to utter ruin and destruction. *Olethros*, a classical Greek word, is also used by Paul at 1 Corinthians 5:5 for the "destruction of (the body, his flesh)." *Apōleia* is more frequently used in the New Testament than in classical Greek; in most cases in the New Testament, when it is used of persons, it has the connotation of "perishing in hell." Thus, not a few commentators speak of "ruin" as being the complete, total ruin of happiness, virtue, and reputation during this life – and "destruction" as having reference to eternal punishment in the next life. "'Destruction' [ruin] refers rather to the wreck and ruin of the body, whilst 'perdition' belongs rather to the more awful ruin of the eternal soul."[42] The soul whose initial motive was a desire to be rich finds that in the end his love of money has eventually marred and ruined him – both for this life and the life to come.

> Note the progressive and climactic character of the movement portrayed [in verse 9]. First, these men are described as desiring the wrong thing, namely material wealth. Soon they lose their footing and fall into temptation and a snare and numerous hurtful and senseless cravings. Finally, these cravings plunge them into ruin and destruction. Wretched men! They have guided their vessel to the very brink of the cataract, which, in turn, plunges them into the awesome depths ... Instead of the *gain* which they were seeking (verse 5), the men whose hearts are set on worldly riches experience only *loss*.[43]

6:10 -- For – "For" shows verse 10 gives a reason for something just said. What happens to the man who desires to be rich – temptations, snares, harmful desires, ruin and perdition -- is true, "for the love of money is a root of all sorts of evil." It leads to other evils!

The love of money is a root of all sorts of evil – Explaining "love of money" (*philarguria*), Kent observes, "Riches can be the source of much that is good. But the desire for riches, which characterizes the lives of those Paul mentions, is evil and only that. We must not forget the words of Jesus which set the service of God as the opposite of the service of mammon, the money god (Matthew 6:24)."[44] Money is not evil, nor the root of evil in itself. It is simply a medium of exchange and a very necessary one. But unrestrained desire for money is a root of all kinds of evil; that is, there is no evil in our world that has not sometimes been committed for money. Covetousness can be the basis of all kinds of crime and wickedness, can lead us away from faith in Christ, and can bring us to eternal sorrow.

---

[42] Spence, *ibid.*

[43] Hendriksen, *op. cit.*, p.200.

[44] Kent, *op. cit.*, p.191.

The KJV reads "*the* root ...." When the English reader reads the expression "*the* root," he gets the idea that money-love is the *only* root of evil. Is this what Paul is saying? Is money-love the only root, or are there other "roots" that can lead to evil? Hebrews 12:15 also indicates that "bitterness" is a root of evil. James 1:15 indicates that there are "lusts" (*epithumia*) that lead to sin. Remember, in 1 Timothy 6:9, the "want to get rich" and "desires" (*epithumia*) are two different things, one following from the other. Elsewhere, selfish ambition, intemperance, debasing lusts, and the hatred of God are roots of evil. Thus, if we read as does the KJV, "*the* root," we may be led by this English rendering to give a faulty explanation to the statement Paul wrote.

On the other hand, if we read "*a* root" (as does the ASV and NASB), we may miss the emphasis that Paul himself has written, for his word order in the original has "root" as the first word in the sentence, so we know he wants us to emphasize it.[45] Evidently what Paul wants us to consider is that money-love is the **source** of other evils. Paul says, Don't forget it! It is not just a product; rather, it leads to other (spoiled) fruit. In the Greek text for "all sorts of evil," *pantōn* ("all") is used distributively (predicate position) with *tōn kakōn*, and thus bears the meaning "all kinds of evils." Alford (*Alford's Greek Testament*) quotes a striking passage from Diogenes Laertius, in which he mentions a saying of the philosopher Diogenes that "the love of money (*hē philarguria*) is the metropolis, or home, of all evil things (*pantōn tōn kakōn*)." We should likely take "all" in its widest sense. There is no type of evil which cannot arise from this money-love root. Theft, armed robbery, embezzlement, extortion, kidnapping, prostitution, drug pushing, child abuse, divorce, murder – are all evils that can sometimes develop from the love of money. Hendriksen (p.200) has well illustrated how money-love leads to other evils.

1) It caused the man with very many flocks and herds (in Nathan's parable) to steal the poor man's one little ewe lamb.
2) It caused the rich young ruler to turn away from Christ.
3) It caused the rich fool (of Christ's parable) to deceive himself into thinking that all was well.
4) It caused the rich man (in another parable of Christ's) to neglect poor Lazarus.
5) It caused Judas to betray his Master and commit suicide.
6) It caused Ananias and Sapphira to tell lies.
7) It caused the rich oppressors of James' epistle to exploit those who worked for them. And none of these escaped punishment!

---

[45] In Greek, Colwell's Rule of Grammar states that a definite predicate nominative has no article [no "the"] in the Greek when it precedes the verb; it does have an article when it follows [a linking] verb. The former is the construction in verse 10 -- "root" precedes the linking verb "is", so strict adherence to this well-known rule would tend to require us to write "*the* root ... is love of money." Still, if this leads the reader to a wrong interpretation, we may need to relax strict rules of grammar as we translate.

And some by longing for it have wandered away from the faith – "It" in the Greek can be a reference either to the "love of money" or to the "money" itself. Commentators are not agreed. Perhaps it refers to the "money" people reach out after. The ASV reads "which some reaching after have erred ...." While the attention of the believer was given to reaching after wealth, he lost contact with Christ and loosed his hold on the faith. Paul is thinking of church members, people who used to be Christians. Even Christians are not free from "love of money," and the woes that attend the desire to be rich are no different for Christians than for non-Christians. The Greek verb translated "wandered away" is passive. Literally, "they were led away."[46] Guthrie suggests they were helpless dupes in the grip of a merciless deception. Was it their love of money that led them away? Or is the devil the understood agent, who behind it all uses their desires as a point of attack, and when they continue to sin, are thereby led to abandon the faith? "Faith" may be either objective or subjective. If subjective, the verse speaks of the possibility of falling away from the personal faith they once had in Jesus. If objective, it says these people have wandered away from the truth confessed by the church.[47] Christians, interested in riches of this world, have wandered away from the faith! Think of it!

And pierced themselves with many a pang – This vivid picture of some who had, for the sake of money, given up their first love – their faith – was evidently drawn by Paul from real life. Did both Paul and the readers know of some in Ephesus who once were faithful, but who have now become wanderers from the faith? Paul does not specify what these "pangs" (*odunais*, griefs, sorrows, painful hurts) are. The commentaries suggest unrest, boredom, dissatisfaction, gloom, envy, remorse, painful reflections on their folly, and the apprehension of future wrath. "They are not the final tortures of the lost, but the present griefs which accompany the avaricious person. Pangs of conscience, disillusionment, spiritual unrest, and many other unhappy accompaniments are the product of this course of life."[48] Seeking material ease, men have forfeited peace of mind, lost friends, alienated family members, destroyed their own character and self-respect, found themselves lashed by conscience and the fear of detection in dishonesty, and ultimately forfeited hope of heaven. The word "pierced themselves" (*periepeiran*), occurs nowhere else in the New Testament. It is from *peiro*, and is made more emphatic by the addition of the preposition *peri*. *Peiro* means to

---

[46] The verb "wandered away" [*apoplanaō*] is often used of the "planets." The ancients saw most of the stars as in a "fixed" position, but the planets seemed to wander around the heavens. That's the word picture -- the man obsessed with riches, having lost his bearings, just wanders around from here to there.

[47] Hendriksen opts for this latter explanation. One holding, as he does, "unconditional eternal security" as a given, must opt for this explanation.

[48] Kent, *op. cit.*, p.191.

pierce through from one end to another, and is used of meat that is pierced through by the spit when it is to be roasted. The addition of the preposition *peri* conveys the idea of doing this all around. It was not a single thrust which was made; they were punctured by penetrating wounds all around. The picture is of a man who is going down the straight, direct path of life, when he notices some poisonous but appealing objects at a distance, but off of the right road on which he is travelling. He wanders here and there, gathering the objects, only to find that he has brought wounds upon himself because the objects have unsuspected thorns. Instead of abandoning the search for these objects, he keeps picking them up, hurting himself in the process. The church at Ephesus is not the only congregation where some who once were faithful, now motivated by a desire to be rich, have wandered from the flock, only to continually hurt themselves.

C. The Charge to Maintain a Proper Walk. 6:11-16

1. The nature of a proper walk. 6:11

6:11 -- But – In contrast to the vices which Paul has just condemned (verses 3-10) stand the virtues which Timothy is now urged to cultivate. In harmony with decisions made at 6:2c, we are using the imperatives found in chapter 6 to help outline this charge to the evangelist himself. Many expositors have noted the KJV's imperatives, "Flee (verse 11a), Follow (verse 11b), and Fight (verse 12)!"

Flee from these things – The present imperative (*pheuge* flee) denotes continuous action. Timothy is commanded to continually flee from unworthy motives which Satan will constantly put in his path. There is no safe distance at which one can stop fleeing. While all preachers must "flee," perhaps especially must the young preacher, who is often underpaid, beware of the temptation of desiring money. Commentaries are not agreed on how much of the earlier portion of chapter 6 is covered by the expression "these things." Some limit the expression to the immediate context, to the allurements of wealth and the sad consequences which the love of money produces.[49] Others think everything since 6:3 is summed up in "these things."[50] Timothy would "flee" the manifold temptations and the ruin and perdition that hurtful lusts might lead to by guarding his heart against the covetousness which is at their root.

You man of God – "Man of God" is a designation regularly used in the Old Testa-

---

[49] The expression "these things" is a little loose, but seems to apply to the love of money, and the desire to be rich, with all their attendant "foolish and hurtful lusts." (Hervey, *op., cit.*, p.121)

[50] Timothy is urged to flee away from such things as wickedness, gold-hunger, error, envy, wrangling, reviling, word disputes, evil surmisings, untruth, the mercenary use of "godliness," etc. (Hendriksen, *op. cit.*, p.202, or Foster, *op. cit.*, p.378)

ment for the prophets (e.g., Deuteronomy 33:1; Judges 13:6; 1 Samuel 2:27; 1 Kings 12:22; Jeremiah 34:4). In the New Testament, the expression is used at 2 Timothy 3:17 and 2 Peter 1:21. If it is used in 2 Timothy 3:17 to refer to Timothy the evangelist, rather than to Christians in general, then it might have a technical meaning here in verse 11. Some have averred that just as the prophet who spoke by inspiration was in a special way "God's man," so Timothy (who had a "gift from God," 2 Timothy 1:6) was in a special sense "God's man." If the term is not used in a technical way, its use is a reminder to Timothy that he belongs to God and represents Him –leaving no time or place for Timothy's heart to be given to the desire for wealth, or for his actions to be other than an exhibition of the qualities about to be listed. "The force of this address is great. It indicates that the money lovers just spoken of were not and could not be 'men of God,' whatever they might profess; and it leads with singular strength to the opposite direction in which Timothy's aspirations should point. The treasures which he must covet as 'a man of God' are 'righteousness, godliness, faith, love, patience, meekness'."[51]

And pursue after – Again the verb (*diōke*) is a present imperative, implying that this "pursuit" is something to be done continually. Not only is Timothy to flee, he is also to "pursue." The verb "pursue" has the image of a hunter pursuing an animal with intensity of purpose, for if he fails to bag the game, he will go hungry. That's the kind of intensity the "man of God" exhibits as he pursues the six qualities or virtues about to be enumerated. Perhaps Kent (*op. cit.*, p.192) is right when he suggests that a good way to flee evil is by deliberately pursuing these six qualities or virtues. The attributes that Paul now lists are given in couplets: righteousness and godliness, faith and love, patience and meekness.

Righteousness – At times in the New Testament (often in Romans), this word speaks of imputed righteousness, God's way of saving man. At other times, it refers to right relationships with one's fellow man. Commentaries are fairly well divided when it comes to choosing one of these meanings to explain this verse in Timothy. Why not talk about right relationships with fellow men, or practical righteousness, for (in the opinion of this commentator) that is the direction the immediate context would point to for the specific idea in this expression.

Godliness – As learned in comments at 1 Timothy 4:8, *eusebeian* refers to the daily life of piety and reverence to God, the attitude that gives to God what is His due. Like a man's relations with other men needs constant attention and thought, so does his relationship with God. With attention focused on these virtues, there will be no time for the "man of God" to be thinking about how to become rich(er).

Faith – Let's speak of "faithfulness" – of being a man of your word when you

---

[51] Hervey, *op. cit.*, p.121.

promise something to someone else. Some writers think we should prefer the subjective sense of the word, of active reliance on God and His promises. However, the context is speaking of how we treat others – lovingly, faithfully, rather than selfishly as was condemned in the previous verses.

Love – The "man of God" is to "pursue" ways to be spiritually helpful to others, for that is what love is -- doing what is spiritually best for the other person. Such love is the fruit of the Spirit (Galatians 5:22), and is the essence of Christ's new commandment (John 13:34).

Perseverance – Some translations use the word "patience" to translate *hupomonē*. A study of Greek synonyms reveals that while "patience" (*makrothumia*) means putting up with people, "perseverance" (*hupomonē*) means putting up with things, "stick-to-it-iveness" in spite of difficulties. "*Hupomonē* (from *menō*, remain, and *hupo*, under) refers to an enduring or a remaining steadfast under trials ... Whatever the difficulty may be, God's child and especially a minister must pursue the development of a patient enduring of the trial."[52] Barclay (*op. cit.*, p.156) illustrates the "brave spirit" involved in *hupomonē* by saying that it "is the virtue which in spite of all things overcomes the world."

And gentleness – *Praupateian*, denotes "gentleness of feeling" or "meekness." It is a rarer quality than "patience," but a precious target for the man of God. "The German is 'sanftmuth' – the meekness of heart and feeling with which a Christian acts towards his enemies. His conduct who 'when He was reviled, reviled not again' best exemplifies this virtue."[53] "The term ... describes the minister's attitude toward opponents and adversity in general. Not only should he endure and not waver (*hupomonē*), but he also must maintain gentleness of temper. He should not exhibit that proud, self-assertive, swaggering demeanor, which unsaved men admire as manly."[54] It speaks of control of strength to produce the best results, rather than using the strength to hurt.

2. The performance of a proper walk. 6:12-14a

6:12 -- Fight the good fight of faith – Both *agonidzomai* (contend, fight) and *agōn* (contest, good fight) are terms derived from the athletic field. Comparing the Christian life with an athletic contest, Paul continues his admonition to Timothy. Simpson (p.87) shows that *agonidzomai* can also be used as a military figure of speech, and that is likely the reason our translators used the word "fight"

---

[52] Kent, *op. cit.*, p.193.

[53] Spence, *op. cit.*, p.265.

[54] Kent, *ibid.*

to translate it. (Recall that Paul used a military battle figure of speech at 1 Timothy 1:18.) But *agōn* is an athletic contest, where strenuous effort is put out to win the wrestling match, or chariot race, or the foot race. That's the kind of energy and effort and dedication Timothy is to give to living the Christian life.[55] Timothy must continue to flee from certain vices and continue to pursue certain virtues, and he must continue to fight this noble fight. It is another present imperative, inculcating continuous action. This contest or fight is a *good* (*kalon*) contest, and contrasts with the love of money which is "evil" (*kakon*). "Paul ... bids the 'man of God' to rise above the pitiful struggles for things perishable and useless, and to fight the noble fight of faith; he bids him strive to lay hold of the *real* prize – life eternal. The emphasis rests here mainly on the words 'the good fight' and 'eternal life'."[56] "Faith" likely stands here for the life (contest) that one enters when he becomes a Christian. The Greek reads "the faith", and "there is nothing to determine absolutely whether *hē pistis* here means faith *subjectively* or 'the faith' *objectively* ...."[57]

Take hold of the eternal life – This is the last of the four imperative verbs introduced by the words "You man of God" (6:11). Unlike the first three (flee, follow, fight) which were present imperatives, this verb is an aorist imperative. It is not so much a course of action as a once-for-all act. Like the aorist imperative that occurs in Romans 12:1 ("present your bodies"), this verb calls for Timothy to make a decisive, once-for-all commitment to lay hold on eternal life.

What is intended by "eternal life"? (1) According to John 3:16,36, "eternal life" is a present possession of the Christian. Is that the sense intended in this passage? If so, Timothy is exhorted to get a good hold on the life he already has, ever since he became a Christian. Such an interpretation might better explain the aorist imperative, "take hold of," than does the interpretation that makes "eternal life" something future, after this life. Hendriksen (*op. cit.*, p.204) writes that making "eternal life" something like a prize to be awarded at the end of a contest, at the end of this earthly race, and which one does not receive in any sense or degree until the conflict is over, hardly does justice to the aorist imperative ("Take hold of"). (2) In other passages, "eternal life" is held out as a reward in the next life. We would affirm that Scripture confirms the idea that every man

---

[55] Perhaps "fight" is not the best possible translation, for the Greek word can be used of a wrestling match or foot race or any of the contests that were popular in Paul's day. Anyone who has entered any such contest would do his best to win; probably the idea of strenuous effort is what Paul has in mind here. Weymouth translates this passage thus: "Exert all your strength in the honorable struggle for the faith." (Adapted from Root, *op. cit.*, p.92.)

[56] Spence, *ibid*.

[57] Hervey, *op. cit.*, p.122. Hendriksen argues that "faith" is used here in the same sense it was in the previous verse. It will be remembered that he explained "faith" to be trust in God and His promises. He is making the article in *hē pistis* an "article of previous reference."

is an eternal soul and will exist throughout eternity to come, either in a state of bliss, or a state of torment. (More will be said on the matter of the immortality of the soul in the comments accompanying verse 16 below.) If this is the meaning here, then "eternal life" is abundant life, something more than mere existence, both here and hereafter. And there is something promised to the believer after this life is over. The Bible speaks of the "crown of life" which the Judge of the living and dead will give to those who have been faithful unto death (James 1:12; Revelation 2:10). 1 Timothy 6:19 will speak of "taking hold of that which is life indeed." What a prize awaits the winner of this "contest": *eternal life*. "Again we must pause to note that the prize is not earned by the athlete. Eternal life is a free gift (Romans 6:23). But God does not give it to anyone who is too lazy to reach out and take it. He does not give it to anyone who does not appreciate it enough to make a strenuous effort to obtain it" (Root, *op. cit.*, p.92).

To which you were called – "Called" has reference to the invitation to become a Christian. According to 1 Thessalonians 2:14, this "call" comes through the gospel. Compare Romans 1:7; 8:28,30; 1 Corinthians 1:29; and Ephesians 4:1 for the "calling" to become a Christian.[58] The aorist tense verb here, a completed act in the past time, points back to the time when Timothy heard the gospel. That is when he was called or invited to share in the "eternal life."

And you made the good confession – In the Restoration Movement, the "steps of salvation" have often been given in this order – hear, believe, repent, make the good confession, be baptized. Some such order or process is inferred here in 1 Timothy since we learn that after Timothy was "called" (invited), he made a confession before many witnesses. "The connection of this phrase with the call to eternal life, and the allusion to one special occasion on which Timothy 'had confessed the good confession' of his faith in Jesus Christ, seems to point clearly to [the time of] his baptism (see Matthew 10:32; John 9:22; 12:42; Hebrews 10:23). The phrase, 'good confession,' seems to have been technically applied to the [pre-]baptismal confession of Christ."[59] The "good confession" Timothy made is easily understood as his confession of his faith in Christ (cp. Luke 12:8). "Confession" is *homologeō*, a compound word that means "to say the same thing." What a person confesses about Jesus is the same thing that God Himself said about Jesus -- "This is my beloved Son ...." Some manuscripts record a "confession" made by the Ethiopian after Philip had "called" him by preaching the gospel to him. Those manuscripts at Acts 8:37 read, "I believe that Jesus Christ is the Son of God." Jesus Himself made a similar statement when He was on trial before

---

[58] See the special study on "Call" and "Grace" at the close of chapter 1 of the author's *New Testament Epistles: Romans*, for an explanation of the Calvinistic language "effectual call" that one often meets in the commentaries when an explanation of Timothy's "call" is proffered.

[59] So Hervey explains it, and so do most commentaries, though a few think it was Timothy's ordination, rather than his conversion, that was the occasion of the confession Paul alludes to here.

Pontius Pilate (see 1 Timothy 6:13). The KJV reads "professed the good profession," but the English word "profession" and the word "confession" are not quite the same in connotation. In the 20th century, "profession" is how one lives, whereas "confession" is something one says. "The profession (confession) of faith that one makes at the beginning of his Christian life is only the beginning. It was for Timothy, and it is for us. The 'fight,' the contest, was ahead of him. He must be faithful to the end, and so must we" (Root, *op. cit.*, p.92).

In the presence of many witnesses – Most initial confessions of faith, and the following baptismal services, were public events, done in the sight of the whole congregation. If Timothy were one of the first converts in his town, then the "witnesses" may well have included some non-Christians who were present for his affirmation of faith and his baptism into Christ.[60] The reminder by Paul to Timothy concerning the "confession" Timothy once made before many witnesses is intended to be another reason why Timothy should "take hold of the eternal life." To fail to "take hold of the eternal life" would be, in effect, to deny what he had once confessed.

6:13 -- I charge you in the presence of God – The sentence which begins here is completed in verse 14. Omitting the witnesses whom Paul reminds Timothy are watching him, the sentence reads "I charge you ... keep the commandment without stain or reproach ...." Apparently verse 13 reminds Paul of two witnesses who are vitally interested in what Timothy does as an evangelist. Solemnly, Paul calls on God and God's Son to witness the charge he is now giving to Timothy. Indeed, these two witnesses are beings in whose presence every minister constantly moves. Paul's calling of these two witnesses increases the solemnity as he approaches the end of the Epistle. In figurative language Paul has charged Timothy to flee covetousness, to follow after righteousness, and to fight. Now he drops the figures of speech and continues his charge in plain language. For "the presence of God," the KJV reads "in the sight of God," which may come closer to reminding us that men's thoughts and actions are matters that are closely watched by God in heaven. (See the same charge at 1 Timothy 5:21.)

Who gives life to all things – In the Greek, this is a present participle, and thus characterizes God as a continuing life-giver. The verb is *dzōogoneō*, which may mean to make alive, or preserve alive.[61] "As an epithet of 'God,' it sets before us the highest creative act of the Almighty as 'the Lord, and the Giver of life'; and is equivalent to 'the living God' (Matthew 26:63), 'the God of the spirits of all flesh'

---

[60] If it is Timothy's ordination when this confession was made, then the witnesses would be the elders and others who were present on the occasion.

[61] Actually, there is a manuscript variation at this place, with the Textus Receptus reading *dzōopoieō*, which also means to "make alive." Both words are used in the LXX as the rendering of the Pi'el and Hiphil of the Hebrew *chayah*, to give or preserve life.

(Numbers 16:22)."[62]   It is not quite clear why Paul reminds Timothy of this attribute of God as a means of enforcing the charge he is about to give.   Perhaps he means that God is the source of life, and that He had given life to Timothy – both natural and spiritual.   Thus, He had a right to require that this life be employed in His service, and that if in the performance of his duties Timothy should be required to lay down his life, he should remember that God had the power to raise him up again.   Perhaps Paul calls attention to this attribute to remind Timothy that he need not fear for his life as he carries out his commission.   "The Preserver rather than the Creator is here brought into prominence.   Timothy is exhorted to fight his good fight, ever mindful that he is in the presence of that great Being who could and would – even if Timothy's faithfulness should lead him to danger and to death – still preserve him, on earth or in Paradise."[63]   Perhaps there is emphasis on the idea that God is sustaining Timothy during his ministry.   "God is not only watching, but is the One who has bestowed eternal life, and is sustaining Timothy as he fulfills his ministry" (Kent, *op. cit.*, p.194).   Perhaps it is to bring out the ever-present character of the Divine witness.

And of Christ Jesus – This is the second great Witness before Whom (in the sight of Whom) Timothy is fulfilling his ministry.   Just like the character of the Father as "the life-giver" was called to mind, so too one of the characteristics of Jesus as "the confessing Christ" is here called to mind.

Who testified the good confession before Pontius Pilate – It will help Timothy to carry out the charge Paul is giving him if he will remember what Christ did when He was testifying before an enemy of the truth.   During His trials, Jesus confessed that He was King of the Jews, the Messiah, the "Son of the Blessed One" (Matthew 27:11; Mark 14:62, 15:2; Luke 23:2,3).   These statements as to who He was were very similar to the confession Peter made, "You are the Christ, the Son of the living God."   If we give the preposition *epi* a temporal signifi-cance, and translate it as "under" (that is, in the days of Pontius Pilate), then the confession made by Jesus during His trials matched exactly what God said about Him.   The majority of expositors construe the preposition to mean "before" (Pontius Pilate), so the testimony must be limited to the scene in the Judgment Hall, to the interview between the prisoner Jesus and the Roman governor (John 18:33-37).   The confession Jesus made during His final trial before Pilate was that He was the king of the Jews, but that His kingdom was not of this world.   He also affirmed that He came into the world on a special mission from God, namely, to bear witness to the truth.   Either way, Paul appeals to the example of Jesus to fortify Timothy.   Before Pilate, Jesus stood firm and bore witness by word and deed.   The confession Jesus made was "good" because it was exactly in harmony

---

[62] Hervey, *op. cit.*, p.122.

[63] Spence, *op. cit.*, p.266.

with God's truth and God's will.   Jesus testified the good confession in spite of personal suffering and in spite of the fact that it would lead to being sentenced to the cross, so His example encourages Timothy to walk courageously in harmony with his confession.   Timothy is reminded that this Witness is the same Christ who confessed Who He was under circumstances which sealed His doom and sentenced Him to the cross.   Timothy's confession of Jesus, as he continues to serve as evangelist, can never cost more than that!   What better example to keep us steadfast in the faith and true to our sacred vows than the example of Jesus?

6:14 -- That you keep the commandment – The charge begun in verse 13 continues.   "I charge you to keep the commandment ..."   "Keep" means to stand guard over, protect, and preserve.   The "commandment" that Timothy must keep has been variously explained as the gospel message (*Ellicott's*, p.267), the injunctions found in verses 11,12 of this chapter (KJV[64]), all of God's commands, or Christ's new commandment.   The most satisfactory explanation is the one that ties "commandment" to Timothy's "commission" to preach the Gospel.[65]

Without stain or reproach – There is a difference of opinion among commentators whether these two adjectives, *aspilon* and *anepilēpton*, modify the word "commandment," or agree with the person, i.e., Timothy, the one being charged. This commentator agrees that the adjectives are intended to describe Timothy's careful living.

> The introduction of *se* ['you'] after *tērēsai* ['keep']; the facts that *tērēsai tēn entolēn*, without any addition, means 'to keep the commandment;' and that in the New Testament, *aspilos* and *anepilēptos* always are used of persons, not things (Jas. 1:27; 1 Pet. 1:19; 2 Pet. 3:14, 1 Tim. 3:2 and 5:7); and the consideration that the idea of the person being found blameless in, or kept blameless unto, the coming of Christ, is a frequent one in the Epistles (Jude 24; 2 Pet. 3:14; 1 Cor. 1:8; Col. 1:22; 1 Thes. 3:13; 1 Tim. 5:23) -- seem to point strongly, if not conclusively, to the adjectives *aspilon* and *anepilēpton* here agreeing with *se*, not with *entolēn*.[66]

"Without stain" says that Paul's expectation for Timothy is that he be "without moral stain."   An evangelist's high aim is that the record of his life will be "spot-

---

[64] The KJV translators inserted "this" so the verse reads "this commandment" because they thought there was particular reference to the imperatives found in verses 11,12 (flee, follow, fight, lay hold on).   Orrin Root, in comments on this passage as found in the KJV wrote, "There seems to be no compelling reason to look beyond verses 11 and 12 for the commandment Paul had in mind."

[65] Hendriksen's suggestion is that the reference is to Timothy's *commission* to preach the Gospel.   "That commission, precept, or mandate, comprises all that he has been ordered to do with respect to the ministry of the Gospel and the government of the church."   Compare what was explained at 1 Timothy 1:18 about the "charge" given to Timothy.

[66] Hervey, *op. cit.*, p.122.   Spence, Alford, Hendriksen, etc., however, refer these adjectives to "the commandment."

less" when he stands before the Judge. We have had "above reproach" at 1 Timothy 3:2, meaning "not laid hold of, irreprehensible, unassailable." It is Jesus Christ Himself, whose keen eyes miss nothing, who makes the decision that Timothy's life is "without reproach". When He makes an assessment of Timothy's life and ministry, it is vital that He find nothing to reproach or assail. "Without reproach" says that it was absolutely requisite that the evangelist in Ephesus should *live* the life he preached. There were those (e.g., the false teachers of whom he had been speaking, well-known to Timothy) whose lives had dishonored the glorious commandment they professed to love and teach. Timothy's life was to be different. A similar command comes to all those upon whom similar responsibility has been conferred. Every evangelist's behavior and fulfilling of his commission to preach ought to be "without stain or reproach."

3. The incentive for a proper walk.   6:14b-16

Until the appearing of our Lord Jesus Christ – There is to be no relaxing of this charge. The charge is valid until Christ comes again. "Appearing" translates the word *epiphaneia*, which means 'to become visible.' Since His ascension, He has been invisible to human eyes, but at His return He will become visible. *Epiphaneia*, "appearing, manifestation," is one of the words used in the New Testament for the second coming of Jesus. While some systems of eschatology try to make a distinction between different "advents" or "comings" of Jesus – because of the different words *parousia* ("coming, presence"), *apokalupsis* ("revelation"), and *epiphaneia* ("manifestation, appearing") – it has been demonstrated in the author's *Prophecy and Revelation Notes* that all three words are but different ways of looking at the same second advent.

Paul does not state unequivocally that Timothy will live until the Lord's appearing. He might, or he might not, for the time of the second advent was not known by Jesus or the angels or the apostles, but by the Father only (Matthew 24:36). Nor should these words be forced into such an interpretation so as to prove that Paul expected the return of Christ in his own lifetime, an expectation or belief in which (it now appears) he was mistaken. To interpret Paul's writings so as to have Paul saying Timothy will live till the second advent impinges on the doctrines of revelation and inspiration, and sows seeds of doubt about the trustworthiness of the New Testament writings in general. That is an exceedingly steep price to pay for what is, at its root, simply an attempt to interpret Scripture in the light of the currently popular philosophy.

We would affirm that *all* the statements about the time of the second coming are couched in such language that readers are required to have the same expectancy that has always been required of Christ's followers. There is what has been called a fine balance between "He is coming quickly" and "after a long time, the Lord comes." This is exactly the tension one would expect when the writer had not been told exactly when His return would be. It is inaccurate to suggest, as have some, that in the early years after the Ascension the Christians and the Bible writers alike looked for a speedy return of the Lord; then, with the passing of nearly a generation, that they had to modify their teaching to "account" for the "delay" they had not foreseen. Justification for such a scenario is often presented on this fashion: in the earlier written New Testament books there is much said about the Lord coming soon, whereas in the books written in the last half or quarter of the first century, the coming is presented as "delayed," or only "possible." But this justification will just not play! 1 and 2 Thessalonians are two of the earliest New Testament books written. When some in Thessalonica misinterpreted Paul's first letter, he wrote the second to correct their misconceptions. In 2 Thessalonians 2, Paul shows that a number of things must happen before the second coming. How can it be said that the earlier New Testament books present only a "soon" return of Christ? Furthermore, 1 Timothy is one of the later books, and Paul can still write in such a way that Timothy is reminded to conduct himself as an evangelist as would one anticipating the appearing of Jesus. There is no proof that in the later New Testament books that "delay" is emphasized, and that perhaps any return at all is explained away.

6:15 -- Which He will bring about at the proper time – Verses 15 and 16 give further details about the "appearing of our Lord Jesus Christ" introduced in verse 14. The second coming of Jesus has not been dated for us. The time of that great event lies in the counsels of God (Matthew 24:36). Over and over again in His eschatological discourse, Jesus emphasized that there are "no signs" by which one can ascertain the near approach of the second coming (Matthew 24:29ff).[67] It is even possible that Revelation 14:14 indicates that the glorified Christ still does not know the exact time of His return, but awaits the command from the Father on the throne to put in His sickle. Not a few writers believe that because the Bible elsewhere seems to say that only the Father knows when the second advent will be, the "He" of verse 15 (*deixei*, "He shall shew" KJV, "He will bring about" NASB) is none other than the Father. They then affirm that the doxology of verses 15-16 is directed to the Father, rather than to Jesus. The phrase "the proper time" (*en kairois idiois*) also occurs at 1 Timothy 2:6 and Titus 1:3. A similar phrase (*kairo idiō*) occurs at Galatians 6:9 and is translated "in due time" in the NASB, and clearly corresponds to the "the fullness of time" (*plerōma tou chronou*) at Galatians 4:4, since the terms are combined in Luke 1:20 and 21:24. The Father is the one who decides the "fitting" or "proper" time. That was true of Christ's first coming into the World, and it is true of His second coming, too.

-- He who is the blessed and only Sovereign – The Person to whom this doxolo-

---

[67] See the author's "Gospels Notes" on Matthew 24-25, or his *Let's Study Prophecy* for details.

gy is addressed has been debated.   Is it addressed to Christ, or to the Father?

> A few writers, among them Chafer and Ironside, have suggested that Christ is
> meant. This is based on a similarity of expression here and in Revelation
> 19:16, in which latter reference the 'King of kings and Lord of lords' is Christ.
> (This is a different expression in the Greek text, however). Also the reference
> to immortality is thought by these advocates to be more applicable to Christ.
>
> Nevertheless, the great majority of commentators ... understand the doxology
> to refer to the Father. The grammatical structure seems to distinguish Christ
> from the subject of *deixei*, and it is best to understand the Father as displaying
> Christ at the appearing.   This harmonizes with the passages previously
> mentioned, where the season of the epiphany is in the Father's authority ...
> Furthermore, some of the descriptions in this doxology (all of which are
> nominative and belong to the subject of *deixei*) apply more easily to the Father
> than to Christ. He is called the One 'whom no one has seen nor is able to see.'
> How can this be Christ? Yet it applies perfectly to the Father (John 1:18), and
> it was the eternal function of the Son to make known the Father (John 1:18).[68]

Just as sublime statements elsewhere in the Pastorals have been ascribed to
various sources (e.g., taken from an early hymn), many guesses have been offered
as the source of this doxology.[69]   As observed earlier, if such a search for sources
stems from a belief that the contents of the sublime statement are inflated and
probably not exactly true, and therefore would not have been written by an
inspired writer, then we are suspicious of such a search for sources.   There is no
reason why this passage cannot be a spontaneous outburst from the heart of Paul,
who was a devout believer in Jesus Christ.   Just as Paul's contemplation of the
first coming of Christ led to a doxology in 1 Timothy 1:17, so also meditation
upon the second coming here in verses 15-16 led to a similar, expanded doxology.

There are seven terms descriptive of deity in this doxology (3 nouns, 2
participles, and 2 relative clauses), and each word stresses the transcendence or
incomparable greatness of God.[70]   In Scripture, the term "the blessed" (*ho
makarios*, not *eulogētos*, as in Mark 14:61) is only here and in 1 Timothy 1:11
(where see note) applied to God.   God is described by the term "the blessed"
because He is the source of all blessedness and happiness (i.e., spiritual prosperity).   Second, He is described as "only Sovereign" (KJV, "Potentate").   God is
"sovereign" and is absolutely incomparable in His right do to as He pleases, for

---

[68] Kent, *op. cit.*, p.197.

[69] See Hendriksen, *op. cit.*, footnote #106, p.206.

[70] We shall apply these terms to God the Father because (as indicated above) we think that is
what Paul is writing. Nevertheless, were we to ascribe any of these characteristics or attributes to
Jesus, who is elsewhere in Scripture shown to be deity, we would not be claiming for the Son
anything other than what his equality with the Father would justify.

example, to choose the appropriate season for Christ's second coming. He is the only sovereign, the only one with such power.[71] Spence thinks there may be an allusion to incipient Gnostic ideas in this expression. "Possibly already in Ephesus the teachers of Gnosticism had begun their unhappy work, with their fables of the mighty aeons and their strange Eastern conception of one God the source of good, and another the source of evil."[72]

The King of kings and Lord of lords – The original reads "the King of those kinging, and the Lord of those lording"; the words translated "kinging" and "lording" are participles in the Greek. Here in 1 Timothy, this is a description of the Father. Likewise, in Psalms 136:2,3, God is spoken of as "God of gods ... Lord of lords."[73] These two phrases are perhaps intended to call attention to God's relation to the universe, and even the rulers in that universe. God is King over those whom men style as kings, and Lord over all those whom men call lords. These titles have been assumed by earthly rulers, each boastfully assuming to be a great king among all kings. They are rightly attributed to God, who is ruler over all kings, and from whom their temporary authority comes (Romans 13:1).

6:16 -- Who alone possesses immortality – The Greek word (*athanasia*) speaks of "deathlessness." It is a different word from "immortal" (*aphthartos*) at 1 Timothy 1:17. Commentators are extremely careful in the wording of their comments at this place, lest they appear to agree with the assertion some make that the belief in "the immortality of the soul" is a pagan idea, not a Biblical one. It is not at all unusual to find this assertion made as part of an argument that there is no such thing as eternal punishment, and only annihilation awaits the wicked. The view that "immortality is a pagan idea" is not correct.[74] In view of this need for extreme care in wording, it is instructive to study several comments offered by way of explanation for this phrase: (1) Barnes explains that *athanasia* properly means "exemption from death, and seems to mean that God, in his own nature, enjoys perfect and certain exemption from death. Creatures have immortality only as they derive it from Him, and of course are dependent on Him for it. He has it by His very nature, and it is in His case underived, and He cannot be deprived of it."[75] To this comment we might compare John 5:26, where we

---

[71] The word *dunastēs* means a powerful one, Potentate. Here it is joined with a word that means "only" or "alone." God is the "alone Potentate." There is no one to compare with Him. Earthly kings and lords may wield some power, but only God is "alone sovereign."

[72] Spence, *op. cit.*, p.268.

[73] The same language (though the Greek uses simply nouns, not participles) is applied to the Son in Revelation 17:14 and 19:16.

[74] Attention is called to the author's article in the 1964 *Sentinel*, titled "Is Man Immortal?" It is included as Special Study #6 following these comments on chapter 6.

[75] Barnes, *op. cit.*, p.202

read "the Father has life in Himself."   (2) Now note how Hendriksen worded it:

> The only human beings who, as far as it is possible for creatures to do so, share this immortality, and thereby become "partakers of the divine nature" (2 Peter 1:4) are believers, though also unbelievers exist endlessly.   It is through the gospel that immortality or imperishability (*aphtharsia*) was brought to light (2 Timothy 1:10) ... While the believer has received immortality, as one receives a drink of water from a fountain, God *has* it.   It belongs to His very being.   He *is* Himself the Fountain.[76]

In the first part of this note, Hendriksen comes very close to wording it just as an annihilationist would -- when he says that the only souls who are "immortal" are the redeemed who have received their immortality from Jesus.   The wicked, the annihilationist would affirm, does not receive this gift of immortality, and that is precisely why it is annihilation that awaits him in the future.

Again we read the word "alone" (cp. comments at verse 15).   The holy angels and the souls of men, since their creation, are immortal.   But one alone, God, can be said to "have immortality."   Unlike other immortal beings who enjoy immortality through the will of another, He derives it from His own essence.

And dwells in unapproachable light – Revelation 4:3 pictures the One sitting on the throne encircled with an emerald sphere of light.   Is "unapproachable light" another description of that dazzling, brilliant sphere of light that surrounds the Father on the throne?   A little bit of that light frightened shepherds in the field near Bethlehem (Luke 2:8,9).   See also Ezekiel 1:4; Psalm 104:2; and Daniel 2:22.[77]   While it is true that intense light hurts mortal eyes, there may be more implied in "unapproachable light" than its mere brilliance.   Perhaps the brilliant light is a reminder of God's holiness, a holiness that cannot tolerate sin.   The book of Hebrews indicates that until men's sins are completely forgiven, they have no access to God's presence.   Even at the present time, the souls of the redeemed are standing on the sea of glass before the throne (Revelation 15:2).   But the day will come, after Jesus returns, when the redeemed will be allowed closer to the presence of the One on the throne than just the sea of glass.   No longer will men find the brilliant light in which God dwells unapproachable.

Whom no man has seen or can see – We've had the word "invisible" at 1 Timothy 1:17 (see comments there).   John 1:18 reads "no man has seen God at

---

[76] Hendriksen, *op. cit.*, p.208.

[77] "The symbolism of the old covenant teaches the same truth, the unapproachable glories in which God dwells; for instance, the guarding of the bounds of Sinai in the giving of the Law; the covering of the faces of the Seraphim in the year that King Uzziah died, when Isaiah saw the divine vision; the veiled darkness of the Holy of Holies in the Tabernacle and the Temple, wherever and anon the visible glory dwelt" (Spence, *Ellicott's, op. cit.*, p. 268).

any time (*pōpote*)."[78]   See also Exodus 33:20-23 and Deuteronomy 4:12.   The use of *pōpote*, which could be translated "ever yet," points forward to that open vision of the Divine which shall be granted hereafter (1 John 3:2; Matthew 5:8). Westcott's notes on John 1:18 are helpful:

> Comp. I John 4:12. In both places the original of "God" is without the article (*theon*, not *ton theon*). By this manner of expression thought is turned to the divine Nature rather than to the divine Person: "God as God." The Theophanies under the OT did not fall under this category (cp. Ex. 33:12ff). Even Christ Himself was not "seen" as God. The perception of His true divine Nature was not immediate, but gained by slow processes (John 14:9). The words ... do not deny the possibility of a true knowledge of God, but of a natural knowledge of God, such as can be described by "sight" ... This verse justifies the claim of the Gospel to be Truth, while it lays down the inherent limitations of human knowledge. It is impossible, so far as our experience goes, for man to have direct knowledge of God as God. He can come to know Him only through One who shares both the human and divine natures, and who is in vital fellowship both with God and man. In Christ this condition is satisfied.[79]

As noted earlier, the presence of this phrase ("whom no man has seen or can see") causes most writers to attribute this doxology to the Father. Men have seen Christ, and have even seen His glory (John 1:14). Yet it applies perfectly to the Father (John 1:18), and it was to make Him known that the Son became incarnate.

To Him *be* **honor and eternal dominion!** – Such a God as has been described is worthy of all honor (reverence, esteem, adoration). We must supply a verb, as the italics show, and it is proper to supply a form that makes this a prayer. "Let honor and eternal dominion be given to Him!" He is worthy to be the One who eternally exercises dominion in the new heavens and earth – to the discomfiture of his enemies and the salvation of His people. (Cp. Romans 11:36.) "This passage is a magnificent embodiment of the attributes of the living God, supreme blessedness and almighty power, universal dominion and unchangeable being, inscrutable majesty, radiant holiness, and glory inaccessible and unapproachable by his creatures, save through the mediation of his only begotten Son."[80]

Amen – We may suppose that as the Holy Spirit led Paul to pen this marvelous doxology that extols the majesty and incomparable greatness of God, Paul himself is moved to add his "So be it!" to the words the Spirit has prompted.[81]

---

[78] The fact that Jesus had seen and could reveal the Father sets Him apart forever from mere men (John 1:18). (Hayden, *Standard Lesson Commentary*, 1953)

[79] B.F. Westcott, "The Gospel of John," in *The Bible Commentary*, edited by F. C. Cook (New York: Charles Scribner's Sons, 1886), p.14,15.

[80] Hervey, *op. cit.*, p.123.

[81] Some believe Paul is quoting a liturgical ascription of praise used in the early church, and is

D. The Charge to Perform a Faithful Ministry.   6:17-21a

1. This is accomplished by directing men toward spiritual goals. 17-19

6:17 -- Instruct those who are rich in this present world – "Instruct" is the way the NASB renders *paraggello*, the very same word translated "charge" in 6:13, 1:3, 4:11, 5:7. This fact explains the wording of the paragraph title. Who are the "rich"? Observe the different way this verse reads compared with verse 9. Not those who are *eager* to become rich (verse 9) are alluded to, but those who are *already* rich. It is implied that in the congregation at Ephesus there were many, owing to birth or other circumstances, already rich and powerful, already in possession of gold and rank in varied degrees. In many places Christianity influences some of the wealthy class. If Timothy is going to carry out his work as an evangelist, he must offer a word of special warning to these people, too.

Many of us, reading these words about some who are "rich in this present world," immediately think of someone else who has more money than we do, and suppose the warning is addressed to them.   Let those of us in the western world, with our high per capita annual income, remember that *we* are the ones who are "rich" in this present age!   People who have a choice about which set of clothes to wear today, or which pair of shoes, or which food to fix for dinner, are the rich people of the world!   "This present world" (Greek. *aiōn*, 'age') is the period of time which closes with the second coming of Christ.   If men do not have treasures laid up in heaven so they are rich in the world to come, they will have missed the whole purpose of living.   Paul does not say that wealthy church members have no prospect of serving God faithfully.   He does say that those who are rich face special perils, and should be warned by the evangelist lest they find themselves "rich" only as far as "the present world" is concerned.

> The persons Paul has in mind are legitimately rich. He gives no suggestion of avarice or dishonesty involved in the acquiring of the wealth. These persons have been entrusted by God with material wealth through some legitimate means. Now Paul challenges Timothy to warn them about the dangers of possessing wealth. Paul does not follow the communist line of denying personal property and wealth. He does not condemn rich men because they are rich, but he does warn them of the false trust which they may easily develop.[82]

Not to be conceited – In the first part of verse 17, Paul gives two specifications as to what the rich man's attitude should *not* be.   The first is "conceited" or "high-

---

simply copying the "Amen" from that ascription.   This is unnecessary.   On other occasions, he used the same word in closing his ringing, climactic periods (Romans 1:25; Galatians 1:5; 2 Timothy 4:8).

[82] Kent, *op. cit.*, p.199.

minded" (KJV),which translates *hupsēlophronein*. The word means to be high-minded, proud, exalted in mind. The word occurs elsewhere only in Romans 11:20. The Greek words compounded with *hupsēlos* have mostly a bad connotation -- 'haughtiness,' 'boastfulness,' and the like. "Those who possess wealth in this present age, as opposed to those who are materially poor, are often deluded into thinking that wealth is a mark of special divine favor ... If a Christian has riches, it cannot be considered as proof that he is more pleasing to God than his poorer Christian brothers."[83] The idea in "not to be conceited" is "that they should not value themselves [above their fellow Christians] on account of their wealth, or look down with pride and arrogance on their inferiors. They should not suppose that they are any better men, or any nearer heaven, because they are wealthy. Property really makes no distinction in the great things that pertain to character and salvation."[84]

Or to fix their hope on the uncertainty of riches – This is a second attitude that the evangelist is to warn the rich against harboring. The expression "the uncertainty of riches" ought to be a sobering one.

> There is uncertainty in riches, because they may soon be taken away. No dependence can be placed on them in the emergencies of life ... A man whose house is in flames, or who is shipwrecked, or whose child lies dying, or who himself is in the agonies of death, can derive no advantage from the fact that he is richer than other men.[85]

> Spence explains this uncertainty which attaches itself to material wealth on two counts. First, the duration of life itself, even for a day is uncertain, and wealth cannot be possessed after death. Second, the shifting circumstances of life, such as commercial depressions and war, make wealth uncertain. How foolish, then, to transfer one's trust from God to riches! Yet men show a preference for trusting a bank account rather than a God in heaven.[86]

The uncertainty is the reason men are not "to fix their hope" on such riches.

> Timothy is to caution the rich to a problem to which they are much exposed. A man who is rich is liable to 'trust' in his riches, and to suppose he needs nothing more (even God!). He feels that he is not dependent on his fellow-men, and he is very likely to feel that he is not dependent on God.[87]

Far from being worthy of trust, material wealth is of a temporary and unsubstantial nature even in the present world (Haggai 1:6; Proverbs 23:5). They that trust in it shut themselves out of heaven (Mark 10:24). Jesus once said, "It is easier for a camel to go through the eye of a needle, than for a rich man to enter the kingdom

---

[83] Kent, *ibid.*   [84] Barnes, *op. cit.*, p.202.   [85] *ibid.*

[86] Kent, *ibid.*   [87] Barnes, *ibid.*

of God". His startled disciples asked, "Then who can be saved?" Jesus answered with a profound truth, "With men this is impossible, but with God all things are possible" (Matthew 19:24-26). God can change a person's heart. He can help the man whose trust is in riches. With God it is possible for even a rich man to live happily and eternally in God's kingdom.

But on God – After the two negative attitudes that are to be avoided, here begins what the rich Christian's attitude should be. The Christian may be rich, and even enjoy those riches, if he retains his Christian principles. Some of those principles are now enumerated. We must supply the verb from the previous phrase. Christian are "to fix their hope on God ...." The KJV reads "in the living God," but the word translated "living" does not appear in the more ancient textual authorities and its removal does not alter the sense of the passage. God is not, like material riches 'uncertain.' He has revealed himself to men so that we may know how He thinks and acts, being confident that what He is today, He will be tomorrow and forever. To trust the money rather than the Giver of the money is tantamount to idolatry!

> When one has all the money he can use, he soon learns that it can buy almost anything he wants. It can supply all the material things necessary to life, plus all the luxuries that appeal to him. It can take him halfway around the world in a chartered jet, and bring him back when he is ready to return. Year after year his wealth never fails him. How can he keep from being *highminded*, from looking down on the people who respond to his every whim? Paul reminds us that riches are *uncertain*. If one uses them unwisely and he becomes an alcoholic, they do little for his hangover. They cannot save him from a crash if he drives when he is drunk. They scarcely dull his grief when a loved one dies. And when cancer strikes, he hurts like a poor man. Or riches may vanish in a crash of the stock market. So the rich man had better keep his priorities straight. It is God, not money, who never fails. It is God, not money, who *giveth us richly all things to enjoy*. Trust is misplaced if it is not placed in God.[88]

Who richly supplies us with all things to enjoy – Paul thus reminds rich people that God is the One who has provided all things, riches included, for us. No man possesses anything that God did not provide. (Cp. James 1:17; Psalms 104:28, 145:16). Furthermore, this is another of the many sayings of Paul in which he urges on the people of God that their kind Father in heaven not only allows men reasonable pleasures and gratifications, but even Himself abundantly provides such for them. Kent (*op. cit.*, p.200) observes, "Here asceticism is branded a lie. God's blessings are not to be shunned, but used as God intended, and when this is done, the user receives a godly satisfaction." How foolish to transfer trust from God to riches, and then miss all the "enjoyment" that God the giver intended His people to experience. Trust the Giver, rather than the gifts, to provide this enjoy-

---

[88] Orrin Root, *Standard Lesson Commentary*, 1985-86.

ment!   "All things" tells us "God is munificent, by virtue of which He provides us with all things necessary both for body and soul, for time and eternity."[89]

6:18 -- *Instruct them* to do good – Having pointed out the dangers connected with being wealthy, Paul now turns to the good things that can be done by those with means.   This verse contains several infinitives which depend on the verb "instruct" from verse 17.   The positive attitudes which Timothy is to inculcate upon his rich brethren (beginning in verse 17b) are here continued.   The attitude the rich Christian is to have is continued, with this difference: in verse 17b, the proper attitude towards God has been pointed out; now the proper attitude towards other people, particularly believers, is set forth.   God wants His wealth in circulation!   Riches are given to people so they may do good.

> Inasmuch as wealth itself is one of the 'all things' which God has richly given, the rich man is then a steward of that which God has bestowed.   In four infinitive phrases Paul shows how proper enjoyment of riches involves using them to bless others.   If a rich man can share his wealth with others and find enjoyment in so doing, he is using his wealth as God intended.   But if the thought of sharing is abhorrent to him, then he has fallen prey to the danger which Paul describes of having his hope on the possession of riches rather than on God.[90]

"Do good" translates *agathoergein*, which occurs here only, for the more common *agathopoiein*.   Wealthy Christians[91] are commanded to be continually doing good; the verb is a present tense infinitive, indicating continuous action.   It is not enough for a Christian to strive to avoid evil.   He must also strive to do good – good deeds, noble deeds, helpful deeds, benevolent deeds.   In verse 17 we were told God richly supplies "all things to enjoy."   This verse points to the way of highest enjoyment for those who have received God's beneficence.   They have the luxury of doing good, of helping others to be happy, and only giving brings an enjoyment that never fails, never disappoints.

To be rich in good works – Compare 1 Timothy 5:10 and comments there. Rather than seeking just to be rich, the Christian is to seek to be rich in good works, in a multitude of attractive and worthwhile works (plural of *ergois kalois*) which their wealth enables them to perform.   "Good works" are the only true wealth, as they are also the only true adornment (Revelation 19:8; 1 Peter 3:3,4). A wealthy man is extremely poor if his only desire is to hoard wealth, but the wealthy man who is "rich in good works" is rich indeed.

---

[89] Hendriksen, *op. cit.*, p.210.

[90] Kent, *op. cit.*, p.200.

[91] The same charge about "do(ing) good" is true for those not so rich, but the rich have more wealth to use for good purposes.   Hence they have a greater responsibility. (Hayden, *Standard Lesson Commentary*, 1953)   A rich man has vast opportunities to do good. (Root, *op. cit.*, p.94)

To be generous ("ready to distribute" KJV) – This word, which is nearly synonymous with the following expression, points to the hand which generously gives, while the next term points to the heart which lovingly sympathizes. *Eumetadotous* occurs only here in the New Testament, and rarely in later classical Greek. The opposite, "close-handed," is *dusmetadotos*. The verb *metadidōmi* means "to give to others a share or portion of what one has" (Luke 3:11; Romans 1:11; 12:8; Ephesians 4:28; 1 Thessalonians 2:8). The evangelist is to teach rich Christians to be quick to give, and ever ready to share what they have with others who belong to the fellowship or community of believers in Christ. The early church must have been taught this truth, for we see the spirit of giving illustrated in Acts 2:42-44 and 4:34-37. It is evident that the church at Ephesus did not practice the community of goods which characterized the Jerusalem church in its early days in Judea (Acts 2:44,45, 4:32), nor was any congregation of believers ever commanded to do so. But those with means are commanded to be generous.

And ready to share ("willing to communicate" KJV) – *Koinōnikous* is used here only in the New Testament, but is found in classical Greek in a slightly different sense. "Communicate" is its exact equivalent, though the word "communicate" now has a connotation narrower than the word originally had. Two words from the same root, *koinōnein* and *koinonia*, often translated "fellowship," are used in passages where they mean "giving" or "participating in a common cause" (Romans 12:13, 15:26; 2 Corinthians 9:13; Galatians 6:6; Philippians 4:15; and Hebrews 13:16). The ASV has a marginal reading, "ready to sympathize." At one time the KJV carried a marginal reading, "be sociable." The idea was that the Christian was to sympathize enough to share his riches with others so as to make them comfortable. When the Christian sees a need he can help meet, he is ready to share. In a sense he is recognizing and participating in the brotherhood and mutual helpfulness that is shared by all believers.

> "Distribute" and "communicate" both mean "share," and a very wealthy man can share much without coming to poverty. But good sharing is not so easy as one might think. If a man distributes money thoughtlessly, he hurts people by destroying their initiative. Wise giving requires much care and thought. Some who are willing to share are not willing to take the time and make the effort to be sure they are really doing good. But the charge is here to challenge them: "Do good ... be rich in good works."[92]

6:19 -- Storing up for themselves – The Greek word is a circumstantial participle in the present tense, indicating a concomitant to the right use of wealth. While the rich are doing good, are being rich in good works, etc., at the same time they are storing up for themselves a very real treasure. This verse contains two main lessons: (1) By doing good works, we build a solid and stable spiritual posses-

---

[92] Root, *op. cit.*

sion – a good foundation.   (2) This foundation provides a stable base for getting a firm grip on eternal life.

The treasure of a good foundation for the future – By giving materially, one enriches himself spiritually and assures himself of future reward.   Compare Mark 10:21, "Sell all you possess, and give it to the poor, and you shall have treasure in heaven."   Compare also the "they may receive (i.e., welcome) you into the eternal tabernacles" that Jesus held out as promise to those who properly manage their riches (Luke 16:9, ASV).   Jesus also commanded His followers to lay up treasure in heaven (Matthew 6:19,20).   So this whole matter of accumulating riches versus sharing riches becomes a matter of priorities.   The Christian's top priority, that which comes before all else in importance, is to be sharing, distributing, doing good – for that is the way to ensure a heavenly destiny.

There is an obvious mixture of metaphors in the phrase, "storing up ... a good foundation."   There is little agreement when commentators try to explain the figures.   Ellicott (*op. cit.*, p.270), following Weisinger, understands "a wealth of good works as a foundation."   This treasure will be an excellent foundation upon which to build when, in the age to come and particularly in the great judgment day, the believer's works are taken into account (Matthew 25:34-40; Romans 1:7,10).   Alford sees no difficulty in considering the "foundation" as a treasure.   Others have made a conjectural emendation of the text, substituting *keimēlion* ("a stored treasure") for *themelion* ("foundation").   Each student of the Word will have to decide whether one of the above explanations should be adopted, or simply admit that Paul was capable of using a mixed metaphor.   Anyhow, the doctrine is clear that wealth spent for God and his Church is repaid with interest, and becomes an abiding treasure.

So that they may take hold of that which is life indeed – As Timothy is told to take hold of the eternal life (6:12) through a faithful stewardship of the spiritual riches committed to his care, so the Christians who have material wealth are to gain the same reward through faithful stewardship.   The treasures may be different, the faith, the faithfulness, and the inheritance are the same.   By storing up this spiritual treasure by using God-given wealth correctly, the Christian is laying hold on the true life which is genuine and lasting.   It is the way to make sure one really "lives" in the age to come.   The KJV reads "eternal life" where the NASB has "life indeed."   The readings reflect a manuscript variation, the older manuscripts supporting the reading "*ontōs dzōēs* -- really life."[93]   Life indeed is that eternal life in Christ which contrasts vividly with the uncertain life supported only by material riches that are temporary.   A proper exercise of one's

---

[93] It was the same adverb, *ontōs*, that was translated "indeed" at 1 Timothy 5:3,5, "widows indeed."   Compare John 8:36, "free indeed" [*ontōs eleutheroi*].

stewardship does not earn salvation, but it is one of the items God looks for when He comes to ascertain whether or not a man has been faithful. Such generosity and participation in the needs of the brethren (verse 18) is the way a person who has been redeemed by the blood of the Lamb may lay hold on that which *in truth* deserves the name "life," because the fear of death will no longer cast its gloomy shadow over it.

2. This is accomplished by guarding the deposit of the faith. 6:20,21a

6:20 -- O Timothy – Is this where, as was his custom, Paul took the pen in hand and personally added a few words in his own handwriting?[94] "It is a beautiful thought which sees in these few earnest closing words the very handwriting of the worn and aged Apostle Paul. [If so,] the epistle dictated by the old man was in the handwriting of some friend of his, who acted as Paul's scribe."[95] "O Timothy" – Paul is no longer addressing church or evangelist, but his own favorite friend and pupil, the loved heir of his God-inspired traditions and maxims, which so faithfully represented the doctrine and teaching of Jesus Christ, the Son of God.

Guard what has been entrusted to you – In 1 Timothy 6:14, Paul said "Keep the commandment (commission)." Now he speaks of "guarding what has been entrusted to you." The picture in the word "guard" is of a sentry keeping watch, and by so doing, preserving safe and uninjured whatever is guarded. The meaning is well brought out in the familiar words of Psalm 121, "He who keeps you will not slumber ... He who keeps Israel will neither slumber nor sleep ... The Lord Himself is your keeper." "What has been entrusted" is a banking term. *Parathēkē* indicates a treasure entrusted, or deposited in, a bank for safekeeping. Some "treasure" has been entrusted to Timothy (perhaps by Paul, perhaps by God) for safekeeping. But what, exactly, has been entrusted to Timothy? The reference is likely to the gospel – God's redemptive truth – and all the responsibilities that Timothy's office as evangelist and this letter have placed on him.

> This deposit cannot be distinguished from the frequent objective use of the terms 'the faith,' the 'commandment,' etc., but its particular significance is found in the preciousness of what is to be guarded ... The metaphor must not, of course, be pressed too far, for the minister of the gospel does not keep the "deposit" from others, but encourages them to come and share in its precious secrets.[96]

---

[94] Compare Colossians 4:18 and 2 Thessalonians 3:17.

[95] Spence, *op. cit.*, p.271.

[96] Guthrie, *op. cit.*, p.118.

> Vincent of Lerins, about 430 AD, explained it thus: "What is meant by 'keep the trust'?   The disciple of St. Paul must keep the sound doctrine of his master safe from robbers and foes ... What is meant by 'the *trust*'?   Something intrusted to you to keep -- not a possession you have discovered for yourself; something you have received from another -- not what you have thought of yourself ... of this trust you are nothing but a guardian ... What then is the meaning of '*keep the trust*'?   It is surely nothing else than 'guard the treasure of the [universal Christian] faith' ... Gold you have received; see that you hand gold on to others.[97]

Likely there is an intended contrast between the treasure of the gospel and the heresy and worthless speculations of false teachers about whom Timothy has been warned.   Although the word *parathēkē* is not employed in the New Testament outside the Pastorals, the idea of the gospel as a sacred trust is found elsewhere in Paul's writings.   For example, 1 Thessalonians 2:4, "But as we have been approved by God to be entrusted with the gospel, so we speak."   The Christian faith is not an invention of men, but a treasure committed by God to men.

Avoiding worldly and empty chatter – The participle with which this phrase begins is circumstantial.   It likely means that the "guard(ing)" is to be done "*by* avoiding ....."[98]   Timothy is to guard the deposit by deliberately turning away from the false teaching.   The same verb *ektrepomai* is applied in 1:6 to the false teachers' defection from truth.   In addition, the participle is in the middle voice; Timothy is urged to avoid these false teachings *for his own benefit*.   Again, the participle is a present tense, requiring continuous action.   It is to be a continual avoiding of worldly and empty chatter.   The expression "worldly and empty chatter" reminds us of 1 Timothy 1:4, 1:7, 4:7, etc., and the contradictions and word battles mentioned in 6:4.   "Worldly" (*bebēlous*) signifies that which is of nonsacred character.   "Empty chatter" (*kenophōnias*, from *kenos*, empty, and *phōnē*, voice) is plural, and refers to empty sounds, empty talkings, arguments with no real content, such as would be the affirmations of the teachers who were espousing the "falsely named knowledge."

> Paul does not tell Timothy to refute these things, but to turn away from them every time.   There is no way to refute a myth or a fanciful fabrication, especially if the proponents themselves are incapable of thinking rationally (1:7).   One is in danger of granting such errorists a measure of respectability by deigning to consider their schemes, and the uninformed may get the notion that their teaching does contain something after all, instead of seeing it for the empty talk which it is (*kenophōnia*).   What must be done is to preach the truth positively, and the

---

[97] Spence, *op. cit.*, p.272.

[98] Verse 20a has indicated what is to be guarded.   Now verse 20b tells us how it is to be guarded.   It is to be guarded by turning away from worldly and empty chatter, and by turning away from the arguments of what is falsely called knowledge.

myths will be shown to be false.[99]

And the opposing arguments of what is falsely called 'knowledge' – The KJV reads "science falsely so called". From this text, many a sermon has been preached about how "science" (the scientific method, and the conclusions reached by this method) is inimical to Christian faith, and is to be avoided by Christian teachers. When the KJV version was translated, "science" (from the Latin *scientia*, to know, to distinguish, to separate) was a term that had the connotation of "special knowledge". Later, after the industrial and scientific revolutions, the word came to have the more limited meaning associated with it in the 21st century.[100] It is "knowledge" falsely so-called, *Gnosticism*, that Timothy is told to avoid. As was noted in the Introductory Studies,[101] care must be exercised here lest the developed Gnostic ideas of the mid-2nd century be thought to be already present in Ephesus, or that this reference is evidence against the Pauline authorship of the epistle, as though the "writer" has in mind 2nd century Gnostic heresies. What likely had already come to the city was an incipient Gnostic teaching, eastern religious ideas, that are contrary to Christian doctrine. Just what was opposed by the "opposing arguments"? Most likely, the "deposit" that had been entrusted to Timothy. The gospel allows no admixture of truth and error (Gnosticism); what Timothy must continue to teach is nothing but pure, holy truth. Eastern religious ideas have always been opposed to the truth revealed in the Scriptures, always opposed to what God is trying to do in His world. The modern cults, and the doctrines behind the New Age Movement, all claim an exclusive grasp of true "knowledge". Yet it does not take much study to see that the old "Gnosticism" has been revived and dressed in modern language; and is, by this admonition, to be avoided by men who would guard the deposit of truth entrusted to them.

6:21 -- Which some have professed – "Which" (a feminine singular pronoun in the Greek) points back to falsely-called "knowledge" (a feminine singular noun). We have had the word "professed" at 1 Timothy 2:10. It is Gnostic knowledge that some have "professed" (espoused and preached). The "some" who were now preaching Gnosticism used to be Christians. But they were attracted by the "falsely called 'knowledge'" and as a consequence were led to deny the great truths of Christianity.

And thus gone astray from the faith – Gnostic doctrines are inimical to faith. Hear it! Paul's instruction is very up to date, especially in this age of influx of

---

[99] Kent, *op. cit.*, p.202.

[100] It is hardly a correct thing to do to use the KJV translation to preach against "scientism."

[101] See "Religion In and Around Ephesus" in the Introductory Studies. There a detailed presentation of incipient Gnosticism in Asia Minor was given.

Eastern religious ideas. The "faith" here is probably objective, standing for a body of doctrine as in 1:6,7 and 6:10. With "gone astray", Paul's "parting shot at the false teachers significantly uses the same word *ēstochēsan* (have erred) to describe their defection as was used at the beginning of the Epistle (1:6)."[102] By promoting false doctrine, the "some" who espoused the falsely called "knowledge" have been aiming in the wrong direction. They have not been advancing toward the true faith at all. Once again, we have a warning that it is possible to be once saved, and then to go "astray from the faith." After commenting on verses 20 and 21, Kent (*op. cit.*, p.203-4) writes,

> Thus Paul recapitulates the content of his letter. Because of false men who are ever active in thwarting the Gospel, Timothy and all ministers must be ever alert to safeguard the true message. This they can do by faithful preaching of its truth, and caring for the organization and needs of the church in the God-appointed way, so that the faith may be preserved in the hearts of believers and may be held forth to the world.

CONCLUDING BENEDICTION.   6:21b

Grace be with you – Nowhere in Paul's letters is there a shorter benediction. This shorter form, *hē charis*, is used in the Pastoral Epistles (2 Timothy 4:22; Titus 3:35) in place of the fuller and more usual form, *hē charis tou Kuriou hēmon Iesou Christou* (Romans 16:20; 1 Corinthians 16:23; 2 Thessalonians 3:18). The short form also occurs in Hebrews 13:25. "You" is plural in the Nestle text.[103] This is one of the indications that though the letter was addressed first of all to Timothy, it was intended for the whole congregation.[104] God's grace is that for which Paul prays in this closing benediction, and he wants it for the entire congregation. "Every reader [be he an evangelist, or a member of some local congregation] may include himself as one of the *humōn* ['you'] if he has responded in [obedient] faith to the sound doctrine proclaimed in Jesus by Paul,

---

[102] Guthrie, *op. cit.*, p.119.

[103] The manuscript authorities for *sou* ("you," singular) and *humōn* ("you," plural) respectively are somewhat evenly balanced. On internal evidence, some have defended the singular found in the Textus Receptus and thus the KJV, since Paul, it is affirmed, is addressing Timothy personally in this closing benediction.

[104] "The concluding benediction is interesting because *with you* is plural. This may mean that the Epistle was designed for others beside Timothy, although examples in the papyri of the plural used for individuals are not uncommon (cf. Moulton, *Expositor*, 6th Series, vii. 107). Both 2 Timothy and Titus close with the same plural greeting, while the conclusion to the Epistle to the Colossians furnishes an exact parallel from Paul's earlier letters." Bruce, *op. cit.*, p.119

and has 'guarded the deposit' of that truth ... as a sacred trust from all attempts of Satan and men to lead astray."[105]

   With these words of prayer for Timothy, Paul ends this Epistle.   This benediction may be brief, but it is rich in meaning, for grace (all the help that God can give a man) is the greatest blessing of all.   With that help, Timothy can carry out all the charges given in this epistle, and so fulfill his task as evangelist at Ephesus.

---

[105] Kent, *op. cit.*, p.204.

SPECIAL STUDY #6

IS MAN IMMORTAL?

What do you think? Is man immortal or is he not? Opinions differ. One of the doctrines currently making the rounds is that the Bible does not teach that the soul is immortal, and therefore, eternal punishment of the wicked is unthinkable, since before eternal punishment could be inflicted, God would have to deliberately keep the soul alive. Well, then, is man immortal or not?

Definition of Terms

One important term is "soul" (Heb. *nephesh,* Grk. *psuchē).* Lexicons give three literal meanings for the word: (1) *Life* on the earth in its external, physical aspects; used in this sense of animals and men; when it leaves the body, death occurs. (2) The *soul,* by which is intended man's desires, feelings, emotions. (3) The *soul* or *immaterial part* of man – which can receive salvation or can be lost, which men cannot injure but which God can hand over to destruction, and which is distinct from the body so far as the body is made up of flesh.[1] It is primarily this third usage with which we are concerned.

It is important to remember that there are two Greek words translated "immortal" in the New Testament. One is *athanasia* (1 Corinthians 15:53,54; 1 Timothy 5:16), which speaks of "deathlessness." The other is *aphtharsia* (1 Corinthians 15:42ff; Romans 2:7; 2 Timothy 1:10) and its cognate *aphthartos* (1 Timothy 1:17; Romans 1:23; 1 Corinthians 9:25; 1 Peter 1:4,24), which mean "uncorruptible, imperishable."

With these brief definitions in mind, let us again consider the question, "Is man immortal?" Is the soul "deathless" and "imperishable"?

Three Modern Attitudes Toward Immortality

Oscar Cullman argues that the idea that the New Testament teaches the soul's immortality is a misunderstanding. He alleges that the immortality of the soul is a Greek, not a Christian doctrine. The Christian doctrine is that of resurrection, not that of immortality.[2]

Hoeksema, while agreeing with the position that soul-immortality is a non-

---

[1] See the lexicons by Arndt and Gingrich, Thayer, Liddel and Scott, and others.

[2] Oscar Cullmann, "Immortality or Resurrection" an article in *Christianity Today,* July 21, 1958, pp. 3-6.

Christian idea, will permit the term immortality to be applied to man, provided the term is defined. His position, in substance, is that only those who are in Christ are immortal.[3]

The third of the modern attitudes is the opinion that in a sense the souls of all men are immortal (i.e., all have an endless existence), but that the term "immortality" is used in the Bible only of the redeemed, since the heavenly life with its blessings is the only life that meets the real sense of the term.[4]

Which of these three is nearest the truth of the Scriptures?

Old Testament Idea of Immortality

The Bible nowhere explicitly mentions the immortality of the soul, and never attempts to prove it in a formal way. Everywhere it assumes man's immortality as an undisputed postulate, in much the way it assumes the existence of God.

The Old Testament teaches immortality, but not with the clarity of the New Testament, chiefly because God's revelation in Scripture is progressive and gradually increases in clearness. Several Old Testament texts imply the immortality of the soul. The translation of Enoch (Genesis 5:22,24). The phrases "to go to his fathers" (Genesis 15:15) or "to be gathered to his people" (Genesis 25:8, 35:29; Numbers 20:24) speak not of burial in a family cemetery, but of a place where the dead dwell connected together in a society.[5] From Genesis 47:9 (and similar passages where life is called a "journey") Paul argues that the patriarchs expected a life after death.[6] And consider Exodus 3:6 in the light of Matthew 22:23. According to Jesus' words, Abraham, Isaac, and Jacob were definitely alive even though their bodies were in the grave. None of them had 'gone out of existence.' All of them were souls that had survived death. Consider further that the dead in the Old Testament descended into Sheol (Greek, Hades), and in Sheol they were in a state of conscious existence.[7] A belief in the immortality of the soul is also evidenced by Old Testament Jews from their practice of necromancy, or consulting the dead – against which God gives frequent

---

[3] H. Hoeksema, *In the Midst of Death,* pp. 98,99.

[4] L. Berkhof, *Systematic Theology,* pp. 672-78.

[5] Lange's Commentary on Revelation, p. 368; McClintock and Strong, *Cyclopedia of Biblical Literature,* V. 4, p. 516.

[6] Hebrews 11:13-16.

[7] Genesis 37:35, Isaiah 14:9ff.

warnings.[8]   Further, the passages that speak of the future resurrection of the dead imply immortality.[9]

Some have attempted to show from the Old Testament that the soul is not immortal. Ecclesiastes 3:19,20 and 9:2-10 are appealed to for proof, since there it is stated that the same thing happens to both men and beasts, in that they all die, and the dead know nothing. Surely, it is alleged, such language speaks of nonexistence.

How does Ecclesiastes answer the question, "Is man immortal?" Ecclesiastes 12:11 tells us that the book is made up of "goads" and "nails." It may be that the "goads" are *problems* raised to stimulate earnest reflection, and the "nails" are the *solutions* to the problems. The goad would be that which perplexes the man who looks at things from the standpoint of the earth ("under the sun"). Thus, the goad problem – Is it not true that men and beasts all die, and that ends things for them? And the nail solution – viewed from the region above the sun, is that man's spirit does not go out of existence. On the contrary, "Then the dust shall return to the earth as it was, and the spirit will return to God who gave it" (Ecclesiastes 12:7). In fact, in Ecclesiastes 3:11 we are told that man's soul reaches out for the life after this life.[10]

And when Ezekiel 18:4,20 says, "The soul that sinneth, it shall die" (ASV), this is not necessarily proof that the soul is mortal. It might mean that sin will *separate* man from God. That is one thing that death is. It is separation.

Certainly, the Old Testament implies the immortality of the soul.

Greek Philosophers on Immortality

It has already been recorded that some are of the opinion that immortality of the soul is not a Christian idea, but a Greek idea. Just what did the Greek philosophers teach on the subject of immortality? At death "the soul departs ... to a divine, immortal ... place ... It lives the rest of the time with the gods."[11] In another place is this note,

---

[8] Leviticus 19:31, 20-27; Deuteronomy 18:11; Isaiah 8:19, 29:4.

[9] Job 19:23-27; Psalms 16:9-11, 17:15, 49:15, 73:24; Isaiah 26:19; Daniel 12:2; Hosea 13:14.

[10] Some interpret Ecclesiastes 3:11 to mean that man is different from the beast in that man is a reflecting, meditating soul, while the beast is not. At least, the "nail" says that "man is not in every respect like the beast."

[11] Adam Fox, *Plato and the Christians,* p. 75.

... the soul is an entirely different thing from the body. In actual life, that which makes each of us what he is, is the soul ... the immortal soul (when we are dead) passes on to other gods to give account of itself, so tradition tells us – an encouraging thought for the good man, but very alarming for the wicked.[12]

The ideas the philosophers taught plainly had come, they said, from "sacred sayings of old" or "tradition." Instead of the Christians getting their beliefs from the philosophers, the Greek philosophers got their teachings from that ancient knowledge which men deliberately allowed to get away as time passed.[13]

It will further help to see whether immortality is a Greek or Biblical idea by examining the doctrine of immortality in the New Testament.

New Testament Teaching of Immortality

The doctrine of immortality is found everywhere assumed in the New Testament. A future state for both righteous and wicked is clearly taught. The continued existence of believers appears in such passages as Matthew 10: 28; Luke 23:43; John 11:25ff; 2 Corinthians 5:1. The survival after death of the wicked is made clear in Matthew 11:21-24, 12:41; Romans 2:5-11; 2 Corinthians 5:10. That even the wicked survive death, and are in a state of conscious existence, is clearly suggested by the narrative of the rich man and Lazarus, Luke 16:19ff. Immortality is implied in all those passages in which the body is represented as a garment which is to be laid aside, or as a tabernacle or house in which the soul dwells.[14] When Jesus Christ appeared in this world, the views about immortality that prevailed were those of the Jews and the Greeks. It was left for Him to advance the revelation of the future state of soul and this He did. Paul says, "Christ Jesus ... abolished death, and brought life and immortality to light through the gospel."[15] By means of the gospel, men have had disclosed to them the life of the future world, and the incorruptibility (*aphtharsia*) of both body and soul.[16] Paul has pointed out that the wicked survive death, and have wrath, indignation, tribulation, and anguish awaiting them.[17] He also taught that one of the things included in the redemptive act of Christ was the redemption of the body. Christ died for the body as well as for the soul. This is why He can

---

[12] *Op. cit.,* p. 86. See similar ideas expressed on pages 88-90.

[13] Romans 1:20ff.

[14] 2 Corinthians 12:1-4, 5:1; 2 Peter 1:14; Philippians 1:23,24.

[15] 2 Timothy 1:10.

[16] See *Barnes' Notes* at 2 Timothy 1:10. See also Hendriksen, *1-2 Timothy and Titus,* pp. 233, 234.

[17] Romans 2:6ff.

speak of the uncorruptible body which awaits the redeemed at the second coming of Christ.[18]

The statement of 1 Timothy 6:16, that "only God possesses immortality," is often used to refute the conclusion to which this paper is tending. On the basis of that passage, it is alleged by some that no soul is immortal. Is this a true inference to draw from 1 Timothy? No reputable commentary so understands it. To quote just a few:

Justin Martyr says,

> God is said only to have immortality, because He has it not by the will of another, as the rest who possess it, but of His own proper essence.[19]

Barnes' note is this,

> It seems to mean that God, in his own nature, enjoys a perfect and certain exemption from death. Creatures have immortality only as they derive it from Him, and of course are dependent on Him for it. He has it by His nature, and it is in His case underived.[20]

One other New Testament doctrine needs to be considered. Briefly, it is this: The word "immortality" is used specifically only with reference to the redeemed, when speaking of men. This seems to imply that the Bible writers put an exalted definition on the term, speaking of the blessedness of heaven. There is a sense in which only the saved have "immortality" since the continued existence of the wicked cannot be called "eternal LIFE" in the full sense of the word "life."

Conclusion

The reality of a conscious life beyond the grave is uniformly assumed and taught by the inspired Bible writers. To this future life they assign no terminus or end. Cullman's assertion that the idea of immortality is "Greek" has been shown to be false. The wicked have been shown to be immortal in the sense that they have continued existence after death. Those who wish to deny the future punishment of the wicked will have to go elsewhere for arguments.

---

[18] 1 Corinthians 15; 1 Thessalonians 4:16ff, etc.

[19] Quoted by Henry Alford, *Greek Testament,* V.3, pp. 362,363.

[20] *Barnes' Notes* on 1 Timothy, p. 202. Compare Hendriksen, *op. cit.,* p. 208.

To the question "Is Man Immortal?" a good answer would be, "Yes, but only in the sense that his existence never ends.   The Bible uses the word "immortal" only for the redeemed.   The soul has been endowed with immortality by the God who alone possesses immortality!"

Commentary On

Titus

ORIENTATION TO THE EPISTLE TO TITUS

Detailed introductory studies for all of the Pastoral Epistles have been included at the beginning of this volume on 1 Timothy, Titus, and 2 Timothy. There it was concluded that there is no reason to doubt the Pauline authorship of this letter to Titus. It may be dated between AD 65 and 67. What we know from scripture about Titus has been reviewed. As Paul's later life was recounted there, it is likely Paul wrote this letter to Titus about the same time as he wrote the first one to Timothy. Paul had been released from his first imprisonment in Rome. He was traveling among the churches as he had done before he was arrested and put in prison. At one point in these travels, Titus accompanied Paul. Together they came to Crete. When it came time for Paul to move on, he left Titus behind to serve as evangelist there among the churches. Titus was to "set in order" the things that were lacking. Titus was therefore to be involved in a correcting and healing type of ministry.

Titus was a man Paul could send on trouble-shooting assignments. Whether it involved a difficult problem like the one at Corinth (2 Corinthians 2:13, 7:5-6,13-14, 8:6,16,23, 12:18), or among the people on the island of Crete who were not an easy people with whom to work, Titus was one who could help troubled churches.

After noting that many of the directions given to Titus are the same as one reads in 1 Timothy, one has asked why was Titus included in the Bible. One possible answer is this – in Titus we learn more about the "message" the evangelist is to preach than perhaps in any other book of the New Testament. It is a very fruitful study to work through the instructions to Titus, just looking for topics the evangelist is to preach as he shares "sound doctrine" with the church members. Another possible answer is that Titus, along with Timothy, gives us a rounded picture of the task of the preacher/evangelist. Any preacher who wishes to have a Biblical job description will find herein plenty to keep him busy for the Lord.

OUTLINE OF TITUS

SIGNATURE, ADDRESS, AND GREETING. 1:1-4
   A. The Writer. 1:1-3
   B. Address and Greeting.   1:4

I.   INSTRUCTION CONCERNING GODLINESS IN CHURCH LIFE. 1:5-16

   A. Godliness In the Selection of Elders.   1:5-9
   B. The Reason Elders who were Sound in Doctrine and Otherwise Qualified were Needed was the Presence of False Teachers.   1:10-16.

II. INSTRUCTION CONCERNING THE PRACTICAL DEMONSTRA-TION OF SOUND DOCTRINE IN THE LIVES OF CHURCH MEMBERS. 2:1-15

   A. Sound Doctrine Involves Corresponding Character Traits to be Developed.   2:1-10
      1. Character traits to be cultivated by older men.   2:2
      2. Character traits to be cultivated by older women.   2:3
      3. Character traits to be cultivated by young women.   2:4,5
      4. Character traits to be cultivated by young men.   2:6-8
      5. Character traits to be cultivated by slaves.   2:9,10

   B. Reasons Why Christians are to Develop Corresponding Character Traits.   2:11-14

   C. Consequent Admonition to Titus.   2:15

III. INSTRUCTION CONCERNING PROPER CONDUCT TOWARDS THOSE OUTSIDE THE CHURCH. 3:1-11

   A. Obligations to Government Officials and Superiors.   3:1

   B. Obligations Toward Fellow-citizens.   3:2

   C. The Reasons for Proper Conduct Toward Non-Christians.   3:3-8a

   D. The Evangelist's Own Conduct Toward Non-Christians.   3:8b-11

CONCLUDING REFERENCES. 3:12-15

TITUS

SIGNATURE, ADDRESS, AND GREETING.   1:1-4

A. The Writer

1:1 -- Paul – This letter begins in the usual way for the 1st century Roman world, with the signature of the author and a brief description further identifying him. First-century letter-writing form also called for an address and a greeting to follow the signature. The writer signs his name ("Paul"). There is no real reason to deny the Pauline authorship of Titus or any of the Pastoral Epistles.[1]

A bondservant of God, and an apostle of Jesus Christ – Here begins the words by which the writer further identifies himself. Many commentators have noted that the opening words of this letter which further identify the writer are among the longest of such further identifications found in any of the New Testament letters.[2] As in the opening words of each of his other epistles, Paul already is introducing some of the key themes and truths which will be unfolded in the body of the letter. The opening words are in harmony with the emphases of sound doctrine, godliness, and the need to do things in the church as God wants them done. Paul claims for himself two roles – bondservant and apostle. When he calls himself a "bondservant of God" (a role he also affirms for himself in Romans 1:1, Philippians 1:1, and Galatians 1:10[3]) he is saying that he recognizes he has stepped into the same function as God's Old Testament "servants" – who are called "my servants the prophets" (e.g., 2 Kings 9:7; Jeremiah 7:2; Zechariah 1:6). That is, he realizes he functions as a mouthpiece for God. It is true that every Christian is in one sense a "servant of God," or a "servant of Christ"; every Christian is one who gives himself up wholly to another's will. But it seems very likely that Paul is using the term "servant"[4] in a special sense as he designates and

---

[1] The arguments against the Pauline authorship are examined in the Introductory Studies.

[2] In the Greek, there are 19 words in the name, address, and salutation of 1 Thessalonians, the shortest such opening found in any of Paul's signed letters. Only Galatians, with 75 words, and Romans, with 93 words, are longer than Titus.

[3] Paul calls himself a "servant of Christ" in other passages. The description he gives himself here, "servant of God," is not fundamentally different.

[4] Translators have had trouble reaching agreement with respect to translating *doulos* at this place, whether it should be "slave" or "servant." Neither word quite conveys the full meaning of the original. When we hear the word "slave," it often carries with it the connotation of harsh and at times inhumane treatment. When we hear the word "servant," it does not carry with it the connotation of harsh treatment, but neither does it carry with it any connotation of the honored position in which God's Old Testament mouthpieces were held.

identifies himself as the writer of this letter. It has sometimes been debated whether or not the apostles knew they were writing Scripture and/or speaking specially for God. The use of "bondservant" certainly says they were aware of being a special tool in God's hands.[5] Paul is God's servant, and as did God's servants in the past, he brings a message from his Master.

When Paul calls himself an "apostle of Jesus Christ," he is using the term apostle in the narrow sense. The original Twelve were called apostles of Jesus, just as in Romans 1:1, 1 and 2 Timothy 1:1. This is the second of two roles he claims for himself. The notes at 1 Timothy 1:1 give detailed information about the office of apostle. Paul received his call and commission as an apostle directly from Jesus Christ (Acts 26:16-18).[6] As an ambassador sent by Jesus Christ (2 Corinthians 5:20), Paul speaks and writes with the authority of Him who sent him and whom he serves. The use of both these designations in one letter is something we do not often find in Paul's other letters,[7] but we can quickly think of several reasons he might use both in this letter to Titus. The designations might show that this is not intended to be simply a private letter. Certainly, Titus would not need to be reminded of Paul's position as servant and apostle, but the church people on the island of Crete might need such a reminder. When there came to be questions about who was telling the truth, Paul or the false teachers who came to Crete and taught a different message than Paul, these "designations" would call attention to the authority with which Paul spoke.

For the faith of those chosen of God – The marginal note calls attention to the fact that the word translated "for" is *kata*, which when used with the accusative, as is the construction here, is quite regularly translated "according to" and indicates a standard with which something is done in harmony or conformity or agreement.[8] This is the only place this phrase "according to the faith" is found

---

[5] Barclay (*op. cit.*, p.259) writes, "this very title, *slave of God, doulous theou*, was the one title that was given to the prophets and the great ones of the past. Moses was the slave of God (Joshua 1:2), and Joshua, his successor, would have claimed no higher title (Joshua 24:29). It was to the prophets, the slaves of God, that God revealed all His will and all His intentions (Amos 3:7)."

[6] Note that "Jesus Christ" here (the order of the words in the better manuscripts) is the reverse of the order found in 1 Timothy 1:1 and 2 Timothy 1:1. For the possible meaning of the expression "Jesus Christ" or "Christ Jesus" see notes at 1 Timothy 1:1.

[7] He does use both designations in Romans 1:1. He uses neither designation in letters which, like Philemon, are strictly personal. Nor do we find either designation in 1 or 2 Thessalonians where other men are named along with Paul in the signature. We do find "servants" used of both Paul and Timothy in the letter to the Philippians. It begins to appear that in each case there is a plausible reason for the presence or absence of such designations that call attention to the authority or position of the writer(s). Peter uses both designations of himself (2 Peter 1:1), and both are used of James (Galatians 1:19; James 1:1). Each of these men held the same position under God and Jesus that Paul did.

[8] Thayer, *op. cit.*, p. 328.

in the New Testament, and its exact meaning is not easy to determine.[9] Further-more, since the word "elect" occurs here, not a few commentators will make their comments harmonize with their ideas about God's unconditional election and predestination of some to salvation.[10] God's "chosen" or "elect" are those who by their own response to God's invitation are "in Christ." God's "elect" in this church age are those who have accepted Christ as their Savior (1 Peter 1:1-5; Ephesians 1:4). God's choice of those who would be his special sons took place back in eternity. As He was planning His creation, He chose or determined that those who were "in Christ" would be those special people. Whether or not a man is "in Christ" depends not on God's sovereign choice, but on the man's response to the Gospel.[11] "Faith" sometimes stands for personal belief, and sometimes for a body of doctrine. Perhaps, in this case, we should think of each person's personal faith in the revealed truths of salvation. Some suppose that what Paul writes here in Titus is similar to what he wrote in Romans 1:5, where he tells us the purpose of his apostleship was "to bring about the obedience of faith among the Gentiles." Perhaps the whole phrase says God's people believe God's message that Paul has delivered, and theirs is no mistaken belief. Paul's commission as a "servant" and an "apostle" were in harmony with the gospel being preached so that men could become believers (faith comes by hearing the Gospel), and so be included among the "chosen" or "elect." No one needs to go to the Gnostics to get extra "knowledge" before he can be one of God's elect.

And the knowledge of the truth – "Full knowledge (the Greek is the compound *epignōsis*) of the truth" is what one learns from God's servants/apostles. One need not look to any Gnostic teachers to flesh out or fill in what Christianity as originally given allegedly had failed to teach.[12] Paul's ministry can be measured by this standard, too. His work as a "servant" and an "apostle" is in harmony

---

[9] Hendriksen, Bernard, and the RSV read "to further the faith of God's elect." Kelly prefers to translate it "in the interest of" and calls attention to John 2:6 where he thinks the preposition *kata* has a similar meaning. Barclay (*op. cit.*, p.261) offers "to awaken faith in God's chosen ones," but this smacks of the Calvinistic doctrines of predestination and unconditional election.

[10] Not a few commentators, following Calvinistic doctrine, comment that Paul's apostleship was carried out "in order to further or promote the reliance of God's chosen ones upon Him," or "it is through Paul's instrumentality that the chosen of God should believe." Some even find a parallel statement in Acts 13:48, which in many versions reads, "as many as had been appointed (ordained) to eternal life believed."

[11] See notes in *New Testament Epistles: Romans*, p. 337. It should also be observed that God's "chosen people" are no longer limited to those of Jewish descent, but in the New Testament include all those who are believers in Jesus, whatever their ethnic backgrounds happen to be. The phrase "elect of God" designates Christians and emphasizes who it was who elected them.

[12] These comments about "Gnostic teachers" reflect the conclusions reached in the introductory studies to Timothy and Titus, as well as what shall be said about "Jewish" teachers in Titus 1:10ff. Incipient Gnosticism was at first a Jewish heresy before it infiltrated the church and became a "Christian" heresy.

with the "full knowledge of the truth" which God wants proclaimed to His world.

Which is according to godliness – For the meaning of "godliness" see comments at 1 Timothy 2:2. It speaks of one's conduct or attitude towards God.[13] It is the way a man lives when he fears and serves God. It is a quality of character that can be developed (2 Peter 2:6). Whether this phrase goes only with the nearest antecedent ("truth") or with both antecedents ("faith" and "truth") is debated in the commentaries. If we take it with "full knowledge of the truth," this phrase distinguishes the truth about God from any other kind of truth. If we take it with "faith," then it is implied that there are some kinds of "faith" that do not lead to godliness. Some make both "faith and truth" the antecedents of this phrase.[14]

These words of this verse, along with those we shall read in the next verse, give us Paul's own perspective on his message and ministry. So far he has said that his position, ministry, and message are in complete accord and harmony with (*kata*) the faith, and with full knowledge about God. Now he says it is also in harmony with (*kata*) godliness. We shall use "godliness" – the promotion of Christian values, the spirit of true dedication to God, the kind of conduct that God tells us He expects – as the "theme" for each of the chapters in Titus.

1:2 -- In the hope of eternal life – This verse continues Paul's longer-than-usual description of himself, of the Gospel, and of his commission to teach it. This first phrase of verse 2 might better be translated "based upon" or "resting on the hope of eternal life," but this still does not settle just what it is that rests on the hope. It may be that this first phrase in verse 2 modifies all of verse 1. If so, then "hope of eternal life" is the thing that energizes Paul's ministry. 1 Timothy 4:10 might then say the same thing, "It is for this we labor and strive, because we have fixed our hope on the living God." It may be that this first phrase in verse 2 modifies "godliness." If so, then the "hope of eternal life" is the incentive for holy living for believers in general. We might compare Romans 8:24,25 and 12:12 where "hope" serves as a similar incentive. In this context, the expression "eternal life" stands for salvation in its fullest development, the abundant life in Heaven (cp. John 17:24; Romans 8:25). It is that endless future life which the believer shares in fellowship with God, and the Savior Jesus Christ (Romans 5:21,

[13] Much is said about "godliness" in these Pastoral Epistles. See 1 Timothy 3:16, 4:7,8, 6:3,5,6,11; 2 Timothy 3:5.

[14] Barclay (*op. cit.*, p.261-2) comments at this place, "The result of faith and knowledge must be a *truly religious life*. Faith must always issue in life. Christian knowledge is not merely intellectual knowledge; it is knowledge *how* to *live*. There have been many people who have been great scholars and whose shoulders have been heavy with the weight of their academic distinctions, and who have been completely inefficient in the ordinary things of life, and total failures in their personal relationships. A truly religious life is a life in which a man is on the right terms with God, with himself and with his fellow men."

6:23; 1 Timothy 1:16, 6:12). "Hope" is a complex emotion of the human mind consisting of a desire for some known object, and an expectation of receiving and enjoying it. If either the desire or the expectation is missing, it is not "hope," it is just "wishing." There is one sense in which "eternal life" is the believer's present possession (John 3:16,36). But there is a sense, just as true, in which "eternal life" is still something just hoped for, since in many aspects it is unrealized. Hope is a confident expectation based upon God's promise.

Which God, who cannot lie, promised long ages ago – God's promise of eternal life will certainly come true, for God cannot and does not lie. Just as each of the phrases in this expanded epistolary opening prepare us for an emphasis to be made later, so "God ... cannot lie" may have been chosen by Paul with reference to one peculiar vice of the Cretans, their tendency to lie ("Cretans are always liars"). Hebrews 6:18 also tells us it is impossible for God to lie. God cannot lie, and therefore we have the soundest possible basis for our "hope of eternal life."

The Greek rendered "long ages ago" can also be rendered, as the margin shows, "before times eternal."[15] (1) It may refer to the ages (Patriarchal and Mosaic) that precede this Christian age. The first promise of salvation is found in Genesis 3:15. Many promises of the salvation Messiah will make possible then follow all through the Old Testament Scriptures. It was promised back then in the earlier ages; now, however, it is manifested. Compare also Romans 16:25,26. (2) It may refer to what God purposed back in eternity, before He even began to create. Salvation was purposed and settled even then, before the world was created and the ages began to roll. In fact, ever since, God has been moving history to the goal He determined ahead of time. Compare 2 Timothy 1:9. Christ was the "Lamb slain from the foundation of the world" (Revelation 13:8). As God planned or purposed (Romans 8:28), "in love He predestined us unto adoption as sons" (Ephesians 1:5). "He chose us for Himself in Christ before the foundation of the world" (Ephesians 1:4). God promised eternal life for people who did not yet exist. None of them were there to hear the promise, but it was made in the mind of God and perhaps in the hearing of angels. The Gospel message which Paul preaches is no new idea, no recent development with little forethought. It has been planned and pledged by God Himself for long ages. Is this intended as a deliberate contrast to the recently-developed doctrine of the false teachers who have invaded the churches of Crete? We think so!

1:3 -- But at the proper time manifested – Here in verse 3, we are still in Paul's epistolary opening, working through the longer-than-usual description of the Gospel which Paul preaches. Paul moves from eternity past to the manifestation in contemporary history of God's promise and purpose. Although God made the

---

[15] The KJV reads "promised before the world began."

promise of eternal life before there was any human being to hear it, and all through Old Testament times human beings had only vague intimations of it (verse 2), it was not until the opportune time arrived that God made it quite plainly known to men through the cross of Calvary and the inspired message that was committed to Paul and the other apostles of Jesus by God's own command. The words "proper time," like "the fullness of time" in Galatians 4:4, speak of the most suitable time in God's program as determined by God Himself.[16] Compare 1 Timothy 2:6 and 6:15. "Manifested" speaks of a clear, public revelation and/or proclamation. It is a word regularly used of the incarnation of Jesus. God's plan, hitherto not clearly seen, can be seen in all of its glory, simply by looking at Jesus Messiah (see 1 Peter 1:10-12 and 2 Timothy 1:10,11).

Even **His word** – The NASB breaks the sentence, adding the word "even." Some of the older translations read that God "manifested His word," that is, the gospel.[17] There is a slight but understandable change in the construction. The relative sentence passes almost imperceptibly into a primary sentence. "His Word" becomes the object of the verb "made manifest," rather than the "eternal life" referred to in the previous verse, as we might have expected. "Word" is used rather coextensively with "the gospel." Peter used the same term in his address to Cornelius, where "Word" is the whole revelation of the gospel, including the Person and work of Jesus Christ (Acts 10:36).

In the proclamation with which I was entrusted – Paul here calls his preaching the proclamation of the Word or gospel of God. "Proclamation" translates *kērugmati*, a word which implies "the open cry or proclamation" made by a herald. Paul is a "herald" in God's service, making the proclamation he was commanded to make. That's what "preaching" is – a herald delivering the King's message. Ever since the Damascus Road experience, Paul has been aware of a sacred trust to be a preacher of the unsearchable riches of Christ. God had given him a precious treasure, and Paul was going to guard it faithfully. We suppose that this phrase, as is true of most of this extended opening to this letter, is deliberately added, as a balance to the "message" one would hear from the Gnostics.[18] Their

---

[16] Lewis Foster has written, "In the fullness of time God sent forth His Son. The Jewish nation had spread the teaching of one God. The Greek people had taken their language to the far corners of the earth. The Roman government had established one rule for practically the whole known world, and tied that world together with roads and communication. Man in general had acknowledged a desperate need for security and for peace in the face of vain and false religions." *Standard Lesson Commentary*, Nov. 1964, p. 409.

[17] Though Paul uses the word *logos* at this place, he is not using the word as it is used in the prologue of John's Gospel, with specific reference to the person of Jesus Christ, the Son of God. We can see this when we note that Paul goes on to explain how this "word" was "proclaimed/preached."

[18] When proper nouns appear in the Greek, such as "I" (*egō*) does here, there is an implied contrast. "I," in contrast to others, was entrusted with the gospel, Paul says. "Entrusted" is a

message wasn't a treasure entrusted to them, as the Gospel was a treasure entrusted to Paul.   People who go off after the Gnostics are going to find they have discovered "fool's gold" rather than a genuine treasure!

According to the commandment of God our Savior – It was no one less than God Himself who "commanded" that Paul be entrusted with the proclamation of the gospel.[19]   (Paul dwells with emphasis on the fact that God commanded he be entrusted with preaching the gospel.   Who "commanded" the Gnostics to deliver their message?)   Paul here writes "God our Savior."   Elsewhere in the New Testament, the term "Savior" is regularly applied to Jesus, though we have "God our Savior" in 1 Timothy 1:1, 2:3, and 4:10.   See also Luke 1:47.   God is "our Savior" in the sense that salvation originated in His mind, and He is the one who made the necessary arrangements for our redemption.   Through Jesus Christ our Savior, God is our Savior.   Paul may speak of "our" Savior, because the readers of this letter[20] need to be reminded that the one who entrusted Paul with the Gospel was their Savior, too.   In fact, if men do not avail themselves of the salvation God offers, there is no salvation for them at all!   Men must let this important fact shape their thinking and acting.

B. Address and Greeting.   1:4

1:4 -- To Titus – According to the usual 1st century format, after signing his name and identifying himself (as Paul did in verses 1-3), the writer then indicates to whom he is writing this letter.   "Titus" is the addressee.   See the Introductory Studies for the Pastoral Epistles, Part X, "Survey of the Life of Titus," where there is a brief sketch of what we know about the life and ministry of this evangelist.

My true child in a common faith – These words of address closely resemble what is said about Timothy in 1 Timothy 1:2 and 2 Timothy 1:2.   Titus was Paul's "child" in a spiritual sense.   It probably means that Paul was the one who converted Titus to the faith, and ever after that, Titus stood to Paul in the position of a son in the faith.[21]   "True" (*gnēsios*) used with "child" means "legitimately

passive form of the verb *pisteuō* (often translated "to believe" when it occurs in the active voice).   "I was believed in by God," says Paul, and that's why He gave me the message to preach.

[19] *Kat' epitagen* means "in accordance with the command."   Paul's role as servant and apostle did not originate from human sources; God Himself ordered it.   In other passages, Paul speaks about the "will of God" being behind his calling to be an apostle (1 Corinthians 1:1;   2 Corinthians 1:1;   Ephesians 1:1;   Colossians 1:1).

[20] Titus knew all these matters that Paul has alluded to in this extended opening of this letter. These things are certainly alluded to for the Cretan's benefit, more than for Titus' benefit.

[21] See notes at 1 Timothy 1:2 for the connotations included in the word "child."   Even if Titus had been led to Christ by someone other than Paul, Paul had taught him, nourished him in mind and spirit, and brought him up in the faith.   That would justify Paul calling Titus "my own son."

born."[22] In Scripture true childhood is synonymous with obedience (1 Corinthians 4:15-17, Philemon 10-13). The appellation "common" describing "faith," is likely included in this extended epistolary opening to contrast with the "faith" which the Gnostics were offering, which was something different from the "common faith." As measured by[23] the common faith taught by the apostles and held by all Christians, Titus was a "true child." This use of the word "common" would serve to remind Titus, the churches on Crete, and the false teachers "of the circumcision," that Paul regards the uncircumcised Titus and himself, a Jew, as sharing the same faith. "Faith" (as in verse 1) can refer either to a body of doctrine, or to one's personal acceptance of the truths included in that body of doctrine. Since the thrust of the whole letter is about a body of doctrine the false teachers were trying to get the Cretans to accept, we suppose that is the thrust here in verse 4. Christians already share a common faith – one delivered to them at the opportune time by God. Why listen to some other doctrine? Throughout all three of these "Pastoral Epistles," there is an emphasis on "faith" that results when men hear and accept the teaching of the Word of God. Local churches ought to be "Bible institutes" where the Word of God is taught systematically and practically.[24] Church members can then continue to share in the "common faith."

Grace and peace -- See 1 Timothy 1:2 for explanations of the words of this prayer for blessing for Titus. Some manuscripts include "mercy" just as 1 Timothy 1:2 and 2 Timothy 1:2 have it, and the critics are divided as to whether or not "mercy" ought to be retained here. This salutation articulates well the essence of what Christians, especially leaders like Titus, need. They need "grace" (God's help to live the Christian life) and "peace" (the child's consciousness of having been reconciled). The next phrase states from whom these blessings are received.

From God the Father and Christ Jesus our Savior – Both the Father and the Son are sources[25] of grace and peace for "true children in the faith." "Savior," the title just given to the Father in verse 3, is now ascribed to Jesus. This is one of the many indications we possess of Paul's belief that the Son was equal to the Father as touching His Godhood. To call Jesus "our Savior" is a rare expression. Jesus is usually called "Lord." But all three members of the Godhead are active in the work of salvation, so it is not surprising that Jesus should be called "Savior."

---

[22] Men and women become the "children" of God by being born again (John 3:3-6).

[23] Four times in the first four verses Paul uses *kata*, "according to": Verse 1, "according to the faith;" verse 1, "according to godliness;" verse 3, "according to the commandment of God;" and now here in verse 4, "according to the common faith," in harmony with it, in accord with it. Paul, Titus, and all of us who become Christians share this common faith.

[24] During B.W. Carrier's ministry at Hessville, Indiana, that church was well taught in the Word of God. The methods Mr. Carrier used are worth studying and emulating.

[25] The preposition "from," which is not repeated, governs both "God" and "Jesus."

Paul may well be anticipating two points he will make, one in 2:11ff, and the other in 3:1ff. In both, he appeals to the saving work of Jesus as a basis for the exhortations he makes.

I.   INSTRUCTION CONCERNING GODLINESS IN CHURCH LIFE. 1:5-16

A. Godliness In the Selection of Elders. 1:5-9

1:5 -- For this reason – Verse 1 has spoken about "godliness," doing things according to God's will out of fear and devotion to Him. The "reason"[26] Titus was left on Crete is about to be stated in the following words – namely, "to set in order what remains, and to appoint elders in every city." If these two things were done, there would be "godliness in the life of the churches on Crete. We observe that Paul's letters to individuals do not have a "thanksgiving section" as do his letters to congregations. When writing to trusted individuals, Paul just plunges immediately into the reason for which the letter is written.

I left you in Crete – The word translated "I left you" is the word used in reference to leaving his cloak at Troas, and leaving Trophimus ill at Miletus (2 Timothy 4:13, 20). It indicates Paul had been with Titus on the island and had left him behind there as he himself travelled on elsewhere. Crete was a well-known large and populous island in the Mediterranean, southeast of Greece. We identify Crete with the Caphtor of the Old Testament (Deuteronomy 2:23; Jeremiah 47:4; Amos 9:7). Very early it was the scene of advanced civilization. In Homer's *Odyssey* it is mentioned as having 90 cities. In the *Iliad* 2.649 it has as many as 100 cities. In 69 BC, the island was added to the Roman dominion. In the days of Augustus it was united into one province with Cyrene. It abounded with Jews of wealth and influence; this we learn from the testimony of Philo and Josephus. We have no other account of this visit by Paul to the island of Crete. According to the history in Acts, Paul briefly touched on this island during his voyage to Rome (Acts 17:7-13), but that is hardly the time alluded to here in Titus 1:5. On the supposition that Paul was released from his first Roman imprisonment, we may well suppose a journey by sea from Rome towards the churches addressed in the Prison Epistles, during which Paul and Titus stopped at Crete.[27] We may

---

[26] The word translated "reason" is *charin*, the accusative of *charis* used as a preposition. When so used it indicates the goal or the reason for which something was done. Arndt and Gingrich, *op. cit.*, p. 885.

[27] Paul's travels after his release from the first Roman imprisonment have been variously reconstructed. See the Introductory Studies for details on whether the Pastorals were written from one journey or several. If there was but one journey – from Rome to Crete to Miletus to Troas to

suppose both worked together with the churches on the island until Paul found it necessary to press on. Titus was then left behind to continue the church work. We have no account of how or when the Gospel was first brought to this island. Some suppose people present in Jerusalem on the Pentecost birthday of the church (Acts 2:11) carried the gospel back to their homeland. Some suppose in the years since Pentecost, preachers came to this island and began the church (much as preachers first went to Antioch and planted a church there, Acts 11:19,20). Perhaps Paul and Titus themselves were successful in evangelizing the cities and planting churches on the island in a six-month or so long crusade.[28] The language of Titus 1:5 presupposes that congregations of Christians already exist on the island, but they are without an "appointed eldership," and there are some other things lacking, as well, that Titus needs to correct. This statement about Paul's leaving Titus on Crete would let the churches know that what Titus was doing had apostolic authority behind it.

That you might set in order what remains – The word translated "set in order" (*epidiorthoō*) is a word full of meaning. The root word can mean "to make straight" or to restore something to its natural and normal condition after something protrudes or has gotten out of line. It is a medical term, for example, used of straightening crooked or misshapen limbs. The same root is used at Hebrews 9:10 ("times of reformation") as a reference to the Christian age as compared to the Mosaic age. Once Messiah has come, He will "set things straight;" that is, He will replace the Mosaic gifts and sacrifices, the food and drink and various washings, the regulations which were good only for the body, but which could not cleanse the conscience or make it possible for the worshiper to be "perfect" (enter into the presence of a Holy God because his sins were atoned for). Exactly what "the remaining things" (*ta leiponta*, neuter plural) were that needed to be "set in order"[29] we have no way of ascertaining. In any new church planting venture, there is a need for new converts to be taught what is expected of them, and a need to guard against the encroachments of false doctrine and careless lifestyles. It is also possible that the instructions in the following chapters of Titus concerning godliness in church life, in home life, and in public life, are some of the things that needed to be emphasized by Titus as he set in order the remaining things.   The *epi-* prefix on "set in order" means "in addition" or to

Macedonia to Corinth to Nicopolis and back to Rome – then it would follow that Paul dropped Titus off at Crete, and then left Timothy behind at Ephesus. On this scenario, the epistle to Titus would be the first of the three Pastoral Epistles to be written. If several journeys were undertaken during the years of freedom between the apostle's imprisonments in Rome, then Titus would be written after 1 Timothy, but before 2 Timothy. See all this explained in detail in the Introductory Studies.

[28] On an earlier missionary tour, Paul spent less than six months in Thessalonica, yet a flourishing congregation was planted there.

[29] The TEV captures the sense well. It reads "put in order the things that still needed doing."

"carry it further" than has already been done. Others had begun the work, now Titus is urged to do additional things.

And appoint elders in every city as I directed you – Apparently, this directive to Titus to arrange for the selection of elders is a separate task from the ones previously identified by the words "the remaining things."[30]   If "set in order" and "appoint" are two different tasks, we would be slow to offer the comment found in many commentaries to the effect that while little groups of Christians had been gathered, and meeting places arranged for, there was no official organization of the congregations.[31]   Not a few commentaries offer the idea that here in Titus we have the germ of an episcopal type of church government, with Titus serving as "bishop" over the many "presbyters" on the whole island, and in turn seeing that the churches on the island were organized completely under his oversight. Groups of Christians in any town can function as a "church" without having elders appointed (e.g., new churches planted on Paul's first missionary journey functioned for several years before elders were appointed for them, Acts 14:23). Groups of Christians do not have to be "organized" (i.e., have an eldership over them) before they can be called a "church."   It is also noted by many that nothing is said to Titus about arranging for the selection of deacons as Timothy was instructed to do (1 Timothy 3:8ff).   This would imply that congregations can function without deacons until the need for their service becomes apparent, at which time they, too, could be selected as was done at Acts 6:1-6.

"As I directed you" indicates Paul had given directions on "just how to do it" (Greek, *hōs*) before he left the island.   These directions likely included emphasis on the qualifications for the office, as well as the manner of selecting them.   It is to our benefit that Paul repeated his directive to Titus in writing.   We thus have a written apostolic directive[32] concerning the selection of elders in case someone should ever dispute how it should be done.   We also have the divinely given qualifications a man must meet before he is appointed to such an important task in the congregation.   The NASB translation "appoint" is probably better than "ordain"[33] in the KJV, since the verb (*kathistēmi*) means to "arrange for, to establish, to put in charge, to cause something to be done."   The verb does not

---

[30] It is possible that *kai* (rendered "and" in the NASB) should be translated "namely" at this place.   If so, then the one thing lacking that needed Titus' attention was the appointment of elders for each congregation.   However, "remaining things" is plural and two different verbs ("set in order" and "appoint") are used.   So we think that the conjunction should be rendered "and" just as the NASB has it.   The selection of elders was one of the things that still needed doing.

[31] In this passage, one's "denominational" polity is likely to influence the comments on church organization and administration.   A commentator must make every effort to read this passage through New Testament glasses rather than through present-day church government glasses.

[32] The word "I" is emphatic in the Greek, to provide full apostolic authority for Titus' mission.

[33] The regular verb for "ordaining," i.e, the "laying on of hands," is *epitithēmi*.

tell how the selection was to be made. Perhaps the congregation was to do the selecting after being instructed by Titus on how to do so.[34] Perhaps in newly planted congregations the evangelist takes more of the lead (i.e., the congregation has less voice in the choice) to appoint only qualified men to be elders.[35] Evangelists should be very hesitant before assuming unilateral power to appoint elders and deacons. Verse 5 which says "that *you* might appoint" is far from Scriptural proof that the evangelist acting *alone* appoints elders over the congregations.

This list of qualifications is hardly given for Titus' benefit alone, but surely is intended as a guide for the Christians on the island of Crete.[36] In light of Acts 6:3 ("appoint") and Acts 6:6 ("prayed and laid their hands on them"), it might be said that evangelists may very well "ordain" (officially install into office) those whom the congregation has selected to be their leaders.[37] In New Testament times, the words "elders" (*presbuteroi*) and "bishops" or "overseers" (*episkopoi*) were used interchangeably for the same task or function or office in the church.[38]

---

[34] The congregation was given a voice in the selection of deacons (Acts 6:1-6). Note the same verb translated "appoint" is used at Acts 6:3. The church also had a voice in the "appoint-ment" of messengers to travel with Paul as they took the offerings from the churches to Jerusalem (2 Corinthians 8:19). Even the passage at Acts 14:23 (where the verb is *cheirotonidzō*, "to stretch the hand," i.e., either in voting or ordination) does not rule out congregational choice as elders were appointed for each of the churches in Galatia. If the congregation always has a voice in the selection of its leaders, then Paul compresses the whole process, speaking only of the last act (the ordination service), rather than relating the whole process that leads up to the last act in the appoint-ment or selection of church leaders. (At the close of the 1st century, Clement of Rome used the same term "appoint" [*cheirotonidzō*] concerning the selection of leaders for the church, and then quickly clarifies the procedure by saying "with the consent of the whole church." I Clement 44.3)

[35] When comparing all the passages dealing with the selection of church leaders, there is just enough question that may be raised legitimately about the method of selection to keep us from dogmatically affirming that there is only ONE way, or ONE pattern, that must be followed every time we propose to select leaders. Nevertheless, this commentator's preference is to include three steps in the selection of leaders: (1) The evangelist calls attention to the necessity of the qualifications. (2) The people are given the opportunity to select qualified men of their own choosing. (3) An official installation service follows, led by the evangelist, during which time the congregation is impressed with the solemnity and responsibility of the tasks just given to the people selected for leadership of the congregation, and of their obligations to those whom they have just chosen to be their leaders.

[36] The list of qualifications in Titus would then serve a similar purpose as the list found in Acts 6:3, when the Seven were selected. The list is intended to guide the Christians in their choices.

[37] Care must be exercised here. The "laying on of hands" in Acts 6:6 may well have been to impart supernatural spiritual gifts to the Seven, rather than just being part of a formal ordination service. After all, Stephen performed miracles (Acts 6:8) and spoke by inspiration shortly thereafter (Acts 6:10); Philip also had the ability to work miracles (Acts 8:13).

[38] See comments at 1 Timothy 3:1 on the meaning of the terms "elder" and "bishop." Certain religious groups think of the church's presiding official as being a "priest." Those groups are accustomed to think of "elder" and "priest" as being the same thing in the New Testament, and commentaries written by adherents of these groups will substitute the word "priest" at this place in the explanations they offer for these verses. It is hardly to be believed that Titus' job on Crete included the appointment of "priests" to serve in the local churches! We know of no New Testament passage where "priest" (*hiereus*) and "elder" (*presbuteros*) are used interchangeably, as we find

How many "elders" were to be selected in each town or city is not specified.   It is a fact that in the New Testament we find a plurality of "elders" in each "church" or "congregation."   Compare Acts 14:23.   A plurality of men so functioning would provide each member with a "shepherd" (1 Peter 5:2), who would have time to care for their needs, and who would also guard against any one elder being tempted to "lord it over the flock" (1 Peter 5:3).   The words "in every city"[39] point out that Christianity is already widely extended on Crete, an island, as noted above, famous for its hundred cities.   The charge to Titus is that he is to see to it that each city that already has a congregation of believers has elders appointed.

1:6 -- Namely – Though we have a broken sentence, the sense is clear.   "If anyone is blameless, etc., then he can be appointed."   Observe that the verb "must" occurs in Titus 1:7 just as it did in 1 Timothy 3:2.   Twice in this list of qualifications (verses 6 and 7), we read the general requirement that the man who would be elder must be "above reproach."   This leads some commentators to outline the qualifications under two points – verse 6 speaks of being "above reproach" in his family life, while verses 7ff speak of being "above reproach" in areas where he is to function as "God's steward."   Others divide the list into three groups – group 1 in verse 6, group 2 in verse 7, and group 3 in verses 8-9.   The lists given in Titus 1 and in 1 Timothy 3 are somewhat parallel.   To avoid unnecessary duplication, the qualifications and their explanations that have already been covered in notes on 1 Timothy will not be repeated here in Titus.   Rather, a cross reference to the appropriate verse in 1 Timothy will be given.

If any man be above reproach – While the Greek could be translated "any one," the context makes it clear that males rather than females are the ones being considered for the function of elder in the church.   Any man meeting the qualifications is eligible to be selected as elder.   This word "above reproach" was used of deacons at 1 Timothy 3:10.   It is one against whom no charges legitimately can be made.[40]   One of the particular areas, as the rest of this verse shows, where no charges can be made concerns the man's family life.

The husband of one wife – See this qualification explained at 1 Timothy 3:2.   It says that marital and sexual fidelity are required of the potential elder.   While

---

"elder" and "bishop" being used interchangeably for the same office.

[39] Literally, the Greek *kata polin* means "city by city."

[40] None of these qualifications are interpreted to mean that the elder must be sinless perfect. That quality was true of only One who ever lived on earth.   But the work of the church is so important that only well qualified men, only men who consistently display in their lives the characteristics enumerated, are to be considered for the office.   For a man to live in such a way that charges about his life and reputation can be legitimately made indicates a serious lack of judgment.   The very lack of judgment that leads to a blameworthy record would in itself render the man undesirable for a place of leadership in the church.

Titus might be read "If he is the husband" (i.e., thus implying that he would not have to be married, though it might generally be expected that most potential elders will be married men), such an interpretation cannot be given to the qualification as found in 1 Timothy. 1 Timothy indicates that only married men are to be considered for the function of elder. Unmarried men are not qualified.[41] As stated in 1 Timothy 3:5, leadership in family life is an important training ground for leadership in the church.[42]

Having children who believe – Another possible source of reproach arises from a man's children. "Elder" means older. For a man to have children old enough to be Christians ("believers") would suggest a man younger than the late 30's or early 40's is too young to be qualified. Children who were still pagans would be a great handicap to any elder. Therefore, for a man to be qualified to become an elder, his children who are above the age of accountability are to have become Christians ("believers"). This requirement suggests that Christianity has been established on Crete for some period of time. Time enough, at least, for not only the father, but also the children to have been won to the Lord.[43] A plurality of children who have become Christians is what this qualification speaks of.[44] The children may be the elder's own, but nothing in this passage would prevent a man and wife from adopting children and rearing them in the nurture and admonition of the Lord, in order for the man to meet this qualification for eldership.

Why is this qualification so important? Something about the experience of seeing one's children through the teenage years (remember each child is different, and each requires a different way of handling) prepares a man to handle all the personality problems and situations that will arise among the different mem-

---

[41] In fact the next phrase here in Titus "having children" ought to cause us to pause before affirming that the previous phrase means "if he is married"!

[42] Mrs. Charles Harris penned this note at the bottom of her Sunday School quarterly at this place: "If he can't keep his marriage together, how can he manage the church?"

[43] The word translated "faithful" can also be translated "believers." In fact, it is translated both ways in the Pastoral Epistles (2 Timothy 2:2; 1 Timothy 6:2). It means more than what some have inferred from the context, i.e., that it here is virtually synonymous with "obedient" (to their parents). (Could a preference for "obedient" be part of an attempt to prove that in order to be qualified to be an elder, a man does not have to be married, nor does he have to have children who are Christians? But conversely, are children who are obedient and submissive to his loving authority all he needs to be qualified?)

[44] If "husband of one wife" requires a man be married, then "having children who believe" requires that a man have at least two children who are Christians. The Bible does not teach infant membership in the church, so the qualification rather requires that the children are old enough to have passed the age of accountability, and have personally accepted the invitation to follow Christ.

Given this understanding of what this qualification requires, this commentator does not personally encourage men with less than two believing children to seek the office of elder. Not all agree with this strict interpretation, but each of us must act on our understanding of Scripture as men who will in the final judgment for how we taught and led the congregations to whom we preach.

bers of the congregation.   Without the experience in his own family, the potential elder would be greatly limited, perhaps even handicapped, in his ability to "shepherd" the members of the flock of God over which he is appointed.

Not accused of dissipation or rebellion – It is the potential elder's children who are not accused of dissipation or rebellion.   It is possible for one's children to be professed Christians but to live so as to belie their profession.   "Dissipation" translates *asōtias*, a word used in Plato and Aristotle for "debauchery" or "profligacy," and is used of the prodigal son's lifestyle after he left home (Luke 15:13).   It could include self-indulgence and reckless expenditure.   The word is also used in the New Testament of drunkenness (Ephesians 5:18) and of vices found in the non-Christian world (1 Peter 4:4).   One of the elder's responsibilities included the superintendence of the church's funds (see Acts 11:30).   The fact that a man was prepared for this responsibility could be seen in the man's children, if they have learned from their father the error of reckless waste and extravagance.

"Rebellion" translates *anupotakta*, which means "not under rule, insubordinate, not under subjection," "undisciplined."   It is used elsewhere in the New Testament of people who are unwilling to be under God's law (1 Timothy 1:9), and of false teachers who turn away from the truth (Titus 1:10).   If a man is not capable of teaching his own children obedience and submission to authority, how can his influence be of value within the church at large?   The true training ground for the eldership is at least as much in the home as it is in the church.

When it comes to making modern application of this qualification, a number of questions have been asked, to which there are no absolute cut-and-dried answers.   For example, is a man unqualified for elder by children who were Christian while living at home but who are no longer living at home and are no longer consistent in their Christian walk?   We may suppose that the children in this directive from Paul to Titus are thought of as still living at home with their parents.[45]   While they are under their father's roof, they are to be practicing Christians, not accused of self-indulgence and insubordination.   On the other hand, should some man, heartbroken by his children's prodigality, conscientiously question his own qualification to serve as elder, we would not insist or even encourage that he go ahead and serve, especially if his conscience bothers him after reading this qualification.[46]   Paul is not asking any more of the potential

---

[45] The verb translated "having" (i.e., "denoting possession of persons to whom one has a close relationship," BAGD, p.332) may imply that Paul is talking only about children who are still rightfully under their father's authority in his home.   Compare what is specifically stated about "ruling well his own house, having his children in subjection" in 1 Timothy 3:4.

[46] These notes about grown children's waywardness should not for a moment be construed as meaning there is something inherently wrong with the man's work at being a good father if somewhere down the way the child rebels and turns away from the Lord.   Each child has his own free

elder and his children than is expected of every Christian father and his children.

1:7 -- For the overseer must be above reproach as God's steward – Verse 7 continues the list of qualifications of the person who would be an elder/bishop. The title "overseer" is explained at 1 Timothy 3:1. "Elder" (verse 5) and "overseer" (verse 7) are the same function/office. The use of the singular "overseer" continues the generic singular that began in verse 6 with "anyone." It is not evidence that "overseer" is an office distinct from that of "elder." "Above reproach" is the same word used at Titus 1:6.[47]

"God's steward" apparently explains the position to which the elder is appointed – he is a responsible administrator of the house, the church of the Living God. In the household of New Testament times the most trusted and best qualified servant was chosen to be the steward or manager of his master's household.[48] The same kind of qualified man is the one to be chosen to be "steward" or "manager" of God's house, the church. Elders do exercise a certain rule or authority over the lives of the members of the congregation that select them. This is implicit in the word "overseer" and also seems to be implied in passages like Hebrews 13:17. At the same time, elders must guard their own hearts against any idea that their position makes them "boss." The idea that leaders are "bosses" is perfectly pagan (Matthew 20:25, 23:11,12). Elders must never think or say of the church, "This is mine!" The word "steward" reminds us that elders are manager of another's possessions or house, and will give an accounting to the owner (Luke 12:42 and 16:1ff). See also 1 Corinthians 4:1,2, where the most important characteristic of a steward is "faithfulness."

The qualifications in this verse and following are some of the areas in which a man must be "blameless" if he is to be qualified for such an important position as "steward" over God's house.[49] As in 1 Timothy 3:2, these things "must be".

Not self-willed – *Authadē* occurs elsewhere in the New Testament only at 2 Peter 2:10, and in the LXX at Genesis 49:3,9 and Proverbs 21:24, though it occurs quite

---

will, and some break their parents' hearts, regardless of all the good training and love they received while still at home. Waywardness in children is not necessarily proof of a poor job by the parents when it came to carrying out their responsibilities when the children were young.

[47] In these letters to Timothy and Titus, Paul uses two words for "blameless" that seem to be synonymous. One, *anepilēmptos*, "never caught doing wrong, irreproachable," is used at 1 Timothy 3:2, 5:7, 6:14. The other, *anegklētos*, which means "to accuse" or "to bring charges against someone" occurs at 1 Timothy 3:10 and Titus 1:6,7. This latter word was used in Acts 23:29 and 26:2 of charges brought against Paul, but which, upon examination, proved to be unfounded.

[48] Perhaps the most famous steward in the Bible is Joseph, who had complete control over all of Potiphar's business (Genesis 39:1-9).

[49] The five negative vices are in the accusative case, in agreement with *episkopon*, the subject of the infinitive *einai*. The negative is *mē*, which is the form an infinitive would normally take.

commonly in classical Greek.[50]   It always has a bad sense – stubborn, harsh, self-pleasing, self-willed.   The contrasting virtue would be "gentle, kind, gracious" (*eipeikēs*).   The man who has this bad quality is a headstrong, stubborn, self-loving man who demands his own way without regard for others.   This describes a man who is intolerant, who thinks there is no way of doing anything except his way.   He tends to be overbearing, always pushing to have his own way.

Not quick-tempered – *Orgilon* occurs only here in the New Testament, though words from the same root are frequent.   A possible contrasting virtue would be the word translated "peaceable" (*amachos*) at 1 Timothy 3:3.   "Quick-tempered" may not be a good choice of words for this adjective which means "prone to anger."   *Orgilos* is not the anger that suddenly blazes up, but rather is the anger or wrath a man has to nurse to keep warm.   It is a long-lived, deliberately nurtured, purposely maintained anger.   A man who nourishes within his heart a long-lasting anger against any man is not qualified to be an elder in the church.

Not addicted to wine – See comments at 1 Timothy 3:3.   The word means "given to overindulgence to wine," but also has a figurative meaning describing outrageous conduct resulting from lack of self-control.   The man who even in sober moments acts with a lack of self-control is hardly qualified to be an elder.

Not pugnacious – See comments at 1 Timothy 3:3.   It speaks of the person who is prone to settle arguments with his fists, or, in its broader sense, with violent speech (i.e., one who "browbeats" his fellow-men).   The man who resorts to violence of action or speech to make his point is not fit to be a leader in the church.

Not fond of sordid gain – See comments at 1 Timothy 3:8, where this word is one of the qualifications for deacons.   See 1 Timothy 3:3, where the man who would be an elder must be "free from the love of money."   It pictures taking from others what one already has an abundance of.   Nathan accused David of this sin when he told the story of a man who had plenty of his own sheep but took the one which belonged to another.   The Greek word describes a man who does not care how he gets money so long as he gets it.   It so happens that Cretans were notorious for this character fault.   Polybius said, "They are so given to making gain in disgraceful and acquisitive ways that among the Cretans alone of all men no gain is counted disgraceful."   Plutarch characterized the Cretans as sticking to money

---

[50] "Aristotle, who always defined every virtue as the mean between two extremes, set on the one extreme the man who pleases everybody (*arēskos*), and on the other extreme the man who pleases nobody (*authadēs*), and between them the man who had in his life a true and proper dignity (*semnos*).   He said of the *authadēs* that he is the man who will not converse or associate with any man.   Eudemus said that the *authadēs* was the man who 'regulates his life with no respect to others, but who is contemptuous.'   Euripides said of him that he was 'harsh to his fellow citizens through lack of culture.'   Philodemus said that his character was compounded in equal parts of conceit, arrogance and contemptuousness."   Barclay, *op. cit.*, p.269-70

like bees to honey. Elders were in a position where the money they got for serving, and the money they were entrusted to administer, could became a serious distraction and temptation. A man whose mind is full of thoughts of amassing money is too preoccupied to be able to function as an honest "steward" should function. One writer has summarized the vices listed in this verse as all forms of selfishness: pride, anger, desire for drink, dominance, and wealth.

1:8 -- But hospitable – See comments at 1 Timothy 3:2. Having named some faults that would disqualify a man from being selected as an elder, Paul now lists some virtues that are to be present in the man who would be selected as an elder. A man who is a "lover of hospitality" is one with real concern for others' welfare.

Loving what is good -- *Philagathon* is rendered as "a lover of good men" in the KJV, a translation perhaps influenced by Hebrew 13:2 ("showing hospitality to strangers"). It likely refers to a virtue different from the "hospitality" just mentioned. If so, "lover of good" denotes a heart that finds room for sympathy and involvement with any good, noble, or generous act. "Good" includes not only good men, but also good books, good music, good causes, and many other good things. It is difficult to believe a man who would be a dedicated leader in the church would deliberately associate with things that are bad for him and his family. Some commentators think Philippians 4:8 gives a list of "good things" the prospective elder is to love. Others speak of how an elder should love to see in people what God wants them to be. It is supposed that this corresponds to *kosmios* in 1 Timothy 3:2, especially if that word means "well-behaved."

Sensible – See comments on the word "prudent" at 1 Timothy 3:2, the same Greek word that is here translated "sensible." The sobriety of a person removed from wine can be extended to mean a balanced judgment in other fields.

Just – *Dikaios* is often understood as describing a man's conduct towards his fellow men.[51] It is the kind of conduct towards others that meets the approval of God. The prospective elder is to be a person who practices the kind of behavior towards others that God has revealed is proper in His children. He is to be a man of integrity who sticks by his word and who practices what he preaches.

Devout – The word here is *hosios*, a word which describes a man's conduct towards God.[52] See comments on this word at 1 Timothy 2:8. It is the kind of conduct towards God which observes the true and established ordinances of the Lord. It is moral and religious behavior in harmony with the God of the universe. The man is "pure" because of dedication to a God who is "pure."

---

[51] Joseph was "just" or "righteous" in his conduct towards Mary (Matthew 1:19).

[52] Contrast "unholy" in 1 Timothy 1:9 and 2 Timothy 3:2.

Self-controlled – This adjective indicates one has his appetites or desires under control,[53] one who is self-disciplined in his habits.[54]   An elder must discipline his time so that he gets his work done. He must discipline his desires. He must keep his mind and body under control.   As is true of several of these characteristics or qualifications, self-control is one of the fruit of the Spirit (Galatians 5:23).   This virtue is listed as one of the steps of Christian character development in 2 Peter 2:6.

1:9 -- Holding fast the faithful word – After listing some of the qualifications expected in a man who would be selected as an elder, Paul now climaxes his list of qualifications with the necessity of strict loyalty to the apostolic teaching that has been delivered and remains unchanging.   The "word" which is characterized as "faithful, trustworthy, or reliable"[55] is none other than the Gospel, the word of salvation.   It seems very likely that the word "faithful" is used because the Cretans needed to hear that the message from God through the apostles was "reliable."   They didn't need any further word, especially some word from incipient Gnostics.   The teachings of the Gnostics could not be categorized as "faithful, trustworthy, or reliable."   The word translated "holding fast" carries the idea of "clinging to."   To be qualified to be an elder, a man must steadily adhere to the Christian doctrine as taught by Jesus and His apostles.

Which is in accordance with the teaching – "The teaching" is the body of Christian truth as taught by the apostles.[56]   At this point of time in the early church, most teaching had been done orally.   Some New Testament writings were already circulating, but people still depended mainly on the oral tradition for their "doctrine."   That "Word" was reliable only when it was in accord with the apostles' teaching.[57]   The elder must have a good grasp of Christian doctrine, and his beliefs must be in harmony with the message[58] delivered by the apostles of Jesus.   Timothy the evangelist was instructed "to hold the pattern of sound words which you have heard from me" (2 Timothy 1:13) and was instructed to "continue in the things which you have learned and become convinced of, knowing from

---

[53] The rendering "temperance" in the KJV has come to have the connotation of "not given to wine."   The Greek term is broader than just controlling one's appetite for alcohol.

[54] 1 Corinthians 9:25 uses the same word for an athlete "exercising self-control in all things."

[55] See the word "faithful" used in the same sense in 1 Timothy 1:12,15, 3:1, and 4:9.

[56] In 1 Timothy 1:10-11, "sound doctrine" is said to be in accordance with the Gospel.

[57] Like the first church at Jerusalem "continued steadfastly in the apostles' teaching," so the men who would be elected elders must do.

[58] The word order in the Greek, which has *kata ten didachen* between the article and the adjective, says the "word" is "reliable" because it is in harmony with the teaching.   This verse likely speaks of what the elder has heard taught, rather than speaking of teaching the prospective elder has been doing.

whom you have learned them" (2 Timothy 3:14). Here in Titus, we learn that what was expected of evangelists when it comes to clinging to the faithful Word is also expected of Christians, especially of those who would be elders!

That he may be able both to exhort in sound doctrine and to refute those who contradict – Two reasons are given why a prospective elder must adhere to God's Word. By adhering to the Word, he will be able to carry out the tasks described in this verse. This qualification is also a "must." One reason for adhering to God's Word is that, once selected to be an elder, he will be expected to "exhort in sound doctrine." For the meaning of "sound" ("healthy") as applied to doctrine, see comments at 1 Timothy 1:10 and 2 Timothy 1:13. Believers benefit from this exhortation[59] in sound doctrine as they are protected from the inroads and errors proposed by the false teachers.[60] The word translated "exhort" is a present tense infinitive, indicating the exhortation in sound doctrine is something an elder will do continuously. "Exhort" means to urge or to encourage, to incite to action. The second reason a prospective elder must adhere to God's Word is so that he may be able "to refute those who contradict" the gospel message. It seems probable that "those who contradict" are synonymous with the "false teachers" discussed in verse 10. The elder must know and cling to the faithful word if he is going to refute the teachings of those who contradict the gospel message.[61] The word translated "refute" is also a present tense infinitive, indicating that refutation[62] of those who contradict the Gospel is something an elder will find need to do continuously. The word means to rebuke a man in such a way that he is compelled to see and to admit the error of his ways.[63] There of course are times when contradictors and opposers of the Scriptures may refuse to change their beliefs, even though they are convicted of the error of their own position. These two functions should be included when one makes a list of tasks an elder performs. The Christian man who has the qualities here listed will be equipped

---

[59] "Exhort" seems to be the proper translation. The sense is that the hearers are being urged by the elders to accept, believe and practice the sound doctrine. 1 Timothy 5:17 speaks of the elders laboring at preaching and teaching. We picture elders exhorting in sound doctrine both publicly and privately.

[60] "The naive church member who says, 'We don't want doctrine! Just give us helpful devotional thoughts!' does not know what he is saying. Apart from truth (and this means Bible doctrine) there can be no spiritual help or health." W. Wiersbe, *Be Faithful* (Wheaton: Victor Books), p.102.

[61] Chrysostom (*Hom. ii on Titus*) commented on this passage, "that he who knows not how to contend with adversaries, and is not able to demolish their arguments, is far from [qualified for] the teacher's chair."

[62] The verb *elegchō* has several connotations, such as "refute," "confute," "convince," "reprove," and "convict." Alongside "those who contradict," what is called for is "reproof" or "refutation."

[63] Barclay (*op. cit.*, p.274) illustrates the word "refute": "Demosthenes said it describes the situation in which a man unanswerably demonstrates the truth of the things he has said. Aristotle said that it means to prove that things cannot be otherwise than as we have stated them."

to exercise the kind of oversight a steward in God's house should exercise.

B. The Reason Elders Who Were Sound in Doctrine and Otherwise Qualified Were Needed Was the Presence of False Teachers. 1:10-16

1:10 -- For there are many rebellious men – "For" introducing verse 10 tells us this verse is intended either to give a reason for something just said, or is further explanation of something just said. Paul has just called for godliness – doing things so as to please God, doing things like God wants them done – when it comes to the selection of elders to administer the churches. These verses may give a reason why elders are needed. Verse 9 has just spoken of "those who contradict." Perhaps verses 10-16 are intended to give us further explanation or identification of those whom Paul had in mind. "Rebellious"[64] suggests these men refuse to submit to the rules God has laid down. They are disobedient to God's Word. "Many" tells us that these false teachers are numerous. The following verses will (1) further describe them and their erroneous teaching (verses 10,14); (2) indicate that their impact on whole families is devastating (verse 11); (3) identify their motives as being purely mercenary (verse 11); and (4) characterize their lifestyle as detestable and disobedient (verse 16).

Who are these "rebellious men"? (a) The false teachers described in Titus 1:10-16 have characteristics similar to the false teachers of 1 Timothy 1:3-11.

- In both passages they are characterized as "rebellious," 1 Timothy 1:9, Titus 1:10.
- In both passages there is emphasis on "futile talk," 1 Timothy 1:6, Titus 1:10.
- In both passages their "teaching" is described as different and as something which ought not be taught, 1 Timothy 1:3, Titus 1:11.
- In both passages they are characterized as "liars," 1 Timothy 1:10, Titus 1:12.
- In both passages there is a concern for the effect the false teachers will have on "sound doctrine" or "sound faith," 1 Timothy 1:10, Titus 1:13.
- In both passages there is an allusion to "Jewish myths," 1 Timothy 1:4, Titus 1:14.
- In both passages there is a concern for "conscience," 1 Timothy 1:5, Titus 1:15.
- In both there is emphasis on a "pure heart," 1 Timothy 1:5, Titus 1:15
- In both passages there is something strongly "Jewish" about the false teachers, 1 Timothy 1:7, Titus 1:10.

(b) In the Introductory Studies to these Pastoral Epistles, Part XI, we have offered an identification of the false teachers who were a threat both at Ephesus and on

---

[64] The same word is used at Titus 1:6 of one of the traits that would exclude a man from being qualified for elder.

Crete.   We have shown that Gnosticism began as a Jewish heresy before it ever infiltrated the churches and became (in a later century) a Christian heresy.

Empty talkers and deceivers – "Empty talkers"[65] says they achieve no useful purpose with their fictitious tales and myths.   They told others what to do, and did not do it themselves (Titus 1:16).   "Deceivers" tells what their teaching does to the minds[66] of those who listen to them.   As 2 Peter 2:14 puts it, the false teachers "beguile unstable souls."   Instead of leading men to the truth, they lead men away from truth.   Instead of establishing men in the faith, they slowly erode away their faith.[67]   It is a tragedy when people are deceived by false teachings!

Especially those of the circumcision – The false teachers on Crete about whom Paul is warning[68] are of Jewish background.[69]   It is probably not correct to speak of them as nominal Christians, or as Jewish church-members.[70]   They likely are not claiming to be church members at all; they are just making church members (among others) the targets of their recruiting efforts.   Several sources indicate that a large number of Jews lived on Crete (Acts 2:11, Philo,[71] and Josephus.[72])

1:11 -- Who must be silenced – *Epistomidzō* is a rare verb.   It means "to stop the mouth by means of a bridle, muzzle, or gag."[73]   Another verb meaning

---

[65] The word used here is from the same root as the word translated "fruitless discussion" in 1 Timothy 1:6.   There are two Greek synonyms for "empty" or "vain," *kenos* and *mataios*.   The first means "empty" and refers to contents.   The second is "aimless, purposeless," and refers to the result.   It is an adjective which was applied to heathen worship.   The word translated "vain talker" (*mataiologoi*) is a compound made up of *mataios* and a word meaning "words" or "speech."

[66] The word here translated "deceivers" is a compound made up of the word for "mind" and another word meaning "to deceive, beguile, cheat."   Thayer reminds us that there is more than "deception" implied by the second word.   It brings out the idea of subjective fancies.

[67] Barclay, *op. cit.*, p.275.

[68] If *malista* means "especially," then the phrase says that most, but not all, of the false teachers about whom Paul is concerned are "of the circumcision."   However, a recent study has shown that in ad hoc documents *malista* may mean no more than "that is."   If that is the meaning in this place, then this phrase does no more than give us a further definition or description of the false teachers.

[69] "Circumcision" is used with several connotations in the Scripture.   It is used of Jews in general (Romans 4:12); of the Judaizers (Pharisees who pretended to become Christians, Galatians 2:4,12); and of Christians of Jewish descent (Acts 10:45, 11:2).   If we have correctly identified the false teachers about whom Timothy and Titus are warned, then we would not identify "the circumcision" of Titus 1 with the "Judaizers" of Acts 15 and Galatians 2 since those Judaizers were zealous for the Law.   The Jewish Gnostics were zealous for their speculations and philosophy and myths, but only secondarily concerned with the Jewish Scriptures.

[70] Some suppose the phrase in verse 14 rendered "turning away from the truth" (KJV, NASB) implies that the false teachers once had embraced the truth of Christianity.

[71] *Legatio ad Gaium* 228.

[72] *Antiquities* XVII.12.1;   *Lives* 427.

[73] Hervey (*op. cit.*, p.3-4) has written, "It may be worth noticing that the horses on Etruscan

"muzzle" or "tie shut" (*phimoō*) is used of the Sadducees at Matthew 22:34, and the word used here is nearly a synonym of that. The one here emphasizes curbing, controlling, preventing of the mouth from speaking. "Stop the mouth" is a very suitable way to express the idea in English. How this silencing is to be done is not spelled out in detail.[74] The context implies it is to be done by Titus and the elders. Verse 9 speaks of the need to "refute" or "rebuke" those who "speak against" what the apostles had been teaching. At the very least, the false teachers are not to be given opportunity to speak to any of the Christian assemblies. In Titus 3:9-11, Paul tells Titus to warn the "factious man" once or twice, and then to reject such a person if the warnings are not heeded. Perhaps the elders, too, are to visit the homes of Christians who have given an ear to the false teachers, and attempt to stop their influence in those surroundings also. This does not suggest Christian leaders may use violence or persecution or physical intimidation to silence the false teachers. While the way to stop the mouths of the false teachers is not specified at this place, it is suggested by what the letter says elsewhere: "rebuke them sharply" (Titus 1:13), "speak the things which are fitting sound doctrine" (2:1), "sound speech which is beyond reproach" (2:8), "remind them to be subject" (3:1), "avoid foolish questions" (3:9), "reject a factious man after a first and second admonition " (3:10). It is dangerous to allow false teachers to thrive unchallenged. It is like a plague that spreads from one member of the family to another until the whole house is infected.

Because they are upsetting whole families – "Whole families" may imply the false teachers went from house to house seeking converts to their heterodox teachings. The meaning of "upset" or "overthrow" is well-expressed by the verb "subvert" found in the KJV. The family members' faith was undermined, and the family members then wandered away from the truth. This devastation of whole families was the reason the mouths of the false teachers had to be stopped. Some think of family life being disrupted by the behavior of those deceived. Some think of the spiritual harmony in the family being subverted by the false doctrines some were embracing. Because some versions read "whole houses" and because the early church met in people's houses, some think whole congregations meeting in various private homes are affected by the false teachings.[75]

---

vases are usually represented as in effect muzzled by the bridle, and have their mouths shut."

[74] Of course, if the false teachers were church members, then the steps of discipline taught in Matthew 18:16-18 would be the proper method of silencing them. But if they are outsiders, such a method of church discipline would be inappropriate and unworkable.

[75] People today who have Bible study classes in their homes must be careful lest visitors come in with strange doctrines. There are sects and cults that look for such classes to infiltrate just for the purpose of winning the whole study group to their cult or sect. Bible study classes, too, must be careful what books they use to guide their studies of various Scriptural topics. It might be a good idea for the home Bible study leader to allow the elders to evaluate the proposed study guides.

Teaching things they should not teach, for the sake of sordid gain – "Teaching ... for the sake of sordid gain" pinpoints the real motives that lay behind what the false teachers were doing. They were acting as teachers simply for the money they could get out of it. Such income for teaching is "sordid" or "shameful" when the teachers are enriching themselves even at the expense of the downfall of their students. We've already been told that one of the qualifications for elder is that he is "not to be fond of sordid gain." The elder will be a teacher, but he is to be motivated by nobler motives than the Jewish false teachers about whom Paul warns. "Teaching things they should not teach" says that Jewish myths and Jewish Gnostic doctrines ought not even be taught. 1 Timothy 1:7-11 indicates that the emphasis on the Jewish law as though it were intended for Christians is something that was totally in error since the Law was never intended to be anything but temporary, its job finished when the goal to which it pointed (the coming of Messiah) had been reached (Romans 10:4; Colossians 2:14). Perhaps the next verse in Titus gives the reason these things should not be taught; namely, they are lies, typical of the lies Cretans were famous for.

1:12 -- One of themselves – Paul here appeals to a source the Cretans themselves would acknowledge as being correct in order to document the fact the false teachers were more than likely being untruthful.[76] The line about to be quoted comes from Epimenides, who was a native of Crete.[77] Epimenides, "one of their own," certainly knew well what his countrymen were like.

A prophet of their own – The primary meaning of the word "prophet" is "one who speaks by inspiration." In the majority of places the word appears in the Scriptures, it designates one who speaks God's message, i.e., a genuine prophet,

---

[76] Paul's knowledge of this pagan writer's work is but one of several instances that occur in his writings which well may indicate his familiarity with secular literature. Such a familiarity is regularly attributed to his studies in post-graduate school at the University of Tarsus before he became a persecutor of Christians, and then an apostle of Jesus.

[77] The words were original with Epimenides, whose date is given variously as somewhere between 630 and 500 BC. The first words of the line from Epimenides' poem are later quoted by Callimachus (c.300-240 BC) in his hymn "To Zeus." Callimachus was not from Crete but from Cyrene, and his poem does not have the entire statement quoted by Paul.

Vincent (*Word Studies*, p.1075) gives a summary of Epimenides. "Legend relates that, going by his father's order in search of a sheep, he lay down in a cave, where he fell asleep and slept for fifty years. He then appeared with long hair and a flowing beard, and with an astonishing knowledge of medicine and natural history. It was said that he had the power of sending his soul out of his body and recalling it at pleasure and that he had familiar intercourse with the gods and possessed the power of prophecy ... He is said to have lived to an age of 157 years, and divine honors were paid him by the Cretans after his death. He composed a Theogony, and poems concerning religious mysteries. He wrote a poem on the Argonautic Expedition, and other works. Jerome mentions his treatise *On Oracles and Responses*, from which the quotation in this verse [in Titus 1:12] is supposed to have been taken." The work alluded to by Jerome is no longer extant.

Diogenes Laertius (I.10) tells us it was this same Epimenides who advised the Athenians to sacrifice "to the appropriate god." This advice from a "prophet" may have led to the erection of the "altar to the unknown God" referred to in Acts 17:23.

speaking by Holy Spirit inspiration. In some cases, where the prophet is labeled a false prophet, he too may be speaking by inspiration, but the source of his inspiration is an evil spirit, not the Holy Spirit. This brings us to the phrase at hand. There is no evidence that Paul calls this man Epimenides a "prophet" in the true sense of the word, i.e., a spokesman for Jehovah-God. When certain ancient men who consulted occult sources for information, most of whom served as priests as well as mediums, were called "prophets" by their pagan contemporaries, it reflects the common belief that these ancients were specially favored by the "gods," were in special contact with the "gods," and "spoke for them." We suppose Paul is using the word "prophet" in the sense that pagans would have used it of Epimenides. It is perhaps an argument ad hominem, appealing to an authority that the readers themselves were accustomed to acknowledge had spoken the truth. In fact, in the next verse, Paul will affirm the truthfulness of what this pagan "prophet" said, since such "prophets" did not always tell the truth.

Said, "Cretans are always liars, evil beasts, lazy gluttons" – "Lying" was such a characteristic of the Cretans that the verb *krētidzein* was used to denote "telling lies"; literally, "to lie like a Cretan."[78] Cretans had a reputation for telling lies for selfish purposes. *Thērion*, the word rendered "evil beasts," is the synonym for "wild beast." When men are called "wild animals," it implies brutality and unreasonableness and a love of cruelty. Not only are they called "wild animals" but they are called "*evil* beasts." Epimenides also stated that the absence of wild beasts from the island of Crete was remedied by its human inhabitants. This implied that Cretans would push anyone out of the way in order to gain an advantage for themselves. "Lazy gluttons" points to a life of dull gluttony and slothful sensuality. The expression is used of those who, by indulging their bodily appetites, become corpulent and indolent.

From the general bad character of the Cretans arose the line, "Cretans, Cappadocians, and Cilicians, three most evil 'C's" (*Krētes, Kappadokoi, Kilikes, tria kappa kakista*). Livy, Polybius, Cicero, and Plutarch alike bear witness to their "covetousness and dishonesty and shameful greed."[79] "When was there ever an upright Cretan?" (*Tis Krēton oide dikaiosunēn*) asks Leonides in an Epigram. What an indictment! Instead of living for the beautiful things of the spiritual life, they lived for their own appetites. Not only are they "gluttons," but Paul calls them "*lazy* gluttons." Some have criticized Paul for being "untactful" in his characterization of the Cretan population. Others have found fault with the slight shift from "those of the circumcision" (verse 10) to "Cretans" (verse 12). But it is not lack of tact to call attention to some well-known truth in order

---

[78] One is reminded that a similar thing was true at Corinth, where the verb "to Corinthianize" was synonymous with immorality.

[79] See Hendriksen, *1 and 2 Timothy, Titus*, p. 352, for the quotes from these ancient writers.

to drive home another truth that needs to be heard and recognized. Nor is the "shift" surprising since it would appear that many Jews who resided on Crete have assimilated some of the worst character qualities of the native population. Otherwise, how does one explain what makes these Jewish false teachers "tick"?

1:13 -- This testimony is true – Paul emphatically endorses the evaluation of Cretans which Epimenides, their countryman, had voiced years earlier. This endorsement helps us to see that Paul used the description "prophet" in a sense the Cretans would have used to characterize Epimenides.[80] Pagan "prophets" did not always tell the truth, but in this case, he spoke aright. Paul had lived long enough among the Cretans to have witnessed their lifestyles, and he writes this personal endorsement of Epimenides' words under the Holy Spirit's influence.

For this cause reprove them severely – "For this cause" may look back to what was said in verse 12, and thus verse 13 gives a reason why a sharp rebuke is needed. It will take sharp, firm action to overcome the regular behavior of the Cretans. "Reprove" is *elegche*, a word used at 1 Timothy 5:20 and 2 Timothy 3:16 and 4:2. It means to "convict a man of the error of his ways," or "rebuking" (as in "rebuking" errors in living[81] and doctrine), to bring the fault home to the offender. Who is to be "reproved" by Titus and the elders[82]? (1) Is it the Jewish false teachers? Since verse 10 began, the topic has been false teachers. Does the command mean that Timothy is to reprove them with a restorative purpose in mind; namely, to try to win them[83] to soundness in the faith? If so, then we may continue to affirm that the false teachers were outsiders, as we have done in previous comments on this section. (2) Is it the Christians on Crete (the "whole families" of verse 11) who are to be rebuked? Does the command mean Titus is to reprove the Christians[84] who have given a willing ear to the false teachers, so

---

[80] Not often is it necessary for an inspired writer to voice such an evaluation of statements made by a genuine prophet of God. Nor do we think that 1 Corinthians 14:29 teaches that the utterances of genuine prophets are to be evaluated. The instruction about evaluating the utterances of prophets in 1 Corinthians 14:29 seems to require those with the ability to discern spirits to determine whether it was the Holy Spirit or an evil spirit that prompted the "prophets" in the church at Corinth to speak. The Corinthians' passage does not seem to suggest that after a prophet of God has spoken, bystanders have a right to sit in judgment and even to reject or ignore truths inspired by the Holy Spirit. What the Corinthian Christians in the audience are to do is "test the spirits," for false prophets and false teachers abound.

[81] Matthew 18:15 uses the same word, where the English reads, "Go and *tell* him his fault ..."

[82] This whole chapter is tightly joined together (see the "for" with which verse 10 begins). Titus has certain responsibilities as he would set the churches in order, and he is to enlist the help of the elders in carrying out those responsibilities.

[83] 2 Timothy 2:25-26 shows that it is possible for false teachers to repent.

[84] The ones to be rebuked seem to be distinguished from "men who turn away from the truth" (verse 14). If so, it is believers who are to be rebuked lest they follow those "men." Further, it could be argued "that they may be sound in faith" seems to fit people who already are believers.

that they might become sound in the faith? If so, then we may continue to affirm that the false teachers were outsiders, as we have done in previous comments on this section. (3) Some broaden the scope of "they" so that it includes both the false teachers and their victims.

When Titus reproves, it is to be done "severely." The same root word *apotomōs* ("severity") is used of God's dealings when He cut off the unbelieving branches (i.e., Jews who rejected Jesus as Messiah) from the olive tree (Romans 11:22). The faithful evangelist or elder must use severity when it is necessary for the spiritual health of the flock, just as the skillful surgeon uses the knife to cut away the diseased and cancerous flesh so as to save the patient's life.

That they may be sound in the faith – The purpose behind the "rebuke" which Paul had in mind is here stated. He wants the ones who are rebuked, the teachers and/or the taught, to become "sound in the faith." "Faith" here probably refers to each person's own personal beliefs and practices. As the next verse will show, such a state of sound faith consists in "the rejection of Jewish myths and the commandments of men." In other words there is a body of doctrine ("the faith") to which each Christian's personal beliefs ("his faith") is to conform. Paul's use of "the faith" and "the truth" as synonymous with "the Gospel" is the same in the Pastoral Epistles as it is in Paul's other letters. See "the faith of the Gospel" (Philippians 1:27), "belief in the truth" (2 Thessalonians 2:13), and "preaching the faith" (Galatians 1:23). "May be sound," (*hugiainōsin*) is a present subjunctive. It does not seem to mean that the sharp rebuke is given to someone who is already healthy. It does seem to mean that the sharp rebuke is administered to someone who is not healthy, in the hopes that they may become healthy ("sound"). The rebuke is administered so that they may become what at present they are not – namely, sound in the faith. The attitude of some church members is, "It makes no difference what you believe, just so you sincerely believe it." Paul would not agree with that foolish philosophy. It makes all the difference between life and death whether or not one believes the truth of the Word or believes lies. A man indeed may choose what he wants to believe, but he cannot change the consequences if he chooses to believe a lie!

1:14 -- Not paying attention to Jewish myths – This verse continues the thought begun in verse 13. The "reproof" that would lead to "sound faith" also includes the deliberate rejection of "Jewish myths" and "commands of men." Concerning "Jewish myths," see comments on 1 Timothy 1:4. The false teachers were the ones who were teaching "Jewish myths," and people who wish to be "sound in the faith" (verse 13) will pay no attention to such teachings.

And commandments of men who turn away from the truth – The "commandments of men" refer apparently to religious practices and everyday lifestyle regulations. They are man-made, rather than God-revealed.[85] Compare what Paul wrote at Colossians 2:21-22 concerning such precepts as "touch not, taste not" being the "commandments and teachings of men." Compare also Titus 1:15, where we gather that something about "purity" is included in these "commandments of men." Comparing the language of 1 Timothy 4:1ff with Titus 1:14-15, several similar expressions provide a good reason to conclude that 1 Timothy 4:1ff ("forbidding marriage, and advocating abstention from certain foods") gives two examples of the kind of rules that Paul calls the "commandments of men." The "men" who turn away from the truth are the false teachers. We have tended to identify them as Jewish Gnostic teachers. "The truth" is used here of "the content of Christianity as the absolute truth."[86] 2 Timothy 4:2 and 4:4 use the terms "truth" and "the word [of the Gospel]" interchangeably. The "turning away" that these men do has been variously explained. The verb translated "turn away" is a middle voice form of *apostrephō*.[87] In the middle voice it means to "reject" or "repudiate." I. Howard Marshall offers the translation "perverting the truth" at this place. Hendriksen offers the suggestion that the false teachers "obscured" the real intent and meaning of God's truth, or "turned their backs on the truth." The verb form here is a present tense, which indicates this "perverting" or "repudiating" is a continuous action, a habit pattern, a repeated action. The expression could be used of those who had never embraced the truth in the first place, and it could also be used of those who once knew the truth, and now have departed from it.

1:15 -- To the pure, all things are pure – The connection with the context seems to be this: the "commandments of men" alluded to in verse 14 have something to do with "pollution" and "ceremonial cleanness." The words "pure" (*katharon*) and "defiled" (*miainō*) are the proper words for ceremonial "cleanness" and "defilement" respectively.[88] Paul addresses this topic of "purity" because it was

---

[85] The same expression "commandments of men" occurs at Matthew 15:9 and Mark 7:7. In that place the *halakhic* rules for daily living which had been propounded by the Pharisees are what Jesus is speaking about, and Jesus flatly says such rules void the Law of Moses, and result in vain worship. Each sect of the Jews had their own peculiar *halakhic* rules, the observance of which automatically separated them from all other sects. While we would not precisely identify the *halakhic* rules of the Pharisees and the rules taught by the Gnostics, there is this similarity – both sets of rules were man-made, rather than being rules God has made and revealed for men to obey.

[86] BAGD, p.35.

[87] This same verb, in the active voice, was used of those in Asia who "turned away from Paul," 2 Timothy 1:15.

[88] The Pharisees were masters at making rules about what was "clean" and "unclean" in regard to articles of food, pieces of furniture, the human body, contact with a Gentile, etc. However, we would not explain the Jewish Gnostic ideas of "clean" and "unclean" as being either identical with Pharisaic ideas or derived from Pharisaic teachings. Remember, even pagans had their taboos. Greek dualism would not be much help either, when it came to what was "good" and "evil."

one of the topics emphasized by the false teachers.[89] "The pure" are those who have been cleansed by the blood of Christ (1 Peter 1:22). "All things are pure" may be explained either by what Jesus taught, or by what Paul wrote. During His earthly ministry, Jesus ended the Old Testament distinctions between clean and unclean foods when He declared all things clean (Mark 7:14-22). In Romans 14:20 Paul repeats what Jesus taught. In 1 Timothy 4:4 Paul indicates that "every creature of God is good for food, if it is received with thanksgiving." In harmony with what he writes there, it seems correct to understand this first phrase of verse 15 as being Paul's own teaching.[90] It will be remembered that God told Peter on the housetop at Joppa that He had ended the old distinction between clean and unclean meats (Acts 10:15). With all these passages to guide them, Christians nourished on sound doctrine know that any teaching about abstinence from certain foods as tending to make a man more holy is in error.[91]

But to those who are defiled and unbelieving – "Those" refers to the false teachers. The last phrase in this verse likely explains in what sense he speaks of the false teachers as being "defiled." Something has happened to both their minds and their consciences.[92] "Unbelieving" tells us the false teachers who are pushing these "purity" codes are not themselves Christians. They have refused to surrender their lives to Jesus who fulfilled the Law, and nailed it to the cross.

Nothing is pure – It has often been said that if a man's beliefs are right, his practice will likely be right. But if his beliefs are wrong, his practice too will in all probability be wrong. That is exactly what has occurred among these false teachers. Without the truth of the Gospel (which indicates the Old Testament rules about clean and unclean are no longer binding) for a guide, the false teachers

---

[89] The suggestion of some that the "proverb" just quoted was a saying the false teachers used to excuse their own immoral teaching and conduct, we think, misses the point of the context here. It is true that some Gnostics were libertines while others practiced rigid asceticism. If the maxim "To the pure all things are pure" are the words of the Gnostic libertines, then we have them claiming to be the "pure ones" who therefore are free to do anything they wanted to do without any worry about being defiled. When we try to make the maxim the words of the false teachers, it is difficult to see the connection with the verse that precedes, or to follow the train of thought in the rest of this verse. If we understand the maxim to be Paul's correct Christian teaching, the train of thought is easily discerned.

[90] Some have called Paul's words here a "proverb," a short saying intended to summarize Christian doctrine on this matter of clean and unclean things.

[91] Obviously this maxim is not intended to offer license to Christians to indulge in all sorts of sensual excesses. See the safeguard against such excesses in 1 Timothy 4:4,5. Only a foolish or untaught person would try to extend the principle "To the pure, all things are pure" to excuse or defend those thoughts and actions that the Bible clearly labels as sin.

[92] In the light of Scripture, the idea taught by many denominations of an inherited sinful nature, inherited from Adam after he fell, is incorrect. This defilement is not to be blamed on Adam. It is the result of each man's own personal sin that he finds himself defiled!   See the Special Studies on "'Sin' in the Bible," and "Original Sin" in the author's *New Testament Epistles: Romans*.

still make human rules concerning what is or is not "pure." How foolish! Without the Gospel to guide them, their beliefs and their rules and their practices (e.g., depending on certain "purity" codes) are wrong.

But both their mind and their conscience are defiled – In spite of the purity rules they proclaim and follow, they still find themselves defiled in two areas: their mind and their conscience. A man's own sins do tend to defile him. And they defile the inside. Rules originally made for the body don't do a very good job of helping a man get a clear conscience. "Defiled" translates a perfect tense of the verb *miainō*. The verb means "to defile, pollute, contaminate, soil."[93] The perfect tense speaks of "past completed action with present continuing results." Their own sins "defiled" them in the past, and they still are defiled. The "mind" is the willing as well as the thinking part of man. Defilement of the mind means that the thoughts, wishes, purposes, and activities are all stained and debased. A man uses his mind to think things out. His thoughts will hardly be true and straight when his mind is "defiled." The "conscience" is an innate faculty that prompts you to do what your mind thinks is right, and criticizes you when you do what your mind thinks is wrong.[94] Defilement of the conscience means that one has ignored the promptings of the conscience so long that the conscience ceases to work. And when it ceases to work, one of the most precious safeguards of the soul has been lost. A man's conscience will become defiled when he lives a double life. Outwardly the false teachers pretended to be very religious, but inwardly their love for money caused them to teach false doctrine and live false lives, and the result was a defiled conscience that no longer made any effort to criticize or convict them when their actions were wrong.

1:16 -- They profess to know God – The description of the false teachers ("they") who "turn away from the truth" (verse 14) and "who are defiled and unbelieving" (verse 15) continues. These false teachers' claims to know God remind us of the claims made by those whom John writes against in his epistles a generation later. Those Gnostics, too, claimed to know God, and by their actions denied Him (1 John 2:4, 4:7). If we may press the verb *oida* here, the false teachers were claiming an intuitive and direct knowledge of God. The false teachers were claiming publicly to "know" God – that is, to have a personal and special relationship with Him or special knowledge from Him. Paul reminds Titus that those who are really foes of the truth will often present themselves under the guise of friends. They use Bible words – often with their own slanted definition – in their teaching, sing the songs that Christians sing, and for a pretense make long prayers.

---

[93] Thayer, *op. cit.*, p.414, where attention is also called to a synonym of *miainō*, namely, *molunō*. The latter means to "smear," primarily in an outward sense. *Miainō* is a stronger verb and speaks of something that sinks down in (like "stain" does when applied to wood).

[94] For more detailed information about the "conscience," see the notes at 1 Timothy 1:5.

But by their deeds they deny *Him* – The NASB has added "Him" as the object of "deny," since the object of the previous verb, God, is naturally assumed in this clause. Paul perhaps specifies some of the deeds by which the false teachers belie their profession in the three adjectives that follow.[95]

Being detestable and disobedient – "Detestable" (*bdeluktoi*) occurs only here in the New Testament, though it occurs in the LXX, and some cognate words are not uncommon. The word often has the connotation of being involved in idolatry, something which is disgusting and detestable to God. It is the root word from which "abomination" comes. Behind this word may be the fact that the Gnostics, as they searched for esoteric truths, were involved with evil spirits. "Disobedient" (*apeitheis*) signifies a stubborn refusal to be persuaded. They stubbornly refused to be persuaded by any teaching based on God's Word. They can be sticklers for the "commandments of men" but that does not justify them in the sight of God.[96] God says they are "disobedient."

And worthless for any good deed – "Worthless" is used to translate a word (*adokimoi*) that often implies that a test has been given and the test has been failed, so the thing that was tested is false, unfit, useless, disapproved.[97] As a result of their hypocritical, selfish, defiled life, these men, when any good or noble work had to be done, were simply useless, worthless. The kind of good works that characterize a Christian life, the kind God expects his children to do,[98] you do not find these false teachers doing. The false teachers have become useless and worthless both to God and to men.

---

[95] All three adjectives are dependent on the circumstantial participle "being." Circumstantial participles can imply any one of several ideas, such as time, manner, means, attendant circumstance, etc. If we treat this as "means" and use the word "by" to introduce this participle, then it says the false teachers deny God "by being detestable, etc."

[96] Again, it should be remembered that the false teachers Titus is warned about are not the Judaizers with whom the people at Antioch and in Galatia had to contend (Acts 15, Galatians 2).

[97] The KJV reads "reprobate." "Reprobate" is a term that means "rejected after testing." Stones that were rejected for building were marked with a capital "A" (the first letter of this Greek word for "reprobate") and tossed aside as being unfit to have any place in the building. The same Greek word is translated "disqualified" or "castaway" at 1 Corinthians 9:27. The word can also be used to describe a counterfeit coin which is below standard weight. It is used of a cowardly soldier who fails in the testing hour of battle.

[98] See Ephesians 2:12 and 2 Timothy 2:21, 3:17, where we learn something about the "good works" God looks for. Matthew 25:31ff and Romans 2:7-10 also come to mind in this regard.

II. INSTRUCTION CONCERNING THE PRACTICAL DEMONSTRATION OF SOUND DOCTRINE IN THE LIVES OF CHURCH MEMBERS. 2:1-15

A. Sound Doctrine Involves Corresponding Character Traits To Be Developed. 2:1-10

2:1 -- But as for you – Note the word of "contrast" ("but") and the emphatic "you" with which this chapter begins. In contrast with the vain talk of the false teachers, Titus[1] is to present the solid, sober teaching of a true man of God, in harmony with the sound doctrine of the gospel of Christ. What germs do to a physical body, false teaching will do to a spiritual body, the church. In chapters 2 and 3 Paul identifies for Titus the proper "antibiotics" that will counteract the germs of false teaching and maintain the health of the church body. One is "sound doctrine" and the other is a corresponding "behavior." In chapter 1, Paul has focused on sound doctrine as it relates to congregational life and polity. Now in chapter 2, Paul emphasizes how sound doctrine will show itself in the everyday lifestyles of the individuals and families in the church. The different age groups, the different sexes, and the different social positions were all to live so as to bring no dishonor upon their Christian profession. There may also be the inference that Titus is to refute the lifestyles of the false teachers (Titus 1:12,16) by presenting the kind of godly lifestyle that sound doctrine requires.

Speak the things which are fitting for sound doctrine – "Speak" is a present imperative, stressing the need for continuing action. Titus is to continue on the same course he has been on, encouraging church members to demonstrate their beliefs with their right actions. Perhaps it speaks of public sermons. Perhaps it speaks of daily conversation with people in their homes and on the streets. Perhaps it speaks of any occasion Titus has to teach.[2] On "sound doctrine" compare notes at Titus 1:9 and 1 Timothy 1:10. In 1 Timothy 6:1, "the doctrine" (*hē didaskalia*) means "the Christian faith," "the doctrine of the Gospel." The varying phrases, "the good doctrine" (*he kalē didaskalia*), "the doctrine according to godliness" (*hē kat' eusebeian didaskalia*), and "the sound doctrine" (*hē hugianousa didaskalia*) all mean the same thing, with varying descriptive qualifications. The "sound doctrine" (i.e., the true teaching of Christianity) Titus was

---

[1] Not only are the elders to do their duty over against the false teachers (chapter 1), but Titus himself is to continue to counteract the evils these false men were disseminating.

[2] "Speak" at Titus 2:15 is virtually synonymous for the verb "teach" used in a parallel passage, 1 Timothy 6:2.

bidden to promulgate in his teaching stands in clear contrast to the sickly, unhealthy teaching of the misleading teachers of Crete. "Which are fitting" (*prepei* means "what is in accord with," "fitting, suitable, appropriate to") certainly suggests that doctrine and life must harmonize. False doctrine inevitably leads to a life characterized by sinning. Sound doctrine, on the other hand, will issue in a godly life. More will be said later in this chapter on the question of whether or not the moral standards Titus is to teach are specifically Christian and timeless, or whether they are simply cultural and perhaps therefore temporary. Verse 1 bears on that question and indicates that the moral standards are "becoming" to sound doctrine (i.e. Christian doctrine). In the following verses, five classes[3] of individuals – aged men, aged women, young married women, young men, and slaves – are to be issued commands by Titus relative to the proper conduct of their lives.[4] Titus himself is to set an example of the kind of conduct that sound doctrine expects (Titus 2:7-8).

1. Character traits to be cultivated by older men. 2:2

2:2 -- Older men – These "older men" (*presbutas*) are not official "elders," but "aged men" in the church.[5] The term regularly used for the official "elder" is *presbuteros* (see Titus 1:5, Acts 11:30, 15:3), though in the similar list found in 1 Timothy 5:1ff "aged men" are also called *presbuteros*. An "older man" is one over 40 years of age,[6] and perhaps, given what is said at Titus 2:6, is over 50.

Are to be – All the Greek has at this place is the infinitive "to be." Perhaps the infinitive is dependent on the verb "speak" in verse 1. If so, Titus is to preach the cultivation of these character traits to every congregation on Crete as he goes about seeing that elders are selected, and things that are lacking are set in order. Perhaps the infinitive is dependent on an implied verb, similar to the verb "exhort" or "urge" found in verse 6. If so, it is still Titus' responsibility as evangelist to encourage the church members to develop these Christian character traits. A.T. Robertson has suggested that the infinitives in this paragraph may well function as imperatives.[7] Here in one sentence we have a quick sketch of what an elderly

---

[3] It is interesting to compare the lists found in 1 Timothy 5-6 and in Titus 2. Both lists include the same groups, but not in the same sequence. Titus has aged men, aged women, young women, young men, and slaves. Timothy has old men, young men, old women, young women, and slaves.

[4] Some of the areas of conduct Titus is to emphasize are in direct contrast to the typical Gentile sins so prevalent in Crete – lying, drunkenness, immorality, and a quick and quarrelsome temper.

[5] The term found here is consistently used in Greek literature for older men. Compare Luke 1:18, Philemon 9.

[6] Hippocrates used "older men" to designate men between the ages of 50 and 56. Philo used the term to refer to a man over 60 years of age.

[7] *Grammar*, p.944.

Christian man ought to be.

Temperate –"Temperate" (*nēphalios*) was one of the qualifications for potential elders (1 Timothy 3:2) and deacon's wives (1 Timothy 3:11). As noted in comments in 1 Timothy, "temperate" literally means "abstaining entirely from wine." Figuratively it means to be "sober in judgment." It is the opposite of over-indulgence. A life of self-indulgence is costly. When a man has reached his years of seniority, he ought to have learned what are, and what are not, real and true pleasures. Titus is to encourage older men to be "temperate."

Dignified – This word (*semnos*) and its cognates occur frequently in 1 Timothy (see 2:2, 3:4, 3:8, 3:11). Frivolity is not becoming to an older man. Older men's actions are to be "dignified," "serious and worthy of respect." An older Christian man should be such a person that younger men can look up to and admire. Older men should recognize that the sin and woe of the world in which we live is in sharp contrast with the purity to which God calls us.

Sensible – This trait, too, was one expected of prospective elders. See Titus 1:8, 1 Timothy 3:2. Older men are to be "thoughtful" (*sōphrōn*) in contrast to the thoughtlessness of careless youth. Over the years of their Christian lives and experience, older men will have learned to keep their thinking wholesome so that their speech will be clean and their actions right.

Sound in faith, in love, in perseverance -- "Sound", a word used at Titus 2:1, suggests the older men are to be living "healthy" Christian lives. There are three areas of life where this "soundness" is to be clearly evident.[8] We have the same three traits listed in 1 Timothy 6:11. The famous Pauline triad often reads "faith, hope, and love," as in 1 Corinthians 13:13. In 1 Thessalonians 1:3, Paul speaks of "work of faith, labor of love and patience of hope." Instead of "hope," the last member of the trilogy here in Titus is "patience." This may signify that patience is more needed in the older person than hope. He may indeed have high hope, but still needs the endurance to meet each day as it comes. We must not miss this important exhortation. Not only are men to have some kind of faith, love, and patience; they are to be healthy and vigorous in their faith, love, and patience. That is something men will have to cultivate as the years go by. Otherwise theirs will be a puny faith, a sickly love, and a misdirected patience.

The first trait is "sound in faith." See notes at Titus 1:13, where this same trait was to be taught. Older men should know what they believe, and their doctrinal convictions should accord with God's Word. A man's doctrinal posi-

---

[8] In the Greek, each term has a definite article. Hence it is "the faith," "the love," and "the perseverance," i.e., the well known faith, love, and perseverance that Christianity teaches as being the Christian's duty and privilege.

tion and/or personal beliefs are not to be adulterated with superstitions, or commandments of men, or Jewish myths. He is to be getting a firm handle on Christian truth. Involved in this trait is one's attitude towards God. Over the years, men should learn not to trust God less, but to trust God more. The second trait is "[sound] in love." Likely in this trait, Paul is speaking of love for the brethren. Older men are to look for ways to be spiritually helpful to others since "love" is doing what is spiritually best for the other person.[9] *Agapē* is a "love" that can be willed, that can be developed and nurtured.[10] Does this suggest that one danger of old age is that men, if they are not careful, may drift into censoriousness, and criticism, and fault-finding? Over the years it is fatally possible to lose one's kindly sympathy and beneficial actions towards others. Older men have to be warned to beware of a possible loss of love! The third trait is "[sound] in perseverance." "Perseverance" or "endurance" or "patience" (*hupomonē*) speaks of how one faces the difficult things that occur in an ordinary lifetime. James (5:7,8) urges Christians to display such "perseverance" on earth while they wait for their Lord to appear. This trait speaks of a man's attitude toward bitter trials that everyone must face from time to time. When one grows old and physical strength begins to fade away, there is a temptation to relax one's moral and spiritual strength as well. Though the body is growing weaker, there is no reason one cannot grow stronger in his fortitude and intention to conquer the slings and arrows of life. The kind of "perseverance" or "patience" Christianity teaches is no mere passive acquiescence to what happens, but it is a brave, active trait. It is taking hold of the misfortune and making something good out of it. "If life hands you a lemon, make lemonade!"

Many of the traits older men are to manifest are also qualifications given for elders and deacons. In other words, many of the qualifications for church office are traits any person older in the faith should be exhibiting in his life.

2. Character traits to be cultivated by older women.   2:3

2:3 -- Older women likewise – "Likewise" means that like Titus was to teach older men what is expected of them (verse 2),   so he is to teach older women in

---

[9] The KJV uses the word "charity" to translate the Greek word *agapē*, but that word now has a limited connotation it did not have in 1611. "Love" also has connotations that are not right for this Greek word. *Agapē* is not romantic love inspired by a moonlit night, nor is it the kind of love that is reserved for one's family and friends. It is a sincere and active goodwill that a Christian feels even toward those who mistreat him.

[10] An old preacher prayed, "O God, help me not to be a mean old man." Older men can become problem children!

the churches what is expected of them.[11] How easy it would be for a younger preacher like Titus to misunderstand or neglect the older members of the congregation.[12] The context indicates "older women" are those whose children are grown. The word translated "older women" (*presbutis*) is a cognate to the word used for "older men" in verse 2. Paul, faithful to what had become one of the guiding principles of Christianity – i.e., the elevation of the status of women – now shows that their new privileges have corresponding responsibilities. "Older women" have character traits that "sound doctrine" indicates should be developed.

Are to be reverent in their behavior – "Reverent" is an attempt to translate *hieroprepeis*, a compound word made up of "temple" and "becoming" or "fitting." The picture is of a priest(ess) functioning about the sacred things in the temple. Though the word is common in classical Greek, it occurs only here in the New Testament, and only twice in the LXX (4 Maccabees 9:25 and 11:20[13]). Detailed instructions to Christian women were given in 1 Timothy 2:9-10, all of which were summarized under the phrase "as befits women professing godliness." Ephesians 5:3 speaks of living "as is proper among saints." Older women are to conduct themselves as if they are servants or priestesses in God's temple. The word translated "behavior" (*katastēma*) includes dress, appearance, conversation and speech, manner. Outward deportment for the Christian is dependent on something internal. *Katastēma* has a much broader meaning than *katastolē* in 1 Timothy 2:7. This word denotes a person's comportment or bearing. *Katastēma* speaks of "a state," or "condition." It speaks of behavior in general, and covers movements of the body, expressions on the face, what is said, and what is left unsaid. The older Christian woman has had time to learn that all of life has a sacredness attached to it. There should be something in the older Christian woman's general appearance, in her dress, in her speech, in her everyday behavior, which her younger Christian sister could respect and reverence – an ideal she might hope one day, if the Master spared her so long, herself to reach.[14]

---

[11] It is possible that the word "likewise" means that the older women were to have the same qualities as the older men, plus the additional ones listed here in verse 3.

[12] One of the strongest forces for spiritual ministry in the local church lies with the older believers. Those who are retired have time for service. It is good to see that many local churches have organized and mobilized these important people. Older saints who know how to pray, teach the Word, visit, troubleshoot, and help build the church should be encouraged to use their abilities.

[13] The words do occur in the LXX, but not in the current English editions of 4 Maccabees since these editions are being based on a text other than the LXX. The word is also used of the conduct of a priest in Greek inscriptions (see BAGD).

[14] Root writes, "Getting up in years and freed from the heavier household work, a woman may begin to feel free from other responsibilities too. She may become careless about personal cleanliness and appearance ... She may no longer guard her tongue, but uses expressions that would have shocked her years ago ... She may cease to be considerate of others." (*Standard Lesson Commentary*, 1977, p.12) Paul says older women are to be reminded of their need for "reverence." They still serve in God's temple. They dedicated themselves to Jesus, a dedication that still stands.

Not malicious gossips – "Reverent" is further explained by several phrases that express what a "reverent" person is "not." For an explanation of "malicious gossips" see comments at 1 Timothy 3:11 where this same qualification was expected of deacons' wives. The danger of such speech (i.e., picking up gossip and spreading it) by older women is obvious. A "malicious gossip" or "slanderer" or "false accuser" (*diabolos*) may be behaving as the old Slanderer himself (the devil, also *diabolos*) has tempted them to do. Further, old age can at times be intolerant, censorious, even bitter, forgetful especially of the days of youth. Older saints must use their voices for better things than "gossip." Make up your mind to say nothing about people unless there is something good to say. Let older women develop a mindset where they will not tolerate the communication of gossip.[15]

Nor enslaved to much wine – Wine is not absolutely forbidden, since in that day and region it was the common beverage, but its dangers were noted. Cp. 1 Timothy 3:8.[16] The word "enslaved" is well-chosen; an alcoholic is thoroughly the slave of this vicious appetite. (Cp. Titus 3:3, Romans 6:16, 2 Peter 2:19.) "Circumstances may make an elderly lady especially vulnerable to alcoholism. She may have time on her hands, and wine now and then may help to relieve boredom. She may find it hard to go to sleep at night, and alcohol is an ancient and effective tranquilizer. She may be annoyed by a variety of petty aches and pains that seem to be lessened by a few drinks. Before she knows it, the lady may be enslaved to much wine." (Root, *Standard Lesson Commentary*, 1977-78, p.9)

Teaching what is good – This phrase further defines what it is for a woman to be "reverent." *Kalodidaskalous* is a word used only here in the New Testament. It is not found in the LXX or in classical Greek.[17] The part of the compound that is translated "good" means "winsome," "attractive." Some specific "good" things the older women were to teach are apparently identified in the next two verses.

---

[15] W.W. Perry shared this illustration. "'Did you hear what I heard that Mrs. Brown said about Mrs. Smith?' How many conversations have begun in such a way? My grandfather did not tolerate that type of communication. He had a way of looking any of the family directly in the eye and cutting short such recitals with a brief and sometimes brusque statement, 'Tell me what you know!' I came to know the value of his practice when I arrived home one day with a wild story of the misdeeds of some of my schoolmates. I was eager to share my information; I began to describe in detail their wrongdoing. My gusto was slowed considerably when Grandfather called me over, sat me firmly on his lap, and said, 'Woodrow, is that information something you saw, heard, or made up?' He stayed with it until I admitted that I had heard it and then added my own interpretation of its meaning. That stern voice, 'Woodrow, only tell me what you know' has an echo in the more modern 'Tell it like it is'." In letters and written communication, which are more permanent than conversations, we strive to make sure we have our facts straight. It would be useful for a Christian to be just as sure he has his facts straight when he is about to share something in conversation!

[16] Also refer to notes at 1 Timothy 5:23 on wine drinking.

[17] Paul is fond of compound words, and even coins some compounds found first in the New Testament.

Where the older women were to do the teaching is not stated. In light of 1 Timothy 2:12, some insist the women were not to be doing public or official teaching at the church assemblies. The older women would be teaching in the home, either their own, or the younger woman's.[18] Others attempt to harmonize 1 Timothy 2:12 and Titus 2:3 by suggesting the older ladies did their "teaching" by their behavior, more than by their words.[19] But it is difficult to see how all the things specified in the next two verses could all be learned simply by watching, using no spoken lessons at all. "The older women can offer helpful, spiritually tested advice and instruction to those who have not traveled so far on the road of life. This teaching need not be in a public place; many grandmothers minister thus in the homes." (Foster, *op. cit.*, p.418) "Most mothers of growing children feel the responsibility of teaching both by word and by example. But when the children are grown, a mother may feel that her teaching days are over. Not so! People still see what she does. Some shape their own doing by it to some extent; others shape their idea of the value of Christianity by what an elderly Christian says and does." (Root, *op. cit.*, 1977-78, p.9)

3. Character traits to be cultivated by young women.   2:4,5

2:4 -- That they may encourage the young women – "That" with which verses 4 and 5 begin, gives the content of what the older women were to "teach" (verse 3). It suggests that no one – not even Titus – would be as well-able to train the young women as were older, experienced Christian women. In many cases, older women who are "sound doctrine" Christians are far better qualified to be wise advisers in problems of married life than young counselors deep in theory but short on experience. "Young women" (*neas*), as the context indicates, are women whose children are not yet grown. In the 1st century, the term covered a longer period of time than the term does today. A slightly different word (*neoteras*) was translated "younger *widows*" at 1 Timothy 5:14. Several of the commands there to the "younger widows" are the same as those here to the "young women."

---

[18] Attention should be given to the comments on 1 Timothy 2:12 lest these notes here be interpreted to mean that women are absolutely forbidden to speak or teach in the public assembly. As noted in 1 Timothy, the prohibition is against habitual, repeated, customary public speaking and teaching by wives in their husband's presence – not against all teaching by women whatsoever.

[19] An oft-used illustration to show that one may teach simply by his "behavior" has Ignatius saying of the bishop of the Trallians, "His very demeanor (*auto to katastēma*) was a great lesson (*matheteia*)." Others appeal to Beza's rendering, "mistresses of honor," which he implies that he thinks aged women should not occupy a position of public instructor, but do their "teaching" more by golden behavior and here and there speaking a word of kind warning. Others refer to 1 Peter 3:1,2, where the non-Christian husband is won by the wife's attractive behavior rather than by constant nagging about things spiritual. Of course, that passage does not teach that non-Christians are won without ever hearing the Word of God, for "faith comes by hearing the Word of God."

Titus 2:4

The word "encourage" (*sōphronidzōsi*), common in classical Greek, is found only here in the Greek scriptures.[20] In classical Greek, the word has the meaning "to correct," "to control," "to moderate," "to restore one to his senses," "to train." "Train them by making them sober-minded." It is not only that the older women show the younger mothers how to make a home, but that they put within their hearts and minds the right spiritual and mental attitudes. The KJV translates "teach them to be sober," but this is a very doubtful way to translate the verb. Even though a cognate of this verb is translated "sensible" in Titus 2:5, "sober" or "sensible" can lead us to miss the spiritual thrust of what Paul is writing. In 1 Timothy, it is the preacher Timothy who would have to make known Paul's wishes concerning "younger widows" as he helps the church to determine those who are "widows indeed." Here in Titus, it is the preacher Titus who will have to teach[21] the older women about an opportunity and responsibility they have to train the "young women." If older women exhibit the qualities listed in verse 3, then the younger women will see what they themselves can become if they will take advantage of the "training" older women can offer. "Godly older women have the responsibility of teaching the younger women how to be successful wives, mothers, and homemakers; and the younger women have the responsibility of listening and obeying. The Christian home was a totally new thing, and young women saved out of paganism would have to get accustomed to a whole new set of priorities and privileges. Those who had unsaved husbands would need special encouragement" (Wiersbe, *op. cit.*, p.110).

To love their husbands – Young Christian women will need to be trained to love their husbands. Think of that! *Philandrous* is a compound of "love" and "husband."[22] "Love" (*phileō*) is the Greek synonym that means "an inclination prompted by sense and emotion."[23] In our Western society, a man and woman fall in love and then get married. In the East, marriages were less romantic. Often the two got married and then had to learn to love each other. The older women who at one time had to learn it, too, could teach the younger women how to love their husbands and children.[24] Young ladies, especially newlyweds, will

[20] The word is related to the word translated "temperate" in verse 2.

[21] It will take more than a sermon, or many sermons, for Titus to "teach" the older women how to take hold of this wonderful work that God calls them to do. Titus will have to give this matter a lot of personal and patient individual effort, if the elderly women will catch the vision of the service they could render to younger Christian wives and mothers.

[22] Adolf Deissmann, *Bible Studies*, p.255f, has shown that this term was even found on a tombstone from Pergamos, from about the time of Hadrian. The deceased was eulogized as "the most sweet woman who loved her husband and her children."

[23] *Agapaō* on the other hand denotes a love founded in admiration, esteem. It is the word that means to do what is spiritually best for someone else, because you think well of that person.

[24] Ephesians 5:18-33 is a good Scripture for a husband and wife who really want to love each other in the will of God.

find that husbands can do many thoughtless things that can wound and hurt; and if the young woman isn't careful, she can let her love for her husband be killed. Older Christian women can show the young ones how to handle those difficult times, and even how to help the young women explain their feelings and needs to their husbands.

To love their children – Young Christian women will need to be trained to love their children. Think of that! *Philoteknous* uses the same synonym for love that the previous compound word did. Little children take a lot of time, and even at times can be so exasperating as to tend to leave the mother cross and irritable. Here is where older Christian women can help the young women know how to handle such crises. It may seem unnecessary to exhort a mother to love her children, but in the pressures of pleasure and work there is often a temptation to neglect love to the husband or children. Careers (such as modern-day mothers pursue) do not excuse mothers from these responsibilities. "Love" can and does include discipline when the children need it. It is an error for a mother to think, "I love my child too much to spank her." In reality, that mother has a selfish love for herself and does not really love the child. "He who spares the rod hates his son, but he who loves him is careful to discipline him" (Proverbs 13:24).[25] "While Paul would never have the women of Christ forget their new and precious privileges in the present, their glorious hopes in the future, yet here on earth he would never let them desert, or even for a moment forget, their first and chiefest duties. Their work, let them remember, lay not in the busy world. Their first duty was to *make home life beautiful* by the love of husband and child – that great love which ever teaches forgetfulness to self."[26] "It is noteworthy that the list of characteristics for young women begins with love for husband and children. This section thereby fills out the instructions to wives in Ephesians, Colossians, and 1 Peter, where the emphasis falls on fulfilling the role of submission and where love on the part of wives is not mentioned."[27]

2:5 -- *To be* sensible – Verse 5 continues the "training" of the young wives which the older women are to be enlisted to do.[28] "Discreet" or "sensible" may be nearer the sense than "sober minded" (as in the KJV). Others suggest the right English word might be "sage," a word which means "characterized by calm foresight, wisdom and prudence." The same word *sōphronas* was used in verse 2, where it was translated "thoughtful" or "sensible." (See also Titus 1:6,8 and

---

[25] If, as in Eastern homes, the father is the one who disciplines the children, the mother dare not try to escape being supportive of the procedure, or else the child will run to its mother for protection.

[26] Spence, "Commentary on Titus," in *Ellicott's Commentary*, p.20.

[27] Knight, *op. cit.*, p.307.

[28] Of course, the older women themselves will need to display these qualities, too.

1 Timothy 3:2.[29]) Outlook determines outcome. If a person is not thinking rightly, he will not act properly. A woman needs a correct and disciplined outlook on her ministry in the home. So thoughtful self-control is needed.

Pure – *Hagnas* suggests the idea of being "chaste" or "pure," not polluted with immorality. Young women must scrupulously avoid any immorality in thought, word, or deed. In look, in speech, in thought, and even in dress, they are to be "chaste." If anyone is tempted to think that it is modern, smart, and exciting to "have an affair" with someone other than her husband, let her note that such a silly notion was exploded nineteen hundred years ago.

Workers at home – There is a manuscript variation here. The text from which the KJV is translated reads *oikourous*, "stayers at home." The Nestle text reads *oikourgous*, "workers at home." The word in the Textus Receptus is found elsewhere only in classical Greek. The word in the Nestle text is found nowhere else in the New Testament, LXX, or classical Greek. Whichever reading was original, the sense of the passage is little changed. "Caring for the home" is the idea. "Guide the house" Paul wrote (1 Timothy 5:14). "Home worker"[30] describes the active wife, whose labors are beyond measure and whose efforts will bless the lives of her husband and children in a thousand ways. (A wide range of activities is described in Proverbs 31:10-31.) Young wives can be shown the value of such home duties by the older Christian women. The wise husband allows his wife to manage the affairs of the household, for this is her special ministry. "Workers at home" does not mean the home is a prison where she must be kept. He did mean that she should not flit about as a busybody and gossip (cp. 1 Timothy 5:13,14).

What about women being career women? What about young mothers working at factory or shop, outside the home?[31] See on 1 Timothy 2:10 and 5:13. When the Scriptures regularly speak of the mother at work in the home, we should be slow to encourage young women to do otherwise. Perhaps young women without children may pursue careers,[32] but mothers hardly should try to be a

---

[29] This quality of "sensible" is one which each of the groups of Christians (old men, young men, old women, young women) are to be encouraged to develop.

[30] Several modern English translations offer "busy at home" as a way to catch the sense of this word.

[31] World War II, when "Rosie the riveter" was joined by thousands of other women at work in the factories turning out war materiel, ushered in a sweeping change in society, and made acceptable the idea that women could work outside the home. That war was one of the greatest causes of social upheaval in the history of the world, and not all the changes have been good.

[32] Young women with husbands will find it stressful to balance the work of the home and the work outside the home. The stress can affect the marriage adversely. It is a high price to pay for a career!

homemaker and on a career track at the same time.[33]   Some have offered the
suggestion that Paul's instructions about marriage and home are no mandate
against working outside the home because women in those days did not ordinarily
pursue careers outside the home.   Paul was simply dealing with society as he
found it.   It may be true that the reason why four of the seven traits the young
women are to be trained to develop relate to marriage and the home is because
Paul is urging Titus to minister to the women in the sphere where they were.   But
it could just as plausibly be urged that the reason for Paul's emphasis is a response
to the error of the false teachers.   If it were the false teachers who were destroying
"home life," then Paul's instructions would continue to be the antidote wherever
people encouraged the women to pursue lives outside the home.   What would
Paul say to mothers who work away from home for pay?   Of course, some
mothers and their children have been abandoned by their husbands and fathers.
They may have little choice but to work to support what is left of the family.   But
where the family unit is still whole, we imagine Paul would tell the mothers to
think earnestly of the children's welfare.   A child does not necessarily lose any
of his mother's love by spending part of each day with a grandmother, an aunt, or
a dear friend.   In some cases it is an advantage to the child to learn to feel secure
and cherished in more than one place and by more than one family circle.   But it
is still true that children who must grow up as "latch-key kids" develop some
character traits and attitudes that are hard on society.   That's a steep price to pay
for working outside the home.

Kind – The word is *agathas*, a word regularly translated "good."   It is possible
to punctuate the verse so that it reads "good workers at home."[34]   However, since
none of the other qualities has a modifier (each is a single word in the Greek), our
translators have chosen to treat this word as a separate quality, too.   Whether we
should use the general idea of "good," or narrow it down to "kind," is also debated
in the commentaries.   Those who prefer "good" comment how the young woman
must be trained in doing that which is good and beneficial to others, even those in
her own home.   Those who prefer "kind," comment how the young woman must
be trained to be gracious, kind, thoughtful to others.   A young woman needs to
be careful lest the constant strain of domestic duties make her irritable and sharp
in her words.   One way for young women to develop this grace of "kindness" is
to pray for grace to remain kind to husband and children, and even the household
slaves.

---

[33] The little babes and young children are affected, too. Working mothers often leave their preschool children with babysitters or daycare centers. The little children, before they are three years of age, have had to learn how to be worldly wise, and scratch and claw to get along. A different personality develops in children who are cared for by their parents versus those who are cared for by strangers or in-laws. It's enough to make a mother want to stay home and "love her children" herself, rather than entrusting them to others to rear.

[34] "Good housewives" is the way TEV renders it.

Being subject to their own husbands – This is the last of six responsibilities that the older women may help train the young women to be and do. The participle is most likely a middle voice, suggesting that this "submission" is something voluntarily done by the woman for her own benefit. Women who really love their Master Jesus should take care that, as far as in them lay, the law of subordination in the family to its rightful head should be lovingly and carefully carried out. While women have equal access to the salvation offered in Jesus Christ (Galatians 3:28; 1 Peter 3:7), God's creation intent regarding a wife's relationship to her husband (Genesis 2:18, "helpmeet") is still the role woman is expected to fulfil. It is no more degradation for the young woman to be submissive to her husband,[35] than it is for men to be submissive to Christ, or for Christ to be submissive to God (see 1 Corinthians 11:3). This directive concerning voluntary submission is in no way contrary to teachings that have elevated the status of women wherever Christianity and Paul's teachings have gone.

> The idea that wives should be obedient to their own husbands is not very popular nowadays. But look what happens when a wife is determined to be the ruler. Sometimes the marriage ends in divorce because the husband refuses to be ruled. If he decides to submit, the couple becomes a joke in the community. People scorn both the wife who dominates her husband and the husband who allows her to do it. Not many people argue that a wife should be dominant, but many say husband and wife should be equal partners. Note, however, that equal partners do not necessarily do exactly the same things. In an ideal arrangement, each partner strengthens the team by doing what his natural talents fit him to do. That is precisely what happens when God's plan is accepted by husband and wife. If the husband is what a Christian ought to be, the wife's submission is a pleasure; if he is not what he ought to be, she only increases her burden by rebelling.[36]

That the word of God may not be dishonored – These words seem to refer specially to the duties being taught young wives.[37] Paul is giving a spiritual motive for such action on the part of the young women. "That the Word of God be not blasphemed" is a good motive for cooperation and submission at home. The "Word of God" is another name for the gospel (2 Timothy 2:9; Philippians 1:14; Titus 1:3). It may be among non-Christians, whose standards for wives are as high as the Christian standards, that the Word of God might be dishonored. If Christianity led wives to be less than what even pagans expected them to be, then

---

[35] Especially is this true when the husband, too, is a Christian. When he is not, then "as unto the Lord" makes her burden bearable (Ephesians 5:22-33; Colossians 3:19; 1 Peter 3:7).

[36] Root, *Standard Lesson Commentary*, 1977-78, p.12.

[37] Scripture elsewhere warns all believers about their lifestyles, lest they give the gentiles occasion to look with disdain on Christianity. (Cp. 1 Timothy 6:1 and Romans 2:24.) For a Christian to live otherwise than a winsome life would be to disobey what Jesus Himself taught (Matthew 5:16).

the name of God would be greatly dishonored. It may be non-Christian neighbors and townspeople who are thought of as blaspheming the Word of God. Wrong conduct or failure in the everyday tasks expected of the wife and homemaker would bitterly reflect on the religion taught by Jesus. It may be the woman's husband who does the blaspheming. If the woman's husband were not a Christian,[38] he would tend to blame the gospel when his wife failed to exhibit the qualities here listed. Her unruly actions were not what she learned from Jesus, but the husband would blame her religion for her behavior. The world usually judges Christianity, not by its doctrines, but by its effects on its followers. The gospel ought to make a woman a better wife. Paul can appeal to the non-Christian's evaluation of misconduct precisely because he regarded their evaluation in these matters as correct.[39]

Now a word or two about the sense of "right" among the pagans. Where did they get their standards? Are these duties for young women, especially the one about "submission," only cultural and temporary? Fee and others identify Paul's prescriptions for conduct as being simply something which was culturally acceptable rather than being something intrinsically right in God's sight. We affirm they are mistaken in this "cultural" identification. Would Fee and others regard all the traits (rather than the last one, "submission") in the list for young women as simply cultural? When Paul is instructing the evangelist Titus about "sound doctrine" (2:1), would they treat the traits listed for older women, older men, younger men as simply cultural? If those are not cultural, why treat this one trait expected of young women as cultural rather than as part of "sound doctrine"? Would Fee and others regard the same kind of motivation for Titus' own behavior (Titus 2:8) simply as temporary and cultural? Paul is certainly giving a Christian perspective in those verses. Would Paul talk about something being "good" simply because society says it is good? Would Paul have no regard for what God consistently says is "good" when he holds up standards by which men are expected to live? If Paul is a servant of God, a spokesman for Jesus, the answer is, "No!" Not only is Paul giving a Christian perspective, he is likewise to be understood to be giving the timeless Christian perspective when he states the virtues and character traits that followers of Jesus are to develop in their lives. Fee is correct when he understands Paul to see a motivation for good behavior

[38] In 1 Peter 3:1-6, the unconverted husband is to be won by the winsome behavior of his Christian wife. If in Titus, the one who might blaspheme the name of God is the husband, and it is the "unbeliever" who is thought of as seeing the Christian wife's behavior, then the instructions to the young wife about her love for husband and children, her purity, kindness, homemaking would be examples of the winsome behavior that Peter speaks about. In this case, Paul's instructions to Titus and Peter's instructions concerning Christian wives behavior would be nearly identical.

[39] It must be very difficult for advocates of "total depravity" to explain how it is that non-Christians can have some standards and expectations in the ethical realm that are exactly in harmony with God's expectations.

in the standards expected by non-Christians in a particular culture. And Paul does list things here that represent the norms of the day. But it is an error to assume the standards by which non-Christians live are simply cultural rather than reflecting a transcultural moral standard, derived from primitive revelation from God. Paul can appeal to Gentile non-Christian standards here and elsewhere (1 Timothy 5:8; 1 Corinthians 5:1) because he regards the non-Christians as having in those cases a proper sense of right and wrong.[40]

4. Character traits to be cultivated by young men. 2:6-8

2:6 -- Likewise urge – Just as the other groups are to be encouraged to develop certain traits, so the young men "likewise" are to be appealed to or taught. Titus was to let older women minister to the younger women, lest he get himself in a difficult situation. But he was to urge the younger men, as well as be an example to the younger men with whom he would easily identify.

The young men – What age limits would be included in the term "young men"? The term usually speaks of those under forty years of age.[41] But then, if "older men" (Titus 2:2) meant those over sixty years of age, we would have a large group (those between 40 and 60) for which there is no admonition. Hence, in this place, "young men" may refer to those, say, under fifty, or even under sixty.[42]

To be sensible – This important virtue for young men, one that will serve to guide all one's behavior, is the same trait of "sound mindedness" or "self-control" (*sōphronein*) expected of all ages and groups of Christians.[43] The instructions in the next two verses to Titus himself about being an example to the younger men may well list several areas where "sensibleness" is especially to be cultivated, both by Titus and his peers. Paul writes more about Titus the "example" than he does about Titus the "exhorter"!

2:7 -- In all things – A problem of how to punctuate and divide this material into verses immediately presents itself. Shall we take "in all things" with verse 6 (so that it reads "be sensible in all things") as Jerome, Moffatt, NEB, and Hendriksen

---

[40] In our comments on Romans 2:15 (*New Testament Epistles: Romans*, p.83), we explain "the work of law written on their hearts" as being a memorized set of rules, handed down by oral tradition, after God first revealed His standards of right and wrong to one of the old patriarchs. Romans 1:32 also indicates an ancient awareness of right and wrong and the penalties for doing the wrong, which could only come by revelation.

[41] See notes at 1 Timothy 4:12 and 2 Timothy 2:22.

[42] See Irenaeus, *Against Heresies* II.22.5, and John 8:56,57. In 1 Peter 5:5, the word "young men" (*neōteroi*) is contrasted with "elders" (*presbuteroi*), as in 1 Timothy 5:1. Here however, the contrast is with "older men" (*presbutidas*).

[43] See Titus 1:8, 2:2, 2:5, etc. The word used here for young men is the same used earlier and translated "temperate" and "discreet" ("sensible").

do, or shall we take "in all things" as the beginning of verse 7, as the NASB does? The arguments for either way of punctuating are rather evenly divided, and the significance of verses 6-8 are about the same either way. Young men are expected to be "sensible" and Titus is to set an example of sober judgment or self-control in all things, so the other young men have a model to copy.

Show yourself to be an example – The language implies that Titus himself is still a "young man."[44] The task of influencing the other young men in the churches belongs especially to him.[45] He is to show them what is expected by his own example.[46] In fact, the evangelist is to continually offer himself (present tense participle) as the pattern[47] or model or example. In that way, the young men in the churches will have a hero to follow. A similar admonition about setting an example was addressed to Timothy (1 Timothy 4:12). Some of the particular characteristics that Titus is to model as he sets his example are delineated in the words following in this verse and the next.[48]

---

[44] This commentator pictures Titus being a few years older than Timothy. Several evidences of Titus' age can be deduced from what we know about him. (1) When we compare what is said to Timothy ("let no one despise your youth," 1 Timothy 4:12) to what is said to Titus ("let no one despise you," Titus 2:15), we might deduce that Titus is no longer technically "a young man." (2) It is doubtful Titus was only in his early thirties when he served as trouble shooter at Corinth. In that difficult situation where even Paul's leadership was rejected, one would hardly expect the Corinthians to accept the leadership of one so young. We would picture him in his late 30's when he served in Corinth. Now it is eight or so years later that Titus is evangelizing on the island of Crete. So perhpas Titus is in his mid-40's as he serves on the island of Crete.

[45] The addition of a reflexive pronoun ("yourself") to a verb in the middle voice ("show") is somewhat unusual. It emphasizes the point that Titus *himself* has this responsibility!

[46] "Example" translates *tupon*, which originally meant "an impression made by a die." Titus was to live so that his life would be like a "spiritual die" that would impress itself on others. Several writers note that this is the only passage in the New Testament where *tupon* is followed by a genitive of the thing. Elsewhere it is followed by the genitive of the person to whom the example is given.

[47] Women who make their own clothes understand what a "pattern" is. It is a model or standard by which something else is shaped. This "example" or "pattern" that Titus is to be is an example to be followed again and again by those looking for a model.

[48] Knofel Staton, *Standard Lesson Commentary*, 1992, p. 443, has written, "Bumper stickers come in many different sizes, colors, and messages. I saw a bumper sticker in our neighborhood that caused me to think about our Christian lives. It said, 'Caution, I drive the way you do.' It made me think about what driving would be like on the highways if everyone drove the way I do.

[T-shirts also come with messages.] Then I transferred that thought into the Christian life. What if every Christian wore a T-shirt that had one of the following messages on it:

'Caution, I study the Bible the way you do.'
'Caution, I pray the way you do.'
'Caution, I talk about people the way you do.'
'Caution, I forgive the way you do.'
'Caution, I give the way you do.'
'Caution, I demonstrate the fruit of the Spirit the way you do.'

In what they do and how they speak, more people are guided by our examples than we can ever imagine." Paul would urge the same exhortation about being an example on all young preachers, just as he has on Timothy and Titus.

Of good deeds – Compare Titus 3:8 and Titus 2:16. Note the stress Paul lays upon Christian practice as the result of sound doctrine (Titus 2:1). While this stress on good deeds certainly reflects against something wrong in the doctrine or lives of the false teachers (Titus 2:16), it is also true that by one's deeds he will be judged in the final judgment (Matthew 25:31ff; 2 Corinthians 5:12). How one lives, what one does, is of supreme importance.

With **purity in doctrine** – "With" is in italics, showing that the translators have added it. Adding "with" causes us to think that the "example of good deeds" is the result of purity.[49] This phrase likely is another area in which Titus is to be a model for other believers. It might have helped us to catch the sense of this if the translators had simply repeated the verb from the previous clause, so that this verse would read "in doctrine *show yourself* pure (uncorrupted)." In fact, the Greek words in the accusative case in this verse ("example," "uncorrupted" and "dignified") all depend on the verb "show yourself."

It has been suggested that the sentence construction is somewhat irregular for brevity's sake. Paul is doing two things at once. He is listing the characteristics young men are to cultivate, and at the same time is admonishing Titus about his particular responsibility as an evangelist for setting the example for his own age group. "Doctrine" is an abbreviated expression, conveying the same meaning as "sound doctrine" in Titus 1:9 and 2:1. The word is *didaskalia*, which emphasizes the content of what is taught.[50] "Purity" is the NASB's rendering for *aphthorian*, the reading found in the Nestle text. The Textus Receptus has a different word, *adiaphthoria*. *Adiaphthoros* is a classical word, which means, among other things, "incorruptible" – not influenced by entreaties or bribes. *Aphthoria* has the best manuscript authority here, but it is the only time the word occurs in the New Testament. Lexicons suggest both words are compounds made up of an alpha-privative (negating what the rest of the word says) plus the root word *phtheirō*, which means "to ruin, corrupt, destroy." In the realm of morals and religion it means to ruin the inner life, often by erroneous teaching or immorality. Donnegan's lexicon gives these meanings for the adjective *aphthoros*: "unpolluted, uncorrupted, unviolated, in a state of virginal purity."

Titus is to present the Gospel in such a clear and courageous way that it will be evident to everyone that he is not motivated by fear or favor, nor has he been infected with the lies and distortions of the Gnostic adversaries. Titus is to continually hold before the young men an example of incorruptness in the teaching of God's Word. Perhaps this term is specially chosen. If Gnostic doctrine is accepted, a person's inner life would no longer be "unpolluted" or "unviolated".

---

[49] So taken, the word "purity" is a quality of the teacher rather than a quality of his doctrine.

[50] See comments at 1 Timothy 1:10 and the footnote on the verb "teach" at 1 Timothy 2:12.

Dignified – *Semnotēs* was used at 1 Timothy 2:2 and 3:4. The word speaks of one's conduct or attitude towards men, a quality of life that earns respect.[51] Dignity ("seriousness") is the consciousness of having the terrible responsibility of being an ambassador of Christ in a world where sinning men are in a desperate predicament. Such seriousness can be seen in the preacher's careful preparation, in practicing the application of what he teaches, and in believing the eternal significance of what he teaches. The evangelist Titus is to set an example for other young men by letting them see this quality of life in action.

2:8 -- Sound *in* speech which is beyond reproach – "Speech" is in the accusative case, still dependent on the verb "show yourself" (verse 7). The same word "speech," when used of the example Timothy was to set (1 Timothy 4:12), referred to his personal conversation as differentiated from his preaching. We suppose the same is true here, that "speech" is different from "doctrine." "Sound" (*hugiē*[52]) means "healthy, practical, restorative."[53] Titus' everyday speech is to be the kind of words that will help spiritually sick people get well. When people hear his words, their spiritual lives are not damaged or hurt. "If any man offend not in word, the same is a perfect man" (James 3:2). By careless or hasty talk, a good man may give bad men an opportunity to find fault, not only with the good man but also with the faith he teaches. A Christian leader cannot refuse to speak, so he must take care to speak truly, charitably, and understandably.

"Beyond reproach" translates *akatagnōston*, literally, "not known against." The word occurs only here in the New Testament and once in 2 Maccabees 4:47. 2 Maccabees is a courtroom scene where, if the judge had carefully examined the witnesses, he would have gained no knowledge of any kind of flaw in the defendant; no one knew anything against the defendant. The word thus emphasizes the care that a Christian teacher must take to say nothing in his everyday language that is rash, or thoughtless, or foul. Paul directs the evangelist to speech that cannot be condemned, and it cannot be condemned if it benefits people, if it brings healing and help to the total well-being of others. Our speech ought to be so true, so uplifting, so helpful that no one can find fault with it even if he wants to.

---

[51] As noted earlier, the construction of this Greek sentence is somewhat irregular. Because of that fact, not a few commentators have opted for a different way of explaining exactly what traits or characteristics Titus is to model. It is possible that the words "uncorrupted" and "dignified" both modify "doctrine" (i.e., the doctrine he presents is to have no taint of heresy or impurity, and his manner of presenting it is with dignity). If so, there are only two traits for Titus to model – doctrine (verse 7) and speech (verse 8). Though the Greek construction is clearer in 1 Timothy 4:10 than here, since Timothy is given 5 areas where he is to be an example to the believers, we suppose that Titus likewise is given several areas where he is to be an example to the younger men. Titus' example is not limited to doctrine and speech, but to other areas of everyday life as well.

[52] The word is a cognate of the word translated "sound" in Titus 1:9 and 2:1.

[53] "Sound" represents the Greek word from which our English word "hygiene" comes. It means well and strong, healthy.

In order that the opponent may be put to shame – The last part of verse 8 indicates the result or purpose[54] of such conduct by Titus and the young men for whom he serves as an example. The words translated "the opponent" are an elliptical expression, "on the opposite (side)" or "of the opposite (party)."[55] The reference might be to any non-Christian on the island of Crete. In Crete were unbelievers, both Jewish and Gentile, who would oppose the church and seek occasion against it. However, it is more likely that there is special reference to the Gnostic false teachers described in Titus 1:9-16. There are "contrary" people with whom the church must deal. Such opponents would be "put to shame"[56] when it is shown in public that their charges of wrongdoing against Titus and Paul and the Christians are baseless, since there is nothing either in the life or the teaching of the Christians which can be fairly criticized as "bad." For a similar sentiment about putting the adversary to shame, see 1 Peter 2:15 and 3:16.

Having nothing bad to say about us – It seems to be implied that the opponent has been spreading malicious gossip[57] about Titus and Paul and the Christians. They had tried to reproach the conduct of the Christians, but it soon became obvious that their insinuations and accusations were all lies. The public knowledge of the teaching and behavior of the Christians was contrary to what the false teachers were saying; so the ones who were "shamed" were the false teachers, not the Christians. The manuscripts followed by the Textus Receptus read "about you", but the older manuscripts read "about us." "About us" associates Paul and others with Titus.[58] The antagonism of the opponents was not directed simply against Titus. It was also an accusation against the apostle Paul, and ultimately a word spoken against Christ and all of His messengers. It is not an easy thing to be the evangelist working with a congregation of people. He is always on duty. He must be careful to practice what he preaches. He must be the same man in the pulpit and out of it. No preacher is perfect, just as no church member is perfect. But the preacher must strive to be the best example possible. A church will never rise any higher than its leadership.

---

[54] Knight (*op. cit.*, p.313) thinks the clause is a purpose clause, and thus sees Paul reminding Titus that his life must be lived purposefully so that it has an effect for God with reference to the gospel on all those who observe the life of the preacher.

[55] The same expression is used of winds that were "contrary" (Matthew 14:24, Mark 6:48), and of Paul's pre-conversion opposition (almost "hostility") to the cause of Christ (Acts 26:9).

[56] The verb is passive voice. In the active voice, it means to put someone else to shame. In the middle voice, it means to "respect or reverence" someone (as in Matthew 21:37). In the passive voice, it means someone or something else has put the subject of the verb to shame. 2 Thessalonians 3:14 is the only other occurrence of the aorist passive of this verb in the New Testament.

[57] The word translated "bad" is *phaulos*, which means "mean, worthless, good for nothing," and is one of the synonyms for "evil" (see Trench, *op. cit.*, section 84).

[58] Unchristian conduct by any Christian, but especially when it is by a leader of the church, will have a negative impact on the reputation of the whole church in the eyes of the outside community.

5. Character traits to be cultivated by slaves.   2:9,10

2:9 -- *Urge* bondslaves – There is no verb in verse 9 so the verb "urge" is supplied from verse 6.   "Bondslaves" (*douloi*) were people over whom masters (*despotai*) had absolute power; they were considered part of their master's property.   Just as the other groups (older men, older women, young women, etc.) Titus is to encourage were Christians, so the "bondslaves" are also Christians.   In comments on 1 Timothy 6:1,2, there is a discussion of the whole institution of slavery in the first-century world.   What is said there is assumed here.[59]   As noted in 1 Timothy, historians usually present the idea that slaves outnumbered free men in the Roman Empire.   Hence, a great percentage of the converts, at least in the cities, would be of this class.   Many of these slaves were well-educated.   In fact, those with skills (doctors, accountants, equestrians, craftsmen skilled in wood and metal working, jewelers, etc.) were the most desirable slaves, and were the ones often taken from their native lands by the conquering Romans and brought back to Rome to be sold as slaves.   With such skills, they would hold responsible positions under their masters.   Paul tells Titus to emphasize the slave's attitude toward his master, gives three common sins slaves must avoid, and then closes with a positive admonition about being reliable.

To be subject to their own masters – In 1 Timothy 6:1,2 Paul distinguishes between masters who were Christians and those who were not as he gave instructions to the Christian slaves.   No such distinction is made here.[60]   The verb "to be subject"[61] is in the middle voice, and speaks of a voluntary submissiveness by those already slaves.   It is not a submissiveness coerced by something on the outside, but a behavior motivated and prompted by something on the inside of the Christian slave.   The slave is not being asked to do something unique.[62]   Any Christian under authority can appropriately be expected to be voluntarily submissive as part of one's responsibility to those in authority.   The Christian is never a man who is above taking orders.   His religion teaches him how to serve.

In everything – Here is another place where textual editors must make a choice.[63]

---

[59] In the notes on 1 Timothy 6, the objection of some to Christianity based on the alleged fact that it condoned slavery, rather than attempting to eradicate this evil, is answered, too.

[60] There is no way to ascertain whether the omission in Titus indicates that fewer masters on Crete were Christian than was the case in Ephesus, or whether the omission in Titus is due simply to Paul's desire for brevity in this letter.

[61] The same verb *hupotassō* is used in 1 Peter 2:18 where Peter gives instructions to domestic slaves.   Elsewhere Paul uses the word *hupakouō*, "to listen" or "to obey."

[62] The same verb *hupotassō* occurs in Ephesians 5:21; 1 Corinthians 16:16; Romans 13:1; Titus 3:1; 1 Peter 2:13; Colossians 3:18; 1 Peter 3:1,5.

[63] A comparison of modern English translations will show both "to be submissive in all things"

Shall we take "in everything" with the verb "to be subject," or shall we take it with the word which follows, "to be well pleasing"?   If we take it with the former, it says that from morning until evening, and in every category of work, the slave is to voluntarily submit to the master's wishes.   If we take it with the following, then it says that from morning until evening, and in every category of work, the slave makes it his purpose not just to submit, but also to please his master.   Some Bible students are convinced to adopt the former by the parallel instruction found in Colossians 3:11, where "in all things" clearly goes with "obey."   Lest it be forgotten what Scriptures say to Christians elsewhere, this phrase "in everything" is hardly to be treated in an absolute sense.   Paul is hardly to be understood as telling the slave to be submissive or to please his master when the master demands that the slave commit some crime or do something immoral.   Verse 10 will instruct the slave that he must "adorn the doctrine of God" in all his behavior. So, of course, if God and slave-master contradict, the slave must obey God![64]

To be well-pleasing – When the word is used elsewhere in the New Testament, it is God who is thought of as being pleased by a person's conduct (Romans 12:1; 2 Corinthians 5:9; Ephesians 5:10).   That might be the meaning here, too.   If so, we may have another phrase in this context that limits how far a slave must go in his submission to his earthly master.   Or, this phrase may say that such voluntary submission is the kind of attitude and action that pleases God who is watching our lives.   It is also possible that in this place the one who is well-pleased with the slave's behavior is the earthly master.[65]   If so, then the passage is asking for not merely external compliance with the master's wishes.   There is no sullen disposition, no growling or grumbling underneath, nor doing the job grudgingly. The slave makes it his aim to be eager to please, to try to satisfy his master.[66] And this even when some unsaved masters would not be thoughtful and might overwork their slaves.   Jesus taught His followers to go the extra mile.   The Christian never puts less than his best into any task given him to do.

Not argumentative – The same word (*antilegontas*) is used in Titus 1:9, where it is rendered "contradict."   It was a common fault of slaves to dispute a master's

---

and "to be well pleasing in all things" being used.

[64] See also Acts 4:19, 5:29, and Ephesians 5:21. It is tacitly understood that obeying God rather than men may well result in a fit of wrath on the part of the man. But Jesus spoke about the blessing that comes to the man who suffers for righteousness' sake.

[65] Interpreted this way, it matches Ephesians 5:7, where the slave is "with good will to render service."

[66] In the introductory studies to these Pastoral Epistles, note was taken of the numerous arguments advanced by some critics why the epistles could not have been written by Paul. It is instructive to note that the adjective *euarestos* is a favorite word with Paul. The only writer in the New Testament to use this word is Paul. The adjective occurs seven times in Paul's signed letters, and once in Hebrews. (In this commentator's opinion, Hebrews should be attributed to Paul.)

25

desires. The Christian slave is to avoid this common fault of slaves. If he is going to be well-pleasing, he is not to resist or talk back to the master. The slave does not set himself against his master's plans or orders. He does not actively disobey or rebel. He doesn't "gripe" about his master to the other slaves. Such sweet conduct towards their earthly master would help greatly (verse 10 says) the heavenly Master's cause. The masters (some of whom at first would be hostile to Christianity) would begin to think there was something special and desirable about a religion which could so powerfully influence the behavior of even slaves.

2:10 -- Not pilfering – The instructions begun in verse 9 which Titus is to give to Christian slaves continue. "Pilfering" or "embezzling" or "stealing" was another common fault of slaves, a fault not to be found in slaves who were Christian.[67] "Pilfering" (*nosphidzomenous*) is a compound word including *nosphi*, which means "apart, aside." It means "to keep back part for one's self" or "to secretly keep apart a portion" which really belongs to someone else. "Misappropriating" or "stealing" are suitable English words to express the idea in the Greek. It is the word used of Ananias and Sapphira (Acts 5:2,3), of Achan (Joshua 7:1, LXX) and of Menelaus (2 Maccabees 4:32). So often the temptation to such larceny is an attitude which says, 'They owe me this because I'm not being paid for all my work. Besides, I'm taking such a small quantity that it will not even be missed.' Slaves did have opportunity for fraud and dishonesty by which they could enrich themselves. Some were entrusted with shops, some were artists, some were physicians, some were stewards. There were hundreds of ways a dishonest slave could "keep back a portion for himself." A Christian slave is to be honest, not stooping to the petty dishonesties of which the world is full.

But showing all good faith – "Showing" translates *endeiknumi*, and the present tense of the participle indicates this is to be the habitual behavior of the Christian slave. He is to "show" or demonstrate or make it perfectly manifest that he is "faithful." The participle is also in the middle voice, suggesting the slave voluntarily does this for his own benefit. Some render *pistis* as "faith" or "faithfulness." Others prefer "fidelity" or "reliability" in this place. Not a few writers treat this word as the positive side of "not pilfering." It is not enough for the Christian to avoid the wrong. There is a positive attitude and action that must be cultivated. "All fidelity" means fidelity in everything where fidelity is required in a Christian servant – care of his master's property, conscientious labor, careful keeping of time, acting behind the master's back the same as before his eyes. The force of the adjective "good" in this place is debated. Bengel's ex-

---

[67] In our society there may be no slaves, but there are employees. Christian workers must obey orders and not talk back. They must not steal from their employers. Millions of dollars are lost each year by employers whose workers steal from them, everything from paper clips and pencils to office machines and vehicles. The preacher will have to constantly remind Christian workers of the expectations God has for them.

planation is that what is required is "fidelity in all good things," that the duty of fidelity does not extend to committing crime or doing anything God says is wrong. Appeal is even made to Titus 3:1 where it is affirmed we have a similar limitation on obedience. Others treat "good" as modifying "faith." The slave is to display "good faith" in all relationships with his earthly master. He must be trustworthy to the utmost. "All" is possibly added to show that this faithfulness or reliability must extend to all areas of the slave's service to his earthly master.

That they may adorn the doctrine of God our Savior – Paul here gives the special reason why slaves in their difficult circumstances should be motivated by Christian standards in their behavior, dispositions, and dependability. "Adorn" means to "beautify" or "embellish with honor." In his letter to Timothy, Paul worded this same reason negatively, "that the name of God and His doctrine be not blasphemed" (1 Timothy 6:1). "Adorning" is like adding jewels and other adornments to something already beautiful in order to draw more attention to it. People are thus drawn to see the true value and precious treasure that lies in the Christian teaching itself. It is sometimes difficult to take Christianity to work with us, but when it is done and done consistently, the result is respect for the worker and respect for the Gospel he follows. The world will regularly come to see that the Christian workman is the only workman worth having! "Doctrine" is used in the same way it was at Titus 2:1 and 1:9. It refers to Christian teaching, the Gospel, that which is taught.

That a slave (or any Christian, for that matter) can "adorn" or "give due credit to" the Gospel is noteworthy. Slaves were considered to be below the rank of men (they were things, like wagons, or cattle, or horses, or tools). Yet God deigns to allow them to make His Gospel look better! Hendriksen writes that obedience, cheerfulness, and integrity in a slave are like precious jewels that serve to ornament the doctrine of God. Kent comments on how slaves living according to Paul's instructions would reflect honor on the Christian faith which they profess. "As a beautiful picture may be enhanced by an appropriate frame, so we (whether slaves, employees, or in other positions) make Christian teaching attractive if we exhibit its power and truth in our lives."[68] In the eyes of men, it makes the Gospel more attractive and appealing when it becomes obvious that it can transform lives, even of those of the lowest social order.

In the Greek, the article "the" that precedes "doctrine" is repeated before the phrase "of God our Savior." Thus the phrase serves as a restrictive attributive adjective. This construction calls attention to the doctrine "of God" and at the same time reminds the reader of the fact that there is also doctrine that is not from God our Savior. "God" the Father was designated as "our Savior" at Titus 1:3.

---

[68] Kent, *The Pastoral Epistles*, p.226.

In every respect – It is the "adorning" that is to be done in every respect, or "in all things" (*en pasin*). Compare 1 Peter 4:11. Paul has written five things about slaves' behavior: their submissiveness, being pleasing, not talking back, not stealing, and being entirely trustworthy. These are some of the "respects" Paul has in mind by which slaves may adorn the doctrine of God.

B. Reason Why Christians are to Develop Corresponding Character Traits. 2:11-14

2:11 -- For – "For" indicates the verse either gives a reason for something just said, or a further explanation of something just said. (1) Some writers opt for "explanation of something just said." Perhaps verses 11-14 explain why God is called "Savior" (verse 10). Perhaps verses 11-14 further explain what is involved in "the doctrine of God" (verse 10). So understood, verse 12 is specifically stating that such character traits as enumerated earlier in chapter 2 are an integral part of "the doctrine of God." (2) Most writers opt for "reason for something just said." Perhaps verses 11-14 are intended to give a reason why slaves should "adorn the doctrine of God" (verse 10). Perhaps verses 11-14 are intended to give a reason why Titus should "speak the things which are fitting for sound doctrine" (verse 1). So understood, this new paragraph in chapter 2 would be a reason why all the character traits emphasized in 2:1-10 should be cultivated – i.e., the grace of God says so! Lewis A. Foster has succinctly summarized the thrust of this whole second chapter written to Titus.

> In the early verses of the second chapter, Paul gives instruction to old men, to old women, to young women and young men, and to slaves. [Titus himself is to be a good example in all he says and does.] This is practical instruction for Christian living; but with the verse before us [verse 11], Paul lays a theological foundation for the ethical demands that he has written down. The beginning point for his doctrine is *the grace of God*; apart from this there would be no *salvation*. God's grace was made manifest in the incarnation of his own Son, Jesus Christ, and in the atonement that He made effective on the cross.[69]

This commentator agrees with the view that verses 11-14 are laying the theological foundation for all that has been written earlier in chapter 2.[70]

The grace of God has appeared – "Has appeared" (*epephanō*) is an aorist tense and points to a past act. The word literally means "become visible [to human

---

[69] *Standard Lesson Commentary*, 1964, p.409-10.

[70] Paul's usual custom is to give the doctrinal basis first and then give the practical application. Here we would have the reverse – first the practical exhortations, then the doctrinal basis on which they rest. We find a similar order in some of Paul's earlier letters, e.g., Philippians 2:12,13.

eyes]," "come to light," "become clearly known."[71] "Appeared" is a word often used with respect to Jesus the Messiah. The English word "epiphany" is a transliteration of this Greek word and is regularly used of Christ's first coming. Though He existed before the birth in Bethlehem, Jesus was not ordinarily visible to human eyes. But between Bethlehem and the Ascension, while He was in the flesh, Jesus (God's way of saving men) was visible to human eyes. "Epiphany" is also one of the synonyms used of Christ's second coming, when He again will be visible to human eyes. However, in this passage it is not Jesus, but the "grace of God" that has appeared. Having noted the use of the word with respect to Jesus Himself, it should be carefully observed that this passage in Titus speaks of the "grace of God" as something distinct from Jesus and as having appeared. Later in Titus 3:4 we will have the word again: "when the kindness of God our Savior and His love for mankind appeared." See also Colossians 1:5,6 and the comparable statement in 2 Timothy 1:9,10. "Appeared" stands first in the Greek sentence, putting emphasis on it. "Appeared, yes actually appeared, has the *grace* of God ...." "The grace of God" here spoken of is "all that God thinks and does to save men."[72] Grace is God's loving favor and tender compassion for the men He created that leads Him to provide for man a way to escape from the guilt and penalty of sin. Through the ages before Jesus' earthly ministry, God gave little glimpses of His grace, but it was not until the coming of His Son to redeem us that the extent of God's grace could be clearly seen. By looking at Jesus and Calvary, one can see with his own eyes how broad and generous God's grace actually is. Writers who believe salvation is "by grace alone" are wont to find that doctrine in this passage. Those writers will emphasize how "grace" brings salvation to men, and how "grace" instructs men how to live. Now it is true that if mankind is to be saved it will have to be by the way God provides, and that way might here be called "grace of God." But this is far from teaching that salvation is monergistic – i.e., something God does to man, something that requires no response from man. This very context (verses 1-10 and verses 12,13) gives instructions concerning several expected responses to "the grace of God." What this passage does say about grace is that it has appeared, it provides salvation, and it instructs. (Calvinistic writers want to add a fourth thing grace does, namely, "it enables people," but it is hard to see where that idea is found in these verses.)

Bringing salvation to all men -- There is a puzzling manuscript variation at this place. (1) Some manuscripts read *hē charis tou theou hē sōtēpios pasin anthrō-*

---

[71] The Greek word translated "appeared" occurs in Luke 1:79, which is a prophecy of the coming of Jesus under the figure of the sun rising and "shining" on people who before had been sitting in darkness. In Acts 27:20, it is used of the inability of the people on the ship to see either sun or stars because of the continuing storm on the Mediterranean during Paul's voyage to Rome.

[72] For a study of the concept of "grace" in the New Testament, see *New Testament Epistles: Romans*, p. 45ff.

pois.[73]   The Textus Receptus repeats the word "the" before the adjective *sōtērios* ("bringing salvation") making "the salvation" an adjective phrase which modifies "the grace."[74]   Alford has offered the suggestion that some scribe mistakenly added the article *hē* before *sōtērios* because in the scribe's opinion it would make this construction clearer.   (2) Some manuscripts read *hē charis tou theou hē sōtēros pasin anthrōpois.*[75]   These manuscripts result in the translation "the grace of God our Savior" (*sōtēros* in the genitive case, agreeing with "God"), just as 2:10 reads.   (3) Some manuscripts read *hē charis tou theou sōtērios pasin anthropois.*   Most modern Greek texts (following Aleph* A C[1] D[1] Syr.) omit the article "the" before *sōtērios.*   In so doing, the resulting reading of the adjective *sōtērios* with no article is a construction that occurs only here in the New Testament.[76]   *Sōtērios* is a singular adjective in the nominative case, and this particular form may be either masculine or feminine.   There is a rule that adjectives agree with the nouns they modify in case, number, and gender.   The only word in the nominative singular in this verse is "grace," a feminine noun.   If we adopt this reading, we must connect *sōtērios* with *charis* when we make our translation.   Our choice of readings will affect how we understand this verse.   Since the majority of manuscripts somehow connect "salvation" with "grace," we shall attempt to do likewise in the comments we offer on this passage.

"Bringing salvation", as the NASB reads, translates the adjective *sōtērios.* *Sōtērios* comes from the same root as the word "Savior" (*sōtēros*) in verses 10 and 13.[77]   One lexicon gives "to bring salvation" or "he who embodies this salvation," or "he through whom God is about to achieve salvation" (Thayer). Another lexicon gives "the means of salvation" (BAGD).   *Sōtērios* is a predicate adjective[78] agreeing with "grace."   "Salvation-bringing grace" seems to be what is required as a translation.   Further, the verse says "salvation-bringing grace

---

[73] The manuscripts which so read are C[3] D[2,3] K L P Clem., Cyr., Jer., Chry., Thdrt., Procl. Damasc.

[74] With the article "the" included, as the Textus Receptus has it, "to all men" can be taken with either "appeared" or "bringing salvation."   Most, however, see that text as meaning "the salvation-bringing grace of God has appeared to all men."

[75] Aleph[1] F vulg., Copt., Aeth., Epiph.

[76] It also occurs in the LXX in Wisdom 1:14 and 3 Maccabees 7:18, and frequently in classical Greek.

[77] What does the suffix *-terios* mean when it is added to a word like "Savior" (*sōtēr*)?   Perhaps the *-ter* indicates the "doer of the action" and the *-ios* is simply the common way of forming an adjective out of a noun.

[78] *Sōtērios* with an article immediately before it, as in the Textus Receptus, is what is called an attributive adjective.   With no article immediately before it, it is what is called a predicate adjective, or stands in the "predicate position."   We normally use "is" (or some form of the verb "to be") to help translate an adjective in the predicate position, but that is exceptionally hard to do in this place. Knight (*op. cit.*, p.319) offers "God's favour has appeared with saving power", but this commentator is not familiar with using "with" as a helper to translate adjectives in the predicate position.

appeared."   It appeared in order to rescue men from the guilt and penalty of sin.[79]

Our English versions have two different readings for "to all men" at this place.   (1) The KJV reads "The grace of God ... has appeared to all men."   (2) Most modern versions connect "to all men" with "salvation" and so read as the NASB does, i.e., "bringing salvation to all men."   One reason for the different readings in our versions is manuscript variation.   Another reason for the different readings may also be found in the word order in the Greek.   Alford, for example argues, that "to all men" goes with "bringing salvation" (the word that immediately precedes it), and that "appeared" is used absolutely.   Probably a further reason the modern translations put "to all men" with "bringing salvation" is a logical one.   It is obvious that the grace of God is not even yet, nearly 2000 years after Paul wrote these words to Titus, known to all men.   On the other hand, Christ died for all, whether Jew or Gentile, bond or free, young or old.   Salvation, universal in scope, is offered to all, is available to all, is within reach of all. "Bringing salvation to all men" (if we so elect to read the verse) does not mean that Paul teaches universal salvation regardless of how men live.   This very context (verse 12) lists some of the requirements of the gospel if men are to enjoy the proffered salvation.   (See the comments at 1 Timothy 4:10 on the misuse of certain passages in the Pastorals to defend the doctrine of universalism.)   It does mean that all men – Jew or Gentile, rich or poor, slave or free, male or female, aged or young – are eligible to enjoy the benefits offered in the Gospel.   Further- more, the "all men" of verse 11 and the "us [Christians]" of verse 12 are somehow closely related in this passage.   This is enough to keep us from embracing a "universalistic" interpretation for "all men."   Alternately, "the grace of God has appeared to all men" (if that is how we decide to read the verse) would mean that all men – Jew or Gentile, aged or young, male or female, slave or free, etc. – who sit in darkness will have the light shine on them (Luke 1:79).   God's grace has appeared to all men in the incarnation of Jesus and in the preaching of the gospel, and it does make salvation available for all men.   Unfortunately, many reject the salvation that is offered, and therefore are not saved.   Perhaps the intimation also is this: since God's salvation-bringing grace has appeared to "all men," no particular group or caste has any reason for not developing the character traits the gospel inculcates.   All are expected to live as the grace of God instructs us to do.

2:12 -- Instructing us – The verb *paideuō* can mean either to "instruct" or to

---

[79] This writer is a bit hesitant about this suggested translation.   Would we not, after all, offer the same translation if the adjective *sōtērios* were in the attributive position like it is in the Textus Receptus?   The usual word order is for the adjective (with or without an article) to be written immediately before or after the word it modifies with no words intervening.   Yet what we have here in the Greek [NA26] is an article, a noun, a genitive phrase ("of God") and then the adjective in the nominative case (with no article).   The usual word order, however, is not always used.   There are times that phrases do appear between the noun and the adjective that modifies the noun, and this likely is the case here since "bringing salvation" is an adjective that is somehow related to "grace."

"correct/discipline." In classical Greek, *paideuō* has as one of its meanings the idea of "correcting, chastening, disciplining." But Alford surely is wrong in saying that the *universal* New Testament sense of *paideuō* is "to discipline," i.e., to teach by correction. In Acts 7:22, 22:3, and 2 Timothy 3:16, the idea of "teaching" but not necessarily that of "correcting" is predominant. Liddell and Scott show that *paideuō* regularly has the meaning of "instruct" or "teach" even in classical Greek. That is abundant justification for a similar rendering in this passage. Perhaps "grace" uses both means to help Christians know what is expected of them. Grace teaches and instructs, and grace disciplines and corrects when that is needed. Perhaps in this context, given the instructions that follow, the chief idea of *paideuō* is its broader meaning of "teach" or "instruct."

God's "grace" (verse 11) does the instructing which this verse talks about.[80] The same attitude (grace) that prompted God to "bring salvation" (verse 11) also prompts God to instruct those who are saved about how they are then to live. Grace teaches us not to tolerate sin in our lives. Salvation is not only a change in position (i.e., set free from the slavery to sin), but is also a change in attitude, appetite, ambition, and action. Men would still be walking in darkness if God had not determined He would reveal how He expects men to live. God did us a favor when He revealed what He expects of men. The verb form is present tense, indicating continuing or repeated action. Grace so instructs over and over again.

To deny ungodliness and worldly desires – The Greek is a *hina* clause. *Hina* may in this instance introduce what is called indirect discourse. If so, the *hina* clause would introduce a phrase that gives the content of what is to be taught. *Hina* is also used in Greek to introduce a purpose clause. With the subjunctive mood verb *dzēsōmen* ("might live") following, it is most likely a purpose clause. Thus grace instructs us "in order that we might ... live sensibly, etc. ...." The instructions "grace" gives have both a negative and a positive side. The negative side is stated first.[81] "To deny" translates *arnēsamenoi*, a nominative plural participle. Thus the phrase beginning with the participle "denying" is subordinate to the main verb "might live," so that this verse says that "denying" (ungodliness and worldly desires) is a condition prerequisite for developing the positive traits (sensibly, righteously, godly) we are called on to demonstrate.

Perhaps neither the English word "deny" nor "avoid" is strong enough to catch the meaning of *arneomai*.[82] Not only should redeemed men refuse to follow after ungodliness and worldly lusts, but they should hate and spurn them as men would the sting of a serpent. It is not enough to refuse to commit sin.

---

[80] The participle "instructing" by its ending in the Greek shows that it has "grace" as its subject.

[81] Paul often gives both negative and positive instructions in the same context.

[82] The verb basically means "say 'no' to."

In the heart as well as in deed, redeemed men should deny all ungodliness and worldly lusts. A change of attitude is demanded. Redeemed men must learn to say "No!" and to say it firmly! Grace instructs Christians about things they are to deny or renounce or reject or spurn if they are to live sensibly, righteously, godly. The aorist tense indicates these evils are to be renounced once and for all. As a growing Christian learns the different things God identifies as "evil," he deliberately renounces them and gives up what would displease God.[83]

"Ungodliness" (*asebeian*) is one thing that will have to be renounced. "Ungodliness" is the opposite of "godliness" (Titus 1:1). Redeemed men reject any way of life that is without reverence and service for God. A vivid description of "ungodliness" is found in Romans 1:18-32 (in fact, the very word "ungodliness" occurs at Romans 1:18). "Worldly desires" are inordinate desires for those things which belong only to this world.[84] Included would be desires for personal pleasure, for personal power, and for worldly possessions (as though a man's life consists of the abundance of the things he possesses). The Devil has something to do with prompting such worldly desires (1 John 5:19). Here is another whole area where the Christian is just to say "No!"[85] Many of Paul's readers have trouble understanding "grace." They mistakenly suppose that Paul's presentation of grace encourages men to go on sinning. "God is gracious," they say. "He will forgive all our sins. So why not keep on sinning and give God more opportunity to make use of His abundant grace?" Paul says that such

---

[83] Hendriksen (*op. cit.*, p.371) has a thoughtful note. "The verb used in the original is from the same stem as the noun *pedagogue*. A pedagogue leads children step by step. Thus, grace, too, gently leads and guides. It does not throw things into confusion. It does not suddenly and forcefully upset the social order. For example, it does not abruptly order masters to free their slaves; nor does it unwisely command slaves to rebel forthwith against their masters. [Instead], it gradually causes masters to see that the encroachment upon the liberty of their fellows is a great wrong, and it convinces slaves that to resort to force and vengeance is not the solution to every problem."

[84] Actually the word "desires" is a neutral word. There are desires for good things and there are desires for bad things – only the context decides how the word "desires" is being used. The context here is of negative things to be renounced, so we speak of "inordinate" desires. See the comments at 2 Timothy 2:22 for a listing of some "sins" that result from such worldly desires.

[85] "JUST SAY 'NO'!" Historians will surely be kind to Nancy Reagan, if for no other reason than her antidrug campaign and motto: *Just Say 'No.'* ... The result is hard to measure, but if even a handful of kids spurn drugs, the effort is worthwhile.

It is ironic that children, whose first clearly-spoken word is often 'No,' need to be taught to say 'No' at the right times. They quite naturally say 'No' to spinach, liver, naps, and all kinds of medication. Yet they (and all of us) must be taught to say 'No' to alcohol, pot, heroin, vandalism, and premarital sex.

The *New International Version* translates verse 12 as, "It [the grace of God] teaches us to say 'No' to ungodliness and worldly passions." By the grace of God, Christians can 'live self-controlled, upright and godly lives in this present age.' We can say 'No' to violent and sexually explicit movies. We can say 'No' to unwholesome television programs that present immorality and deviant life-styles as acceptable. We can say 'No' to humanism and materialism.

We *can* say 'No' – and we *must* say 'No'." Richard W. Baynes, *Standard Lesson Commentary*, 1992, p.444.

thinking is wrong (Romans 6:1-2). Grace does not teach that at all! God's forgiveness is not an act of blindness to let us keep sinning; it is an act of kindness to bring us to repentance (Romans 2:4). Rather than teaching us to increase our ungodliness, grace teaches us to be denying ungodliness and worldly lusts.

And to live sensibly, righteously and godly – There is no "and" in the Greek, but the NASB has worded the verse so that we see both the negative and positive sides of the instructions which grace gives. We now take up the positive qualities a Christian is to demonstrate in his life. "Live" is the main verb in this *hina* clause. This shows that the main thing grace teaches is the positive lesson about how Christians are to live. "Sensibly" is a word used numerous times before in Titus (see 2:2,4,5,6). "Sensible" is our familiar word for "self-control, prudence, restraint" (see 2:2). The "sober" or "sensible" man is the one who has learned to be thoughtful, who has learned how to master his own desires, who is in control of himself. "Sensibly" emphasizes the redeemed man's relationship to himself. "Righteously" speaks of the redeemed man's relationships with other people. Involved are fairness, honesty, justice, and integrity as we deal with others. Living righteously is living in accordance with the permanent, eternal ways established by the Creator. "Godly" is an adverb from the same root as "godliness" (Titus 1:1), and speaks of the redeemed man's relationship to the Lord. This word speaks of giving God what is due to Him. Reverence and worship to Him who alone is the proper object of worship are included. So is gratitude to the One who provided salvation, and an awareness that we live in the presence of the Eternal God to Whom we must one day answer for the deeds done in the body.

In the present age – Two nuances are probably intended by the phrase "the present age." (1) God's grace does not simply teach us about the age to come. It also teaches about living in this present age. (2) God's grace also teaches us that this present age is not the one that is most important. These words, plus what will be written in the next verse, remind the readers that the present world is transitory. The outward form of this world and its lusts are in the process of passing away (1 Corinthians 7:31, 1 John 2:17). The temporary nature of "this present age" is something that grace instructs us about. Grace also instructs us that for a man to be wholly interested in "this present age" is a great fault (2 Timothy 4:10; 1 Timothy 6:17). Scripture makes a sharp contrast between "this present age" and "the age to come" (Ephesians 1:21, Mark 10:30). Christians live "in this present age," but they are not to live *like* it or *for* it. Christ has redeemed us from this present evil age (Galatians 1:4), and redeemed men must not be conformed to this present age (Romans 12:1-2). Neither are they to walk according to its standards (Ephesians 2:2). In harmony with the Scriptural doctrine of the surpassing importance of the age to come, we will read in verse 13 that grace also instructs us to set our affections on the grace that will be brought to us at the second coming of Christ. Christ never intended for his followers to shut themselves away from other people in order to avoid committing sin. But as they live in this present age and try to win this present age, they also must guard themselves against the present age's attitudes and mores and evil actions.

2:13 -- Looking for – The connection with the whole thought of verses 11ff is this: Although the grace of God teaches us how to live in this present world, it also points us beyond this present world. The word *prosdechomenoi* is a present participle, indicating a continuous "expectant waiting" or "looking forward to." The participle is a circumstantial participle and has as its subject the "we" in the verb "we might live." The circumstantial participle might emphasize "attendant circumstance." If so, the verse means that our living in the present age is accompanied by a lively expectation of what the future will bring. The circumstantial participle might emphasize "means" or "manner." If so, the verse says that whether we are old men, old women, young men, young women, or slaves, we can live victoriously – eliminating the negative and accentuating the positive virtues listed in verse 12 – because we are motivated by the anticipation of what the future holds. Whenever a royal visit was expected in the ancient world, everything was cleaned and decorated and made fit for the royal eye to see. In a similar way, the Christian always keeps his life prepared (by denying ungodliness and living sensibly, verse 12) for the coming of the King of kings.[86]

The blessed hope – "Hope" and "appearing" are what Christians are "looking for." Sharp's rule of grammar[87] leads us to understand that "the ... hope" and "appearing" are two descriptions of the same single event. The thing hoped for and the appearing are the same thing. Each noun is qualified: the hope is called "blessed" and what is to "appear" is explained as being "glory." The One to whom the "glory" belongs is further expressed by a phrase that makes up the rest of verse 13 and part of verse 14. The event Christians are looking for is none other than the second coming of Christ! "Hope" in this place means "the thing hoped for."[88] Scripture elsewhere gives some of the details about this "thing hoped for," for it embraces several elements:

---

[86] When Jesus comes, we shall be like Him. Everyone who has the hope of becoming like Christ starts that process here and now (1 John 3:2,3).

[87] Sharp's rule reads, "When two nouns in the same case are connected by the Greek word 'and,' and the first noun is preceded by the article 'the,' and the second noun is not preceded by the article, the second noun refers to the same person or thing to which the first noun refers, and is a further description of it." (K.S. Wuest, *Treasures from the Greek New Testament*, p.31). That is exactly the kind of construction we have in the phrase being commented upon.

[88] In Scripture, "hope" sometimes is the subjective hope each person holds, and sometimes it refers to the thing hoped for. In Acts 24:15, both ideas are included, as the whole verse shows. The word is used both ways in Romans 8:24,25. In Galatians 5:5 and Colossians 1:5 ("the hope laid up for you in heaven") and Hebrews 6:18,19, the word can only refer to the "thing hoped for."

- There will be a trumpet blast and a shout of the archangel.
- Christ suddenly becomes visible and slowly descends from Heaven, accompanied by the souls of the righteous dead and by multitudes of angels.
- The bodies of dead in Christ are raised in a glorious new and heavenly form and reunited with their souls.
- The living are transformed.
- At the Judgment, Jesus will confess their names once and for all before the Father.
- Then, upon the invitation to "Come, enter with me into the joy of My Father," hand in hand and arm in arm the redeemed will move toward the new Jerusalem with its streets of gold and its river of living water flowing from the throne of God.

The thing hoped for is also called "blessed" (*makarian*). When something or someone is called "blessed" in Scripture,[89] that thing or one is regularly thought of as *receiving* the blessing. Perhaps in this place (it would be one of the few times in the New Testament where it is so used) "blessed" means that what happens at the second coming (i.e., the thing hoped for) will be a *source* of blessing for the Christian.

And the appearing of the glory – "Appearing" (*epiphaneian*) is the word already encountered in verse 11, but with this difference. This "visible appearance" is Christ's second coming.[90] Just as *epiphaneia* was often used by the Greeks to refer to the intervention by their deities into human affairs, so the second coming of Jesus will be a real intervention of a real Deity into human affairs. "Epiphany" is used exclusively of the appearance of Jesus in our world; it is never used of God so appearing.

"Glory" is not an easy term to explain. (1) Perhaps the phrase serves as an adjective modifying "appearing", so that we could read "glorious appearing."[91] The KJV, Berkeley version, and Goodspeed so translate it. Treating the genitive "of the glory" as an adjective phrase modifying "appearing" would be the same as is done at Luke 16:8 where "the steward of the unrighteousness" (as the Greek

---

[89] There are two words translated "blessed," *makarios* and *eulogētos*. Of the 50 passages where the word *makarios* occurs, in 43 it is applied to persons; twice it is applied to God (see notes on 1 Timothy 1:11 and 6:15); three times to parts of the body (the virgin's womb, and the eyes and ears of those who saw and heard Christ), and once it is used impersonally (Acts 20:35). This is the only passage where "blessed" is applied to something like "hope" (i.e., the thing hoped for).

[90] When "appearing/appearance" occurs elsewhere in the New Testament, the reference is regularly to Christ's second coming. The only exception is 2 Timothy 1:10, which refers to Christ's first coming. It will be recalled that in Titus 2:11, it was the grace of God which appeared. Though that concept includes Christ's first coming, it is not limited to it.

[91] In technical language, the construction is called a Hebraism. It was the way adjectives were written in Hebrew.

has it) is translated "the unrighteous steward."   (2) Perhaps this phrase refers to what will be seen ("epiphany") when King Jesus comes again, namely, His "glory."   (a) Perhaps it is the *shekinah* "glory" that Paul has in mind, that brilliant sphere of unapproachable light in which God dwells.   In Matthew 16:27 and Mark 8:38 we are told that "the Son of man shall come in the glory of the Father." So Weymouth renders it, "the appearing in glory."   (b) Perhaps it is Christ's own personal glory that Paul has in mind.   In Matthew 25:31 we are told what will happen "when the Son of man comes in his glory."   In Matthew 24:30 and Mark 13:26 we are told that when the Son of Man comes, people will see Him coming "in clouds with great power and glory."   See also Luke 21:27.   Jesus will be seen no longer in "the form of a servant" (Philippians 2:7), but as the Son of God who is both Savior and Judge (Matthew 25:31-46).   Luke 9:26 speaks of both the Son's glory and the Father's glory being displayed at the second coming.   2 Thessalonians 1:9,10 also speak of this glory that is Christ's.   In His high priestly prayer, Jesus prayed that he might be glorified with the "glory" that He ever had before the foundation of the world (John 17:5, and cp. Luke 24:26).   In fact, Jesus prayed that those who believe in Him through the words of the apostles might one day behold His glory (John 17:24).   (3) Jesus has a personal glory (or splendor or majesty).   He is called "the Lord of Glory" (1 Corinthians 2:8).   It may well be that very glory about which Paul writes, a glory which will finally and openly be manifest for all to see when Jesus returns.

Of our great God and Savior Christ Jesus -- The natural meaning these words convey is that Christ Jesus is called "our great God and Savior."   Through the years, however, two other interpretations have been given to these words.[92]

(1) One of these other and different interpretations says that in this phrase there is reference to two persons: [i] our great God, and [ii] our Savior Christ Jesus. This view is presented in the Wycliffe, Tyndale, and Cranmer English versions, in the KJV, the ASV (text), Moffatt, RSV (margin), and Phillips.[93]

(a) Some opt for the "two-person view" out of what they admit are dogmatic reasons.   They just do not think that Paul would call Jesus "God"!   As early as the Arian controversy, an attempt was made to blunt the force of this verse. Arians, who viewed Jesus as a created being and therefore not co-equal and co-eternal with the Father, did not want Him being called "our great God" in this passage.   They thought they got around it by affirming that it was the

[92] See Murray J. Harris, "Titus 2:13 and the Deity of Christ," in *Pauline Studies: Essays Presented to Professor F.F. Bruce on His 70th Birthday*, ed. by Donald Hagner and Murray Harris (Grand Rapids: Eerdmans, 1980), p. 262-277.

[93] Readers who wish to study this view in greater detail could consult Alford, Dibelius-Conzlemann, Jeremias, or N.J.D. White.

Father, not Jesus, who is here called "God."   But Arians get no support for their low view of Jesus from this verse, or this chapter, or this epistle, or the Scriptures as a whole!   Elsewhere, Paul certainly calls Jesus "God" (see Romans 9:5; Philippians 2:6; Colossians 1:15-20, 2:9; and see Hebrews 1:8-9, where it is God Himself who calls Messiah "God"), and so do other New Testament writers (John 1:1,18 and 2 Peter 1:1).   In this, the apostles are simply reflecting accurately Jesus' own claims (John 5:18ff, et al.).   Further, the New Testament writers ascribe to Jesus qualities and attributes that the Old Testament ascribes to Jehovah (for example, see Titus2:14).

(b) Some opt for the "two-person view" after explaining why, in their opinion, Sharp's rule of grammar is not valid at this place, even though "Savior" is anarthrous.   Alford[94] valiantly tries to explain why "Savior" here must be a reference to a second person, even though there is no "the" preceding it in the Greek.   But his explanation that, as time passed, "Savior" (without the article) was gradually becoming a quasi-proper name for Jesus does not fit what we find in the Pastorals.   Letters written late in Paul's life have "the Savior" (Titus 1:4, 3:6; 2 Timothy 1:10), while a sermon from early in Paul's life has anarthrous "Savior" (Acts 13:23).

(c) Some opt for the view that it is the Father who is alluded to here because "great God" was a LXX way of referring to the Father.   While it is true that we know of no other place where Jesus is called "great God," there could be a very good reason – considering the false teachers Titus and the Christians on Crete were facing – for Paul to so designate in this way our Jesus who elsewhere is called God.   (See this explained below.)   We have found no compelling reasons why this "two-person view" should be accepted as the interpretation of this disputed passage.[95]

(2) The other and different interpretation is one that makes the verse say that Christ Jesus is the "glory of our God and Savior."   We might call it "the appositional view."

(a) The verse is punctuated so that "Christ Jesus" is in apposition to "glory" – as though He were the "glory" of the Father (i.e., it is the Father who is here called "our great God and Savior").[96]   It is then God's glory that is manifested

---

[94] Volume 3 of *Alford's Greek Testament*, p. 420,421.

[95] While it is true that the second coming of Jesus our Savior will bring us into the presence of the Father as well as the Son, that does not seem to be the emphasis here.   On the whole, the evidence will favor this passage being a reference to one person, Jesus Christ, who is both God and Savior.   This interpretation fits better the reference to His "appearing."

[96] This apparently is what the translators of the NASB have tried to show, by placing the comma after "Savior," thus setting "Christ Jesus" apart from the words "Great God and Savior."   Students

in the coming appearance of Jesus. In favor of this view is that it combines several of the strong features of this text. There is only one appearance, namely, God's glory. The titles "God" and "Savior" do go together, as Sharp's rule of grammar shows. They would both refer to the Father, and without doubt in many verses elsewhere both those titles apply to the Father. This verse therefore would harmonize with those verses. A further evidence in favor of taking "Christ" and "glory" in apposition is the claim that "glory of God" was soon to become a Christological title.

(b) This "appositional view" also makes the verse refer to two persons – Jesus Christ, and the Father whose "glory" Jesus is. Some opt for this "two-person view" on the basis that, just as "Savior" is regularly applied to the Father elsewhere in Scripture (e.g., Titus 1:3, 2:10, and 3:4), so it would be here, too. This argument is somewhat weakened by the fact that Jesus has already been called "Savior" in Titus 1:4, and will be again in Titus 3:6.

(c) Against the "appositional view" these things can be said: (i) It seems to make too sharp a distinction between the Father and the Son, since it could be argued from this interpretation of the verse that Jesus is presented not as Deity, but merely as the "glory" of God. (ii) The emphasis of the whole context is on Jesus. Isn't "glory" sufficient to tell us how great God is? Isn't it almost redundant to have Paul pausing to tell us in even more words ("our great God and Savior") about His surpassing nature? Yet that is exactly what the "appositional view" requires. (iii) The hypothesis made by some that "glory of God" was a primitive Christological title has inadequate evidence to sustain it. And even if it is a Christological title, it is difficult to see how this in any way bolsters the "appositional view" of this passage.

When all the arguments for the other views have been examined, there is found no real reason to set aside the traditional view that the reference here is to one Person, Jesus Christ, who is called both "God" and "Savior." This view is presented in the ASV (margin), Weymouth, Goodspeed, Berkeley, RSV, NEB, TEV, LNT, NIV, NRSV. This is the way, scarcely without exception, that the Greek church fathers understood it.[97] Sharp's rule of grammar applies here just as it did earlier in this verse, and thus "great God" and "Savior" refer to the same

---

who wish to do more research on this view could consult Hort (*Epistle of James*, p. 47, 103ff), Fee, and Parry.

[97] "To select two examples out of the long chain of [church] fathers ... who have thus understood the text: 'St. Paul here calls Christ the great God, and thus rebukes the heretical blasphemy which denies his Godhead' (Theodoret). 'What can those persons say,' asks Chrysostom, referring to this passage, 'who allege that the Son is inferior to the Father?'" (Spence, "Titus" in *Ellicott's Commentary*, p.27). Readers wishing to do further research on this view may consult Barrett, Guthrie, Hendriksen, Simpson, or Hiebert.

person.[98]   That person without doubt is then named. He is none other than
Christ Jesus!   The fact noted above, that "appearing" is used in the New
Testament only of Jesus, lends support to the view that He is the one person this
passage speaks about.   The fact that the next verse (verse 14) carries on the
thought of what Jesus Christ has done, tends to support the view that it is Jesus
who is called "the great God and Savior."   In view of all that has been written, it
still seems obvious that the interpretation of the early Greek fathers is correct. It
is Jesus who is called "our great God and Savior."   And it is His appearing in
glory that is the blessed hope that sustains believers in this present age.   The
translators of the NEB have attempted to catch the thrust of this whole verse by
rendering it, "Looking forward to the happy fulfillment of our hopes when the
splendour of our great God and savior Christ Jesus will appear."

See what Jesus is here called! (a) **God**. This verse boldly affirms that
Jesus Christ is "God"!   He is not just a prophet, or an exalted angel. He is one
of the members of the Godhead.   (Review what was said above about Jesus being
God, in the rebuttal to the "two-person view.")   Not only is Jesus called God, but
elsewhere in the Scriptures He has the attributes of God. He even receives
worship, something no angel is permitted to do.

(b) **Great God**. Grundmann[99] notes the Old Testament use of "great" to proclaim
Jehovah's greatness. He notes the examples in Hellenism where "great" was
applied to pagan gods and goddesses (cp. Acts 19:28,34). He then offers the
hypothesis that Jesus is called "great" as a direct counter to contempor-ary pagan
claims about their "gods."   Hendriksen offers the view that the unexpected use of
"great" may reflect the fact that in the 1st century there were others who wanted
to be called "god" and "savior."   Several Greek rulers (Ptolemy I was called
"savior" and "god"; Antiochus IV was called "god manifest") and even Roman
emperors accepted homage as "gods."   But for the Christian, there is only One
who is "our great God and Savior"!   If indeed Gnosticism is the false teaching
being refuted, "great God" applied to Jesus Christ would be exceedingly apropos.
"Great God" was a late Jewish term for God (and Gnosticism was a Jewish heresy
to begin with).[100]   Christian doctrine would say that Jesus is "great God"
whatever Jewish Gnostics might say about Him.

---

[98] "No valid reason has ever been found which would show that [Sharp's] rule does not apply
in the present case. It is generally admitted that the words which in the original occur at the close
of 2 Peter 1:11 refer to *one* Person, and must be rendered, 'our Lord and Savior Jesus Christ.' But
if that be true, why should not the *essentially* identical idiom in 2 Peter 2:1 and here in Titus 2:13 be
rendered, 'our God and Savior Jesus Christ' (or 'Christ Jesus')?" (Hendriksen, *I and 2 Timothy, Titus*,
p.375).

[99] *Theological Dictionary of the New Testament*, edited by Kittel. Vol. IV, p. 538-40)

[100] See Jeremias, who refers to the LXX, Enoch, Philo, and Josephus, as examples where
"great God" is found as a designation for Jehovah.

(c) **Savior**. Here Christ is called savior, not only as the one who gave Himself for us in order to redeem us (verse 14), but because He also is the one who brings the hoped-for blessedness when He appears the second time, "without sin, unto salvation" (Hebrews 9:28). Compare also Philippians 3:20,21.

(d) **Messiah ("Christ")**. Jesus is everywhere in the New Testament presented as the long-awaited Messiah, who had been promised as coming ever since Adam and Eve sinned. The qualities and attributes of Jesus to which attention is called must certainly have been chosen because they were doubted and denied by the false teachers about whom Paul warns Titus and the churches on the island of Crete. The whole point of this verse is that anticipation of the return of Jesus Christ (a blessed event, a glorious event, a vindication of who He actually is – our God and Savior) is a motivation to Godly living. That is an event so glorious that people who are not properly prepared for it will be eternally sorry!

2:14 -- Who gave Himself for us – These words express part of all that is involved in the word "Savior" in verse 13.[101] A statement of Jesus' redemptive work very similar to this is found in 1 Timothy 2:5,6.[102] He gave nothing less than "Himself." Jesus' death was voluntary. For the great truths contained in the words "who gave Himself" compare John 10:11,17,18; Galatians 1:4; Ephesians 5:2,25; 1 Peter 2:24; Hebrews 9:11-14. He redeemed us with His own precious blood (1 Peter 1:18,19).

"For us" translates *huper hēmōn*, "on our behalf." Jesus' death was sacrificial. It was "for us." In Scripture, when it speaks of our redemption by Jesus Christ, we find two different phrases often rendered "for us." One is *huper hēmōn* and the other is *anti hēmōn*, "in our stead." The literal meaning of *huper* is "in defence of," and hence generally "on behalf of," or "for the good of." The primary meaning of *anti* is "standing opposite," and hence it denotes "exchange," "price," "worth," "instead of," "in the place of." We find *anti* in Matthew 20:28 and Mark 10:45, where Jesus Himself explained His own mission to this world – He came to seek and to save the lost, and "to give His life a ransom for many").[103]

---

[101] The antecedent of "who" with which this verse begins is "Christ Jesus," the "great God and Savior" about whom the previous verse spoke.

[102] It would be well to review what was there written about the atoning, substitutionary death of Christ, and the ransom that His death provided.

[103] In comments at 1 Timothy 2:6, it has been suggested that Paul is actually echoing the words of Jesus, both in Timothy and here in Titus. Of course, Paul has made a few minor changes so that the words fit the sentence and time he is writing. Jesus used a present tense verb; Paul uses past tense (since the crucifixion was past when Paul wrote). Jesus said that He was giving "His soul"; Paul says Jesus gave "Himself." Jesus said His ransom was "for many"; Paul writes that it was "for us." The preposition "for" in Matthew is *huper*; the preposition Paul uses is *anti*. The two prepositions are virtually equivalent in meaning (see for example M. Harris, in the *New International Dictionary of Theological Terms*, Vol.3, p. 1196f).

We also find *anti* compounded with the verb "redeem" (*lutreō*) in 1 Timothy 2:6. We find *huper* here in Titus 2:14 and in Luke 20:19,20; John 6:51, 10:11,15, 11:50-52, 15:13, 18:14; Romans 5:6,8, 8:32; 1 Corinthians 5:7; 2 Corinthians 5:14,15,21; Galatians 1:4; Ephesians 5:2,25; 1 Thessalonians 3:10; Hebrews 2:9; 1 Peter 2:21, 3:18, 4:1; 1 John 3:16.

> Anyone who doubts the necessary, objective, voluntary, expiatory, propitiatory, substitutionary, and efficacious character of the act of Christ whereby he gave himself for us should make a diligent, contextual study of the [above passages, plus the following]: John 1:29, Acts 20:28, Rom. 3:25, I Cor. 6:20, 7:23, Gal. 2:20, 3:13, Eph. 1:7, 2:16, Col. 1:20-22, Heb. 9:22,28, I Pet. 1:18,19, Rev. 5:12, 7:14.[104]

As this verse continues, we are told that His giving of Himself for us was in order that He might redeem us, and make it possible for us to live as verse 12 has instructed.

That He might redeem us from every lawless deed ... – Christ gave Himself for a two-fold purpose: (1) to redeem us, and (2) to purify a people for Himself. These purposes are stated in language drawn from several places in the Old Testament including Psalm 130:8,[105] Ezekiel 37:23, 2 Samuel 7:23, Exodus 19:5, and Deuteronomy 14:2. Since verse 11, we have had the instructions that the grace of God "teaches" us as the controlling theme. Verse 12 especially has spoken both of behavior to be renounced, and a positive lifestyle to be developed. Now we are reminded that these two sides of Christian living are exactly the intended results our redeemer Jesus had in mind when He gave Himself for us. Christ's intention for us was to separate us from something (iniquity) and also to unite us to something (good works). "Redeem" is *lutrōsētai*. In 1 Timothy 2:6 the verb used was *antilutron*. In the active voice the verb means "to release upon receipt of a ransom." Here in Titus the verb form is middle voice, which means "to release by payment of a ransom."[106] The thrust of the word is conveyed by any one of several English words: "set free," "redeem," "rescue." In the phrase "from every lawless deed," the singular Greek word "every" means "everything belonging in kind to the class designated by the noun (i.e., lawless deeds)." *Anomia* is a general word for sin, and sin is "transgression of the law" (1 John 3:4). Such "lawless deeds" may be either deeds of omission (a failure to do the

---

[104] Hendriksen, *op. cit.*, p. 376.

[105] The words "redeem ... from every lawless deed" are found in Psalm 129:8 in the LXX. The chapter numbering of the LXX is 1 less than in our English versions, because what is Psalm 1 and 2 in our Bibles are combined as Psalm 1 in the LXX. What is Psalm 3 in our Bibles then becomes Psalm 2 in the LXX, etc.

[106] Concerning to whom any actual ransom price was or may have been paid, see the author's *New Testament Epistles: Romans*, at Romans 3:24.

positive things God's law commands) or deeds of commission (a failure to avoid the things God's law[107] prohibits). Several meanings are possible in the words about being redeemed "from lawless deeds." Perhaps this means that the effect of Christ's redemption is deliverance from the penalty of these lawless deeds. Perhaps this means that the effect of Christ's redemption is deliverance from bondage and slavery to these lawless deeds.[108] Perhaps this means that the effect of Christ's redemption is deliverance from the defilement of these lawless deeds.

And purify for Himself a people for His own possession – As was the previous phrase, this phrase is part of the two-fold purpose for which Christ redeemed us, and it is still couched in the language of the Old Testament (see Exodus 19:5; Deuteronomy 7:6, 14:2, 26:18, and also Ezekiel 37:23). Just as Jesus died to rescue us from sin, so also He cleanses and purifies us so that we may live as God's holy children (see Hebrews 10:19-22; Titus 3:5; 1 John 1:7). The "purification" picks up the theme of verses 12 and 13, where we have been told that grace instructs us that while denying ungodliness and worldly desires, we should live sensibly, righteously, and godly in this present age, while at the same time anticipating the glorious return of the Savior. Purification is something that occurs first when a man becomes a Christian, and then it continues on through his Christian life (cp. Ephesians 5:26,27). This process of purification is called "sanctification," and its goal is to make believers more like Jesus Christ (Romans 8:29). Care should be taken that "purify", or "cleanse", not be taken in simply a ceremonial sense, as it might be in the Old Testament. While "the blood of bulls and goats and the sprinkling of the ashes of a heifer sanctified for the cleansing of the flesh, the blood of Jesus cleanses the conscience from dead works so people may serve the living God" (Hebrews 9:13,14). Perhaps we should say that "redeem" had reference to the freeing of people from the slavery to sin, whereas "purify" speaks of removing the defilement of sin (cp. 2 Corinthians 7:1).

A "people for His own possession" suggests Jesus wants a people that are uniquely His. This expression "a people for His own possession" is taken from the LXX translation of the Hebrew Scriptures, where the words occur several times (e.g., Exodus 19:5; Deuteronomy 14:2).[109] The use of the Old Testament language "a people for his own possession," both here and in 1 Peter 2:9, suggests

---

[107] Men have broken God's laws in Patriarchal times (Romans 1:32 implies a revelation to the Patriarchs that explained exactly what God's expectations were), in Mosaic times (God's rules as given through Moses), and in New Testament times (God's laws and standards as revealed through the New Testament apostles and prophets after they were first spoken by His Son).

[108] Compare what Romans 6 says about the old slavery to sin being broken when a person is immersed into Jesus Christ.

[109] In Jeremiah's classic New Covenant prophecy, we have the words "I will be their God, and they will be my people." Not a few Bible students think that "a people for his own possession" means the same thing as "they will be my people," i.e., "a people who are specially His very own."

that the church now constitutes God's (Christ's) peculiar people, whereas in Mosaic times believing Israel had been that people. (On this side of the cross, people who are Israel after the flesh can still be a part of God's special people, His chosen people, if they embrace Jesus Messiah as their savior and redeemer, and allow Him to purify them. They would then be part of "the Israel of God," Galatians 6:16.) "A peculiar people"[110] or "a people for His own possession" reflects the idea that something very common and ordinary becomes special when it belongs to a famous person. For example, a stove-pipe hat, or an umbrella used by Abraham Lincoln has special value. Likewise, when we belong to Jesus, we have special value. One way of illustrating the idea in *periousios* is to note it was used especially for that part of the spoils of a battle or a campaign which the king who had conquered set apart especially for himself. King Jesus has won a great battle for the control of the whole universe. He has set aside a people for His very own! Another way of illustrating the idea in *periousios* is to think of jewels on which a man sets a special value, and places them safely in his treasury, and uses them only on special occasions. Christians are Jesus' "precious jewels."

Zealous for good deeds – Christ's people are to be characterized by zeal for good deeds.[111] They are to be eager or enthusiastic to perform the good works He expects. Christians should be different from non-Christians, and it is in holy living, including a zealousness for good works, that the difference should be marked. The man who hopes to live in glory after the epiphany of his Lord is to be a "zealot"[112] for goodness, doing his utmost for Christ's cause because he knows that is what Christ his redeemer and Savior desires. At Titus 2:7, attention has already been called to the Biblical emphasis on "good deeds" or "good works." Indeed, several of the character traits that Titus is to instruct the various groups to develop (Titus 2:2ff) could be categorized under the heading "good deeds." The same is true of the three positive traits given in verse 12.

C. Consequent Admonition To Titus.   2:15

---

[110] In the antique English of the King James Version, the word "peculiar" is used to describe personal property. It is something that is "one's very own."

[111] "Peculiar" does not mean that Christians are to be odd in dress or manners. The distinguishing feature of God's people is that they "keep all his commandments" (Deuteronomy 26:18), are "zealous for good works" (Titus 2:14), and "show forth the praises of Him who has called [them] out of darkness into His marvelous light" (1 Peter 2:9).

[112] "Zealot" is singular in the Greek, in apposition with the collective noun "people." In Acts 21:20 this same word is used of the members of the church at Jerusalem who are characterized as still being "zealous for the Law." The word also came to be the name of the fanatical sect (the Zealots) whose zealous actions precipitated the Jewish rebellion that led to the destruction of Jerusalem in AD 70. ("Canaanean" [Matthew 10:4; Mark 3:18] is the Hebrew word for "zealot.") Christians are bursting with eagerness to do good deeds.

2:15 -- These things speak and exhort and reprove with all authority – Verse 15 is likely the conclusion of chapter 2, rather than the beginning of chapter 3. Recall that chapter and verse divisions were not part of the original, but were added later. Sometimes the ones who made the divisions perhaps made faulty choices. Here, it seems that the break following verse 15 is likely correct. If verse 15 is the conclusion of chapter 2, then "these things" would recall all that has been said in chapter 2 – the instructions to the different age groups (verses 2-10), and the reason why the different age groups could be expected to respond (verses 11-14).[113] The admonition to Titus contained in verse 15 is based on the instruction the grace of God gives, just as much as is the duty of church members to practice what grace teaches. Because Jesus wants people who live right and who are zealous for good works (verse 14), Titus has a consequent responsibility to help his listeners bring their lives into harmony with Jesus' wishes (verse 15).

The command to "speak" given to Titus in 2:1 is repeated. The verb is a present tense imperative, indicating continuing action. "These things" are something that Titus must constantly talk about! The directives for Christian conduct must continually be urged upon the people. This is part of the preacher's job! The verb ("exhort") used at Titus 2:6 is repeated. An "exhortation" is an appeal to the will of the listener. This verb is also a present tense imperative, indicating continuing action. "These things" must constantly be urged on the people, whenever the occasion demands. The verb "reprove" used at Titus 1:9,13 is repeated. When people have erred and need to repent, a "rebuke" is in order. In some cases, people who have been doing their duties begin to neglect them. In other cases, people are slow to respond or fail to respond altogether. Then a "rebuke" is in order. This verb is also a present tense imperative, indicating continuing action. When church members have so lived as to need reproof concerning "these things," it is Titus' continuing responsibility to administer the reproof. In the phrase "with all authority," the word translated "authority" (*epitagē*) is the same word translated "commandment" in Titus 1:3 and 1 Timothy 1:1. Thus, when Titus "speaks, exhorts, reproves," his presentations are to be accompanied by (*meta*) the appropriate command from the Lord. The preacher has no authority of his own. The word of God is the preacher's only authority. "All" suggests that Titus is to bring to bear the full weight of all God says on the subject, as he speaks or exhorts or reproves.

Barclay[114] suggests that the three imperative verbs in this verse are a good way to highlight some of the important tasks an evangelist is expected to do:

---

[113] The Greek word translated "these things" sometimes, in the Pastoral Epistles, refers to that which precedes, and sometimes to that which follows. See 1 Timothy 4:11 and 6:2c. "These things" in this place serves as the object of all three imperative verbs.

[114] *The Daily Study Bible*, on Timothy and Titus, p.295-296.

It is a task of *proclamation*. There is a message to be proclaimed. There are some things about which argument is not possible, and on which discussion is not relevant. There are times when the preacher ... must say, "Thus saith the Lord!"

It is a task of *encouragement*. Any preacher who reduces his audience to bleak despair has failed in his task. Men must be convinced of their sin, not that they may feel that their case is hopeless, but that they may be led to the grace which is greater than all their sin.

It is a task of *conviction*. The eyes of the sinner must be opened to his sin. The mind of the misguided must be led to realize its mistake. The heart of the heedless must be stabbed [wide] awake. The Christian message is no opiate to send men to sleep; it is no comfortable assurance that everything will be all right. It is rather the blinding light which shows men themselves as they are and God as He is.

Here are instructions for all who preach. The things we learn from God's grace, and the things we learn from Jesus' apostles, we are to *speak* plainly and clearly. We are to *exhort*, urge, and persuade those about us to live by those teachings. We are to *rebuke* those who fail to do so. And this we are to do *with all authority*.

Let no one disregard you – Titus is to present the "command of the Lord" as he speaks, exhorts, and rebukes (verse 14a). Titus is also to be careful how he lives, lest he live in such a manner that people think they may safely ignore[115] what he says when he delivers the "thus saith the Lord." God's truth is at stake. That's why Titus must be careful lest he give people any excuse to disregard it. Of course this admonition was directed first of all to Titus, who must put it into practice. But when this letter was read among the churches, the preacher would be helped in his duties, for the Christians would hear not only what the preacher was to do, but what their response to authoritative preaching was to be. Church members must not disregard the Word of God, or think of ways to ignore what the preacher says when the preacher has the authority of God behind his message.

---

[115] The verb used here for "disregard" is *periphroneitō*, "to think around" or "to by-pass in heart or mind." In 1 Timothy 4:12 and 6:2, Paul used a slightly different word, *kataphroneo*, which means "to think down" or "to despise."

III. INSTRUCTION CONCERNING PROPER CONDUCT TOWARDS THOSE OUTSIDE THE CHURCH. 3:1-11

A. Obligations to Government Officials and Superiors. 3:1

3:1 -- Remind them – A part of living "soberly, righteously, and godly, in this present world" (Titus 2:12) lies in the Christian's fulfillment of his responsibilities towards those outside the church. The instructions in chapters 1 and 2 (with the possible exception of those concerning the slave towards his earthly master) have all dealt with how a Christian lives among fellow Christians. Yet there is also life outside the circle of Christian fellowship. How are followers of Christ to order their behavior when dealing with the pagan world? Titus 1:5 indicated that Paul and Titus were together for a time on Crete, likely doing evangelistic work among the cities on the island. This verb tells us that Paul and perhaps Titus spoke about the obligations of Christians towards outsiders. Now Titus is to remind the Christians about those obligations.[1] "Remind" is a present tense imperative. The reminder is something that is to be given over and over again.

To be subject to rulers, to authorities – The verb "to be subject" (*hupotassō*) is in the middle voice, and so speaks of voluntary submission[2] (see Titus 2:5). To be "subject" does not mean blind obedience, but it does mean to give up our self-centered interests for the well-being of others. Of course, submission to author-ities does not give us permission to follow them if they ask us to be involved in evil work. The Textus Receptus reads "and" (*kai*) between the words "rulers" and "authorities," and while many uncials omit the word, it almost seems neces-sary to the sense. The only other option is to separate the words by a comma as the NASB does, showing two different classes of officials to whom Christians are to be submissive. "Rulers and authorities" are two words which Paul regularly juxtaposes (1 Corinthians 15:24; Ephesians 1:21, 2:10, 6:12; Colossians 1:16, 2:10,15). The words also occur in 1 Peter 3:22. In all these examples the two words apply to angelic hosts. But it is doubtful that Paul is here teaching submis-sion to angels, whatever their rank or station. Elsewhere the words "rulers" and "authorities" are used separately to refer to officials who hold positions in the civil government.[3] In Luke 20:20 they are applied together to the authority of the Ro-

---

[1] Compare the reminder given at 2 Thessalonians 2:5 and the instructions given to Timothy at 2 Timothy 2:14.

[2] If the verb were in the passive voice, the submission would be forced or coerced by some external agent. The Christian doesn't wait to be forced into submission.

[3] See Romans 13:1,2,3.

man governor in Judea.   In Luke 12:11 they are applied together to the authorities before whom Christians may find themselves due to persecution.   These terms in Titus would refer to all civil officials on the island, governors and their subordinates, Roman and otherwise.   Towards such government officials what the Christian's attitude is to be is quite clear.   He is to be "subject."

> He is to obey the law and treat officials with respect.   Some officials may be corrupt, taxes may be high, some injustices may be evident; but this is no excuse for the citizen to change his attitude.   Armed rebellion is not the answer of Paul, and neither is "civil disobedience" or "passive resistance."   Paul was well aware of corruption and injustice.   Not many years before he wrote this [instruction about attitudes toward government], Paul was a prisoner for four years, though no substantial charge was made against him – and for half of that time he was held by a governor who was hoping for a bribe (Acts 24:26,27; 28:16).   Through all that injustice Paul did not try to break jail, he did not disrupt courtroom proceedings by shouting obscenities or sulk in his cell and have to be carried to the courtroom.   He was *subject* to the ruling *powers.*[4]

To be obedient – *Peitharchein* occurs only here and in Acts 5:29,32, 27:21.   The word in its classical use means "to obey a superior."   The KJV tried to catch this meaning when it used "to obey magistrates" to translate this term, but the addition of that word tends to limit or restrict the "superiors" whom Christians are to obey only to one group, which is hardly correct.[5]   Some have wondered if the different emphasis found in the instructions given to Timothy (1 Timothy 2:1ff) about "praying" for government leaders, in contrast to the instructions given to Titus about "submission" to government leaders, is significant.   Ellicott suggests that the writings of some of the ancients, such as Polybius and Plutarch, give us a clue why Titus is to emphasize submission and obedience to the Christians on Crete.   Those ancient writers tell us that Cretans were quarrelsome, and stubbornly and impatiently resisted control by any authority.   He reminds us that when Paul wrote, the island had been under Roman domination for about 125 years.   Before the Romans came, the government of the island had been democratic.   There was unrest now that some of their freedoms were gone and they were under the Roman yoke.   There were also many Jews on Crete, many of whom were eager to assert their right to be free from the hated rule of Rome.   Titus is to teach the Christians that Christianity was not to get a reputation as being a tool for political agitation.[6]

---

[4] Root, *Standard Lesson Commentary*, 1977-78, p.18.

[5] Knight and Parry suggest the construction in Titus 3:1 is a double asyndeton (omission of "and").   Both infinitives ("to be submissive" and "to obey") govern the two words in the dative case ("rulers" and "authorities"):   Christians are "to be submissive to and obey rulers and authorities."

[6] One would think that certain 20th-century liberation theologians, who teach that active Christian involvement in the forceful overthrow of the existing oppressive government in their lands is exactly what Jesus meant when He taught about bringing in the Kingdom of God, should hear these words in Titus.

Besides the statements about the Christian's relationship to civil government officials found in Timothy and Titus, there are corresponding instructions elsewhere in the New Testament. Jesus said that His followers were to "render to Caesar the things which are Caesar's, and to God the things which are God's" (Matthew 22:15-22).[7] He also taught Peter that taxes are to be paid (Matthew 17:24-27).[8] In Romans 13:1-7 Paul gives a detailed exposition of the Christian's relationship to civil government. Government is ordained of God, so to resist governmental authority brings condemnation. Christians also have an obligation to help support their government.[9] The apostle Peter likewise has instructions concerning the Christian's relationship to civil authority (1 Peter 2:13-17). Peter's instructions, in fact, may have as their immediate background the problem of how Christians are to react when called on to suffer in the Neronian persecution (1 Peter 1:6, 3:14ff, 4:12, 5:8-10). It was important that Christians be good citizens without compromising the faith. Their pagan neighbors might chafe and rebel under authority, but Christians must submit to the authority of the state, as long as they can do so without at the same time disobeying God. Obedience to civil government obligates Christians to observe all civil laws, from traffic regulations to payment of taxes.[10]

To be ready for every good deed – "Be ready" tells the Christians to be willing, prepared, and alert to the opportunities to do whatever good deed may need to be done (cp. 2 Timothy 2:21 and 3:17). Paul is likely still speaking with special reference to submission and obedience to government officials.[11] If rebellion is

---

[7] In the light of Jesus' distinction between obligations to Caesar and obligations to God, it is obvious that the general principle of obedience and submission to civil government is not absolute. When the rules the government makes are obviously contrary to God's rules and standards, then the Christian will quietly disobey the government, and be obedient to the consequences. Compare Acts 5:29 where Peter refused to obey a command that was contrary to the commission he had received from God, and Acts 5:40 where there was a punishment joyfully endured. Also, see notes on the last phrase of Titus 3:1 which may limit how far one's obedience to superiors is to go.

[8] It may properly be affirmed that Jesus' words were the model for all the later teaching by the apostles on this topic of the relationship of Christ's followers to government authorities.

[9] Most writers pause to express an initial surprise at Paul's words about submission to government officials, especially when they recall that Nero was the reigning emperor, and that Paul himself, at times, suffered at the hands of government officials. If our dating of Romans and the Pastoral Epistles is correct, then Romans was written before the Neronian persecution of Christians. But the Pastorals (written after AD 64) were written after the city had burned and Nero had tried to shift the blame onto the Christians.

[10] Commenting on "submission and obedience" in v.1, Staton inquires, "How are we doing in little things like our speed on the highway, paying income taxes, saving water during water shortages, and other requirements that seem inconvenient?" (*Standard Lesson Commentary*, 1991-92, p.445)

[11] Among the commentaries, there is no agreement when the topic changes from "government officials" to "outsiders" in general. Some make the break after "obedient" in verse 1. Some make the break "uncontentious" in verse 2. Some make the break between verses 1 and 2. There are no convincing reasons which help us decide the matter with any degree of certainty.

not the proper behavior for the Christian, neither is doing nothing! Though he is not willing to do wrong, the Christian is ready and eager to do right. If the topic is still the Christian's attitude towards those in authority, then perhaps this phrase means that the Christian "submits and obeys" when what the government asks for is "good deeds." Otherwise, when the government asks for something that is not "good," the Christian obeys God. If so, then this instruction tells the Christian to be ready cheerfully to aid all lawful authority, municipal and otherwise, in their public works undertaken for city or state. Christians were to demonstrate that they were good citizens, always ready for any duty to which they were called. Augustine could boast that when the emperor Julian asked Christians to sacrifice and offer incense to the gods, they, at all hazards, sternly refused. But when he summoned them to fight for the empire they rushed to the front. "They distinguished between their Eternal Lord and their earthly ruler, and yet they yielded obedience to their earthly ruler for the sake of their Eternal Lord."[12] If, on the other hand, Paul has already shifted to the Christian's responsibility to non-Christians in general, then this phrase would instruct the Christians to be ready to be helpful whenever opportunity presents itself. Whether epidemics, tornadoes, earthquakes, fires – Christians must be ready to show their good spirit by getting involved in helping people who are hurting, even if those people are not brothers in Christ.

B. Obligations Toward Fellow-Citizens. 3:2

3:2 -- To malign no one – Verses 2 and 3 together show that the "fellow-citizens" in view are those who are not Christians. Paul first tells the Christians to be good citizens (verse 1), then he encourages them to be good neighbors (verse 2). There are four requirements given concerning the Christian's behavior towards people outside of the church. "Malign no one" (*mēdena blasphēmein*) or "blaspheme no one" or "speak evil of no man" (KJV) says the Christian is not to revile or to heap curses upon or speak reproachfully of anyone. Those who think the topic is still the Christian's relationship to civil authorities read this obligation to mean that the Christian, even if he is oppressed by the government, is not to speak evil of the government officials (cp. 2 Peter 2:10 and Jude 10). In such a context, what Paul and Peter both inculcate is that the Christian is to reflect the spirit of Christ, who, "when He was reviled, reviled not again." "Paul is not saying by this admonition that Christians must be naive and never correctly evaluate or speak out about the evil they see in anyone, since this is what he himself does in 1:10-16."[13] Those

---

[12] Quoted by Spence in *Ellicott's Commentary*, p.29.

[13] Knight, *op. cit.*, p.333. Obviously this prohibition does not forbid God's people to expose falsehood or rebuke wrong.

who think the topic is the Christian's relationship to his non-Christian neighbors read this obligation to mean that the Christian is not to use insulting and abusive language even when his neighbors are difficult to get along with. Loud denunciation is not the Christian answer. Picking a quarrel adds to the world's wrong instead of ending it. "Let all bitterness and wrath and anger and clamor and slander be put away from you, along with all malice" (Ephesians 4:31). It is very difficult to witness to a man concerning Christ after we have just spoken reproachfully to him or in his presence.[14]

To be uncontentious – This is the second requirement concerning the Christian's behavior towards those people who are outside the church. The Greek is literally "to be not fighting" (*amachous einai*). The same word was used at 1 Timothy 3:3. The word is likely used here in its figurative sense (we wouldn't think of Christians literally getting into fist fights and pitched battles with their neighbors, would we?), meaning "peaceable" or "uncontentious" (as the NASB has it). The Christian is not to be quarrelsome or contentious with their non-Christian neighbors. A quarrelsome attitude makes a poor witness for Christ.

Gentle – This is the third requirement concerning the Christian's behavior towards those people who are outside the church. English versions have struggled to find an equivalent English word for *epieikeis*. Attempts include "sweet reasonableness," "helpfulness," "generosity (in attitude toward others)," "forbearance (no domineering attitude)," "gracious," "fair," and "mild."[15] It is possible that "uncontentious" and "gentle" go together and that the one infinitive "to be" governs both these terms. It is also possible that "to be" is understood with the second virtue, "gentle."

Showing every consideration – This is the fourth requirement concerning the Christian's behavior towards those people who are outside the church. "Showing" translates *endeiknumenous*, and "consideration" translates *prautēta*. "Showing" is a word Paul uses frequently (Romans 2:15, 9:17,22; Ephesians 1:7; and Titus 2:10). It means to "demonstrate something openly" for all to see (cp. 2 Corinthians 8:24). It is a present tense participle, suggesting the need for continuous action. *Prautēs* (the Textus Receptus reads *praotēs*) is also a word Paul uses frequently. See 1 Corinthians 4:21; 2 Corinthians 10:1; Galatians 5:23;

---

[14] Indeed, the Christian will find it difficult to pray for any government official (1 Timothy 2:1,2) while at the same time he is speaking with contempt about that same official. Even if this first phrase in verse 2 no longer has specific reference to the Christian's conduct toward government officials (like verse 1 did), the general principle here given could apply to government officials as much as to one's next-door neighbors.

[15] This word was used for one of the qualifications for elder in 1 Timothy 3:3. One writer suggests that the opposite of "gentle" is "making no allowances for weaknesses and infirmities in others."

1 Timothy 6:22; and 2 Timothy 2:25, where it is sometimes rendered "gentleness" or "meekness" or "control of power" (when one has the power to crush his opponent[16]), or "courtesy."[17]   "Meekness" was one of the characteristics taught by Jesus (Matthew 5:5).   This precept is given its widest extension by the double use of the word "all" – showing "all" (consideration) to "all" (men).   To show some consideration to some people might not be so difficult.   But to show all consideration to all people is something that will require the Christian's whole-hearted cooperation with the Spirit's promptings.   The precepts here taught to Christians were new virtues.   No heathen moralist ever urged these qualities.   Thus, they were not common in 1st century society, let alone on Crete.

For all men – All men, whatever their station, the highest or the lowest, are to receive gentle and considerate treatment from the Christian.   That these men are not yet Christians is evident from what is said in the next verse, where Christians are to remember how we ourselves were once just like our neighbors, before we became Christians.   Orrin Root asks, "What Can We Do?"

> None of us are entirely satisfied with the conditions or the society in which we live.   So many things are wrong!   We can hardly name or count them all.   Our government is sometimes too repressive, sometimes not repressive enough, and always too costly.   Sometimes we think 'big business' is using its economic power to cheat us, and sometimes we think 'big labor' is doing the same.   We are distressed by crime in the streets, by increasing indecency in books and magazines and movies, by vandalism and littering and pollution.
>
> What can we do?   Constantly we are urged to vote; but when election time comes we have so little information and such a flood of biased propaganda that we hardly know which way to vote – and sometimes we feel that our voting makes no difference anyway.
>
> What can we do?   Often there is a temptation to take things into our own hands, ignoring the law; and many people do just that.   Frequently we read of organized groups that resort to bombing and shooting.   Many business firms recently have admitted illegal campaign contributions and bribes.   Labor leaders have been convicted of various crimes, including murder.   A woman recently was convicted of trying to assassinate the President of the United States.   Are these good ways of protesting against the many wrongs we see?

---

[16] The word *prautēs* describes the man whose temper is always under complete control.   It describes the man who knows when to be angry and when not to be angry.   It describes the man who recognizes his absolute dependence on God and who gains his strength from that relationship.   At the same time it is the man who patiently bears wrongs done to himself, but who is ever chivalrously ready to spring to the help of others who are wronged or injured.

[17] The two terms "gentle" and "considerate" are synonyms.   Lenski (*op. cit.*, p.982) distinguishes the former as referring to outward conduct which yields our rights to the other person, and the latter as the inward virtue which produces such conduct.   The opposite of "consideration" is rudeness, bad temper, sudden anger, brusqueness.

What can we do?   Christians are expected not only to be good themselves, but also to have a good effect on the society in which they live.   That seems to be the clear meaning of the Master's parable of the leaven (Matthew 13:33).   How shall we go about it?[18]

The six things emphasized in Titus 3:1,2 give us some thoughts and directions on this subject.

C. The Reasons for Proper Conduct Toward Non-Christians. 3:3-8a

3:3 -- For we also once were foolish ourselves – The first of two reasons for proper conduct (note the "for" with which the verse begins) is stated in this verse: Christians must remember that we were once just like what our non-Christian neighbors now are.   Seven characteristics are enumerated to remind us what our state then was like.   The time indicated by "once" or "formerly" (*pote*) is the time before our conversion, and for some of Paul's readers and Titus' hearers, that was not so long ago.   "We" includes Paul, Titus, and the readers.[19]   We know of Paul's Jewish background before he became a Christian from the book of Acts and Galatians.   We know also of Titus' background, coming from a Gentile family (Galatians 2:3).   The unevangelized people on the island of Crete had a bad reputation even among themselves (Titus 1:12, 13).   "All have sinned" (Romans 3:23).   This inclusion by the writer of himself among his readers, as to what they formerly were, is an effective way to appeal to the readers.   It shows the writer understands them and stands on common ground with them.   The unsaved person is called "foolish" (*anoētoi*) because he lacks understanding of God's truth.   Sometimes it is because he has not been taught (Romans 1:14).   Sometimes a person was taught, but he didn't listen (Luke 24:25).   Sometimes it is because his mind has been darkened (Ephesians 4:18).[20]   Sometimes a person is "foolish" because he has been "bewitched" (Galatians 3:1,2).   The same word was used at 1 Timothy 6:9 of behavior that cannot be defended rationally.

Disobedient – *Apeitheis* denotes being unwilling to do what is right, a stubborn refusal to do what God commands.   This same is word used at Titus 1:16 and Luke 1:17.   In a context where submission to authority has just been a topic, one might also think of disobedience both to civil and parental authority being charac-

---

[18] Root, *Standard Lesson Commentary*, 1977-78, p.18.

[19] The Greek is emphatic.   "We *ourselves* (not somebody else) were ..." is the idea.

[20] Discernment must be exercised by the Bible student as he makes his way through the commentaries at this point.   Calvinistic writers who hold the idea of an inherited "sinful nature" as axiomatic are likely to use that as an explanation of why the unconverted are "senseless."   It is a man's own transgressions that result in his mind being darkened (Romans 1:21,28; Ephesians 2:1).

teristic of the unconverted. Before conversion, men's lives are characterized by disobedience to God.

Deceived – The Greek word *planōmenoi* is a present passive participle. Someone else (the Devil? a false religion?) has deceived them, and led them astray, encouraging them to wander from the path of truth and right.[21] The Greeks used the same root word for certain bodies in the heavens. They called them "planets" because to them it seemed that the planets "wandered" around the heavens, not following a fixed path like the "stars" did. Instead of following the narrow road which leads to life, before the non-Christian's "deception" is ended, he wanders every which way.

Enslaved to various lusts and pleasures – "Enslaved" is a present participle, indicating a continuous "slaving" to his old desires. The Bible pictures the man who has committed his first sin as being "sold under sin," as being a "slave to sin" (Romans 6:6, 7:14). Jesus said, "Whosoever [habitually] commits sin is a slave of sin" (John 8:34). That same idea is here called to mind. "Various" is one rendering of *poikilais*. It could also be rendered "manifold," "many colored." This adjective governs both nouns, "lusts" and "pleasures". "Lusts" translates *epithumiais*, the same word earlier translated "desires" (Titus 2:12). In this context, the "desires" or "lusts" are evil, and have been stirred up in men's bodies by the devil's temptations. "Pleasures" translates *hēdonais*, from which we get our English word "hedonism." This word always has a bad sense in the New Testament (see Luke 8:14; James 4:1,2; 2 Peter 2:13). The unconverted world seeks "pleasures" first here and then there, only to find out that they don't really satisfy the hungry soul. Instead, the "lusts" and "pleasures" become terrible masters, a slavery that only gets more galling as time passes.

Spending our life in malice and envy – "Spending our life" is *diagontes*, a present participle meaning "to lead" with "life" understood.[22] Compare 1 Timothy 2:2. The attitudes of "malice" and "envy" are an everyday occurrence among the unconverted. The word translated "malice" is *kakia*, a word sometimes used for "wickedness" in general, but frequently in the New Testament (see Ephesians 4:31; Colossians 3:8) it denotes "malice" (i.e., the desire to do harm to others), or "ill will." "Envy" (*phthonō*) is a word Paul uses in several lists (Romans 1:29; Galatians 5:21; Philippians 1:15; 1 Timothy 6:4). It speaks of

---

[21] The participle could also be identified as being a middle voice participle. If so, it says that those who are disobedient may come to the point where they deceive themselves and believe that they are doing what is right. This is one of the terrible dangers of sin.

[22] It is common in Greek writers to find this verb both with and without the object "life" actually stated. Nevertheless, it is uniformly rendered "to spend one's life."

looking with ill will on another person because of what he is or has.[23]   There is no impulse to rise to the level of or to gain what the other has.   There is only the desire to depress the envied to his own state.

Hateful – *Stugētoi* occurs only here in the Greek Scriptures, but the word is used in classical Greek and in Philo.   It means "offensive, disgusting, repulsive."   By his attitude and actions, the unconverted man leaves others disgusted with him. They find him repulsive or "odious" (NEB).   The unconverted continue on in their selfish ways and become detestable even to those who know them, if not to God, too.

Hating one another – This is a participial phrase (*misountes allēlōn*) in the Greek.   The present tense participle indicates continuous action.   Such a wrong attitude is a regular thing among the unconverted.   *Miseō* means to hate or detest. Perhaps in some places in the New Testament it means "to love less," "to postpone our love or esteem," "to slight."[24]   It is an attitude that treats the other fellow with indifference or disregard.   Unconverted people live in close proximity, and they pass each other and meet each other a thousand times, but they don't even learn each other's names, or hurts, or needs.   It is a mutual distrust, a mutual indifference.   The seven vices just named give a sad but too true picture of human life among the unconverted.   Christians were once like them.   But for the Christian, accepting and following Jesus should make all the difference in the world.   No longer will the Christian behave like the unconverted do.   That's why the Christian will demonstrate toward the unconverted the virtues listed in Titus 3:1,2.

3:4 -- But – Here begins the second of two reasons for proper conduct towards the unconverted.   Reason #1 was that we should remember we once were where they are and needed someone to help us.   Reason #2 is that God has saved us, and we must be careful lest we reflect poorly on our Heavenly Father.   Four expressions ("kindness," "love," "mercy," "grace") characterize God's attitude and action towards lost men.   The "but" with which verse 4 begins contrasts the characteristics of God with the characteristics of lost men (verse 3).   It also introduces the contrast between what "we" were "once," and what we are now.

When the kindness of God our Savior ... appeared – Here "God our Savior" (as in 1 Timothy 1:1 and Titus 1:3) has reference to God the Father.   We usually think of Jesus when we hear the word "Savior," but the Father who sent Jesus is our Savior too.   "Appeared" means to come into public view, as it did in Titus 2:11 and 2:13.   Christ came to earth as the "appearance" of God's kindness and

---

[23] "Jealousy" is afraid of losing what it has.   "Envy" hates to see another person have something.   Trench, *Synonyms*, p. 86-90.

[24] See Thayer, *op. cit.*, p.415.

love. And then God's "kindness" was specially visible when His Son died on the cross. "Kindness" (*chrēstotēs*) is an attitude towards others that expresses itself by trying to do good to those others (Romans 2:4, 3:12, 11:22).[25] "Kindness" is a spirit which is always ready and eager to give whatever gift may be necessary. This is one of God's attributes. He is benevolent, benign, essentially generous. He does what is useful or beneficial to others. "Malice" (verse 3) is an antonym.

And *His* love for mankind – The original reads "the love for man" (*hē philanthropia*), with the article. Sometimes the article serves as a possessive pronoun, so the NASB has used the word "His." *Philanthropia* (transliterated into English, we get "philanthropy") occurs only twice in the New Testament, here (where it is used of God) and in Acts 28:2 (where it is used of men's love for other men). When we consider that the word for "love" in this compound is *phileō*, we see that it is a special love.[26] Men are dear to God! This word would also serve as a quiet but solemn reminder to those Christians who might hesitate to display the virtues towards their non-Christian neighbors that Titus 3:1,2 call for. *Kai* might better be translated "even" in this place, rather than "and," since the verb "appeared" is singular. If we do this, then God's kindness, even (or especially) His special love to man, is the thing that became visible when Christ our Savior came to earth and provided for men's justification. God's kindness also becomes visible when each of us responds to the Gospel invitation to become Christians and heirs of eternal life (verse 7, cp. 2 Timothy 1:9,10).

3:5 -- Not on the basis of deeds which we have done in righteousness – The point of the whole passage apparently is this – in order to prevent Christians from ever saying "Why should I?" when instructed how to behave before non-Christians (Titus 3:1,2), Paul stresses the fact of how God behaved when we were unsaved and needed someone to help. God didn't say "Why should I?" Rather, He demonstrated His kindness and love and mercy and grace.

"He saved us."[27] Each Bible student who undertakes to study this passage should pause to ask God's help to understand it, and then should go very slowly and thoughtfully as he considers what others have written on these verses. Why do we say this? Because not a few of us will be tempted simply to make this

---

[25] A beautiful illustration of "kindness" is found in 2 Samuel 9 where we read of David's treatment of Mephibosheth, a little lame prince. Because Mephibosheth was part of King Saul's family, he expected to be slain. But David, in kindness, spared him and treated him as one of his own sons, even sittingat the palace table.

[26] *Agapaō* denotes the love of reason, 'esteem.' *Phileō* denotes the love of feelings, 'warm instinctive affection.' G.R. Berry, *A Greek-English Lexicon to the New Testament*, p.1. The former is the word used in John 3:16.

[27] Because this verse has been and continues to be a theological battlefield, it has seemed best to comment on some of the subordinate clauses before offering comments on "He saved us."

passage harmonize with whatever we think the Bible teaches elsewhere about salvation. For example, if we believe salvation is *monergistic* (that is, man is wholly passive, while God does it all), we will emphasize those phrases that seem to harmonize with that thesis. If, on the other hand, we believe salvation is *synergistic* (that is, that God provides it, and man must meet certain conditions set by God, before man enjoys it), we will emphasize those phrases that seem to harmonize best with this thesis. Even translators have at times chosen words to use in their translations which reflect their biases, so that even the popular translations must be used with caution. In addition, most of us are struggling with a legacy of centuries of Roman Catholic or Reformation theology, not all of which is totally in harmony with God's own Word. It is not easy to come to this passage with an open mind, with no preconceptions, and attempt to see just what it says, no more and no less. Still, this we must try to do.

"On the basis of" represents the preposition *ex* followed by a word in the genitive case. "Works which we did" seems intended to recall the acts we were doing all the time we were unsaved (Titus 3:3). Just like the behavior of the unsaved has nothing in it to win the kindly consideration of the Christian, so there was nothing in our behavior before we became Christians that would make us appealing to God, either. It was "not" on the basis of works, Paul affirms.

We have studiously attempted to avoid several ideas as we have offered the above comments: (1) Monergistic theologians have been accustomed to use this phrase to prove there is nothing man can do, no conditions he must meet, in order to be justified by God.[28] Such comments, in this commentator's opinion, are out of place, and in direct opposition to what the Bible plainly teaches elsewhere about "faithfulness" being the condition God looks for before He justifies anyone. (2) Protestant theologians, rightly objecting to Rome's system of meritorious works, have been accustomed to write at this place that the "works which we did" do not merit salvation. It is true that salvation is not merited by men, but in this commentator's judgment, this is not the verse to prove it. Therefore we think it wise not to talk about meritorious works or "earning salvation" at this place. (3) Some commentaries write paragraphs about "works of Law" as they try to explain what does not contribute to salvation in this Christian age. This commentator is not convinced that "works of Law" should even be imported into the notes of explanation offered on this passage.[29]

---

[28] In this writer's commentary on Romans, it is shown that behind the monergistic theory of salvation lies the belief in an inherited sinful nature and total depravity. Of course, if man is totally bad, he could do nothing right, not even respond to some condition God lays down for him. In those same comments on Romans the whole idea of inherited sinful nature and total depravity are rejected as being contrary to what Scriptures themselves teach.

[29] The passages usually alluded to which are alleged to show that "Paul rejects works as a basis for God's salvation" are Romans 3:27,28, 4:2-6, 9:11; Galatians 2:16; Ephesians 2:9; and 2

"In righteousness" (*tōn en dikaiosunē*), because of the genitive article, modifies the word "works" which is also in the genitive case. *En dikaisunē* is a construction in the dative case. May we identify it as a dative of sphere? Is it the sphere in which the "works" were being done? "Righteousness" is used several ways in Scripture: (1) Sometimes, it refers to God's way of saving man (Romans 1:17, 3:22). (2) Sometimes it refers to one of God's attributes (Romans 3:25). (3) Sometimes it refers to a saved man's standing in God's sight (Luke 1:6). (4) Sometimes it refers to man's right behavior towards his fellow man (Romans 6:13, 14:17; 2 Timothy 3:16). The context here in Titus 3 would seem to suggest that we opt for number 4, man's right behavior towards his fellow man.[30] It wasn't because we were doing anything right towards our fellow men that God's kindness appeared on the stage of history. We were once behaving just like our non-Christian neighbors are still behaving.

But according to His mercy – The adversative "but" introduces a strong contrast to the preceding negative. It was *not* because *we* were behaving right. It was because of God's attribute of mercy that we were saved. The construction is *kata* followed by an accusative case.[31] Thayer says that with the accusative *kata* denotes "reference, relation, proportion." It denotes agreement or conformity to a standard "according to," "in proportion to," "agreeably to," "according to the measure of." It is sometimes used of cause, "in consequence of."[32] BAGD speaks of "the norm [which] is at the same time the reason [that something is done]."[33] "Mercy" – God's attribute of mercy – is the measure or standard to which His actions were conformed. Mercy is *eleos*, on which see comments at 1 Timothy 1:2. Mercy is kindness or pity for those in need or distress, and that kindness manifests itself in action more than in words.[34] Salvation came not only because of God's kindness and love, but also because of His mercy.

Timothy 1:9. None of these passages should be interpreted so that they stand in direct contradiction to the "faith" (understood as doing what God says) on which the Bible everywhere conditions salvation! Since the publication of the Dead Sea Scroll 4QMMT (*Miqsat Ma'aseh Ha-Torah*), it has become clear that "works of Law" which Paul insists do not save are the *halakhic* rules the Pharisees and Sadducees made in an effort to help people understand what the Law required. These *halakhic* rules were nit-picking and, said Jesus, caused men to ignore the Law of Moses (Matthew 15:2-9).

[30] Option 2) would make no sense at this place. Option 3), which requires walking blamelessly in all the commandments and requirements of the Lord, is excluded by what is said in Titus 3:3. Option 1) would be out of place, for we are talking of unjustified people's behavior, not of works done when the doer was already in a state of righteousness.

[31] The same construction was encountered at Titus 1:1 ("for the faith"). What was said there about the meaning of *kata* followed by the accusative would also be true here.

[32] *Lexicon*, p.327-328.

[33] *Greek-English Lexicon of the New Testament*, p.408.

[34] To get a sense of the broadness of this attribute of God, one should study the passages in the Old Testament where the Hebrew *chesed* (translated sometimes as "lovingkindness," sometimes as "mercy") is used. The LXX translators used *eleos* where the Hebrew has *chesed*.

He saved us – This is what God did when He acted according to His mercy. This is the main subject and verb of the whole long sentence that stretches from verse 4 to verse 7 (a sentence that gives a second reason why we should behave towards outsiders as 3:1,2 teach us to). "He saved us" should not be treated as though these were the only words in this sentence. The very context (verses 5, 7 and 8) ought to warn us not to think that salvation is all God's doing, and that man is wholly passive. God did take the initiative. He is the One Who planned for and provided the means of salvation, and without that initiative there would be no salvation available. "Saved," as we shall see in comments on verse 7, is synonymous with, or involves, "justification."[35] Everything said in Romans about "justification by faith" (i.e., justification on the condition of faithfulness) would be involved in the terms "saved" and "justified" used in this passage. In brief, Romans tells us that God's way of saving men ("righteousness" or "justification"[36]) is revealed in the gospel, which is God's power to salvation. Everyone, Jew and Gentile alike, needs the salvation offered in the gospel. The universally needed salvation offered in the gospel has been provided by God for believers through the redemption that is in Jesus Christ. That universally needed salvation also has the most blessed effects – peace with God, complete deliverance through Christ from death and sin, the help of the Holy Spirit to live the Christian life, all culminating in ultimate glorification. In fact, God's dealings with men all through history have been in harmony with the doctrine of justification by faith.

By the washing of regeneration and renewing by the Holy Spirit – The Greek reads *dia loutrou paliggenesias kai anakainōseōs pneumatos hagiou*. Several things must be noted: (1) The preposition *dia* is a different preposition than any other encountered so far in this verse. Our English translations do well when they distinguish between *ex* and *kata* and *dia* in this verse. (2) Since both the words "regeneration" and "Holy Spirit" are in the genitive case, one should be slow to use two different prepositions to translate here (as the NASB translators have done). If one preposition is translated "of," so is the other. If one is "by," so is the other. (3) "By" (*dia* followed by the genitive case) means "through," expressing the instrument or means by which something is effected.[37] We are now being told how God saves us, after His kindness and love (i.e., Jesus Christ) appeared in history. (4) Commentators are in agreement about the difficulty of

---

[35] In addition, comments on "to save sinners" at 1 Timothy 1:15 and on "salvation" at Titus 2:11 should be reviewed.

[36] Both "righteousness" and "justification" are used to translate the Greek root *dikaio-*. The word "justification" apparently is a forensic word, picturing what a judge does when a case comes before him. He considers the defendant either "guilty," or "not guilty," as the case may be.

[37] Thayer, *Lexicon*, p.133. Kent (*op. cit.*, p.233) writes that "the channel whereby salvation reaches us is expressed by two phrases."

understanding just how to construe this passage. The problem is this: the construction at Titus 3:5 is ambiguous. "Regeneration" (*paliggenesias*) is in the genitive case, and is related somehow to "washing." But is *paliggenesias* an objective or subjective genitive? That is, is "washing" the thing that makes "regeneration" possible, or is "regeneration" the thing that makes "washing" possible? "Holy Spirit" (*pneumatos hagiou*) is in the genitive case and qualifies "renewing" (*anakainōseōs*). But it is uncertain whether it should be construed as a genitive of agent or a genitive of source. And it remains uncertain whether the genitive *anakainōseōs* depends upon the preposition *dia* or upon the noun "washing" (*loutrou*). Worded another way, are "regeneration" and "renewal" regarded as two separate acts or processes, or are both part of the "washing"? The latter is the interpretation adopted by the Vulgate (*per lavacrum regenerationis et renovationis*), and is followed by Spence and Hendriksen. The former is supported by codices D*EFG which repeat *dia* before *anakainōseōs*, and is followed by Bengel, Alford, Wuest, Guthrie and Lenski.[38] We shall study the individual words, and then try to make a decision.

"Washing" is used to translate *loutron* both times it appears in the New Testament (here and at Ephesians 5:26 where it reads "washing of water"). Some commentators have written about the "laver of regeneration" as they have tried to explain this verse, but "laver" is a different Greek word (*loutēr*). So the use of the word "laver" in the margin of the ASV could be misleading if one immediately begins to think of the "place" where the washing takes place. Thayer says that *loutron* is used both in the New Testament and in ecclesiastical writers of "baptism."[39] The connection between "washing" and "baptism" has been made because a number of passages seem to use the two words interchangeably: (1) Acts 22:16 speaks of having one's sins washed away as he is being baptized.[40] (2) Ephesians 5:26 speaks of a "washing of water" accompanied by a spoken word, or based on the Word [of God].[41] Not all Bible teachers are happy with the identification of "washing" and "baptism in water."

[38] Knight opted for the former in his *Faithful Sayings*, p.96f. He changed his mind and opts for the latter in his *Commentary on the Pastoral Epistles*, p.344.

[39] *Lexicon*, p. 382. Similar are the comments in BAGD, p.481. Did the ecclesiastical writers use the term "baptism" because that is what the church had long been doing, learning it first from Paul? Or did the ecclesiastical writers add something to what Paul really intended when he wrote "washing"? The monergists and the synergists offer different answers to these questions, and it is difficult to determine when either the monergist or the synergist is simply offering a special plea to defend a doctrine held dear, and when they are representing faithfully what the evidence will support.

[40] Lest this be misunderstood, it is not the water that washes away sins. It is God who "washes them away" at the time the person is being immersed. As Peter puts it, when a man obeys the truth, that is the time the blood of Jesus becomes efficacious in his life (1 Peter 1:2).

[41] It seems to be a case of special pleading when some attempt to make "water" and "word" both refer to the same thing (i.e., Scripture) as they explain Ephesians 5:26. That is certainly not the first, nor the most natural, understanding a man would get as he reads the passage for himself.

Monergists[42] are especially adamant that no such identification should be made. The reason is not what this verse may actually say. It is their *a priori* view that salvation never was and is not now conditioned on any works a man does. If that is true, of course, "washing" cannot be a reference to baptism. It must be a reference to something God does to us as "He saves us." Indeed, many of the monergistic efforts to explain how God saves a man at first sound plausible. These theologians even offer verses that seem to corroborate what they say, as they explain away the verses that (on the surface, at least) make baptism one of the conditions of salvation.[43] So while it may be admitted that "washing" *might not* be a reference to "baptism in water," recognize also that if the reference *is* to baptism as the channel through which God's salvation comes to man, this passage says nothing other than what the New Testament everywhere affirms about baptism in water being one of the conditions of salvation.[44] Whatever this "washing" is, it is one of the means (*dia*) by which "God saves us."[45]

---

[42] Monergism is the theological term for the belief that in salvation man is wholly passive. God alone does all that is needed for regeneration, with no human co-operation expected or needed.

[43] Wiersbe (*op. cit.*, p.118) appeals to the conversion of Cornelius to attempt to show that Cornelius was saved before he was baptized in water. He writes "I do not think that 'washing' here in Titus 3:5 refers to baptism, because in the New Testament times, people were baptized *after* they were saved, and not in order to be saved (see Acts 10:43-48)." It would seem to this commentator that this confuses the "baptism with the Holy Spirit" that Cornelius and his house experienced with the new birth (or the begetting work of the Spirit).

Wiersbe then appeals to Ephesians 5:26 when he writes, "Paul related this same cleansing experience ['washing'] to the Word of God." Now it is necessary to read Ephesians 5:26 carefully. It reads, "having cleansed her [the church] by the washing of water **with** the Word." These words of Paul do not equate "water" and the "Word." Instead, the cleansing is attributed to both the water and the Word. F.F. Bruce suggests the rendering, "the washing of water accompanied by a spoken word" (either the baptismal formula, or the word of confession of Jesus Christ as Lord spoken by the candidate).

[44] Does "washing" have reference to baptism? It has already been noted that neither the words "baptism" nor "water" is explicitly mentioned in Titus 3. Washing is associated with water in Ephesians 5:26, but even there the word "baptism" is not explicitly named. In 1 Peter 3:20,21, however, baptism in water is directly connected with salvation. After pointing out that Noah and his family were saved by water, Peter adds, "And corresponding to that [the only possible antecedent of "that," a neuter relative pronoun in the Greek, is "water," the only word in verse 20 that is neuter] baptism now saves you ...." It seems likely, therefore, that this passage in Titus is also a reference to baptism in water. This does not minimize the need to believe what the Gospel says about Jesus any more than the mention of "belief" minimizes baptism.

[45] Some religious groups teach a doctrine of conversion that can be called "baptismal regeneration." What is meant by this phrase is that a person is regenerated simply by means of baptism. The rite itself produces the result. Some have affirmed that Titus 3:5 ("He saved us by means of the washing [read 'baptism'] that produces regeneration") teaches baptismal regeneration. This is hardly what Paul is writing. We would not treat the parallel language of the very next phrase as though it affirmed that "renewal produces the Holy Spirit." It would be improper, then, to affirm that the "washing" produced or effected the "regeneration." Hear this clearly! When Restoration Movement teachers affirm that immersion is essential to salvation, they are not teaching baptismal regeneration. What they are saying is this: when we speak of the conditions on which God saves a man, He has made immersion just as important as repentance or belief or confession.

"Regeneration" is the translator's choice to render *paliggenesia* both times it appears in the New Testament, here and at Matthew 19:28. *Paliggenesia* is a compound word made up of two parts, *palin* meaning "again" and *genesis* meaning a "birth." In Greek usage before New Testament times, *paliggenesia* was used with several meanings: (1) the transmigration of souls; (2) the restoration of the world at the time of the flood; (3) the change in life of one who becomes a convert to the Jewish religion. "Commonly the word denotes the restoration of a thing to its pristine state."[46] Interpreters of Matthew 19:28 have, for some reason, been rather in agreement that *paliggenesia* there has reference to the cosmic renovation that accompanies the second coming of Christ.[47] But in point of fact, there is no grammatical or lexical reason to think Matthew 19:28 refers to some far-off future time. Jesus may well be saying, "In the age when men are born again [regenerated], the Son of man will sit on His throne ...., etc." So explained, both Matthew and Titus would be using the word *paliggenesia* of the same thing, namely, the new birth.

In Titus, *paliggenesia* refers to something that happens when men are "saved" or "justified." It is something that happens in this life. But theologians have had a difficult time explaining exactly what is involved in "regeneration."[48] (1) The early church fathers made the term synonymous with remission of sins. (2) Augustine and the Reformers explained regeneration as being "prevenient grace." (3) 17th century Reformed theology made regeneration synonymous with the whole process of conversion.[49] (4) Later Reformed theology returned to Augustine's "prevenient grace" or "first work of grace" when they explained regeneration as being the implanting of the seed from which faith and repentance spring. (5) Lutheran theology defines regeneration as the kindling of saving faith in the heart of the sinner. (6) Modern religious liberalism thinks of regeneration being the same as a man's desire to better the world in which he lives. This commentator sees no reason why we cannot use "begotten,"[50] "begotten of the

---

[46] Thayer, *Lexicon*, p.474. Some modern source critics have searched diligently for a source of Paul's use of this word in, say, the mystery religions. But even Dibelius-Conzlemann (p.150) acknowledge that there are points of difference between the use of the word in the mystery religions and its use in the New Testament. Machen long ago (*The Origin of Paul's Religion*) put to rest any notion that Christianity is simply a rehash of some of the distinctive features of the mystery religions.

[47] Likely, such an interpretation is based on an eschatology that has Christ's reign occurring during a millennium following this church age, and that presentation may not at all accurately reflect what the Scriptures say about when Jesus reigns at the right hand of the Majesty on high.

[48] See James I. Packer, "Regeneration" in *Baker Dictionary of Theology*, p.441.

[49] Alexander Campbell, whose writings still influence many in the Restoration Movement, understood that "baptism" completes the process of regeneration. *Christian System*, p.228ff.

[50] John 1:13. The Greeks did not have different words for "conception" and "birth." *Gennaō* had to do double duty. It was used to refer both to conception and to birth. Each time they come to the word *gennaō*, it is up to the translators to decide whether the reference is to "conception" or

Spirit,"[51] "born again [from above],"[52] "begotten of God,"[53] "born again (*anagegennēmenoi*),"[54] and "regeneration" as interchangeable terms. 1 John 5:1 says that the man who believes that Jesus is the Christ has been begotten. John 1:12,13 tell us that the man who receives Jesus (that is, believes in His name) has been begotten of God. While the exact relationship between all the words in the genitive case in this clause is not certainly clear, this much is apparent: no doubt, "regeneration" somehow is related to the word "washing" that immediately precedes it, since a word in the genitive case ordinarily follows the word it is grammatically related to. We opt for the genitive of source, since that is a meaning that will satisfy both members of this parallel construction.

Tentatively, we are ready to offer a translation for *dia loutrou paliggenesias*. It is "through the washing that results from regeneration" (i.e., a "washing" that follows [or results from] "belief" in who Jesus is).

"Renewing" is *anakainōseōs*, a word which occurs only here and Romans 12:2, and not at all in the LXX or in classical Greek. *Anakainōseōs* is also a compound word, made up of the preposition *ana*, which in compounds often means "again," and *kainoō*, "to make new, to change, to alter." It helps to grasp the meaning of *kainos* if we compare it to its synonym *neos*. *Neos* denotes the "new" primarily in reference to time; *kainos* denotes the "new" primarily in reference to quality.[55] There is no way to be sure just when the "renewing" alluded to here in Titus is thought of as occurring. It certainly occurs at the time when God initially "saves us," but is it limited to that time? Could the "renewing" be something the Holy Spirit does after a person has been saved by the washing of regeneration? Parallel passages can be found for both ideas:

(1) Passages that seem to refer to something "new," beginning when a person becomes a Christian (i.e., it is part of the conversion process) are those that speak of becoming a "new creature" (*kainē ktisis*)[56] who walks in "newness of life" (*kainotēs dzoēs*)[57] and "newness of spirit" (*kainotēs pneumatos*),[58] who is no

---

to "birth." In the KJV, when the translators think the reference is to "conception," they used "begotten" to translate it. When they think the reference is to "birth," they used "born."

[51] John 3:6

[52] John 3:3,7.

[53] 1 John 5:1

[54] 1 Peter 1:23.

[55] Thayer, *Lexicon*, p.318.

[56] 2 Corinthians 5:17; Galatians 6:15.

[57] Romans 6:4.

[58] Romans 7:6.

longer an "old man" but is a "new man" (*kainos anthrōpos*).[59] Perhaps some other passages also refer to the same "beginning again." When Jesus tells Nicodemus that he must begin over religiously (i.e., "be born again" or "from above"), He goes on to explain how it occurs.[60] Jesus talks about being born of water and Spirit, and He further elucidates what He means when he says "that which is begotten of Spirit is spirit." The "spirit" part of man is begotten or born again, and the Holy Spirit has something to do with that new beginning. The writer of Hebrews encourages his readers to continue to draw near to God in full assurance of faith. He reminds them of how they became eligible to draw near to God when he says that they have had their hearts sprinkled from an evil conscience, and their bodies washed with pure water.[61] Not a few Bible students would relate "hearts sprinkled from an evil conscience" to "renewing of the Holy Spirit" and "bodies washed with pure water" to the "washing of regeneration."

(2) Then there are passages which speak of a "renewing" as occurring all through the Christian's life here on earth. It follows the new birth and is a gradual renewal of heart and life into the image of God.[62] Romans 12:2, the only other place where *anakainōseōs* occurs in the New Testament, surely is one. The verb from the same root, *anakainoō*, is used in 2 Corinthians 4:16 and Colossians 3:10. Those passages refer to something that happens all during life after one becomes a Christian. Indeed, there are those who affirm that what is said in Titus 3:6 limits us to the interpretation that the work of the indwelling Holy Spirit is what is in Paul's view as he writes about the "renewing of the Holy Spirit."

Since parallel passages exist for both ideas about when the "renewing" occurs in God's saving process (i.e., both when a man initially becomes a Christian, and then through his Christian life), perhaps[63] we might say "The renewing of the Holy Spirit is experienced both in regeneration and later as the abiding Holy Spirit continually refreshes the Christian all through the Christian's days here on earth."

The reference in "of the Holy Spirit" is to the third person of the Godhead.

---

[59] Ephesians 4:22-24.

[60] John 3:3-8.

[61] Hebrews 10:22.

[62] As one reads Titus, it would seem that the "renewing" is a thing looked on as happening in the past, rather than a gradual thing going on in the present. To alleviate this apparent difficulty, those who explain "renewal" as being a gradual progressive change are accustomed to explain that all this was potentially involved in our initial salvation.

[63] Whether the "renewing" has reference to what precedes initial salvation or has reference to the Christian life following initial salvation depends on how we read the whole difficult phrase. See more on this matter in the commentary following, beginning with the last paragraph on page 407.

In fact, all three members of the Godhead – God our Savior, Jesus Christ our Savior, and the Holy Spirit – are all alluded to as having a part in our salvation. Since we explained the first genitive construction in this clause (*loutrou paliggenesias*) as a genitive of source, it seems proper to construe the second genitive in the same way, namely, as a genitive of source. Thus, we would suggest that the "renewing" is the result of the Holy Spirit's work. In the light of the fact that the exact timing of the "renewal" is disputed, the Holy Spirit's part in this "renewal" is also variously explained.

(1) Those who think the "renewing" occurs when a person is initially saved point to passages elsewhere in Scripture where the Holy Spirit is active in a man's conversion. This rendering lends no support to the Reformed doctrine called "first work of grace," or "prevenient grace." Reformed doctrine says that because we are all totally depraved, that we inherited a sinful nature from Adam, God has to perform a first work of grace on the elect before they can even want to believe the Gospel. While the Bible does not teach all that Reformed theology says it does, the Bible does show that the Holy Spirit works through the word to produce conviction of sins in the heart of the potential convert as he hears the Gospel, and the Holy Spirit also prompts or encourages the Gospel hearer to respond to the claims and requirements of the Gospel.[64] Could that help and encouragement to become a Christian be the same as what is referred to as "renewal of the Holy Spirit" here in Titus? Could the "spirit" part of man, which before conversion was dead in trespasses and sins, but in conversion becomes "alive" again, be what is referred to as "renewal resulting from the Spirit's work" here in Titus?

(2) Those who think the "renewing" is a gradual thing which occurs all during a Christian's life point to passages elsewhere in Scripture where the indwelling Holy Spirit is given as a helper to aid the man to live the Christian life. Among others, Acts 2:38, Romans 6:12ff, and 8:12ff come to mind.

So how shall we construe this whole phrase "the renewing of the Holy Spirit"? As a second element in God's saving us? Or as a further explanation of the one element "washing" by which God saves us? As indicated above, because this whole phrase begins with *dia*, it describes the instrument, or the means, God uses when He goes about saving a man. But just how many elements are included in those means? (1) Arguments are used to show that "washing" (i.e., a cleansing from sins once committed) is accomplished by "regeneration and renewal," both of which are the work of the Holy Spirit. Monergists are almost

---

[64] 1 Peter 1:2 speaks about the sanctifying work of the Holy Spirit that leads a man to obey the truth and then be sprinkled with the blood of Christ. 1 Corinthians 12:13a tells us that the Holy Spirit leads us to the place where we want to be immersed into the body of Christ.

forced to accept this view. It is the only way they can continue to insist that no works (for they call baptism a "work") are involved in salvation. It does permit them to say that "regeneration" and "renewing" are all the work of the Holy Spirit. (2) Other arguments are used to show that when God saves men, there are two separate things that occur: [a] a "washing that results from regeneration," and [b] a "renewal that results from the Holy Spirit." Synergists[65] prefer this way of explaining the verse. It no longer leaves totally out of the picture any response on the part of the man who would be saved. Against this view (that "washing" results from both the "regenerating and the renewing") it has been argued that such a construction results in a very long rambling thought, one which is not completed till the close of verse 6. But the fact that the word "and" separates "washing of regeneration" from "renewing of the Holy Spirit" favors the view that there are two separate things involved.

If we had only Titus 3:5, it would be difficult to conclusively decide upon one interpretation or the other. But with Scriptures elsewhere to guide us, it becomes evident that salvation has two sides, God's provision and man's response. If Titus 3:6 limits the "renewing of the Holy Spirit" to the Holy Spirit's work in the life of the Christian (as distinct from His work in the conversion process), then it is rather obvious that we must say there are two things involved in this "channel" through which God saves us. The idea in the word "renewing" is that of a continuing process of "making new." The "washing of regeneration" marks the entrance into the new life, while renewing is a continuing quality of that life. This word for "renewing" is only used elsewhere at Romans 12:2, "Be ye transformed by the renewing of your mind." Renewing is associated here with the work of the Holy Spirit. Since the gift of the Spirit accompanies a person's immersion in water, washing and renewing probably are closely connected but distinct elements in the process God uses to save men. Salvation is first accomplished when men are immersed ("the washing that results from regeneration"), and then the Holy Spirit helps immersed believers to live the Christian life that such a salvation entails ("the renewing that results from the Holy Spirit").

This phrase has led to a very long study of what the Scriptures say about how God saves a man. The long study is necessary, not because the Scriptures themselves are so difficult to understand when they present the process of salvation, but because theologians and preachers have imported doctrines which have led to confusion and misguidance. This commentator wishes to add nothing to the confusion, but simply attempts to speak as the oracles of God speak.

---

[65] Synergism is the doctrine that in salvation God and man cooperate. God provides it, and specifies the conditions on which salvation is granted. But man must cooperate by meeting the conditions God has laid down. This cooperation is what the Bible everywhere calls "faith" or "faithfulness."

3:6 -- Whom – Some manuscripts read *hou*, a genitive case; others read *ho*, an accusative case. The accusative would be the expected form for this pronoun, but the majority of manuscripts read genitive. Grammarians explain that it has been attracted to the genitive in order to match the case of its antecedent, and the pronoun's antecedent is the "Holy Spirit"[66] in verse 5. To further show the impropriety of the question "Why should I have right behavior before non-Christians?" (see notes at verse 4), Paul reminds his readers of the gift of the Holy Spirit. The Spirit is involved in "renewing" the believers, and this renewing certainly involves the proper behavior before unbelievers called for in 3:1-2.

He poured out upon us richly – "He" is God, the one who saved us (verse 5). God not only gave His Son to demonstrate his "kindness" (verse 4), but He also gave the Holy Spirit. "Poured out" (*execheen*) is the same word applied to the Holy Spirit in Acts 2:17,18,33, and in the LXX of Joel 2:28,29. There is little agreement among the commentaries at this point concerning the measure and occasion Paul has in mind when he writes about the Spirit being poured out. (1) Because the verb "poured" is common both to Joel's prophecy and to Pentecost, not a few writers say the reference is to Pentecost (Acts 2). That is when the Spirit was poured out upon the church, says Hendriksen. Some Pentecostal/Charismatic writers appeal to this verse from Titus as proof of another outpouring of the Holy Spirit exactly like that given the apostles on the day of Pentecost, an outpouring that every Christian may be expected to receive. A problem with this explanation is that the writers who so believe rather expect miracles and supernatural spiritual gifts to be part and parcel of every Christian's life. Now the problem is this: what would such abilities have to do with the point of this whole passage, namely to give a reason for living a proper lifestyle before unbelievers (remember how verses 3-6 are connected to what was said in verses 1,2)? (2) Others, noting that the recipients of this "outpouring" are identified as "us,"[67] insist we must look for some measure of the Holy Spirit that was received in common by both Paul and his readers. And then when they observe the aorist tense of the verb "poured out," they immediately point to the measure of the Holy Spirit each person receives when he initially becomes a Christian (Acts 2:38, 19:2), the measure commonly called "the indwelling of the Holy Spirit." Romans 8 is the chapter that explains in more detail than any other passage how the indwelling Spirit helps the Christian with his walk, so that his walk is pleasing to God. It is the Father who pours out the Holy Spirit upon each new-born Christian. The Spirit prompts the Christian concerning his lifestyle. Paul seems to be saying, 'Listen to the Spirit's promptings, and you'll be led to the proper kind of lifestyle before the non-believers.'

---

[66] Both "Holy Spirit" and "washing" are in the genitive case. "Whom" refers to the nearest antecedent, "Spirit," as the context seems to show.

[67] "Us" speaks of the same people identified as "we" in verse 3, and "us" in verse 5.

"Richly" translates the adverb *plousiōs*, indicating the generosity of God's giving of the Spirit.   Compare notes at 1 Timothy 6:17, where the same word is used, and also the use of *ploutos* at Ephesians 1:7, 2:7.   God was "lavish" in His granting of the Spirit.   The continual abundance of the Spirit's presence is why the Christian dispensation is called the "ministration of the Spirit" (1 Cor. 3:8).

Through Jesus Christ our Savior – *Dia* with the genitive denotes the intermediate agent through whom God has worked.   We've already suggested that the God who saves us is also the One who lavishly pours out the Holy Spirit.   What then does the phrase "through Jesus Christ our Savior" mean?   What has He had to do with this outpouring from the hand of God?   Perhaps the title "Savior"[68] added to "Jesus Christ" indicates that if Jesus had not offered as an atoning sacrifice for men, there would be no measure of the Spirit available to help them live the Christian life (cp. John 7:37-39).   Acts 2:33 says that the exalted Christ, after He had received from the Father what the Holy Spirit had promised (i.e., He wasn't abandoned in Hades, nor was His body in the grave long enough to begin to decay, Psalm 16:8-11), poured out the Holy Spirit on the day of Pentecost.   Some suppose that Acts 2:33 (Christ did the pouring) and Titus 3:6 (God did the pouring) can be harmonized in this manner: God did it through the agency of Jesus Christ, only after Jesus was glorified and exalted to God's right hand.[69]   Perhaps this phrase indicates that it is when we are immersed into Christ, when we are united with Christ so as to share the benefits of His death, burial and resurrection (Romans 6:4,5), that we are entitled to receive the Holy Spirit.   Compare also the promise recorded at Acts 2:38.

3:7 -- That – Verse 7 continues the long sentence begun in verse 4.   This is a *hina* clause, and evidently is intended to show us the purpose[70] God had in mind for saving us.   He intended that we be heirs according to the hope of eternal life.   The hopeless and lost state described in verse 3 is no longer true of Paul's readers.   They have been born again and immersed and have received the Holy Spirit and have been justified.   Now they have the position of "heirs ...."

Being justified by His grace – Not only have Christians been "saved by the washing of regeneration and the renewing of the Holy Spirit."   They have also been "justified."   Those who were once sinners (verse 3) are now "righteous" in God's sight.   "Justified" is the "courtroom word" we are so familiar with from

---

[68] Here the Son is given the same title of "Savior" which in verse 4 was applied to the Father. The title can rightly be applied to both the first and second persons of the Godhead.   The Father is the architect of our salvation, while the Son is its builder.   One planned it; the other carried it out.

[69] Students should not miss the clear reference to all three persons of the Godhead in verse 6.

[70] It seems better to interpret this as a purpose clause, than as a result clause.   *Hina* clauses are, at times, "result clauses."   If verse 7 were a result clause, it would tell us the result of God's kindness, love, mercy, and justification by grace.

Romans. God declares men righteous when He sees their faithful response to His offer of salvation.[71] "Justification" is the opposite of "condemnation" (Romans 8:33,34). The man who is justified has peace with God, and access to grace, and a hope of experiencing the glory of God (Romans 5:1,2). "His" translates *ekeinos*, the demonstrative pronoun that points to the farther antecedent. It is the Father's grace that is talked about. "Grace" speaks of God's attitudes and actions to bring about the redemption of lost men. Remember what was said about grace in Titus 2:11-16. While men were still sinners and alienated from God, God's mercy went before and provided the needed sacrifice so that sins could be forgiven. "By grace" should not, as is done by certain theologians, be interpreted to say that men are wholly passive in the matter of salvation.

We might be made heirs according to *the* hope of eternal life – This is the purpose or goal God had in mind when He set about to provide lost men with an opportunity for forgiveness and salvation. He intended that we become "heirs."[72] The same action that renders us just makes us heirs. Romans 8:17 develops the idea of "heir." Christians are God's reborn children who will inherit all He has in mind for us. Christians are joint-heirs with Christ. They will receive the same thing Jesus received when He returned to Heaven – i.e., a glorified body, and an opportunity to have intimate access to the presence of the Father.[73] While he is still in this world, full possession of the inheritance is not yet the Christian's experience. But his inheritance is, through faithfulness, reserved in heaven for him (1 Peter 1:3-5). This idea of being made heirs is in accord[74] with the hope of eternal life.

There is some debate about the punctuation of this final phrase in Titus 3:7. (1) Some would add some commas, so it reads "heirs, according to hope, of eternal life." This makes "eternal life" depend on "heirs," and would suggest that for Paul's readers eternal life was something still in the future. Since the Scriptures elsewhere suggest that in some sense "eternal life" is a present possession of each Christian (see John 3:16,36), the commentators must then write an explanation of how Paul's "eternal life" that was still future does not contradict what Scriptures say about "eternal life" being a present possession.[75] (2) Others would punctuate

---

[71] In theological language, God's righteousness (justification) is an imputed righteousness, not an infused righteousness. See all this discussed in the author's commentary on Romans.

[72] Elsewhere it is given as God's purpose that Christ "might be the firstborn among many brethren" (Romans 8:29).

[73] Christians do not become "gods" any more than Jesus for the first time became "God" when He ascended to Heaven after His resurrection. But Jesus did return from earth to glory (John 17:5), and that glory the Christian, too, may enjoy after a life of faithfulness to Jesus.

[74] See footnote #23 at Titus 1:4 for the meaning of the preposition *kata*, "according to."

[75] The expression "eternal life" has occurred in 1 Timothy 1:16 and 6:12, and in Titus 1:2.

as does the NASB. This makes "eternal life's hope" the thing in harmony with which Christians are heirs. While already possessing "eternal life," there are some things still hoped for that go along with that "eternal life" – things which will make it a blessed and happy experience. More than likely this verse picks up the phrase "in the hope of eternal life" that Paul used at Titus 1:2. Hebrews 6:17-20 also says much about the "hope" which Christians enjoy. When a man knows by revelation what God's plans and purposes are for His children, those children are encouraged thereby to "behave before non-Christians" in the way God has instructed (see v.2ff). No Christian would chance to forfeit his hope!

3:8 -- This is a trustworthy statement – Five times[76] this formula occurs in the epistles to Timothy and Titus. Detailed notes concerning the meaning of the formula are found at 1 Timothy 1:15. We have opted for the conclusion that they were memorized summaries of Christian doctrine.[77] The question here in Titus is what exactly are the words of the "faithful saying?"[78] Shall we look to verses 4-7, or shall we look to some words later in verse 8? The majority of writers identify the saying as verses 4-7 or some part of that long sentence.[79] The sketch of God's program of redemption included in those verses would be one of the memorized summaries of Christian doctrine. If we look to the words following, we must pick those that begin with *hina*, as introducing an indirect discourse statement. Thus, the saying would at least include "Those who have believed in God are to be careful to engage in good deeds."[80] It might also include the last phrase in the verse, "These things are good and profitable for all men."[81]

---

[76] See 1 Timothy 1:15, 3:1, 4:9, and 2 Timothy 2:11 for the other four.

[77] We tend to reject the view that each of these sayings just sprang up accidentally in the church, and caught on because they were catchy lyrics or were accompanied by catchy tunes. We doubt that, for example, Titus 3:5-7 is simply a "formula" repeated as part of the baptismal service of new converts. There is little evidence these "faithful sayings" were to be memorized and repeated only on certain special occasions. They were intended to help the Christians in their everyday beliefs and witness.

[78] The student who wishes to pursue this matter in detail will find help in Knight's *Faithful Sayings* and also in his commentary on the Pastoral Epistles in the *New International Greek Testament Commentary* Series (*op. cit.*, p.347f).

[79] Alford, Barrett, Bernard, Ellicott, Hendriksen, Kent, Simpson, Vine, Wuest, Knight all pick verses 4-7. A few limit the saying to verses 5-7, and some limit it to 5b-6, and Dibelius-Conzelmann pick verses 3-7 (because of the use of the first person plural all through those verses).

[80] Hervey in *Pulpit Commentary* (p.45) so explains the "faithful saying." He calls attention to the fact that a similar *hina* clause occurred at Titus 2:12, and that frequently, after words of "commanding", *hina* introduces a clause that gives the words of the command. If we take these few words as the "faithful saying," then this "faithful saying" nicely concludes the topic begun in Titus 3:2 about the Christian's behavior towards the non-Christians.

[81] In comments offered below, we address the matter of whether or not this last phrase – printed as part of verse 8 in our versions – goes with what precedes, or with what follows. Only if it goes with what precedes could the words be thought of as perhaps part of the "faithful saying."

And concerning these things I want you to speak confidently – Since one of the special emphases in Titus is the message the evangelist is to deliver, the wording of the "faithful saying" is of some importance. When Paul says "these things," does he tell the evangelist to emphasize the ideas found in verses 4-7, or to emphasize the need for "winsome living among the outsiders" (verse 8), or both? Over and over again in the hearing of the congregation, Titus is to speak confidently of these things.[82] Paul's "I will" or "I want you to" is urgent! "Speak confidently" (*diabebaiousthai*) means "to stoutly maintain and urge." "Orthodox preachers of the gospel must be no less forceful in their presentation of the truth than are the errorists in their falsehoods (same word is used of false teachers in 1 Tim. 1:7)" (Kent, *op. cit.*, p.236). If the words following are the words of the "faithful saying," then Paul uses this phrase to add extra weight to it.

So that those who have believed God may be careful to engage in good deeds – "So that" translates *hina*, which may indicate the purpose for which Titus is to speak confidently, or it may introduce the "statement" that Titus is to repeat over and over. If the former, then the reason Titus is to affirm the truths rehearsed in verses 5-7 is so that believers will have a good foundation for their conduct. Right beliefs[83] should lead to right actions. If the latter, then this phrase is the gist of the "faithful saying." "Believed" is a perfect participle, and the phrase does not say "believed in God" since there is no preposition after "believe" in the Greek[84]. It *does* say that these people have believed what God has said. They did so in the past and continue to do so (i.e., past completed action with present continuing results is the force of the perfect tense). If we indeed believe what God says, then we'll be careful to engage in good deeds. What has God said about "engaging in good deeds"? One is rather quickly reminded of Matthew 25:31-46 and Ephesians 2:10, among others. The Christian's continuing good works are the necessary evidence – more than that, they are the active living part – of his faith (James 2:17-26). "Be careful" is *phrontidzōsi*, a word used only here in the New Testament, but common in the LXX. The word means "to give thought" about a thing," to "be careful" or "anxious" to do it. "To engage" trans-

---

[82] Both "I will" and "to affirm confidently" are present tense verb forms, indicating continuing action.

[83] Hendriksen, with his usual Calvinist emphases, outlines the "truths" as being four in number: a) The kindness of the Father and His love toward man; b) The work of the Holy Spirit in regenerating and renewing man; c) The grace of Jesus Christ considered as the effective cause of our justification; d) The purpose of all this, that we might become what we are today, heirs-in-hope of life everlasting. We list these in order to stir up our own attempts at summarizing the key ideas in verses 4-7.

[84] "The meaning is not the same as *pisteuein en*, or *epi*, "to believe in," or "on," but "to believe" (as Romans 4:3,17 and 1 John 5:10, where the context shows that it is the act of believing God's promise that is meant" (Hervey, *op. cit.*, p.45). See also Machen's *New Testament Greek for Beginners*, paragraph 184. (Some have questioned this note of grammar, and have appealed to Acts 16:34 as an example of the verb "believe" followed by the simple dative, which is still [in their opinion] to be translated "believed in God.")

lates *proistasthai*, a word meaning "to stand before, preside, superintend, take the lead."[85] The same word was used at 1 Timothy 3:4,5,12 and 5:17. "Be careful" and "engage in" emphasize the fact that Christian living is not automatic. It takes constant effort. It also emphasizes the fact that a good beginning is not enough. The race must be run with endurance to the end (Hebrews 12:1,2; Revelation 2:10). "Good deeds" or "good works" (cp. Titus 2:14 and 3:1) refer to practical and helpful deeds of all kinds towards others.[86] The only difference between verse 1 and verse 8 is that the word translated "good" at verse 8 is *kalē*, and implies that the Christian's works are "winsome," "attractive," "beautiful." Christians are not only in a changed position, "heirs" of God, but they are also to be manifesting a change in practice – "engaging in good works."

D. The Evangelist's Own Conduct Toward Non-Christians. 3:8b-11

3:8b -- These things – A word needs to be said about the suggested outline for Titus. The NASB does not offer a paragraph break until verse 12. That tends to leave the main part of Paul's instructions to Titus without a fitting conclusion. The more one studies these closing lines of Titus, the more attractive the suggestion becomes that a new point in the outline should begin with the last phrase of verse 8. Verses 8b-11 then become the final point of emphasis in this letter to Titus. This final point thus includes both positive and negative emphases and forms an impressive concluding exhortation to the evangelist Titus.

The KJV reads "These are the things that are good and profitable to all men." There is a slight manuscript difference at this place. The Textus Receptus reads *tauta estin ta kala ... k.t.l.* Inserting the article *ta* before *kala* makes "good" a predicate adjective, so we use some form of the verb "to be" to help translate it. The manuscripts which are older than those from which the Textus Receptus was derived omit the article *ta* before *kala*, resulting in the reading found in the NASB.

If we treat this closing sentence of verse 8 as the beginning of a concluding summary to the letter,[87] we have several options for explaining "these things."

---

[85] The reading offered in the ASV margin, the NEB, and RSV margin, "profess honest occupations," seems an unwarranted rendering of this verb, for it requires *kala erga* to be a reference to "honorable occupations." It is doubtful whether any instance can be found of this meaning in the Greek literature. Barclay (*op. cit.*, p.302) shows the word literally means "to stand in front of" and was used for a shopkeeper standing in front of his shop crying his wares. Likewise, by his good deeds, the Christian advertises what the Christian life is for the benefit of those not yet converted.

[86] As observed before, Paul's ideal Christian must be a generous, public-spirited man. In the eyes of Paul, the cloistered ascetic would have found but little favor.

[87] Whether we can treat this as the beginning of a concluding summary depends on several

(1) "These things" could refer to the same "these things" (earlier in verse 8) concerning which Titus is to speak confidently, namely, the truths highlighted in the faithful saying (verses 4-7). "Such doctrines are really good and profitable for those whom you are commissioned to teach," Paul tells Titus. "Leave alone the foolish and unprofitable controversies" (verse 9), he continues.

(2) Perhaps "these things" is comprehensive, referring to the entirety of Paul's instructions to Titus since Titus 1:5. The things then that would be good and profitable would be: (a) The importance of setting the church in order, seeing that properly qualified leaders are selected who will be able to guard the congregations against the incursions of teachers like the Jewish-Gnostics; (b) Instructions to the different age groups about practical Christian living; (c) Instructions about the Christians' behavior towards outsiders.

Are good and profitable for men – If "good things" looks back to the faithful saying in Titus 3:4-7,[88] then the two adjectives "good" and "profitable" would refer respectively to the two parts of that entire saying. The teaching about how God has provided salvation is "praiseworthy" ("good"). The good deeds done to men would be "profitable," i.e., they would benefit the non-Christians who were the objects of those good deeds. If we take the comprehensive view where "these things" summarizes the instructions in the whole epistle, then "good and profitable" would refer to how all that is included in the letter is really "good and profitable" both for the listeners and for Titus. This summary statement may be intended as much for the Cretan churches, among whom this letter would be read, as it was intended for the evangelist Titus. The immediately drawn contrast (verse 9) would make all the more obvious the worthlessness and unprofitability of the Gnostic-Jewish teachings. When the differences between sound Christian doctrine and the unhealthy teachings of the false teachers are so plain, surely the Cretan Christians and the preacher himself will want to hear and preach only the good and profitable message God has given through Jesus Christ, and will be only too happy to avoid foolish Gnostic ideas.

3:9 -- But shun foolish controversies and genealogies and strife and disputes about the Law – Following the positive directions that are profitable given in the last part of verse 8, now we have certain things that are to be avoided by Titus as

---

decisions made earlier. Which words are the "faithful saying"? Where do we make a paragraph break (not till after verse 11 as the NASB, or may we insert one earlier)?

[88] Of course, if the faithful saying is found in verse 8, then we must give a slightly different emphasis to "these things." "These things" would have reference to the teaching which bids Christians to distinguish themselves among their unconverted fellow-citizens and countrymen in all generous and useful enterprises – in all good deeds, whether public or private. In fact, Hervey (*op. cit.*, p.45) believes that the last phrase of verse 8 implies that "good works" is the subject of the faithful saying, rather than what was written in verses 4-7.

unprofitable.[89] "But" creates a contrast with what was said in the close of verse 8. Titus is to do the one, he is to avoid the other. "Shun" (*periistaso*) occurs also at 2 Timothy 2:16. When Titus sees "heresies" or "heretics" coming, he is to turn and flee! The verb, a compound of *peri* and *histemi* in the middle voice, means "to go around so as to avoid." The present imperative indicates continuous action. Paul identifies both the heresies and the heretics that are to be avoided. Thus our outline speaks of Titus' behavior towards "non-Christians."

    "Controversies" and "genealogies" were explained at 1 Timothy 1:4. The use of those same words here indicates that the same sort of false doctrine was troubling the churches on Crete as troubled the church at Ephesus. In the comments at 1 Timothy 1:4, we noted that these genealogical tables were expanded and interwoven with fanciful tales. The Talmud includes unnumbered instances of these strange and curious inquiries about which men gravely disputed and wrangled. They used the words of the Old Testament family lists in a mystic sense to establish new and hidden teachings, which then became the subject for doctrinal discussions. The Dead Sea Scrolls, especially the Temple Scroll and the manuscripts found in Cave 4, show that such controversies were rampant both in the century before and the century after the coming of Jesus to earth. The controversies and genealogies were "foolish" (*mōras*, "silly," "stupid," "moronic") because they were utterly impractical in nature, consuming time and energy which were needed for other and better things. "Strife and disputes about the Law" also points to the Jewishness of the troublemakers on Crete. Remember, the Gnostic heresy began as a Jewish heresy before it ever invaded the church. Concerning "strife" (*eris*), see 1 Timothy 6:4. All the matters just mentioned led to "strife" or "contentions" between the people who held differing views.[90] Concerning "disputes about the Law" (*machas nomikas*), see the expression "disputes about words" at 1 Timothy 6:4. See also Titus 1:9,10,14 and 1 Timothy 1:3-7,19,20, and 6:3-5, or the disputes between the Sadducees and Pharisees (and among the Pharisees between the schools of Hillel and Shammai) over *halakhic* rulings (all of which were "pertaining to the Law"). Endless hours were spent discussing what could and could not be done on the Sabbath, and what was and was not clean, and who could and could not bring offerings to the Temple.

For they are unprofitable and worthless – What a contrast between the doctrines of the Gnostics and the very useful matters about which Paul has just spoken in this letter. Here Paul gives some reasons why the false teaching of the Jewish Gnostics should be avoided. "Unprofitable" (*anōpheleis*) means not

---

[89] At the close of our comments on verse 8, we offered the suggestion that verse 9 really continues the new point in the outline that begins with the last sentence of verse 8.

[90] Christians are to contend for the faith (Jude 3), but they are not to get involved contending for this or that sect's *halakhic* rulings!

useful, not helpful, not beneficial. Fightings disturb those who are not well-grounded in the faith, and do not produce purer conduct in older Christians. Note that the results of the Gnostic activities are the opposite of "profitable" in verse 8. "Worthless" (*mataioi*) says these controversies about the Law produce no results. They are utterly useless for the production of Christian virtues.

3:10 -- A factious man – The KJV reads "A man that is an heretick ... reject." The Greek word translated "heretick"[91] in the New Testament occurs only here, though the cognate term "heresies" occurs twice (1 Corinthians 11:19; Galatians 5:20). Originally the word translated "heresy" simply meant "that which one chooses for himself." Then it came to mean "a group of persons who hold the same opinions," hence a "school" or a "party," e.g., "the party (or "sect") of the Sadducees," Acts 5:17. Since in our time the word "heretic" signifies a fundamental doctrinal error, it may give a slightly wrong idea if we retain that word in our English versions. Now, in our language, the "heretic" is one who forsakes the truth always taught by the church, and "chooses" some doctrine of his own devising. Indeed there were some deviate doctrinal problems in the Jewish Gnostic system of teaching, but there is more to *hairetikon* than doctrinal error. The NASB uses "factious" and this comes closer to conveying the meaning of the Greek. Remember that in Corinth there were "factions" ("I am of Paul," "I am of Apollos," etc.). When Tertullus called Paul "a ringleader of the faction of the Nazarenes" (Acts 24:5), he was accusing Paul of introducing doctrine that had led to a "split" in the Jewish religious ranks. So a "factious man," or one we might call a "sectarian," is one who gathers around himself other discontented spirits and establishes what might be called a rival congregation, all of whose members hold the same views and opinions on the matters dear to the sect.[92] The "factious man" often goes from person to person, or group to group, forcing people to make a choice. "Are you for me, or are you in agreement with that other person?" And when choices are forced, divisions result.

Whether or not these "factious" people were ever members of the church on Crete is debated. Some commentators picture a church member who became dissatisfied with the congregation of which he was a part, one who perhaps considered himself in some way slighted, and who withdrew himself and began a new "party." Others picture the "factious man" as an outsider who came to town, taught his own special rules and doctrines, and attempted to gather around himself a group of like-minded people. Still others think the "factious man" is not so much the leader of the group, but rather a follower. He was once a church mem-

---

[91] In the years since the KJV was translated the spelling of the word has changed. Now, usually, the word is spelled without the final "k."

[92] Remember how the sect of the Pharisees traveled over land and sea trying to make converts to their position (Matthew 23:15).

ber, but has now been "roped into the new party" by these false teachers.

Reject ... after a first and second warning – How is Titus to deal with "factious men?" He is to "warn them" and then "reject them." "Reject" means "have nothing further to do with," "shun," "avoid." See 1 Timothy 4:7, 5:11 where the same word is used. If the "factious man" is a church member, it likely points to excommunication from church membership, as Jesus taught in Matthew 18:16-18. If the "factious man" is a non-member, then Titus is told to cease efforts at correcting and/or trying to win the man. Perhaps this is Paul's application of Jesus' statement about not casting pearls before swine. If the "factious man" is a non-member seeking membership into the church, Titus is to "refuse them."[93] "A first and second warning" suggests Titus' first obligation is to point out the error of the action or doctrine to the "factious man." Titus need not make more than two attempts at correcting the man's errors. "Warning" is *nouthesia*, a word used at 1 Corinthians 10:11 and Ephesians 6:4. It might be rendered "admonition" or "counsel." The word suggests that truth is clearly shown, followed by encouragement to embrace it. Two sessions with the factious man will likely show whether further remonstrance will be a waste of time, and to spend more time with the offender is merely to give the offender undeserved publicity. Verse 11 will give further reasons why Titus is to cease to admonish, and instead to shun or to have nothing further to do with the factious man.

3:11 -- Knowing that such a man is perverted and is sinning – "Such a man" refers back to the "factious man" who has been warned once and again. "Knowing" is a circumstantial participle. It gives the attendant circumstance that results from spending time with the "factious man," trying to counsel or admonish him. The factious man's true state soon becomes obvious to the evangelist, especially when the evangelist's warnings are not heeded. Thus is explained how the evangelist can without compunction "reject" the factious man. The word "perverted" (*exestraptai*) is found only here in the New Testament, but is common in the LXX and is also found in classical Greek, where it means "to turn inside out," "to root up," and the like. The same word is used in the LXX at Deuteronomy 32:20, the "*very froward* generation." The factious man is not living and seeing straight. He is mentally turned and twisted. The passive voice[94] suggests a cause outside the "factious man." He has been caused by someone else (by the Devil, or by demons, or by human religious leaders?) to become twisted and perverted. The present tense verb "is sinning" (*hamartanei*)

---

[93] Of course, the man is not refused fellowship without first being given fair and repeated hearings and warnings.

[94] The verb form can be either perfect middle or perfect passive. If we take it as middle, it means "he has turned himself aside" or "perverted himself." Either way we take it, the factious man has rejected the apostolic message by his own choice and actions.

pictures a course of action. The verb means to miss the mark, to fail to fulfill God's demands. To have been shown the right way and then refuse it is sin (James 4:17). He continues to sin against the light of God's Word which the evangelist has presented to him as the first and second admonitions were given. What makes his sin so bad is that after being instructed by Titus, the man knows that he is sinning and persists in his chosen course anyway.

Being self-condemned – By his continual sinning, the factious man condemns himself (*autokatakritos*). This word is found only here in the New Testament, and is not found in the LXX or in classical Greek. Cicero says of C. Fabricius that he was *suo judicio condemnatus*, condemned by his own judgment. Fabricius was self-condemned because he had left the court in confusion at a critical part of his trial.   Such a self-condemnation (he couldn't clearly give evidence to defend himself), Cicero says, was a heavier condemnation than even that of the law and the judges ('*Pro Cluentio*,' 21, at the end). The factious man does not need any judgment to be passed by the evangelist. By deliberately rejecting God's word and continually sinning against the light, the factious man condemns himself. He has shown himself to be clearly guilty, and has thereby provided the basis for his rejection.

With these words the main body of the letter to the preacher on the island of Crete closes.   There are yet some personal directions concerning Titus' continuing and future ministry which follow.

CONCLUDING REFERENCES.   3:12-15

3:12 -- When I send Artemas or Tychicus to you – The letter concludes with a few personal notes and instructions to Titus. We wonder whether Paul has followed the custom indicated in 2 Thessalonians 3:17.   Did one of Paul's helpers serve as the penman as Paul dictated the body of the letter? Is this the place where Paul picked up the pen and added a few notes in his own hand?

Paul is contemplating that either Artemas or Tychicus will come to Crete and replace Titus as the evangelist. When the new preacher comes, Titus is then to join Paul for the winter. Apparently, at the time he was writing this letter, Paul had not yet decided which of the two men he would send, nor exactly when he would send him. Perhaps both men were at the moment busy in some other ministry, and when they could be sent would depend on the circumstances connected with that ministry. Of "Artemas" nothing more is certainly known since this is the only mention of the man in the New Testament. It would not be out of place to suggest he was one of Paul's young preacher boys. Tradition has him at a later date as the bishop (evangelist[95]) at Lystra. "Tychicus" is mentioned five times in the New Testament (Acts 20:4, Ephesians 6:21, Colossians 4:7; 2 Timothy 4:12, and here). Tychicus seems to have been one of the star graduates of "St. Paul's Bible College." Paul speaks of him as a beloved brother, a faithful minister and fellow-servant in the Lord, and the importance of the missions with which he was entrusted by Paul shows us how high this disciple stood in Paul's estimation. (He had been sent to Colossae, Colossians 4:7, and to Ephesus, Ephesians 6:21.) We may conclude that Artemas was the person who eventually came to Crete since Tychicus we know went to Ephesus (2 Timothy 4:12). However, at the time Titus was written, it was not yet clear which would be sent to Ephesus. By the time 2 Timothy was written, it had all become clear.[96]

Make every effort to come to me at Nicopolis – After the new evangelist arrives, Titus is to make every effort to leave Crete and join Paul. (1) Most commentators tend to insert notes at this place which are agreeable to the church polity practiced by his particular church or denomination. For example, those churches which have a monarchical episcopate form of government find justification for their practice in Paul's dispatching and directing preachers as to their place of service. Or to appeal to another example, Hervey (*Pulpit Commentary*, p.46) writes, "The action of Paul in sending Artemas or Tychicus to take the place of Titus in Crete is exactly the same as he pursued with regard to Ephesus, where he sent Tychicus to take Timothy's place (2 Timothy 4:11,12). He would not leave the presbyters in either place without the direction and superintendence of one having his delegated apostolic authority. This led to the final placing of a resident bishop in the churches, such as we find in the second century." We think it likely that an apostle of Jesus had authority over the congregations that no other office had in the church. What an apostle had the authority and right to do hardly is precedent for someone without apostolic authority to suppose he can exercise the same oversight over local elders and preachers. (2) Others find guidance for the establishment of indigenous churches in lands that are evangelized. "As soon as the replacement arrives, Titus can leave, but not before. Note that Paul does not say, 'The Cretans can easily take care of themselves during your absence.' He realizes that churches cannot be made indigenous over-night. As long as leadership 'from the outside' is necessary, it must be provided."[97]

---

[95] See Kim Mallette's unpublished thesis, *The Evangelist* (shelved in the library of Central Christian College, Moberly, MO) where he affirms that the evangelist (not some elder) is the one who is called "bishop" in Early Christian Literature.

[96] In the Introductory Studies, it was noted that this verse has a bearing on the date of writing of the Pastoral Epistles. It evidently shows that Titus was written before 2 Timothy. In fact, when 2 Timothy was written, Titus has visited with Paul and was off again to minister in Dalmatia (2 Timothy 4:10).

[97] Hendriksen, *op. cit.*, p.397-98.

Zahn lists nine cities named "Nicopolis."[98]   The Greek word means "victory city."   The most famous and the most likely city is the one located in Epirus – the western part of Greece, across the Adriatic Sea from the heel of Italy. This city was built by Caesar Augustus after the battle of Actium (31 BC) to commemorate the great naval victory Augustus won over Antony and Cleopatra, from whence it derived its name, "The City of Victory."[99]   "Make every effort"[100] suggests that one just doesn't up and leave a ministry.   There are tasks to finish, loose ends to tie up, and work to be done so the transition to the new preacher will go smoothly.   Whether or not Titus can conclude all these in time to join Paul for the winter is something at which Titus will have to work diligently.

For I have decided to spend the winter there – "I have decided" (perfect tense of *krinō*) indicates that, after careful planning, Paul had come to this decision, this judgment.   It is likely the winter of AD 67.[101]   Paul's plans to winter in this place seem related to his next planned evangelistic work.   Paul regularly seems to have tried to spend the winters with Christians in locations strategic for his ministry as apostle to the Gentiles.   Nicopolis would be a good place from which to launch a new work in whatever unevangelized place the Lord might lead him since it was on the western-most edge of the area where Paul's earlier evangelistic efforts had been accomplished.[102]   Paul is not yet in Nicopolis.[103]   Perhaps he is somewhere in Macedonia (Philippi?) when he writes this letter to Titus.   Paul desires to spend the winter with Titus.   Nicopolis would be a suitable meeting place, more or less centrally located between where Paul and Titus are at the moment this letter was written and received.   Nicopolis was a fine place to spend the winter, for the winter months were not suitable for sea-travel.

3:13 -- Diligently help Zenas the lawyer and Apollos on their way – It is very likely that these two men were the bearers of this letter from Paul to Titus.   This is the only reference to "Zenas" in the New Testament.   Hippolytus says he was one of the "seventy" (Luke 10:1), and that in later years he was the bishop (i.e.,

---

[98] *Introduction to the New Testament*, Vol.2, p.53,54.   Those nearby where we last saw Paul during his journeys at this point in his life are the cities in Cilicia, in Thrace, and in Epirus.

[99] The city now lies in complete ruin, uninhabited except by occasional visiting shepherds, but with vast remains of broken columns, baths, theaters, etc.

[100] The same verb is used at 2 Timothy 2:15 and at 4:9,21.

[101] On the question of whether the winter here referred to is the same winter mentioned in 2 Timothy 4:21, see the Introductory Studies.

[102] 2 Timothy 4:10 will tell us that Titus has gone to Dalmatia.   We suppose he went because Paul so directed him.   Since no previous word has been given about evangelistic work done in the Roman province of Dalmatia, this may have been the next area Paul intended to evangelize. Nicopolis would have been a good base from which to evangelize the province of Dalmatia.

[103] Thus, the subscriptions on some manuscripts, which say that this letter to Titus was written from Nicopolis, are not accurate.

evangelist) at Diospolis (i.e., Lydda in Palestine). Whether "lawyer" means he was a converted "Jewish scribe" or a converted "Roman legist" – one learned in Roman civil law – cannot be decided. (1) Some urge that he likely was Jewish, both because of his association with Apollos and because of the frequent use of the term "lawyer" (*nomikos*) in the New Testament for the Jewish scribes and lawyers (Matthew 22:35; Luke 7:30, 10:25, 11:45,48,52, 14:3). If he were Jewish, now that he is converted he would no longer be a "lawyer," for Jewish rabbis who became Christians would not continue to function in their old vocation. Since Apollos before his conversion was a Jew who was "mighty in the Scriptures," and since Zenas is here designated as a "lawyer," some suppose that both of these men, now Christians, were just the kind of experts in Jewish Law and lore as were needed in places like Crete where Jewish Gnosticism was beginning to be a threat to the church. (2) Others suppose he must have been a Roman since he has a Greek name, a name which might even be an abbreviation of Zenodorus, meaning "gift of Zeus." If he were a converted Roman,[104] he could still practice law, for that would not be at odds with a Christian profession.

"Apollos" is known to us from the other references to him found in the New Testament. From Acts 18:24, where we are introduced to him for the first time, we learn he was an Alexandrian Jew, an eloquent speaker, one who knew the Old Testament Scriptures well, and one who had embraced the "good news" as taught by John the Baptist. When he came to Ephesus, about AD 54, he was taken aside and instructed more accurately in the way of the Lord by Aquila and Priscilla. Aquila and Priscilla converted him to Christianity; embracing the Messiah once He came is something John's preaching would have prepared Apollos to be ready to do. He then moved to Corinth and served as an evangelist[105] in that city (Acts 19:1, 1 Corinthians 1:12, 3:4-6,22, 4:6). He was able to powerfully and publicly confute the Jews by showing from the Old Testament Scriptures that Jesus was the long-awaited Messiah (Acts 18:27,28). At the time Paul wrote 1 Corinthians from Ephesus, Apollos was involved in a ministry somewhere near the city of Ephesus (1 Corinthians 16: 12).[106] The factions at Corinth (1 Corinthians 1:12)

---

[104] The fact that the man has a Greek name is no real proof he was not Jewish. "Paul" and "Apollos" and "Philip" and "Andrew" are all Jews with Greek names.

[105] The Scriptures do not specifically name any office or function held by Apollos, but the fact that he appears in this passage in Titus to be subordinate to Paul suggests Apollos did not hold the office of apostle. With no evidence that Apollos had an apostle's hands laid on him before he went to Achaia and began to preach, we may well suppose he was serving as an evangelist, rather than, say, a prophet or teacher. His being named by the Corinthians as one of their party favorites (alongside Paul and Peter) does not require that he must, like them, have been an "apostle of Jesus."

[106] Martin Luther conjectured that Apollos is the unnamed writer of the Epistle to the Hebrews. If Luther were correct in this, we would have to suppose that the Hebrew letter was written some time between AD 57, the time Apollos is ministering nearby to Ephesus, and AD 70, the date of the destruction of Jerusalem, which is the *terminus ad quem* for the dating of Hebrews. See the author's *New Testament Epistles: Hebrews* for reasons for rejecting Luther's suggestion about the

might consider Paul and Apollos rivals, but Paul had no ill feelings towards Apollos. Here in Titus they appear as close associates in the work of Christ.

"Help on their way" (*propempson*) is a technical expression, both in the New Testament and in the LXX, for helping persons to continue onward on their journey by supplying them with money, food, letters of recommendation, escort, or whatever else they might need. We do not know the destination of the journey Apollos and Zenas were on. Lewin has conjectured that Apollos was on his way back to Alexandria, to preach there in his hometown. He would be a handy "postman" to carry this letter to Titus since Crete was on the way between the place where Paul wrote this letter and Alexandria, Apollos' ultimate destination. "Diligently" (help them on their way) means "Do everything you can" or perhaps it also means "do it quickly" or "with haste, with a sense of special urgency."

So that nothing is lacking for them – When missionaries visit, it gives the congregation's members an opportunity to practice doing good and being hospitable. Knowing one has helped a messenger of God on his way, with all his earthly needs met, is a very satisfying thing. "Nothing lacking" reflects the result of appropriate Christian generosity towards Christian workers.

3:14 -- And let our *people* also – Titus is to take the lead in seeing that Zenas and Apollos have all the provisions they need to continue their journey, but he is not expected to meet all the missionaries needs by himself.[107] Titus likely would not have the funds personally to provide all that was involved. It does not appear that the church already had a special fund to help travelers that was at Titus' disposal, otherwise there would be little need to call on Titus to "train" the Christians to contribute for this occasion. The NASB renders hoi hēmeteroi as "our people" whereas the KJV simply has "ours." The people[108] Paul has in mind are those who along with Titus on Crete call upon the name of Jesus.

Learn to engage in good deeds to meet pressing needs – The verb translated "engage" is the same verb used in Titus 3:8. The Christians on Crete were "to take the lead" in good deeds. Such helpfulness and thoughtfulness is something a person can learn to do. When opportunities, such as helping missionaries or evangelists on their way, present themselves, the people are given an occasion of

---

authorship of Hebrews.

[107] "Also" says that the Cretan Christians are to do something just like someone else is to do. We suppose that someone else is their preacher, Titus. We are not very excited about the suggestion that says, "Let our Christians learn to do what the Jews do, or what even the unconverted gentiles to, viz., provide for the real wants of their own."

[108] The Greek has a nominative plural article followed by a possessive pronoun in the nominative plural, and we must supply some noun that agrees with the nominative case. "People" is a suitable choice.

learning this grace. The expression "Let [them] learn" would seem to suggest that Titus is to "train" the church members in the wise and thoughtful performance of deeds of mercy and charity. The verb tense means that this is something the Christians can "keep on learning." Learning through practice is one of the best ways to get an education. Here we read about "good deeds" again. In the few chapters included in the Pastoral Epistles, there are no less than eight special reminders to be earnest and zealous in good works.[109] Is it possible that this large number of exhortations reflects the very real possibility that Christians who profess a love of Jesus and who may know the doctrine about Him very well, may also fail to practice one of His great teachings? "Pressing needs" (*eis tas anagkaias chreias*) means "urgent necessities," the "indispensable wants." In classical Greek, the expression *ta anagkaia* means "the necessary things of life."

That they may not be unfruitful – By teaching Christian believers to grasp such opportunities for doing good, they become fruitful. Compare 2 Peter 1:8, where "brotherly kindness and love" are qualities that keep a Christian from being unfruitful. Is it fruit the Christians produce, or is it fruit the Christians will receive? In Philippians, which is a thank-you letter for a missionary offering he received from the Philippian Christians, Paul speaks of "fruit that abounds to your account," a phrase that suggests God takes note of the generous offering given by the Philippians and will reward them accordingly in Heaven. It is also true that when we help a missionary on his way, and he wins men to Christ, the ones who made it possible for him to go are just as involved in the fruit being produced as the missionary himself is. Several commentaries call attention to what happened to the unfruitful branches in John 15, to call attention to the danger any Christian puts himself in when he fails to respond to "pressing needs."

3:15 -- All who are with me greet you – The farewell greeting consists of three short statements. First, Paul's associates join with him in sending greetings to Titus ("you" is singular in the Greek). It is not certain where Paul was when he wrote this letter, so we have little to help us identify his associates who joined in this greeting.[110] Paul regularly had young "preacher boys" who travelled with him (cp. Acts 20:34), learning how to serve the churches which Paul and others planted. Perhaps these fellow workers are the ones who send their greetings (cp. Philippians 4:21). Another possibility is that "all" refers to the Christians in the town from which Paul writes this letter (cp. 1 Corinthians 16:20).

---

[109] See Titus 1:16, 2:7,14, 3:14; 1 Timothy 2:10, 5:10, 6:18; 2 Timothy 2:21. The adjective translated "good" in these places is sometimes *agathon*, and sometimes *kalon*. We doubt there is any difference in meaning, nor do we see any reason (as sometimes has been done) to suppose that one or the other of the expressions should be used as a "proof" that the writer of the Pastorals was not Paul.

[110] On two different occasions, Paul actually names his associates as he closes a letter (2 Timothy 4:11,21 and Philemon 23,24).

Greet those who love us in *the* faith – This second statement tells Titus to relay the greeting from Paul and his associates to all the church which loved and respected Paul and the other preachers.   By this language those who have remained loyal to the Gospel of Christ are distinguished from those who are disloyal to the Gospel and to Paul's preaching.[111]   The reader's love for Paul was based upon the common faith[112] in the Lord Jesus Christ.   Those who recognized Paul as an earnest preacher of the faith once for all delivered to the saints are to be told how much Paul appreciates their affection for him.   Before Titus could extend this greeting, he would have to make an appraisal of the church members on Crete with regard to their relationship to "the faith" and "to Paul."   Titus who was in a position to know where each of the Cretan church members stood.[113]

Grace be with you all – In comments on 3:12 we noted Paul's custom of adding a short note in his own handwriting at the close of each of his letters.   If that was not the place where he picked up the pen, then surely this final prayer for the readers is the place.

"You" in this statement is plural in the Greek, so this greeting is addressed to the whole church.[114]   It shows Paul intended that this letter be read out loud at the public service.   The "grace"[115] which Paul prayed would continue to be with the whole church may well be connected with the general thrust of this whole letter.   Church members who listened to the false teachers would shortly quit the church and forfeit any access to the grace of God.   What Paul wishes for all is that they may continue in the sphere of God's grace.

So, with but slight variation, end all of Paul's epistles.   The Textus Receptus has "Amen" as the final word of this letter, as do most of the other epistles.   The greater number of the ancient authorities for the text omit the "Amen" here in Titus.   It was probably added by a copyist early in the history of the transmission of the text.

No other forty-six verses of the New Testament contain quite so much valuable instruction to preachers as this short letter addressed to Titus.

---

[111] Compare the even more forthright statement in 1 Corinthians 16:22 concerning those who reject the Lord Whom Paul has been sent to preach.

[112] "The faith" is a right rendering.   See 1 Timothy 1:2.   See also "common faith" in Titus 1:4.

[113] Such "appraisals" are not at all prohibited by Jesus' prohibition against hypocritical judging (Matthew 7:1ff).

[114] The plural "you" occurs in the closing benedictions of each of the Pastoral Epistles.   See comments on 1 Timothy 6:21.

[115] See "grace" explained in notes at 1 Timothy 2:2.   The Greek reads "the grace," so it refers to the grace of God.

Commentary On

2 Timothy

ORIENTATION TO 2 TIMOTHY

Detailed introductory studies for this letter have been covered in the Introduction to the Pastoral Epistles found at the beginning of this volume. It was concluded that there is no reason to doubt the Pauline authorship of this letter. It may be dated about AD 67. The historical allusions in 2 Timothy indicate that Paul is a prisoner as he writes this letter (1:8, 2:9), that he is in Rome (1:16-18), that his first defense is past (4:16,17), and that he knows he shortly will be executed (4:6).

Paul writes this letter to Timothy, who is an evangelist in Ephesus, pleading with him to come to Rome to visit before Paul is executed (4:9,21). Timothy is to bring Mark with him on the journey to Rome.

Helpful to our understanding of the background of 2 Timothy would be a brief review of Paul's travels after his release from the first Roman imprisonment. About AD 63 he was released (see introductions to the Prison Epistles). He travelled to visit the churches addressed in the Prison Epistles. He also visited Ephesus (see 1 Timothy) and Crete (see Titus). Rome burned in AD 64 in the month of July. By October the blame had been placed on the Christians by Nero. Now Christian leaders were being arrested and brought to Rome for trial and execution. Paul had intended to spend the winter in Nicopolis (Titus 3:12), perhaps the Nicopolis in Epirus, across the ocean from the heel of Italy's "boot". Perhaps it was there that Paul was arrested and taken to Rome a second time. From Rome he addresses this second letter to Timothy, who likely was still in Ephesus, as he was when 1 Timothy was sent to him. Paul urges him to bring winter clothes to Paul, and to also bring Mark (4:11,21). One purpose for writing is to encourage Timothy in the face of this new danger presented by the Neronian persecution. Another theme running through the letter is a further warning about the evil men and impostors with whom Timothy must deal and a call to "guard ... the treasure which has been entrusted to you."

The theme of the letter has been summarized in this succinct statement: "It's always too soon to quit!" After Paul is gone, someone will have to carry on the gospel preaching. Timothy, don't quit the ministry! Instead, prove your faith (chapter 1), protect your faith (chapter 2), practice your faith (chapter 3), and preach and proclaim your faith (chapter 4).

Outline of 2 Timothy

APPEALS TO STAY IN THE MINISTRY

I. The First Personal Appeal – Prove Your Faith.   1:1-18
    A. A Call for Courageous Enthusiasm.   1:1-7
    B. A Call for Shameless Suffering.   1:8-12
    C. A Call to Spiritual Loyalty.   1:13-18

II. The Practical Appeal – Portraits of the Evangelist.   2:1-26
    A. The Torch Bearer.   2:1,2
    B. The Soldier.   2:3,4
    C. The Athlete.   2:5
    D. The Farmer. 2:6,7
    E. His Teacher.   2:8-10
    F. The Faithful Saying. 2:11-13
    G. The Workman.   2:14-19
    H. The Vessel.   2:20-22
    I. The Servant.   2:23-26

III. The Prophetic Appeal – Practice Your Faith.   3:1-17
    A. Turn Away from Those Who are False.   3:1-9
    B. Follow Those Who are True.   3:10-12
    C. Continue in God's Word. 3:13-17

IV. The Second Personal Appeal – Preach and Proclaim Your Faith!   4:1-18
    A. Preach the Word!   4:1-4
    B. Fulfill Your Ministry.   4:5-8
    C. Be Diligent and Faithful.   4:9-18

Final Greetings and Benediction.   4:19-22

2 TIMOTHY

APPEALS TO STAY IN THE MINISTRY

I. The First Personal Appeal – Prove your Faith. 1:1-18

A. A Call for Courageous Enthusiasm. 1:1-7

1:1 -- Paul – In accordance with the custom of the day, and in common with the majority of New Testament letters, this letter opens with the signature of the writer, the name of the recipient, and a greeting. This letter carries Paul's signature. There is no believable reason to doubt the truthfulness of this claim.

An apostle of Christ Jesus – Concerning himself Paul references his apostleship, for it is the basis of the authority he exercises. Paul begins 5 of his letters (1 and 2 Corinthians, Ephesians, Colossians, and 2 Timothy) with this identification. Paul was Christ's called apostle. Jesus appeared to Paul on the Damascus road to call him to become an apostle to the Gentiles (Acts 26:16-18).

By the will of God – As in the epistles to Corinth, Ephesus, and Colossae, Paul describes his apostleship as being something that God willed to be. Compare Romans 1:1 and Galatians 1:1, too. When Jesus appeared to Paul on the Damascus road, Paul had not been aspiring to the office of apostle, nor wishing for it. The reference to the "will" of God Almighty not only in this place but throughout this whole epistle is singularly in harmony with the spirit of calm resignation which Paul breathes through this whole letter. It was God's will that led Jesus to call him to be an apostle, which guided him through an eventful life, and which brought him to the prison of Nero Caesar, where, face to face with death, he wrote this last letter to his friend and disciple, Timothy.

According to the promise of life in Christ Jesus – *Kata* may be translated "according to" or "with a view to." If we opt for the former, the verse says Paul's apostleship was in accordance with, was in harmony with, God's promise of life[1] in Christ Jesus. Gnostics cannot say that their mission is in harmony with what God is doing in His world. If we opt for the latter, then this use of *kata* is similar to its use in Titus 1:1. "With a view to the fulfillment of the promise," *kata* expresses the aim or goal God had in mind. In these first words of this letter, written as he expects shortly to be executed, Paul dwells upon the promise of life,

[1] For the expression, "promise of life," see 1 Timothy 4:8.

the life in Christ.   Several times in the letter, Paul's keen awareness of the life to come stands out (1:10, 2:8,9, 4:6-8,18).   Only when a man remains faithful to Jesus, remains in Christ Jesus, is such a promise of life meaningful.

1:2 -- To Timothy – A sketch of Timothy's life and ministry has been included in the Introductory Studies to these Pastoral Epistles.   At the time Paul addressed this letter to him, Timothy was the evangelist working with the church in Ephesus.

My beloved son – Here is where Paul expresses his love for Timothy.   Compared with the words of 1 Timothy "my true (genuine) child (*gnesiō teknō*) in the faith," this language is more loving.   It is because Paul knows that in spite of his earnest request for Timothy to come to him with all speed, these lines just might be in reality his farewell to his trusted friend who is more than a son.[2]   Timothy was Paul's convert, his a "son" in the faith.   Further, the years have forged a deep bond of friendship between the two.   In addition, Timothy's faith and life mirror well his spiritual father's faith and life.

Grace, mercy and peace from God the Father and Christ Jesus our Lord – Compare the "greeting" Paul wrote in Romans 1:7.   These words are a prayer from Paul's heart for Timothy.   He prays a three-fold blessing on Timothy, and asks that both the Father and the Son conjointly confer those blessings.   Observe that Christ Jesus is here designated with a term that denotes deity, "Lord."   That view of Jesus, that He is "Lord," is not one – as current liberal theology would have us believe – that gradually grew[3] as worshipers' estimations of Jesus in later generations took on accretions never dreamed of by Jesus or His early followers.

1:3 -- I thank God – Now we begin the two verses that tell us about Paul's prayers for his young preacher friend.   For what does Paul thank God?   The grammar of the sentence which follows is difficult and ambiguous, so the answer to that question is disputed.   It seems as though there is a long parenthesis which intervenes between the verb[4] about thanking God and the content of his prayers. If this is correct, then, as Paul reflects on his own service to God, what Paul expresses thanks for is his remembrance of the unfeigned faith of Timothy and of Lois and Eunice (verse 5).   First-century letters usually included a formal thanks-

----

[2] Observed how a dying person, with meaning and intensity, says his final farewell to a loved one, knowing full well this is the last time they may get to talk with each other in this world.

[3] See Maurice Casey's work *From Jewish Prophet to Gentile God* (Louisville, KY: Westminister/John Knox, 1991) where the use of redaction criticism on the New Testament actually leads writers to believe the idea that Jesus is "Lord" is only a late superstition, and a wrong one at that.

[4] Instead of the usual verb *eucharisteō* for "giving thanks," Paul begins his thanksgiving here and in 1 Timothy 1:12 with *charin exō*, "I have thanks."   This more literary expression (Simpson, *Pastoral Epistles*, p.121) may well reflect the fact that Luke, the highly educated Greek physician, was Paul's amanuensis.

giving right after the greeting.   Paul follows this regular custom in all his letters save Galatians and Titus, offering a thanksgiving right after the greeting.[5]

Whom I serve with a clear conscience – The conscience is an innate faculty which prompts us to do what our mind thinks is right, and condemns us when we do what our mind thinks is wrong.[6]   The present tense verb "serve" ("whom I am serving") may be a statement that anticipates the thrust of this letter.   A man who quits the ministry may have a troubled conscience with which to contend.   But Paul's conscience was clear; it did not condemn him for failing to keep serving God.   Of course, it does not mean that Paul never committed any acts of sin.   It does say that his motives were to obey and please God, to continually serve[7] Him, and in that his conscience didn't bother him.

The way my forefathers did – Literally it reads "from my forefathers."[8]   How can Paul serve God "from his forefathers"?   Perhaps Paul means his immediate parents and grandparents had served God and had set an example for him how to serve God with a clear conscience.   Perhaps it means that his ancestors for generations have been steadfast to the historic faith revealed to the patriarchs Abraham, Isaac, and Jacob, and revealed to Moses.   Paul has not turned his back on that sacred religious heritage now that he has become a Christian preacher and apostle.   He is not worshipping and serving some other God when he recognizes and worships Jesus as the promised Messiah.   He is walking in the very path his forefathers did when it came to responding to God's overtures.   Just as there is a linkage to ancestors in Paul's religious life, so there is one in Timothy's life, too.

As I constantly remember you in my prayers night and day – These unstudied words tell us something of Paul's prayer life.   He prayed regularly for the churches (cp. Philippians 1:3,4) and for those who had once been his preacher boys.   The word "constantly" or "unceasing" (ASV) does not mean Paul prays 24 hours a day.[9]   Rather it tells us that each time in that lonely prison when Paul prays, he expresses to God his wishes for Timothy and his own wish – the Greek word for "prayers" is petition or begging – to see Timothy again.   The Greek

---

[5] In 1 Timothy, before stopping to thank God, Paul talked to Timothy about the urgent task that faced him in Ephesus.   But he still had a thanksgiving section in that letter (1 Timothy 1:12-14).

[6] See comments at Acts 23:1; Romans 2:15; and 1 Timothy 1:5.

[7] The word translated "serve" is *latreuō*, a word also often translated "worship."   Cp. Philippians 3:3, Hebrews 12:28, Romans 1:9 and 12:1.   A man's "worship" is not just something limited to two hours on Sunday mornings.

[8] *Progonoi* means "born before."   It occurs elsewhere in the New Testament only at 1 Timothy 5:4 where it refers to one's immediate parents or grandparents.   In other literature it also has the more remote sense of "ancestors" or "forefathers."

[9] See notes at Romans 9:2.

sentence is a broken.   Being about to say that he remembered Timothy's faith (see verse 5, "I am mindful"), the thought arose in Paul's mind that he was thinking more than just about Timothy's faith.   He was thinking about how grand it would be to see him again in person.   The words "night and day" come at the very end of the verse in the Greek.   Some think they should be taken with verse 4, so that it speaks of Paul's longing night and day to see Timothy.   It is also possible our translation has it right, that Paul went to God in prayer several times a day.

1:4 -- Longing to see you – Paul wanted badly ("night and day," verse 3) to see Timothy.   Many of his helpers were a long way away, and some were even "deserting him" (2 Timothy 4:10), so we can understand Paul's desire to see one on whom he could count to remain faithful – Timothy.   A man with many years in the ministry will often recall things that were part of his grand expectations in earlier years.   Of all those dreams and ideals, he will dwell on one or two young men who have entered the ministry and who came close to fulfilling those expectations.   They can carry on the work for which the older man has given his life.

Even as I recall your tears – When were tears shed by Timothy?   Was it a year or so earlier,[10] the last time Paul and Timothy had parted?   It was not uncommon for men to express their emotions by weeping (e.g., Acts 20:37,38).   Has Paul simply understood what Timothy's reaction would have been when he heard the distressing news that Paul had been arrested again and deported to Rome?   Close friends often know how the other will respond.   Paul's language seems to infer that he had personally seen Timothy as he was crying, not just imagined it.   Were Timothy's tears shed years earlier, when their relationship was just beginning, at the time when Paul was stoned at Lystra (on the first missionary journey, Acts 14:19) and left for dead?   When Paul awakened, was one of the first sights he saw none other than young Timothy standing over his body, crying at what had happened to his teacher?   Whenever they were shed, they were tears of love and loyalty to Paul and to the Lord, and so were cause for joy in Paul's heart.

So that I may be filled with joy – Probably this is to be connected with the first phrase of the verse: "longing to see you ... so that I may be filled with joy."   Paul would be filled with joy if he and Timothy, one whose genuine love and faith were expressed in tears, just once more could spend some time together.[11]   Paul will express again this wish to see Timothy in 2 Timothy 4:9.

1:5 -- For I am mindful of the sincere faith within you – Literally, "I have been

---

[10] According to 1 Timothy 1:3, Paul had left Timothy behind to be the evangelist at Ephesus while he himself went on to Macedonia to serve Jesus there.

[11] To be sure, when Timothy arrived in Rome (and we hope he did get there before Paul was executed) and stepped through the door into Paul's cell, tears would have filled the eyes of both and emotions would have welled up.   But they would have been tears of joy!

reminded."[12]   Something – a letter, a visitor, a news report – has been a most pleasant reminder of Timothy's sincere faith.   "Sincere" or "unfeigned" means that Timothy's faith was genuine.   During a time of persecution such as Paul and the church were facing, a genuine faith, one that would not waver even in the face of serious difficulty, was so very important.

Which first dwelt in your grandmother Lois, and your mother Eunice – Paul had come into contact with this family during his early missionary journeys to southern Galatia (Lystra and Derbe, Acts 16:1-3).[13]   Lois and Eunice[14] were devoutly Jewish, though Timothy's father was a Greek.   We may even suppose his grandmother[15] lived in the house with her daughter and son-in-law, and so was nearby to exert a positive religious influence on Timothy.   Timothy and Eunice had become Christians during Paul's first visit to their town (Acts 16:1,2); at least Luke designates them as "believers" when Paul returns to their town at the beginning of his second missionary tour.   Faith, of course, comes by hearing the Word of God.   The Scriptures had made son, mother and grandmother "wise unto salvation" (2 Timothy 3:15 KJV) and they responded.   Timothy's faith, and theirs, was a result of long teaching and growth.

And I am sure that it is in you as well – One way to encourage another person to do as you wish is to express your confidence in them that they will.   Paul wants Timothy's faith to remain steadfast, so he expresses his own belief and confidence in him.   There is no greater inspiration than to feel that someone believes in us.   The fear that we may let down those who love us is a healthy fear.   Timothy is walking in a fine family tradition.   Let him thank God for it, and let him never bring dishonor to it!

1:6 -- And for this reason – In the light of Paul's remembrance of Timothy's past

---

[12] Bengel notes that *hupomnesin lambanein* means to be reminded of any one by another, as distinguished from *anamnesin*, which is used when any one comes to your recollection without external prompting.

[13] Since Paul shows such an intimate knowledge of Timothy's family, a few writers have speculated concerning whether Lois, Eunice, and Timothy were kinsfolk of Paul.   Indeed, Lystra was not a great distance from Tarsus from whence Paul came, and it might be possible.   But such a possible relationship is nothing more than supposition.

[14] Both "Lois" and "Eunice" are examples of the frequent use in the first centuries BC and AD of Greek or Latin names by Jewish people.   That Eunice is married to a Greek may indicate her Jewish family was not as strict as some 1st century Jews were, for many 1st century Jews would not have tolerated such a mixed-faith marriage, nor would they permit sons to grow up uncircumcised.

[15] The word for "grandmother" (*mamme*, like our "mama") which Paul uses, was in classical Greek used for "mother."   The regular classical word for "grandmother" was *tethē*.   However in the papyri and in inter-testamental literature (4 Maccabees 16:9), the word Paul uses also appears, so it must have already been a child's name for "grandmother."   In any case, the context, which also uses "mother" for Eunice, indicates what sense Paul gives to the word *mamme* in this place.

faith and his family's, in light of the confidence that Timothy will stay faithful ...

I remind you – One doesn't remain faithful without effort. One doesn't stay at a task without effort. Timothy has been told this before, and now Paul reminds him again. Paul has been fondly reminiscing about Timothy: first his family and their faith, then Timothy's tears, now the time when Timothy had been commissioned to the work of God.

To kindle afresh the gift of God – The exhortations to boldness and courage which begin here in verse 6 were the natural results of the danger to which Paul's own life was exposed, and the dangers which faced the church to which Timothy was to minister. It is in such times when a man might get discouraged and dejected that the word "kindle afresh" often occurs.[16] It is a word used of fanning the smoldering embers of a fire into a blaze.[17] But just what was the "gift" (*charisma*) that Timothy is to stir up? Should we try to identify it as one of the "spiritual gifts"[18] like "teaching" or "exhortation" or "leading"? Or is Timothy's gift his ministry, the office of evangelist (Ephesians 4:7-12)?

Which is in you through the laying on of my hands – Spiritual gifts (*charismata*) were conferred by the laying on of an apostle's hands (Acts 8:14-18, 19:1-6; Hebrews 2:4). Is this "laying on of hands" how Timothy was enlisted into the office of evangelist? Did it require the laying on of an apostle's hands before one could be an evangelist? If so, how would this impact the question of whether or not there are evangelists in the church today?[19] Or through the apostle's hands was Timothy given some supernatural gift, such as the ability to work miracles or speak by inspiration, which could be used in his work as an evangelist?

Another issue concerns how we are to relate what is here written to what we find in 1 Timothy 4:14, where "elders" laid hands on Timothy and gave him a "gift" (*charisma*). Was it on the same occasion when the elders ordained Timothy that Paul laid hands on him? Or was it a separate occasion?[20] Either

---

[16] See Genesis 45:27 and I Maccabees 13:7.

[17] Anyone who has tended a fireplace fire knows that it needs to be stirred up occasionally. The Greek infinitive here is present tense. This "kindling afresh" is something that speaks of continuous action, not just a one-time act.

[18] Romans 12:6-8, 1 Corinthians 12-14, 1 Peter 4:10-11.

[19] Several times in our study of the Pastoral Epistles (including the Special Study #5, *J.W. McGarvey's Concept of the Ministry*), the matter of whether or not today's "preacher" is comparable to the New Testament "elder" or the New Testament "evangelist" has been discussed. If "evangelist" were a supernatural gift bestowed by the laying on of an apostle's hands, we would not have the office in the church today since no one today is qualified to be an apostle of Jesus (Acts 1:22).

[20] This commentator tends to put together the verse in 1 Timothy 1:18 about Timothy's future work for Jesus being the subject of a prophecy, and the verse in 1 Timothy 4:14 about the elders

way, Paul is giving Timothy another reminder of his past in order to encourage him to keep his courage high and his efforts strenuous. Paul reminds Timothy about his ordination service, and the dreams and hopes and prophecies made then. Timothy is not going to fail them now, is he? Think of all those who would be disappointed if Timothy were not faithful to his ministry! With such encouragement, surely Timothy will make full use of the abilities, responsibilities, and privileges that had been conferred on him.

1:7 -- For God has not given us a spirit of timidity – A verse beginning with "for" either explains something just said or gives a reason for something just said. Is Paul explaining of what he has just said about a "gift"[21] given by the laying on of his hands? Should we use a capital "S" (as does the TEV), making it a reference to the Holy Spirit who here would then be called the "Spirit of... power, love, and discipline"? Or is Paul giving a reason why Timothy should kindle afresh his gift – i.e., there is no reason to have a timid or cowardly spirit. If so, the lower case "s" in "spirit of timidity" refers to an attitude or spirit or feeling a man may harbor. It is not easy to decide exactly what this verse is saying.

Not only do we not know whether "spirit" is Holy Spirit or a human attitude, we do not know who is included in "us," nor can we determine with certainty when the gift was given. Perhaps "us" refers to Paul and Timothy. If so, it may say Paul and Timothy both have a special "gift" of the Holy Spirit given at some time in the past,[22] or it may say that Paul and Timothy share the same attitudes.[23] Perhaps "us" refers to all Christians. If so, the reference is far broader than a gift of the Holy Spirit conferred on Paul and Timothy at their ordination into ministry.

If it is a reference to the Holy Spirit, it might be the indwelling gift given at the time of conversion. Or perhaps it should be affirmed that every Christian gets some "spiritual gift" at conversion,[24] a "gift" in addition to the indwelling

---

laying hands on him (an ordination service, wherein the elders set Timothy apart to the office of evangelist). This commentator also tends to think Paul laid hands on Timothy after that ordination service was complete, giving him a supernatural spiritual gift beyond what the elders could confer.

[21] If this verse is a further explanation of the *charisma* received by the laying on of an apostle's hands, then this verse will likely cause us to have to rethink all of our explanations about how miraculous gifts were received (see 1 Timothy 4:14, too). Indeed, we would need to rethink just what is included in the *charisma* that could be received by the laying on of hands, whether an apostle's or an elder's.

[22] The time when Timothy received his "gift" (*charisma*) would have been when Paul laid hands on him. The time when Paul received his "gift" (special Holy Spirit powers to enable him to do the work of an apostle) would have been perhaps during his stay in Arabia for those three years immediately following his conversion.

[23] It is not easy to explain just how God "gives" a person his attitude – in this case an attitude of power, love, and sound judgment.

[24] Compare 1 Peter 4:10, Romans 12:6, 1 Corinthians 12:13b.

Holy Spirit. If, on the other hand, it refers to an attitude, it would be a grave reminder to Christians of every age that all cowardice, all dread of danger, all shrinking from doing one's duty for fear of man's displeasure, proceeds not from sober and correct thinking. "Fear" is a paralyzing timidity or cowardice that wants to stop acts of Christian ministry or service.[25] The gift of God in Timothy, whatever its manifestation may have been, did not include a spirit or attitude of fearfulness, even when persecution threatened. A fear of the earthly consequences of being faithful to Jesus has its source with someone other than God.[26]

But of power and love and discipline – The Holy Spirit, whether He manifests himself in His indwelling gift or in spiritual gifts, helps a man be other than timid and cowardly. How we explain the three terms in this phrase depends considerably on decisions made about the meaning of the word "spirit" in the first phrase of this verse.

- If "us" speaks of Paul and Timothy, and if "spirit" speaks of Holy Spirit, then "power" (*dunamis*) might refer to the miraculous power the Holy Spirit imparted to special servants of Christ (cp. Acts 1:8, 6:8; Luke 4:14; Acts 10:38; 1 Corinthians 2:4).
- On the other hand, if "us" is all Christians, there are verses where "power" seems to be an effect of the indwelling Holy Spirit (Ephesians 3:16, Romans 15:13). The Holy Spirit works in those to whom He is given, producing *strength* to fight the fight of God, *power* not only to endure but also to strike good blows for Christ, *power* of steadfastness in resisting temptations, *strength* to discharge the tasks allotted, *power* to combat foes and dangers, *power* to withstand trials, *power* to triumph in persecutions.
- If "spirit" speaks of an attitude, it is the nature of the gospel to inspire the mind to holy courage. While we might think of "power" as being a miraculous power, it is difficult to think of "love" as being a miraculous power. Love is regularly one of the fruit of the Spirit (Galatians 5:22). Love – doing what is spiritually best for the other person – leads to noble deeds of self-surrender. It never shrinks from any sacrifice which may benefit the friend or neighbor. 1 Corinthians 13 explains that to be without love for the other person renders all service valueless.
- For the third of this verse's three terms, Spence suggests that instead of rendering the word "sound mind" (KJV) or "discipline" (NASB), we ought

---

[25] Compare Romans 8:15, "a spirit of fear." See also 1 Peter 3:14, written about the same time as 2 Timothy, and also in the face of the same Neronian persecution. Timothy is not to be cowardly nor shrink from the daily difficulties which the Christian meets during the warfare for the kingdom of Christ.

[26] Is it the devil who fills the heart of would-be servants of God with fear, so they are unable to think or act effectively?

to use "self-control" (*Ellicott's*, p.283). A person who has self-control is able to live in and mix with the world, to be exposed to its varied temptations and pleasures, and still be able to regulate and to keep in wise subjection his passions, desires, and impulses. A person whose attitudes are "power, love, and discipline (self-control)" has attained a level of spiritual maturity that comes only by persistent growth and patient striving. It is never attained simply by wishing for it.

If these three qualities characterize Timothy's attitude, Paul is confident he will continue to kindle afresh the gift of God he has received, and will continue to be faithful to the Christian beliefs and practices he has learned from Paul.

With these words Paul has finished the first emphasis of his personal appeal to Timothy, namely, that he should exhibit courageous enthusiasm in his ministry. The second emphasis begins with the next verse.

B. A Call for Shameless Suffering.   1:8-12

1:8 -- Therefore – The word gathers up all that has been said thus far. Both men share a promise of life in Christ Jesus. They share a faith that matches what God has been revealing during ages past. They share a gift, a special ministry, from God. They both have a spirit of power, love, and discipline (i.e., self-control).

Do not be ashamed of the testimony of our Lord – The "testimony of our Lord" is a long name for the gospel, which is both a testimony about Jesus and a testimony that Jesus gave.[27] The gospel was proclaimed by Jesus Himself during His earthly ministry, and then by those who were eye-witnesses of His ministry (Hebrews 2:3). There were two ways to write prohibitions in Greek: one prohibits the continuance of an action already going on, the other prohibits even beginning an action. The latter is the construction here. Timothy is not even to begin to be ashamed or embarrassed. Paul wants his young preacher friend to have the same attitude he himself expressed in Romans 1:16, "I am not ashamed of the gospel ...." Remember, the gospel includes the sufferings and the shame Christ experienced, to the Jews a stumbling block, and to the Greeks foolishness (1 Corinthians 1:23). Timothy is not to shrink from telling about these. Neither Timothy, nor any Christian, is to shrink from openly espousing the (often unpopular) cause of the Crucified, or from publicly declaring their sympathy with its hated martyrs.[28] Jesus Christ is here designated as "Lord," a term of deity

---

[27] It is difficult to decide whether it is a subjective genitive ('testimony borne by our Lord') or an objective genitive ('testimony about our Lord').

[28] "We would not hesitate to read a newspaper on a bus, but few of us would have the courage

that was learned from the lips of Jesus Himself (John 13:13; cp. notes at 2 Timothy 1:2).   As he warns Timothy not to be ashamed of Christ, he also reminds Timothy who Christ is; He is the "Lord."

Or of me His prisoner – Paul was imprisoned in Rome, his second Roman imprisonment,[29] as he writes this letter to Timothy.   When Paul calls attention to his status, he does not say he is man's prisoner, or a prisoner of Rome, but rather a prisoner of Christ; "His" refers back to "Lord".   It is implied, perhaps, that all Paul would have had to do to avoid this imprisonment was to have stopped preaching the gospel and gone into seclusion.   But had he done this, he no longer would have been a servant of Christ.   Because of his devotion to Christ he was in prison.   This will give Timothy a proper perspective concerning Paul's imprisonment.   Timothy must not, in any of the days to come, be afraid to confess before men that he had been the disciple and friend of the prisoner Paul, who paid so dearly for the courage of his convictions concerning Jesus Christ.

But join with me in suffering for the gospel – Instead of injuring the good cause by fainthearted conduct, Timothy should rather be ready to suffer, if need be, with Paul,[30] ready to bear the same shame with him, ready to incur sore danger for the gospel's sake.   If Timothy wanted the glory and happiness that went with the gospel,[31] he must be ready to endure the hardships it brought.

According to the power of God – What was to be done "according to the power of God"?   And what does the phrase mean?   Does "power" in this verse have any connection to what was written in the previous verse about "power" (the power of the Holy Spirit, *charisma* or indwelling gift) given by God?   Or, does it say that one can get through persecution and suffering for the gospel because God supplies the means, the "power," to endure these sufferings?   Does it say that God exerts power on our behalf while we suffer?[32]   Or does the verse say that the "gospel" is a demonstration of the power of God (like Romans 1:16)?

---

to read our Bibles every morning on the bus as we go to work.   How much more, then, Paul needed to encourage Timothy not to be ashamed when Paul was in prison for having preached this same Gospel."   Cecil Thomas, *Standard Lesson Commentary*, 1961.

[29] See 2 Timothy 1:17, and 4:16-17, as well as the discussion of the "Place of Writing" in the Introductory Studies.

[30] The ASV reads "suffer hardship with the gospel."   This is a possible rendering of the Greek, but an unnatural one, and not at all in harmony with the context.   What Paul manifestly wants Timothy to do is "join with him" in suffering afflictions that the cause of the gospel may prosper.

[31] Paul uses the term "gospel" elsewhere in these epistles to Timothy and Titus at 2 Timothy 1:10, 2:8, and 1 Timothy 1:11.

[32] "The apostle evidently supposes that they who were subjected to trials on account of the gospel might look for divine strength to uphold them, and asks Timothy to endure those trials, relying on that strength, and not on his own," is how Barnes (*op. cit.*, p.214) explains this phrase.

1:9 -- Who has saved us – In this and the following phrases, so that Timothy will never have any reason to feel ashamed of the gospel, Paul enumerates some of the salient facts of the gospel, and thus reminds Timothy about some of the ways in which the power of God has been displayed.[33] "Saved us" probably has reference to what was done at Calvary, where Jesus offered a perfect sacrifice so that men's sins could actually be forgiven.[34] Paul, and Timothy, and all who obey the gospel, are included under "us."

And called us with a holy calling – Once the sacrifice had been provided at Calvary, the next step in saving men is to offer an invitation to participate in that salvation. God's invitation to salvation is offered through the gospel (2 Thessalonians 2:14). The Holy Spirit works on the heart as the Word is preached, convicting of sin, and leading to repentance and obedience. Whether the "holy calling"[35] is the means God used ("*with* a holy calling"[36]), or is a dative of interest ("*to* a holy calling"), is not easy to determine. Either way, the use of the word "holy" implies that God's call is intended to lead us to live a holy life, to fellowship with Christ Jesus (1 Corinthians 1:9).

Not according to our works – Paul here denies that God's saving and calling us is "on the basis of" our own works.[37] In the next clause of this verse Paul will affirm on what basis it actually is that God saves and calls us. No religious actions that men can devise can ever be the basis of salvation. God himself must plan it and provide the means. Bible students must exercise extreme care when trying to understand what is here asserted in the words "our works." A similar phrase, "works of the Law," occurs at Romans 3:20,28 and Galatians 2:16. That expression refers to man-made religious rules based on some verse in the Law (Jewish *Halakhah*).[38] By parity of reasoning, and by the very context here in 2

---

[33] If verse 8 spoke of the power of God to sustain man in the face of all trials and afflictions, then this verse is intended to show that power is proved by the fact that God has had power to save man from the beginning. As long as we remain in the fold of Jesus Christ as people of His kingdom, we are saved, for God "has delivered us from the power of darkness and has transferred us into the kingdom of his dear Son" (Colossians 1:13).

[34] As so often in the Pastoral Epistles, God, the first person of the Godhead, is referred to as the Savior.

[35] The words "holy calling" are in the dative case, with no preposition in the Greek. We will have to supply one as we translate.

[36] If we take it as a dative of means, the call would then be called "holy" because it comes from God, who is holy. Care must be exercised here, lest we begin to think that Calvinistic ideas of unconditional divine election and irresistible grace are somehow implied in this expression.

[37] Protestant commentators, in an effort to deny the Catholic doctrine of salvation by "meritorious works," tend to comment at this place that "we do not earn our blessings by doing good works." It is not at all certain that Paul is here even dealing with the topic of "meritorious" works.

[38] See the Special Study, "4QMMT and Paul's 'Works of Law' " in the author's commentary, *New Testament Epistles: 2 Corinthians & Galatians*. The Dead Sea Scroll 4QMMT shows that

Timothy which speaks of God's "purpose and grace," "our works" would be religious actions devised by men, rather than those commanded by God. Similar language, denying the efficacy of "works," is found at Ephesians 2:9 and Titus 3:5. If our explanation of "works" (i.e., man-made rules) which do not save is correct, then a man's faith, repentance, and baptism are not to be classified as "works." Those conditions for salvation have been laid down by God himself. They are not just man-made rules or religious actions.

But according to his own purpose – Rather than our own works being the basis of salvation, God's purpose and grace are the basis. Back in eternity, before He ever set about creating a world and men to live in it, God made a "plan" (purpose) about redeeming men should the men need redemption. See this explained in detail in Ephesians 1:4ff and Romans 8:28-30.[39] Now, in time (Titus 1:3), that plan has been put into operation, and our salvation and call have been accomplished, just as God planned. "His own" emphasizes that the plan is God's own plan, and no one else's.

And [according to] grace which was granted us in Christ Jesus from all eternity – "Grace" is almost equal to "mercy" in Titus 3:5-7, "according to His mercy" He saved us. Grace speaks of God's attitude or intention. Back in eternity[40] before He ever began to create, God looked with favor on the man He was about to create. He determined that He would provide in Jesus Christ – His death on Calvary and His resurrection and living to make intercession for us – the means for man's salvation to be accomplished.[41] If the man of his own volition chooses to surrender his life to Christ, then God's grace is available to that man.

1:10 -- But now has been revealed – God's eternal purpose and grace can now

---

"works of law" and *Halakhah* are interchangeable terms. *Halakhah* are rules like the Pharisees and Sadducees made up for the Sabbath, for ceremonial cleansing, and the like.

[39] God wanted a family who would love Him, not because they had to, but because they wanted to. Having formed his "eternal purpose," He set about to bring it to fruition.

[40] The Greek in "from all eternity" is *pro chronōn aiōniōn*, and it probably has the same meaning as *pro katabolēs kosmou*, "before the foundation of the world," in Ephesians 1:4, for the general context is the same. We say "probably" because the same phrase used here in 2 Timothy also occurs in Romans 16:25 and in Titus 1:2 (the time indicated in Titus is after the creation of men). Putting all the passages together in which a similar phrase occurs – and there are many listed, for example in *Pulpit Commentary, in loc.* – and adverting to the classical meaning of *aiōn* and its Latin equivalent, *aevum*, a "lifetime," we seem to arrive at a primary meaning of *aiōn* as being a generation, and then any long period of time analogous to a man's lifetime. Hence *chronoi aiōnioi* would be times made up of successive generations, and *pro chronōn aiōniōn* would mean at the very beginning of the times which consist of human generations. *Pulpit Commentary* then suggests this expression may allow room for the different ages (*aiōnes*) or dispensations we sometimes speak of -- Patriarchal, Mosaic, Christian (cp. 1 Timothy 1:17).

[41] "Which" is feminine, and both "purpose" and "grace" are feminine, and both can be antecedents. Both were "granted" in Christ Jesus.

be clearly seen. In Old Testament ages they were somewhat hidden from men, but since Calvary they are clearly revealed. Compare Ephesians 3:1-12.

By the appearing of our Savior Christ Jesus – Paul likely has the first coming of Jesus in his mind at this place.[42] The word "appearing" (*epiphaneias*) is a word which the Jews repeatedly used of the great saving manifestations of God. The Greeks used it of the accession of a new emperor to his throne. Both ideas are true of Jesus' first coming to the world – it was God's great saving manifestation, and it was the beginning of the rule of Christ. Jesus' "appearing" includes more than His birth. His whole mission, including the death, resurrection, and coronation are included. In these we are able to see clearly both God's purpose and His grace. Paul often refers to Jesus as "Savior" in his letters (see comments at 1 Timothy 1:1).

Who abolished death – It was at Jesus' first coming that he rendered powerless him who had the power of death, namely, the devil (Hebrews 2:14). *Katergeō* means to put out of commission, render inoperative. The death that Jesus conquered can be either physical death, spiritual death, or the second death. All have been rendered harmless to the Christian. Of course, physical death for mankind is not yet eliminated from the world, but all men will one day be raised from the dead, so physical death is conquered (1 Corinthians 15:22ff). Spiritual death, the result of committing sin, is overcome, and even in this life men can "rise to walk in newness of life." And only the unrepentant and wicked will be cast into the lake of fire. Christ has abolished death!

And brought life and immortality to light through the gospel – "Life" is the abundant life, true life in its highest and completest sense.[43] "Immortality" (*aphtharsia*) means incorruption, and is a word that is applied to the body at 1 Corinthians 15:42 and Romans 2:7.[44] "Brought to light" means that the ideas of "life" and "incorruption" have had light thrown on them; they are illuminated so they can be better seen and understood. Before Christ came, "life" and "incor-

---

[42] It is probable that in most passages where the Greek word used here for "appearing" occurs, it refers to the second coming of Christ. However, in this passage, it clearly refers to His first coming. The related verb meaning "to appear" was used in a similar sense in Titus 2:11 and 3:4.

[43] Other references to this "life" include Ephesians 2:18 where Gentiles were alienated from the life of God, Romans 8:2,6 which speak of life in Christ Jesus, and 2 Corinthians 2:14-16 where to be saved is to live. For a full description of the abolition of death and the introduction of eternal life in its stead through the death and resurrection of Jesus, see Romans 5 and 6, especially 6:8-11.

[44] In three other epistles Paul uses this word for "immortality" or "incorruption," but more often he uses the word "resurrection" to signify life after death. Resurrection emphasizes the raising of the body, while this word emphasizes the non-decaying nature of the new body. Bible students should be aware that certain teachers of annihilationism use this verse in 2 Timothy to prove that only the redeemed have immortality. For more information on this, consult the study "Is Man Immortal?" included in this commentary at the close of comments on 1 Timothy 6.

ruption" were subjects about which men were in the dark, so to speak.[45] Christ
has illuminated them so they are as bright as day.   What was not clearly revealed
in the Old Testament is now made clear and plain by the gospel, which both
declares the death and the resurrection of Christ, and calls us to share in their
benefits.   The kind of glorified body He now has and the sharing of the presence
of God which Jesus now enjoys are what His visit to earth has shown to be
possible for us all.[46]

1:11 -- For which – That is, to preach the gospel, referred to in the previous verse.
In an effort to further encourage Timothy, Paul now gives his own example of not
being ashamed of the gospel.

I was appointed a preacher and an apostle and a teacher – Having pointed out
what the purpose and grace of God has done for us all through Jesus Christ, Paul
now adds his own word of personal testimony.   He has a special relationship to
the gospel that not all men are privileged to have.   He has been called to several
different tasks: preacher, apostle, teacher.[47]   These three terms are but different
aspects of the ministry Paul was called to perform.   He is privileged to act as a
preacher, a "herald" who proclaims the good news, delivering the message from
the King, just as the King gave it to him, with no additions or subtractions.   He
was an authorized messenger for the King.   He had been commissioned as an
"apostle,"[48] an ambassador, missionary, envoy, one who has special tasks of
leadership and guidance, one who represents another kingdom to the country in

[45] Remember the trouble the Jews had trying to ascertain the Biblical teaching about resurrection when all they had were the (not very clear) teachings of the Old Testament to go by (Matthew 22:23ff).   Now that Christ has risen and the gospel is preached, the somewhat nebulous information men had about life and immortality has given way to much clearer concepts.   No longer is man's knowledge somewhat obscure at best.   It now has fact and truth behind it.

[46] Certain editions of the Greek text (including Nestle-Aland 26) and certain English versions in recent years have set verses 9 and 10 in verse form, as if it were a statement from some other source that Paul simply quotes.   Other editions of the Greek text (for example, UBSGNT) do not treat these as a quotation, but as Paul's own composition in the course of his argument.   What is discouraging and disheartening is to read the number of authors who think this lofty designation of Jesus the Christ is simply some uninspired song or verse included by the writer of 2 Timothy, along with the concomitant implication that the lofty ideas are likely false.   How foolish to talk about the "power of God" in verse 8, and then to treat verses 9 and 10 in such a way as to deny He has any such power at all!

[47] The same three words were used at 1 Timothy 2:7.   It was noted there how the higher office includes the functions of the lower.   The KJV has likely interpolated the words "of the Gentiles" after "teacher" here in 2 Timothy because that is the way the phrase reads in 1 Timothy.   The better and older manuscripts of 2 Timothy do not include the extra phrase found in the TR and KJV.

[48] There is likely reference to his calling to be an apostle to the Gentiles, Romans 11:13; Galatians 2:7-9; Acts 26:16,17.   The passive voice verb "appointed" causes the reader to intuitively grasp that "by God" or "by Christ" is to be understood.   While some men might be "apostles of churches" (2 Corinthians 8:23), Paul was an apostle in the special sense of one directly called by Christ.

which he is stationed. And Paul was made a "teacher," ready to impart instruction about things pertaining to salvation, such as the glory and grace of God and the necessity of faith and obedience in man.

1:12 -- For this reason – Namely, because he had been appointed preacher, apostle, and teacher.

I also suffer these things – The reason for all his present sufferings[49] – the prison, the chains, the solitude, the hate of so many – is to be found in his fulfilling the task to which Christ had called him.[50]   If we translate *kai* as "also," then this verse says that sufferings were included in his appointment to be an apostle ("I will show him how many things he must suffer," Acts 9:16).

But I am not ashamed – Here is the reason Paul touches on his fortunes and situation. When Timothy is tempted to be embarrassed about being a preacher and a friend of Paul's, let him think of Paul and of Paul's sufferings, and Paul's reason for courage in the midst of difficult circumstances. Though Paul's involvement in spreading the gospel had entailed suffering, there is no sense of regret or repining, only a sense of joyous confidence in the One whom he has come to know intimately and trust completely. What he was asking Timothy to do (verse 8) was something he was actually doing himself, without any wavering or hesitation or misgiving as to the result.

For I know whom I have believed – Paul gives a two-fold reason why he is not ashamed. First, he knows Christ, and second (next clause), he is convinced what Christ is able to do for him. Commentators do not agree on the identification of the one "whom" Paul knows and believes.[51]   Some think it refers to God the Father, and they have Paul stressing the fact that he knows God personally, on the basis of a close fellowship with Him. Others (with whom we tend to agree) think it refers to Jesus Christ, who appeared to Paul on the Damascus Road and several times since. Paul knows Jesus personally! "Believed" is a perfect tense verb. It is something Paul has done for a long time and still continues to do. He trusts

---

[49] "Suffer" is a present tense verb and points to what Paul was experiencing even as he wrote.

[50] The punctuation of the text has some bearing on the meaning. Several Greek Testaments and English versions place a comma at the end of verse 11 and put a period in the middle of verse 12 after "I suffer these things." They think everything from verse 8 to the middle of verse 12 is one long sentence. They then begin a new thought with the new sentence starting in the middle of verse 12. The comments in this place are based on the punctuation found in the NASB.

[51] Some have supposed that "whom" is a reference to Timothy, and that the rest of the verse expresses Paul's conviction that Timothy will be able to guard the "deposit" (gospel) that he has entrusted to Timothy. They have Paul preparing for his last long journey, and therefore depositing his valuables with a friend before the journey begins. However, since both God and Christ are mentioned in the preceding verses, it is likely that the antecedent of "whom" is one of those persons. Christ is the nearer antecedent, and is likely the One "whom" Paul knows believes and trusts.

Christ implicitly.

And I am convinced that He is able to guard what I have entrusted to Him –
"Convinced" is also a perfect tense verb. This is something of which Paul has
been convinced for a long time. Commentators differ over the interpretation of
"what I have entrusted." Literally the phrase is "my deposit." Is this deposit the
responsibility that Christ has entrusted to Paul[52] in carrying the gospel to the
world?[53] Or is it Paul's very soul and salvation which he has entrusted[54] to
Christ's care? The latter interpretation seems more likely. And this statement
becomes even richer when we realize that Paul is in a prison cell as he writes, and
is aware that his execution is pending and certain. Notwithstanding that, Jesus
can still take care of me, Paul affirms!

Until that day – If we interpret "deposit" to be something Christ has entrusted to
Paul, then this verse promises Christ's protection for His chosen messengers until
the day of the second coming. If the "deposit" is Paul's very soul and salvation,
the "day" would be the day of Paul's execution by the Roman government.
Execute him, they may, but Jesus still cares for him and assures him there will be
a crown of life awaiting him.[55]

C. A Call to Spiritual Loyalty.   1:13-18

1:13 -- Retain the standard of sound words which you have heard from me –
It was not enough for Timothy to kindle afresh his gift of God (verse 6) or brace
himself to join with Paul in suffering for the Gospel (verse 9). Timothy will also

---

[52] Some would translate it, "what He has entrusted to me" (cp. RSV). Appeal is made to 1
Timothy 6:20 and 2 Timothy 1:14, the only two other places the word "entrusted" is used, as evidence
that this is the meaning here. The truth of the gospel ("the testimony of our Lord," verse 8), and the
responsibility to be a missionary who heralds and teaches it, would comprise the deposit that had
been entrusted to Paul.

[53] If it is a deposit given to Paul, then the verse promises Christ's protection to Paul so that the
deposit be not lost. Interpreted this way, there would be something very similar to what was said in
verse 7, that there is no reason to be timid. Jesus will be there to protect what He had committed
to human messengers. RSV, TEV, NEB interpret it as a deposit entrusted to Paul. See this view
defended in Bernard, Guthrie, Jeremias, Kelly, Lenski, Stott, Barrett.

[54] This is the interpretation of the phrase accepted by those who translate it "which I have
entrusted to Him." This explanation of "deposit" causes us to find the same metaphor used in two
different ways in the same context (verses 12 and 14), but that need not cause hesitation or difficulty.
That it is a deposit entrusted to God is how NASB, NIV, and the margin of RSV, TEV, and NEB treat
it. See this view presented and defended in Alford, Calvin, Fee, Hendriksen, Kent, Robertson,
Simpson, Barclay, Knight.

[55] It is true that "that day" elsewhere in Paul's letters refers to the day of God's final judgment
(see 2 Timothy 1:18, 4:8), so not a few writers have Paul affirming that Jesus will care for Paul up to
and including the time of the final judgment.

need to keep in mind the solemn apostolic standard (pattern, model)[56] of sound words[57] as he teaches others.   Just how much is included in "standard of sound words" is debated.   One writer thinks Paul has in mind such "words" as the "faithful sayings" referenced so often in these epistles to Timothy and Titus.   Another writer alludes to the "truth content of the gospel message."   Before long in this letter, Paul will turn directly to the special threat to this truth content which they and other Christian teachers faced from the teaching given by false teachers (2:14ff, 3:1ff, 4:3ff).[58]   The least this passage demands is that there are certain great Christian verities which must always be preserved intact.[59]   There were certain facts that were the heart and soul of the gospel message.[60]   Paul identifies his own teaching as an example of the sound words which Timothy is to use as a pattern or model.[61]   These truths cannot be compromised, Paul tells Timothy.[62]

---

[56] See this word explained in comments at 1 Timothy 1:16 where it was translated "example."

[57] "Sound words" is an expression already explained at 1 Timothy 6:3.

[58] In the Introductory Studies to these epistles to Timothy and Titus, we have identified the false teachers as Jewish-Gnostics.   Their unique handling of certain passages of Scripture and their denial of certain basic facts of the gospel would certainly be in Paul's mind as he urges Timothy to hold on to the "standard of sound words."

[59] In a postmodern era built on the idea that all truth is relative, that there are no absolute standards, this passage needs to be emphasized.   "Historically, evangelicals held that God communicated truth through men in such a way that it could be understood and serve as a divine guide for thought and life.   This objective truth was expressed in statements that were to be believed and obeyed by all people.   The Bible was given in historic contexts, so some of it, though true and to be believed, was limited in its intended audience for expected obedience, in which case the Bible itself would indicate its intended audience.   If people followed reasonable guidelines for getting at the meaning intended by God and expressed in the text, they could understand objective, unchanging truth.   Their understanding would bear an adequate and reliable correspondence with ultimate reality.   Although Scripture is infallible, one's interpretation of it is not infallible in every detail because understanding is limited by one's pre-understanding, spiritual receptivity, level of intellectual acumen, mastery of and faithful adherence to the disciplines of hermeneutics (classically defined) and the amount of hard work invested in the effort."   McQuilkin and Mullen, "The Impact of Postmodern Thinking on Evangelical Hermeneutics," JETS 40:1 (March 1997), p.69.   While some modern scholars believe that this older optimism is naive and unwarranted, it is nevertheless the correct approach to the "standard of sound words" heard from the apostles.

[60] Consult the chart (footnote #61 on chapter 1) of the author's New Testament Epistles: Romans, where the gospel facts to be believed, commands to be obeyed, and promises to be enjoyed, are listed in table form.

[61] This passage should be heard by those who are enamored with Redaction Criticism's method of handling Scripture.   That method suggests there are three levels of information in our New Testaments – the sayings and deeds of Jesus (of which we know very little), the apostolic preaching (of which we do not have much), and the beliefs and teaching of the early church (where the post-apostolic church changed and edited and adopted the kerygma as they saw fit).   Beware of writers who glibly say, "It was the belief of the early church that ...."   They may well be denying the validity of those beliefs for us, thinking they were different from what Jesus or the apostles taught.   This passage insists that Paul passed on exactly what he received from Jesus, and that Timothy himself passed the "PATTERN" on, and that faithful men also are to pass it on, unchanged!

[62] In a day when new "definitions" are being given to old Gospel words, to the detriment of the gospel, Paul's admonition needs to be heard.   Giving the old words new meanings – like Christian

The very frequent reference to "sound (healthy) words" in these epistles by Paul to Timothy and Titus, and from which he urges his disciples and successors never to depart, indicate to us the deep importance Paul and the first generation of believers attached to the very words and expressions used by the apostles and those who had been with the Lord.[63]

In the faith and love which are in Christ Jesus – Paul virtually repeats the language he had used in 1 Timothy 1:14. Timothy, in the days to come, must not only hold the correct doctrine. He must hold it in faith and love.[64] The spirit in which the doctrine is held and taught to others is very important, too. The truth must be taught by one who is being faithful to Jesus,[65] and who loves men like Jesus loved them.[66] Jesus Himself is the example of faithfulness and love essential to preserve the apostolic standard.

1:14 -- Guard [the treasure] through the Holy Spirit who dwells in us – Guard the treasure so that it is not lost or destroyed. The word "guard" is used of guarding a place against marauders and possessions against thieves. There were false teachers abroad, bent on corrupting the gospel and so robbing the church of her priceless treasure. There is a difference between "retain(ing)" (verse 13) and "guard(ing)" (verse 14). Not only is Timothy himself to retain the pattern of sound words, he is to guard that same treasure so that others don't make off with it or corrupt it. The indwelling Holy Spirit, received at conversion[67] (Acts 2:38),

---

Science, and New Age teachers do, for example – robs the old gospel of its power to save. Of course, as he declared the message he learned from Paul, Timothy did not have to imitate Paul's mode of presentation (e.g., the raised hand gesture so familiar when Paul got up to speak). He could hold fast the "standard of sound words" without mimicking Paul's mode of presentation. Nor when he went to a different culture did Timothy have to avoid new terms from that culture that might help the listeners understand, simply because Paul had not used those precise terms.

[63] One cannot help but contemplate whether the emphasis on "sound words which you have heard from me" may not have some bearing on the whole question of the accuracy of "oral tradition" by which the gospel was at first passed on from person to person. Instead of being surprised that the "Synoptic Gospels" are so much alike, it is rather what we would expect of people who were passing on precisely what they had learned, even to the very expressions used by Jesus when He taught God's truths and standards of living. Compare 1 Corinthians 15:2, where it is stated as important to "hold fast the word (very expression) which I preached (the gospel) to you." See also Luke 1:2, about those who were "eyewitnesses and ministers of the Word." That word "minister" is a special term indicating responsibility to see that the tradition was passed-on precisely and exactly.

[64] We suppose the phrase "in faith and love" goes with the main verb "retain," rather than with the subordinate verb "heard."

[65] The Christian leader must always be true and loyal to Jesus. He must never be ashamed to show Whom he serves.

[66] To love men is to see men as God sees them. It is to refuse ever to do anything but seek their highest good. It is to meet bitterness with forgiveness. It is to meet hatred with love. It is to meet indifference with a flaming passion which cannot be blunted or quenched or dulled.

[67] It seems better to speak of the indwelling measure of the Holy Spirit, a measure each

will help Timothy to know how to hand down the deposit to the next generation.

The treasure which has been entrusted to you – The "treasure", the deposit, entrusted to Timothy is likely different from the "deposit" that Paul entrusted to Christ (verse 12).[68] In the Greek, the gospel, the "standard (pattern) of sound words," "the sound doctrine," "the treasure," deposited with Timothy is called "the good deposit" (see NASB margin).[69] The precious deposit of the gospel is committed to followers of Christ like Timothy, not only to be kept and guarded but also to be proclaimed. There are two sides to this matter of a precious "treasure." Not only do we entrust our life and our work to Christ (as Paul did, verse 12), but Christ puts His trust in us! And that idea is staggering! The idea of God's dependence on men is never very far from the New Testament thought. Very often, when God wants something done (such as the gospel guarded and proclaimed), He has to find a man to do it, a man He can trust.

1:15 -- You are aware of the fact – The connection of verses 15-18 to the rest of the argument is debated. Some think this paragraph goes with chapter 1, and gives examples of those who were ashamed, and of one who was not. If this is the connection, then Paul is explaining why he is so anxious for Timothy to guard the deposit. Not all have been doing as good a job guarding it as Paul would wish. Others think this paragraph forms the background to what Paul writes in 2:1ff. Since others (with one notable exception) have turned away, you therefore, Timothy, must be strong in the grace that was granted us in Jesus Christ.

That all who are in Asia turned away from me – We do not know what happened in Asia[70] to cause brethren to turn away from Paul. Has he been in jail once too often? Are they afraid they too will be accused of complicity with him in the burning of Rome, if they own up to being in fellowship and sympathy with

---

Christian receives, rather than to speak of some special measure of the Holy Spirit (e.g., baptism of the Holy Spirit, or spiritual gifts) received by such special leaders as apostles and those, like Timothy, on whom the apostles laid their hands to impart the spiritual gifts.

[68] In comments on verse 12, we've noted that the NASB so translates the verses that the "treasure" in verse 14 and the "deposits" of verse 12 are different. The RSV, on the other hand, so translates that the "deposits" in verse 12 and "treasure" in verse 14 are the same.

[69] Just what the "treasure" was that had been entrusted to Timothy has been discussed at 1 Timothy 6:20, "the faith which was once for all delivered to the saints."

[70] Not all commentators agree that the turning away from Paul was something that happened in Asia (the Roman province of Asia, in what is now Western Turkey). Instead, many – including the great Greek expositors such as Chrysostom – have maintained that "all who are in Asia" is a Hebraism which actually means "all those from Asia," and so refers to certain Asiatic Christians who happened to be in Rome at the time Paul was arrested and brought there as a prisoner. Instead of offering the apostle any comfort or help, they were terrified for themselves and forsook him and fled. Compare 2 Timothy 4:16. The more simple and obvious meaning to be preferred here is that the forsaking took place in the province of Asia itself. Large numbers of Christian leaders, if not whole churches, repudiated any connection with Paul.

him? Comparing verse 15 with verse 16, it seems that in contrast to Onesiphorus, those who forsook Paul did so because they were, as he words it later, "ashamed of my chains."[71] How Timothy became aware of this turning away from Paul is easier to explain. Timothy is in Asia himself, preaching at Ephesus. How Paul learned of the defections that were happening in far-away Asia is not here explained. Perhaps he learned it from Onesiphorus (verse 16,17).

Among whom are Phygelus and Hermogenes – Timothy would know these men and the congregations they were involved with, assuming they were persons in the position of evangelist similar to Timothy's position at Ephesus. But no tradition has been preserved which throws any light on the lives and actions of these men who were once friends and supporters of Paul.[72] That Paul names these two shows that perhaps he had expected better treatment from them.

1:16 -- The Lord grant mercy to the house of Onesiphorus – In striking contrast to those false friends who turned away from him, there was another man, well-known to Timothy, probably an Ephesian, who had helped Paul often. His name was Onesiphorus. Verses 15 and 16 tell us this about him. Early in Paul's second Roman imprisonment, Onesiphorus arrived in Rome (on matters of business?). Having arrived in the capital city, he heard of Paul's arrest and sought him out in prison, in order to "refresh" the apostle. He could have made excuses for staying away from Paul the prisoner, but he didn't. He braved the danger to do as Jesus taught about "visiting those in prison" (Matthew 25:36). Paul here offers a prayer for Onesiphorus' family back in Ephesus (2 Timothy 4:19) while Onesiphorus is absent from them.[73] Onesiphorus' "household" likely enabled Onesiphorus to provide for Paul's needs. Now Paul prays to the Lord (Jesus[74]) they may receive "mercy" (i.e., have their needs met) in return.

---

[71] Since what these men did is contrasted with what Onesiphorus did, the idea seems to be that they failed to offer needed personal help to Paul when they could have, rather than that they fell away from or repudiated Christian doctrine.

[72] It is a sad thing when the only record made of a man, the only evidence which we have that he ever lived at all, is that he turned away from a friend, or he forsook the paths of true religion.

[73] There is the possibility that Onesiphorus' visits to Paul had cost the man his life. In fact, it may be that his death has just recently happened. Bible students who think that his ministry to Paul cost him his life note in support of their supposition that Paul does not offer a prayer for Onesiphorus himself, but rather prays for mercy on his house, who may now be without their breadwinner. The past tenses in verse 17 ("when he was in Rome") seem to say that Onesiphorus' ministrations and visits to the prison in Rome are concluded – either by his death, or by his departure for home. If Onesiphorus' loyalty to Paul actually cost him his life, then there is something strangely touching in this loving memory of one who, in his trouble, did not forsake Paul. And what a contrast to those who did forsake Paul. Even if his ministry did not cost his life, it was still extremely dangerous for him to show loyalty to Paul. That, too, is an example to be emulated.

[74] "Lord" in the previous verses, 2 Timothy 1:8,12, was a reference to Jesus. There is no reason to think it is any different here. It was not unheard of to address prayers to Jesus, as well as to the Father. Jesus is deity, too.

For he often refreshed me – The Greek word means "to cool again." Onesiphorus' ministry was like a breath of fresh air.   Not only did he minister to the apostle's bodily needs for food and clothing while Paul was in prison, but the word "refreshing" could include cheer and sympathy that a visit would bring to one who was lonely while in prison.[75] People need someone to share spiritual matters with; spiritual souls can become very lonely if there is no one like this nearby with whom they can share spiritual matters.   What a blessing, that Onesiphorus' visits to Paul were frequent!

And was not ashamed of my chains – Implied is the idea that there was some personal danger to Onesiphorus as he came to visit the apostle.   Open friendship with a prisoner charged with treason and arson, as was Paul, was an invitation to receive suffering similar to the prisoner's.   "My chains" tells us that during this second Roman imprisonment Paul was kept in chains.   He was manacled to a Roman soldier 24 hours a day.   In these examples in verses 15 and 16 there is an implicit appeal to Timothy.   Paul needs him to do as Onesiphorus has done, and before this letter is finished he will beg Timothy to come to Rome.   Onesiphorus was not ashamed of Paul's chain; neither should Timothy be.

1:17 -- But when he was in Rome – Instead of fear and far from being ashamed, when Onesiphorus arrived in Rome, he went looking for Paul in order to minister to him.   We suppose he was in Rome on a business trip of some kind, for the language does not appear to mean that he deliberately came to Rome for the sole purpose of ministering to Paul.   This is the verse that tells us that Paul was in Rome when this letter to Timothy was penned.

He eagerly searched for me, and found me – The second Roman imprisonment must have been a much more rigorous captivity than the first Roman imprisonment alluded to in Acts 28, where Paul dwelt in his own hired house and visitors freely came to him and went from him.   Now, in his second imprisonment, Paul was kept in secure confinement, and the very place of his captivity was not, apparently, easily found.   It was with no little difficulty that Onesiphorus had tracked him down.   He went to the effort because he was not ashamed of Paul's chains, but rather was determined to help Paul if he could.   P.N. Harrison has drawn a vivid picture of Onesiphorus' search for Paul in Rome:

> We seem to catch glimpses of one purposeful face in a drifting crowd, and
> follow with quickening interest this stranger from the far coasts of the Aegean,
> as he threads the maze of unfamiliar streets, knocking at many doors, following

---

[75] "These must have been lonely hours for the aged apostle in prison, facing almost certain death and forsaken by his friends.   It is difficult for us to understand why God's servants who have given themselves in sacrificial service to others should suffer like this at the end.   But Paul knew that the glory of the next life would repay it all."   Earle, *Expositor's Bible Commentary*, v. 11, p.398.

up every lead, warned of the risks he is taking but not to be turned from his quest; till in some obscure prison-house a known voice greets him, and he discovers Paul chained to a Roman soldier. Having once found his way, Onesiphorus is not content with a single visit, but true to his name [which means 'profitable' or 'help bringer'], proves unwearied in his ministrations. Others have flinched from the menace and ignominy of those chains; but this visitor counts it the supreme privilege of his life to share with such a criminal the reproach of the cross.[76]

"It is not every one, even among professors of religion, who in a great and splendid city would be at the trouble to search out a Christian brother, or even a minister, who was a prisoner, and endeavor to relieve his sorrow."[77] As noted earlier, the past tense verbs used of Onesiphorus' ministry to Paul in verses 16 and 17 indicate that the ministry was a thing of the past when Paul writes this letter.

1:18 -- The Lord grant to him to find mercy from the Lord on that day – The unusual double occurrence of the word "Lord" in this prayer is best explained by taking the first "Lord" in the sense in which the term is regularly found in Paul's epistles (i.e., as a title for Jesus Christ), and taking the second "Lord" as a reference to the Father to whom is ascribed, as in Romans 2:5,16 and Hebrews 12:23, judgment at the last day. Paul can never repay now, not even with thanks, the kindness which Onesiphorus showed him in his hour of need. So he prays that the Judge of the living and dead may remember on the day of judgment.[78] "Mercy" can be requested for a man without asking God to violate His own principles of holiness, righteousness, and justice. Once again it is necessary to pause and consider whether or not Onesiphorus is still living or whether he is dead.[79] If Onesiphorus is dead, this verse would be a prayer that God would be merciful to him. Such a prayer is really a hope expressed that God will remember Onesiphorus' act of unrequited and devoted love. While verse 16 was a prayer that God would bless his household now, verse 18 is a prayer that God will

---

[76] Quoted in Barclay, *op. cit.*, p.178-179.

[77] *Barnes' Notes.* p.219.

[78] Paul makes a play on the word "find." May he who "found" me "find" mercy from the Lord. Likewise, we tend to interpret "day" here in verse 18 as a reference to the same "day" spoken of in verse 12, the day of God's final judgment.

[79] This passage is famous because it is the one generally quoted from among the very rare statements in the New Testament which seems to bear on the question of the Roman Catholic doctrine of praying for the dead and offering masses for the deliverance of souls from purgatory. Among Roman Catholic interpreters and among the majority of the later writers of the Reformed Church, it is common to assume that Onesiphorus was dead when Paul wrote 2 Timothy. Many early church writers, however, held quite another opinion, namely, that Onesiphorus was still living when Paul wrote. The language ("household," "that day") used in this paragraph is not conclusive proof that Onesiphorus is dead, for the household of a man who is still living is spoken of in 1 Corinthians 1:16, and "that day" is used in 2 Timothy 1:12 and 4:8 of people who are still alive.

bless Onesiphorus in the future.   So viewed, it hardly becomes an example of the kind of prayers for the dead (e.g., to get them out of purgatory) that have been wont to be defended by appeal to this passage.[80]   If Onesiphorus is still living, then Paul is praying that his act of kindness will be remembered by the Lord on the day when men are rewarded for the good deeds done in the body (cp. Matthew 25:34-40, Romans 2:7).[81]

And you know very well what services he rendered at Ephesus – Not only during his recent trip to Rome but also at another time in Ephesus, Onesiphorus has on several occasions shown great kindness to people who had special needs. Timothy, who has been living and ministering in Ephesus, would know about Onesiphorus' services.   The passage does not specify the recipients of Onesiphorus' ministry or when they were rendered.   Perhaps before his recent trip to Rome he regularly helped any church members at Ephesus who had special needs of his services.[83]   Perhaps Paul was the recipient of Onesiphorus' ministry. One might conjecture that at some time before this imprisonment in Rome, during Paul's ministry at Ephesus on the third missionary journey, Onesiphorus came to his aid.   Or we might conjecture that after he returned to Ephesus from his recent trip to Rome, while Paul was still in prison in Rome, Onesiphorus sought to procure the apostle's acquittal and release by lobbying the principal persons at Ephesus to intercede with the Roman government on behalf of the apostle.   Or we might conjecture that Onesiphorus, after his trip to Rome is over, has organized a "care-package" ministry to make sure that while Paul is in prison, someone from the churches will continue to minister to him.   In any case, the point is that the memory of Onesiphorus' courageous friendship moves Paul still, and provides just the example he needs to illustrate his appeal to Timothy – lest Timothy become ashamed of either the gospel or of Paul the prisoner of Christ. Paul's very next words (2:1ff) will appeal directly to Timothy.

We have completed chapter 1, with its personal appeal from Paul to Timothy to stay in the ministry.   Paul gave a call for courageous enthusiasm, a call for shameless suffering, and a call for spiritual loyalty.

---

[80] It is extremely precarious to interpret this passage as if Onesiphorus is dead, and then base a doctrine of prayer for the dead on it, especially if this is the only passage in the New Testament which can be found that even remotely touches on the subject.

[81] Another explanation of this prayer for Onesiphorus, one which assumes he is still alive, is also possible. Suppose he was arrested for being a Christian while he was helping Paul. This prayer would be a request that God in His providence will so work it that Onesiphorus will not have to pay the supreme penalty for helping Paul, but that instead he will be treated leniently when the day of his trial comes and be allowed to return to his family at Ephesus.

[83] Because the word translated "services" is the same root translated "deacon," some have inferred that Onesiphorus was a deacon. However, a man does not have to be a deacon to be engaged in many services to people who need help.

II. The Practical Appeal – Portraits of An Evangelist. 2:1-26

A. The Torch Bearer.   2:1-2

2:1 -- You therefore, my son – The words "you therefore" serve to connect verse 1 with what has just been said in 1:15-18.[1] Briefly stated, Timothy is to leave Ephesus for Rome as soon as possible. The work he is doing in Ephesus must now be delegated to others in order that he may accept the summons to suffer with Paul and Christ in Rome. The form of address, "my son," suggests Timothy is one of Paul's converts (see notes at 2 Timothy 1:2).

Be strong in the grace that is in Christ Jesus – After the reference to the Asiatics who are turning away from Paul, and considering what has taken place in Paul's life (i.e., he was reduced to needing the faithful ministrations of Onesiphorus), Timothy is implored to be strong. Is "grace" the sphere in which Timothy is to be strong, or the source where he is to find strength? If it is the sphere, then "grace" might stand for the Christian religion, as it does in 1 Peter 5:12. Timothy is to take pains to continue to be a strong Christian. If it is the source, then grace in this passage may be synonymous with the power and gifts of the Holy Spirit to which chapter 1 has already referred.[2] Such grace is available only "in Christ Jesus," that is, as one stays true to Jesus.

2:2 -- And the things which you have heard from me – Not only is Timothy to be strong himself (verse 1), he is to share the gospel with others (verse 2). Like an Olympic torch bearer, he is to hold the torch high while it is his to carry; then he is to pass it on to others he trusts will do well carrying it. "The things which you have heard from me" would be the gospel, the sum of Paul's teaching about

---

[1] It is also possible that the "therefore" gathers up all the concerns, commands, and examples alluded to in the whole of chapter 1. The emphatic "you" in the Greek contrasts Timothy with those who have turned away from Paul (1:15). At an earlier place in these notes, we have indicated our doubt as to how to outline this material – whether or not verses 15-18 of chapter 1 go with what precedes them, or with what follows them. Some think that verses 15-18 of chapter 1 interrupt the appeal Paul began at verses 13 and 14. They see the appeal taken up again in 2:1. Others find the idea first written in 1:8 ("Join with me in suffering for the gospel") still continued in 2:3ff. If Timothy is to demonstrate that he is not ashamed of the testimony about Christ, or of Paul the prisoner of Christ, then Timothy will have to suffer with Paul (1:8), retain the standard of sound words (1:13), guard the deposit (1:14), be empowered by grace (2:1), entrust the gospel to faithful men (2:2), and learn some lessons about stick-to-it-iveness from the soldier, athlete, and hardworking farmer. We might then begin a whole new point of the outline with 2:8, "Remember Jesus Christ!"

[2] Some, having noted that the verb translated "be strong" is a present passive imperative form in the Greek, are thereby persuaded that "in the grace" is to be treated as a dative of means. "Be continually strengthened by the grace ...."

Jesus Christ.[3] "Heard" reminds us that until just a few years earlier than this in the church's history, the teaching would have all been oral. By such language Paul shows he is aware that his message had authority and a permanent significance. With him, such an awareness has been true from the first (cp. 1 Thessalonians 2:13). After all, his message did not have its origin in men, but in a revelation from Jesus Himself (Galatians 1:12).[4]

In the presence of many witnesses – Timothy had been associated with Paul for about fifteen years. He had heard the teaching of Paul over and over, as he and many audiences sat together listening to the apostle.[5] This same teaching that he had heard over and over Timothy was now to pass along to a new generation, to men who had the ability to communicate it to others. The appeal to the "many witnesses" would tacitly remind Timothy that if he changes anything (like the false teachers often did), there were plenty of Christians who had heard Paul preach who would know the changes when they heard them, disapprove of them, and indict Timothy himself for his failure to be true to the Word.

These entrust to faithful men – "Faithful men"[6] are not merely men who were believers in Jesus Christ. This, of course, was intended, but the "faithful men" denoted here are loyal, trustworthy, dependable souls, men who would not, whatever the temptation, betray the deposit committed to them.[7]   Timothy is to

---

[3] Some suggest that there was but one occasion when Timothy had "heard things" from Paul which he was to pass on to faithful men, namely, the time of Timothy's ordination service (2 Timothy 1:6). The suggestion is made that on that occasion there was a rehearsal of the great fundamental truths of Christianity given by Paul before the elders and congregation who were witnessing Timothy's ordination. It is difficult to see how we may limit the occasions of hearing to but one time.

[4] Paul also speaks of his teaching as something to be held and followed by Christians at 2 Thessalonians 2:15, 3:6-7. He praises the Corinthians for holding firmly to the "traditions" (oral teachings) just as he delivered them (1 Corinthians 11:2). He says that the things he writes are "the Lord's commandment" (1 Corinthians 14:37). He commands that his letters be read in public worship services and then shared with other churches (1 Thessalonians 5:27; Colossians 4:16). Peter will shortly speak of Paul's letters as "Scripture" (2 Peter 3:15,16).

[5] While it might be possible to translate this phrase "the things you heard from me through many witnesses," such a translation would hardly be true. To know what Paul taught, Timothy surely did not have to depend on the ministry of others who heard Paul and then had to relay what they heard to Timothy. He himself personally had heard Paul often enough, beginning with the preaching that led to his own conversion, to know what Paul taught.

[6] A commentator's beliefs about the permitted role of women in the church will likely influence comments offered on this verse. The word translated "men" is *anthrōpois*, a word that usually denotes mankind in the general sense, rather than "males" as contrasted to "females." Those who think the context is talking about ordaining teaching elders are confident that *anthrōpois* here must be used of men, adult males, since the office of elder requires males. They can even point to passages (such as Matthew 19:5; 1 Corinthians 7:1; Ephesians 5:31) where the term does refer to adult males in contrast to women. Those who think the context is not limited to ordination services of elders are not so adamant that women are excluded from the term *anthrōpois*.

[7] Bible colleges are by no means the only way young people can be trained for church

search out men who, as far as he knows, would yield neither to persecution nor to error. "These (things)," which refers back to "the things which you have heard from me," means that Paul wants all that he has taught to be passed on. Once the authority and permanent significance of Paul's teachings are understood, it is not surprising to hear instructions that those teachings are to be handed on carefully by generation after generation. "Entrust" is a verb which means 'hand over for safe keeping.' How is that to be done? Typical of many who explain the passage in the same way, Barnes believed that the whole context speaks of ordination services, so he sees in the word "entrust" a command to Timothy to *ordain* other evangelists or elders after giving them the same summary[8] of fundamental gospel facts which Paul had given to him.[9] In other words, Barnes thinks this command mandates the continuation of a line of ordained bishops and their successors, a succession intended to last down through church history. Certainly, we encourage present church leaders to search out at least two people whom they can enlist and train and encourage to serve in the cause of spread of the gospel.[10] What bothers us about comments like Barnes' is the unwarranted emphasis on the doctrine of apostolic succession of ordained clergy.

---

leadership roles. But whether potential leaders are trained in the local church or at a Bible college, the requirement that they be "faithful men" before they are entrusted with the sacred deposit is certainly true. The American Association of Bible Colleges encourages its member colleges to enroll only "committed Christians." We are about to the place where we agree. If Bible colleges are in the work of entrusting the sacred deposit of gospel truth to the next generation, then certainly those people need to be "faithful men," either before they enroll, or certainly before they are graduated.

[8] Some religious groups see evidence in 2 Timothy 2:2 that there was a "standard of sound words" (something in the nature of a creed, or certain items that must be memorized and confessed) which was the deposit placed in Timothy's charge when he was ordained, and which he must in turn pass on. Consult again the comments on 2 Timothy 1:14 concerning the treasure entrusted to Timothy. It is reading too much into the text, in this commentator's opinion, to state that such a memorized list of items "I believe" is specifically what is intended by these instructions to Timothy. At the same time, there is much wisdom in questioning the candidate before he is ordained as an evangelist or elder, to ascertain whether his beliefs are in harmony with the teachings of Jesus.

[9] This passage has been used by many to give Biblical sanction to the idea that the way to preserve the faith once for all delivered in a pure and unadulterated form is to be found in apostolic succession – the doctrine that there must be an unbroken line of ordained religious officials clear back to the apostles. The Eastern Church, for example, insists that their doctrines are guaranteed to be true because they can show an unbroken line of ordained officials clear back to the apostles, and in the very cities where apostles planted churches. The Roman Catholic Church, too, has guaranteed "truth," preserved in the curia, or the college of cardinals, or in the bishops. We in the Restoration Movement would appeal to the Scriptures as the guarantee for truth, not to an unbroken line or succession of ordained "clergy." There is a succession in the New Testament. It is the *message* that is passed on intact, not that there is a line of clergy that extends back intact to Christ.

[10] Why cannot each Sunday school teacher and superintendent, each elder, each deacon, and each evangelist make it their sacred purpose to enlist and train at least two people to do the jobs they are doing in the church? That way the church will have an unbroken chain of leaders when those leaders are needed. The tragedy and harm that results to the life of the church when present leaders do not pass on the torch must not be allowed to continue! Paul's instructions to Timothy about looking out for faithful men need to be heeded by today's leaders.

Who will be able to teach others also -- Not only must the Christian teachers to whom Timothy is to give this deposit of truth be trustworthy men, they must also possess the skills to be able to communicate the knowledge to others. Once they have been trained and entrusted with Paul's teachings, then they too are expected to teach.[11] And so the gospel is handed down from one generation to the next. The great Christian truths must never be allowed to be handled recklessly. The Church is dependent on a chain of teachers. Each teacher, each current torch bearer, has a responsibility to see that it will be passed on to the following generation. Do not break the chain by quitting the ministry, Timothy! Do not break the chain by failing to enlist someone to serve in your place when your years of ministry come to a close.

B. The Soldier.   2:3,4

2:3 -- Suffer hardship with *me* – The second portrait of the preacher is a metaphor drawn from the soldier's life. The Greek doesn't specify "with whom" Timothy is to endure hardship.[12] Some would render it "Take your share of hardship," leaving the English as indefinite as the Greek. Others would add the object "me," as does the NASB, as if Paul were asking Timothy to follow in his teacher's tracks, putting up with the same hardships Paul has been. The point of this verse and the ones following seems to be that if Timothy is to be true himself, and to pass on the deposit, it will cost him something.[13]

As a good soldier of Christ Jesus – Paul highlights three areas of comparison between the ministry and soldiering. Both must be willing to endure the rigors of arduous campaigns. Both must recognize the impossibility of engaging in military service and at the same time maintaining a civilian occupation. Both must have it as their ambition to satisfy their commander. Barnes notes that soldiers often endure great privations. Taken from their homes and friends; exposed to cold, or heat, or storms, or fatiguing marches; sustained on coarse fare,

---

[11] Shall we understand this charge to Timothy as local or universal? Some have imagined that these directions about handing down the lamp of Christian truth to others were given to Timothy with a view to his leaving Ephesus – the present scene of his labors – in order to join Paul in Rome. In this view, they were temporary and local instructions, true only in Timothy's case. Others understand that this verse contains a universal principle. It is far better, in this commentator's judgment, to understand Paul's charge to Timothy as a *representative* leader of the church, and to understand that Paul's instructions were addressed to generations of torch bearers to come. The runners in the Christian race must take good care, before they fall out of the race, that their torches, still burning, are handed on to the runners who will take their place.

[12] The Greek verb is the same one Paul used at 2 Timothy 1:8.

[13] "Many people have the idea that ministry is a soft job. Preachers are often the butt of jokes that suggest that preachers are lazy and should be ashamed of accepting their salaries. But a dedicated Christian minister is in a battle that requires spiritual endurance." (Wiersbe, *op. cit.*, p139)

or almost destitute of food, they are often compelled to endure as much as the human frame can bear, and often, indeed, sink, under their burdens, and die. If, for reward or their country's sake they are willing to do this, the soldier of the cross should be willing to do it for his Savior's sake, and for the good of the human race. Let no one enter the ministry who is not prepared to lead a soldier's life, and to welcome hardship and trial as his portion. What kind of soldier, at his enlistment, makes it a condition that he should be permitted to sleep on a bed of down, always be well clothed and fed, never exposed to peril, or never compelled to pursue a wearisome march? Yet do not some men enter the ministry setting such conditions? Would they enter the ministry on any other terms?

2:4 -- No soldier in active service – After discussing the hardship a soldier (and a preacher) suffers, there is another point of comparison: neither the soldier nor the preacher should be encumbered with the everyday affairs of life. The picture of a soldier would have been very familiar to Paul's readers, most of whom dwelt under the shadow of the Roman power and Roman occupation soldiers.

Entangles himself in the affairs of everyday life – No soldier on active duty gets himself so entangled[14] in the affairs[15] of civilian life that he shirks his military responsibility. The good Roman soldier was concerned only in the military affairs of the empire; the legionary was wrapped up in his service, with no thought or care outside the profession of which he was so proud. None of these sworn legionaries would have anything to do with buying or selling, with the Forum, or any of the activities of civilian life. This is always a condition of becoming a soldier.[16] He gives up his own business during the time he is enlisted, and devotes himself to the service of his country. The farmer leaves his plough, the mechanic leaves his shop, the merchant leaves his store, the student leaves his books, and the lawyer leaves his brief. None of these expected to pursue such things while engaged in the service. It would be wholly impracticable to carry

---

[14] The word used here presents the picture of a sheep whose wool is caught in the thorns.

[15] The word translated "everyday life" is common in the LXX and in classical Greek, where it means, as here, business, affairs, occupation, trade, and the like.

[16] Tent-making ministries are not totally excluded by this dehortation to Timothy. Paul himself, in the early years of his missionary journeys, often found it necessary to work at his trade in order to support himself or the mission. Paul did not pursue the trade of tent-making all the time, but he did so only when the young churches were incapable of supporting him. In fact, churches and communities that require their preacher to be a tentmaker find that there is little spiritual or numerical growth in the congregation. It is certain that the preacher who regularly must work long hours at secular employment finds that he has little time or energy left to accomplish the needed tasks of the ministry. Paul never intended that his example should become the rule for the church down through the centuries. In fact, he gives very plain directions in 1 Corinthians 9:1-15 that the people who benefit from the ministry of Christian teachers are to provide the teachers with a living wage. Paul's instructions to Timothy, and to us, are that preachers should not become so loaded with the affairs of this world that they neglect the things of God.

on the plans of a campaign if each one undertook to prosecute his own private business.   Grotius calls attention to the "Rules of War among the Romans." Roman soldiers were not allowed to marry, or to engage in any agriculture or trade; they were forbidden to act as tutors to any person, or curators to any man's estate, or proctors in the cause of other men.   The general principle was that they were excluded from those relationships, agencies, and engagements, which it was thought would divert their minds from that which was the sole object of pursuit. Likewise, God's servant must place priority on his calling, and refuse to allow business or home to become a hampering entanglement (cp. Mark 10:29,30).

So that he may please the one who enlisted him as a soldier – Only those soldiers who with heart and soul devote themselves to their military work will win the heart of their commander.[17]   Only the preacher whose loyalty and devotion are preeminently to the person and work of Jesus Christ can please his commander.   The soldier's will is absorbed in the will of his commander; his purpose is accomplished if he meets with the commander's approval.   Nowhere else is it so true that the will of one becomes lost in that of another as in the case of a soldier.   In the army it is contemplated that there shall be but one mind, one heart, one purpose – that of the commander.   The whole army shall be obedient to it, as the members of the human body are to the one will that controls all.   The application of this to the minister of the gospel is obvious.   His one grand purpose is to please Christ.   He is to pursue no separate plans and have no separate will of his own.

C. The Athlete. 2:5

2:5 -- And also if any one competes as an athlete – Paul uses a third metaphor to give a portrait of the ministry.   Athletes were well-known to all the dwellers in the great cities of the empire.   As with the case of the soldier, if the athlete aspired to victory[18] he must "suffer hardship."   Before the athlete ever competes in the games there is a period of long and careful training.   And the contests themselves, whether wrestling, running, chariot-racing, or hand-to-hand contests, all required an exertion of energy.

He does not win the prize – In the athletic contests, only one was crowned as

---

[17] In ancient armies the commanding officer was often the one who was responsible to see that there were sufficient numbers of men to fill the ranks.   The word "enlisted" occurs only here in the New Testament, and is not found in the LXX, but is common in classical Greek, and it means "to levy an army," "to enlist soldiers."

[18] The KJV reads "If a man also strive for masteries."   This is old English.   "Strive" means to contend with an antagonist. "Mastery" is an old English word for "superiority, victory."

winner.[19]   In the Christian effort, all will be winners who strive for Christ, loyal to His rules and discipline (2 Timothy 4:8).   No less than any athlete who wants to win must Timothy subject himself to personal disciplines and self-denial, some of which may be alluded to in verses 24 and 25, if his efforts are to be rewarded by the Heavenly Judge.

Unless he competes according to the rules – This phrase indicates the athlete in view is a professional as opposed to an amateur.   For the professional the competition was not just a spare-time thing, as it might be with the amateur.   For the professional, it was a whole-time dedication of his life to excellence in the contest he had chosen.   The rules[20] concern not only the game itself, but also the months of training – a schedule to keep, a strict regimen to build muscles, and the proper diet to follow.   The application to the Christian preacher is easy to understand.   The preacher's life must be concentrated upon his ministry just as the professional athlete's life is concentrated upon his chosen contest.   Barclay comments (*op. cit.*, p.185) that as the athlete must keep his schedule of training and let nothing interfere with it, and so with the Christian leader.   There will be days when he would like to drop his training and relax his discipline, but he must not do so.   There will be pleasures and indulgences which he would like to allow himself, but he must refuse them.   There will be times when he is tired, and when he would like to stop, but the great athlete knows that when he thinks he can go on no longer, he must go on for another 10 minutes.

D. The Farmer.   2:6,7

2:6 -- The hard-working farmer – The fourth portrait of the preacher is drawn from the world of agriculture.   Farmers work hard!   Remember the idea being illustrated is to "suffer hardship" (verse 3).   The synonym used here for "hard-working" is one that emphasizes the weariness that results from long, hard work.[21]

---

[19] The victor was crowned with a wreath, given as a prize on the day of the games.   Compare 1 Corinthians 9:24-25.

[20] The Greek reads "lawfully" (*nomimōs*).   The reference is to the laws and usages of the athletic event.   The athlete must compete according to rules governing the contest if he is going to gain the desired victory.   The same word "lawfully" was used at 1 Timothy 1:8.   At this place it is a great error to think it refers to the "Law of Moses," as though Christians must compete according to the rules in the Law.   The New Testament everywhere shows that the Law was temporary, has been nailed to the cross, and is replaced by the rules and directives from Christ's own lips.

[21] Once more attention is called to the point being made in each of the metaphors.   Not every soldier wins his commander's praise, but only the veteran who has devoted himself heart and soul to his profession.   Not every athlete wins the crown or prize, but only he who trains and competes with anxious, painful care.   Not every tiller of the ground gathers the earth's fruits, but only the patient toiler.   So it is in the Christian leader's life.   Stay at the job!   Endure the hardship!   Let your devotion be single-minded devotion to Christ and his work!   Live the life you say you love!

Ought to be the first to receive his share of the crops – It is not easy to translate the Greek into smooth English.[22]   Probably what it is intended to say is that for his patient efforts and hard work the farmer is ultimately compensated by the joy of benefiting personally from the harvest.   The farmer must work *first* before he receives a harvest.   The same is true of the preacher of the gospel.   He must work first, hard work resulting in weariness, before he receives his reward.   This being understood, it should encourage Timothy to persevere in his toils for the gospel.   But what "share of the crops" does the preacher receive?   Is there a financial application?   As the local church grows, the people ought to faithfully increase their support of their preacher?   Is there a spiritual application?   Does Paul have in mind the truth that the preacher and teacher always get more out of the sermon or lesson than do the hearers, because they put more into it?   Does Paul have in mind the joy a preacher feels when he sees planted seeds begin to bear fruit in the lives of others?   Does Paul have in mind the time in the future when the preacher's joy will be to see some of his converts walking along the streets of heaven (cp. 1 Thessalonians 2:19,20), converts who wouldn't have been there but for his long, hard toil to get the gospel to them?   Whatever the "share of the crops," this much is true of several of these portraits of the preacher.   The thing that motivates the preacher to struggle or "suffer hardship" is the goal.   It is not a pointless effort.   Like the soldier has thoughts of victory, the athlete has hopes of the crown, and the farmer anticipates the harvest, so the Christian preacher can be very certain after a life of effort in Christian service, there comes the joy of heaven.   And the greater the struggle the greater the joy.

2:7 -- Consider what I say – Preacher, are you thinking of leaving the ministry?   Before you make a firm decision, think over and take note of the point Paul is making![23]   The problem facing commentators is whether it is verses 3-6 that Timothy is to think over,[24] or verse 8ff.[25]   If we take verse 7 with what precedes, then Barnes' note is a good explanation: "Think of the condition of the soldier, and the principles on which he is enlisted; think of the aspirant for the crown in

---

[22] The question is whether the word "first" applies only to the metaphor of the farmer, or whether it carries over into the preacher's life, too.   And if it does carry over to the preacher, does "first" speak of something the preacher receives in this life before he shares in his future reward?

[23] The verb "consider" is in the imperative in the Greek.   Timothy is commanded to consider or contemplate what Paul writes.

[24] Several times in these notes, we have called attention to the problem of trying to outline Paul's thoughts in chapters one and two.   When we come to verse 7, the whole matter of outline is once again thrust upon us.   The difficulty some feel with taking verse 7 with what precedes is why Paul would say "The Lord will give you understanding."   Are not the metaphors rather obvious?   Does it take special comprehension to understand them?   Ellicott tries to get around this seeming difficulty by explaining verse 7 as Paul's directions to Timothy to be careful to make personal application of each of the pictures or metaphors.

[25] The weightier words which follow have seemed to some to be the ones that will require special thought by Timothy and some enlightenment from the Lord before they are fully appreciated.

the Grecian games; think of the farmer, patiently toiling in the prospect of a distant harvest; and then go to *your* work with a similar spirit." (*Barnes' Notes*, p.223) If we take the exhortation with what follows, then the idea is this: Paul has set before Timothy some earthly examples to show the necessity of enduring perseverance in the face of hardships. Now he is about to set before Timothy the greatest example of suffering hardship – the example of Jesus Christ Himself.

For the Lord will give you understanding in everything – Paul suggests a reason why Timothy should think these things over carefully. Paul is confident that where there is careful meditation upon a spiritual truth, there too is known divine illumination.[26] "Lord" is likely, as often in this letter, a reference to Jesus Christ.[27] Paul promises Timothy that Jesus will help him see the force of the everyday portraits, and/or the force of the example of Jesus Himself. When the preacher of the gospel is looking at the hardships and the struggle it takes against the evils of the world, let him think of the soldier, the athlete, the farmer, and be content! How patiently they bear it all, and yet for what mundane rewards. When the preacher of the gospel is looking at the hardships, and the struggle it takes, let him consider Jesus!

E. His teacher. 2:8-10

2:8 -- Remember Jesus Christ – Here is the greatest incentive for Christian service: remember the One Who is the central subject of the Christian message. Right from the beginning of this letter, Paul has been trying to inspire Timothy to the task. He has reminded him of his own belief in him, of his godly parentage from which he has come, the men who ordained him, and the portraits of the torch bearer, the good soldier, the good athlete, and the farm laborer. Now we have the example of Paul, Timothy's teacher, who gets his inspiration from the greatest example of ministry one can imagine – "Jesus Christ!" Remember Jesus Christ, and he will have ample reason to work hard at his own ministry. In several short phrases following, Paul asks Timothy to remember much concerning Jesus.[28]

---

[26] Perhaps a similar presentation of the Lord's help is found in 1 Corinthians 2:14ff where the idea of help to understand the wisdom of God, which was given by revelation (2:10ff) and spoken by inspiration (2:13), is also promised to the believer.

[27] "It is a mark of the exalted meaning of the term 'the Lord' as the early Christians used it that it is not always easy to see whether they meant Jesus or the Father" (Leon Morris, *New Testament Theology*, p.167). Some commentators appeal to the analogy of Scripture to suggest that "Lord" here in verse 7 is a reference to the Father, since He is the One elsewhere who gives understanding (cp. Ephesians 3:2-4; Proverbs 2:6 LXX).

[28] The KJV reads "Remember that Jesus Christ of the seed of David was raised from the dead according to my gospel." The way the KJV reads, Timothy is to remember the resurrection of Jesus. Actually, there are many more things Timothy is to remember about Jesus, not just His resurrection. The verb is a present imperative; it is something Timothy is to think about regularly.

First, keep in mind that Jesus is the long-promised Messiah ("Christ").

Risen from the dead – A second thing Timothy is to bear in mind is the bodily resurrection of Jesus[29] from among the dead.[30]   Jesus is the living, victorious Messiah.   To contemplate Jesus' victory would remind Timothy that he too can share in that victory and glory.   There is perhaps also an emphasis on the work Jesus performed on behalf of others, an example for Timothy.

Descendant of David – A third fact Timothy is to remember is the incarnation. Paul words it with triple advantage: stressing Jesus' true humanity,[31] His Messianic lineage,[32] and his sovereign authority.[33]   Jesus has trod this road, lived this life, faced this struggle, and therefore knows what we are going through.   He has given us an example to follow in His steps.

According to my gospel – This phrase means "according to the Gospel which I preach."   It does not mean that Paul made up what he preached, that it was dif-ferent from what Jesus or the original apostles preached.[34]   Paul's gospel and the

---

[29] "Risen" is a perfect tense verb, and underscores the fact that not only has Jesus risen, but He continues to be alive.   The resurrection was not an event that occurred once and was restricted in its significance to that point in time.   Rather, Jesus Christ was raised once, and remains a risen Savior forever.   The word "risen" is one that occurs frequently in our Lord's own teaching (as He predicted His coming death and resurrection) and in the Gospel accounts of His resurrection.   Paul's use of the word here and in 1 Corinthians 15:4,12, and elsewhere, carries the testimony back to its earliest form.   See B.B. Warfield's *Lord of Glory*, p. 184-196, concerning how Paul emphasized the apostolic message of Jesus Christ *risen*.

[30] "Dead" is an adjective and it is plural.   We supply the noun "dead people" or "dead bodies." Jesus was among them for a while (after He died on the cross).   But he rose "out from among them," the first-fruits.   Paul preached that Jesus Christ died, was buried, and then arose, thereby eliminating any figurative interpretation that might be given to "risen" or "dead."

[31] The thought of Jesus' incarnation would ever be whispering to Timothy, "Yes, and the risen and glorified One sprang, too, like himself, from mortal flesh and blood."   There also might very well be a refutation of the Gnostic (Docetic) doctrine that Jesus "just seemed" to be human, and "just seemed" to suffer.   "Jesus became a man; He suffered as man suffers; He was tempted as man is tempted; He died as man must die.   Jesus' existence in the flesh was real." (Foster, *op. cit.*, p.393)

[32] The long-promised Messiah was to be of the house and lineage of David.   The "Risen One" was not merely born of flesh and blood, but He belonged to the very line which the promise made to the chosen people specified would be the lineage of Messiah.   Compare Jeremiah 23;5,6 (KJV), "Behold, the days come, saith the Lord, that I will raise unto David a righteous Branch, and a King shall reign and prosper, and shall execute judgment and justice on the earth. ... and this is His name whereby He shall be called, THE LORD OUR RIGHTEOUSNESS."   See also Romans 1:3; Acts 13:23; and 2 Samuel 7:12ff.

[33] The prophecies of the coming Messiah indicated He would be of the royal line and would "sit on David's throne."   Paul's usual term for this idea of sovereign authority is "Lord."   Compare John's presentation of the same doctrine (Revelation 3:7, 5:5, 22:16) and Peter's (Acts 2:30,36).

[34] Already in 2 Timothy, Paul has emphasized that the gospel he preaches he was commissioned to preach (1:10,11); it is the "testimony of our Lord" (1:8).   In the light of such affirmative statements, it will hardly do to read "my gospel" as though Paul considers himself the

gospel preached by the other apostles was exactly the same (Acts 15; 1 Corinthians 15:1-12).   The same designation ("my gospel") for what Paul habitually preached is found frequently in Paul's letters.[35]   Some, as long ago as Jerome,[36] have even suggested that the Gospel we call "the Gospel of Luke" may be referred to in this expression.   The tradition is that Luke's Gospel reflects what Paul regularly preached about Jesus.[37]   Thus it would not be out of order to affirm that what Luke's Gospel says about the incarnation and resurrection of Jesus the Messiah is substantially what Paul preached on these topics, too.

2:9 -- For which I suffer hardship – Preaching the gospel has cost Timothy's teacher considerable hardship.   Paul is giving Timothy his own brave example of suffering while discharging his office as a preacher of the gospel.[38]

Even to imprisonment as a criminal – At the time he writes this letter Paul is a prisoner in a Roman jail, confined as an evil-doer,[39] chained up as a common criminal.[40]   Rome took no chances that her prisoners should escape.   They were bound by a length of chain to a Roman soldier.   The prisoner was bound around the clock, with soldiers taking turns being the one to whom the prisoner was manacled.   There was a reason Paul should be regarded as a "criminal," having to do with the burning of Rome in AD 64.   To divert suspicion from himself, Nero had blamed the Christians for the conflagration.[41]   Paul was a Christian.

---

source of some particular brand of good news that differs greatly from what others may be preaching. These comments are intended to call attention to the fact that liberal theology has supposed it can detect a Pauline theology, a Petrine theology, a Johannine theology, and perhaps others in the pages of our New Testament.   This whole approach to the study of theology is misguided!   It cannot be justified by appealing to statements like Paul's "my gospel."

[35] See Romans 2:16, 16:24; 1 Timothy 1:11; 1 Corinthians 15:1.

[36] Jerome's remark was this: "As often as St. Paul in his Epistles writes 'according to my Gospel,' he refers to the volume of Luke."

[37] Luke himself tells us that he got his information about Jesus from others who were eyewitnesses and ministers of the Word, and that he was not himself an eyewitness of the earthly ministry of Jesus (Luke 1:1-4).

[38] It is not easy to determine the antecedent of the relative pronoun "which."   The nearest antecedent is "gospel;" the farther antecedent is Jesus Christ.   Making a comparison with 2 Timothy 1:12, it seems likely that "which" refers to "gospel."   The troubles, opposition, and imprisonment Paul experienced stemmed directly from his unswerving testimony to the incarnation and resurrection.   See J. Oliver Buswell, *Behold Him!*, p.42-49.   See also Acts 24:16-21.

[39] *Kakourgos* (cp. Luke 23:32,39) is the same word used in Luke's Gospel for the two thieves ("malefactors," "revolutionaries") crucified with Jesus.   The word has incidental bearing on the time and place of the writing of this second epistle to Timothy.   This description is ill-suited to the situation portrayed in the closing chapters of Acts, during the first Roman imprisonment.   It does fit with what we know of a second Roman imprisonment.

[40] "Imprisonment" translates *desmōn*, "bonds, chains."   The same word appears in Acts 26:29; Philippians 1:7,13;   Colossians 4:18.

[41] Let Tacitus, the Roman historian, tell us how it was done.   "But all human efforts, all the

More than that, he was a great leader of the Christians.   And he had been to Rome (two years in custody, Acts 28:30) just before the fire began.   Is it not possible that he was somehow responsible?   So Paul was arrested, brought to Rome, and held in chains as a criminal,[42] a political prisoner, member and leader of the sect charged with arson in the burning of the city.

But the word of God is not imprisoned – The "word of God" is used to designate the message and teachings that come from God, namely, the gospel.   He may be a prisoner in chains, and (as he tells us later on in this letter) expecting to be executed rather than freed; yet Paul still could write and pray, speak to his captors – both those who guard him, and before whom he will be tried – and from his prison encourage others to speak.   Surely Timothy, still free, ought to work on with undiminished spirit and zeal.   The thought of his own bonds, likely soon to be exchanged for the martyr's death, awakens the comforting thought, "Though they bind me with an iron chain, they cannot bind the gospel.   While I am here, shut up in prison, the Word of God, preached by a thousand tongues, is giving life and liberty to myriads of my brethren in the human race.   The tyrant can silence my voice and confine it within the walls of my dungeon; but all the while the sound of the gospel is going through all the earth, its saving words to the ends of the world; and I therein rejoice, yea, and will rejoice; and not all the legions of Rome can take this joy from me."[43]   That the gospel should prosper was the great matter.   His own imprisonment was of comparatively little consequence.   What may befall us is of secondary importance.   The grand thing is the triumph of the truth on earth.   And well may we bear privations and sorrows, if the gospel moves on in triumph!   Tertullian gives testimony that he was drawn to investigate further the message of the Christians because he saw the way Christians died.   The messengers may be executed and buried, but the gospel is not buried with them!

---

lavish gifts of the emperor, and the propitiations of the gods did not banish the sinister belief that the conflagration was the result of an order [from Nero].   Consequently, to get rid of the report, Nero fastened the guilt and inflicted the most exquisite tortures on a class hated for their abominations, called Christians by the populace." *Annals*, 15:44.

[42] Tradition has it that late in their lives, both the apostles Peter and Paul were held in the Mamertine Prison at Rome.   The place is still shown to tourists as the place where they were confined.   The Mamertine prisons are of great antiquity.   They consisted of two compartments, one over the other, built with large, uncemented stones.   There was no entrance to either, except by a small aperture in the roof, and by a small hole in the upper floor, leading to the cell below, without any staircase in either (an entry into the upper cell has now been made so tourists can view and enter the lower through the opening).   The upper room is about 27 feet by 20 feet, and the lower one is elliptical and measures about 20 feet by 10 feet.   In the lower one is a small spring, which tourists are told arose at the command of Peter, to enable him to have water to baptize his keepers and fellow prisoners.   No certain reliance can be placed on any part of this tradition, though there is no improbability of the apostles converting some of their jailers.

[43] Hervey, *Pulpit Commentary*, p.20.

2:10 -- For this reason – This expression may look back to what was just said. When you remember Jesus Christ, and that the Word of God cannot be confined by chains, he just goes on sharing it. Perhaps this verse looks forward to what follows.[44] No hardship is considered too great when the blessing of those who are the chosen of God is involved. Endurance means more than not complaining, more than bearing up under adversity. It means carrying on despite all the obstacles that are put in the way.

I endure all things – The cognate noun *hupomonē* for patience, so frequently attributed to the suffering saints of God, means patience under trials, putting up with things. Like a faithful soldier at his post, Paul would bear up with a quiet, patient courage against suffering. Paul has been doing what he was urging Timothy to do, suffering hardship for the gospel. Paul says he could "endure" because he was certain that what he was going through would in the end be a help to other people. There was a purpose behind his behavior. He was suffering to make it possible for others to have the opportunity to hear and believe, and to have an example of encouragement when the way becomes hard.

For the sake of those who are chosen – The word translated "chosen" is also sometimes translated "elect." Briefly, as far as salvation[45] is concerned, the doctrine of election is that back in eternity God *chose* that those who were "in Christ" would be saved, and those who were not in Christ would be lost. The question has been asked whether the "elect" for whom the apostle endured his sufferings were, when he wrote these words, already believers. If they were already believers, then Paul views his own sufferings and hardship as an example for others to emulate. Those who have already been called and responded to the invitation to follow Christ would be in need of encouragement and strengthening along the road of trials. Paul is going to be whatever encouragement he can be. If they were not already believers, but would become such if only they had the opportunity to hear, then Paul views his own sufferings and hardship simply as part of the price he gladly pays to give people the opportunity to hear and obey.[46] Timothy must understand that Paul's suffering is a suffering on behalf of others, just as Christ loved the church and gave himself for her (Ephesians 5:25-27).

---

[44] Some appeal to 1 Timothy 1:16 and Philemon 15 where "for this reason" clearly refers to the words that follow, and insist those are a model to understanding this verse in 2 Timothy.

[45] God also chooses people for service when He has a special job He wants done. For example, in Old Testament times the Jews were the "chosen people," chosen to be the channel through whom the knowledge of Jehovah was kept alive in the world, and through whom Messiah would come into the world.

[46] Of course, Calvin found his own peculiar doctrine of the unconditional election of certain individuals to salvation confirmed in this verse. Those who reject the doctrine of unconditional election or reprobation take the "election" to be in a potential sense, similar to how Acts 18:10 ("I have many people in this city") is understood.

Paul was committed to enduring suffering if that was what was required so that others might hear and believe!

That they also may obtain the salvation which is in Christ Jesus – This clause gives the purpose in view behind Paul's endurance. "They also" – in effect, "they as well as I" – shows that Paul has not only his own salvation but also the salvation of others in view. Although man is unable to earn salvation, this is another passage of Scripture that indicates man must do something to accept or "attain" or "obtain" the salvation that God makes available in Jesus Christ.[47] If the "chosen (elect)" are already Christians, then "salvation" is the ultimate entrance into heaven,[48] and the thing that must be done by the elect is to be faithful until death. Paul is modeling that truth for others to copy. If the "chosen (elect)" are not yet converts, then "salvation" is the initial deliverance from the guilt and penalty of sin, and the thing that must be done if they would become one of the "chosen" is to hear and obey the gospel. Paul will do whatever he can, even if it means suffering hardship, to give lost men that opportunity.[49]

And with it eternal glory – Defining what all is involved in "eternal glory" is not easy. Bernard Ramm has given us a delightful volume, *Them He Glorified!* (Grand Rapids: Eerdmans, 1963). Among other things, "eternal glory" includes the resurrection body and all the blessings of the New Jerusalem, the New Heavens, and the New Earth.[50] Eternal glory is the end, the goal of the salvation which is in Christ Jesus. This it is which the apostle will help others to win, regardless of any suffering it may cost him.

F. The Faithful Saying.   2:11-13

2:11 -- It is a trustworthy statement – There are five of these "faithful sayings"

---

[47] "In Christ Jesus" may say that salvation belongs to those who by their own free choice obey and are thus in Christ Jesus, or it may mean that Jesus is the instrumental cause why salvation can be offered to any man.

[48] Both body and soul are involved in the salvation God provides. When a man first becomes a Christian, his soul is saved; when the second coming of Christ occurs and he receives his resurrection body, the body is saved. If a person is not faithful until death, both these benefits are forfeited.

[49] There is an interesting parallelism in verses 9 and 10. "Suffer hardship" answers to "endure all things." "Word of God is not imprisoned" answers to "that they also may obtain the salvation." The Bible elsewhere teaches that the Spirit works through the Word to lead men to conversion (John 17:20; 1 Peter 1:18ff).

[50] Because "eternal glory" seems to be something distinct from the "salvation" spoken of earlier in this verse, not a few writers opt for the view that the "elect" are not yet believers, and have before them both the prospect of present deliverance from sin, and glory in the future life, too.

in the Pastoral Epistles.[51]   They were short summaries of Christian doctrine, memorized by believers in order to have a content to share when they were involved in personal evangelism, especially in the absence of a personal copy of the New Covenant Scriptures.   This one deals with the fact that all believers are aware of the fact that they must endure for Christ.[52]   Timothy is being reminded of the truths contained in this saying since they will prove to be a good motivation for his suffering hardship in order to continue in the ministry.

For if we died with Him, we shall also live with him – This line reminds us of what Paul wrote at Romans 6:8, "Now if we have died with Christ, we believe that we shall also live with Him."   Both passages speak concerning the death of the individual as he is baptized into Christ and puts on Christ: "For if we have become united with Him in the likeness of His death, certainly we shall also be in the likeness of his resurrection" (Romans 6:5).[53]   Perhaps we can understand Paul's reason for writing this first line to be this:[54]   the reason many recoil from "suffer(ing) hardship" is because they have never died with Him or risen to walk in newness of life.   People like Paul and Timothy, who have risen to walk in newness of life have that as a motive for faithful service!

---

[51] See 1 Timothy 1:15, 3:1, 4:9; and Titus 3:8.   In the comments at 1 Timothy 1:15 the matter has been discussed of whether or not these faithful sayings were quotations of a Christian hymn well known to the church in the 1st century, or whether Paul composed these lines as he wrote this letter.   Almost all commentators call attention to the overall balanced structure of verses 11-13 (each line begins with an "if" clause, the first two conclusion clauses are worded somewhat alike, so are the last two), and offer suggestions to explain such a structure.

[52] This comment presupposes that the actual words of the "faithful saying" occur in the verses to follow.   Some writers, thinking that "For" is a peculiar way to introduce the actual faithful saying have tried to find the content of the "saying" in one of the preceding verses (e.g., verse 8 or verse 10 or verses 4-11), but the effort has not proven satisfactory.   Commentators cannot even agree on whether verse 13 was part of the faithful saying, or whether verse 13 was added as a climax to drive home the point.   Barrett, Lenski, and Guthrie regard all of verses 11b-13 as the faithful saying, as do the translators of the NASB.

[53] Some suppose that Paul, as he and other Christians were facing physical death for their faith, turned his thoughts to the life with Jesus that they would have in a new way after their martyrdom. Spence (*op. cit.*, p.300), for example, appeals to 1 Corinthians 15:31 as being parallel.   There Paul, speaking of apostolic suffering incurred because of his belief in the resurrection, writes, "I die daily." Spence then adds that the meaning is still further illustrated in 2 Corinthians 4:10 where we read how Paul and his companions were always "carrying about in the body the dying of Jesus."   While it is certainly true that the apostles and preachers had given themselves up to a life that involved exposure to sufferings, bitter enmity, cruel persecutions, and even death, nevertheless, in this commentator's opinion, comments about such physical sufferings should be saved for our comments on verse 12ff.

[54] Attempts to explain the "for" with which this line begins include: (1) Translate it "namely," so that it emphasizes what follows.   (2) The word occurred in the hymn Paul is quoting and he just picked it up and included it.   (Some even suggest the early words of verse 8 are also part of the hymn.)   (3) The "for" introduces a reason why Paul suffers hardship and endures all things for the gospel's sake.   (4) The "for" introduces a reason why Timothy should suffer hardship (verse 4).

2:12 -- If we endure – The faithful saying continues with this stirring declaration about how we live for Christ once we have become dead to sin and live to walk in newness of life. "Endure" is the same word we have had before, as in verse 10, where Paul said "I endure all things." As distinguished from the aorist tense in "died," mark the present tense verb "endure." It betokens the patient continuance in endurance under difficulties and tests.

We shall also reign with Him – This second line of the faithful saying is similar to Romans 8:17. How can a believer in Christ shrink from suffering, or whatever else "endure" may involve, when he knows what the glorious consequences of faithfulness will be? If we endure in this life, we shall, in the life to come, *reign* with Him; it is more than just *live* with Him. See Romans 5:17, 8:17; 1 Corinthians 4:8; and Revelation 1:6, where Jesus is especially spoken of as having made us "kings." See also Luke 19:11ff where the faithful servants are made "rulers" over cities. The future "reign of the saints with Christ" gives us a strangely glorious hope, a marvelous outlook, concerning the active and personal work with which Christ's redeemed will be entrusted in the ages of eternity to come.

If we deny Him – The third line of this faithful saying turns from steadfast endurance to the opposite kind of living, namely, the denial of a Person with whom we had a prior relationship. We are reminded of Matthew 10:33, "Whosoever shall deny Me before men, I will also deny him before My Father who is in heaven." There is this other side to the words of the Blessed Christ. To the faithful, the one who endures so the Word may be spread, Christ will grant to sit down with Him in His throne. The denier, the one who does not endure for the Word's sake, will have no share in the glories of the life to come. While denial of Christ can be manifest in various ways,[55] in Timothy's case the "denial" would include quitting the ministry rather than suffering hardship.

He also will deny us – We see a plain warning in the closing proposition of this verse. Not only do the words remind us of Luke 9:26, they also include something of an expectation on man's part that Jesus will recognize us as His friends. They are an echo of the Lord's own sad reply to those many who will say to Him in that day, "Lord, Lord, have we not prophesied in your name? ... And then will I will profess unto them, I never knew you; depart from Me, ye that work iniquity" (Matthew 7:22,23 KJV). In the lines of this faithful saying there is a double incentive to remain faithful: the hope of reigning with Him, and the certainty that if we deny Him by not enduring faithfully, He will deny us. And Christ's denial at the final judgment has a finality to it! It is permanent and decisive.

---

[55] Remember Peter's denials of Christ, when Jesus was on trial before Annas and Caiaphas. He rejected the truth of statements made by the maid and others; he denied any knowledge of Jesus; he denied any relationship with Jesus.

2:13 -- If we are faithless – In this context, "faithless" may speak of being untrue to our vows, our Christian profession,[56] a failure to "endure" so that the gospel may be spread (cp. verse 10). Rather than speaking of unbelief in one of the fundamental doctrines of the faith, such as the resurrection of the Lord or His divinity, it seems to speak about letting hardships cause one to abandon his opportunities to preach and minister.[57]

He remains faithful – In the closing line of this faithful saying, Paul gives an extreme warning and at the same time a solid hope. There is a warning that we may fail, but there is also a promise that in spite of everything Christ[58] will be faithful. We can depend upon Christ to be true to His word[59] and remain loyal to His promises. Jesus will keep His promises about rewarding those who remain loyal to His calling, and He will keep His promises about punishing those who deny Him.[60]

For He cannot deny Himself – Here we are told why Jesus is faithful.[61] Christ must always act in harmony with His holy character. It would be out of harmony with His character to save those who were unfaithful. It is impossible even for the compassionate Redeemer to forgive in the future life those who have proven faithless in this. He cannot act as though faithfulness and faithlessness were one and the same. The Christian teacher, such as Timothy, and the members of his flock likewise, must remember that sure and certain are the promises of glory and happiness to those who love the Lord and live their lives to serve Him, and so surely will fall the punishment on all who are faithless and untrue. All the lines of the faithful saying are quoted to Timothy so that they may have their impact

---

[56] The verbs are present tense, and speak of what Christians like Timothy might do or be in the present.

[57] *Apistoumen* could be translated either "unbelief" or "unfaithfulness." The latter is what the context here calls for. It answers to Christ's "faithfulness" in the next clause.

[58] While some treat the pronoun "He" as a reference to the Father, we think the whole passage has had Jesus Christ in view as the subject. "Remember Jesus Christ!" Furthermore, the whole faithful saying has had Christ in view.

[59] There is a passage in Romans 3:3,4 that has a similar thrust, though it speaks of the Father rather than the Son. It says "Let God be true!" That is, recognize that God is absolutely true to His word, absolutely consistent in His behavior. No action of His will ever conflict with His character.

[60] Those who have understood these words to contain soothing, comforting words for the impenitent sinner, or for the faithless Christian who has left his first love, are gravely mistaken. It would be contrary to everything He has spoken to interpret these verses to mean that we may live in habitual and unrepented sin, and yet He will certainly save us (as if He had made some promise to the elect, or formed a purpose that He would save them, whatever be their conduct). Has He not just said that He will deny us if we deny Him?

[61] In the first three lines of this faithful saying, the conclusion clause is the result of the *If* clause. Here it is different. The conclusion clause is the opposite of the *If* clause. So the last clause of the verse gives a reason why the conclusion must be opposite.

on Timothy as he has been called on to suffer hardships and endure for Christ.

G. The Workman.   2:14-19

2:14 -- Remind *them* **of these things** – In verse 2 of this chapter Paul has given Timothy this command: "The things you have heard from me ... these entrust to faithful men."   He now continues his instructions to Timothy by urging him to remind these reliable men[62] of the things he has been writing, perhaps especially the things written since verse 8 about Jesus Christ and the essentials of being faithful to the gospel ministry just enumerated in the faithful saying.   The verb is a present tense imperative, meaning keep on reminding them or constantly give them reminders.   If there is a difference in emphasis as we begin this verse, it might be this: in earlier verses, Paul's exhortations were in the context of how the non-Christian world sees Christianity; now, beginning in verse 14, the context is that of the Gnostic false teachers.

And solemnly charge *them* **in the presence of God not to wrangle about words** – Not only is Timothy to remind these reliable men of things already written, but he is to charge them[63] "in the presence of God"[64] not to wage useless word battles that only disturb or upset those who hear.   The same word (*diamartureō*) is used again at 2 Timothy 4:1.   Timothy was to give others the same charge Paul was giving him, and the present tense of the verb indicates this solemn charge was to be repeated over and over.   It is a very sobering thought to every public teacher like Timothy, that what he says to his listeners is also heard by the living God!   Such a reminder is calculated to deepen the life and the sense of solemn responsibility of the one who would be a teacher.   From 1 Timothy 6:4 we learn that "disputes about words" is one of the special characteristics of the false teachers with whom Timothy and Titus had to deal.   We have concluded that the false teachers were Jewish Gnostics.[65]   What were they doing that could be called a fight over words?   Were they giving esoteric definitions to certain

---

[62] It seems better to think of the faithful men as being the ones who are to be reminded, rather than this being instructions to Timothy what he is to preach to all the members of the church where he serves as evangelist.

[63] There is also a manuscript variation here.   Some manuscripts read *logomochei*, as if this command is addressed to Timothy himself.   But the infinitive *logomaxein* is supported by the better manuscripts and agrees best with the context.   This is something Timothy is to address to the faithful men.

[64] The KJV reads "before the Lord" and commentaries based on the KJV explain that it is Christ Jesus our Lord who is the witness when this solemn charge is given.   The NASB reads "God" because the manuscripts seem to testify this was the original reading.

[65] See the Introductory Studies (p.lxiv and following) to these epistles to Timothy and Titus for the identification of the false teachers.

Biblical words,[66] and then claiming that their occult practices were actually similar to what one reads in the Bible, and that therefore their practices must be true Christianity? Is the Gnostic handling of the "resurrection" (see 2 Timothy 2:18) an example of such battling over words?[67] "Paul certainly does not advocate retreat in face of false doctrine, nor does he urge a silence that would condone denial of Christ or His word; but he plainly advocates that one avoid prolonging a discussion that leads only to further confusion. A good positive presentation of the truth is far better than a labored denial of foolishness."[68]

Which is useless – Such "wrangling" was spiritually profitless to the disputants and their hearers. It provides no food for the soul. It serves no good purpose.[69]

And leads **to the ruin of the hearers** – This "ruin" (*katastrophē*) is a catastrophe,[70] the very opposite of "building up" the hearers. Not only were Gnostic arguments and disputes over words useless and profitless, they were positively mischievous. The wrangling over words unsettles and turns men away from the truth.[71]

2:15 -- Be diligent – Especially for preachers, 2 Timothy 2:15 is a good verse to memorize, and then let it become one's motto for life! The KJV reads "Study to shew thyself approved ..." and this translation has given rise to countless sermons

---

[66] In numerous New Age writings, in certain fringe groups such as Christian Science and Unity School of Christianity, and in the Emerging Church movement, one finds new definitions being given to standard Biblical words. It is only as one is in the know about these special meanings that one understands what the groups are actually teaching.

[67] The 1st century Jewish Gnostics were not the last people who used words after giving them peculiar definitions. Certain 20th century neo-liberal and neo-orthodox theologians have done a similar thing. One teacher called them "weasel words," used to cover the real meaning of the speaker's mind and heart, and yet deliberately used so the listeners (who used the standard definitions for the same words) would not really "hear" the real views of the speaker and as a result over a period of time the listeners' faith would be destroyed. Two common examples of weasel words: (1) "Resurrection" is used to mean that the memory of someone lives on after they are dead and gone. Thus speakers can deny the bodily resurrection of Jesus, and yet say "I believe in the resurrection of Jesus." (2) Another says "the Bible is trustworthy" and means that in his opinion it is trustworthy only in matters of salvation, not in matters of history or science. Yet the listener, at first, doesn't "hear" this limited definition given to "trustworthy."

[68] Foster, *op. cit.*, p.394.

[69] Who of us hasn't been in a meeting where two disputants get to wrangling over semantics? The debate just kills any interest on the part of others.

[70] The same Greek word is translated "destruction" or "overthrow" at 2 Peter 2:6 where Peter is describing what happened to Sodom and Gomorrah when God rained fire and brimstone on them.

[71] There is always the danger that pupils will be worse than their teachers. What the teacher says "may be" the pupil often affirms "is" or "must be." The pupil's audiences are soon distracted from genuine Christianity.

on the need for careful Bible study.   But while careful Bible study by the preacher before preaching is an absolute must, this may not be exactly what verse 15 means at all.   The same word *spoudason* occurs at 2 Timothy 4:9,21 where it is rendered "make every effort."   The Greek word speaks of persistent zeal or earnest effort.[72] In the preceding verses Paul has included admonitions to Timothy concerning his own personal life and work (the torch bearer, soldier, athlete, farmer, teacher, workman), and the need to entrust the gospel to faithful men who will then teach others.   What Paul says here in verse 15 is this, 'Now, Timothy, be very diligent to attend to the things I have been speaking about to you.   Remember that God is watching what you do (verse 14).   Make certain that your work habits are such that you have God's approval in your life and teaching.'   Timothy's handling of the Word of truth is to be a positive example for those to whom he is entrusting the same message.

To present yourself approved to God – "Present" is *parastēsai*, a word that means "to commend" or "to show yourself" to someone else, in order to gain his approval.   Barclay (*op. cit.*, p.198) even says the word characteristically means "to present oneself for service."   "Approved" is *dokimon*, something or someone who has been tried and tested and found to be sterling or genuine.   And just when does one "present" himself to God for His approval?   Perhaps the point is that God is watching Timothy every day, and is passing judgment on Timothy's work every day.[73]   Others would suggest that while it is true God watches our lives every day, the testing and the approval would come at the final judgment.[74]   The rest of this verse gives two qualifications Timothy must have if he would appear "approved" before God: (1) a workman who does not need to be ashamed, and (2) one who handles accurately the word of truth.

As a workman who does not need to be ashamed – How very natural was this "workman" figure of speech in Paul's mouth.   He himself "worked" at his trade with Aquila and Priscilla (Acts 18:3), and he "kept working night and day" at Thessalonica that he might earn his own living and support the missionary team (2 Thessalonians 3:8).   A good workman is known by the quality work he does.   A poor workman is known by the shoddy work he does.   Timothy is to be a la-

---

[72] If you must translate it "study," then think about studying your work habits.   It is the opposite of quitting the ministry!

[73] The idea that God is watching is certainly Biblical.   But whether or not it is the idea in this verse may certainly be questioned since the verb "present" is an aorist tense, speaking of something done once and for all.   The same verb "present your bodies" is written to all Christians at Romans 12:1.

[74] Some have appealed to 1 Corinthians 3:10-15, where every teacher's work would be tried by fire at the time of the Second Advent.

borer whose workmanship is quality. In the ministry, even more than at Ford
Motor Company, "quality is Job #1."   A workman has no cause to be ashamed of
his work when it is being inspected if he has made every effort to do his work
well. It is the workman who has skimped, who has worked carelessly, or who
has been dishonest and so has produced an inferior product, who is rightly
ashamed when his work is examined by others and found out to be shoddy.   Such
shame Timothy would never feel if he went about entrusting the gospel to faithful
men as Paul is instructing him, and if he reminded them and charged them as verse
14 has directed him to do.

Handling accurately the word of truth – The "word of truth" certainly has
reference to the whole of Christian teaching, the gospel which has been entrusted
by Paul to Timothy.[75]   "Handling accurately" is an attempt to translate
orthotomeō which signifies the cutting of a straight line or to cut a road cross-
country in a straight direction so the traveler might go directly to his destination.[76]
The conscientious Christian teacher wants to so present the Word of God that the
travelers on the road may get to their destination without becoming lost or taking
side-roads to nowhere.

What is "handling accurately" the word of truth? Different answers are
offered: (1) In the Restoration Movement, this passage, especially the KJV's
"rightly dividing the word of truth", has been used as a proof text for
distinguishing between Old and New Testaments as our rule of faith and practice.
Such a distinguishing must be made if we would rightly understand God's
progressive revelation to men, since, after all, the Law of Moses was never
intended to be anything but temporary (i.e., it was good only till Calvary).[77]   In
fact, within a passage written to counteract Jewish Gnostics, the Jewish emphasis
on the permanence of the Law would hardly be accurate handling of the Word.
(2) "Devious interpretations" of Scripture are here objected to, writes another.
This, too, fits the context, which has spoken of "wrangling about words."   The
exact opposite of right dealing with the Word might be expressed in 2 Corinthians

---

[75] There is no difference between "word of truth" and the expression "word of God" which Paul used in verse 9.

[76] Other suggestions have been offered to explain this metaphor. "Drawing a straight-cut furrow" would fit the context about the hard-working farmer. If we speak of a bricklayer, we would say "he lays a straight course of bricks." Or if we might speak of a stone mason so cutting his stones that he achieves perfect symmetry in his work, it would fit a context about a building or a temple.

[77] One-covenant theologians, who are loathe to distinguish between Old and New Covenants, object strenuously to the usage made of 2 Timothy 2:15 to support "dispensation theology." John Gerstner has even entitled his book which critiques dispensational theology *Wrongly Dividing the Word of Truth* (Woglemuth and Hyatt, 1991).

2:17 (KJV), where Paul speaks of "many which corrupt the word of God."[78]   (3) Another takes this occasion to speak of the need for careful exegesis of Scripture. (4) A fourth writer understands this passage to warn preachers about the danger of getting on a hobby horse in one's sermon or lesson content.

2:16 -- But avoid worldly and empty chatter – This is a strong contrast to the conduct just urged on the workman who would have God's approval.   In Paul's first letter to Timothy he has already warned Timothy about "avoiding worldly and empty chatter" (1 Timothy 6:20).[79]   "Avoid" is a strong word, and signifies literally to make a circuit so as to avoid, to stay out of the way of (see notes on *periistaso* at Titus 3:9).   The present tense imperative suggests this is something Timothy is constantly to do.   "Worldly" speaks of something not consecrated to God, profane.[80]   "Empty chatter" in this context refers to the useless and profitless discussions or utterances (the word translated "chatter" is plural in the Greek) the Jewish Gnostics loved to use as they tried to promote their false teaching.   How the "resurrection" was handled (see verse 18), saying it is past, is an example of such chatter.   Behind the chatter were philosophical concepts that, once held, robbed the gospel of its power.[81]

For it will lead to further ungodliness – Here is one reason Timothy is to avoid the chatter: where it leads is tragic and dangerous.[82]   As the marginal reading shows, the Greek verb is third person plural, "they will lead ...."   Because it is plural, some suppose it speaks of the false teachers as leading to more and more ungodliness, rather than their empty utterances.   The Greeks had a favorite word for making progress, *prokoptō*.   It literally means "to cut down in front."   It speaks of removing obstacles from a road or pathway so that straight and uninter-rupted progress can be made.   Recognize that the progress the profitless talkers

---

[78] For 2 Corinthians 2:17 to be "opposite" of "handling accurately," the Greek word *orthotomeō* must be understood to have already in the time of Paul lost its primary meaning of "cutting" and as having a meaning simply "to manage rightly" or "to treat truthfully without falsifying."   The word had changed meaning by the 3rd century AD (Clement of Alexandria, *Stromata* vii, for example), but we are not sure it had already lost its primary meaning in Paul's time.

[79] That Paul uses the same language both here and in 1 Timothy 6 probably indicates he is dealing with the same false teaching in both places.

[80] It is the same word translated "profane" at 1 Timothy 1:9.

[81] One cannot help but wonder whether what the Jewish Gnostics were doing is similar to our time when theologians are attempting to interpret the gospel through philosophical glasses, trying to make everything fit the current popular philosophy (e.g., the attempts of the Heilsgeschichte school, neo-orthodoxy, neo-liberalism, etc. to make everything match French existentialism).

[82] Paul has two reasons for giving this warning.   One is introduced by "for" in the latter part of verse 16, and the second is introduced by "and" at the beginning of verse 17.

are making is progress in reverse! They, or their hearers, or both,[83] are going more and more in the wrong direction, towards ungodliness! A number of times in Paul's writings, there is a connection between right doctrine and right living, on the one hand, and false doctrine and loose living, on the other. So we have the latter here. "Ungodliness" is a lack of reverence toward God, or ungodly thoughts and deeds that show disregard for the person of God. The erroneous teachings divert the attention from solid truth, and this is followed by errors in conduct.   What a tragedy!   People need to cease their ungodliness.   The Gnostic words, while sounding plausible and helpful, actually contribute to people sinking further into ungodliness. If you doubt this is true, take into account the case of Hymenaeus and Philetus, about to be called to Timothy's attention (verses 17,18).

2:17 -- And their talk will spread like gangrene – Here is a second reason Timothy is to avoid the chatter of the false teachers.   "Their talk" seems to refer to the teachings of those who engage in "profane and empty chatter."   There is likely a deliberate contrast between "their talk (word)" and "the word of truth (verse 15).   "Gangrene" translates *gaggraina* (from *grainō*, "to gnaw, or eat," "to devour," "to corrode"[84]) and refers to a disease that continually attacks other parts of the body and eats away at it till the body dies.   Another contemporary word might be "cancer."[85]   The word translated "spread" is *nomē*.   The same word is translated "pasture" (a place where flocks graze) at John 10:9.   The word is also applied to a fire which "feeds" upon all around it.   Pastures can be eaten down so close to the ground the remaining grass dies.   The fire burns till all combustible material is consumed.   The false teachings are pictured as eating and eating at the healthy life of the church till all is eaten away and the whole body is killed.

Among whom are Hymenaeus and Philetus – Paul here names two glaring examples of the false teachers he has in mind.   In the words "their talk" earlier in this verse, it was suggested there were a number of these teachers.   Now two are singled out so Timothy will know exactly the kind of teacher Paul is warning him about.   Hymenaeus is also named at 1 Timothy 1:20.   Regardless of the

---

[83] Some have supposed it is the false teachers themselves who become more ungodly.   Others have supposed that it is their hearers who become more ungodly.

[84] Contemplate how a rusted area on an automobile grows and grows.   The hole gets bigger and bigger.

[85] The life of a cancer sufferer may be prolonged for months or years.   A few hours, however, is sufficient to put an end to the life of the patient attacked with "gangrene" unless the limb affected by it is at once amputated.

severe disciplinary action taken against him indicated by that verse, he was apparently still continuing in his error.   Sadly, some people will not repent. Philetus is not mentioned elsewhere; nothing more is known of him than what we learn here.

2:18 -- Men who have gone astray from the truth – Compare what is said in 1 Timothy 1:19,20 ("made shipwreck concerning the faith" ASV) and 6:21 ("gone astray from the faith").   These men missed the true end of "the truth" – the purity of heart and conscience and life available through the gospel, something that is healthful and health-giving spiritually.   Note this carefully.   It is possible to miss what one aims for.   It is possible to once have embraced the truth and then to go astray from it.   It is the usual way with heresy like Judaistic Gnosticism to corrupt and destroy gospel truths under the pretense of improving them.

Saying that the resurrection has already taken place – This is one example of "empty chatter", an example of giving a Biblical word ("resurrection") a meaning other than its intended meaning.[86]   The resurrection that Hymenaeus and Philetus explained away was not the resurrection of Jesus from the dead, but rather the future resurrection of the body that is promised to all ("as in Adam all die, so also in Christ all shall be made alive," 1 Corinthians 15:21,22).   That the dead will be raised is a truth grounded on Jesus' own words (John 5:28,29).   Paul often emphasized this truth, as for example his words to Felix in Acts 24:15 and his argument in 1 Corinthians 15.   Prompted by the Holy Spirit, Paul taught men that the future state of rewards and punishments was intimately bound up with the "resurrection of the body" at the time of Jesus' second coming.   The Jewish Gnostics, perhaps influenced by Greek philosophy that saw the body as evil and that it would be a boon to get rid of the body, explained the word "resurrection" as though it meant something other than getting a new body at the Second Advent. At times, the Bible does use the word "rise" in a figurative sense, when at baptism a person "rises to walk in newness of life" (e.g., Romans 6:1-11; Colossians 2:12). But it will not do to make all instances of the use of the word "rise" or "resurrection" a reference to the new birth.   Yet this is apparently what the Gnostics tried to do.   They tried to say there was no future resurrection body to look forward to, because the "resurrection" has already taken place when you were immersed and came up out of the water.[87]

---

[86] Peter has a word for such handling of Paul's words.   He calls it "distort(ing) Scripture" at 2 Peter 3:16.

[87] More elaborately presented, but still scarcely disguised, a denial of the future bodily resurrection was a characteristic of the widespread Gnostic systems of the 2nd and 3rd centuries AD. The false teachers allegorized away the doctrine of bodily resurrection.   We wonder if the 20th century emphasis on "symbolism" used to explain away everything supernatural in the Bible isn't also condemned by Paul's exposition against the allegorizing by the Gnostics of his day!

And thus they upset the faith of some – Just like the gangrene spreads and destroys everything if not checked, so this doctrine pertaining to the future resurrection of the body, unless checked, would destroy[88] people's Christian faith and life.[89]   Some people,[90] not well-grounded in Christian doctrine, would be easy targets for these false teachers to proselytize to their distorted doctrines.

2:19 -- Nevertheless – That is to say, though some may go astray from the truth and upset the faith of others, yet assuredly God's firm foundation stands unshaken. This comment reflects a decision to treat verse 19 with the metaphor about the workman that began in verse 14, rather than treating verse 19 as though it were part of the metaphor in verse 20ff.[91]

The firm foundation of God stands – In harmony with the decision to treat verse 19 with what precedes, it is likely "the firm foundation" has reference to the truth of the gospel,[92] the foundation of men's faith.   Part of this foundation[93] was the doctrine of the resurrection, the very doctrine the false teachers have twisted as they mishandled the word of truth.   In spite of the false teachers, the foundation stands!

[88] The word "upset" is used also at Titus 1:11.

[89] An error concerning the future resurrection and the concomitant final judgment can seriously affect how one lives in the present.   A poor view of the value of the human body, a poor view of how the body should be the object of self-control, and soon one's relationship to Christ and to Christ's children is badly warped and twisted.

[90] It is heartbreaking to see the sects and cults luring out of the church unsuspecting souls. Many do not try to win the unconverted.   They instead go after those already involved in a church somewhere.

[91] As has been noted several times in these comments on chapter 2, there is little agreement about the outline.   As far as verse 19 is concerned, the decision about which outline we shall adopt also has an influence on how some of the phrases in verse 19 are explained.   Especially is this true of the phrase about the "firm foundation of God."

[92] Several other interpretations have been suggested for "firm foundation."   (1) A number of commentators speak of the "foundation" being the church itself.   Appeal to support this view is derived both from the "house imagery" in verses 20-21 and from 1 Timothy 3:15 where Paul has spoken of the church as the "pillar and support" of the truth.   Commentators then observe that the church on earth is but the beginning of the Glorious Temple which God is building, which in the fullness of time will be completed.   Others comment that the verse means the church stands firm in spite of the waywardness of some of its members.   (2) Some think that Christ Himself is here called the foundation of the truth about a future resurrection.   This group of commentators calls attention to 1 Corinthians 3:10-12 as being a parallel passage in Paul where Christ is designated as the foundation.   (3) Another group thinks we should let Ephesians 2:20 guide our comments here, and find the "foundation" in the apostles and their teachings.   Whatever the false teachers may assert, what the apostles have taught is still the truth.   (4) Finally, another interpretation says that the "faithful in the church" are the foundation, yea, the useful vessels, as compared to those who have gone astray from the truth and those "some" whose faith has been upset.

[93] "Foundation" is used both of the foundation of a building, and of the elementary beginnings of a thing.   The comments offered for this verse combine both ideas.

Having this seal – It was a custom, which dates from the very earliest times, when a building or monument was erected, to chisel upon it an inscription which told of its origin and purpose. Such inscriptions have been found on the ziggurats in Babylon and on the temples and monuments and tombs from ancient Egypt. In similar fashion, on the "foundation" of which Paul is now speaking there was carved a legible inscription containing two sentences.[94] The writing is called a "seal" here instead of an "inscription" since "seal" best conveys the idea of the solemn binding character of the writing. Hervey suggests it is called a "seal" to emphasize the immutable condition of the facts indicated in the two sentences written (*Pulpit Commentary*, p.22).

"The Lord knows those who are His" – This is the first sentence of the inscription graven on the foundation stone. The words are probably taken from the LXX of Numbers 16:5.[95] Timothy the workman has been encouraged to present himself to God for His approval (verse 15). Now we have a verse from Scripture that teaches in no uncertain terms that God does indeed pass judgment on the actions of men; some He approves, and some He disapproves.[96] False teachers such as Philetus and Hymenaeus do not have His approval, in this life or the next!

And, "Let every one who names the name of the Lord abstain from wickedness" – This is the second sentence of the inscription graven on the foundation stone. The first sentence of the inscription is easily found in the Old Testament, but the second sentence is not. (1) Some suggest it is a rather loose rendering of Numbers 16:26, a passage that deals with Korah's rebellion. At that time, Moses' command to the people was "depart now from the tents of these wicked men, and touch nothing of theirs."[97] In this case, Paul would be giving Scriptural precedent to "avoid worldly and empty chatter." (2) Some suggest

---

[94] The demonstrative pronoun "this" points to the statements which follow.

[95] The only difference between Paul's sentence and Numbers 16 is that Paul uses "Lord" where the Greek has "God." The Hebrew here reads YHWH (Jehovah), and that should probably guide our understanding concerning which person of the Godhead is in Paul's view.

[96] "Know" is used in the sense of "approve," much like it is in Jesus' well-known conclusion to the Sermon on the Mount. He is speaking of how things will be in the final judgment. The Judge says "Depart from me ... I never knew you." That is, I never approved of your actions. It is also noteworthy that in the same context Jesus talks about a wise and foolish builder, just as Paul has been talking about a workman and the foundation.
(The Bible student should exercise caution here. Reformed theologians have been accustomed to find in the words "the Lord *knows* those who are His" a corroboration of the doctrine of unconditional election. See the author's commentary on Romans [at 9:14] for a refutation of the doctrine of unconditional election.)

[97] How far we may press the parallels between Korah's mutiny and the heretical activity of Hymenaeus and Philetus and the Gnostics is not certain.

this second sentence of the inscription is a conflation of several Old Testament passages (such as Isaiah 52:11, 26:13) which warn about staying away from wickedness. (3) Still another suggestion is that this second sentence is another of those "faithful sayings" like the five others referred to in the letters to Timothy and Titus. Whatever the source, "wickedness" here includes the teaching of those false men alluded to above, and the lax and evil way of life to which their teaching inevitably led. To "name the name of the Lord" would be tantamount to "confessing Jesus as Lord."[98] No person who has confessed with his heart that Jesus is Lord can commit iniquity deliberately. The two are utterly incompatible. So the second inscription with its "abstain" is an imperative call to holiness. Stay away from such (Gnostic) teachers like Hymenaeus and Philetus! Stay away from the lifestyle their teaching encourages!

H. The Vessel.   2:20-22

2:20 -- Now in a large house – Here Paul begins a new metaphor as he appeals to Timothy to protect the faith.[99] The emphasis is on the "vessels" in the house, and on Timothy's options as he himself chooses what kind of vessel he will be.[100] As archaeologists have excavated 1st century houses, artifacts found in "large houses" (villas) differ greatly from those found in small (one to four-room) houses. It was a fact of life that only in large houses were to be found such a variety of dishes (vessels) as Paul here lists.[101]

---

[98] As they have offered comments on "names the name of the Lord," some writers have called attention to the very similar expression "to call upon the name of the Lord" found at Joel 3:5, Acts 2:21, and Romans 10:13. Whether it be confession or conversion alluded to, the person who has become a follower of Jesus has an obligation to live carefully.

[99] If it be thought a new metaphor begins at verse 20, then it would not be quite right to say that "the purpose of this analogy is to elaborate on the second part of the inscription (verse 19)." What we think Paul is doing in this whole chapter is giving Timothy portraits of the evangelist so Timothy can keep his life headed in the proper direction a faithful servant should go.

[100] The metaphor or analogy is given in verse 20, and the application is made in verses 21- 22.

[101] Here again, any decision made about the outline of chapter 2 affects the comments offered. For example, Barclay (*op. cit.*, p.204-5) thinks verses 19 and 20 go together. He identifies the "firm foundation" as being the church and offers these comments: "The connection between this verse and the ones immediately preceding is very practical. Paul had just given a very great and high definition of the church. It consists of those who belong to God, and of those who are on the way to righteousness. Now the obvious question is this: If this is so, how do you explain the existence of the chattering heretics in the church? How do you explain the existence of Hymenaeus and Philetus in the church? Paul's reply is that in any great house there are all kinds of vessels and utensils. There are things precious and things base. So long as the church is an earthly institution, the church must be a mixture." Think about Barclay's comments. Is there not an undercurrent that sounds suspiciously like the Calvinist doctrine of eternal security? These heretics are still "in the church"! How can this commentator say that? Has not verse 18 told us they have gone astray from the truth? Has not 1 Timothy 6:20 told us they have gone astray from the faith? Might it not have been such an unsuitable conclusion (which resulted from identifying the large house with the

There are not only gold and silver vessels, but also of wood and earthenware – "Vessels" are utensils, dishes, incense altars, weapons, and the like.[102] Archaeologists have unearthed gold and silver platters and rhytons (drinking vessels). They have also found golden daggers and silver forks and spoons. They have even found household idols made from gold and silver. Bowls and spoons were made of wood. So were children's toys. Jars, bowls, pitchers, plates, and storage containers were made of clay and fired in a kiln.[103]

And some to honor and some to dishonor – Paul uses the same figure in Romans 9:22,23. "Honor" and "dishonor" speak of the *use* to which the vessels are put – some to noble purposes and some to ignoble.[104] Further, as verse 21 shows, it is usefulness in this life that is in Paul's mind.[105] To Timothy this metaphor would at once suggest that some teachers (e.g., the Jewish Gnostics like Hymenaeus and Philetus) put themselves to a dishonorable use, while other teachers (i.e., those who handle accurately the word of truth) put themselves to an honorable use.[106]

2:21 -- Therefore – This is the application to Timothy's life and service of the metaphor about the vessels. Since some vessels are for honorable use, one should "therefore" seek to be one of them.

---

church) that led the early church fathers to hold that the "large house" refers to the world rather than to the church? If we begin a new metaphor with verse 20, it saves us from all such unsatisfactory implications.

[102] Some who think the figure of a building is being continued from verse 19 have been wont to compare verse 20 with 1 Corinthians 3:12 where materials used to erect the superstructures of buildings were designated by some of the same terms – "Gold, silver ... wood ...." That passage goes on to speak of the Final Judgment, and it seems therefore to be out of place to compare it with this passage in 2 Timothy.

[103] "Ostracon [plural, ostraca]" (a transliteration of the Greek word rendered "earthenware") is the term used in archaeology for fragments of ancient pottery.

[104] Some writers have supposed the vessels of gold and silver are the "honorable" vessels, while the wooden and earthenware ones are those which are "dishonorable." This commentator sees little to be gained by making this distinction. In fact, it may cause us to miss the point of the metaphor. After all, a golden vessel (say an idol) can be a dishonorable thing, whereas a wooden dish dedicated to sacred purposes can be an honorable thing. What might be better is to note that among vessels (teachers) not all are equal. Some few may be golden mouthed or silver-tongued orators; most are likely to be of more common material but none the less useful.

[105] Neither this passage nor Romans 9:22,23 refers to rewards and punishments in the next life. "Honor" and "dishonor" should not be interpreted so that this verse is made to teach that God predestines certain men to be saved ("honor") and certain to be lost ("dishonor") regardless of how they live. Certainly, when the day of Final Judgment comes, whether or not a man has fulfilled his God-intended noble service or not will have some bearing on the sentence God pronounces. The point of this passage, however, is "usage" in this life, not how things will be in the Final Judgment.

[106] Instead of suggesting that all the members of the church are "vessels" of some kind, in this passage it seems best to limit the term "vessels" to the *teachers*, some of whom serve noble purposes, and some dishonorable purposes. Further, it seems best in this context, having begun a new point of the outline with verse 20, not to speak of these "vessels" being two distinct classes in the church, the genuine v. spurious members.

If a man cleanses himself from these *things* – What "man" does Paul particularly have in mind? Is it the faithful brethren (to whom Timothy has entrusted the gospel message) who are to cleanse themselves, and thus become useful vessels? Is it an appeal to the heretical teachers to give up their erroneous doctrines in order to become useful vessels? Is it Timothy? In the light of the next verse, which is addressed to Timothy, it seems best to understand that this metaphor is aimed particularly toward him. "Things" is in italics, so we cannot be certain whether it is "false teachers"[107] or "false doctrines"[108] that Paul has in mind. Perhaps Timothy is being warned to separate himself[109] from the Jewish Gnostic teachers if he wants to be a useful and honorable vessel. Perhaps Timothy is being warned to separate himself from vain babblings, ungodliness, and the gangrenous words of the heretics, if he wants to be an honorable and useful vessel.

He will be a vessel for honor – This is the same language used in verse 20. The teacher of false doctrines (like Hymenaeus and Philetus) was a vessel in dishonorable use. The teacher of essential and correct doctrines (like Paul urges Timothy to be) is a vessel in honorable use.[110] Which kind of vessel will Timothy choose to be?

Sanctified -- The Greek word is a perfect passive participle, which indicates past completed action with present continuing results. Perhaps there is a reference to Timothy's ordination service when he was set apart for sacred service.[111]

Useful to the Master -- "Useful to the Master" suggests Timothy will be a vessel

---

[107] This view takes "some to dishonor" as the antecedent of "these."

[108] This view understands that the topic of the whole paragraph since verse 14 is the antecedent of "these."

[109] The compound word "cleanse" or "thoroughly cleanse" probably speaks of "separation from." It is something a man does to his own heart and soul, not something done to others, say by excommunication. The reflexive pronoun "himself" indicates that the action called for affects the subject of the verb.

[110] Chrysostom's note on these words is thought provoking. He points out the possibility of the vessel once engaged in dishonorable use becoming a vessel for honorable use, and the reverse. He refers to Paul, once an earthen vessel, who became a vessel of gold. He refers to the traitor Judas, who, on the other hand, from being a vessel of gold became an earthen vessel. (Chrysostom's idea is right, but his use of gold for honor and earthen for dishonor seems to be wide of what Paul wrote.) In modern times, Etta Linneman, a student of Bultmann, a thoroughly neo-liberal proponent, has been converted. She has repudiated the doctrines she taught when she was a "vessel" in dishonorable use, and now teaches conservative Christian views about the Gospels. See her books *Historical Criticism of the Bible* (Baker, 1990), and *Is There a Synoptic Problem?* (Baker, 1992) in which she thoroughly repudiates and demolishes the faith-destroying things she once taught.

[111] Some writers speak of having been cleansed from the defilement of sin, as they offer comments on this word. But it seems to this commentator that this is not quite right, for the word used for such "cleansing" is *katharidzō* (as in Ephesians 5:26), not the *hagiadzō* used here.

his Master Jesus can find a good use for. "Master" (*despotēs*, "absolute owner") is an expressive divine title used of Jesus.[112]

Prepared for every good work – That is, Timothy will be ready to take advantage of any opportunity which may offer itself to do a generous, noble action, which will have eternal significance.[113] "Every good work" speaks of the wide range of good deeds one is called to do as a preacher. People have needs to be ministered to, or salvation to be furthered, and the glory of God to be increased.

2:22 -- Now flee from youthful lusts – If Timothy would continue to be a vessel for honor there is something more he will need to do besides separate himself from communion and friendship with men who, by their teaching and in their lives, did dishonor to the Master's religion (verse 21).[114] There is something to flee and several things to pursue. "Flee" is a present tense imperative and indicates continuous action. Timothy must constantly flee youthful lusts.[115] At the time Paul writes this to Timothy, the preacher is in his early manhood, somewhere between 30 and 40 years of age.[116] That's the age when men are likely to feel most strongly the temptations to covetousness, self-assertion, pride, ambition, as well as the fatal excesses summed up in the 7th commandment. Young preachers will have to consciously work at self-control over all those passions to which youth is particularly liable.

And pursue after righteousness, faith, love and peace – "Pursue" likewise is a present imperative. If Timothy would be a vessel for honorable use, he will have to keep on pursuing (and that eagerly) these positive virtues. Paul nearly repeats the same exhortation he gave in 1 Timothy 6:11.[117] "Righteousness" likely has

---

[112] Compare the use of the word at Luke 2:29, Acts 4:24, 2 Peter 2:1, Jude 4, and Revelation 6:10.

[113] Chrysostom spoke of any emergency which would enhance the glory of the Lord Jesus – ready even for death or (any painful) witness.

[114] The "Now" with which the NASB begins this verse may be a bit strong for the conjunction *de*. Perhaps the translators were intending to treat verse 22 as the beginning of the next metaphor, rather than the continuation of the one about "vessel for honor" as we have chosen to do. A number of modern translations do not even translate the *de*, treating verse 22 as a simple continuation of the thought already started in verses 20-21.

[115] Paul does not actually identify what he means by "youthful lusts (desires)." Some have supposed that the characteristics named in verses 23 and 24 are examples of such youthful desires, but the things there listed are not unique to young men.

[116] See comments on 1 Timothy 4:12.

[117] Paul was fond of listing the "virtues" that Christians in general and preachers in particular need to cultivate. See 2 Corinthians 6:6-7; Galatians 5:22,23; Colossians 3:12-15; 1 Timothy 6:11; 2 Timothy 2:22 and 3:10.

reference to right relationships with one's fellow men or right conduct toward other men. In 2 Timothy 3:17, Paul will indicate that Scripture is the place to look for the standard of such righteousness. "Faith", or "faithfulness", tells Timothy to be a man of his word, loyal and reliable. Or perhaps it means to continue to be a man of the Word, faithful to the gospel. "Love" talks about doing what is spiritually best for the other person, seeking the highest good for our fellow man, no matter what they do to us. "Peace" signifies the absence of contention, the tranquil state of the soul at one with God and men.

With those who call upon the Lord from a pure heart – How this phrase is connected to the rest of the verse is not quite clear. Perhaps it is connected with the verb "pursue," so that Timothy is instructed to pursue these virtues in partnership with other Christians, those who call upon the Lord. The Christian preacher must never seek to live alone, detached and aloof from his brethren. He must find his strength, his joy, his support in the Christian fellowship. Perhaps it is connected with "peace," so that Timothy is to pursue peace only with those who call upon the Lord with a pure heart. He does not have to try to pursue peace with enemies of the cross.[118] The words "from a pure heart" contrast those holy and humble men who serve God without any ulterior motive, with those false teachers who dare to make their religion a means of personal gain or a source of profit.

I. The Servant. 2:23-26

2:23 -- But refuse foolish and ignorant speculations – Here begins the last of this series of portraits of the preacher, metaphors to help Timothy understand his responsibilities as a preacher. This one calls attention to how a good "bond-servant" thinks and behaves. The word here translated "speculations" (*dzēteseis*) is translated "questioning" in John 3:25, "debate" at Acts 15:2, "speculation" at 1 Timothy 1:4, and "controversial questions" at 1 Timothy 6:4. It seems to speak of an angry debate, a controversy. In John's Gospel, written against incipient Gnosticism, the word is used in a context over purification. In Acts, the word is used in a context dealing with a controversy about the need for observing Pharisaic *halakhah*. Does it have a similar meaning in the letters to Timothy, also written against Jewish Gnosticism? Unlearned or uninstructed is a good way to translate the word behind "ignorant." It speaks of someone who is poorly educated in the topic at hand. "Foolish" speaks of being dull or sluggish of mind, and sometimes also indicates that the action is sinful and culpable. If Timothy

---

[118] If this second way of connecting the verse is correct, then there is a difference between love and peace, as Theodoret long ago pointed out. Timothy was to love all, but he did not have to be at peace with all.

is going to be a good bond-servant, he will have to make it a point to refuse to get involved[119] in such angry debates.[120]

Knowing that they produce quarrels – Probably this is intended as the reason why Timothy should refuse to get involved in angry debates. The only thing that heated debates with a Jewish Gnostic gives birth to is conflicts or fights,[121] and such activities never are spiritually edifying. Out in the world, people have enough of these. They should not come to church only to find conflicts and fights there, too.

2:24 -- And the Lord's bond-servant – While there is a sense in which every Christian is a servant of Christ,[122] it is also true that the term seems to be used especially to describe those whose office it is to preach the gospel – either as apostles[123] or as evangelists.[124] In this context it seems likely that the term is used to designate those "teachers" to whom Timothy entrusts the deposit of the gospel, as well as to Timothy himself. In a special sense they are Christ's bond-servants. They let Jesus determine their conduct and behavior.

Must not be quarrelsome – It appears Paul is instructing the bond-servant Timothy and other preachers how to minister and relate to people caught up in the error of the false teachers. The preacher just "must"[125] not be quarrelsome! This is a conclusive exhortation against engaging in a foolish and heated argument with someone who just wants to fight. Not a few writers call attention to the example of the Suffering Servant in Isaiah, who "shall not strive, nor cry; neither shall any man hear His voice in the streets" (cp. Matthew 12:19,20). Jesus did

---

[119] See comments at 1 Timothy 4:7 and Titus 3:10 where this same strong verb "refuse" is used.

[120] One cannot help but wonder whether Paul's advice to Timothy reflects a sad experience of his own some years earlier. There was the debate with the unconverted Pharisees over circumcision at Antioch (Acts 15). It was finally settled by an appeal to the words of the apostles. Paul did not just permit the false teachers to freely take over the church, but perhaps he learned that heated debate is not the way to settle such momentous issues.

[121] The same word translated "quarrels" occurs at Titus 3:9 ("fightings [disputes] about the Law" ASV) and at James 4:1,2 ("fightings" KJV). "Nothing can be more emphatic than Paul's warnings against foolish and angry controversies ... and yet nothing has been more neglected in the Church in all ages." (Hervey, *op. cit.*, p.23)

[122] Ephesians 6:6, 1 Peter 2:16, and Revelation 19:2,5 and 22:3 are examples where the word is applied to Christians in general.

[123] The term "bond-servant" used of the apostles Paul (Romans 1:1, Galatians 1:10, Philippians 1:1, Titus 1:1), James (James 1:1), Peter (2 Peter 1:1), and John (Revelation 1:1). It is also used of Jude, the Lord's brother (Jude 1:1).

[124] Epaphras, an evangelist (or minister) is styled as a "bond-slave" (Colossians 4:12).

[125] It is the same word used at 1 Timothy 3:2 when speaking of qualifications for elders. There were some "musts" for them. Likewise, there are some "musts" for preachers!

respond to those who were opposed to Him, but He did it in a way designed to win the hearts and allegiance of His opponents, not just win an argument.

But be kind to all – "Kind" (*ēpion*) does not mean the preacher is a pushover who never takes a stand for what is right. A nurse does not meet the child's waywardness by blows or threats, but firmly takes charge and does what is needed in gentleness and love. So Timothy may point out faults and correct waywardness, but he must be careful about his attitudes as he does so. The preacher is firm and kind, not only to those belonging to the brotherhood of Christ, but as is expressly mentioned, "to all." When it is remembered that we are coming near to the close of the last directions given to those whose responsibility it would be to see that the gospel is handed on from generation to generation, these instructions take on new importance. How does the preacher behave himself before the church and in his relations with the unconverted? "Conciliation" might be a good way to express it. Paul would impress upon Timothy and the following generations of preachers "the great truth that it is the Master's will that the unnumbered peoples who sit in darkness and in the shadow of death should learn, by slow though sure degrees, how lovely and desirable a thing it was to be a Christian; should come at length to see clearly that Christ was, after all, the only lover and real friend of man" (*Ellicott's*, p.309).

Able to teach – The preacher must aim at being a teacher rather than a controversialist. The preacher, as well as the elder (1 Timothy 3:2), is to be an able teacher. When confronting a false teacher like the Jewish Gnostics, the preacher is hardly quiet and passive. He communicates the Word of Truth to them, with the intent of correcting their false views and leading them to repentance.

Patient when wronged – *Anexikakon* literally means "bearing up against ill treatment," "bearing evil without resentment." The preacher must be able to accept insult and injury, slights and humiliations. The false teachers may make slanderous insults against the preacher as they engage in their wordy strifes, but the preacher does not retaliate in kind. He controls his temper, he measures his responses, he keeps his cool when provoked. There may be greater sins than touchiness, but there are not many that will do greater damage to the congregation to whom the preacher is ministering.

2:25 -- With gentleness correcting those who are in opposition – *Prautēs* is not an easy word for which to find a suitable English equivalent, though "gentleness," "meekness," "courtesy," and "considerateness" have been used. There is included in the term the idea of controlled power. Think of a surgeon whose hand is unerring to find the diseased spot, yet who never for a moment causes unnecessary pain. The preacher does not become angry with persons who embrace error, nor denounce them at once, nor hold them up to public reproach and scorn. Without causing unnecessary pain, he goes about the business of instructing and training[126] them. The preacher must remember that he are not likely to convince a man that he is right and the other man is wrong, if he first makes the other man angry; nor is he very likely to do it if he enters into harsh contention. And who is intended by the phrase "those who are in opposition"? Shall we understand that the people intended are different from the leading teachers of false doctrines? Are the ones intended those who have been led astray by the teachers? Perhaps the preacher is to "correct" those who were taught rather than the false teachers themselves. After all, in Titus 3:10 we read how the false teachers were, after a first and second admonition, to be shunned, were to be left to themselves.[127] And here in this very chapter (verse 21) are instructions that the leaders are to be avoided. But the treatment of the duped followers is to be a gentler one. Nothing is said about a first and second admonition; nothing is hinted that these are just to be avoided. The preacher instead tries to instruct them and help them learn like one must teach a little child.

If perhaps God may grant them repentance – Repentance is something a man must do himself. It is not something God does for a man or to a man. However, when we read in Acts 5:31, 11:18, and here, that God "grants" repentance, what it means is that God may[128] give the men time and opportunity to repent.[129] The "repentance" here signifies an abandonment on the part of those in opposition of the wrong course on which they have entered. It is the abandonment of the doctrines taught by the Jewish Gnostics.

Leading to the knowledge of the truth – In the Johannine literature the word "knowledge" (*epignōsis*) is used in a distinctively Gnostic setting, suggesting that Christianity as taught by the apostles and evangelists already offers full knowledge. Whatever their claims to the contrary, one need not join the Gnostic sects to get "knowledge." We would be inclined to see a similar usage here.[130] Only as the doctrines taught by the false teachers are abandoned does one have any real possibility of arriving at the truth taught in the gospel. The first part of

---

[126] The verb *paideuonta* means to "educate" or "bring up" or "train" a child. Sometimes the idea of teaching predominates; sometimes the idea of correcting or chastising predominates.

[127] Paul did not give up on the false teachers without trying to rescue them (1 Timothy 1:20).

[128] Note the verb is subjunctive, "may grant." There is no guarantee that God will give men unlimited time to repent.

[129] Some writers use the expression "God may grant them repentance" to corroborate their belief in what is called "a first work of grace." In their belief, man is totally depraved, and before a man can even want to believe, God must change the heart and turn the person around. That is more than the phrase "grant repentance" implies!

[130] See comments on this phrase "knowledge of the truth" at 1 Timothy 2:4.

this verse shows the preacher at work. The last part of the verse shows the outcome he is seeking as he teaches. One of the things that keeps the preacher at work is to have responses to the invitation he offers to men to obey the gospel. An expectancy that this visit and gospel presentation may result in a changed life gives zest to the preacher's work.

2:26 -- And they may come to their senses – The literal meaning of the Greek *ananēpsōsin* is to "return to soberness," or "be recovered from drunkenness." A man who has been following the false teachers like those Paul warns Timothy about has been "spoiled of his senses." He is "out of his mind" and doing something crazy.

And escape **from the snare of the devil** – As the italics indicate, "and escape" has been added in the English text. All the Greek says is "they may return to soberness out of the devil's snare." It is not alcohol that has caused them to be "drunken." The devil has used a snare that has caused them to be duped, to be out of their minds. The doctrines taught by the false teachers did not look like a trap, but that's one of the deadly things about "snares" – they are designed to deceive the unwary, to capture them before they even know what is happening. The introduction of the name "devil" throws a brilliant light on what has been happening on the human level. There are false teachers and there are people duped by them, but behind it all is the work of the real enemy of mankind, the devil.

Having been held captive by him to do his will – One suggested explanation of these words is that the whole phrase refers to the devil.[131] While the dupes were held captive[132] by the devil they were obliged to do the devil's will.[133] The margin offers another possible translation, "having been held captive by him, to do His will." The difference is that in the Greek there are two distinct pronouns, and some think the first refers to the devil ("held captive by *him*") while the second pronoun ("to do *His* will") refers to God. When the captivity to the devil is escaped, the convert is free to do the will of God. That is one of the blessed benefits of conversion. There is a change of masters.

---

[131] Those who think the whole phrase refers to the devil appeal to a passage like John 1:7,8, where, though there are different pronouns used, the whole passage talks about the same person.

[132] In classical Greek the word has the sense of "to take alive." It is used of prisoners of war, who, if not ransomed, always became slaves of the conqueror. (Interestingly, the only other place the word appears in the New Testament is at Luke 5:10, where Jesus promises the fishermen he has just called to the ministry that from henceforth they would "catch" men. They will "take them alive" and make them servants of a new Master.)

[133] This interpretation has implications. May it then be said that the devil's captives were deprived of their own will? While they were subservient to the will of the devil, was there what has been called a "bondage of the will"?

We have finished the portraits of the preacher. These portraits show how demanding the work of being a preacher truly is. There are enemies to fight, tasks to be completed, false teachers to be warned about, opponents to be corrected, erring souls to be rescued, Christians to be encouraged, and new workers to be recruited for Christ. All the while the preacher must handle accurately the Word of Truth, and at the same time be careful about his own faith and life, that they are pleasing to the Lord. There are not only duties to be performed, but attitudes to be cultivated, so the preacher does the duties in the way most likely to be beneficial and winsome.

III. The Prophetic Appeal – Practice Your Faith.   3:1-17

A. Turn Away from Those Who are False.   3:1-9

3:1 -- But realize this – Paul has just encouraged Timothy to be strong and not to let any hardship he may have to suffer paralyze his efforts in the Lord's cause (2:1-13). He has detailed how Timothy's efforts were to be directed against the false teachers and their duped followers (2:14-26). Now Paul will describe how some of Timothy's severest opposition would come from those who have a form of godliness only. In this third appeal[1] to stay in the ministry, Paul will tell Timothy how to have an effective ministry. He must turn away from those who are false, follow those who are true, and continue in God's Word. Grave dangers face the church; this serious fact is something Timothy must keep in mind, lest the opposition discourage him from continuing in the ministry.

That in the last days – The expression "last days" in Bible terminology refers to the whole Messianic age, from the first to the second comings of Christ.[2] While many commentators explain "last days" as a reference to the period immediately preceding the second coming, rather than the whole church age, such a view will hardly satisfy here. Timothy himself is going to experience the difficult times those days hold, and he is hardly still alive and preaching some 2000 years after Paul writes. No, Timothy was already living in the "last days."[3]

Difficult times will come – *Chalepos* is a very picturesque term. It was used by Plutarch to describe what we would call an "ugly" wound. It was used by astrol-

---

[1] The outline for 2 Timothy suggested in these notes has Paul making four appeals to Timothy to stay in the ministry. There are other suggested outlines for this material. One suggests that 3:1-9 are closely related to the metaphor of 2:20,21 – about the great house with vessels both useful and unuseful. The faithful, useful vessels have been described in 2:22-26. Now the vessels of dishonor – men of corrupt mind and counterfeit faith – are described in chapter 3. Another suggests that the grave dangers that 3:1-9 warn Timothy about are part of the hardship he will face (2:3,11,12).

[2] The expression "last days" comes from the Old Testament (e.g., Isaiah 2:2; Micah 4:1). In Peter's quotation of Joel 2:28 on the day of Pentecost (Acts 2:17), the expression clearly refers to the Messianic Age which had already begun, for Peter declared that the prophecy was being fulfilled that very day. (Even 2 Peter 3:3 which uses "last days" as it predicts something future does not necessarily have reference to only the period immediately preceding the Second Advent, since a few years later Jude 18 says that what was predicted in Peter has already come true.) Paul's own kinsmen were accustomed to speak of two great periods of the world's history – "this age" and "the age to come." The first term included all the periods up to Messiah's first advent. The latter, "the age to come" covers all the periods subsequent to His first coming.

[3] The words of 2 Timothy 3:5, "avoid such men as these," would require certainly a strained interpretation if we are to suppose that the "last days" referred to a time immediately preceding the end of the church age. Further, the present tense verbs in 3:6-8 picture the activity of the false teachers as already occurring in Timothy's own time.

ogers to describe what they called a "threatening" conjunction of heavenly bodies. In Matthew 8:28 the word is used for the "violent" demoniacs. Other terms are "trying," "perilous," "dangerous." The times that Timothy is warned are coming will produce grief. The very existence of the church would be menaced by the Jewish Gnostic heresy. "Will come" says the Jewish Gnostic attack on the church was just in its beginning stages. It will get worse as Timothy gets older.[4] History now tells us, it got even more difficult in the 2nd and 3rd centuries.

3:2 -- For men will be lovers of self – Verse 1 has set the theme about difficult times coming. Verses 2-5 list some of the characteristics of the false teachers who will be such a threat. Verses 6-9 will describe how those teachers will operate. In verses 2-5 we have a list of no fewer than 19 vices,[5] and the "for" with which this verse begins explains the reason why Timothy will face difficult times. When people, be they teachers or their followers, exhibit these vices in their lives, no wonder the preacher faces dangerous times! The future tense verb "will be" indicates what will be true for Timothy, and likely also "will be" true all through the church age. The identity of these "men" is a matter of some importance because of the command (verse 5) that these men are to be avoided. When the illustration of Jannes and Jambres (verse 8ff) is taken into consideration, a case can be made that the "men" are specifically those who are false teachers. If so, then it is just the teachers who are to be avoided.[6] "Selfishness" or "self-centeredness" is another way to characterize the men who are "lovers of self." What a dreary word with which to start a dreary list! The word "love" occurs several times in the list – "lovers of self," "lovers of money," "lovers of pleasures more than lovers of God." The heart of every problem is a problem in the heart, namely, misdirected love. God has commanded us to love Him supremely and our neighbors as ourselves (Matthew 22:34-40); but if we love ourselves supremely, we will not love God or our neighbors.[7]

---

[4] Paul wrote about this same subject at 1 Timothy 4, but its importance leads him to advert to it again.

[5] Several attempts have been made to produce an outline under which to categorize these vices. (1) For the 18 vices listed in verses 2-4, Hoffman and others have suggested three groups consisting of five, six, and seven terms respectively. (2) Another way of handling the material is to suggest that the first one listed (or the first two) are the parent sins from which all the rest of the wretched brood are begotten. Nute takes the first two – lovers of self and lovers of money – as the sins from which the others develop. Wycliffe takes just the first one – lovers of self – as the principle from which the others come. (3) Knight (*op. cit.*, p.430) presents a chiastic arrangement of matched groupings at the beginning and end of the list. (4) Still others suggest that all such efforts at producing an outline are artificial.

[6] This identification of the "men" as referring in this passage to the false teachers should not be taken to mean that their followers needn't worry about such heart problems too, for Scripture elsewhere indicates that men in general are liable to have many of the same vices.

[7] "In the universe there is God, and there are 'people' and 'things.' We should worship God, love people, and use things. But if we start worshiping ourselves, we will ignore God and start

Lovers of money – This word is used elsewhere in the New Testament only at Luke 16:14 where it is used of the Pharisees. A word of similar root[8] is found in 1 Timothy 6:10. People whose driving motives are love of self and love of money soon banish God from their lives. Barclay (*op. cit.*, p.212) notes that Ephesus in the 1st century "was a town of a prosperous, worldly, materialistic civilization." A large part of the population was affluent. Those who were not so well off could easily let the good life become the only thing important in their quest. It was the kind of town where a man could easily lose his soul.

Boastful – Plutarch uses the word *aladzōn* of a wandering, quack doctor. He wanders over the country with medicines and spells and methods of exorcism, which, he claimed, were panaceas and cure-alls for all diseases. They were much like the "medicine men" who huckstered patent medicines in the old west. Aristotle defines the *aladzōn* as "the man who pretends to creditable qualities that he does not possess, or possesses in a lesser degree than he makes out."[9] If the derivation of the word is *alē*, "wandering," then perhaps we may compare the "strolling Jews" of Acts 19:13. Such vagabonds were usually boasters. They were involved in religion the way they were only for the sake of getting something or making some gain. Paul has already in 1 Timothy 1:7 and 6:4 characterized the false teachers with the same vice.

Arrogant – One who is arrogant contemptuously looks down on others as beneath them, either in social position or wealth, or perhaps in natural gifts. The same Greek word is often translated "proud," especially in those verses which say that God receives the humble but resists the man who is proud. Both "boastful" and "arrogant" refer to man's conduct toward his brother man, with this difference: boastful has reference to words and actions; arrogant speaks of the thoughts in the heart. In the heart there is contempt for others.

Revilers – *Blasphēmos* means to speak in an insulting way. Sometimes a man speaks insultingly towards God. But a man can also speak insultingly towards other men. Pride begets insult. Contempt of men often issues in hurting actions and wounding words. Paul uses this word of his own behavior before he became a Christian (1 Timothy 1:13). He has also used "abusive speech" to characterize the false teachers in 1 Timothy 6:4.

---

loving things and using people. This is the formula for a miserable life; yet it characterizes many people today. The worldwide craving for 'things' is just one evidence that people's hearts have turned away from God." (Wiersbe, *op. cit.*, p.152-3)

[8] The KJV has "covetous" in this place, but the Greek word *philarguroi* is not the usual word rendered "covetous."

[9] *Nichomachean Ethics* 7.2. The Latin translators chose *ostentatiō* ("ostentatious") to translate "boasters."

Disobedient to parents – If, as seems likely, Paul is listing some of the vices that drive the false teachers, this one is unexpected. Isn't it children and teens, rather than people who are old enough to be teachers, who are disobedient to parents? Yet a little thought will show that older people can be "disobedient to parents," too. The ancient world set duty to parents very high on their list of virtues. The oldest Greek laws disenfranchised the man who struck his parents. To strike a father was in Roman law as bad as murder. In the Jewish Law, honor for father and mother comes high in the list of the Ten Commandments. Have these false teachers utterly repudiated the guidance their parents would give them in things religious? Have they lost all respect for age? Are they so interested in self and money that they fail to recognize the unpayable debt and basic duty owed to those who gave them life?

Ungrateful – The vice of ingratitude, of being unthankful to others who have shown kindness along life's journey, is a hurtful sin because it is blind to sin. King Lear's words, as far as they go, are true: "How sharper than a serpent's tooth it is to have a thankless child!" It is just as hurtful when adults are thankless.

Unholy – There are several Greek synonyms translated "holy" (or with an alpha-privative added, "unholy"). The word here is *anosios*, a word used of persons or things, describing that which is out of harmony with the divine constitution of the moral universe.[10] It is to be out of harmony with what is generally and by common consent felt to be right. The teachers here characterized as "unholy" are men who offend against the unwritten laws which are part and parcel of the very essence of community life. As examples of *anasios*, the Greeks regarded a marriage between brother and sister as "unholy," and a failure to properly bury the body of a relative was a thing "unholy." Another word that might translate this term is "disrespectful." The false teachers are disrespectful toward other people.

3:3 -- Unloving – Of the synonyms for "love," this one is used primarily of the natural affection of parents to their children and children to their parents. The word speaks of being careless and without regard for the welfare of those connected with them by ties of blood. It is family love or human affection. The epidemic of child abuse and spouse abuse today would be examples of men who are "unloving." Men are so set on self that even the closest of human ties mean nothing.

Irreconcilable – *Aspondos* speaks of the man who is so bitter and truculent and unappeasable in his hatred that he will never come to terms, will never make a

---

[10] The word was used at 1 Timothy 1:9.

truce,[11] with the man with whom he has quarreled.[12] They are unyielding and must have their own way.

Malicious gossips – "Slanderer" might be a better translation.[13] The same word in the singular (*diabolos*) is one of the regular names used for the Devil, who is the "accuser of the brethren." The false teachers are characterized as slandering their fellow men. There is a sense in which slander is the most cruel of all sins. If a man's goods are stolen, he can set to and build up his fortune again. But if a man's good name or reputation is taken away, irreparable damage has been done to him.[14]

Without self-control – It means to be intemperate in the pursuit or use of anything, whether it be money, or the tongue, or pleasure, or the appetite.[15] It describes a man who is easily led into sin; he puts up little or no resistance to the devil's solicitations to evil; he is without strength.

Brutal – *Anēmoros* is a word often applied to the wild beast. It denotes a savagery which has neither sensitiveness nor sympathy nor mercy.[16] Aeschylus uses the word to warn about an ancient people who lived in Pontus. He wrote "Beware of the Chalubes, for they are savage (*anēmeroi*) and cannot be approached by strangers."[17]

Haters of good – The word means to have no love for good things or good persons.[18] There can come a time in a man's life when the company of good

---

[11] The KJV rendering "trucebreakers" is not justified by any example we can find in ancient Greek literature. The word does not mean to "break a truce." It rather means that one will not make a truce.

[12] The idea in the word might be illustrated by some folk today involved in marital breakups. They just will not forgive. No amount of counseling will result in a "truce" or in reconciliation.

[13] The KJV reads "false accusers," and in the margin has "makebates." That marginal term speaks of one who excites contention and quarrels. It is the very kind of ill feelings towards another that "slander" is intended to produce. The same word is used at 1 Timothy 3:11.

[14] This is a vice that leaders must be careful lest they exhibit. Unfortunately, some of this slanderous activity goes on even among professed Christian leaders, who accuse one another in the pages of their publications and in their public sermons. If the accusation is true, it is not "slander." It is when the accusation is made simply to destroy the other in the minds of one's listeners that this vise is so reprehensible.

[15] The KJV's "incontinent" expresses only one part of the meaning of the word, for "incontinent" means "having no control over the passions."

[16] The KJV has "fierce" which comes from the Latin *ferus* which meant "wild, savage, not tame."

[17] *Prom. Vinct.* 734.

[18] The KJV follows the Vulgate when it offers "despisers of those that are good" as a translation for this word. The positive side, "lovers of what is good" occurs in Titus 1:8.

people and the presence of good things is to him simply an embarrassment. The devotee of cheap music has no pleasure in listening to good music. He who feeds his mind on cheap literature can in the end find nothing in the great masterpieces. The false teacher who fills his mind with Jewish-Gnostic ideas will shortly come to have no love for what God says is good.

3:4 -- Treacherous – *Prodotai* might better be translated "betrayers." It is used of Judas Iscariot at Luke 6:16 and of the Jewish religious leaders at Acts 7:52. The KJV uses "traitors" but the Greek word used here does not mean someone who betrays his king or country. It speaks of someone who betrays the persons who trust in him, or of the cause committed to him.[19]

Reckless – "Headstrong" is the idea. It denotes obstinacy which will not be influenced by wise advice. The "reckless" person acts from impulse, without considering the consequences or weighing principles. The town clerk at Ephesus, speaking to the mob, used this word as he encouraged them to do nothing "rash" (Acts 19:36).

Conceited – The same word was used at 1 Timothy 3:6. As noted there, included in the root of this Greek word is the idea of "smoke." Then it comes to mean "lightness," "emptiness," or "elation." The false teachers are "wrapped in clouds of delusion."[20]

Lovers of pleasure rather than lovers of God – The Greek word behind "pleasure" can be translated "hedonism." Anything producing a feeling of pleasure is what the false teachers love. Men should be lovers of God. It is a sad substitute when men choose to love pleasure rather than God. The false teachers were men who would make any sacrifice to procure a fleeting pleasure, and who would give nothing up in order to do honor to the eternal but invisible God.

3:5 -- Holding to a form of godliness – This is the last in the long list of vices that characterize the false teachers whom Timothy and the church will shortly be confronting. Notwithstanding the long list of sins, yet these people are externally

---

[19] If the context were not characterizing the false teachers whom Timothy would have to confront, the suggestion would be that "betrayers" speaks of those who inform on or turn in their brethren in times of persecution. "In the days of Timothy, and for many a long year thereafter, to inform against the believers in Jesus of Nazareth, to give information of their places of meeting in times of persecution, was often a profitable though a despicable work" (Ellicott). Such informers often did it just to gratify an old grudge, or revenge themselves on an old enemy. The informer was selfishly thinking of paying back an old score, satisfying an old hatred, winning a moment's cheap reward – and that is why he would inform against the Christians to the Roman government.

[20] Ellicott renders it "blinded by pride." Barclay (*op. cit.*, p.219) reads "inflated with conceit."

religious! Amazing! "Form" is *morphōsin*, the synonym which speaks of 'outward semblance' as contrasted to inner essence. "Godliness" or "piety" says they were keeping up a show of observing the outward forms of the Christian religion.[21]   Some of the forms they kept are likely the same items called attention to in 1 Timothy 4.

Although they have denied its power – "Denied" is a perfect tense participle. The false teachers had denied it a long time ago, and still were. It is a strong word, implying knowing and yet decisively rejecting the truth. In the word "power" most commentators see a reference to the Holy Spirit. Compare 2 Timothy 1:7,14 where the Spirit's power has been emphasized. The false teachers knew little about the indwelling of the Holy Spirit, and little about the validation of the genuine gospel message that was afforded by distributions of the Holy Spirit (Hebrews 2:4). They know little of the empowering the Spirit gave apostles of Jesus (Acts 1:8, 1 Timothy 1:12). The false teachers were professing to be Christians and engaging in actions that looked "Christian," but they did not know the reality of the Christian religion!

And[22] avoid such men as these – Timothy was to have nothing to do with such men ("these") as just described. He was continually to avoid such teachers who had an outward form of Christianity.[23]   "Repel them away from you" like a good soldier repels a foe.[24]   As noted in verse 1, this command indicates that Paul thought of these evil teachers as already present, as needing a certain behavioral response in the present by Timothy, even though he calls the time when they appear "the last days".

3:6 -- For among them are those who enter into households – Verses 6-8 tell

---

[21] As the years pass, Gnosticism, which began as a Jewish heresy, becomes a Christian heresy. How did that happen? Did the Christians not see the false teachers for what they really were in part because the Gnostic teachers had a "form of godliness"? It is sobering and distressing that people can go through the motions of accepting Christianity while at the same time their lives and doctrine dishonor and ruin the very religion they have professed to embrace.

[22] "And" likely connects the imperative verb here in verse 5 with the one in verse 1. "Know this ... and avoid them!" The KJV does not translate the *kai*; it reads simply "from such turn away."

[23] Paul here repeats the command he has already given to Timothy in 2 Timothy 2:22,23.

[24] We see different ways to treat "sinners" in the New Testament. The unconverted pagan was to be courteously entreated, for there was always the possibility he would be convicted of his sins and become a convert. The Christian who had been seduced by false teachers away from the school of the apostles (where the life as well as the doctrine of Jesus was taught) was to be gently instructed. Perhaps he could be led back to faithfulness. But these false teachers, who, while pretending to belong to Jesus and who refused to change after one or two admonitions, were to be shunned. Timothy the preacher had no further responsibility at trying to win them back, nor was he to give any appearance that he in any way approved of their doctrine or lives.

how some of the false teachers[25] liked to operate as they tried to peddle their false religious wares. The "for" with which this verse begins tells Timothy another reason why he should "avoid" such people. The Greek word translated "enter" carries the idea of "sneaking into" or "insinuating themselves into." The idea is that they worm their way into people's homes. While "sneak into homes" sounds perfectly natural in the Western world when used of the method by which bad people surreptitiously enter and plunder the house, it has a more sinister turn when we remember Paul and Timothy lived in the Eastern world. Since the next phrase speaks of how the teachers influenced the women in these households, we must recall that in many societies the women's apartments were separate from the men's living area. The false teachers would have to go to great pains to get access to the women of the house.

And captivate weak women – *Aichmalōtidzontes*, used also at Ephesians 4:3, describes the blind surrender of the will and conscience to such crafty teachers. It represents these women as wholly under the influence of these bad men, to the utter destruction of all true, healthy, home life. Paul uses the diminutive form of "women" here. He does not describe them as "ladies" but as "little women."[26] There was immaturity in some area of these women's lives that made them susceptible to the wiles of the false teachers. This very term is used in later literature to refer to the women who were made use of by the later Gnostic false teachers.[27] Irenaeus draws a vivid picture of the methods of Marcus who dealt in magic and spells:

> He devotes himself specially to women, and those such as are well-bred and elegantly attired, and of great wealth. He tells such women that by his spells and incantations he can enable them to prophesy. The woman protests that she has never done so, and cannot do so. He says, "Open your mouth, speak whatever occurs to you, and you shall prophesy." The woman, thrilled to the heart, does so, and is deluded into thinking that she can prophesy. She then makes the effort

---

[25] Some commentators have used the words "from among them" to help try to determine who the "men" (verse 2) are whose characteristics are described and who are to be avoided. Those commentators think it is "men in general, who are professing Christians" and that from this larger group verse 6 now speaks of their leaders.

[26] The KJV renders the *gunē* diminutive as "silly women." The NIV uses "weak-willed women." Knight (*op. cit.*, p.433) offers "childish women." This does not mean all women are like this, or that men are not vulnerable to the wiles of false teachers. Whether men or women, people who fall for the kind of false religious systems threatening the 1st century church have the same characteristics.

[27] Irenaeus I.13.3 speaks of the women influenced by the Valentinian Marcus. Epiphanius (*Haer.* 26:12) and Jerome (Ep. 133 *ad Ctesiphontem* 4) cite a number of instances of Gnostic influence over women converts. Simon Magus was accompanied by the wicked Helen. Nicholas of Antioch gathered around himself what Jerome calls a "chorus of women." Montanus is associated with the well-known names of Maximilla and Prisca. Donatus is linked with a woman named Lucilla. Marcion, Arius, Priscillian, and other heresiarchs, famous in the annals of the early churches, are spoken of as intimately associated with or supported by female influence. (*Ellicott's*, p.315)

to reward Marcus, not only by the gift of her possessions (in which way he has collected a very large fortune), but also by yielding up to him her person, desiring in every way to be united to him, that she may become altogether one with him.

Satan began his work of temptation with Eve rather than with Adam, and the advocates of error often follow Satan's example.[28]

Weighed down with sins – The "weak women" are further described as "loaded down" or "overwhelmed"[29] with sins. This phrase and the next gives us some insight into the means by which the false teachers acquired some degree of control over these women of Ephesus (and elsewhere), who were Christians, but who were either babes in Christ,[30] or else not strong Christians. The nearly helpless victims these false teachers focused on were women who had trouble mastering their passions and desires, so were habitually sinning.

Led on by various impulses – Here is an added description of the "weak women." They are "swayed" by all kinds of carnal and selfish desires (for *epithumia*, see "desires" at 1 Timothy 6:9 and 2 Timothy 2:22). Such women are easy prey for the false teachers.

3:7 -- Always learning – Is this another way in which the immaturity of the women exhibited itself? Once they have been captured, they run from teacher to teacher[31] to see if they can learn some desired truth. The context indicates that some of the things they were learning dealt with occult lore. Perhaps, too, the women had never learned to master their passions and lusts, and their consciences bothered them. The false teachers, by their lying doctrines, could offer them a false peace. In their school, they could no doubt show the women how they might still be Christians and yet indulge their divers lusts.[32]

---

[28] The exploitation of spiritually immature women for immoral and irreligious purposes is seen also in Acts 13:50, 16:16-18; Revelation 2:20; and 1 Timothy 5:13. On the other hand, spiritually mature women were useful and active in many good works, as seen in Acts 9:36, 16:13-15, 17:4,12,34, 18:18; Romans 16:1-4; 1 Timothy 3:14; and Titus 2:3-5.

[29] The perfect passive of the verb *soreuō* which means "to heap upon." See the same word at Romans 12:20.

[30] Compare 2 Peter 2:14-18, where the false teachers Peter warns about used the same methods: they enticed unstable souls, they used sensuality as bait, and they focused their efforts on new converts (those who have "just escaped" their old way of life).

[31] The RSV translates this phrase, "they will listen to anybody."

[32] Remember that the false teachers in Timothy's day were Gnostics. One basic principle of Gnosticism was the philosophy that spirit was altogether good and that matter was altogether evil. Such a dualistic philosophy could issue in one of two lifestyles, either asceticism or license. Some Gnostic heretics taught that since matter was evil, a rigid asceticism must be practiced, and the body and all the things of the body must be as far as possible destroyed and eliminated. If the Gnostics at Ephesus were ascetic, they would teach these doctrines to impressionable women. The result would be that the woman would break off all married relationships with her husband in order to live

And never able to come to the knowledge of the truth – A hope of penetrating into the mysteries not revealed by God's true teachers spurred these female learners on.[33] There is a constant interest in the secrets that can be learned by astrology or scrying or spiritism. In Paul's analysis, some of the false teachers laid claim to occult arts, to a knowledge of magic and sorcery; this is clear from the statement contained in the next verse, where certain sorcerers of the time of Moses are compared to them. The Gnostics promised more "knowledge" than they could deliver. They never themselves came to, nor could they bring their followers to, a "*full* knowledge[34] of the truth."[35] The women fell prey to these teachers because the teachers were laying claim to a higher and deeper wisdom, which, if learned from them, would give the women knowledge of profound and hidden mysteries and would ease their guilt feelings resulting from their sins and lusts. It is a sad and traumatic time when one who has been duped eventually learns he or she has not really come to a "knowledge of the truth."[36]

3:8 -- And just as Jannes and Jambres opposed Moses – "Jannes and Jambres" are the traditional names of the magicians who opposed Moses in the court of

---

the ascetic life. Or, if the Gnostic teachers were libertine in their application of the principle, they would teach that it did not matter what one did with the body. It was only the spirit that was important. The desires of the body could be sated and indulged to the limit because they did not really affect the soul. If the Gnostics at Ephesus were libertines, they would teach these doctrines to impressionable women. The result would be that the woman would give the lower instincts full play, and abandon herself to promiscuous relationships with men. In either case home life would be destroyed.

[33] How like what one sees in the New Age Movement. Shirley MacLaine, for example, keeps going to gurus and self-acclaimed ascended masters to learn truths about her inner self, and how to get into harmony with the universe in which she lives. There are things to be learned about reincarnation, karma, communication with astral-plane entities through psychic mediums, spiritual channeling, UFO's, and extraterrestrials. The goal is to become a "Christ" (an ascended master who doesn't need to be reincarnated again) in some future life.

[34] Gnostics used several words for "knowledge," both *gnōsis* and *epignōsis*. The compound Greek word means "full knowledge" as opposed to knowledge. "Knowledge" you might get in Christianity. But the Gnostic claim was that only by joining their group and learning all the false teachers had to teach you could have "full knowledge" that would mean salvation.

[35] It should not be missed that Paul here says that "never," "never at all" will Gnosticism with its dabbling in the occult bring a person to the truth. What pupils of the false teachers get is the exact opposite of what they expected.

[36] A young lady involved in Satanism heard the same promises of peace from the head witch that she did from Christian counselors who were trying to help her. The thing that finally cleared her mind was this question: If those in the coven have peace, why do they continually use drugs to feel at peace? One doesn't have to use drugs to have peace in Christ! See 1 Timothy 2:4 for more on the expression "knowledge of the truth" and how it relates to gospel salvation.

Pharaoh.   This is the only place in the Bible where their names are given,[37] though Exodus 7:11,22 speak of Egyptian magicians who were called upon by Pharaoh to oppose Moses and Aaron.   "The Pharaoh also called for the wise men and the sorcerers; and they also, the magicians of Egypt, did the same with their secret arts."   They "opposed Moses."[38]   It should be observed that those involved in the occult are always opposed to the right ways of God.   They may claim to be God's servants, but they are perverting the ways of God (Acts 13:10).

So these *men* also oppose the truth – "These men" are the Jewish Gnostic false teachers about whom Paul is warning Timothy.   Hear it – Gnosticism is not true Christianity, even though some sects then and today try to affirm it is.   It is in opposition to Christianity.   Note the points of comparison between the false teachers of Ephesus and the magicians of Egypt: both were involved in the occult; both were opposed to the truth – were deadly enemies of the truth.[39]   We can well imagine the comparison Paul here makes between the magicians of Egypt and the Gnostics flooding into Asia being repeated in many an assembly of the faithful, long after the apostle's death.

Men of depraved mind – *Katephtharmenoi* is used at 2 Peter 2:12 of wild ani-

---

[37] There are some extra-Biblical references to these men.   If Origen can be trusted (*Against Celsius*), there was an apocryphal book called by their names.   Theodoret ascribes their names here to an unwritten (oral) Jewish tradition.   Their names are found in the Targum (Aramaic paraphrase) of Jonathan on Exodus 7:11 and 7:22.   Spence (*Ellicott's*, p.316) informs us that these traditions as recorded in the Targum are full of contradictions and anachronisms.   These traditions relate how these men, Jannes and Jambres, were the sons of Balaam, were alive before Moses was born, and interpreted a dream of Pharaoh so as to foretell the birth of Moses and cause the opposition and oppression of the Israelites.   The traditions have Jannes and Jambres being the teachers of Moses, and then subsequently his enemies and opponents.   One tradition has them perishing in the catastrophe when the waves of the Red Sea overwhelmed the armies of Egypt.   Another tradition has them becoming proselytes to the Jewish religion, and leaving Egypt at the time of the Exodus among the mixed multitude.   They are the ones who instigated Aaron to make the golden calf, and then the tradition speaks of their perishing in the slaughter after the worship of the golden calf.   Another tradition has them slaughtered during the occasion connected with the name of Phinehas.   Jannes and Jambres are also mentioned, in connection with Moses, though with some variation in the spelling of the name Jambres, by Pliny (*Natural History* 30.1.11), who probably got his information from a work by Sergius Paulus on magic, of which the materials were likely furnished by Elymas the sorcerer (named in Acts 13:6-8).   The Pythagorean philosopher Numenius (2nd century AD) speaks of Jannes and Jambres as Egyptian *hierogrammateis* or "sacred scribes."   The Hebrew word translated "magicians" at Genesis 41:8 and Exodus 7:11 is *hartummim*, and means sacred scribes who were skilled in the sacred writing, that is in the hieroglyphics.   They were a variety of Egyptian priests, all of whom were involved in the occult.

[38] The same word ("opposed") is used of Elymas' occult activities in Acts 13:8.   Observe, too, that Paul treats Moses as an historical character, and the Old Testament record as fact, not myth.

[39] Compare Acts 19:18-20.   At an earlier time in Ephesus, when Christians were shown the error of being involved in the occult, they ceased their involvement and came confessing and showing their deeds.   And let it be noted that after the occult involvement is broken, that is when the Word of the Lord grows mightily.

mals who must be "destroyed."[40]   Does this verse imply that continued involvement in the occult affects men's minds till their minds no longer work, that they are 'destroyed' or they have 'perished'? That seems to be the case. The devil may be the one who ultimately is behind their minds being ruined. The false teachers' minds are gone, so they are in a place where they have little likelihood of being won back to the faith. If their minds don't work, it would be vain for Timothy to hope that by working with them he might win them to Christ.

Rejected as regards the faith – "The faith" equals "the gospel."[41] "Rejected" is a word Paul applies to the very same kind of false teachers at Titus 1:16. Whether it is Christians who reject their claims to being Christians (i.e., they cannot be trusted to teach the truth), or whether by inspiration Paul tells us that God has rejected them,[42] is difficult to decide. These false teachers were tried and tested[43] and were found to be counterfeit. Verse 8 has given further reason for the command of verse 5 to "avoid such men."

3:9 -- But they will not make further progress – "Progress" is the same idiom used at 2 Timothy 2:16 (where it was translated "lead"). Paul's encouraging message is that, as the truth of God prevailed against the tricks of the magicians of Egypt, even so the gospel will triumph over the Jewish Gnostic error Timothy faces. The false teachers would proceed further into ungodliness, as he said in 2 Timothy 2:16 and 3:13, but not up to the point of destroying the gospel. History has shown Paul's prediction here was fulfilled exactly. Gnosticism's influence did grow in the centuries following Paul's death, but the various forms of Gnosticism have been regularly overcome, and the gospel remains. To human eyes, the great mischief already accomplished by the false teachers would appear to be cause for despair. It would seem as though a deadly and incurable cancer was eating away the whole life of the community. But Timothy need not despair; the evil would only be allowed to advance to a certain point.

For their folly will be obvious to all   –   We have here the reason why the false

---

[40] Does this verse simply say that these false teachers' minds or understandings are gone, like the one who is *diephtharmenous tēn akouēn*, meaning "one whose hearing is gone"? Compare Paul's similar assessment of the fix the false teachers are in at 1 Timothy 6:5.

[41] "Faith" here likely should be understood in its objective sense rather than being a reference to the subjective beliefs of the false teachers.

[42] The Bible does teach that men are either in a saved or lost condition while they live on this earth (see John 3:36).   So if Paul here says they are in a lost condition, rejected by God, this would not be an unscriptural idea.

[43] Just as *dokimos* (translated "approved") at 2 Timothy 3:15 means "tried and tested and found to be genuine," so *adokimos* used here means just the opposite, "tried and tested and failed the test."

teachers would fail to make progress.[44]   "Their folly" refers to the teaching of the false teachers.   Men will be able to see the foolishness of what they are teaching, and no longer be such easy souls to fool and capture.   Paul does not say how soon their folly would become obvious, so interpreters have tried to pinpoint when this did or will happen.   Some reformers identified the Roman Catholic Church as being the false teaching predicted, and pointed to the Reformation as the time when the folly became obvious and the impact of the false teaching ceased to grow or make further progress.   Still others have attempted to put 2 Timothy 3:9 together with 2 Thessalonians 2:8 and then suggest that when the "man of lawlessness" (2 Thessalonians 2:3) is revealed that is when the folly of the false teachers will finally become obvious.

As also that of those two came to be – Paul seems to be alluding to the last references to Jannes and Jambres in the Old Testament (Exodus 8:18,19 and 9:11). They could not duplicate the miracles God worked through Moses and Aaron. Their enchantments were shown to be folly.   If any of the traditions about how these magicians died alluded to earlier are true, that too demonstrates their folly. Not only was there public ridicule to be endured when folly becomes obvious, there is also the judgment and eternity separated from God to be considered. Timothy might take comfort by considering what Holy Scripture had placed in the record respecting the Egyptians "whose folly was manifest to all men."   With these words, the first personal appeal – to turn away from the false, to avoid Gnostic occultism – has been concluded.

B. Follow Those Who are True.   3:10-12

3:10 -- But you followed my teaching – Here Paul begins the second part of his prophetic appeal to Timothy to stay in the ministry.   It seems from the emphatic "But you" that it is with a measure of relief that Paul turns from the gloomy survey of the false teachers, their lives, their corrupt doctrines, and the consequences of their conduct, to address these words of appeal to Timothy.   "Followed" (*parakoloutheō*) is a word which has a magnificent depth of meaning flowing from the literal translation of "to follow alongside."[45]   One meaning is to follow a person *physically*, to stick with him through thick and thin, to be at his side in fair weather and foul.   Another meaning is to follow a person *mentally*, to attend

---

[44] The phrase is reminiscent of Exodus 8:18,19 and 9:11.

[45] There is a slight manuscript variation here, the readings fluctuating between an aorist tense and a perfect tense.   The evidence for the two readings is evenly balanced.   Paul used the perfect tense when he wrote this word at 1 Timothy 4:6; it seems highly improbable that he here used the aorist, for that would convey a rebuke to Timothy by insinuating that he had once followed, but that he was doing so no longer.   The perfect tense would imply that Timothy has been following all along, something Paul wants him to keep doing.

diligently to his teaching, and to understand fully the meaning and the significance of what he says.[46]   The word may also mean to follow a person *spiritually*, not only to understand what he says, but to carry out his ideas, and to be the kind of person that he wishes his followers to be.   Timothy had followed alongside Paul for enough years and through enough circumstances to know what Paul taught and how he lived.   Timothy could know that what Paul is about to say is the truth. "In order to challenge Timothy to loyal service, Paul calls attention to certain things in his own service to the Lord.   We have enough writings from the pen of Paul to recognize that Paul never calls attention to his own life in any sense of bragging; but when he can use a personal experience to prove the very point he is attempting to establish, he does so."[47]   Paul lists a series of nine things in which Timothy has been his follower and disciple.   In this list we find duties, qualities, and experiences of an apostle.   "Teaching" (doctrine) is the first one listed, for this is the place it occupied in the mind and writing of Paul.   Timothy knew very well what Paul had been teaching and preaching.   Paul had given years of his life to the clear setting forth of Christian doctrine (gospel); it was one of his chief contributions to the church.   How different was Paul's teaching from that of the false teachers who were poisoning the stream of Christianity!

Conduct – *Agōgē* is used only here, but we can learn its meaning from the LXX where it was used in Esther 2:20 for "her manner of life", and from classical Greek.   It speaks of a person's conduct, or mode or manner of life.   What a contrast between Paul's conduct and the conduct of the false teachers as just delineated in 2 Timothy 3:6ff.   Paul's conduct, whether in the public eye or in the privacy of his most intimate circle of friends, displayed nothing out of perfect harmony with the gospel he taught.

Purpose – "My aim in life" will remind Timothy of the sense of purpose which dominated Paul's whole life.[48]   Years earlier on the road to Damascus, Paul had seen the risen Lord.   Jesus had called him to be an apostle.   That call was never forgotten or disobeyed.   Paul never swerved from remaining true to the gospel or to his mission to the Gentiles.   The purpose or chief aim in life is important to our judgments along the way, too.   Without a specific purpose, without a resolute plan for ministry, people will drift like derelicts upon the high seas.   Like Paul did, so Timothy was to hold in view the purpose or end to be attained in life.

---

[46] Adapted from Barclay (*op. cit.*, p.224).   The KJV translation, "thou hast fully known," gives this sense fully and clearly.   It is interesting to note the same Greek word occurs at Luke 1:3, where the NASB has "having investigated everything carefully" while the KJV version has "having had perfect understanding."

[47] Foster, *op. cit.*, p.401.

[48] *Prothesis* is that which a person sets before himself as the end to be attained.   See Acts 11:23, 27:13; 2 Maccabees 3:8, and examples in classical Greek.   The very same word is often used of God's eternal purpose (2 Timothy 1:9 and Ephesians 1:11).

Faith – It might speak of trust in God, or absolute dependence on God. It might speak of Paul's faith or belief in the fundamental doctrines of Christianity, i.e., Paul's loyalty to the Christian faith. It might speak of "faithfulness" in our every-day contact with people, being a person who does what he promises he will do.

Patience – *Makrothumia* is the Greek synonym that means "putting up with people." It speaks of "forbearance," that certain patience that is necessary in one's dealings with other people. It is the ability not to lose our patience when other people are foolish, not to grow irritable when people seem unteachable. It is the ability to put up with perversity, blindness, and ingratitude on the part of others and still to remain gracious, and still to toil on. It is a quality needed by those who, like Timothy, minister in difficult situations.

Love – *Agapē* is doing what is spiritually best for the other person. According to 1 Corinthians 13 this quality has a number of facets, all of which will have to be displayed at one time or another as we minister to hurting and lost people. It was the reason Paul could, in the realm of Christian liberty, "become all things to all men" that he might, somehow, win some to Christ (1 Corinthians 9:22).

Perseverance – *Hupomonē* is the synonym which means "putting up with things."[49] It is not the passive endurance of the hard and bad things that occur during the course of one's life. It speaks of steadfast perseverance. It is the triumphant conquering of those difficult things, and turning what could have been a tragedy into something beneficial. It is the mindset behind the maxim, "If life hands you a lemon, make lemonade!" Perhaps the next several words in this list are examples of some of the trials through which Paul had to "persevere."[50]

3:11 -- Persecutions – Timothy knew about some of these because some of them had taken place in or near his home town, and others had happened on the missionary tours that he had made with Paul. On each occasion, when life's circumstances became difficult, Paul persevered. Though his ministry to one group of people might be ended, his ministry to others was just beginning.

Sufferings – Some of the persecutions resulted in personal, literal, physical hurt to Paul. Perhaps here too is the idea that at times Paul got sick during the arduous missionary journeys. He persevered through these times, too!

Such as happened to me at Antioch, at Iconium, *and* at Lystra – "Such as"

---

[49] Earlier in the verse Paul used the synonym for "patience" that has to do with relationships to people, rather than to adverse conditions.

[50] The first seven words in the list are singular. The two that follow in verse 11 are plural, and so may be giving concrete examples of what Paul means when he writes about "perseverance."

indicates Paul selected these as examples of many such persecutions and suffer-ings. For an account of some of these persecutions and sufferings during Paul's first missionary journey, before Timothy became a member of the missionary team, see Acts 13:50,51, 14:1-6,19,20.[51] No doubt Timothy had heard Paul preach during the apostle's first missionary journey to Timothy's hometown. It is also more than likely true that Timothy had witnessed firsthand some of Paul's trials, including his stoning and being left as dead (Acts 14:19). Timothy was aware of these when he agreed to become a preacher and join Paul in the ministry.

What persecutions I endured – "What" demonstrates the gravity of the persecutions.[52] Paul willingly and firmly endured[53] these great persecutions.[54] He did not quit because of the persecutions he endured for the work he was doing. He had been called by the Lord to his ministry, and minister he would!

And out of them all the Lord delivered me! – This is the second point Paul wishes to make. Not that the Lord kept unpleasant things from happening, but rather that the Lord helped him through them! Think of Paul's miraculous recovery from the stoning at Lystra, for example.[55] "Out of them all" says that in every instance the Lord delivered or rescued him.[56] To encourage Timothy, Paul recalls his own readiness to endure persecution and sufferings for the sake of the gospel. He also reminds Timothy that the Lord never left him alone.[57]

---

[51] The persecutions and sufferings during the first missionary journey were not the only such experiences Paul had. See 2 Corinthians 11:21-33. Bible students, therefore, have speculated as to why Paul refers to events that happened to him before Timothy became a fellow-missionary. (1) One suggestion is that these are events with which Timothy would be personally familiar. What happened to the apostle in Timothy's own sight before Timothy was ever ordained to be a gospel preacher would have been a never-to-be-forgotten experience. They served as warnings to the soon-to-be-ordained preacher of just what he might expect in the ministry. (2) It has been observed in the Introductory Studies to these Pastoral Epistles that they are intended for the churches as much as for the evangelists to whom they are addressed. So another suggestion is the things that happened in the cities of Galatia are referred to precisely because the book of Acts is already circulating among the readers of 2 Timothy. They will know about the persecutions and sufferings from that source, just as much as Timothy knew from personal experience.

[52] The Greek word agrees with "persecutions" and is slightly different than the relative "such as" with which the verse began. The exclamatory translation given by the NASB catches the right idea.

[53] On the verb *hupēnegka*, "endured," compare 1 Peter 2:19 where it is rendered "bears up."

[54] *Diōgmoi* is used in the New Testament of "persecutions" suffered for religious reasons.

[55] Acts 18:9,10 is another example of such deliverance.

[56] The verb is *hruomai*, which means to "deliver" or "rescue." In every instance Jesus preserved His servant. Even in the last event in Paul's earthly life, Paul is confident that Jesus will "deliver me from every evil deed and will bring me safely to His heavenly kingdom" (2 Timothy 4:18).

[57] Some have observed that Paul may have had in mind the clause in Jesus' model prayer, "deliver us from evil" (Matthew 6:13), where the resemblance is very close. See also 2 Timothy 4:18.

"Lord" is very likely a reference to Jesus.[58]   Observe the testimony to Christ's omnipotence and providence in this statement about Him.   Even when Paul was being stoned or mobbed, Jesus still cared for him and helped him endure it and overcome its intended ill effects.[59]   It was as though Paul said to Timothy, as he ends this list of areas where Timothy has "followed," "Surely no danger, no trouble, however great, need appall you.   You know what I have gone through, yet in all the Lord was with me and has helped me through.   Be sure He will be with you too!" (*Ellicott's*, p.319)

3:12 -- And indeed – On the one hand, in verse 11 Paul encourages Timothy with the word about "deliverance".   But on the other hand, in this verse he warns him that everyone who is determined to live a godly life must anticipate persecution. "And indeed" indicates that Paul's was not a solitary example of a servant of Christ being persecuted.

All who desire to live a godly life in Christ Jesus – In this context, "godly life" involves the aggressive kind of witness Paul gave at Lystra, which aroused opposition in addition to winning souls.[60]   "In Christ Jesus" highlights the intimate relationship between the servant of Christ and his Savior.[61]   The persecution, suffering, and purpose that one sees in Christ's life become a challenge and example for the lives of His servants.   "Desire" seems to pick up the word "purpose" used earlier in verse 10.   There is will, resolution, purpose of heart driving the preacher's lifestyle.

Will be persecuted – The "godly life" is no easy way.   There is no guarantee to apostles or preachers that things will be easy.   Just the opposite!   Persecution is subjecting a person to injury or disadvantage because of his convictions and lifestyle.[62]   Jesus warned his disciples, "because you are not of the world ... the world hates you" (John 15:19; see also Matthew 10:22, 38,39).[63]   The ungodly

---

[58] That the "Lord" here is a reference to Jesus, rather than to the Father, seems required by the verse that follows where Jesus is specifically named.

[59] This echoes the language found so often in the Psalms.   E.g., 25:17, 17:1-5, 91:1-11.

[60] In a sense each Christian is to live a "godly" life.   But in this place, the comparison is between the false teachers and those who teach the truth.   Timothy is to be one of the latter, at whatever the price.

[61] This expression causes the reader to recall the introductory statement in this letter, 2 Timothy 1:1.

[62] Christians must be careful lest they confuse well-deserved ridicule with undeserved persecution.   Those who adopt some mode of dress irresistibly ludicrous, or who have boorish manners, or who are uncivil in their conduct, or outrage all the laws of social life, may well be ridiculed and held in contempt.   But they should not think of themselves as martyrs, as being persecuted because they are "real" Christians.

[63] This truth is affirmed again and again in the Scriptures.   See Matthew 5:10-12; John 16:1-

find various troublesome ways to oppose the advance of the gospel. Paul is simply repeating what Jesus had already taught. Paul is not telling Timothy to go out and seek suffering to prove that he is a Christian. Rather, Paul is saying that if Timothy is resolute in his work as an evangelist he will not be able to escape suffering. "When a person refuses to compromise with the world in his living, when a person refuses to countenance in silence the propagation of false teaching, when a person refuses to condone practices that lead away from Jesus Christ, he is sure to arouse resistance and to experience persecution. If the going is too easy, it is time to examine the strength of the current in which one is moving and to take note whether he is drifting with the world."[64]

We have come to the close of the paragraph about "you followed my teaching."[65] Paul has reminded Timothy of their long personal association, of Paul's own suffering of persecution and experience of deliverance, and of the inevitability of persecution for those involved in the work of Christ. It is all part of Paul's appeal to Timothy to remain in the ministry!

C. Continue in God's Word. 3:13-17

3:13 -- But evil men and imposters – Here begins the third part of Paul's prophetic appeal to Timothy to stay in the ministry.[66] The thrust of this paragraph is found in the imperative verb "continue!" in verse 14. "Evil men," a reference to the false teachers described in 3:2-9, tells us they are deliberately being harmful to the good. The adjective "evil" (*poneroi*) shows these men are not merely satisfied at being evil themselves, but they try to get others to be evil, too. "Imposters" indicates people who are involved in the occult, who utter incantations, and work magic tricks to deceive people.[67] It calls to mind what was said in verse 8 about the Egyptian magicians Jannes and Jambres.

Will proceed *from bad* to worse – History has borne witness to the accuracy of

---

4,33; Acts 14:22; 1 Thessalonians 3:3,4.

[64] Foster, *op. cit.*, p.402.

[65] Several characteristics of true teachers have been emphasized: their lives are open for all to see, they teach true doctrine, they practice what they preach, their purpose is to glorify God, and they are willing to suffer to accomplish their ministry.

[66] Not all Bible students would insert a paragraph break between verses 12 and 13. Those who do not have comments like this: "This verse seems to be a reason why men who desire to live godly lives will be persecuted. There's going to be no scarcity of persecutors!"

[67] The Greek word speaks of a "wailer, howler" – and then "a juggler, enchanter" – because incantations used to be uttered in a kind of howl. Then it came to mean "deceiver, imposter" (Thayer). The KJV uses the word "seducer" to translate at this place, perhaps because the false teachers misled others both in religion and morals.

these prophetic words.   The false teachers known to Paul and Timothy developed[68] into something worse,[69] namely, the leaders of the various wild and speculative Gnostic sects that the church had to battle in the 2nd and 3rd centuries,[70] and later.   One wonders whether the modern revival of interest in the occult and Gnostic ideas (under New Age dress) is not a further historical fulfillment of this prediction about waxing worse and worse.

Deceiving and being deceived – "Deceiving" says the false teachers make others believe that what was false and wrong was really true and right.   Recall what 2:17 says about gangrene spreading!   "Being deceived" shows that the advocates of error are often themselves as really under deception as those whom they impose upon.[71]   Occultists very often do believe that what they say is true.   They would not only lead others into error, but they themselves are victims of the same errors. "It seems that man, once he is determined to cast his life at variance with the ways of God, becomes all the more entangled and misled in his own evil ways. 'And even as they did not like to retain God in their knowledge, God gave them over to a reprobate mind, to do those things which are not proper (Romans 1:28).'"[72]

3:14 -- You, however – The "you" is emphatic in the Greek.   There is to be an obvious contrast between Timothy (this verse) and the "evil men and imposters" (previous verse).   They may get worse and worse, but Timothy was to keep right on being faithful to his ministry!

Continue in the things you have learned and become convinced of – These words almost pair up with those of verse 10.   Timothy was to continue in the things he had learned from Paul,[73] for what Paul had taught was the gospel truth received directly by revelation and preached by inspiration.   Paul appeals to Timothy to remain loyal to all the teaching which he had received.   He is not to be like the seducing heretics, blown about by every wind of doctrine, and always

---

[68] The verb here rendered "proceed" is the same verb used at 2 Timothy 2:16 ("lead to further ungodliness") and at 3:9.

[69] *Cheiron* is the comparative degree of the adjective *kakos*.   The false teachers will "make progress to the worse."

[70] There is no contradiction between this verse ("will proceed from bad to worse") and verse 9 ("they will not make further progress").   Paul looks at the progress of the false teachers from two different perspectives.   Yes, the doctrine will become worse.   No, the church will not be overcome, even though the opposition becomes more intense.

[71] The Greek form can either be middle (self-deceived) or passive (deceived by someone else). Paul has already spoken of how the devil captures people (2 Timothy 2:26).   The false teachers are deceived by the devil and by his evil spirits (1 Timothy 4:1-2).

[72] Foster, *op. cit.*, p.402.

[73] "The things" refers to the gospel, the truths of Christianity.   From whom Timothy learned "the things" of the gospel will be explained in the next phrase.

seeking some new thing. Timothy is to abide in the old truths which he learned from the Scriptures before Paul ever came to bring the Good News that the promises had been fulfilled in Christ. Paul admonishes Timothy to proceed carefully in the way in which he had been instructed in the past. A thing is not to be preferred simply because it is new. Whether it is true or not is the final test. Timothy was "convinced" of the truth of Christianity's claims in the past. Those claims had the marks of truth upon them. No such validation or guarantee accompanied the doctrines of the false teachers. Timothy should not lightly or unadvisedly give up what he has already been made sure of.

Knowing from whom you have learned *them* – Convictions are not to be lightly jettisoned, for two reasons. The first reason is given in this phrase; the second reason (that Timothy's convictions rest squarely on the solid foundation of the Scriptures) is given in verse 15. The first reason involves Timothy's teacher or teachers. There is some question whether the Greek rendered "whom" is singular or plural.[74] If we read it plural, the reference might be to Lois and Eunice,[75] or Paul and Barnabas, or all of them.[76] If we read it singular,[77] the reference might be to the Holy Spirit,[78] or to Paul himself. Timothy's confidence in the Christian faith – as he had been taught it, and not as the false teachers were teaching it – was made deeper and more secure because of his confidence in those who had taught him that faith. Truthful people give assurance to the truth.[79]

3:15 -- And that from childhood – Here is the second reason why Timothy's Christian convictions must not be just quickly jettisoned. His convictions rest squarely upon the solid foundation of the Scriptures. "From childhood" denotes that Timothy's instruction in the Holy Scriptures began at a very early age.[80] Timothy had been taught the Scriptures as soon as he was capable of learning

---

[74] The Textus Receptus has it singular.   The Nestle-Aland and UBS texts have it plural.

[75] See 2 Timothy 1:5.

[76] A few writers add the name Silas as another distinguished teacher in addition to Paul and Barnabas. Silas travelled with Paul on the second missionary journey, at the time when Timothy was ordained and began his internship or apprenticeship to learn how to be an evangelist.

[77] This is the way the Syriac version reads.   So do Chrysostom, Augustine, and the Vulgate.

[78] Timothy had received some "gift" by the laying on of the apostle's hands (2 Timothy 1:6). If Paul had the Holy Spirit in mind as Timothy's teacher, there would be great force in reminding Timothy that he had received the gospel under the immediate teaching of the Holy Spirit. That would make it even more shameful for him to turn aside from his evangelistic ministry simply because the going got hard.

[79] Pay some attention to the character of the teacher who teaches you.   You are ill advised to forsake people of spiritual stature and holy living simply to follow the latest religious quack.

[80] *Brephos* denotes a babe unborn (Luke 1:41,44), or an infant, a suckling (Luke 2:12,16; Acts 7:19).

anything.[81] His mother and grandmother had been careful to follow the Jewish custom of teaching the Law to Jewish children at a very early age, and to cause them to commit parts of it to memory.[82] At the age of five, when he was old enough to go to the synagogue school, it is likely Timothy was enrolled, and there continued his schooling in the Scriptures.[83] Jewish children learned to read from the very words of Scripture. With such a beginning as this, surely Timothy would not quickly throw away such a precious heritage.[84]

You have known the sacred writings – "Sacred writings" or "Holy Scriptures" is an expression used in Philo[85] and Josephus[86] to designate the Old Testament canonical writings. The Scriptures studied by Timothy from childhood were the Old Testament.[87] An ordinarily-educated child learns "letters" (*gramata*, John 7:15), in contradistinction to the "uneducated" (who are *agramata*, Acts 4:13). But Timothy had learned *ta hiera gramata*, "letters" or "writings" whose excellence is described in the following phrases. Jews used "sacred" or "holy" to indicate the special association of their writings with God. They did not use the word "writings" for anything other than those works which had the mark of Divine inspiration on them.

Which are able to give you the wisdom – The present participle translated "which are able" is notable, here used to express the ever-present power of the Scriptures on the human heart. The Holy Scriptures had not completed their

---

[81] If the previous verse did not include his mother and grandmother among his teachers, this verse certainly does.

[82] "This is a good place to admonish Christian parents to teach their children the Bible. In our home, my wife and I use Kenneth Taylor's *Bible Stories with Pictures for Little Eyes*; in fact, we wore out two copies! What a joy it was to see our older children who had learned to read share the stories with the younger ones, and help them answer the questions. Little by little, the children graduated to older Bible storybooks and then to Bibles of their own. We were fortunate that our Sunday School included a Bible memory program. As soon as your child is born, surround him with the Word of God and prayer. You will not have this opportunity after he grows up." (Wiersbe, *op. cit.*, p.159)

[83] See the Mishnah tractate *Pirke Aboth* 5:21 for information about schooling of Jewish children.

[84] "A person's starting point is a most important factor in the conclusions of his thinking and living. Starting points can be changed in life, but not without great struggle and much effort. Timothy had a good starting point." (Foster, *op. cit.*, p.395)

[85] *Life of Moses*, III.39.

[86] *Ant.* X.10.4. In *Contra Apionem* 1.39ff, Josephus enumerates the books of the Hebrew canon that comprise the Jewish "holy writings."

[87] While Christians might well call the New Testament canonical books "sacred writings" or "holy Scripture" (cp. 2 Peter 3:16), the term as used here in 2 Timothy does not have reference to the New Testament writings. At the time when Timothy was a child and was being instructed in the "sacred writings," none of the New Testament books had yet been penned. In the author's *New Testament Survey Notes*, it is documented that the books of the New Testament were written between AD 45 and 96.

work on Timothy when, in his boyhood, he first mastered their contents. It was still going on (*Ellicott's*, p.322). From 1 Corinthians 1:30 we learn that the "wisdom from God" includes "righteousness, sanctification, and redemption." From the Scriptures Timothy received teaching or instruction about the Savior, the Christ who was to come and become the sacrifice that would provide the way of salvation ("righteousness"). He learned about the corresponding expected lifestyle ("sanctification") to be lived by one who had accepted Christ as Lord and Savior. And he had learned about the future "redemption" of the body and the believer's ultimate glorification.

That leads to salvation – This marks the glorious end and destination of the true wisdom that is gained by a study of the sacred books of the Old Testament. There are many prophecies in the Old Testament as well as things of a typical nature which point to the coming of the Messiah. Paul here reflects Jesus' own use of the Old Testament Scriptures (Luke 24:25-27,44-47; John 5:39,46). These Holy Scriptures were used by the earliest preachers to convince men that Jesus is the Christ, the expected Messiah of the Jews (Acts 2:14-36, 8:26-36, 17:1-4). Paul's preaching to Jewish audiences placed much emphasis upon the prophecies and deeds of God recorded in the Old Testament which pointed to Christ. (See an example in Paul's sermon at Antioch of Pisidia, Acts 13:16-39).

Through faith which is in Christ Jesus – Salvation is conditioned upon faith in Christ Jesus,[88] and as Romans 10:17 tells us, "faith comes by hearing ... the Word of Christ." Or as Galatians 3:24 words it, "The Law has become our tutor to lead us to Christ, that we may be justified by faith." Wisdom gained from the Scriptures helped Timothy to believe in Jesus so that he could share in the salvation Jesus came to make available to mankind.[89] "Faith ... in Christ Jesus" is the regular way in Scripture of expressing an obedient faith.[90] This reminder of Timothy's personal experience in conversion is intended to stimulate his confidence in the trustworthiness of the Scriptural message.

3:16 -- All Scripture is inspired by God – This verse gives the reason why Timo-

---

[88] What Paul writes here corresponds to what he has written elsewhere – e.g., Romans 3:22; Galatians 2:16, 3:26; Philippians 3:9

[89] This verse does not say salvation was to be found in obedience to the Jewish Scriptures, for the Old Testament (Mosaic covenant) was but valid only from Moses to Christ, and has been nailed to the cross. But this verse does show how wisdom gained through a wise and judicious use of the Old Testament Scriptures points a person to Jesus Christ. Then once the promised Messiah has been identified, a commitment of one's life to Him results in salvation.

[90] The word for "believe" or "faith" is followed by a prepositional phrase. That designates an obedient faith as compared to simple mental assent (expressed in the Greek by a word for "believe" followed by the one believed, with no preposition). See Machen, *New Testament Greek for Beginners*, p. 85, paragraph #184.

thy should continue in God's Word.   Scripture is of divine origin!   That accounts for the excellence of the holy writings, both Old and New Testament Scriptures.[91]   When God went about helping men produce the Scriptures, He had a purpose in mind, namely, that the Scriptures were to be useful to men.   Verse 16 has no verb in the Greek, and "is" has to be inserted somewhere in our English translations to make sense.[92]   The ASV did it this way: "Every Scripture inspired of God *is* also profitable ...."   The NASB did it another way: "All Scripture *is* inspired by God and profitable ...."   Both translations affirm that Scriptures[93] are "God breathed."   It is another way of saying that Scripture is God's Word.[94]   "Inspired" may not be the best choice of English words for

---

[91] In verse 15 Paul has used the expression "sacred writings." Is the expression used in verse 16 co-extensive with that earlier expression, or is it possible that "all Scripture" is a larger body of writing than the previous expression "sacred writings" included. After all, in 1 Timothy 5:18 Paul has called Luke's Gospel "Scripture," and 2 Peter 3:15-16 includes Paul's writings among the body of literature called "Scripture." Paul himself has numerous references to the fact that his writings are authoritative, are to be read in the churches, are to be obeyed, and are to be held fast as "the standard of sound words." What Timothy has learned from Paul is to be passed on to faithful men, and all are to "handle accurately" the word of truth. A case might be made that verse 16 (with its "all") is a wider reference than just the Old Testament sacred writings alluded to in verse 15.

[92] In technical language, the debate is whether "inspired (God breathed)" is to be considered part of the subject of the sentence, or part of the predicate. Scholarly works have been produced defending both views, and none has been absolutely convincing. See Knight, *Commentary on the Pastoral Epistles*, p.446 for a recent summary of the scholarly works covering this issue. He opts for "God breathed" being a predicate adjective, which is the NASB's treatment.

[93] A furious debate rages among scholars whether to translate it "all Scripture" or "every Scripture." (1) One reason for the debate is theological. "Every Scripture inspired by God" has been interpreted by some higher critics to mean there are some Old Testament books that are not inspired. (Just as "every good work" implies that there are some works which are not good; and just as "every spiritual blessing" implies that there are some blessings which are not spiritual; and as "every evil work" implies that there are some works which are not evil, so "every inspired Scripture" is interpreted to mean there are some scriptures which are not inspired.) In many cases the reason conservative scholars have opted for "all Scripture" is to defend the inspiration of the whole Old Testament canon (each individual part of it, all of it). (2) Another reason for the debate is grammatical. Conservatives advance their choice of "all Scripture" by appealing to the grammar. With respect to the rendering of *pasa graphē*, there is no doubt that strict grammar given the absence of a definite article in the phrase favors the rendering "every Scripture." Yet, "Scripture" may be a technical name, and so it would be common to use it with or without the article. This would admit "all Scripture" as a proper translation. Just as *pasa Ierosoluma* (Matthew 2:3) means "all Jerusalem" and not "every Jerusalem," so we incline to take *pasa graphē* as "all Scripture." Examples of *graphē* without the article are 2 Peter 1:20 and Romans 1:2; and of *pasa* not followed by the article and still meaning "all" are Ephesians 32:21 and 3:15. Simpson (*The Pastoral Epistles*) has a forceful defense of the translation "all Scripture." A good source for further study is H. Wayne House, "Biblical Inspiration in 2 Timothy 3:16," *Bibliotheca Sacra* 137 (1980), p.54-63. Bernard (CGT) and White (EGT) defend the translation "every Scripture" but do not (as some writers do) use it to deny the inspiration of any of the Old Testament books. After all, "every Scripture inspired of God" in the context is a reference to the "sacred writings" i.e., the whole Old Testament canon.

[94] Compare Jesus' use of "Scripture" and "word of God" in apposition to each other (John 10:35). If the earlier observation is correct, that "all Scripture" includes also New Testament writings in circulation before 2 Timothy is written, then this is a statement about the origin of both the Old Testament sacred writings and the origin of New Testament writings, too.

theopneustos which means literally "God breathed." The Latin word behind "inspired" means to "breathe in" whereas the Greek word means to "breathe out." God breathed out as He prompted holy men of old to speak and write (cp. 2 Peter 1:21 and Jeremiah 36:1-6,22-32).[95] It must be noted also that Paul here deliberately calls attention to the divine origin of Scripture. The Scripture itself is the result of God's action.[96] The Gnostics had their own fanciful and fantastic books; the heretics all produced their own literature to support and to expound their claims. But Paul regarded these things as merely man-made things.[97] It is not their books or books like them which will help men. The great books for a man's soul are the "God-inspired books." The divine origin of Scripture is a guarantee of both its truth and its usefulness.

And profitable for teaching – Since the Scriptures are inspired, they are useful ("profitable"). Some of the various uses that may be made of "God breathed Scripture" are now enumerated. This does not say that every verse in the Old and New Testament writings is profitable for all the uses enumerated. Rather, one may be profitable for teaching, another for reproof, and so on. But the whole of Scripture is useful in one or the other of these ways; the whole of Scripture equips the man of God (verse 17).[98] One of the uses is "for teaching."[99] Teaching (i.e., instructing people about God, His Son, His will, and His way for men to live), of which the Holy Scriptures is the only infallible source, is the basis and test of true Christian belief.

---

[95] The best New Testament passage explaining how "inspiration" worked is 1 Corinthians 2:13.

[96] Scholars have debated whether "God-breathed" is active or passive in meaning. These comments take it as passive. Cremer in his *Biblico-Theological Lexicon of New Testament Greek* took the position that it is active, and that Scripture is filled with God's breath and that it breathes out the Spirit of God. Warfield argued for the passive signnificance in *The Inspiration and Authority of the Bible*. While Warfield's arguments appear to be convincing for this passage, it should not be forgotten that the Holy Spirit does work through the Word in conversion and in leading believers to right living. It is just that "inspiration" is not a synonym for such convicting, converting, and leading work.

[97] When we speak of the false teacher's writings being "man-made," we are not discounting the possibility that some were produced by the help of spirit writing (i.e., appealing to demons for help). But they still are a far cry from Scripture when it comes to how they were produced. Scripture is *God* breathed!

[98] A question that deserves careful attention has to do with the use Christians make of the Old Testament, especially since the Mosaic covenant was temporary and nailed to the cross, and people now live under the new covenant. Though it deals with Christians in general, rather than the use preachers in particular might make of the Old Testament, and therefore needs to be read with care, a helpful and extended treatment of 2 Timothy 3:16,17 can be found in F.E. Gaebelein, *The Christian Use of the Bible* (Chicago: Moody Press, 1946).

[99] The KJV reads "for doctrine." The Pastoral Epistles are full of emphasis on what teaching or instruction men are to be schooled in. See notes at 1 Timothy 1:10 for more explanation of the term "teaching" or "doctrine." A similar idea is expressed in Romans 15:4 where we are told that "whatever was written in earlier times was written for our instruction."

For reproof – This is a second use that may be made of Scripture. The idea in the word is that of "convicting" or "convincing" a man of the error of his ways. See Matthew 18:15, where the sinner is to be "convicted" of his fault, and 1 Timothy 5:20, where Timothy is to publicly "rebuke" those who sin. Errors of doctrine and personal conduct are to be reproved by the truths revealed in the Holy Scriptures. "For reproof" suggests that not only does the Scripture point out error, but it is also the agent to be used in refuting the error.

For correction – A third use of Scripture is that it has the power to set a person straight, to restore a person to an upright position before God. "Correction" has special reference to conduct. There are many illustrations concerning how Scripture has come into men's hands and changed their lives. Men are shown the errors of their ways by Scripture, and are led into the correct or right way. No change of conduct is permanent which is not based on the principles of Scripture.

For training in righteousness – After a person is rebuked and pointed in the proper direction, Scripture is able to hold a man steady on the right path. This is a fourth way in which Scripture is useful. Scripture will instruct[100] a man in regard to what is right.[101] It will teach him what is required in order that he may lead a holy life. The Scriptures are God's textbook for instruction in all personal relations.[102]

3:17 -- That the man of God may be adequate – A *hina* clause may express either purpose or result. Perhaps verse 17 expresses the purpose for which God intended the Scripture to be useful. Perhaps it expresses the result of such usefulness in a person's life. And who does Paul have in mind when he speaks of the "man of God"?   Is it a general term for all Christians, or a specific term for the Christian preacher? If we take it as a general term, then the passage says the Scriptures may be useful to any Christian. That certainly is true. Scriptures not only lead a person to Christ (2 Timothy 3:15), but they also nourish his spiritual life so he may grow as a Christian. Without a knowledge of the Word, Christians are not prepared to be laborers together with God. If we take it as a reference to the preacher, and in this context perhaps this is how it should be inter-

---

[100] The word "training" is also translated "nurture" in Ephesians 6:4 and "chastening" in Hebrews 12:5,7,8,11.

[101] "Righteousness" here probably means "right living" – giving both God and men their due.

[102] Some suggest the four words defining the way Scripture is useful can be arranged in two pairs – the first pair dealing with belief, the second with action. This arrangement can be seen, for example, in the New English Bible, which reads "for teaching the truth and refuting error," and "for reformation of manner and discipline in right living." John R.W. Stott (*Guard the Gospel: The Message of 2 Timothy*) sums up the importance of what this passage says. "Do we hope, either in our own lives or in our teaching ministry, to overcome error and grow in truth, to overcome evil and grow in holiness?   Then it is to Scripture we must ... turn, for Scripture is 'profitable' for these things."

preted,[103] then the passage tells Timothy by what means in particular he can continue to be "adequate" and "equipped" for ministry.[104] He must continue in the Word, for it is this tool that God intended preachers and teachers to find useful. "Adequate"[105] talks about being adequate to the task a "man of God" must do. It is the Scriptures that enable the Christian leader to do the task which God has placed him in a certain place to do. From the Scriptures the "man of God" must document the doctrine he teaches. From the Scriptures the "man of God" must draw his reproofs for the ignorant and erring. The Scriptures must be the source, the one source, from which he derives the instructions he gives to teach Christians how to grow in the grace and knowledge of our Lord and Savior Jesus Christ.

Equipped for every good work – The idea is that the man of God, with the Scriptures, is equal to any opportunity[106] which may arise for engaging in good works.[107]   The Scriptures, handled accurately, give the preacher the equipment needed to make him ready for every aspect and task of the ministry that he is called to do. Scripture in the hands of one who can handle it aright is a powerful instrument for good. God indicates in Scripture what should be done. With these words of encouragement Paul comes to the close of his prophetic appeal to Timothy to stay in the ministry. Since with the Holy Scriptures you are so well equipped for the job, Timothy, it is always too soon to quit the ministry!

---

[103] "Man of God" is the regular OT title for the prophets who were in the immediate service of God. (See comments at 1 Timothy 6:11.)   A good case can be made that the usage of the phrase elsewhere in the New Testament (i.e., 1 Timothy 6:11 and 2 Peter 1:21) is in this technical sense. Further, this sentence finishes the thought begun at 2 Timothy 3:14, "You, however, continue in the things you have learned ..." and this thought was addressed specifically to the evangelist Timothy.

[104] This interpretation results from taking verse 17 as a purpose clause.

[105] The Greek word here is *artios*. The KJV reads "perfect" in this place, using the same English word it uses to translate another Greek word, *teleios*. Of course, readers of the KJV must be careful lest they mistakenly suppose the word "perfect" means the Christian can get to the place where he is without sin or fault of any kind. That is not what "perfect" means. "Perfect" (*teleios*) means "mature, full grown." If the Greek word were *teleios*, then commentators might correctly speak of how the Scriptures serve to complete the character and service of the man of God, and how through teaching, reproof, correction, and instruction in righteousness, the Christian is brought from infancy, through childhood, to spiritual maturity. But the word is not *teleios*; it is *artios*.

[106] The word translated "equipped" (*exartidzō*) is a compound form built on the same root as the previous word "adequate." In classical Greek the verb means "to equip fully." The word here in 2 Timothy is nearly synonymous with *katartidzō*, the word translated "prepare" in Matthew 21:16, "fully trained" in Luke 6:40, "be made complete" in 2 Corinthians 13:11, "equip" in Hebrews 13:21, and "perfect" (adjust what is lacking) in 1 Peter 5:10.

[107] If "man of God" means any Christian, then "good works" are any of the generous and self-sacrificing acts so often referred to in the Pastoral Epistles. If we take "man of God" in a technical sense, then "good works" are tasks specially with reference to the labors of Timothy and his fellow evangelists. "Good works," in any case, are exactly opposite the "works" the false teachers were advocating and doing. Cp. 2 Timothy 2:21, where the vessel of honor was useful for good works.

IV. The Second Personal Appeal – Preach and Proclaim Your Faith!   4:1-18

A. Preach the Word!   4:1-4

4:1 -- I solemnly charge you – The word "charge" has been explained at 2 Timothy 2:14.   Giving a charge or command to pass on Divine testimony is emphasized in outstanding Scriptures: Moses charged Israel (Deuteronomy 20:11,16, 29:1,10); Moses charged Joshua (Deuteronomy 31:7,8,23); Joshua charged Israel (Joshua 23:1,6, 24:1,26,27); Samuel charged Israel (1 Samuel 12:1-25); David charged Solomon (1 Kings 2:1-9, 1 Chronicles 28:2-10,20); Ezra charged Israel (Nehemiah 8-10); Jesus charged the apostles (John 13:34, 14-17).   Now, in some solemn last words,[1] Paul gives a serious charge to Timothy.   The actual things Timothy is charged to do are set forth in verses 2, 5, and 9.   The very fact that they are addressed by one anticipating martyrdom to a younger colleague upon whom heavy responsibilities will soon devolve gives them an air of gravity.

In the presence of God and of Christ Jesus – It may mean Paul thinks of God and Jesus as watching him as he gives this charge.   It may mean that Paul thinks of God and Jesus as watching Timothy as he receives and carries out this charge.[2]   God and Jesus are present with Paul in Rome and present with Timothy in Ephesus.   God and Jesus are divine witnesses to this solemn command, and that adds weight to the solemnity of the charge.   Timothy is to realize that Paul's commands have heaven's authority behind them.

Who is to judge the living and the dead – Jesus Christ, the One Who became flesh, and lived before God on earth while accomplishing the task God sent him to do, is here identified as the judge,[3] and the time when the judging will be done is the final judgment.[4]   Timothy and Paul are both to realize that they are answerable at the final judgment for their words and actions.   When Jesus returns, some folk will still be living on earth, and others will have died and then be raised to

---

[1] "A great person's last words are significant.   They are a window that helps us look into his heart, or a measure that helps us evaluate what is important in his life.   In this chapter we have Paul's last words to Timothy and to the church. ... The apostle gave three final admonitions to Timothy, and he backed each of them up with a reason."   (Wiersbe, *op.cit.*, p.163)

[2] Paul used this same phrase in 1 Timothy 5:21, and there includes the elect angels as well.

[3] "Who" has "Christ Jesus" as its nearest antecedent.   In some passages, it is God the father who judges.   In other passages, it appears that the Father entrusts the task of judging to the Son (John 5:25-30; Matthew 7:21,22).

[4] This same final judgment is alluded to in Matthew 25:31ff, 2 Corinthians 5:10, and Revelation 20:11ff.

stand at the judgment seat of Christ. Being alive or dead will make no difference in their status. The whole human race is included into "the living and the dead." There is a judgment to be faced. All men will stand before the judgment seat of Christ.[5]   Looking forward to the judgment morning must surely be a spur to any faint-hearted, dispirited servant of the Lord disposed to temporize, or reluctant to face the dangers which regularly accompany a faithful discharge of duties.   Just as a thought of having to answer in the judgment motivated Paul (2 Corinthians 5:9-11), so he wanted that thought to motivate Timothy.   A Christian preacher's work must be good enough, not to satisfy men, but to satisfy Jesus.   He must do every task in such a way that he can take it and offer it to God.

And by His appearing and His kingdom – There is a manuscript variation here. The Textus Receptus reads "who will judge the living and dead *at* his appearing and kingdom."[6]   The older manuscripts have "and" rather than "at" so that the verse reads "I charge you in the sight of ... Jesus Christ who will judge the living and the dead ... *and* (I charge you) by His appearing and by His kingdom."[7]   The judgment, the appearing of Christ[8] at His second coming, and the ushering in of the eternal kingdom,[9] are all events in the light of which the preacher must live his life and render his service.[10]   God and Christ are divine witnesses; Jesus is

---

[5] "Paul, in his divine wisdom, charges Timothy (and other teachers of the church?) to be faithful and zealous in his work, by the thought, which must be ever present that *they* – either alive on the day of the coming of the Lord, or, if they have tasted physical death already, raised from the dead incorruptible (cp. 1 Thessalonians 4:17) – must stand before the Judge and give an account of their stewardship ... [O]n that awful morning must every man and woman render up, before the Judge who knows all and sees all, a strict account of the deeds done in the body." Spence, *op. cit.*, p.324.

[6] This reading, represented in English by the KJV, makes such excellent sense, as it tells *when* the final judgment will take place, that it is difficult not to believe it is the right reading.   In addition, commentators are far from agreeing what the reading "and" (as in the NASB) actually means.

[7] This reading, the one more ancient and at first sight, the one more difficult, actually adds immeasurable strength and power to the solemn charge Paul is giving to Timothy.   The problem with this reading is that there is a change of case in the Greek, from the genitive ("in the presence of God and Jesus") to the accusative ("and His appearing and His kingdom" is how the Greek literally reads).   As a result commentators struggle to explain the precise meaning of this accusative phrase.

[8] "Appearing" (*epiphaneia*) is a word used both of Christ's first coming (2 Timothy 1:10) and of His second coming (2 Timothy 4:1,8; Titus 2:13).   It means that something not visible to human eyes becomes visible or manifest.

[9] "Kingdom" is also a word that has several meanings.   At times it has reference to the church, the present rule of God over the hearts of men (1 Corinthians 15:20-28; Colossians 1:13; Revelation 1:5,6).   At times it has reference to the future reign of the Godhead after the second coming (Acts 14:22; 1 Corinthians 6:9,10; Galatians 5:21; Ephesians 5:5; 2 Thessalonians 1:5; Revelation 22:3; 2 Timothy 4:18).   It would appear that "kingdom" in this passage means the eternal kingdom in the new heavens and new earth.   It is the "kingdom prepared ... from the foundation of the world" (Matthew 25:34 KJV).   That kingdom will commence at Christ's glorious return, when "the kingdom of the world has become the kingdom of our Lord and of His Christ; and He will reign forever and ever" (Revelation 11:15).

[10] Note that the NASB adds the preposition "by" before both "appearing" and "kingdom."   The

the judge; the appearing and the kingdom are the most solemn incentives to fidelity.[11]   If Timothy hopes to share in the glorious state, he has a responsibility to fulfill and some obligations to discharge, some of which are specifically spelled out in the imperatives that follow.

4:2 -- Preach the word -- This is the first of a series of imperatives – five in this verse, and several more later – that spell out precisely what Timothy is solemnly charged to do.   Of course a preacher preaches, but what does he preach? Timothy is here commanded, not to air his own opinions like the false teachers were doing, but to proclaim God's eternal, authoritative word of truth.[12]   There are two words most often used for "preach" in the New Testament.   One, *euaggelidzō*, emphasizes the "good news" that is being proclaimed; the other, *kērussō*, the word used here in verse 2, emphasizes the manner of proclamation, like a herald announces the message the king sent him to publish.[13]   Timothy was to herald God's word with the authority of King Jesus behind him.   It is impossible to exaggerate the dignity and importance here given to preaching by its being made the subject of so solemn and awful a charge as that in verse 1.

Greek words "appearing" and "kingdom" are in the accusative case, and perhaps are to be understood as being the usual accusative used with verbs of swearing or adjuration, as in Mark 5:7, Acts 19:13 and Deuteronomy 4:26 (LXX).   On the other hand, some express surprise that anyone would "swear by" or "solemnly charge by" Christ's epiphany and kingdom.   Because treating this as an accusative of adjuration is so without example elsewhere in Scripture, others urge that the verb *diamarturomai* should be repeated, so the verse reads "I charge you ... and I call to witness Christ's epiphany and kingdom."   However, this approach treats *diamarturomai* in two different senses in the same verse, which normally would be against such a handling of this very disputed passage.   Ellicott explains that whereas "in the presence of" (in the Greek) requires the genitive case ("God" and "Jesus" are in the genitive) when *persons* are involved, it would not be natural to use the genitive case of *events* like the epiphany and the kingdom, so those words naturally were attracted to the accusative case.

[11] Barclay (*op. cit.*, p.233) reminds us of the 1st century word picture that "appearance" would convey to people's minds.   It was the word used of a new emperor's accession to his throne.   It was also the word used of the visit by the emperor to any province or town.   Obviously, when the emperor was due to visit any place, everything was put in perfect order.   The streets were swept and garnished; all work was up-to-date.   The town was scoured and decorated to be fit for the expected visit of the emperor.   So Paul says to Timothy, "You know what happens when any town is expecting a visit by the emperor.   Well, you are expecting the visit of Jesus Christ.   Do your work in such a way that all things will be ready whenever He arrives."   The Christian preacher so orders his life that at any moment he is ready for the Coming of Christ.

[12] The "word" that Timothy is to herald is the "gospel," as has been learned in 2 Timothy 2:9,15. This word of God is what both sinners and saints need to hear.   It is sad, even tragic, when churches and preachers substitute other things for the preaching of the Word.   "I have seen what the preaching of the Word can do in churches and in individual lives, and I affirm that *nothing can take its place*." (Wiersbe, *op. cit.*, p.164)

[13] In the 1st century world, rulers commissioned certain special messengers to travel throughout their realm, to make special announcements from the king to the people.   The herald would make his announcement in a loud, clear voice so everyone could hear.   He added nothing to the message; he subtracted nothing from the message; he simply repeated what the king sent him to say.   Not to heed the king's messenger was serious; to abuse the messenger was even worse.

Be ready in season and out of season – The second imperative in Paul's solemn command, *epistēthi* (KJV, "be instant," NASB, "be ready"), is not an easy verb to translate.[14]   Marshall offers "be attentive."   The idea seems to be that Timothy is to be ready to preach at any moment, whenever the opportunity presents itself, or even if the preacher has to make an opportunity to teach and instruct and guide in following God's Word.[15]   The work of preaching must be done at all hours and at all times.   It has to be done not only when meeting in the assembly of the saints, not merely in times of security and peace, but it must be carried on in the midst of dangers, even if you are a prisoner and in chains, even if death threatens you.   What do the adverbs "seasonably" and "unseasonably" suggest?   Spence (*Ellicott's*, p.325) quotes two ancient writers to answer this question. Chrysostom, who used Paul's words here as an urgent call to preachers to labor on in spite of discouragement and apparent failure, tells them in his own eloquent way how fountains still flow on though no one goes to them to draw water, and rivers still run on though no one drinks at them.   Augustine asks and answers the question to whom "in season" and to whom "out of season" refers: "in season" to those willing, "out of season" to those unwilling.   Whether the occasion comes conveniently to the herald, or whether the circumstances are inopportune (e.g., he is tired and worn down, or faces dangers and bitter opposition), God's preacher is ready to preach and serve.[16]

Reprove, rebuke, exhort – If the second imperative in this verse was related to preaching, then perhaps so are these three.   There is a good possibility that all three appeals – to the reason, to the conscience, and to the will – are to be included in each instance of preaching.   "Reprove" (see 2 Timothy 3:16 and Titus 1:9,13) means to convict the offender of his fault.   This is the appeal to reason. "Rebuke" means to censure, warn, admonish.   The word involves telling those doing wrong to stop doing it.[17]   The word has the idea of an implied demand for restitution when error is pointed out.   This is the appeal to conscience. "Exhort" can also be translated "encourage" or "comfort" or "appeal to" (cp. Titus 2:15 and 1 Timothy 6:2).   Here is the other side of the matter.   Hand in hand

---

[14] Another meaning offered is "stand by."   In the 20th century, some people instead of having fixed reservations for a seat on an airplane do what is called "Flying stand by."   They wait in the terminal until almost the moment of take-off, for if there is an empty seat, their name may be called and they must hurry to get on board before the plane leaves.

[15] The explanation is offered in general terms, for it is not certain whether the timeliness (seasonableness) for preaching is viewed from the perspective of the preacher, or from the perspective of the hearers, or both.

[16] "It is easy to make excuses when we ought to be making opportunities.   Paul himself found an opportunity to share the Word, whether it was in the temple courts, on a stormy sea, or even in a prison.   'He that observeth the wind shall not sow; and he that regardeth the clouds shall not reap' (Ecclesiastes 11:4).   Stop making excuses and get to work!"   (Wiersbe, *op. cit.,* p.164)

[17] Trench, *Synonyms*, p.13ff.

with the conviction of the sinner and reprimanding him, must be the exhortation or encouragement that comes from love and concern.   No rebuke, no conviction should ever be such that it drives a man to despair and takes the heart and the hope out of him.   Not only must men be rebuked, they must also be encouraged. Encouragement is at least as much a part of preaching as rebuke.[18] Encouragement is addressed to the will.

With great patience and instruction – There is some question concerning the relation of this prepositional phrase with the rest of the verse.   In these notes it has been suggested that "preach the word" is the dominant idea, and that the other four imperatives in this verse are somehow related to the charge to preach.   If that is true, then the prepositional phrase is also related to the command to preach. Every time a man preaches, he must display patience and painstaking instruction. The listeners may be slow to learn, or provocative in their refusal of the message, but the preacher must patiently put up with people[19] who so need what he has to offer and don't even realize their need.   The preacher will not always see immediate results, but he goes right on teaching.[20]   Patient teaching is the most solid basis for ultimate success in the ministry (cp. 2 Timothy 2:25).

4:3 -- For the time will come – "For" shows that Timothy is here given a reason why there will be a need for patience as he preaches and teaches.   Timothy will shortly have to deal with the difficulties this verse describes.   The age indicated in "the time will come" dawned before Timothy's ministry was completed.[21] Perhaps there is also an implicit prediction that, as the church gets centuries older, things will ever grow worse as men reject the gospel and prefer everything else to the gospel.[22]

---

[18] "To quote an old rule of preachers, 'He should afflict the comfortable and comfort the afflicted.' If there is conviction but no remedy, we add to people's burdens.   And if we encourage those who ought to be rebuked, we are assisting them to sin.   Biblical preaching must be balanced."   Wiersbe, *op. cit.*, p.165.

[19] The synonym here translated "patience" was explained at 1 Timothy 1:16 & 2 Timothy 3:10.

[20] Paul has frequently emphasized "teaching" in the Pastoral Epistles.   See 1 Timothy 1:10, 4:6,13,16, 5:17; 2 Timothy 3:10,16.   *Pulpit Commentary* suggests that the use of *didachē* here puts emphasis on the act of teaching.   Titus 1:9 suggests that it is by teaching that one goes about "exhorting" and "rebuking."

[21] The conditions that Paul has been describing, with false teaching and deceitful teachers, were already in evidence to a certain degree as he wrote to Timothy.   However, Paul looked forward to a time when conditions would be still worse, and in the following verses warns Timothy not to be deterred by such worsening conditions from the work he is supposed to be doing.

[22] In most every society, one can see this same history repeat itself.   At first, there is a hunger for the gospel.   People respond quickly.   But as time goes on, it becomes harder and harder to win more converts.   And then the people become hardened, and look for teachers who will satisfy their own desires, rather than for teachers who teach God's Word in all its purity.

When they will not endure sound doctrine – As regularly in the Pastoral Epistles, "sound doctrine" is a reference to the gospel (see 1 Timothy 1:10, Titus 19, 2:1). The idea is that the listeners reject the message because they think its demands are too great. They won't want to hear or listen willingly to gospel preaching. When Timothy sees this happening, he may well be experiencing one of the "unseasonable" times in the ministry. Instead of being caught off guard or disillusioned, Timothy is to just keep on preaching!

But *wanting* to have their ears tickled – One sees the image of an old dog who could be out on the hunt, but who is lying at his master's feet having his ears scratched. The smile on the dog's face betrays his feelings: it just feels so good, and nothing is expected of me. The time comes when the preacher will find that his audience just wants to have their ears scratched. They do not want the preacher suggesting any changes they should be making in their lives, or any duties they should be pursuing.[23]

They will accumulate for themselves teachers in accordance to their own desires – The only teachers they want are those who will scratch or tickle their ears. The verb "accumulate" is a contemptuous word implying the indiscriminate multiplication of such teachers. J.B. Phillips translated this phrase as "They will collect teachers who will pander to their own desires." The expression "their own desires" gives some insight into the reason why the audience will not endure sound doctrine. "Their own desires," at all risks, they would gratify. That would be their first priority, and any preacher who would call for stern morality and purity of doctrine would not be tolerated. Instead, they would seek out teachers who would be more indulgent, who would flatter and gratify their hearers, without expecting the hearers to live pure and saintly lives.[24]

4:4 -- And will turn away their ears from the truth – The curious listeners no longer want a preacher who "tells them the old, old story of Jesus and His love." There will be preachers who still teach the truth,[25] but these listeners turn away

---

[23] "Tickling the ear" is a participle that agrees with the subject of the sentence. Arndt and Gingrich (p.423) suggest that the unusual Greek phrase here (literally, "feeling an itching in the hearing") is a figure of speech signifying "curiosity, that looks for interesting ... bits of information." The next verse would then explain how the false teachers would satisfy this itching.

[24] Preachers who deliberately structure their worship services to be "seeker sensitive" must be careful that they are not just pandering to the desires of the unconverted. A man may build a huge following with seeker sensitive type services, but if he never offers the listeners "sound doctrine," he has failed in his mission as a preacher. Somewhere along the way the "unchurched Harrys and Marys" who are wooed by the well-planned entertainment must be confronted with sound doctrine – and be reproved, rebuked, and exhorted by the preached Word.

[25] Very wonderful is the Bible's constant orientation to *truth*, a comprehensive word for God's revelation centering in Jesus Christ. This is the third expression in this context to designate the gospel – it has previously been called "the word" and "sound teaching." See notes at 1 Timothy 2:4

from listening to it.   It is implied that there was a time the listeners listened to the truth, but no longer.[26]   Timothy should not be discouraged or tempted by this to quit preaching.   The solemn charge is to keep on preaching in spite of the fact that some reject the truthful message being preached.

And will turn aside to myths – At Titus 1:14 there has been a careful explanation of what these "myths" (or "fables"[27] KJV) were and concerning their Jewish origin.   What Paul is warning Timothy (and Timothy's listeners) against is incipient Jewish-Gnosticism that the false teachers would present.   When men leave revealed religion,[28] they usually go into some form of witchcraft (what the Bible calls idolatry).   The Jewish-Gnostics certainly were involved in witchcraft, as indicated in the word "imposters" at 2 Timothy 3:13.[29]

B. Fulfill Your Ministry.   4:5-8

4:5 -- But you – Here begins the second paragraph of Paul's second personal appeal to Timothy to stay in the ministry.   "But you" is an emphatic contrast to what some people may want in their preacher (verses 3,4).   Timothy must not be one who becomes the kind of preacher who simply tickles men's ears.   The four imperatives in this verse will conclude Paul's instructions to Timothy regarding Timothy's work as evangelist at Ephesus.   There will be some personal instructions in the following paragraph.   We suppose that the four imperatives in this verse rather summarize all the things taught in 2 Timothy.

Be sober in all things – Literally the word *nēphe* means to "abstain from intoxi-cating drinks," but Timothy was hardly in danger of needing this command (1

---

and 2 Timothy 2:15,18,24, 3:7,8, where the "truth" is emphasized.   "Truth" is in stark contrast to what the false teachers were offering to their listeners.

[26] This is in harmony with Titus 1:14 and 2 Timothy 1:15, both of which imply a prior relationship with the truth that has been jettisoned or abandoned.

[27] The word "fable" is the English name given to the fanciful stories of the happenings of the "gods" in idolatry.   A "myth" is something that is not true, not historical, and lacks reality.   See 1 Timothy 1:4 for a discussion of the possible content of these myths.   The Greek here at verse 4 reads "the myths," and the definite article may specify the particular myths that are associated with the false teaching Timothy will have to combat.

[28] See comments on "turn aside" at 1 Timothy 2:6.

[29] One cannot help but observe that America, having turned away from the truth of God, has popular literature and media filled with "myths" such as Erik von Daniken's theories, and UFOlogy (with flying saucers and space aliens having crashed at Roswell, New Mexico, and emphasis on "intelligent masters" who would like to impart their advanced knowledge to our civilization).   In a slightly different vein, Lewis Foster (*op. cit.*, p.403) has written, "In view of the popular usage of the word myth in certain theological circles today, this verse takes on special significance.   Some theologians have singled out some of the truths of God and labeled them myths.   [They then set about to 'demythologize' the Bible.]"

Timothy 5:23). So the word likely must be taken in its metaphorical sense. 'Keep your head,' or 'Do nothing to dull your thinking.' In this context, being "sober" might have to do with watching out for the temptation to be a popular preacher (he could be one if he just tickled the ears of the people). Or, being "sober" might just have to do with priorities. There are so many demands on the time of an evangelist. Which one needs to be done now, so the whole work progresses? Timothy will have to be alert and keep his wits about him.[30]

Endure hardship – We have had this word at 2 Timothy 2:3,9. Timothy must be willing to suffer, if need be, for the gospel. Christian ministry is costly, and the preacher is to pay the price of it without grumbling and without regret.

Do the work of an evangelist – Evangelists in the early church seem to have been preachers of the gospel. Sometimes we find them working as church planters (like Philip, Acts 21:8) and sometimes we find them preaching to an already established congregation (like Timothy at Ephesus, 1 and 2 Timothy).[31] We agree with the suggestion that the "exhortation here consists in more than the duty resting on every Christian to tell or spread the good news." There was and is an office or function of evangelist in the church, and the tasks connected with that office or function are what Timothy was to concentrate his efforts upon. Those tasks are here especially termed "work" to remind Timothy that to perform rightly this task he would need zeal, close work, much study, thought, and prayer. It was by persistently performing the duties of an evangelist that some would be stopped from turning away to myths, and perhaps others might be won back from following the false teachers who were teaching those myths. What people needed to hear was the great facts of the gospel placed side by side against the fables taught by the false teachers.

Fulfill your ministry – "Fulfill" is a rather weak rendering of the Greek *plērophorēson*.[32] The KJV "make full proof of thy ministry" also does not

---

[30] The present tense imperative is used for "be sober." This is a change from the series of aorist imperatives that have been part of the solemn charge to Timothy. Perhaps the present tense is used because there will be numerous situations and circumstances that will require "well-balanced, careful thinking."

[31] See the special study on "Evangelists" following 1 Timothy 4. Timothy may be working with the local congregation at Ephesus, he may be their preacher each time the brethren assemble for worship, but there still is evangelistic work to do (i.e., souls to be won to Christ), and Timothy will have to keep at this task. When this commentator was an associate preacher at Lockland, Ohio, he was given the charge, "We expect you to be making evangelistic calls, along with your task as youth minister. Do not go to bed on Saturday night until you are certain there will be at least one response to the invitation on Sunday morning." In this commentator's experience, growing churches are the ones in which the preacher is diligent at personal evangelism and soul winning.

[32] The phrase is likely to be taken metaphorically, but it is uncertain whether the metaphor is that of a ship being borne along by full sails, or of full measure being given.

communicate the idea very well. What Timothy is to do is carry out to its completeness whatever God wants him to do.[33] Included in Timothy's ministry would be the committing of the gospel to faithful men, who would be the next generation of gospel teachers. Included would be faithfully continuing to preach even when his patience is being tested, and when folk preferred some "ear tickler" to Timothy. Included also is the idea that Timothy is not to quit the ministry.[34] Timothy is to keep on preaching the gospel, and to pack his ministry to the full with the things he has been exhorted to do in these two letters from Paul. Timothy's ministry might not be exactly like any other preacher's, but it would be important to the cause of Christ! No God-directed ministry is small or unimportant.[35]

4:6 -- For I am already being poured out as a drink-offering – Observe the verse begins with "for." Just like Paul gave a reason for the first charge to "Preach the word" (verses 3,4), now he gives a reason for the charge just given in verse 5. It was because Paul could no longer minister and travel as he once did; his martyrdom had already commenced and his death was close at hand. Now Timothy would have to carry on! The "drink-offering" was a cup of wine, commonly poured on the sacrificial victim at the conclusion of the sacrifice.[36] Paul viewed his whole ministry as a sacrifice he was offering to God.[37] In Philippians 2:17, from the first Roman imprisonment, when his martyrdom was just a possibility, he wrote "if I am poured out." There is no "if" in 2 Timothy. Here he says "I am already being poured out."[38] As he writes this letter the legal

---

[33] Archippus, the preacher, was given a similar exhortation at Colossians 4:17.

[34] The nine imperative verbs in 2 Timothy 4:2-5 begin "preach the word" and end with "fulfill your ministry." "Paul calls on Timothy to proclaim and apply God's word with much patience and careful instruction, to be clearheaded in every situation, to bear whatever difficulties such a ministry may involve him in, to evangelize, and to do whatever is necessary to accomplish the ministry to which Christ has called him." Knight, *op. cit.*, p.458.

[35] In the final chapter of 2 Timothy, Paul names several co-laborers about whom we know nothing other than what is here said. Yet each had a ministry to accomplish. Wiersbe (*op. cit.*, p.166) offers this illustration: "A young preacher once complained to Charles Spurgeon, the famous Baptist preacher, that he did not have as big a church as he deserved. 'How many do you preach to?' Spurgeon asked. 'Oh, about 100,' the man replied. Solemnly Spurgeon said, 'That will be enough to give account for on the day of judgment'."

[36] The wine poured out over the sacrifice, the drink offering it sometimes was called, was a sweet savor to the Lord. See Exodus 29:40-41; Numbers 15:1-10 and 28:4-8.

[37] Paul had dedicated every part of his being, his money, his scholarship, his energies, his mind, his service to the Lord. He had done what he urged others to do in Romans 12:1,2.

[38] The KJV reads "I am now ready to be offered." This language could be interpreted to mean that for him death held no terror. But that would miss the point of the figure of speech Paul uses.

process[39] that would result in his death is already beginning to be carried out.[40] His martyrdom would be like a drink offering, the conclusion of his life of sacrifice. "My sacrificial work," Paul says in effect, "is now finished and ended, and the last solemn sacrificial act has already begun."[41]

And the time of my departure has come – There is a beautiful word picture in the word "departure." It is the word used of a ship about to weigh anchor and sail away, or of a soldier preparing to strike camp so as to move on. It is the word for unyoking an animal from the tongue of the cart or the plow. Death to Paul was rest from toil. He would lay his burden down. It was a departure from this life to make a journey to the next world. He'll soon be casting off the lines which fastened his vessel to the dock, and weighing the anchor so he can proceed on his destined voyage.[42] The time for Paul to go is "at hand," that is, it is already present. Paul knows exactly how this second imprisonment at Rome will end. He will be executed. But physical death was not the end – it was just a "departure." He would be setting out for new lands! That the time of Paul's "departure" is at hand is all the more reason why Timothy must stay in the ministry and take over some of the things Paul has been doing.

4:7 -- I have fought the good fight – Paul has just told Timothy that the conclusion of his own ministry is at hand. This leads Paul naturally to reflect back over that ministry. Three very vivid expressions are used to characterize his ministry for Christ. It had been a struggle[43] but he had given his all in the struggle.[44] The "fight" or 'contest' or 'struggle'[45] is characterized as "good" or

---

[39] The processes (arrest, trial, sentencing, appeal, etc.) that would lead to his death are already in the course of happening. It was just a matter of time.

[40] While his death is certain, it will not take place immediately. Paul can ask Timothy to come to him (2 Timothy 4:9,21) and expect to be alive when Timothy arrives. But that delay does not mean he will escape being executed.

[41] Several writers have called attention to the fact that "am already being poured out" is a passive voice verb. Paul is not voluntarily committing suicide. His life is being taken from him.

[42] The same figure for "death" was used by Paul in Philippians 1:23. Jesus (Luke 9:31) and Peter (2 Peter 1:15) spoke of death under a similar figure of speech, where they called it an "exodus."

[43] The English word "fight" does not adequately express the meaning of *ton agōna*, a word which embraces all kinds of "contests" – the chariot race, the foot race, wrestling, boxing, etc. I.e., any of the athletic sports that required the participant to strain and sweat and exert great amounts of energy just to participate. The same word is translated differently at Philippians 1:30; Colossians 2:1; 1 Thessalonians 2:2; Hebrews 12:1; and 1 Timothy 6:12. There are also places where the term is used of the kinds of fights one gets into in the army, but perhaps we should limit any comments about Paul's being a good soldier to 2 Timothy 2:3ff.

[44] The verb is a perfect tense. It is a past completed action with present continuing results.

[45] There are two ways of interpreting the metaphors in this verse: (1) Take all three clauses as referring to three different things: the first military, the second athletic, and the third religious (stewardship). Cf. Simpson, p. 159. (2) Take all three clauses as a reference to athletics: they

'honorable.'[46] People sometimes ask the preacher, "Why are you wasting your life? Why not be a doctor, or some other profession?" Paul looks back over his life, evaluates it, and says, "I have been engaged in an honorable struggle. Others may be OK as well, but this is the best one!"

Just who were Paul's opponents in the struggle? He has been in a fight against Satan, against principalities and powers not of this world. He has been in a fight against Jewish and pagan opposition and devices. He has been in a fight against the false teaching, the bitterness, the jealousy and strife within the churches. He has been in a fight against the incipient Jewish Gnosticism, their unbiblical lifestyles and their personal bitterness against him. There has even been a struggle against bodily temptations so that he had to buffet his body daily and keep it in subjection (1 Corinthians 9:26,27). Against these opponents Paul has struggled and won, and he feels a deep sense of satisfaction in his heart.

I have finished the course – With an air of triumph and almost of relief, Paul says he had completed the course Jesus had marked out for him.[47] The word picture is that of the stadium, or the Olympic race course. The runner in a race had a definite "course" to run, that is marked out for him. It is from Acts 20:24 that we get the idea that the "course" for Paul was the ministry he had received from the Lord Jesus. Again we have a perfect tense verb. How can it be said that he had finished his course (i.e., past action with present continuing results) when he is not dead yet? Wycliffe likens this figure to a lap in a relay race. Paul has received the gospel from Jesus, has run his lap, and has passed it on to the next runner. The figure of a relay race seems to fit the following verse, too, for not Paul only, but the whole "team" will receive the prize. Paul makes no claim to having won the race by himself, but he does refer to the fact that in a mighty effort he has done the best he can.

I have kept the faith – If this is still an athletic metaphor,[48] the idea is "I have kept the rules." "I have not fouled out" and so been disqualified from winning.

---

are all figures of speech from the world of athletics.

[46] See the word explained at 1 Timothy 1:18 and 6:12.

[47] Compare Acts 13:25 where Paul speaks of John the Baptist as "completing (finishing) his course."

[48] It might be a religious metaphor. If so, there may be a reference that corresponds to the earlier references to "guarding the deposit" (1 Timothy 6:20; 2 Timothy 1:12,14). He had faithfully carried out the stewardship entrusted to him. Hervey (*op. cit.*, p.59) is of the opinion that Paul has dropped metaphorical language and in plain words explains the thrust of the preceding figures: "Through his long eventful course, in spite of all difficulties, conflicts, dangers, and temptations, he had kept the faith which Jesus Christ committed to him, inviolable, unadulterated, whole, and complete. He had not shrunk from confessing it when death stared him in the face; he had not corrupted it to meet the views of Jews or Gentiles; with courage and resolution and perseverance he had kept it to the end. Oh! Let Timothy do the same!"

"Kept" means not only to "guard" but also to "observe and do." The "faith" is the whole gospel testimony, going back to the words of Jesus, which He committed to His followers.[49] Paul has been loyal to that which was delivered to him.[50] He has lived according to the rules. He has endured to the end. To encourage Timothy to stay in the ministry Paul alludes to his own example. Paul didn't quit. Neither should Timothy, his beloved child in the faith.

4:8 -- In the future – Scripture elsewhere designates when that future time[51] will be. It is at the Second Coming of Christ when faithful servants will be invited up to receive their rewards (Philippians 3:14).

There is laid up for me the crown of righteousness – There are two words for "crown" in the Greek language. One is *diadēma* ('diadem'), the crown worn by kings, the royal crown. The other is *stephanos*, the laurel wreath given to the winner of a Marathon race. It is this latter word that is employed here.[52] The whole passage, it seems, has spoken of an athletic contest; now we are at the ceremony where the awards are given to the ones who were victorious. The phrase "crown of righteousness" may be taken in either of two ways. Perhaps the crown consists of the perfect righteousness that is granted at last to those who have finished the course. Or, perhaps the crown is all the heavenly blessings granted to those who have been righteous (justified) in God's sight.[53]

Which the Lord, the righteous Judge, will award to me on that day – The one who is identified as "Lord" and "Judge" is none other than Jesus Christ.[54] Just why Jesus should be characterized as a "righteous" judge is debated. Some think the athletic contest is still in the background, and unlike human judges who were sometimes partial, Jesus is impartial and absolutely fair in His awards to those

---

[49] Romans 10:17; Hebrews 2:3,4; Revelation 14:12.

[50] The careful reader will notice that we are struggling to decide whether to take "faith" as objective or subjective. Is it a body of doctrine, or is it Paul's own personal faith? In a letter which warns Timothy about false teachers, and encourages him to retain the pattern of sound words, it might seem likely that Paul is offering himself as an example of one who has stayed true to the truth that is in Christ Jesus.

[51] The Greek word is *loipon*, the same word used at Hebrews 10:13.

[52] Other passages where the laurel wreath is mentioned are 1 Corinthians 9:25; Philippians 4:1; 1 Thessalonians 2:19; and 2 Timothy 2:5.

[53] We have no way of knowing whether there are different crowns given to different victors or not, but there are several expressions used to describe the crowns: (1) crown of glory, 1 Peter 5:4; (2) crown of life, James 1:12; Revelation 2:10; (3) crown of exultation (rejoicing), 1 Thessalonians 2:19; (4) a crown of twelve stars, Revelation 12:1; and (5) crown of righteousness, here in 2 Timothy 4:8.

[54] Compare notes at 2 Timothy 4:1 concerning who does the judging at the final judgment. Acts 10:42 says that Jesus is ordained by God to be the Judge of the living and the dead.

who had fairly won them. Some think Paul's own trial before Roman judges is in the background. Many of the decisions Paul has received from Roman judges in this life were unfair and even deliberately twisted, but the Lord is a Judge who will make no mistake, either accidental or deliberate. Perhaps there is a deliberate contrast to Paul's recent trials in Rome; remember, he was charged, along with other Christians, of arson in the burning of Rome. It would not be improbable to think that Paul spoke of the Lord as "the righteous Judge" in deliberate contrast to the unrighteous judge who had condemned Paul, and in accordance with whose unjust sentence he would presently be put to death. The day of the final judgment is in view in the words "that day."[55] The Bible seems to point to one judgment day, when all men will be judged for the deeds done in the body.

And not only to me, but also to all who have loved His appearing – This crown of righteousness is not a crown to be enjoyed by Paul alone. It will be awarded to all those who, in love and obedience, have responded positively to His incarnation.[56] People whose lives have been influenced and controlled by the knowledge that the incarnate Christ has lived on this terrestrial ball are the ones who will be crowned.[57] The verb form "loved" ('who have set their love upon') implies a steadfast maintaining of love for Christ's appearing. Those who have loved His appearing are those who struggle to live their lives according to the course He has marked out for them (verse 7) and fulfill their ministry for Him (verse 5). That is precisely what the Jewish Gnostic teachers were not doing. They would soon be explaining away the incarnation. They would soon stop loving His appearing. And they would be disqualified from being awarded the crown of righteousness. With these words Paul gives a gentle reminder to Timothy. He, too, with any others who really loved Christ's appearing, might win the same glorious crown for which Paul is looking.

---

[55] This is the third time the words "that day" are used in 2 Timothy. See 1:12,18.

[56] We have had the word "appearing" at 2 Timothy 4:1. There we learned it is sometimes used of Christ's first coming into the world, and sometimes of His second coming. In our comments we opt for verse 8 being a reference to Christ's first coming.

[57] It might also be possible to make "appearing" a reference to the second coming here. What would be required is to explain "loved" from the standpoint of the time of the judgment. With reference to that judgement, they loved His appearing. That is, they looked forward to the return of Christ. They fought the good fight because they were looking forward with hope and desire for their Lord's appearing and kingdom. They will be able to say on that day, "Lo, this is our God; we have waited for him, and he will save us: this is the Lord; we have waited for him, we will be glad and rejoice in his salvation" (Isaiah 25:9 KJV).

C. Be Diligent and Faithful.   4:9-18

4:9 -- Make every effort to come to me soon – Paul now begins the third appeal in this second section of personal appeals to Timothy to stay in the ministry. Its general form is similar to the first two – first the appeal, and then the reason for the appeal. As the reason for the appeal is given, we learn about some of Paul's personal needs which he hopes Timothy can take care of. Earlier in this letter (1:4), Paul had expressed his longing to see Timothy again, and now this is crystallized into a specific and urgent request, one which is repeated in verse 21. "Make every effort" is a translation of *spoudason*, the same verb we had at 2 Timothy 2:15. Much of what Paul has written in this letter was obviously put in writing in case his death should intervene before Timothy could complete the journey to Rome, but that does not make the visit unnecessary. Paul is lonely. Several factors contributed to that solitariness, some of which are listed in the verses following. "Come to me soon!" As an aged father of a large family lies dying, he may wish to see all the children just once more. As the last one gets to the bedside, he reaches out and touches the child's hand, and then dies. This is what Paul is asking for – to see his children, just one more time before he dies.[58]

Such a request as this would, had we no other arguments, tell us that no forger ever wrote this epistle.[59] Who would have ever dreamed of putting into the letter such a request as this, *after* those solemn expressions of the last few verses, in which the apostle spoke of himself as even then *already* being poured out as a drink offering? He was writing with full awareness that he would not be released from this imprisonment save by a martyr's death. This request to Timothy to come to him, *after* he had written such thoughts down, is at first sight strange, and one which certainly no forger would have appended to this writing. But though a forger would never have thought of such a summons, Paul might! He still lived, and the thought of life and the hope of life still burned in his heart; whether he lived or died he would serve Christ! In the Roman judicial system, there was a time lapse between sentencing and the execution of the sentence. Paul expects the winter months to have passed before he is actually executed (2 Timothy 4:21).   Though he knew he would be executed eventually, Paul's writing to Timothy presumes there will be enough time for the letter to get to Timothy and for Timothy to get to Rome. Perhaps days and months might drag on their slow, weary length, and still find the old man languishing and solitary in his chains in prison.   He longed to see some of his faithful companions once

---

[58] On the natural human longing for sympathy as the hour of death approaches, compare our Lord's words to Peter, James and John (Matthew 26:38), "My soul is deeply grieved, to the point of death: remain here, *and watch with Me.*"

[59] Spence, *op. cit.*, p.330.   In the Introductory Studies we have noted the widespread opinion among many modern critics that the Pastoral Epistles are not genuine works from Paul's own hand.

more, and for the last time to bid them with his own mouth to be faithful and brave.   So, as if he were hoping against hope, he dictates on the last pages of this letter, "Make every effort to come to me soon!"   Paul, though he begged Timothy to hasten his journey as much as possible, and though he still hoped to live long enough to see him again, framed this final appeal in his letter in such a way that Timothy, if when he reached Rome he should find that the apostle's life had been ended, might know what were his mentor's last wishes and directions.

4:10 -- For – Paul now begins to list some of the reasons behind his request for Timothy to hurry to Rome.

Demas, having loved this present world, has deserted me and gone to Thessalonica – Nothing more is known about Demas than what can be learned about him from Colossians 4:14 and Philemon 24.   From those passages we learn that he was at one time a fellow-laborer with Paul, just as were Luke and Mark (Colossians 4:10).   "Having loved this present world" tells us Demas has quit Paul and quit the ministry; perhaps he also has quit Jesus.   Whether or not Demas was apostate from the faith, it is not reading too much into the account to see that Paul felt his defection keenly.   Right when Paul needed companionship and someone to carry on the ministry, Demas left.   "Having loved this present world" and "deserted" show there was something blameworthy in Demas' actions.   Was the cause for his desertion the hardships which one in the ministry is called on to endure, as Timothy was called on to endure in this letter?   Some have supposed Thessalonica was chosen by Demas because it was a city of excitement and opportunities.[60]   Others have supposed Thessalonica was Demas' hometown.[61]

---

[60] Thessalonica was a great mercantile center, one of the most populous cities in Macedonia, and one of the great cities of the Empire.   Did Demas go there looking for business connections that would give him an opportunity to support himself now that he has left the ministry?   Did he have rich and prosperous friends there, whose company he preferred to that of the condemned and dying prisoner?   (Spence, *Ellicott's*, p.331)

[61] The coupling together of Demas and Aristarchus in Philemon 24 suggests that Demas as well as Aristarchus (Acts 20:4) came from Thessalonica.   One tradition has it that in later years Demas became a religious leader in an idol's temple at Thessalonica.   Chrysostom speaks of Demas being "at home" when he describes his later years in Thessalonica.   (Some have noted that "Demas" is a shortened form of "Demetrius" and this has resulted in some fanciful reconstructions of this man's life.   Barclay [*op. cit.*, p.244-246] has one where he suggests that the Demetrius who led the riot of the silversmiths at Ephesus [Acts 19:25] later became a Christian.   Then for a while he followed Christ, but without really counting the cost.   Then, as the years took their toll, he began to do less and less, till he finally dropped out.   He then suggests that in later years he again took up a leading place in the church, and is to be identified with the Demetrius who showed hospitality and had a good report [3 John 12].   He suggests that Demas' defection was short lived, and that later he again became a servant of the truth.   Barclay, it will be remembered, does not accept the conservative dating of the books of the New Testament.   If the conservative dating and authorship conclusions are accepted, there is not enough time for all the things Barclay has happening to "Demas" to take place.)   There is another interesting thing to be noticed.   It is one of those quirks of history that the name of the patron saint of Thessalonica is Demetrius, who was martyred about AD 290.   What are we to think of the fact that two men connected with Ephesus had the same name,

Crescens *has gone* to Galatia – Nothing is known of this friend of Paul's, save what is here said of him. He has a Latin name, and the tradition[62] that he preached the gospel in Galatia is probably derived from this passage. Instead of "Galatia" (*Galatian*), two old manuscripts, Sinaiticus and Ephraemi, have "Gaul" (*Gallian*).[63] "Galatia" is a province in the land we call Turkey. "Gaul" is the name of the land we now call France. Whether Crescens went to Galatia or to France is therefore uncertain. There is a tradition that he planted the church in the town of Vienne in Gaul. We presume that Paul has selflessly dispatched him on a missionary tour, rather than, like Demas, that he has deserted Paul.[64] If Crescens was sent to France, this would reflect Paul's interest (still) that the unevangelized peoples hear the gospel.

Titus to Dalmatia – A summary of what we know about this man is included in the Introductory Studies to these Pastoral Epistles. The last we heard of Titus is that he was the evangelist on the island of Crete. This verse would imply that Titus had completed his work on Crete (Titus 1:5) and had joined Paul, perhaps at Nicopolis (Titus 3:12), or perhaps at Rome,[65] only to be sent (we presume) elsewhere to do missionary work. Dalmatia is a portion of the land we know as Yugoslavia. It was a district in the Roman province of Illyricum, lying along the eastern shore of the Adriatic Sea, across from southern Italy. Paul seems to have sent Titus to work in this new territory where he himself had had very little time or opportunity to evangelize.

4:11 -- Only Luke is with me – With all his fellow workers and companions having gone elsewhere, except for Luke, Paul is lonely. That's one reason why he wants Timothy to come visit him. About ten years before this, Luke was with Paul on his voyage to Rome which is so vividly recorded in the closing chapters of Acts. He was with Paul during the first Roman imprisonment when the letters

---

one who deserted Paul, and one who became so influential that his name eclipsed that of Paul in the very city where Paul had first planted the church?

[62] *Apos. Const.* VII.46.

[63] From the first century on, Greek writers commonly used "Galatia" for Gaul (modern France, northwest of Italy), as well as for Asiatic Galatia (which is how we are accustomed to use the term, after we have studied Acts and Paul's epistles). See footnote #176 in Hendriksen (*op. cit.*, p.319) for help on the problem of "Galatia" versus "Gallia."

[64] Observed that the verb in the NASB is in italics, indicating the verb must be supplied from the context. We hope that all that must be supplied is "has gone" and that in Crescen's case it is not proper to also supply the verb "has deserted."

[65] We have no way of determining whether Paul was arrested at Nicopolis before Titus could join him (as instructed in Titus 3:12), or whether he was arrested after Titus arrived. If before, then Titus has followed the prisoner to Rome. If after, then perhaps Titus accompanied the prisoner as he was being taken to Rome. In any case, at some time or another, 2 Timothy 4:10-11 implies that Titus and Paul have been together in Rome before Titus went off to Dalmatia.

were written to Colossae (Colossians 4:14) and to Philemon (Philemon 24). It is this commentator's conviction that Luke composed the "Acts" during Paul's two years in custody (Acts 28:30) in that first Roman imprisonment.[66] How Luke spent the time between Paul's release from that imprisonment and this mention of him during Paul's second imprisonment, we have no knowledge. It looks as though he may have been in close personal attendance upon Paul at all times during these latter years of the apostle's life.[67]

Pick up Mark and bring him with you, for he is useful to me for service – The expression "pick up Mark" seems to imply that Timothy is to stop in the nearby town where Mark is,[68] and get Mark to join him on the way to Rome. This is the same Mark – John Mark – who is the author of the second Gospel, whom Paul thought it not good to take along on the second missionary tour because he had left the missionary team before the first journey was over (Acts 13:13 and 15:38). There is something strangely touching in this message of Paul to Timothy to get Mark and bring him on that last solemn journey to Rome. One whom Paul judged so severely some 20 years earlier, and on whose account he had separated from his beloved friend, Barnabas the apostle, is now one whom Paul really longs to see. Since that hour when the young missionary helper had quit and gone home, Mark had, by steady, earnest labor, won back his place in Paul's heart. Barnabas, the son of encouragement, had rescued the young man for the ministry.[69] In fact, some five years earlier than this, by the time of the *first* Roman imprisonment, Mark is with Paul at Rome (Colossians 4:10, Philemon 24). Paul has seen Mark at work; he regards him as his "fellow worker" (Philemon 24).   Paul now gives the reason Timothy is to bring Mark with him in these words, "Mark ... is useful[70] to me for service."   Bible students

---

[66] Paul's two years of imprisonment at Caesarea, before his voyage to Rome, would have given Luke ample opportunity to do the research he did (Luke 1:1-4) before he wrote the "Gospel according to Luke." Whether the third gospel was published in Caesarea, or later in Rome, scholars are not able to decide.

[67] We wonder why Luke stayed with Paul till the end of Paul's life. Was it out of Paul's need for a doctor's ministrations? Was it out of deep personal devotion to Paul? With whom do we have such a relationship – that we are there to encourage and help when we are needed most?

[68] Just where Mark is, when Timothy is to pick him up, is not known. Perhaps as Colossians 4:10 indicates, Mark is working in Colossae, a town just a few miles east of Ephesus. The implication in Paul's instructions to Timothy is that it would not be too much out of his way for Timothy to stop by and get Mark, so Mark must be somewhere in Asia, or Macedonia, or Greece, or the like.

[69] Barclay (*op. cit.*, p.251) tells us that Harry Emerson Fosdick has a sermon with the great and uplifting title, "No Man Need Stay the Way He Is!" Mark was the living proof of that. Mark is our encouragement and our inspiration, for Mark was the man who failed and who yet made good. Still to this day, Jesus Christ can make the coward spirit brave, and nerve the feeble arm for fight. He can release the sleeping hero in the soul of every man. He can turn the shame of failure into the joy of triumphant service.

[70] We had the same word at 2 Timothy 2:21 (a "vessel of honor ... useful ..."). "This testimony

have been unable to decide whether "service" (*diakonia*, "ministry") is used technically of the ministry (cp. Colossians 4:17; 1 Timothy 1:12; 2 Timothy 4:5), or is a general term of "serving," acting as an assistant to Paul in his apostolic labors (cp. Acts 19:22).[71]   There is every evidence that Paul's desires were granted and that both Timothy and Mark arrived in Rome before Paul was executed.[72]

4:12 -- But Tychicus I have sent to Ephesus – "To Ephesus" has considerable bearing on the destination of 2 Timothy. We agree with those writers who understand that Timothy is still in Ephesus when this letter was written to him.[73] Tychicus was evidently one of Paul's trusted "young preacher boys." We know he had been with Paul during the third missionary journey, and had been, during Paul's first Roman imprisonment some six or seven years before this letter is written, sent on a mission trip by Paul to Colossae (Colossians 4:7).[74] A year or two before 2 Timothy is written, according to Titus 3:12, Paul had debated sending either Artemas or Tychicus to Crete to relieve Titus so that Titus could join Paul in Nicopolis. We suppose this verse has a similar thought in the background, and we therefore presume "I have sent" is an epistolary aorist. It would imply that Tychicus is carrying this very letter to Timothy. And it would also imply that Tychicus has been sent to replace Timothy as evangelist with the Ephesian church,[75] so that Timothy will be free to leave and come to Rome to

---

to Mark's ministerial usefulness, at a time when his faithfulness and courage would be put to a severe test, is very satisfactory." (Hervey, *op. cit.*, p.60)

[71] Grotius suggests Mark would have been specially useful in Rome because of his knowledge of the Latin tongue. This is possible, but it is just as likely that what Paul has in mind is the assistance in everyday tasks (cp. Acts 13:5, "John" here is John Mark) at which Mark was so good.

[72] According to our dating of the books of the New Testament, where we have 1 Peter written from Rome after 2 Timothy was written, the reference to Mark in 1 Peter 5:13 also has him in Rome, helping Peter. In fact, tradition has Mark composing the Second Gospel in Rome, either shortly before, or shortly after, Peter is martyred there. So there is every evidence Mark came to Rome, just as Paul requested him to do.

[73] See the discussion of "Destination" in the Introductory Studies to these Pastoral Epistles. It is certainly the natural inference from these words that Timothy is in Ephesus, though some suggest "to you" would be a welcome addition to this sentence if it really meant that Timothy is in Ephesus. Appeal is even made to Colossians 4:7 and Titus 3:12 where "to you" is specifically said. *Pulpit Commentary* suggests that this objection would be removed if we suppose that 2 Timothy was carried by another hand than that of Tychicus. Timothy would then wait at Ephesus till Tychicus arrived, and then could leave for his visit to Rome. (For arguments for and against Timothy being at Ephesus at the time 2 Timothy is written, see the introductory studies in Alford's *Greek Testament*.) Knight (*op. cit.*, p.466) suggests that the place name, rather than the words "to you," was written in this form simply to continue the pattern from verse 10.

[74] On that trip, he was the bearer of the circular letter we call "Ephesians" (Ephesians 6:21) and the letter to Colossae (Colossians 4:7,8).

[75] What bearing does our explanation of Tychicus' being sent to relieve Timothy have to do with our idea of church polity? Did apostles have the power to order evangelists to the churches, and

visit Paul. Tychicus can take over the task of "training faithful men ..." (2 Timothy 2:2). Later in this chapter we will see that this letter was intended for the whole Ephesian church, as well as for Timothy. That being so, it is not hard to consider this verse as Tychicus' "letter of commendation" to the church.

4:13 -- When you come – Not only does Paul ask Timothy to come and to stop by and get Mark, but there is also something else he wants Timothy to do. He is to stop at another place along the way and get some things Paul needs.

Bring the cloak which I left at Troas with Carpus – This is the only mention of Carpus in the New Testament, and nothing more is known of him other than what we may learn from this place. He was presumably a Christian and evidently was in sympathy with Paul and his work, so gladly made storage space available when the apostle needed it.[76] "Cloak" (*phailonēn*[77]) was a thick overcoat or poncho,[78] a large, heavy, cape-like garment very useful to provide warmth in the cold, wet, winter months. The apparently trivial nature of this request[79] in an epistle containing such weighty matter, and also the fact of such a wish being made at all, and by one expecting death, is at first a little puzzling. But upon further reflection, such a request is just what could be expected from Paul. Let us suppose that when Paul left his cloak (perhaps with some of his other possessions) at Carpus' house in Troas,[80] that it was summer, and he was not

---

did the churches have no local autonomy in the matter? Or is Tychicus not an evangelist? May we think of Timothy's work at Ephesus (he's been there for several years) as something other than what an evangelist normally does, and thus when Tychicus arrives, Timothy can resume the work of an evangelist? Can we say that the church has such rapport with Paul, and Paul with them, that the man he sends is exactly the one they would have chosen, had local autonomy been practiced? (It is easy to see how some have slipped into the belief that Timothy is a sort of apostolic delegate, a sort of district bishop, who is moved here and there at the wishes of the senior officials in the hierarchy. However, this commentator has never been convinced that it is proper to compare the authority of an apostle of Jesus with the authority some human dignitary claims for his position.)

[76] H.C.G. Moule suggests that the room used for the church service in Acts 20:6ff was none other than a room in Carpus' house.

[77] The Latin term for this garment is *paenula*, and at one time the Greek was spelled *phainolas*. As the years passed, the letters were transposed, so the spelling became *phailonēs*.

[78] It was a "large, sleeveless outer garment, made of a single piece of heavy material, with a hole in the middle through which the head was passed." (J.N.D. Kelly, *A Commentary on the Pastoral Epistles*, Grand Rapids: Baker Book House, 1963, p.215)

[79] Those who have been wont to attack the inspiration of New Testament books sometimes focus their attention on just such "trivial requests" as proof that the works are not inspired. At another extreme is the idea that the "cloak" was not just a warmer garment for winter, but was some garment Paul was in the habit of wearing when performing certain sacred functions; in other words, what today is called a "vestment". Such desperate efforts to find Biblical proof for the use of vestments in the primitive church is certainly a long way from what this passage can rightly bear.

[80] Troas was a seaport city located in the northwest portion of the land we call Turkey, very near the Hellespont. In the Introductory Studies, we have noted how scholars have attempted to reconstruct Paul's post-imprisonment travel itinerary from such scattered notices as this. There we

inclined to burden himself in his journey with any unnecessary weight. Instead of being able to return for his winter clothes as he had planned, he had been arrested and taken to Rome.[81] Now winter was coming on, and the aged prisoner in the cold, damp prison, with few friends and scanty resources, remembered and wished for his cloak. It is just such a request which the master would make of his disciple, who, knowing well the old man's frail health, would never be surprised at such a request even in an epistle so solemn.[82]

And the books, especially the parchments – "Books" would likely refer to scrolls, written on papyrus. "Parchments" would likely[83] be scrolls, written on leather or vellum (i.e., animal skins). Suggestions trying to identify what was written on the books and parchments are nearly as numerous as there are commentators. For the "books" we find suggestions they were blank rolls so that Paul would have something on which to write further letters; or perhaps copies of several Old Testament books (cp. Luke 4:17, Galatians 3:10); or perhaps copies of several New Testament books (e.g., a gospel or two, and the several epistles Paul had himself written); or perhaps his diary which could contain information that would serve as evidence at his second hearing (cp. notes at 2 Timothy 4:16); or perhaps copies of the literary and poetic writings of some of the famous men like Cleanthes or Aratus (cp. Acts 17:28) to be used as something to read to pass the time in prison.[84] As for the "parchments," there is rather general agreement

---

have shown the evidence for a release from the first Roman imprisonment and the travels that followed. We have weighed the arguments that the Pastoral Epistles were all written from one long journey, and the arguments that Paul made several journeys in the years between his two imprisonments.

[81] J. Russell Morse, when arrested by the Chinese communists out in front of his house, was not even allowed to go into the house to get a toothbrush! Perhaps Paul was arrested in some such manner.

[82] As noted when commenting on an earlier request, this one too is a mark of genuineness. No forger of the epistle would dream of putting down such a request if he wanted his work to pass as the real thing. Instead of proof of a forgery, these personal requests are a mark of the authenticity of the letter. In fact, many critics of the Pauline authorship, outstanding among whom is P.N. Harrison, have felt it necessary to ascribe these personal requests as being fragments of genuine material incorporated by some unknown writer into the letters as they now stand. But the possibility of the survival of such a fragment, and the decision to incorporate it, would seem highly unlikely.

[83] The codex, or book form like we know it, with the parchment pages fastened along one edge instead of being glued together and rolled on a roller, was invented by the Christians very early in the history of the church. But we are not sure it would have been as early as this reference to "parchments."

[84] Not satisfactory at all is the suggestion that through the years Paul has been working on his theological masterpiece, wherein he gave exegetical and explanatory and mysterious senses to many of the Jewish sacred books. His preliminary ideas and some of his polished ones are what, supposedly, were contained in the "books" he wants Timothy to bring to him. Part of this implausible idea is that Paul's handling of Old Testament verses was not straightforward exegetical stuff, so he had to come up with some torturous explanations in order for folk to believe what he was telling them

that these were scrolls of various Old Testament books.[85]   On an earlier occasion, Festus had made the charge "your much learning is making you mad," which really reads "your many writings are making you mad" (Acts 26:24). Festus seems to be saying Paul had in his possession many books that he kept referring to, and it would not be too much of a stretch of the imagination to believe that the writings to which Festus referred, and the parchments Paul left with Carpus, were the identical same things, his copies of various Old Testament books.   There is an interesting historical parallel to Paul's request.   William Tyndale, who translated the first New Testament printed in English, was imprisoned in Vilvorde Castle near Brussels before his execution in 1536.   In the year preceding his death, he wrote to the governor, begging for warmer clothing, a woolen shirt, and above all his Hebrew Bible, grammar, and dictionary.   (Earle, *op. cit.*, p.415)   Erasmus remarked on this request from Paul, "Behold, the Apostle's goods and moveables: a poor cloak to keep him from the weather, and a few books!" (*Ellicott's*, p.334)

4:14 -- Alexander the coppersmith – The word *chalcheus* originally referred to someone who worked with copper, but it came to signify a "metal worker" in general, one working with any kind of metal, silver, gold, copper, even a blacksmith.   Apparently Alexander was an Ephesian, as appears from the words in the next verse, where Timothy is warned to beware of him also.   He is likely the same Alexander named in 1 Timothy 1:20.[86]   If he is, then the "delivery to Satan," which was intended to lead the man to repentance, didn't work.   Instead, it made him vindictive against Paul.

Did me much harm – The question naturally arises, when and where did Alexander thus injure Paul?   Some, after identifying this Alexander with the one whom the Jews put forth at the time of the riot at Ephesus (Acts 19:33), say that Paul still remembers what Alexander did at the time of the riot, and knows his hostility to Christianity is unabated.   Some suggest Alexander did his harm to Paul just after Paul led out in the delivery of Hymenaeus and Alexander to Satan. Some suggest Alexander had been an informer,[87] and had given Roman author-

---

those Old Testament verses really said.   On the contrary, the apostles simply repeated the explanations, the correct ones, given to those Old Testament passages by Jesus Himself (cp. Luke 24:44-49).   Christianity is not some wild aberration from Jewish Scriptures, dreamed up by feverish and warped minds.

[85] We suppose the phrase "especially the parchments" indicates which of the books among all those stored in Carpus' house Timothy is to bring.   Not many private citizens had their own copies of Old Testament books.   That Paul had some among his possessions speaks volumes to us about their importance to him.

[86] See the notes at 1 Timothy 1:20 for further attempts at identification of Alexander, and whether or not he is identical with the Alexander of Acts 19:33.

[87] Some have tried to show the verb used here does have the legal meaning of "inform against."

ities information as to the whereabouts of Paul which led to the apostle's arrest and deportation to Rome at the beginning of this second imprisonment. Some suggest it was at Rome, during Paul's first trial. The suggestion is that Alexander served as a prosecution witness.[88] In some way or other, Alexander, likely one of the leaders of the Jewish Gnostic heresy, opposed Christian teaching, as is said in the next verse.

The Lord will repay him according to his deeds – The KJV reads "The Lord reward him ..." and it sounds as though Paul were wishing the Lord would hurriedly repay Alexander for the evil done.[89] The older text has a simple future tense verb, and thus this is a prophecy of what will happen to Alexander. "His deeds" were the bitter injuries he had done to the cause of Christ, rather than to the apostle himself, as the next verse shows. "The Lord will repay" is in harmony with Paul's writing in Romans 12:19, and in harmony with Psalm 62:12. The time when the Lord Jesus will do this repaying is at the final judgment (2 Corinthians 5:10), when He sits as righteous judge (verse 8).

4:15 -- Be on guard against him yourself – The inference from this caution to Timothy is that Alexander is now somewhere in the area where Timothy is or will be. Most think it is implied that Alexander has left Rome and returned to his native Ephesus.[90] Just what does it mean to "be on guard" against someone like Alexander? Does it mean that Timothy is to avoid Alexander, keeping out of his way? Perhaps it warns Timothy that Alexander hasn't changed, that he is still an enemy of the cross. The present tense imperative indicates Timothy must constantly be on his guard.

For he vigorously opposed our teaching – "For" shows this is the reason Timothy should be on guard against Alexander. We've had the word "opposed" at 2 Timothy 3:8, where Jannes and Jambres "withstood" Moses. The same

---

[88] If we suppose Alexander, like the Alexander of Acts 19, was a Jew, his testimony might be along this line: Now that it is becoming increasingly clear that there is a difference between Christianity and Judaism, Alexander might emphasize his Jewish heritage and insist that Christianity is not Jewish. (Remember, Christianity at first was looked upon as just another sect of the Jews. But that was before the burning of Rome and other recent events, where Jews have tried to urge in Roman courts that Christianity is an illegal religion.) Christianity is an illegal religion, Alexander might insist, and fellows like Paul should be punished.

[89] The Byzantine text has an optative form verb at this place, a mood that expresses a wish, or in this case an imprecation. Though Paul could be very generous towards people who opposed him personally, he was not above offering an imprecatory prayer for justice on those who opposed the gospel and the cause of Christ. See a further discussion on "imprecatory prayer" in the comments offered at Acts 4:29 in the author's *New Testament History: Acts*.

[90] Another suggestion, made by Spain, is that (since Alexander is mentioned just after Paul has asked Timothy to get some things from Troas) Alexander is in Troas. When Timothy goes there to get Paul's belongings, he should be alert to avoid Alexander.

word is used at Acts 13:8, where Elymas "withstood" Paul and Barnabas.   What is meant by "our teaching"?   Some understand, in the light of the verse following, that Paul especially referred to his "defense" before the Roman tribunal.   But why would Paul designate his "defense" as "*our* teaching" when no one stood with him at his first trial?   Would not "my teaching"[91] be a better way to word what happened on that occasion?   It seems likely that Paul says "our teaching" because he knows that he and Timothy have been preaching the same gospel message, the very thing Alexander opposed with his Judaizing-Gnostic emphases.   After Alexander's efforts to torpedo the gospel at Rome, Timothy can be sure that when opportunity presents itself, Alexander will make an effort to sink the gospel at Ephesus, too.   It was not the last time that enemies of the gospel have made determined efforts to keep the church from growing, and even to close a church in a given community or area.

4:16 -- At my first defense – In the midst of this personal appeal to Timothy, Paul relates some of the things that are happening to him which have made the appeal all the more urgent.   "Defense" (*apologia*[92]) is a courtroom word.   It is the classical Greek word for an answer to an accusation.   It seems likely that "first defense" means Paul's initial trial during this second Roman imprisonment.[93]   If so, Paul has had a great public trial before the city prefect, an official who was a nominee of the Emperor Nero.   If "first defense" means Paul's first trial of this second imprisonment, has the second trial taken place yet?   Has he already been condemned at a second trial, and so writes as he does in 2 Timothy 4:6-8?   Or is he just a realist about what the outcome will be when he comes to the second trial, since he was not released after the first hearing?

No one supported me – The word *paragineto* has a technical sense here.   In a legal setting it speaks of someone who "stands by" an accused person as friend or

---

[91] Paul might use "teaching" as a synonym for "defense," since it was his custom whenever on trial not to omit preaching the gospel to his courtroom audience.

[92] Our English word "apology" comes from this Greek word, but our English word has changed meaning in common usage.   Whereas now it means "I was wrong," it originally meant a speech in defense which asserted "I was right."   This original sense survives in our term "apologetics," a defense of one's position because it is *right!*   The word is regularly used in the New Testament with its "courtroom" connotation (Acts 25:16, Philippians 1:7,16, and 1 Peter 3:15).

[93] Zahn (*Introduction to the New Testament*, II, p. 12-14) and others have tried to argue that this speaks of something that happened during Paul's *first* Roman imprisonment, some years earlier. This allows those commentators to explain the central phrases of verse 17 as reference to Paul's continued missionary work after that first imprisonment had ended.   The arguments that have been marshaled, both for Zahn's view and the view presented in the comments above, are nicely summarized in Knight (*op. cit.*, p.469).   Both the inference that Paul is informing Timothy about recent events (not something that happened years earlier) and the expression "delivered out of the lion's mouth" fit well if this is a recounting of something that happened during Paul's second imprisonment.

assistant, to aid and abet them in their defense.   Powerful men sometimes brought such a multitude of assistants as to overawe the magistrate, as Orgetorix the Helvetian, when summoned to trial, appeared with 10,000 followers, and so there was no trial.   No one stood by Paul in his hour of trial: no "advocate" pleaded his cause; no "procurator" (an official who performed the functions of an attorney in a court) helped him in arranging and sifting the evidence; no "patronus" of any noble or powerful house in the eyes of the Romans gave him his countenance and support.   The Christians in Rome, who on another occasion might have stood by him, were not in a position to do so at this trial.

But all deserted me – Where was Luke?   Where were Titus and Crescens?   Not one friend stood by him.[94]   Not a few commentators are reminded of the trial of Jesus at this point.   Just as Paul stood alone in his trial, Jesus, too, in His hour of deadly peril, stood alone before his accusers.[95]   And like his own Master, who proceeded to say, "And yet I am not alone, because the Father is with Me," so Paul went on to tell Timothy in the next verse that neither was *he* alone, for One greater than any friend on earth stood by him.   Paul uses the same word "deserted" that he earlier used for Demas (verse 10).   As bad as it was having no one beside him in the courtroom, Paul does not put the action of these who failed to stand by him in the same category ("loved this present world") as the action of Demas.   Perhaps he knows that his friends failed him out of fear, just like Jesus' disciples temporarily lost their faith and failed Him (Matthew 26:31; Mark 14:50).

May it not be counted against them – Someone should have stood by Paul, and the implication is that it was someone well-known to Timothy.   That's why Paul adds this word about not holding it against them.[96]   Disappointment, perhaps; understanding of the mitigating circumstances, perhaps; but no bitterness is discernible as Paul recalls the experience of having to make his defense all alone. Indeed, there were some mitigating circumstances to help explain the behavior of Paul's friends.   The position of Paul, the well-known Christian leader, accused

---

[94] Just when (verse 10) did Titus and Crescens leave Rome for their new missionary works? Was it after Paul's first trial?   Were they there and too faint-hearted to stand by Paul in the courtroom?   When did Demas quit?   Was it before or after Paul's first trial?   If he was in Rome at the time of Paul's trial, did his failure to stand by Paul have something to do with his decision to leave Rome and head for Thessalonica?   Verse 11 has told us that Luke is with Paul.   Why didn't he stand by Paul at that first trial?   Was he there and lacked courage to accompany Paul into the court room?   Or did Luke not arrive in Rome until after that first trial was over?

[95] Jesus had predicted it would be so.   "Behold, an hour is coming, and has already come, for you to be scattered, each to his own home, and to leave Me alone."   John 16:32.

[96] In the notes offered on this verse, this word about possible ill-feelings is taken as a word to Timothy.   There is also another way this phrase can be read.   Perhaps Paul in his compassion wishes that the Lord will not count this desertion against his friends when they stand in the final judgment.

in the year AD 66-67 was a critical one, and any friend who dared to stand by him would himself be in great danger. Christians have been accused of the fire that had burned Rome in AD 64, and anyone who showed any interest in Paul the Christian might just be another of those arsonists who ought to be arrested and punished for their great crime. Paul was conscious of what peril any display of friendship toward him might cost his friend. He was magnanimous toward them; he could and did forgive his deserters for their weakness in fearing to stand by him. And, lest Timothy and others treat the friends who failed to stand up for Paul with ill-will and an ostracizing spirit, Paul urges that their faint-heartedness and failure to stand by him not be a cause of ill-treatment towards these friends. "Don't count their behavior against them," he tells Timothy.

4:17 -- But the Lord stood with me – There is a sharp contrast between Paul's timid, faithless earthly friends who failed him like a deceitful brook (Job 6:15) and the faithfulness of Jesus, Who was a very present Help in the time of trouble. Jesus[97] was present and stood alongside Paul to offer His help when Paul recently had to appear in court.

And strengthened me – *Enedunamosen* means "poured power into me, made me dynamic."[98]   Paul seems to be claiming that when it came time to speak, he was empowered by the Holy Spirit regarding what to say, thereby giving him courage and readiness. As a result, the following phrases indicate the Gentiles in Caesar's court heard the gospel, which thereby got wider publicity in Rome.

In order that through me the proclamation might be fully accomplished – This phrase tells what happened as a result of the strengthening Jesus provided. Paul was enabled to accomplish his assigned ministry. Instead of just defending himself, Paul used his trial as an opportunity to preach the gospel to his judges. He practiced his own commandment: in season and out of season, he pressed the claims of Christ on men. He looks back on the experience of preaching to the court as the fulfillment of his commission to publicly herald the gospel.[99]   Up to

---

[97] As regularly in these verses, "Lord" is a reference to Jesus. See verse 8 and verse 14. Compare what is said at Acts 23:11 and Philippians 4:13 about how the "Lord" stood by Paul.

[98] Compare what Paul says about being empowered by the Lord at Philippians 4:13, 1 Timothy 1:12, and 2 Timothy 2:1. Each time this verb is used, it is in a context of enabling someone to accomplish their assigned ministry even in the face of difficult circumstances.

[99] When the Lord directed the preacher Ananias to go minister to blind Saul following the latter's Damascus Road experience, Jesus said, "He is a chosen instrument of Mine, to bear My name before the Gentiles and kings ...." (Acts 9:15). There have been kings in Paul's audience (Acts 25:11,12, 26:32) before the time of his last trial, but none were as high or mighty as the emperor of the whole Mediterranean world. Now his job of "proclaiming" (the word is "heralding" or "preaching") is "fully accomplished" (the word means "completed, fulfilled"). "Fulfill" is the same verb used in 4:5 to encourage Timothy to "fulfill his ministry."

the time of the writing of this letter, that courtroom audience was the last time Paul had opportunity to publicly herald the glad tidings he had been called by Jesus to preach. It was the culminating point of his labors as an apostle. It was the climax of his ministry. His last sermon!

And that all the Gentiles might hear – Here Paul makes reference to the audience[100] who crowded the courtroom and had listened on this solemn occasion to Paul's *Apologia pro Christo*. It is probable that Paul's trial took place in the Forum, in one of the Pauline Basilicas, so called after L. Aemilius Paulus. There would be room for a huge audience. The brave, unselfish spirit of the apostle, thinking more of the needs of the audience and the proclamation of the gospel than his own life, is truly admirable. Some have thought Paul's language here to be a bit extravagant, but if it be considered possible that even Nero was in the audience when Paul made this proclamation, then we can begin to feel Paul's sense of elation at the opportunity to preach to this audience.

And I was delivered out of the lion's mouth – Expositors through the ages have dwelt upon the question of whether to take "lion" literally or figuratively. Taken figuratively, it says Paul was delivered temporarily from the jaws of death.[101] This commentator is inclined to take it literally, and see in it a reference to the literal lions in the Circus Maximus. Paul's final presentation of the gospel won enough sympathy that he was spared having to face the lions; instead he was sentenced to execution by the sword.[102]

4:18 -- The Lord will deliver me from every evil deed – Verse 6 has indicated that Paul is expecting to be executed. What then does "deliver" mean? It can hardly mean "exemption from," unless we are prepared to say that Paul was mistaken in this belief, for he was executed in the spring of AD 68. Some have supposed it means that the Lord would protect Paul from *doing* any evil deed,

---

[100] "All the Gentiles" can refer to all ethnic groups (Jews included), or it can refer to "all nations" as distinguished from the Jews. There would be nothing prohibiting Jews (unconverted ones) from being in attendance at the trial, along with numerous folk from all other ethnic backgrounds.

[101] Compare similar language in Daniel 6:20 or Psalm 22:21. Some early church fathers have understood "lion" to be a reference to Nero. (Josephus, *Ant.* 18.22, wrote "the lion died" when speaking of the death of the emperor Tiberius.) Thinking "first trial" to allude to his first imprisonment, the Early Church Fathers understood "deliverance" to mean he was set free by Nero on that first occasion.

[102] We may well compare what Peter writes in 1 Peter 5:8, and be reminded that one of the trials Christians faced after a trial before Nero was to be fed to the lions (or to be burned as torches in Nero's gardens at night). When Christians faced such a fearsome way of dying, they were to remember that behind the fiendish decision to feed living people to the lions was none other than Satan himself. (A.T. Robertson thinks a literal interpretation of "lion" is not possible for a citizen like Paul, since, he claims, Roman citizens were exempt from such punishment. He does not, however, document his assertion.)

such as failing (out of fear) to preach when he had opportunity.[103]   But if this is
what he has in mind, why not use the word "empower" again, rather than
"deliver"? Instead, it seems that Paul expects the Lord to deliver him by means
of death from any further evil deeds being done to him. Once Paul is in the
"heavenly kingdom" (see the next phrase), the evil designs and actions on the part
of Paul's enemies (such as Alexander, or the Judaizers, or even the devil and his
demons) will no longer have to be faced.[104]   Without exception, evil deeds that
might be done to him will all be things of the past. Jesus would bear him safely
through the execution and by means of it introduce him to the heavenly kingdom.
Of that, Paul is confident.

And will bring me safely to his heavenly kingdom – Sometimes the Lord
delivers His people from death, and sometimes He delivers them *through* death
to something better.[105]   In an earlier imprisonment, Paul had expressed a longing
to depart and be with Christ (Philippians 1:23).[106]   "Heavenly kingdom"[107] may
have reference to the intermediate state, where the souls of the redeemed are with
Jesus, waiting the Second Advent. The reference may be to the final state, where
the souls of the redeemed, united with a resurrection body, are with Jesus
eternally, living in the new heavens and new earth. Men may kill the body, but
they cannot harm Paul's indomitable soul. Whichever way we understand
"heavenly kingdom" – i.e., as intermediate or final state – note that the verse is
inexplicable unless we understand that the soul continues to exist after the body
is killed!

To Him *be* the glory forever and ever – This doxology is addressed to the Lord,
whom we have identified as Jesus in this context.[108]   Paul was fond of breaking
out into spontaneous praise now and then in his letters. How delighted Paul was
with the way Jesus was doing things in his life, and how Jesus would continue to

---

[103] We must be very careful here.   Those writers who think Paul means that Jesus would keep him faithful, keep him from ever sinning in any way at all, may be saying more than the verse or the context implies.

[104] On one occasion (Luke 12:4) Jesus said, "Do not be afraid of those who kill the body, and after that have no more that they can do."

[105] Literally the Greek reads, "He will save me into His kingdom, the one which is in heaven."

[106] Paul's confidence simply is that the Lord would, in His own good time and way, transfer him from this present evil world, and from the powers of darkness, into His eternal kingdom of light and righteousness.

[107] When we have the word "kingdom" by itself, the reference can be either to the church, or to heaven (see notes at 2 Timothy 4:1).   But with the addition of the qualifier "*in* heaven" ("heavenly") the expression has reference to Christ's kingdom in a realm different than here on earth.

[108] For a similar ascription of praise to the Second Person of the Godhead, see Hebrews 13:21 and Romans 9:5.

see him through all his troubles and perplexities, never leaving him friendless or desolate. This prayer that praise will be offered to Jesus while the ages of eternity roll[109] seems to suggest that one of the activities of heaven will be to give constant praise to Christ and to the other members of the Godhead.

Amen – After the Holy Spirit has led Paul to write the doxology to Jesus, Paul here adds his own solemn word of agreement. "Amen" means "I concur," or "Those are my sentiments, too," or "So be it!" Its inclusion by Paul is probably intended to invoke the same response from his readers. In fact, in the early church as these letters were read out loud in the public worship service, when the public reader read one of these "amens," the hearers were accustomed to respond with their own "Amen."

What a picture of Paul these final words give us. He is brokenhearted when people quit the ministry (Demas), and he delights in the continuing work of his fellow-workers (Titus and Crescens). He expresses a need for the tools of his ministry (the books and parchments). He is aware of the danger that false teachers and opponents (like Alexander) pose to the cause of Christ, and he warns Timothy to be on his guard also. He is aware that all men will answer in the judgment for the deeds done in the body (whether it be Alexander, or those who have loved his appearing). He is keenly cognizant of the lordship of Jesus Christ. That lordship was expressed in the power from Jesus that has been displayed in his ministry. That lordship had also been displayed in Jesus' ability to deliver His servants out of the mouths of lions. It would be displayed again in the future when Jesus would save him into the Heavenly Kingdom. When it is such a Lord he is serving, Paul is only too happy to take any opportunity he has to fulfill his ministry of preaching the gospel, even in a packed courtroom where he is on trial for his very life. He feels keenly the fact that none of his human friends stood by his side at his first defense. Though he is disappointed over such human frailties, he still wants to see Timothy and Mark one more time. Whether or not he is allowed to live long enough to see his dear friends, his final wish is that people will offer praise to Jesus for ever and ever.

---

[109] The Greek, "unto the ages of the ages," pictures a plurality of ages stretching out through the future. 1 Timothy 1:17 employs similar language, but has this difference: in 1 Timothy the doxology is addressed to the Father.

FINAL GREETINGS AND BENEDICTION. 4:19-22

4:19 -- Greet Prisca and Aquila – As is his custom, Paul concludes this letter with a few personal matters, and then the benediction. One thing Paul asks Timothy to do is to give a special word of remembrance to Priscilla and Aquila. This implies this couple is somewhere in the same vicinity where Timothy is. Either Timothy will greet them at Ephesus, assuming they are there, or Paul knows that on his trip to Rome, Timothy will pass through the town where this husband and wife live and work. Because of the close connection with Onesiphorus' household in this same verse, the former is more likely. That household was in Ephesus. Prisca is everywhere else always called Priscilla.[110] She is named before her husband, as here, in Acts 18:18 and Romans 16:3. Not a few take her being named first, regularly, as an indication that she was the principal worker of the two in the cause of Christ. Others suggest she is named first because, as her name suggests, she was of the equestrian class before her marriage to Aquila and her conversion to Christ.[111] These two were some of Paul's earliest friends after he began his great missionary work. Originally Aquila, a Jew by birth who came from Pontus, had taken up abode at Rome, where he exercised his trade as tentmaker. Driven out of Rome by the decree of Claudius which banished the Jews from the capital, both came to Corinth, where Paul first became acquainted with them. They evidently were already Christians when Paul joined them, about AD 51 or 52, in Corinth. When Paul left Corinth at the close of his second tour, they went with him as far as Ephesus, where they took up residence (Acts 18:18ff), and where shortly they would have opportunity to teach "the way of God more accurately" to Apollos. They were still in Ephesus in AD 57 when 1 Corinthians was written (1 Corinthians 16:19), and a church was meeting in their house. In the year AD 58, when Paul sends greetings to the folk he knows at Rome, Priscilla and Aquila are included among them, as then living at Rome (Romans 16:3). If we have the destination of 2 Timothy correct, they have now returned to Ephesus. In those days, prosperous Jewish businessmen travelled a great deal from city to city.[112]

---

[110] Acts 18:2,18,26, Romans 16:3. A similar variation in names seen in Drusa and Drusilla, Livia and Livella, etc.

[111] Wm. Ramsay, *The Cities and Bishoprics of Phrygia*, Vol. 1, p.637, gives an example in which a woman is named before her husband presumably because she was of higher rank. Knight (*op. cit.*, p.475) offers another suggestion. "It is also possible that placing Prisca's name first is an expression of Christian courtesy extended to her because she is a woman."

[112] See the author's commentary on Romans at 16:3 for further information about this couple. There, too, is discussed the "problem" the couple's movements have caused for those who would hold to the integrity of Romans 16 and to the Pauline authorship of 2 Timothy. Their numerous travels are not so unusual as to cause one to doubt the truth of either Romans or Timothy.

And the household of Onesiphorus – We have already become acquainted with this man and his household in our study of 2 Timothy 1:16-18. Most exegetes think the repetition of the "household of Onesiphorus" is almost conclusive as to the recent death of Onesiphorus himself. Either this, or Paul is aware that Onesiphorus was at that time absent from Ephesus, so this peculiar greeting is addressed to his "household" rather than to Onesiphorus himself. If Onesiphorus has recently died, this special word of salutation to his family is intended to comfort them in their time of bereavement. If Onesiphorus is still alive, Paul singles out this household because he is particularly grateful for the services Onesiphorus and his household have rendered to him.

4:20 -- Erastus remained at Corinth – Verse 10 has explained to Timothy about some of Paul's usual companions who are not now with him. This verse will explain to Timothy why two other of Paul's usual associates are not with him in Rome. An "Erastus" is named in Acts 19:22 as being involved with Timothy on a mission to Macedonia to help organize the benevolent offering for the poor at Jerusalem, which was delivered at the close of the third missionary journey. We learn from Romans 16:23 that an "Erastus" was "treasurer" of the city of Corinth. Perhaps this reference in 2 Timothy and the other two references all refer to the same man (though it is true that "Erastus" was a fairly common name). If this is the same Erastus named in Romans, it might explain why "Erastus remained at Corinth" on their last trip through the town. It was his home. The language clearly implies that Paul, accompanied by Erastus, not long before his arrest and deportation to Rome for imprisonment, had recently travelled through Corinth.[113]

But Trophimus I left sick at Miletus – We first meet Trophimus, a Gentile Christian, during Paul's third missionary journey. He is named at Acts 20:4 as being one of the men who helped carry the offering to Jerusalem. We learn more definitely in Acts 21:29 that he is an Ephesian, being also the one Paul was accused of taking into the exclusively Israelite portion of the Temple at Jerusalem. It was this accusation by the Jews of Asia which led to Paul's arrest on that occasion, and eventually to his first Roman imprisonment. Indeed, Paul passed through Miletus on his third journey, on his way to Jerusalem, but that is not the time Trophimus was left there sick, for Trophimus appeared with Paul in Jerusalem at the end of that journey. We lose sight of Trophimus after that visit to Jerusalem in AD 58 until we meet him here again in this passage. Following the analogy of the first part of verse 20, we suppose Trophimus has been travelling

---

[113] Again, refer to the Introductory Studies to these epistles, where the whole matter of Paul's travels while leaving Timothy at Ephesus and Titus on Crete, and then writing letters back to them from other locations, is discussed in detail.

with Paul and others on a journey[114] among the churches between Paul's two Roman imprisonments. Traveling, that is, until sickness made him too weak to travel, and it became necessary to leave him behind till he recovered. Miletus[115] was a seaport of Caria, about 30 miles from Ephesus.[116] Telling where Trophimus was, and what his condition was, served two purposes. It cleared him of any charge of neglect. It also may have been intended as information to the church at Ephesus so they could render whatever assistance the sick preacher might need. It has also been made a point of interest that Trophimus was left behind "sick," despite the presence of a doctor and an apostle in the company. Though on other occasions Paul had been the instrument through whom God healed people,[117] it is not always God's will that sick people be immediately healed, or that the ministrations of the medical profession result in a quick restoration to full health. This indication of the whereabouts of these two co-workers who are not with Paul makes the following request for Timothy's companionship all the more urgent.

4:21 -- Make every effort to come before winter – "Make every effort" is the same word commented on before at 2 Timothy 2:15 and 4:9. Were Timothy's tasks such that he would have to hurry to get them done before he could leave to join Paul in Rome? Did he have to wait for Tychicus to settle down in the work of "transmitting the deposit" before he could leave? Instead of the adverb "soon" used before (4:9), now Paul says "before winter."[118] "Before winter," lest when winter storms come, it be impossible to make the trip. Remember, the sailing season on the Mediterranean was closed during the winter. Too, if the cloak were still in storage at Troas, it would be a "cold, damp winter" for Paul. If our chronology is correct, that Paul is executed in the spring of AD 68, then this could be the winter of AD 67, or perhaps even the winter of AD 68.[119]

---

[114] It is very difficult, as has been noted in the Introductory Studies, to reconstruct Paul's travels. It is implied that Timothy was not along on the trip just mentioned or he would have known of Erastus' whereabouts, and of Trophimus' being left behind. Therefore, we presume the occasion of leaving Trophimus was not the same as the one which brought Timothy to Ephesus immediately before the writing of 1 Timothy (see 1 Timothy 1:3).

[115] The KJV spells the town's name "Miletum." Beza's text spells the name *Melite*, which is regularly translated "Malta," but there is precious little manuscript evidence to support that reading.

[116] It was at Miletus, it will be recalled, where, on an earlier occasion, Paul met the elders from the church at Ephesus (Acts 20:15ff).

[117] Acts 14:9-10, 19:11-12, 20:10, 28:8-9; 2 Corinthians 12:12.

[118] Plans and procedures leading to Paul's execution are under way (2 Timothy 4:6), but it will not be carried out immediately. In the meantime, the cold wintery months must be gotten through.

[119] Since we believe 1 and 2 Peter were written from Rome, and that Peter arrived in Rome after Paul wrote 2 Timothy, we are inclined to believe it was the winter of AD 67 that is here spoken of, or perhaps even as early as the winter of AD 66. We just do not have evidence how long it was between Paul's arrest, his being "delivered out of the lion's mouth," and then finally his execution.

Eubulus greets you – Of this person nothing is known, for he is not mentioned anywhere else in the New Testament.   The name was not uncommon as a Greek name.   Perhaps we may assume from the mention here that he is a mutual acquaintance of both Paul and Timothy, perhaps even one of that group of young men who joined Paul as a sort of apprentice to learn how to become an evangelist.[120]

Also Pudens and Linus and Claudia – Most writers suggest that "Linus" is probably the same man named by Irenaeus and Eusebius as the first bishop at Rome.[121]   Some identify him with a certain Llin in Welsh hagiography, said to be the son of Caractacus (Hervey, *op. cit.*, p.63).   Caractacus, a king of the Silures, who inhabited South Wales, was one of the most persistent enemies of the Romans in Britain.   For nine years he warred gallantly against the invaders, but at length was completely overthrown.   His wife and daughters fell into the hands of the victors, and his brothers surrendered.   Caractacus himself fled to Cartimandua, queen of the Brigantes, who delivered him up to the Romans.   He was carried to Rome, AD 51, and exhibited to the people by the Emperor Claudius.   When Caractacus approached the imperial seat, we are told, he addressed Claudius in so noble a manner that he and his relatives were immediately pardoned.   They appear, however, to have lived during the remainder of their lives in Italy.   Some commentators identify "Pudens and Claudia" with the couple whose marriage is celebrated in two of the *Epigrams* by Martial.   In the *Epigrams*,[122] Pudens was the son of a Roman senator.   Claudia, who bore the cognomen of *Rufina*, was a foreign princess who came from Britain, and after arriving in Rome was married to Pudens.   Other interesting facts surface. Tacitus tells us that in AD 52, in the reign of the Emperor Claudius, certain territories in southeast Britain were given to a British king called Cogidubnus as a reward for his loyalty to Rome.   Cogidubnus was an ally of the Roman governor of Britain from AD 43-52, Aulus Plautius, whose wife Pomponia is said by Tacitus to have been impeached for the crime of embracing a "foreign superstition," which was probably Christianity.   Further, in 1723, a marble tablet (the Goodwood inscription) was dug up in the city of Chichester, England.   It commemorates the erection of a heathen temple by Cogidubnus, the king, and by

---

[120] The four people named in this verse are somehow differentiated from the ones named in verses 10 and 11.   Nor, apparently, are they at fault for not standing up with Paul at his first trial (verse 16).

[121] Irenaeus (*Haer.* III.3.3) says, "When the apostles, therefore, had founded the church [of Rome] they entrusted the office (*leitourgian*) of the episcopate to Linus, of whom Paul makes mention in his Epistles to Timothy."   Eusebius (H.E. III.2) wrote, "Linus was ordained the first bishop of (*prōtos kleroutai tēn episkopēn*) Rome after the martyrdom of Paul and Peter."

[122] IV.13;   XI.54.   Martial flourished in Rome from AD 66 to 100.   The dates of the *Epigrams* in question would agree with the identification here made, but it is, at best, only a supposition.

Puden, his "son."   In the inscription, the full name of the king is given, and, no doubt in honor of the Roman Emperor, we find that the British king had taken the name of Tiberius Claudius Cogidubnus.   Now if a king of this name had a daughter, her name might well be Claudia.   Furthermore, when a foreign king entered into an alliance with Rome, as Cogidubnus had done, some members of his family were always sent to Rome as hostages and pledges for the keeping of the agreement.   Now may we piece together how this all developed?   Claudia is the one who comes to Rome as the hostage.   She certainly would be welcome to stay in the home of Aulus Plautius, the ex-Roman governor to whom Cogidubnus had rendered his faithful service.   The wife of Plautius was a lady called Pomponia, who came from a distinguished branch of the gens Pomponia which bore the name of Rufus.   Martial says this woman adopted Claudia, and thus the cognomen *Rufina*.   One more thing remains to be suggested.   If the "foreign superstition" was Christianity, then it would have been from Pomponia that Claudia learned about Jesus.   And it is also possible that it was from Claudia that Pudens learned about Jesus.[123]   And now a decade or so later, they both are Christians, known to Paul and Timothy,[124] and they, too, send their greetings.[125]

And all the brethren – Just as greetings have been sent to Timothy from some of Paul's friends at Rome, so here we have greetings from "all the brethren." Perhaps "the brethren" are the missionaries who have been sent by Paul to Dalmatia, Galatia, etc., and who, knowing Paul was composing this letter, asked to have their greetings to Timothy included.   Perhaps "the brethren" are the members of the church at Rome, who were aware Paul was sending this letter to Timothy and to the church at Ephesus.   Perhaps "the brethren" are fellow Christians, imprisoned with Paul, during the Neronian persecution.   In fact, the four named, as well as "all the brethren" may be in prison with Paul awaiting execution.

---

[123] Pudens was still a pagan, as the Goodwood inscription shows, when he gave the site for the temple of Neptune and Minerva, which was built in honor of the imperial family under the authority of Cogidubnus.   The theory also has it that Pudens was not yet married to Claudia when the temple site was given.   And while the inscription calls him "son," he was really "son-in-law."

[124] The four who are named may have a close relationship with Timothy that goes back to the time of Paul's first imprisonment, since Timothy is named in the opening verses of the Prison Epistles (Philippians 1:1; Colossians 1:1; and Philemon 1).

[125] While these attempts at identifying Linus, Pudens, and Claudia have many interesting coincidences to the characters in Martial's *Epigrams*, it cannot be said that the identifications are certain.   See Alford's *Greek Testament*, "Introduction to 2 Timothy," and Conybeare and Howson's *Life and Epistles of St. Paul*, p.780.   Lewin, *Life and Epistles of St. Paul*, V.2, p.392, warmly espouses the identification, but hesitates between Caractacus and Cogidubnus as the father of Claudia.   (If Linus were the son and Claudia the daughter of Caractacus, they would be brother and sister.)   Farrar, *Life of St. Paul*, V.2, p. 569, rejects the whole reconstruction "as an elaborate rope of sand." (Hervey, *op. cit.*, p.63)

4:22 -- The Lord be with your spirit – This is a prayer for Timothy offered by Paul. The manuscript readings vary on this last verse. Some read "The Lord be with you (singular). Amen. Grace be with you (singular)." Others, the better ones, read, "The Lord be with our (singular) spirit. Grace be with you (plural)." Once more Paul refers to Jesus as "Lord." He prays that Jesus will be with Timothy's spirit just as he has been with Paul (verses 17,18). It would appear that this is another place[126] where "spirit" speaks of the disposition or attitude which fills one's mind and governs the behavior.[127] Paraphrased, Paul says, 'Timothy, the Lord will be beside you just as He has been beside me, so there is no need to be disheartened or to do anything but continue on vigorously in the ministry!'

Grace be with you – It is a peculiarity of the benediction here in 2 Timothy that it is double: part is addressed to Timothy personally, and the other to the church. The latter part of this benediction is identical with the one which ends 1 Timothy, the plural pronoun being used there also. And just as in 1 Timothy, so here, we affirm the plural shows that Paul intended these letters just as much for the congregation to which Timothy was preaching as they were for Timothy personally.

* * * * * * * * * *

SUBSCRIPT

"The second epistle unto Timotheus, ordained the first bishop of the church of the Ephesians, was written from Rome, when Paul was brought before Nero the second time."

As we have said often, these subscriptions were not part of the original letter, being added much later. Sometimes they are right; more often they are wrong in what they claim. How shall we judge this one?

"Unto Timotheus" is certainly correct, for that is what 2 Timothy 1:2 says.

---

[126] See notes at 2 Timothy 17.

[127] One of the Kiamichi missionaries was accustomed to use a homey old benediction when it came time to part and each go his separate way. With eyes that looked into your soul, and a slight but beneficent smile, he would say, "God bless your ol' gizzard!" One couldn't help but think about that parting word. You knew he had prayed for God to bless you both body and soul, and you also knew he expected you to keep right on working for Christ as you received those blessings. Is this not exactly what Paul is saying to Timothy?

What are we to think of "ordained the first bishop of the church of the Ephesians"? How is "bishop" used? Of the evangelist (if so, it might be right), or a diocesan bishop (if so, it is an anachronism)? Who ordained him?

What does "the second time" mean? Does it speak of a second imprisonment when Nero was emperor? Was there any actual trial before Nero during Paul's first imprisonment? Was not his case just dismissed because his accusers failed to show?   Does "second time" reflect what was said in 2 Timothy 4:16, and assume that Paul has actually had his second trial before this letter was written to Timothy?

The Bible does not record the final days of Paul. Tradition tells us that he was found guilty and sentenced to die. It also has him taken outside the city and beheaded. (The site shown today is covered with a church building called "St. Paul's Outside-the-Walls".)

Who can measure the impact of one life dedicated to God? Who can begin to calculate the influence of Paul? Who can begin to calculate the usefulness of Timothy, whose name appears so frequently in the New Testament? How *does* one evaluate the contribution of a faithful preacher?

Among Paul's most moving appeals are his words to Timothy, "Come before winter." Writing from a Roman prison, he realized his execution could not be far away. He specifically states, "The time of my departure is at hand." Wanting to see Timothy, and not knowing how long his execution might be postponed, he appeals to Timothy to come soon.

We do not know if Timothy came in time, but I like to think that he did. I like to think that, before Paul left his cold dungeon followed by the headsman down the Appian Way, Timothy and Paul had embraced each other and wept together. And I like to think that before the headsman's axe glinted in the noonday sun, the great apostle bowed his head and thanked God for some people back in the little town of Lystra who noticed a young man named Timothy.

Be on the lookout for a "Timothy" whom you can encourage to the ministry. And if you are a preacher like Timothy, remember, "It is always too soon to quit!"

With eternity's values in view, Lord; with eternity's values in view,
May I do each day's work for Jesus, with eternity's values in view!
                                                            -- *Alfred B. Smith*

SELECTED BIBLIOGRAPHY

Alford, Henry, "The Pastoral Epistles," in *Alford's Greek Testament*. Vol. 3. London: Rivingtons, 1871. Reprinted at Chicago: Moody Press, 1958.
> Alford's introductory studies and comments are still recognized as the standard for commentaries based on the Greek text. Every student who knows Greek should study Alford.

Barclay, William, "The Letters to Timothy, Titus, and Philemon," in *The Daily Study Bible*. Philadelphia: Westminster, 1961.
> Includes a translation made by the author who made use of Moffatt, Weymouth, and Knox's translations. Denies the Pauline authorship, and regards the letters as the work of a Paulinist. Helpful illustrative material when it deals with contemporary historical matters, but often gives a liberal theological interpretation to the verses being commented upon. Barclay offers the opinion that the treatment of women (1 Timothy 2) reflects a particular contemporary situation, and cannot be regarded as a paradigm for the church's attitude to women now.

Barnes, Albert, "The First Epistle of Paul to Timothy," "The Second Epistle of Paul to Timothy," "The Epistle of Paul to Titus," in *Notes on the New Testament*. Grand Rapids: Baker Book House, 1955.
> A verse-by-verse coverage of the text, with practical applications of the chapters given at the close of each. Barnes (1798-1870) was an American Presbyterian minister. In the division between strict Calvinists and New School Presbyterians, he sided with the latter. He preached total abstinence from alcohol, the abolition of slavery, and an unlimited atonement. He advocates a faith-only doctrine at times, holds to unconditional election, and to the Calvinistic doctrine of the perseverance of the saints. He dated the Pastorals from the third missionary journey of Paul, and this improbable dating of the letters colors his comments on numerous verses.

Barrett, Charles K., *The Pastoral Epistles*. The New Clarendon Bible. Oxford: Clarendon Press, 1963.
> A critical study based on the NEB. Barrett attempts to provide solutions to the problems of date, authorship, and historical background of these epistles. He believes that the letters contain fragments of Paul's letters, compiled by a lover of Paul, and expounds them with little thought of any unifying theme.

Bernard, John H., *The Pastoral Epistles*. Cambridge Greek Testament for Schools and Colleges. Cambridge: University Press, 1922. Reprinted in Grand Rapids: Baker Book House, 1979.
> The complete Greek text of the three epistles (based primarily on the critical texts of Tischendorf and Tregelles) is printed consecutively. The author's comments follow on subsequent pages. The introductory studies cover the literary history of these epistles, their place in Paul's life, their style and vocabulary, heresies referred to in them, bishops and presbyters in the primitive church. The author unequivocally affirms the Pauline authorship.

Berry, George R., *A New Greek-English Lexicon to the New Testament*. Chicago: Wilcox & Follett, 1948.
> Bound in the same volume is his work, *New Testament Synonyms*, a very helpful tool. The same two works are included in Berry's *Interlinear Greek-English New Testament*.

Calvin, John, *Commentaries on the Epistles to Timothy, Titus, and Philemon.* Translated by William Pringle. Grand Rapids: Wm. B. Eerdmans, 1948.
>   Calvin, the greatest of the Reformation scholars, wrote commentaries on all of Paul's epistles.

Camp, Daniel, *God's Blueprint for Leadership: A Study of 1 and 2 Timothy and Titus.* Wabash, IN: C. & S. Printers, 1979.
>   An excellent collection of essays and studies intended to help in the training of leadership at the local level. Includes materials prepared by Seth Wilson, Roy Weece, Woodrow Phillips, and others. Invaluable!

Clarke, Adam, "Epistles of Paul ... to Timothy and Titus," *Clarke's Commentary.* New York: Methodist Book Concern, nd. Vol.2
>   An old standard, written in the early 1800's. Arminian in theology.

Denzer, George A., "1 and 2 Timothy and Titus," in the *Jerome Biblical Commentary,* edited by R.E. Brown, J.A. Fitzmyer, and R.E. Murphy. Englewood Cliffs, NJ: Prentice Hall, 1968.
>   Designed to meet the needs of educated readers who wish to study the Scriptures for themselves, it reflects recent scholarly research by Roman Catholic theologians. It has an ecumenical thrust, and often gives interpretations at variance with accepted Catholic dogma. The brief notes on the pastorals are done well, but they are very brief. Denzer upholds Paul's authorship, and dates the letters after Paul's release from the first Roman imprisonment.

DeWelt, Don, *Paul's Letters to Timothy and Titus.* Bible Study Textbook Series. Joplin, MO: College Press, 1961.
>   Several scholars' attempts at outlining these epistles are included in the introductory studies, which also uphold the Pauline authorship. Thought questions, MacKnight's paraphrase, and comments on each verse follow. The volume includes special studies on "Scriptural Elders and Deacons" by H.E. Phillips, "Must Elders be Married?" and "Elders and Children" by W. Carl Ketcherside, and extracts by Frank Hamilton from Farrar Fenton's *The Bible and Wine.*

Dibelius, Martin, and Conzlemann, Hans, *The Pastoral Epistles,* in the Hermeneia Series. Translated by P. Butolph and A. Yarbro. Edited by H. Koester. Philadelphia: Fortress Press, 1972.
>   A commentary built on the premise that these epistles are unauthentic, and that form-criticism is indispensable to exegesis. The writers work from the standpoint that in the historical background of these letters the monarchical episcopate is in the process of emerging. The writers are not quite decided if 1 Timothy 2:8-15 arises from a contemporary church situation, or from the writer's wish to combat asceticism. There is a generous use of Jewish and pagan materials in the discussion on the new birth (Titus 3:4-7). 1 Timothy 3:16 is treated as a hymn, part of which is missing.

Earle, Ralph, "1, 2 Timothy"; and Hiebert, D. Edmond, "Titus," in *The Expositor's Bible Commentary,* edited by Frank E. Gaebelein. Vol. 11. Grand Rapids: Zondervan, 1978.
>   The conclusions in introductory matters, as well as the comments offered in this series of commentaries is usually a bit more conservative than most present-day evangelicals. Thus it serves as a delightful volume to read after one has worked through some of the other commentaries, learned the problems, and the usual solutions offered.

Ellicott, C.J., *The Pastoral Epistles of St. Paul*. London: Longmans, 1864.

Ellis, E. Earle, *Paul and His Recent Interpreters*. Grand Rapids: Wm. B. Eerdmans, 1961.
> The argument over the Pauline authorship (other than in introductory studies in commentaries that have appeared since Harrison's book) was continued in academic journals: *The Expository Times* 67 (Dec. 1955): 77-81; 71 (Dec.1958): 91-94 by Bruce M. Metzger; *New Testament Studies* 2 (1956): 250-61 by Harrison; 6 (Oct.1959): 1-15 by K. Grayston and G. Herdan; *The Evangelical Quarterly* 32 (1960): 151-161 by E. Earle Ellis. The validity of the statistical method is questioned, and the argument is continued in the work here cited.

Fairbairn, Patrick, *Commentary on the Pastoral Epistles*. Grand Rapids: Zondervan, 1956. Reprinted in Minneapolis: Klock and Klock, 1976.
> A fine example of the use of exegesis in the exposition of the text. While much of Fairbairn's material has been superseded (this commentary was first printed in 1874), his methodology is worthy of study, for this is an old standard commentary.

Fee, Gordon D., *1 and 2 Timothy, Titus*, in Good News Commentaries Series. San Francisco: Harper and Row, 1984. (The same volume was reset and some of it rewritten for inclusion in the New International Biblical Commentary Series, Peabody, MA: Hendrickson, 1988.)
> A stimulating and readable conservative commentary. Regarding authorship, Fee tends to see the similarities to Paul more clearly than the dissimilarities. He more or less by-passes the problems some find in language and vocabulary, falling back on the secretary-hypothesis to explain the observable differences when compared with the accepted Pauline writings. Fee thinks the letters to Timothy reflect a situation in which the prophecy of Acts 20:30 has come true: the "heresy" comes from within the Ephesian church, and from some of its own elders. The heresy, he thinks, has had particular success among women, especially younger widows. This is why 1 Timothy 2:8-15 evinces such an anti-feminist attitude; it must be read in the light of their support of the false teachers. The question of how far this attitude is valid for the church of all time is raised in additional notes, but not pursued very far.

-----, "Reflections on Church Order in the Pastoral Epistles With Further Reflection on the Hermeneutics of *Ad Hoc* Documents," JETS 28/2 (June 1985), p.141-151.
> Challenges the widely accepted assumption that the Pastoral Epistles are intended to serve as a "church manual" by which congregations are to be administrated, or that they are models for evangelists to serve as did Timothy and Titus.

Gealy, Fred D., "The First and Second Epistles to Timothy and the Epistle to Titus," Vol. 11 in *The Interpreter's Bible*, edited by Nolan B. Harmon. New York: Abingdon Press, 1955.
> The presentations in *The Interpreter's Bible* are generally inimical to belief in the inspiration and authenticity of the books of the Bible. Gealy writes the introductions and the exegetical notes, while Morgan P. Noyes does the exposition. Gealy proposes that the Pastorals are post-Pauline and an early second-century composition. Church structure is more like the time of Ignatius than that of Paul; bishops are not just elders, and Timothy and Titus are something like metropolitans. The heresy attacked is Gnostic or even Marcionite. On the differences in language, Gealy does not accept that Paul's increasing age or the difference in subject matter are sufficient explanations for the alleged discrepancies. On women in 1 Timothy 2, both

Gealy and Noyes face the hermeneutical problem. Gealy suspects an attempt to counter an over-enthusiastic movement, an attempt which arises from a more conservative piety than that of Paul or that of Acts. Noyes thinks that, as it stands, this passage is not a word for today, and contrasts it with much elsewhere in the New Testament, and with later Christian practice, which he insists is the real norm.

Gromacki, Robert G., *Stand True to the Charge: An Exposition of 1 Timothy*. Grand Rapids: Baker, 1982.

In his first letter to Timothy, Paul gives specific directions to the young minister at Ephesus. These charges set forth principles for the dependable, faithful servant of God. They also contain guidelines for the life of the local church. Divided into thirteen chapters, it is suitable for adult Sunday school classes or Bible study groups.

Guthrie, Donald, *New Testament Introduction: The Pauline Epistles*. Chicago: Inter-Varsity Press, 1961.

This volume will be found combined with the other two that originally made up the series – one on the Gospels and Acts, and one on Hebrews to Revelation. Generally conservative, it provides a detailed, up-to-date discussion of many and varied historical problems. A valuable refutation of the usual arguments offered by some as "proof" that the Pastorals are not Pauline.

-----, *The Pastoral Epistles*. The Tyndale New Testament Commentary. Grand Rapids: Wm. B. Eerdmans, 1957.

Contains much valuable material based on a detailed knowledge of the Greek text and a wide acquaintance with previous commentaries. Has a special study refuting the linguistic arguments against the Pauline authorship of the Pastorals which were introduced by P. N. Harrison. The clear differences are not denied, but are explained by Paul's advancing age, different subject matter, and different recipients of the letters. The church order is not that of the Ignatian episcopate, for bishops and elders are the same, while Timothy and Titus are more like apostolic delegates than monarchical bishops. The historical events behind the letters occurred after Paul was evidently released from his first Roman imprisonment. On women in 1 Timothy 2:8-15, he does not soften the rigor of the treatment, but notes that local circumstances need to be taken into account.

Hanson, A.T., "The Pastoral Epistles" in *The New Century Bible Series*. Grand Rapids: Eerdmans, 1982.

While Hanson concedes a distinct possibility of two Roman imprisonments for Paul, he argues against Pauline authorship of the Pastorals, though he allows the possibility that some Pauline material is incorporated. In the discussion on church government, he suggests the probable identity of bishops and elders, but sees the figures of Timothy and Titus as reflecting a move towards the monarchical episcopacy. He treats 1 Timothy 3:16 as a hymn. In the bibliography, the commentaries section is annotated.

Harrison, Everett F., *Introduction to the New Testament*. Grand Rapids: Wm. B. Eerdmans, 1964.

A sound work prepared primarily for students after Harrison had spent 25 years teaching the subject. Either this work, or Guthrie's, would be considered the best of modern conservative introductions.

Harrison, Percy Neale, *Paulines and Pastorals*. London: Villiers Publications, 1964.
> A sequel to *The Problem of the Pastoral Epistles*, in which the writer still rejects the Pauline authorship of the Pastorals. Harrison has been ably answered by Hendriksen, Guthrie, Kent, Knight and others.

-----, *The Problem of the Pastoral Epistles*. London: Oxford University Press, 1921.
> A critical work, with emphasis on the linguistic arguments against the Pauline authorship of the Pastorals. Modern arguments against Paul's authorship of the Pastorals stem from this study. Serious students of the problem must master the linguistic arguments here set forth.

Hawthorne, Gerald F., ed., *Dictionary of Paul and His Letters*. Minneapolis: InterVarsity Press, 1993.
> A reference work focusing on Pauline theology, literature, background and scholarship. In-depth articles focus on individual theological themes (such as law, resurrection and Son of God), broad theological topics (such as Christology, eschatology and the death of Christ), methods of interpretation (such as rhetorical criticism and social-scientific approaches), background topics (such as apocalypticism, Hellenism and Qumran) and various other subjects specifically related to Pauline theology and literature (such as early catholicism, the center of Paul's theology, and Paul and his interpreters since F. C. Baur).

Hayden, W.L., *Church Polity*. Chicago: S. J. Clarke, 1894. Reprinted in Kansas City, MO: Old Paths Book Club, nd.
> This work, by a second-generation Restoration Movement leader, is subtitled "A practical treatise on the Organization and Regulation of the Kingdom of God on earth." Its chapters deal with the offices of apostle, evangelist, elder and deacon, and with woman's work in the church, among others. Standard reading in the Christian Churches for years.

Hendriksen, William, *Exposition of the Pastoral Epistles*. New Testament Commentary Series. Grand Rapids: Baker Book House, 1957.
> Firmly contends for the credibility of the Pauline authorship of the epistles and provides a good basic exposition of the text. Hendriksen makes no concessions to viewpoints other than the conservative. For example, there is uncompromising acceptance of 1 Timothy 2:8-15's teaching about women: women should no more teach or lead worship than a fish should try to live on land, for it is according to the order of nature that man leads and woman follows. He treats 1 Timothy 3:16 as a hymn. He explains the role of incipient Gnosticism and of pagan dualism in discussing the belief that the resurrection is already past (2 Tim. 2:14-19).

Hervey, A.C., "1 Timothy, 2 Timothy, and Titus" in *Pulpit Commentary*. Grand Rapids: Wm. B. Eerdmans, 1962.
> The introductory studies and comments on the text, verse-by-verse, is regularly found to be helpful for the books of the New Testament, and often proves to be a good source to begin an in-depth study of a Bible book.

Hiebert, David E., *First Timothy*. Chicago: Moody Press, 1957.
> A brief exposition, true to the text and fully abreast of the most recent scholarship.

-----, *Second Timothy*. Chicago: Moody Press, 1958.
> Deals with the historical and critical problems, emphasizes the need for two imprisonments, and expounds the text in the light of Paul's impending death.

-----, *Titus and Philemon*. Chicago: Moody Press, 1957.
> A careful blending of exegesis with a capable exposition of the text. All three of these volumes are part of the Moody Colportage Library series.

Higgins, A.J., "The Pastoral Epistles," in *Peake's Commentary on the Bible*, edited by M. Black and H. H. Rowley. New York: Thomas Nelson and Sons, 1963.
> First published in 1924, but since updated. Includes the "generally accepted results of Biblical Criticism, Interpretation, History and Theology." Higgins thinks Paul is not the author of the Pastorals, but allows the possibility of there being genuine fragments of Paul's writings included in the epistles as we now have them. He finds a church order (polity) developed beyond the polity of the Pauline period and says bishops are not the same as elders. His section on the "widows" (1 Timothy 5:3-16) is helpful.

Houlden, J.L., *The Pastoral Epistles: 1 and 2 Timothy, Titus*. The Pelican New Testament Commentaries. London: Penguin Books, 1975.
> Exceedingly brief, this biased interpretation attempts to establish a non-Pauline authorship for the Pastorals.

Huther, Joh., ed., *Critical and Exegetical Handbook to the Epistles to Timothy and Titus*. Vol.9 of Meyer's Commentary on the New Testament. Edinburgh: T & T Clark, 1883. Reprinted at Winona Lake, Ind.: Alpha Publications, 1980.
> Following Meyer's example (from Meyer has come the Historical-Grammatical method of interpreting), Huther produced this commentary after Meyer's death. He specially studied the commentaries of Van Oosterzee, Plitt, and Hofmann, and often is replying to or refuting those earlier works. A knowledge of Greek is helpful in the study of Meyer's commentaries.

Ironside, Henry Allan, *Timothy, Titus and Philemon*. Neptune, NJ: Loizeaux Brothers, 1947.
> An explanation of these personal letters, perhaps best suited for new converts.

Jackson, John, *Timothy and Titus, The Pastoral Epistles*, in The Bible Commentary, edited by F. C. Cook. New York: Charles Scribner's Sons, 1886. Reprinted in Grand Rapids: Baker Book House, 1978 and 1981.
> Noted for outstanding expository studies, the commentary is designed to assist preachers and Bible students come to grips with the essence of the Bible's teaching. Has "additional notes" on the difficult and disputed passages.

Johnson, Philip C., *The Epistles to Titus and Philemon*. Grand Rapids: Baker Book House, 1966.
> Separates Titus from its traditional position as a part of the Pastoral Epistles, and also rejects the Pauline authorship. Shows little awareness that the epistle has any overall theme.

Karris, R.J., *The Pastoral Epistles* in New Testament Message Series. Wilmington, Del.: Michael Glazier, 1979.
> This commentary is addressed primarily to the non-specialist Roman Catholic readership. Post-Pauline authorship is simply assumed. Karris thinks that church government was still fluid at the time the letters were written, and that the Pastorals do not present one unified model of polity. The value of this commentary is the writer's attempt to show the sequence of thought in the letters – the use of traditional materials, catchword linkages, positive state-

ments balanced against negative ones, etc. Karris views the statements about women in 1 Timothy 2 as reflecting the real world of the readers, a world which included a Gnostic threat, but since this is not our world, we must not therefore take such statements as timeless truths.

Kelly, John N.D., *The Pastoral Epistles* in Harper's New Testament Commentaries. New York: Harper and Row, 1963.
> An able defense of the Pauline authorship (with some problems of vocabulary and style to be solved by postulating the use of an amanuensis). It is critical of the "fragment hypothesis," and Kelly quite reasonably poses the question why, if the Pastorals are pseudonymous, there are *three* of them. Kelly presents a vivid and thorough picture of first century church life, and dates the letters from after the imprisonment recorded in Acts 28. The work is based on the Greek and made understandable to those who do not know Greek through the author's own translation. He treats 1 Timothy 3:16 as a hymn, following Jeremias' ideas in this. He makes no efforts to soften the statements on the place and duty of women (1 Timothy 2:8-15).

Kelly, William, *An Exposition of the Two Epistles to Timothy*. London: C.A. Hammond, 1948.
> This is a reprint of an able exposition by a Plymouth Brethren writer, originally published in 1889.

Kent, Homer A., *The Pastoral Epistles: Studies in 1 and 2 Timothy and Titus*. Chicago: Moody Press, 1958.
> A work of quality and applicability to 20th century "pastoral" needs. Introduces the reader to the possible solutions for most of the problem exegetical passages. Comes out strongly for the Pauline authorship, and gives a possible itinerary (including maps for study) from which the books were written.

Kidd, Reggie M., *Wealth and Beneficence in the Pastoral Epistles: A "Bourgeois" Form of Early Christianity?* Atlanta: Scholars Press, 1990.
> The burden of this dissertation is to assess the scholarly consensus that derives from Dibelius to the effect that the Pastoral Epistles represent a kind of *burgerlich* (= middle-class) Christianity that had adjusted to so-called bourgeois values, with little or none of the eschatological urgency that pervades the earlier Pauline "acknowledged" letters. Kidd's concern is twofold: to urge much greater methodological precision in looking at the sociology of early Christianity as a whole, and of the Pastoral Epistles in particular; and to assess the data of the Pastoral Epistles in this regard at one specific point, the attitude toward wealth and beneficence with a basically two-level sociology, where people are either above or below in two-term relationships.

Knight, George W., *The Faithful Sayings in the Pastoral Epistles*. Nutley, NJ.: Presbyterian and Reformed Publishing Co, nd.
> Studies of the five "faithful sayings" found in the Pastoral Epistles. For the student who knows or can read Greek.

-----, *Commentary on the Pastoral Epistles* in the New International Greek Testament Commentary. Grand Rapids: Eerdmans, 1992.
> One important aim of the NIGTC is to interact with the wealth of significant New Testament research published in recent articles and monographs. Knight does this, as he concludes the traditional views (Pauline authorship [with Luke as an amanuensis], from a date after the imprisonment recorded in Acts28, etc.) are still the correct ones. The reader will find it useful

to be at home in the Greek language. The emphasis in the commentary is on the exegesis of the Greek text and the flow of the argument. The Pastorals are treated in this order: 1 Timothy, Titus, and 2 Timothy. There are excurses on early church offices and leaders (cp. 1 Timothy 3:1-13), and on motivations for appropriate conduct (cp. Titus 2:1-10). Traditional, too, is the author's approach to the interpretation of the role of women in 1 Timothy 2:11-15, in which he argues strongly that the commandment to be silent and the prohibition from teaching and authority in the church are addressed to all women of all times.

Lenski, R.C.H., *The Interpretation of St. Paul's Epistles to the Colossians, to the Thessalonians, to Timothy, to Titus, and to Philemon*. Columbus, Ohio: Wartburg Press, 1937.
> A conservative Lutheran exposition based on the Greek text. Tends to be wordy at times, but the student who will take time to read it will grow in his appreciation of Paul's letters.

Liddon, Henry P., *Explanatory Analysis of St. Paul's First Epistle to Timothy*. London: Longmans, Green and Co., 1897. Reprinted in Minneapolis: Klock and Klock, 1978.
> The "first century message to twentieth century pastors" is a helpful treatment based on the Greek text.

Lipscomb, David, and Shepherd, J. W., *A Commentary on the New Testament Epistles*. Vol.5. Nashville: Gospel Advocate Co., 1942.
> This series of commentaries was written for the Sunday School teacher who is looking for help in greater detail than what a lesson quarterly would give. Lipscomb's notes are expanded by Shepherd.

Lock, Walter, *A Critical and Exegetical Commentary on the Pastoral Epistles*, in The International Critical Commentary. New York: Charles Scribner's Sons, 1924.
> Scholarly presentation based on the Greek text, it is one place to begin for those who are ready for detailed comments based on the Greek text. The introductory studies include an account of the later influence of the Pastoral Epistles, especially on the liturgy of the church, and on church orders. Lock is inclined to support the Pauline authorship, allowing for the use of an amanuensis (he thinks it was Luke). There are sections on the nature of the heresy (Judaeo-Gnostic), on church organization and ministry (bishops may be identical with elders, but perhaps a bishop is an elder when functioning as an overseer). The statement that women will be saved through childbearing may well arise as a protest against the asceticism of the false teachers, but it may also refer to *the* child-bearing, that of Mary at the incarnation. On 2 Timothy 2:18, and the resurrection as already past, he suggests that a spiritual resurrection at baptism is intended.

McGarvey, John W., *A Treatise on the Eldership*. Murfreesboro, TN.: DeHoff Publications, 1956. A reprint of the edition of 1870.
> A series of editorial articles that originally appeared in the *Apostolic Times*. The chapters deal with an explanation of the titles for the office of elder, duties of the office, how to be examples, shepherds, overseers, how to practice church discipline, qualifications, and methods of selection and appointment.

Merkel, Helmut, *Die Pastoralbriefe*, in the NTD series.   Gottingen: Vandenhoeck & Ruprecht, 1991.

This contribution to NTD replaces Joachim Jeremias' commentary on the Pastoral Epistles. Jeremias embraced the Pastorals' prima facie *Sitz im Leben*, not only accepting the Pauline authorship, but interpreting this Paul in continuity with the Jesus tradition.   Merkel rejects each of these views.   He believs the Pastoral Epistles emerged during the third generation of the church (ca. AD 100) as an attempt by a student or school of Paul to establish the apostle's legacy for that generation.   Merkel envisions a situation late in the first century where a vacuum of authority has emerged in some churches in Asia Minor, which has allowed the incursion of an incipient form of Gnosticism characterized by asceticism, speculative exegesis of the Old Testament, and realized eschatology.   1 Timothy finds the churches governed by a council of elders.   The author of the Pastorals intends to overlay on this holdover from the Synagogue government Paul's system of bishop(s) and deacons (a system he had derived from the Hellenistic associations, and one which had served him well in the mission churches). The council of elders is pushed into the background, while the bishop is granted disciplinary power over the elders (5:19-21).   [Is Timothy a "bishop" or an "evangelist?   And how does Merkel explain that in Acts and Titus, "bishop" and "elder" are the same office?]   2 Timothy seeks to rehabilitate the person of Paul as one worthy of emulation by congregational leaders. [Does a "pseudepigraphical" letter encourage its readers to give attention to its theme?]   The letter to Titus, the *Sitz im Leben* for which is a missionary situation, is designed to ensure the support of Pauline itinerants.   This work is more in step with consensus scholarship since Jeremias, and that whole consensus is sad!

Moffatt, James, "Pastoral Epistles," *Encyclopedia Britannica*.   New York: Encyclopedia Britannica, 1911.

The article on "Pastoral Epistles" directs the reader to other areas in the set, where Moffatt rejects the Pauline authorship in favor of a Lukan authorship for the Pastorals.

Moule, Charles F.D., *The Problem of the Pastoral Epistles: A Re-appraisal*. Manchester: John Rylands Library, 1965.

The Manson Memorial Lecture for 1965, reprinted from the *Bulletin of the John Rylands Library*.   Rejects the Pauline authorship.

Moule, Handley C.G., *The Second Epistle To Timothy*.   London: Religious Tract Society, 1905.

A short devotional study of 2 Timothy.

Oden, Thomas C., *First and Second Timothy and Titus*.   Louisville: John Knox Press, 1989.

Part of the Interpretation series of commentaries, it is an exposition, not an exegesis, of the text.   All three books are mixed together in the exposition.   There is no systematic development of each book individually.   Oden acknowledges his conversion to the view that the three works are genuine epistles of Paul, written during a second Roman imprisonment. The author supports his exposition with comments from classic Christian interpreters, such as Augustine, Luther, Calvin and Wesley.   What may be observed is how one scholar proposes to make the teachings of the Pastorals applicable to current issues.

Patton, William, *Bible Wines: or The Laws of Fermentation and Wines of the Ancients*. Fort Worth, TX: Star Bible and Tract Corp,. 1976.
> A reprint of a volume first issued in 1874. In the 1976 reprint an outline of the material, prepared by Stanley B. Niles, is included, and it is a great help to the reader for following the train of the argument. Included also is a scholarly analysis of the use of the word "wine" as found in the Bible. It deals with Jesus being called a winebibber, and His turning water to wine, and with the passage in 1 Timothy 5:23 where Paul gives advice to Timothy to take a little wine for his stomach's sake.

Perkins, Pheme, *Gnosticism and the New Testament*. Minneapolis: Fortress, 1993.
> It was inevitable after the discoveries at Nag Hammadi that new surveys on the theme of Gnosticism and the New Testament would be provided. This book is a good place to start for such an overview. Analysis of treatises from Nag Hammadi have led to a kind of consensus; namely, that forms of Gnosticism (especially "Sethian" Gnosticism) with roots in late Jewish exegesis and thought existed apart from Christianity and provided the groundwork for more refined versions of the Gnostic myth in later Christian circles. In this she seems to be on solid ground. Perhaps, too, in her presentation of the view that the world of Paul can be illuminated by a better knowledge of the history of incipient Gnosticism. Other major conclusions are disappointing: (1) that the Gospel of Thomas occupies an important place alongside the Synoptic Gospels and can be used fruitfully to help sift the traditions about Jesus in the Synoptic Gospels; (2) Paul's Christology is rooted in a mixture of speculation on Wisdom and Adam like that found in Gnosticism.

Phillips, H.E., *Church Officers and Organization*. St. Petersburg, Fl.: Cypress Press, 1948.
> The author's stated purpose in writing this book was to awaken the elders, deacons, and the church to a full realization of the work designed for them by the Lord. The book studies the qualifications for elders and deacons as found in Timothy and Titus, and also handles the standard questions and objections to meeting these qualifications given in the 20th century.

Plummer, Alfred, *The Pastoral Epistles*. Vol. 6 of The Expositor's Bible, edited by W. Robertson Nicoll. New York: A.C. Armstrong and Son, 1908. Reprinted in Grand Rapids: Eerdmans, 1943.
> Worth consulting on the problem passages. Plummer is usually good on whatever book he is commenting.

Roberts, J.W., *Letters to Timothy*. The Living Word Study for Adults. Austin, TX: R.B. Sweet, 1964.
> A series of 13 lessons intended for Adult studies in Bible school classes. Non-instrument author makes application to the 20th century church's needs. Questions to stimulate thought and discussion included with each lesson.

-----, *Titus, Philemon, and James*. The Living Word Study for Adults. Austin, Tex.: R. B. Sweet, 1963.
> Three of the lessons included in this booklet cover the Epistle to Titus. A helpful analytical outline is presented.

Robertson, A.T., *Word Pictures in the New Testament*. Vol. 4. Nashville, TN.: Broadman Press, 1931.

> Robertson's handling of the Greek words of Paul's fourth group of epistles is brief, but would remind a student who has had Greek of some of the vocabulary and grammar and the light that knowledge sheds on understanding

Russell, Bob, *God's Message For a Growing Church*. Cincinnati: Standard, 1990.

> This is a book of sermons based on Paul's epistle to Titus. Message #3, "Guard Against Legalism," tends to follow a presentation of "legalism" that is more easily harmonized with Reformed theology's handling of "works of Law" than what one reads in Titus 1 or elsewhere in Paul.

Rutherford, John, "Pastoral Epistles," in *The International Standard Bible Encyclopedia*, edited by James Orr. Grand Rapids: Eerdmans, 1939.

> Helpful beginning place for the student who would get a grasp of the problems of Introductory Studies relative to these epistles. Defends the Pauline authorship of the Pastorals.

Scott, Ernest F., *The Pastoral Epistles*, in Moffatt New Testament Commentary. New York: Harper and Brothers, nd.

> Written from the standpoint of a more advanced criticism, it denies the Pauline authorship.

Simpson, Edmund K., *The Pastoral Epistles*. Grand Rapids: Eerdmans, 1950.

> Ably defends the Pauline authorship, carefully examines the external and internal evidence which bears on the authenticity of these letters, draws on an extensive knowledge of classical literature, and expounds the text in a scholarly way.

Spain, Carl, *The Letters to Timothy and Titus*. Living Word Commentary, edited by Everett Ferguson. Austin, TX: R.B. Sweet, 1975.

> The usual introductory studies are included, followed by comments on the verses. This series of commentaries, based on the RSV, is a project by a group of Church of Christ scholars.

Spence, H.D.M., "The Epistles to Timothy and Titus," V.8 of *Ellicott's Commentary on the Whole Bible*, ed. by Charles J. Ellicott. Grand Rapids: Zondervan, 1959.

> The comments in *Ellicott's Commentary* regularly are refreshing to study. He brings to light the nuances of the Greek text.

Staton, Knofel, *Timothy - Philemon* in Standard Bible Studies (Unlocking The Scriptures for You). Cincinnati: Standard, 1988.

> Intended for Sunday School teachers and disciples serious about spiritual growth, this series avoids a verse-by-verse treatment, and focuses more on the main ideas of the Scripture being studied. A workbook by Mark Plunkett accompanies this volume. Staton tends to follow the lead taken by his wife Julia Staton, *What the Bible Says about Women* (Joplin: College Press, 1980), and urges that 1 Timothy 2:8ff deals with "wives" and not all women; "husbands" and not all men. His chapter on the qualifications of elders and deacons is a good treatment of this topic.

Stott, John R. W., *Guard the Gospel: The Message of 2 Timothy*. Downers Grove, IL: Inter-Varsity Press, 1973.
> This first volume in a new series titled *The Bible Speaks Today*, presents helpful reasons for continuing to live dynamically for Christ, rather than getting discouraged and quitting the ministry.

Taylor, Thomas, *An Exposition of Titus*. Grand Rapids: Christian Classics, nd.
> This is a reprint of a work that first appeared in 1658.

Thiessen, Henry C., *Introduction to the New Testament*. Grand Rapids: Eerdmans, 1943.
> Provides a good conservative approach to the introductory matters relating to the New Testament, both Special and General introductions. Elementary but scholarly and sufficiently comprehensive.

Treblico, Paul, *Jewish Communities in Asia Minor*. Cambridge: Cambridge University Press, 1991.
> More is known about the Jews of Asia Minor than of any other part of the Diaspora in the early centuries AD. Treblico takes us through a whole corpus of Jewish inscriptions from Asia Minor, archaeological evidence of synagogues, and ancient literature (Josephus and the New Testament). Two interesting points are the alleged prominent role Jewish women played in synagogue administration and direction, and non-Jewish women holding civic titles in Asia Minor.

Van Oosterzee, J.J., "The Pastoral Epistles," Vol.8 of *The New Testament, A Commentary on the Holy Scriptures*, edited by John P. Lange and Philip Schaff. Grand Rapids: Zondervan, nd.
> Lange was one of Germany's greatest Biblical scholars. His notes, and those by authors included in the set, are long, brilliant, and sometimes arbitrary. Philip Schaff, the American translator and editor happily remedies the defects in Lange's commentary in footnotes and complements him in an original way. For the advanced student with a knowledge of Greek.

Vine, William Edwyn, *The Epistles to Timothy and Titus: Faith and Conduct*. Grand Rapids: Zondervan, 1965.
> Basing his studies upon the premise that the epistles were written in order that men might know how to behave themselves in the house of God, Vine expounds them in the light of the needs of the local church or assembly.

Wallis, Wilbur B., "1 and 2 Timothy, Titus," in *Wycliffe Bible Commentary*, edited by Charles F. Pfeiffer and Everett F. Harrison. Chicago: Moody Press, 1963.
> This is one of the better one-volume commentaries on the whole Bible. The brief notes and outlines often prove helpful to the student who would grasp the overall message of the books quickly.

Ward, Ronald A., *Commentary on I & II Timothy and Titus*. Waco, TX: Word Books, 1974.
> The introductory studies deal with the usual arguments for and against the Pauline authorship, and also summarize the doctrine found in the epistles on such topics as God, Christ, Holy Spirit, and Church. Comments are included for each verse in the letters.

White, Newport J.D., *The First and Second Epistles to Timothy*, in Expositor's Greek Testament, edited by W. Robertson Nicoll. Grand Rapids: Eerdmans, 1967.
> For the student who knows Greek. Defends the traditional Pauline authorship of these letters.

-----, *The Epistle to Titus*, in Expositor's Greek Testament, edited by W. Robertson Nicoll. Grand Rapids: Eerdmans, 1967.
> As stated above, a study through the comments in the *Expositor's Greek Testament* with understanding is possible for the student who previously has studied Greek. These notes will remind him of many of the grammar and syntactical notes he was introduced to, and their meaning for the immediate book at hand.

Wiersbe, Warren W., *Be Faithful: An Expository Study of the Pastoral Epistles*. Wheaton, IL: Victor Books, 1981.
> A series of sermons on 1 and 2 Timothy and Titus. Wiersbe writes from the standpoint that Paul is the author, and that the epistles date from after the imprisonment recorded in Acts 28.

Woychuk, Nicholas A., *An Exposition of Second Timothy*. Old Tappan, NJ.: Fleming H. Revell Co., 1974.
> An original and creative exposition which abounds in illustrative material. Inspirational and practical.

Wright, Noble E., *Notes Concerning the Eldership*. Petersburg, Ind.: Published by the author, 1977.
> Major sections of this work cover the office, the work, and the qualifications for the office. The last part of the book deals with methods of selection of men to be elders.

Wuest, Kenneth S., *The Pastoral Epistles in the Greek New Testament*. Vol.2 in Word Studies in the Greek New Testament. Grand Rapids: Eerdmans, 1952.
> Featuring Wuest's own expanded translation, and comments on the nuances of the Greek text to make them understandable to the non-Greek student.

Young, Frances, *The Theology of the Pastoral Letters*. Cambridge: Cambridge University Press, 1994.
> The New Testament Theology Series (edited by J.D.G. Dunn) aims to provide theological discussions of the individual writings of the New Testament, since so much published material concentrates on historical, philological, and literary issues, and New Testament theologies focus on major figures like Jesus, John, and Paul, neglecting other witnesses. Young denies the Pauline authorship of the Pastorals (she valiantly tries to make "pseudonymity" acceptable) as she explains how the theology of the Pastorals differs from Paul. She thinks the Pastorals address the concerns of the generation after Paul's, and were produced by loyal followers of Paul who wished to preserve his heritage from distortion. She attempts to show how contemporary sociological approaches to the New Testament world can help us understand

the Pastorals better. She also offers instruction about the reader-response approach to arrive at a modern value for the Pastorals. At one time, the "assured conclusions" of scholars was that the author of the Pastorals was (1) no theologian; (2) interested above all in church organization; (3) simply lifted ethical codes from his Greco-Roman environment. Each of these views is rebutted by Young.

Zahn, Theodor, *Introduction to the New Testament.* Vol.2. Grand Rapids: Kregel Publications, 1953.
These introductory studies defend the Pauline authorship of the Pastorals in a chapter titled "The Last Three Epistles of Paul."

NOTE: Further Bibliographies are included with the Special Studies found from time to time at the close of comments on the individual chapters of the Pastoral Epistles. Bibliographies on topics such as Women's Work in the Church, Elders and Deacons, Evangelists, Widows, etc., are included there.

INDEXES

INDEX OF TOPICS

Roman numerals refer to pages in the Introductory Studies.   Arabic numerals refer to pages in the commentaries on Timothy and Titus.

INDEX TO BIBLICAL NAMES

www.ingramcontent.com/pod-product-compliance
Lightning Source LLC
Chambersburg PA
CBHW061957090426
42811CB00006B/967

9 780097 176522 1